To Our Graduate Students,
Our Future

Brenda DeVore Marshall

COMMUNICATION
VIEWS FROM THE HELM
FOR THE 21ST CENTURY

JUDITH S. TRENT
Editor
University of Cincinnati

ALLYN AND BACON

Boston • London • Toronto • Sydney • Tokyo • Singapore

Vice President, Editor in Chief: Paul Smith
Series Editor: Karon Bowers
Editorial Assistant: Leila Scott
Marketing Manager: Kris Farnsworth
Editorial Production Service: Omegatype Typography, Inc.
Manufacturing Buyer: Suzanne Lareau
Cover Administrator: Jennifer Hart

ISBN: 0-205-28167-2

Printed in the United States of America
10   9   8   7   6   5   4   3   2   1   02   01   00   99   98   97

CONTENTS

PREFACE

The idea for the "At the Helm" series presented during the 1996 San Diego convention of the National Communication Association was, at least in the beginning, really quite simple. There were a number of communication scholars I wanted to hear and see at our 82nd annual convention. (I guess I took it for granted that other NCA members would view the Helm programs as opportunities to hear "some of our best" in areas of study other than their own.) Thus, as the primary convention planner I took the occasion to fashion a series of programs that would highlight the research and scholarship of some of the discipline's most respected scholars.

The topics for the seventeen Helm programs presented at the San Diego convention and reproduced for this volume were selected because, as we approach the twenty-first century, they are primary among the major areas of research and instruction in the communication discipline. And yet, it was difficult to determine just how to define the contours of our disciplinary knowledge base. How would (or some would argue, why should) interpersonal theory, for example, be separated from communication theory or from rhetorical theory? Why distinguish between group and organizational communication or between mass communication and the rhetorical analysis of public discourse? Can theory be set apart from practice, and why distinguish among research methodologies? The answer is that the frequently artificial distinctions had to be made because of the need for discrete convention programs. And once formed, the convention programs became convenient chapters for this volume. But I recognize, of course, that many of the distinctions are questionable.

As a series, the Helm programs were well attended. (The panel on Gender Studies in Communication must have broken all NCA attendance records for a panel presentation not part of a general or keynote session.) I like to think that they were successful in attracting large audiences because they addressed important theoretical issues/topics and that the panelists, some fifty-nine of them, are practicing scholars with new and bold ideas—ideas that clearly help position the discipline intellectually for the new millennium.

The Helm participants were invited to share new ideas, reaffirm earlier work, comment on current theoretical perspectives, or predict future trends in the research/scholarship in their areas of expertise. Among these essays you will find that the authors have taken all of these approaches to their assignment and more. Some have chided the field, some have challenged, some have congratulated—and all have stimulated.

As I began this project it became abundantly clear that no single person was sufficiently knowledgeable about all of the areas of communication research and instruction to build seventeen programs across the diverse intellectual terrain that now defines us. But I had friends with good ideas whom I thank. They are, in alphabetical order: James Chesebro, Gail Fairhurst, James Gaudino, Dennis Gouran, Robert Ivie, and Jimmie Trent. I also want two former graduate students, Cady Short-Thompson and Caitlin Young, and one current graduate student, Gay E. Gauder, to know how much I appreciate their careful and conscientious work in all stages of the project. Finally, of course, I am indebted to each of the contributors to the volume, the authors of the essays and the introductions. I am pleased that seventy-five of the seventy-seven people who were part of the Helm programs in San Diego are a part of this volume. And without question, great appreciation is due Allyn and Bacon, especially President Bill Barke and Vice President and Speech Communication Editor-in-Chief, Paul Smith. Their goodwill and demonstrated regard for our discipline are evidenced not only by publication of this volume, but also by the provision that, after their costs, any income from the sale of the volume will be used to fund graduate student travel to NCA conventions.

Initially, I recognized that each of the Helm programs would be primary for some NCA members attending the convention, but it is my hope that readers of this volume will sample liberally other divisions of the field where they will find additional leading thinkers and scholars.

Enjoy!

Judith S. Trent
University of Cincinnati
1997 NCA President

CONTRIBUTORS

Deborah F. Atwater
Pennsylvania State University

Leslie A. Baxter
University of Iowa

Charles R. Berger
University of California, Davis

Cynthia Berryman-Fink
University of Cincinnati

Edwin Black
University of Wisconsin, Madison

Arthur P. Bochner
University of South Florida

Robert N. Bostrom
University of Kentucky

Jennings Bryant
University of Alabama

Judee K. Burgoon
University of Arizona

Michael Burgoon
University of Arizona

Brant R. Burleson
Purdue University

Carolyn Calloway-Thomas
Indiana University

Karlyn Kohrs Campbell
University of Minnesota

James W. Carey
Columbia University

James W. Chesebro
Indiana State University

Clifford G. Christians
University of Illinois

Celeste M. Condit
University of Georgia

Vernon E. Cronen
University of Massachusetts

Donald P. Cushman
University of Albany SUNY

Sheron J. Dailey
Indiana State University

John A. Daly
University of Texas

Stanley A. Deetz
Rutgers University

L. Patrick Devlin
University of Rhode Island

Lewis Donohew
University of Kentucky

Steve Duck
University of Iowa

Walter R. Fisher
University of Southern California

Mary Anne Fitzpatrick
University of Wisconsin, Madison

Robert V. Friedenberg
Miami University

Alberto González
Bowling Green State University

H. L. Goodall, Jr.
University of North Carolina, Greensboro

Dennis S. Gouran
Pennsylvania State University

John O. Greene
Purdue University

Richard B. Gregg
Pennsylvania State University

Bruce E. Gronbeck
University of Iowa

Lawrence Grossberg
University of North Carolina, Chapel Hill

Dan F. Hahn
New York University

Roderick P. Hart
University of Texas at Austin

Lynda Lee Kaid
University of Oklahoma

Kathleen E. Kendall
University of Albany SUNY

Wendy Leeds-Hurwitz
University of Wisconsin, Parkside

Thomas R. Lindlof
University of Kentucky

James C. McCroskey
West Virginia University

Lynn C. Miller
University of Texas at Austin

Peter R. Monge
University of Southern California

Paul A. Mongeau
Miami University

Dennis K. Mumby
Purdue University

Paul E. Nelson
Ohio University

W. Barnett Pearce
Loyola University

Della Pollock
University of North Carolina, Chapel Hill

Marshall Scott Poole
Texas A&M University

Linda L. Putnam
Texas A&M University

Scott C. Ratzan
Emerson College and Tufts University
School of Medicine

William K. Rawlins
Purdue University

Everett M. Rogers
University of New Mexico

Michael E. Roloff
Northwestern University

Thomas Rosteck
University of Arkansas

Alan M. Rubin
Kent State University

Rebecca B. Rubin
Kent State University

Teresa Sabourin
University of Cincinnati

David R. Seibold
University of California, Santa Barbara

Barbara F. Sharf
University of Illinois at Chicago

Stuart J. Sigman
University of Albany SUNY

Nancy Signorielli
University of Delaware

Jo Sprague
San Jose State University

John R. Stewart
University of Washington

Mary S. Strine
University of Utah

David L. Swanson
University of Illinois

Dolores V. Tanno
California State University, San Bernardino

Teresa L. Thompson
University of Dayton

Phillip K. Tompkins
University of Colorado, Boulder

Douglas M. Trank
University of Iowa

Jimmie D. Trent
Miami University

Philip C. Wander
San Jose State University

Julia T. Wood
University of North Carolina, Chapel Hill

David Zarefsky
Northwestern University

Contributors' essays were delivered at the National Communication Association Convention, "Communication: Taking the Helm," San Diego, November 1996. Reprinted by permission.

CHAPTER 1

PERSPECTIVES IN COMMUNICATION THEORY: TAKING THE HELM IN THE TWENTY-FIRST CENTURY

Introduction

Jimmie D. Trent
Miami University

During the 1970s, what is now referred to as the "Great Paradigm Debate" involved a number of young associate professors disputing the merits of laws, rules, and systems as a foundation for communication theories. The debate started at an NCA-sponsored Post-Doctoral Honors seminar hosted by W. Charles Redding at Purdue University in June 1975 (Pearce, 1977). Prominent in this debate were Charles Berger, Peter Monge, Donald Cushman, Leonard Hawes, Jesse Delia, W. Barnett Pearce, and Vernon Cronen. The debate was continued at the NCA Convention in Houston in December 1975, where Berger defended the laws perspective, Cushman the rules perspective, and Monge the systems perspective.

Two decades later, the matured perspectives of Monge, Cushman, Berger, and Cronen were presented in an NCA program chaired by Jesse Delia. Those perspectives compose the four essays which follow.

Dr. Peter R. Monge is Professor and Chair of The Annenberg Doctoral Program at the Annenberg School for Communication, University of Southern California. His academic record includes conducting 13 research projects funded by grants totaling $1,179,138. He has authored or co-authored 17 books or book chapters and published

26 articles in professional journals. He has presented one to three research-based papers at all but one of the International Communication Association (ICA) conventions held since 1972. And in seven of those years, he presented papers at NCA and Academy of Management conventions. In addition, his record includes one or more papers at the conferences of the Western Communication Association, the World Conference on Cybernetics, the American Institute for Decision Sciences, the International Association for Mass Communication Research, the Institute for Management Science, and the International Network for Social Network Analysis. He has done extensive public and private sector consulting. Dr. Monge is the current (1997–1998) President of the International Communication Association.

Dr. Donald P. Cushman is Professor of Communication at The State University of New York at Albany. He has won five Outstanding Teacher awards, one from each of the five universities at which he has taught. In 1992, he won both the National Communication Association's Teacher on Teacher Award and the Donald M. Ecroyd Award as the Outstanding Teacher in Higher Education. With 14 books and more than 100 journal articles or book chapters, he has been recognized repeatedly for his scholarship. In 1996, Professor Cushman was named by the National Communication Association to receive the Gerald M. Philips Award for Distinguished Applied Communication Research. He was named a Senior Research Scholar by the Ford Foundation, the National Endowment for the Humanities, and the National Institute of Mental Health. The National Communication Association named him to receive the Charles Woolbert Award "for research of exceptional originality and influence which has stood the test of time." He has been named a Distinguished International Scholar by the East-West Center in Hawaii, the United States Fulbright Commission, Canberra University and Warrnambool Institute of Advanced Education in Australia, Fudan and Beijing universities in the People's Republic of China, Tokyo University in Japan, Warsaw University in Poland, Yugoslavian/Croatian InterUniversity of Post Graduate Studies, and Yonsei University in Korea. He has presented more than 100 papers at conventions of the National Communication Association, the International Communication Association, the InterUniversity Conference, the Corporate Communication Conference, and the Eastern States Communication Conference. In addition, Dr. Cushman has served as consultant to 62 industrial and business firms, unions, or governments in the United States, Poland, Italy, Australia, Indonesia, Egypt, Saudi Arabia, Korea, Canada, Malaysia, Thailand, and Bolivia.

Dr. Charles R. Berger is Professor and Chair of the Department of Communication at the University of California, Davis. Professor Berger's research focuses on a variety of issues related to the cognitive processes that underlie communication exchanges. He is known internationally for his pioneering work on uncertainty reduction theory and his seminal studies on strategic planning. With his co-author James J. Bradac, he received the NCA's Golden Anniversary Award for their book *Language and Social Knowledge: Uncer-*

tainty in Interpersonal Relations. In addition, he has authored, co-authored, or edited 5 other books, 32 book chapters, and 36 journal articles. He has presented 58 papers at national or international conventions, 15 of which were competitively selected for inclusion on NCA or ICA "top three" convention panels. He was named the Van Zeltz Research Professor at Northwestern University (1987–1988) and elected as a Fellow of the International Communication Association (1987). He was editor of *Human Communication Research* (1983–1986) and has co-edited *Communication Research* since 1993. Dr. Berger was President of the International Communication Association during the 1995–1996 academic year.

Dr. Vernon E. Cronen is Professor of Communication at the University of Massachusetts, Amherst. Professor Cronen's primary research interests concern the development and application of the theory "Coordinated Management of Meaning" (CMM) as methodology for: (1) analysis of situated communication, (2) critique of the forms of life that are created, recreated, and sustained by communication, and (3) helping practitioners join with clients for creative change. Dr. Cronen is a scholar who uses his theoretical, interpretive, and critical work in practical applications. He has published 19 books or book chapters and 34 journal articles, and presented 51 convention papers. Applications of his scholarship include seminars, workshops, interdisciplinary meetings, and addresses in the areas of "theoretical issues and their applications" (12 applications in the United States, England, Denmark, and Italy), family interaction and family therapy (16 applications in the United States, England, Italy, and Belgium), intercultural and cross-cultural issues (2), and organizational settings (3).

Pearce, W. Barnett (1977). Preface. *Communication Quarterly,* 25(1), 2.

Communication Theory for a Globalizing World

Peter R. Monge

University of Southern California

Few would argue with the proposition that we live in a globalizing world. Further, it is difficult to dispute the claim that these processes are creating major world-wide changes that will significantly impact the future of the human community. Yet, little is known about globalization processes or their implications for communication theory. Much collective intellectual work is required to (1) articulate the processes by which globalization occurs, (2) identify their humanity building and destroying impacts, and (3) determine the integral roles of communication and communication theory in those processes.

As a complex process globalization must be examined from multiple, diverse perspectives that encompass communication, cultural, economic, legal, political, psychological, social, and religious issues. Globalization creates increasing interconnectedness of all forms of human endeavor due, in large part, to the compression of space, time, and human culture (Robertson, 1992). Although the processes of globalization have been unfolding for centuries, they recently have reached new levels of intensity, occurring at much faster rates than earlier points in human history (Dicken, 1992). Perhaps more important, many commentators believe that we are observing changes of unknowable magnitude that are fundamentally irreversible (Barnet & Cavanagh, 1994).

Communication is located at the center of many theories about globalization. Innis (1951) and McLuhan (1960) were among the first to draw our attention to the pivotal role of communication processes and media in shaping the way we deal with fundamental properties of time and space. More recently, Dyan and Katz (1992) argued that people around the world see, hear, and experience the same historical events through the telecommunicative and computing extensions of their senses. Research by Liebes and Katz (1993) demonstrates that spectators of televised global "media events," such as the Olympics, moon walks, and military conflicts, realize that they share the experience of the moment with millions of other humans; further, this sense of communal experience itself affects the way they see and interpret these events. Similarly, the Internet connects people in worldwide chat rooms, discussion groups, and various other on-line virtual communities that are as yet little understood. And digital cellular phone technology makes it possible to contact others at any time or any place on earth, thus making people around the world instantly connectable (O'Hara-Devereaux & Johansen, 1994). Other theories examine the role of popular culture in facilitating globalization through research on television, movies, popular music, magazines, and other means of importing and exporting culture (Barnet & Cavanagh, 1994). Yet other theories explore how organizations use communication technology to link suppliers, customers, and their own international divisions, thereby creating global network organizations (Monge & Fulk, in press).

IMPLICATIONS OF GLOBALIZATION FOR COMMUNICATION THEORY

The processes of globalization and the numerous opportunities they raise for research also entail important imperatives for communication theory. Three issues seem paramount. The first is to explore the diversity of perspectives on what constitutes communication in the various communities and cultures around the globe. The second is to ex-

3

pand our notions of theory to accommodate multiple forms of knowledge. The third is to address the systemic aspects of our theory and research. In many ways, these three are intertwined.

The first issue for developing a global communication theory centers on the diversity of perspectives that are required by a global perspective. There can be little doubt that the preponderance of contemporary communication theory has been developed from the singular perspective of the United States. Although there are many interesting books and articles that describe communication processes in diverse cultural settings, few examine them from the explicit perspective of communication theory. An important book that explores this crucial issue is Kincaid's (1987) *Communication Theory: Eastern and Western Perspectives*. The book contains a number of original chapters describing communication theory as viewed from Chinese, Indian, Japanese, Korean, and American viewpoints. Each chapter describes a unique aspect of what is taken as communication in that particular society. For example, the Japanese practice of *ishin-denshin* as communication without language, the Korean neo-Confucian practice of *uye-ri* that governs ingroup and outgroup communication, and the role of the Indian Hindu law of *Karma* in cross-caste communication are all communicative practices for which there are few if any equivalents in Western countries and, equally important, almost no account in communication theories developed in the West. As Kincaid (1987) points out, Eastern and Western views of communication differ on several important theoretical dimensions, including the units of analysis, the role of purpose and intention, the limits of language and cognition, the role of emotion and rationality, and the nature of human relationships in communication. It is important to document differences in communication practices around the globe and to make them the explicit subject of future theorizing.

The second issue for communication theory and globalization is to seek multiple ways of knowing. For years, many theoreticians have adopted Hempel and Oppenheim's (1948) covering law or hypothetico-deductive model as the criterion of ex-

planation, and, therefore, as the touchstone of scientific knowledge. Explanation consists of using a known deductive logic to derive statements of fact from universal premises or laws. If the derived conclusions, taken as hypotheses, are observed in the natural world, the theory is said to explain the observations (Berger, 1977; Blalock, 1969; Land, 1971). For many, this was the *only* valid form of scientific explanation (Kaplan, 1964). Yet from the beginning and despite the importance of this perspective, scholars have challenged the covering law model and offered other important alternatives. For example, von Wright (1971) and Toulmin (1974) argued that understanding was an equally if not more important way of knowing about human actions than explanation. Understanding consists of placing people's actions into a web of their personal accounts so that the observed actions are logical and sensible choices given the circumstances of the moment and the intentions of the individuals (see Cushman, 1977, and Pearce & Cronen, 1980).

Another major form of knowledge that has emerged in communication studies over the past decade is metaphor. Interpretive, cultural, and critical studies have made extensive use of this knowledge form. Typically, metaphoric knowledge consists of using one entity to represent a second, the first one the source, the second the target (Black, 1962). Knowledge about the source is taken as an account or interpretation of the target, although constructionists examine the interaction of two entities to identify "the meaning that emerges from that interaction" (Palmer & Dunford, 1996, p. 703), and thus, how each defines the other. These and other alternative forms of knowledge have the potential to provide the new level of breadth that will be required of communication theory if it is to incorporate the diverse processes that constitute globalization.

The third issue for communication theory and globalization pertains to exploration of the systemic interconnectedness of the globalization process. Virtually every scholar who addresses the question of globalization emphasizes that it must be examined as interdisciplinary, interconnected systems (Giddens, 1990; Robertson, 1992). Historically, systems theory focused on homeostatic, self-regulating, functional systems and explored important issues such as stability and control, part-whole relations, and the universal-particular debate (Monge, 1977). While that perspective is certainly important, developments over the past decade have shifted the emphasis to examining autopoietic (Krippendorff, 1987), self-organizing (Contractor, 1994) systems, and those operating under principles of chaos (Prigogine & Stengers, 1984). These perspectives focus specifically on systemic processes of self-referentiality (auto-catalysis), dynamic causality, historicity, and discontinuity (Contractor, 1994). Indeed, as Krippendorff says, these new systems perspectives account for "…processes of communication that make a society see itself as distinct and that make it retain its indigenous form of organization, culture, or mind. In the description-realization cycle, communication becomes the timeless bridge (which thereby transcends the difference) between cause and effect, between creator and the created, and between the observer and the observed. Such organizational processes of communication are explainable only from within a social form and are in the true sense self-referential. Living systems, indigenous culture, self-government, or organizationally autonomous social systems exemplify the empirical domain of this paradigm" (p. 208). Contractor (1994), Krippendorff (1987), Poole (1995), and others have urged the field of communication to examine these new developments in systems theory and apply them to communication theory. Nowhere would this be more appropriate, and in the long run more beneficial, than in the development of communication theory to account for globalization processes.

AN EXAMPLE OF GLOBALIZATION AND COMMUNICATION THEORY

Recent developments in communication network theory and research illustrate these three issues in a globalization process. Communication networks have been an important subject of communication research for many years, particularly in organiza-

tional communication (Monge, 1987; Monge & Contractor, in press). Most of the earlier research was conducted within single organizations in the United States and to a lesser extent, England. Little thought was given to whether these results represented communication processes in organizations in other countries. As Hickson (1996) has so eloquently phrased it, "As an islander (England), my mind was boggled in the sixties at any suggestion of trying to comprehend what organizations might be like anywhere else but on the island. It was quite enough to try and understand them a little just there" (p. 221). Further, little early research was conducted on the communication networks that link organizations together, as, for example, in the case of strategic alliances and interlocking boards of directors. Thus, communication networks in organizations were traditionally viewed as individual entities that were assumed to be (1) like all other organizational communication networks, and (2) themselves unconnected to other organizations.

Over the past decade this view of organizational networks has changed dramatically, especially in the context of a lively theoretical debate over the emergence of a new organizational form called the network organization (Miles & Snow, 1986), which differs in important ways from traditional organizational forms, such as hierarchies, multidivisional firms, markets, and matrix organizations. The defining feature of the network organizational form is the operation of a dense multiplex network, including communication, that ties together many highly specialized organizations to produce the products or services previously produced by a single large organization. Global network organizations, then, interconnect firms from many countries around the world to produce goods and services that are globally distributed (Monge & Fulk, in press).

Research on global network organizations has shown that many countries have unique network forms. For example, the Japanese *keiretsu,* Korean *chaebol,* and Taiwanese *jituangiye* are national network organization forms that differ from each other because their financial, social, familial, and political ties utilize different organizing principles and processes. As Biggart and Hamilton (1992) point out, "The South Korean economy is dominated by networks that on the surface resemble Japan's, but in fact have substantial differences" (p. 475). Thus, global network organizations must take this diversity in national communication networks into account when establishing global alliances. This illustrates the diversity in communication practices that communication theory must account for in globalization processes.

Monge and Contractor (in press) review 11 different theories that have been used to account for the formation, operation, and dissolution of organizational networks and global organizational forms, including exchange theory, collective action theory, uncertainty reduction theory, and social support theory. But these are not the only types of knowledge that exist about networks. Reich (1992) and Stohl (1995) use metaphors like "spiderweb organizations" and "value constellations" (Norman & Ramirez, 1993) to help us understand how network organizations work. Others, such as Boje (1991) relate stories about how networks operate. Yet others, such as Valente (1995) and Stokman and Doreian (in press) use mathematical models and computer simulations. None of these theories by themselves have provided adequate explanations, understanding, or other insights into network phenomena. While each form of knowledge individually provides an interesting and useful way to view global network organizations, collectively they provide a broader and richer knowledge than any one alone, though, to date, it is certainly not a coherent picture. This illustrates some of the variety in knowledge forms that communication theory must incorporate in order to account for processes of globalization. The challenge ahead is to develop a creative theoretical synthesis which can integrate the various types of knowledge or at least provide meaningful theoretical bridges among them.

Finally, this example also illustrates the role that communication systems theory should play in any accounts of globalization. Though national networks display interesting differences, they must be integrated into a coherent whole for the entire global network organization to work. As Monge

and Fulk (in press) point out, global network organizations are virtually impossible without systemic communication and computing infrastructures. Further, they typically operate as self-organizing, self-referential, autopoietic systems (Contractor, 1994; Monge & Contractor, in press) and frequently display chaotic properties. Communication theory must capture and account for these and other systemic aspects of globalization processes.

CONCLUSION

Among the greatest challenges that will confront humanity during the next century are the collective forces known as globalization. The interplay among cultural, economic, environmental, legal, political, social, and religious forces will significantly alter the world as we know it, some for the better, much for the worse. Communication is central to all these processes, and therefore a vital element in globalization. More than at any point in our collective history we need theoretical explanations, understandings, and insights that will enable us to influence the ways in which these processes unfold, hopefully for the good of all humankind. The importance of the potential contribution that communication theory can make to globalization process should lead us to place it at the top of our collective scholarly agenda.

REFERENCES

Barnet, R. J., & Cavanagh, J. (1994). *Global dreams: Imperial corporations and the new world order.* New York: Touchstone.

Berger, C. R. (1977). The covering law perspective as a theoretical basis for the study of human communication. *Communication Quarterly, 25,* 7–18.

Biggart, N. W., & Hamilton, G. G. (1992). On the limits of firm-based theory to explain business networks: The Western bias of neoclassical economics. In N. Nohria & R. G. Eccles (Eds.), *Networks and organizations: Structure, form, and action* (pp. 471–490). Boston, MA: Harvard Business School Press.

Black, M. (1962). *Models and metaphors: Studies in language and philosophy.* Ithaca, NY: Cornell University Press.

Blalock, H. M., Jr. (1969). *Theory construction: From verbal to mathematical formulations.* Englewood Cliffs, NJ: Prentice-Hall.

Boje, D. (1991). The storytelling organization: A study of story performance in an office supply firm. *Administrative Science Quarterly, 36,* 106–126.

Contractor, N. S. (1994). Self-organizing systems perspective in the study of organizational communication. In B. Kovacic (Ed.), *New approaches to organizational communication* (pp. 39–66). Albany, NY: State University of New York Press.

Cushman, D. P. (1977). The rules perspective as a theoretical basis for the study of human communication. *Communication Quarterly, 25,* 30–45.

Dicken, P. (1992). *Global shift: The internationalization of economic activity* (2nd ed.). New York: Guilford.

Dyan, D., & Katz, E. (1992). *Media events: The live broadcasting of history.* Cambridge, MA: Harvard University Press.

Giddens, A. (1990). *The consequences of modernity.* Stanford, CA: Stanford University Press.

Hempel, C. G., & Oppenheim, P. (1948). The logic of explanation. *Philosophy of Science, 15,* 135–175.

Hickson, D. J. (1996) The *ASQ* years then and now through the eyes of a Euro-Brit. *Administrative Science Quarterly, 41,* 217–228.

Innis, H. (1951). *The bias of communication.* Toronto: University of Toronto Press.

Kaplan, A. (1964). *The conduct of inquiry: Methodology for behavioral science.* San Francisco, CA: Chandler.

Kincaid, D. L. (Ed.). (1987). *Communication theory: Eastern and Western perspectives.* New York: Academic Press.

Krippendorff, K. (1987). Paradigms for communication and development with emphasis on autopoiesis. In D. L. Kincaid (Ed.), *Communication theory: Eastern and Western perspectives* (pp. 189–208). New York: Academic Press.

Land, K. C. (1971). Formal theory. In H. L. Costner (Ed.), *Sociological methodology 1971* (pp. 175–200). San Francisco, CA: Jossey-Bass.

Liebes, T., & Katz, E. (1993). *The export of meaning.* London: Oxford University Press.

McLuhan, M. (1960). *Explorations in communication.* Boston, MA: Beacon Press.

Monge, P. R. (1977). The systems perspective as a theoretical basis for the study of human communication. *Communication Quarterly, 25,* 19–29.

Monge, P. R. (1987). The network level of analysis. In C. R. Berger & S. H. Chaffee (Eds.), *Handbook of Communication Science* (pp. 239–270). Newbury Park, CA: Sage.

Monge, P. R., & Contractor, N. S. (in press). Emergence of communication networks. In F. M. Jablin & L. L. Putnam (Eds.), *Handbook of organizational communication* (2nd ed.). Thousand Oaks, CA: Sage.

Monge, P. R., & Fulk, J. (in press). Communication technologies for global network organizations. In J. Fulk & G. DeSanctis (Eds.), *Communication technologies and organizational form.* Thousand Oaks, CA: Sage.

Norman, R., & Ramirez, R. (1993). From value chain to value constellation: Designing interactive strategy. *Harvard Business Review, July-August,* 65–77.

O'Hara-Devereaux, M., & Johansen, R. (1994). *Globalwork: Bridging distance, culture, and time.* San Francisco, CA: Jossey-Bass.

Palmer, I., & Dunford, R. (1996). Conflicting uses of metaphors: Reconceptualizing their use in the field of organizational change. *Academy of Management Review, 21,* 691–717.

Pearce, W. B., & Cronen, V. E. (1980). *Communication, action, and meaning: The creation of social realities.* New York: Praeger.

Poole, M. S. (1995). A turn of the wheel: The case for a renewal of systems inquiry in organizational communication research. Paper presented at the Southwestern Texas State University Conference on the Future of Organizational Communication, Austin, TX.

Prigogine, I., & Stengers, I. (1984). *Order out of chaos: Man's new dialogie with nature.* New York: Bantam.

Reich, R. B. (1992). *The work of nations: Preparing ourselves for 21st century capitalism.* New York: Vantage Books.

Robertson, R. (1992). *Globalization: Social theory and global culture.* Newbury Park, CA: Sage.

Stohl, C. (1995). *Organizational communication: Connectedness in action.* Thousand Oaks, CA: Sage.

Stokman, F. S., & Doreian, P. (in press). Evolution of social networks: Processes and principles. In F. N. Stokman & P. Doreian (Eds.), *Evolution of social networks.*

Toulmin, S. (1974). Rules and their relevance to human behavior. In T. Mischel (Ed.), *Understanding other persons* (pp. 9–30). Oxford: Blackwell.

Valente, T. W. (1995). *Network models of the diffusion of innovations.* Cresskill, NJ: Hampton Press.

von Wright, G. H. (1971). *Explanation and understanding.* Ithaca, NY: Cornell University Press.

Visions of Order in Human Communication Theory

Donald P. Cushman

University of Albany SUNY

The primary purpose of human communication is to share symbolic information and commitments in order to establish, maintain, and terminate relationships among people and their social institutions. The primary purpose of human communication theory is to develop warranted public expectations regarding the principles which govern and guide the manipulation and outcomes of human communication processes. Thus, to assert that one has developed a human communication theory is to make a public claim which can be redeemed only by the presentation of evidence and reasoning of a very specific type which can meet very specific tests of reproducibility and completeness. To my knowledge no complete explication and demonstration of the appropriate character of such a theoretic evidential and reasoning process exists in our literature.

It will be the purpose of this essay to attempt to map the evidential and reasoning processes involved and the tests to be applied in evaluating the validity and completeness of such theoretic claims. In so doing, neither time nor space allows me on this occasion to broadly survey the theoretic research programs in the field which have attempted to make and redeem theoretic claims over an extended period in time. However, such an approach has been attempted by this author elsewhere (Cushman and Kovacic, 1995) and will be utilized in illustrating the analysis provided. Such an analysis divides itself into two stages: (1) an explication and illustration of the appropriate steps and types of evidence and reason required in redeeming theoretic claims and (2) the drawing of some conclusions regarding the current state and future prospects for taking the helm in developing human communication theory in the twenty-first century. Let us address each of these issues in turn.

An Explication and Illustration of the Appropriate Steps and Types of Evidence and Reasoning Involved in Redeeming Theoretic Claims

Ultimately, developing a human communication theory involves three specific stages of analysis. *First,* one must justify a *philosophic perspective* from which to reason and guide the collection of evidence in focusing one's research activity. *Second,* one must locate one or more central *theoretic constructs* which can guide the research process in providing evidence and arguments for specifying the relationship between significant communication activities. *Third,* one must articulate the *practical* communication activities and levels of skills required to manipulate these activities in order to yield predictable communication outcomes (Cushman, 1995:1–4).

Justifying a Philosophic Perspective from Which to Reason in Guiding One's Research Efforts

Every way of looking at a communication process is also a way of not looking at other elements in that process. Thus a theorist must justify what can be gained from taking a given perspective. Two sets of decisions are involved: one *metaphysical* and one *epistemological*. Metaphysical decisions involve the selection of a preferred communication reality to focus one's research efforts. Four such alternatives are available. One can choose to focus on (a) individual interpretations of symbolic interactions, (b) collaborative interaction sequences, (c) nonverbal communication behaviors, and (d) the influence of one or more of these perspectives on one another. In each case a focus on one of these perspectives elevates that perspective to prominence while minimizing the influence of the others and thus requires justification.

Epistemological decisions involve the selection of one or more preferred research methodologies. One can systematically research a preferred metaphysical reality through a wide variety of well-established research methods, be they observational, inferential, interpretive, or critical. Findings which are common through the use of diverse research methodologies are considered well grounded and not merely an artifact of the methodology employed.

Once one has justified through evidence and reasons one's preferred metaphysics and epistemologies, one can put this evidence and reasoning process to a critical test by using the perspective to locate powerful theoretic constructs which yield significant theoretic relationships between communication activities.

For example, Cushman, Valentinsen, and Dietrich (1982) selected a philosophical perspective which focused on the preferred reality involved in (1) choice-oriented and purposeful activities which (2) required the coordination of others to fulfill those purposes, and (3) thus employed a standardized usage or common set of communication rules for coordinating the participants' communication behaviors in fulfilling those purposes. Since social communication rules for achieving coordination must be known by all the members of society who employ them, ethnographic and/or empirical research methodologies could be employed to locate such communication activities and specify their relationships. Two types of such coordination processes are the mate and friendship formation, maintenance, and termination processes. Cushman and Kovacic (1995) then argue that the central construct in these two types of interpersonal relationships are types of self-concept support which the participants provide one another. Evidence and reasoning are then provided for specifying the relationships between entry and intensity communication behaviors in establishing, maintaining, and terminating mate and friend relationships in a variety of cultures (Moemeka and Kovacic, 1995: 141–177).

Locating One or More Central Constructs for Locating Significant Communication Activities and Developing Evidence and Arguments for Specifying the Relationships Between Activities

Human communication is one of the most creative, flexible, and thus anti-theoretic processes in which human beings engage. Multiple cultures and social goals, multiple individual interpretation and personal goals, multiple languages, grammars, and pragmatics make repetitive symbolic interaction difficult to locate. Yet this is exactly what human communication theorists must do. From a theorist-preferred philosophical perspective, one must reason to some controlling generative mechanisms or constructs which constrain the regularity of symbolic interaction. This reasoning must proceed in such a manner as to allow researchers to provide evidence for specifying the type of relationships which exist between communication activities and to develop accurate expectations on the strength of those relationships. For example, Delia, Clark and associates select cognitive complexity; Pearce, Cronen and associates select rule hierarchies; and Philipsen and associates select cultural rituals as their central constructs.

In order for a researcher to have a fully specified relationship between key communication activities, evidence and reasoning must be provided which resolves five issues in regard to a single relationship (Zetterberg, 1963:15). *First,* one must provide evidence and reasoning as to whether the relationship between two communication activities is (a) *reversible* (X influences Y and Y influences X) or *irreversible* (X influences Y but Y does not influence X). *Second,* is that same relationship (a) *sequential* (if X, then later Y) or *coextensive* (if X, then also at the same time Y). *Third,* is the relationship (a) *sufficient* (if X, then Y regardless of anything else) or (b) *contingent* (if X then Y, but only if Z). *Fourth,* a researcher must provide evidence and argument that the same relationship is (a) *necessary* (if X, then and only then Y along with other elements) or (b) *substitutable* (if X then Y, but also if Z then Y). *Finally,* the researcher needs to assess the *strength* of each *relationship* (how much of Y is accounted for by X, 20 percent, 90 percent?).

If the complete specification of relationships between communication activities locates relationships which are contingent, substitutable, and account for only a small part of their effect on each other, we have a *weak theory*. If the evidence and arguments locate relationships which are sufficient, necessary, and account for a large part of the influence on each other, they are *strong theories* (Zetterberg, 1963). For example, Berger in his research program aimed at specifying the relationship between initial interaction and uncertainty reduction posited a relationship which was sufficient, necessary, and accounted for why all people undertook initial interaction. However, Gudykunst and others demonstrate that the relationship was contingent, substitutable, and had a small influence on initial interaction (Gudykunst, 1995: 67–101). Conversely, Gottman investigated the pattern of communication activities predictive of divorce. He located a central construct, husbands stonewalling, and specified the relationship between that construct and divorce as irreversible, sufficient, necessary, sequential, and strongly predictive with better than 87 percent accuracy of divorce (Gottman, 1993: 57–75).

Articulating Practical Communication Activities and the Level of Skill Required to Manipulate These Activities in Order to Yield Predictable Communication Outcomes

Human communication research and theory development can be a political, self-deceptive, and artificial process. In order to protect against these distortions, we must ultimately put our theories and the evidence and arguments which back them to the test of real-world manipulation and outcomes prediction. The issues here are simple— (1) Are the theoretic claims redeemed through a replicable process? (2) Have the advocates of a theory corrected for significant critiques? (3) Do actors in the real world function in the manner the theory suggests? and (4) Can skilled communicators apply the theory in important ways to produce predictable outcomes?

Two issues require evidence and argument in support of the practical claims of a theory. *First,* one must know the communication activities advocated and be aware of the practical outcome predicted. *Second,* one must know the level of communication skills required to employ the theory correctly. When both conditions are met, then a communication theory can be put to a practical test in everyday communication activity.

For example, Cushman (1989:100–103) argues that one of the most significant communication activities involved in an interpersonal relationship is how the participants handle interpersonal conflict. He goes on to point out that the most commonly used sequence for handling conflict is destructive of interpersonal relationships. He then outlines a sequence for dealing with conflict which is constructive and which can build and deepen a relationship. However, only 20 percent of the communicators tested had the skills and control to use the positive sequence. The constructive sequence has skill requirement levels which are unique in a normal population. This theory is applicable in the real world but only when two participants in an interpersonal relationship have reached the appropriate skill levels (Cushman, 1989:87–105).

Gottman, on the other hand, has produced an entire book which details how to change the destructive communication patterns involved in divorce and the skills levels for modifying the communication patterns which are common to most participants. This research program is thus not only predictive with high accuracy of those communication patterns which produce divorce, but also of those interventions which can avoid divorce as an outcome (Gottman, 1994).

The primary purpose of human communication theory is to develop warranted public expectations regarding the principles which govern and guide the manipulation and outcomes of significant human communication processes. We have attempted to outline and illustrate how such theoretic claims can be redeemed by the presentation of evidence and arguments of a very specific type which can meet very specific tests at the philosophic, theoretic, and practical levels of analysis.

Having outlined and illustrated the steps and types of evidence and reasoning involved in redeeming theoretic claims, we are now in a position to draw some conclusions regarding the current state and future prospect for taking the helm in building human communication theory in the twenty-first century.

The Drawing of Some Conclusions Regarding the Current State and Future Prospects for Taking the Helm in Developing Human Communication Theory in the Twenty-First Century

There are several retarding and several catalytic forces influencing the current state and future prospects for taking the helm in developing communication theory in the twenty-first century. Let us explore these.

Retarding Forces.   Three trends have converged to produce retarding forces to the development of significant communication theory in the twenty-first century.

First, the increased politicalization of intellectual inquiry over the past decade has created an anti-thematic and/or ideological insular approach to inquiry. This has in turn created a lack of respect for theoretic inquiry and a mistrust of modes of inquiry which are alternative to one's own preferences. In addition the rise of destructive dialectics such as deconstructionism and treating all forms of inquiry as more or less equally distorted have served to undermine respect for quality theoretic claims and the evidence and reasoning which support them.

Second, the field of communication has experienced dramatic growth in size and the scope of topics considered relevant to the field. This in turn has led to the rapid expansion of undergraduate and graduate programs and an increase in the breadth of courses required for a given degree. This in turn has led to the erosion of in-depth training in the various skills required to develop human communication theory. For example, when I was a graduate student at Wisconsin in the 1960s, I had six courses in rhetorical theory and an equal number in communication theory. When I took a job at Michigan State, most students received six to eight courses in research methods and analytic tools. Students with this kind of background are rare today.

In addition, there has been a significant decline in individuals within the field with well-developed skills in constructive argumentation. It is important to realize that ultimately significant theory development is primarily an exercise in constructive argumentation. It is noteworthy that many of our most significant communication theorists came to the field through extensive participation in intercollegiate debate. Debate forces participants to learn how to develop, research, and defend affirmative cases. Pearce, Cushman, Philipsen, Delia, and many others applied the skills they acquired in debate to their research programs in theory construction. The field no longer attracts such students in large numbers nor do we provide any comparable training or experience in these skills.

Third, within the field of speech communication a tension has developed between those individuals with a desire to conduct basic research and teach communication theory and those individuals with a more practical skills-based approach. This conflict has led members of the practical camp to believe the former activities are either not as important or even irrelevant to the development of practical strategies and skills in specific areas of the field. Programs have emerged which focus on one of these perspectives to the exclusion of the other. Unfortunately knowledge of one is dependent upon or tested by knowledge of the other.

The convergence of these three trends has created a pool of communication researchers and theorists who are ideological, divided in their allegiance to either theoretic or practical inquiry, and have limited scope and depth in the skills necessary for mounting focused research programs which can develop communication theories with philosophic, theoretic, and practical grounding.

Catalytic Forces. Similarly, three trends have converged to improve the prospects for developing significant communication theory at present and in the future.

First, today there exists a significant realization on the part of all people of the importance of human communication for the success of a wide range of interpersonal, organizational, and cultural communication activities. This in turn has created both a demand and respect for significant communication theory which can in turn positively affect these various activities.

Second, within the academic community, researchers in psychology, sociology, political science, philosophy, biology, linguistics, and computer science have developed theoretic and research interest groups for inquiry into the intersection of their disciplines and human communication processes. Because many of these intellectual areas still provide in-depth training in theory development, research methodology, and argumentation, these researchers are filling the void which exists in our field and developing significant research programs and human communication theories.

Third, theorists both in and outside our field have contributed to a broad-based and at times in-depth literature from which we can learn and synthesize in pushing forward our own theoretic research programs. More and more our own scholars are being asked to participate in discussions and research programs across fields and nations providing a new energy source or raw data and to motivate the development of more powerful communication theories.

In short, the demand and respect for the importance of communication across a broad domain of practical activities, and the new demand and respect for communication theory across dis-

ciplines in academia and the extended data bases being developed both within and outside our field are acting as a catalyst for significant new theoretic communication activities. Communication theorists and researchers are positioned along with researchers from other disciplines at the nexus of significant individual and collective societal processes to influence the development of significant communication theories. We have a unique opportunity to take the helm in advancing our understanding and influence over these important societal activities.

REFERENCES

Cushman, D. P. (1989). Communication in establishing, maintaining, and terminating interpersonal relationships: A study in mateship. In S. S. King (Ed.) *Human Communication as a Field of Study.* Albany, NY: SUNY Press.

Cushman, D. P., and Kovacic, B. (1995). *Watershed Research Traditions in Human Communication Theory.* Albany, NY: SUNY Press.

Cushman, D. P., Valentinsen, B., and Dietrich, D. (1982). The rules theory of interpersonal relationship. In F. E. Dance (Ed.), *Human Communication Theory: Comparative Essays.* New York: Harper Row.

Gottman, J. (1993). A theory of marital dissolution and stability, *Journal of Family Psychology,* 7:57–75.

Gottman, J. (1994). *Why Marriages Succeed or Fail.* New York: Simon & Schuster.

Gudykunst, W. (1995). The uncertainty reduction and anxiety-uncertainty reduction theories of Berger, Gudykunst, and associates. In D. P. Cushman and B. Kovacic (Eds.), *Watershed Research Traditions in Human Communication Theory.* Albany, NY: SUNY Press.

Moemeka, A., and Kovacic, B. (1995). The rules theory of interpersonal relationships by Cushman, Nicotera and associates. In D. P. Cushman and B. Kovacic (Eds.), *Watershed Research Traditions in Human Communication Theory.* Albany, NY: SUNY Press.

Zetterberg, H. (1963). *On Theory and Verification in Science.* San Francisco, CA: Berkeley Press.

Big Questions and Communication Theory: Finding the Cure for Communication

Charles R. Berger
University of California, Davis

As a survivor of the great meta-theoretical debates concerning the relative merits of covering law, systems, and rule-governed approaches to the study of human communication that took place at the 1975 NCA convention in Houston, Texas, and subsequently in the pages of a 1977 issue of *Communication Quarterly,* I am here to engage in the sport of revisionist history by announcing that the exercise in which we all engaged some 21 years ago was an abject waste of time. This debate was premised on the dubious notion that a particular meta-theoretical approach to the study of human communication would somehow prove to be the Rosetta stone for the field and, as a result, produce conceptual breakthroughs of monumental proportions in our quest to understand "how communication works" (Schramm, 1954). If only we were to make the meta-theoretically "correct" choice, we would all gain privileged access to that sacred crypt where the secrets of human communication are stored. Unfortunately, I see scant evidence that these meta-theoretical debates produced such insights. Consequently, I will address the following two questions: (1) Where did we miss the boat? and (2) Are there more productive ways we can pursue the development of communication theory?

MISSED BOATS

I do not wish to spend much time bemoaning past mistakes; however, because learning itself is frequently failure-driven (Schank, 1982; Schank, 1986), understanding why meta-theoretical forays of yesteryear failed to produce results commensu-

rate with the vigor with which they were pursued is itself an important endeavor to undertake.

The Pinnacle May Not Afford the Clearest View. Standing atop the large observation tower that is itself situated at the summit of South Mountain (Nam San) near the center of Seoul, Korea, provides the sightseer with a dramatic and panoramic view of one of the world's largest cities. However, one could intensely observe the landscape of Seoul from Nam San tower for a lifetime, but fail completely to apprehend the nature of the people and society that inhabit that impressive landscape. Likewise, highly abstract discussions of meta-theory may be so far removed from the normal activities of communication researchers, who are generally focused on trying to understand the details of communicative action in specific social contexts, that the view from these lofty heights is generally uninformative. This is not to say that meta-theoretical discussions are not potentially informative in their own right; however, it is to say that these discussions may have precious little purchase for researchers who are rightfully occupied with trying to decode the messy and occasionally chaotic world of human interaction.

That's an Interesting Perspective. So, Where Are Your Data? Here, I echo a refrain from my mentor and friend, the late Gerald R. Miller. As the meta-theoretical juggernaut of the 1970s rolled on, Gerry repeatedly asked a question similar to the following: Arguing about the relative merits of these allegedly competing meta-theoretical perspectives is an interesting exercise in academic debate, but when will their research productivity be compared (Miller & Berger, 1978)? Gerry always preferred the pool room of data to the drawing room of debate, and his frustration was occasioned by the tendency for advocates of these various perspectives to make all manner of unsubstantiated claims concerning the virtues of their particular brand of meta-theory, as well as the terrible vices inherent in the other perspectives. In Gerry's view, the problem was that although it should be possible to conduct research in accordance with the tenets of each of these perspectives and then compare the insights about communication produced by each approach, such explicit comparisons were not undertaken. Consequently, even the discerning researcher had precious little *evidence* on which to make a judgment about the relative value of these perspectives.

Roads Not Taken.   As the study of interpersonal communication began to move beyond the experimental study of persuasion during the late 1960s and early 1970s, a number of critical questions concerning important theoretical and empirical issues were marginalized by these meta-theoretical debates. As a result, many of these issues still remain unaddressed. For instance, as interest in the study of nonverbal communication began to gain momentum during this period (Knapp, 1972), a critical question that should have been raised at that time concerns the integrative study of verbal and nonverbal interaction. Researching these two aspects of human action as if they are separable is highly misleading. Seriously addressing this issue at both theoretical and empirical levels at that time may have encouraged researchers to raise basic theoretical questions about the mechanisms responsible for producing both kinds of action and directed their research efforts to the simultaneous study of both of these communicative facets. Instead, with some exceptions (e.g., Patterson, 1983), the nonverbal communication literature mainly grew up around the "channel orientation." This research tradition features studies of such individual channels of nonverbal communication as facial expressions, eye behavior, and gesticulation, while ignoring their relationships with each other

and the verbal messages that, more often than not, accompany them. Issues like these, that are cast at a considerably lower level of abstraction than lofty meta-theoretical issues, are of potentially more relevance to researchers than are their more arcane counterparts, and they very directly lead to theory development, hypothesis generation, and data collection, the kinds of things researchers love most.

Thus, my current view of meta-theory and its relationship to communication research is captured by the following aphorism:

> *Ask not what research question the "proper" meta-theoretical perspective will prompt you to pose. Ask what important, consequential, and interesting question about human communication you can devise.*

POTENTIALLY PRODUCTIVE PATHS

How does one know what is an important, consequential, and interesting question about human communication? I recognize from the outset that such terms as "important," "consequential," and "interesting" have considerable latitudes of acceptable meanings associated with them. However, I will not attempt to address the myriad of potential nuances associated with these terms; rather, my objective here is to provide an alternative to the view that "good" communication theory and research are driven by a particular or "correct" meta-theory.

Even cursory study of a variety of research endeavors reveals that frequently research is organized around "big questions." I have in mind here massive research efforts associated with such diseases as cancer, heart ailments and stroke, HIV/AIDS, and other illnesses. Also included here are efforts to map the human genome. In many of these cases, groups of researchers located around the world organize their research efforts around a small number of big questions with the aim of solving a particular problem. These researchers may embrace competing perspectives; nonetheless, they focus their efforts on the same question. Unfortunately, it is difficult to find groups of communication researchers similarly organized around such big questions about human communication. Of course, there are a few exceptions. For example, there has been continuing concern expressed over the role that depictions of violence on television and in movies may promote aggressive behavior in consumers of such media fare. These concerns have produced an avalanche of research and considerable public attention. However, outside of these few instances, it is difficult to find more than a handful of communication researchers working on the same "big question." Rather than trying to answer the question of why this is so, I will offer some examples of "big questions" that might help us organize our theory development and research activities along more productive lines.

Question One: Whatever happened to the notion of accuracy in the way the media and public officials portray the state of affairs in society? What can be done about it? There is mounting concern from a number of points on the intellectual compass about the way the media report so-called "news." For instance, in 1995 John Paulos, a Temple University mathematician, published a book titled, *A Mathematician Reads the Newspaper,* in which he catalogued many news stories that demonstrated serious factual distortions arising from faulty and misleading data presentations or faulty reasoning about probability. For example, it is not uncommon to witness television news reporters describe increases in such crimes as carjacking and homicide in terms of frequency data, when rate data, that take into account population size, might actually show decreasing crime rates because of increased population. What is even more stunning is that reporters proffering such dramatic stories sometimes refer to the frequency data they have just described as an increase in the "rate" of a particular type of crime. The distinction between frequency and rate data is one that some of us mastered in sixth grade arithmetic.

Egregious examples of statistical misrepresentation can even be found in the advertising of charitable causes soliciting donations from the public. One outstanding example concerned a

Sacramento, California-based organization dedicated to providing services to the homeless. An ad run by this organization that appeared in the West Coast editions of a number of national news magazines proclaimed, *Of 27,000 homeless kids in Sacramento, we feed, shelter, educate and love as many as we can.* During the ensuing furor created in the Sacramento social services and political communities, it was suggested by other equally concerned advocates for the homeless that perhaps there are as many as 500 homeless children in the greater Sacramento area at any given time.

It hardly requires knowledge of differential and integral calculus to understand that which is necessary for making informed decisions in most domains of public affairs. The kinds of errors made by the news media and politicians of all stripes do not even involve basic algebra. The question of why actors and actresses in these domains feel so little responsibility for presenting data to the public in a way that provides a clear depiction of the issue or problem is one that needs to be answered. I believe that researchers in our field are in a unique position to provide answers to this and related questions and to seek solutions to this pressing problem.

Question Two: Whatever happened to studies of the basic processes subserving message production and message comprehension? At first blush, this question would seem to have little relevance to any pressing social concerns; however, I hope to show that it most certainly does. I think most would agree that a significant part of the study of communication processes focuses on how people generate and understand messages. Yet, the amount of research devoted to achieving an understanding of the basic processes underlying message production and message understanding within our field is very small. Although such terms as "sense-making," "meaning-making," and "management of meaning" appear in our field's literature, detailed accounts of the structures and processes responsible for sense- and meaning-making are almost nonexistent. These terms are facilely invoked as if the details of the processes to which they refer are well understood. Curiously, while message comprehension would seem to be a "natural" focal construct for communication theory and research, the number of studies that seriously examine message comprehension in our literature is very small.

By focusing our research energy on basic production and comprehension processes, certain questions get asked about communication that are highly relevant to members of the public. For example, a host of social ills from which this country suffers have been attributed in one way or another to "communication breakdowns," whether these problems involve interactions between doctors and patients, old people and young people, teachers and students, females and males, husbands and wives, parents and children, or members of different ethnic and cultural groups. Within some of our own literature it has recently become fashionable to invoke the notion of "culture" to explain all manner of these communication difficulties. Thus, because males and females, young people and old people are from different "cultures," they are likely to have difficulties making sense out of each other's messages. I do not want to get into the potential problems associated with the mindless invocation of culture (as ill-defined as the construct is) to explain the myriad communication difficulties that arise between people who happen to be members of different social or cultural categories, but I cannot resist pointing out the similarities between this kind of exercise in knee-jerk "explanation" and Abraham Kaplan's Law of the Instrument (Kaplan, 1964).

By focusing attention on message comprehension and production processes, questions about miscommunication and its repair come to the fore. And, while individual differences associated with categorical membership may sometimes be implicated in miscommunication episodes, observing such group differences is not a substitute for a detailed understanding of the basic processes and structures responsible for message production and comprehension. After all, miscommunication and communication breakdowns can occur when people from the same sociological and/or cultural categories interact, and even when these categorical differences between people are potentially implicated in miscommunication, they are mediated through individual psychological processes. Members of the public who experience these misunderstandings and communication breakdowns eagerly await our answers.

Question Three: Why do we believe that we as a people are speaking and treating each other less civilly?   Social commentators representing a wide variety of points along the ideological spectrum seem to feel that public discourse in America is becoming significantly less civil. Examples of this belief abound. Some retiring members of the United States Senate and the House of Representatives, who could very likely run again and win, cite increased lack of civility in the comportment of their peers as one reason for their departure from service in these bodies. Political attack ads have also become the focus of considerable concern. Only detailed historical analysis can reveal whether political discourse in the United States has ever been conducted on a higher plane than it is today. History no doubt contains more than a few examples of unseemly communicative conduct on the part of public officials. It may be our unique penchant as Americans to suffer from national amnesia that makes today's public discourse seem so terrible.

Exercises in "social commentary" presented under the rubric of "talk shows"—where guests make a regular habit of screaming and whining at each other—reinforce the view that uncivil conduct is hardly confined to public officials. Again, I would guess some people might well have exchanged less than cordial greetings when their horsedrawn carriages crossed paths back in the "good old days". And, as I understand it, in the gold rush towns of the Sierra Nevada foothills in the middle 1800s, most people wore side arms and some of them were not very kind to each other.

In my very modest attempt to shed some light on this issue, I sometimes ask people, whose line of work brings them into contact with a large cross-section of the public, to estimate the percentage of customers or clients they encounter who mistreat them, especially verbally, in the course of doing their job. I have asked this question to emergency room physicians, nurses, food service people, store clerks, hotel clerks, and others who have many interactions with a diverse cross-section of the public. In the main, their estimates are very similar. Generally, I am told that between 95 percent and 98 percent of their encounters with the public are relatively pleasant and cordial. Unpleasant, "in-your-face" interactions are quite rare in the lives of these workers. I would be the first to point out the haphazard nature of the sample on which my estimates rest. Nonetheless, in the lives of these people, uncivil discourse appears to be relatively rare. Perhaps it is because uncivil comportment is a statistical anomaly that it has become common fare on those carnival sideshows we now call "talk shows."

My intent is not to dissuade believers from the view that public discourse and action are less civil today than they have ever been in the relatively brief history of the United States. For even if our deportment is more exemplary than that of our forebears, the question is why we believe and talk as if we have become less "civil" in our treatment of each other. Thus, if there has been a discernible decrement in the civility of our discourse, we should seek to find why this has happened, and if there has been no such decrease, we should ask why, at this point in time, we believe there has been one. Either way, there is a "big question" to be addressed here.

My list of "big questions" is far from complete. Perhaps some will not agree that some or all of the questions I have posed here are really all that "big." If this is the case, I have two suggestions. First, feel free to generate your own set of "big questions" for communication research. And second, if you take it upon yourself to critique my list, please be civil.

REFERENCES

Kaplan, A. (1964). *The conduct of inquiry: Methodology for behavioral science.* San Francisco: Chandler.

Knapp, M. L. (1972). *Nonverbal communication in human interaction.* New York: Holt, Rinehart and Winston.

Miller, G. R., & Berger, C. R. (1978). On keeping the faith in matters scientific. *Western Journal of Speech Communication, 42,* 44–57.

Patterson, M. L. (1983). *Nonverbal behavior: A functional perspective.* New York: Springer-Verlag.

Paulos, J. A. (1995). *A mathematician reads the newspaper.* New York: Basic Books.

Schank, R. C. (1982). *Dynamic memory: A theory of reminding and learning in computers and people.* New York: Cambridge University Press.

Schank, R. C. (1986). *Explanation patterns: Understanding mechanically and creatively.* Hillsdale, NJ: Erlbaum.

Schramm, W. (1954). *The process and effects of mass communication.* Urbana: University of Illinois Press.

Editor's Note: Portions of this paper were presented as part of the author's presidential address at the annual conference of the International Communication Association in Chicago, Illinois on May 26, 1996.

Communication Theory for the Twenty-First Century: Cleaning Up the Wreckage of the Psychology Project

Vernon E. Cronen
University of Massachusetts

In the mid-1970s, Barnett Pearce and I began working together on what has become one of the longer-enduring communication theories, "Coordinated Management of Meaning." While the work has evolved in many ways, our original orientation has remained. That was to create a *communication theory, not* a theory *about* communication from the perspective of another discipline. We sought a way of analyzing human action that treated communication as the "Ur" form of human experience. After all these years this orientation still surprises many scholars in NCA.

Last year I was in San Marcos, Texas, with Barnett Pearce and the co-principals of KCC International, London, Peter Lang and Martin Little. We were presenting a short version of our yearly Oxford International Summer Workshop on systemic management. Toward the end of the afternoon on the first day a participant observed that our way of working could be described as "anti psychological." We acknowledged that she was quite correct with respect to mainstream psychology. This did not come as good news to everyone in attendance. Some thought our rejection of psychology could be liberating, but others found it appalling. Those in the latter group said they could not understand how we could offer a principled account of communication without appealing to psychology to supply causal principles.

Whether rejecting psychology evokes a feeling of joyous liberation or appalling threat depends on the context in which one receives the news. It leads me to think of a story about how to deliver such news:

Every afternoon Herr Gutman went to play pinochle with his friends. One afternoon while playing he suddenly fell forward and died. The group decided that his best friend, Herr Lubin, should tell the poor widow.

"Guten tag, Herr Lubin," greeted Frau Gutman, "How are things?"

"How should they be? Fine."

"Have you seen my husband in the Cafe?"

"Sure. Where else?"

"No doubt playing cards?"

"He was, what else would he be doing?"

"And he lost his money?"

"Who else's money would he lose?"

"He lost his money again? That bum! May he be struck dead!"

"Ah," said Lublin brightly, "that's what I've come to see you about."

Like Herr Lubin in the story, I want to set a positive context for hearing news about communication without psychology. Like Herr Gutman, psychology has not proven to be a very good provider. Rather than giving communication scholars a respected place in the social disciplines, it has made us participants in creating a mess. In this paper I want to do three things: 1. Offer a brief review of the received view of social research and the way it moves communication to the margins. 2. Provide an overview of the intellectual and social wreckage that the psychology project has created. 3. Discuss how we can start cleaning up the wreckage left behind by the psychology project. This cleanup task is both our social responsibility and our opportunity for repositioning communication at the center of social research and informed practice.

PSYCHOLOGIZED THEORY: WHAT HAPPENED TO COMMUNICATION?

Psychology rose to prominence in western academic life along with other elements of enlightenment thought. The Oxford English Dictionary traces the English word *psychology* to 1693, *psychologist* to 1727, and *psychological* to 1776. It is probably no coincidence that these multiple forms came into use as British thought adopted the Cartesian program of distinguishing mind from body. It is well to remember that "mind," in our contemporary sense, was a creation of Descartes. It was one of three Cartesian substances, the others being body and God. The British thinkers Locke and Hume criticized important aspects of Cartesian thought, particularly the notion of innate ideas, but they continued the emphasis on individual thought and on a mind-body dualism. This was also the period during which Newtonian science came to be the western scientific paradigm.[1] Newtonian mechanism owed much to dualistic thinking and it is well to recall that Descartes himself was involved in important scientific work.

Kant's nineteenth-century contributions have become the inspiration for the contemporary "cognitive revolution" in psychology. However, while Kant differed greatly from Locke and Hume, his work remained in the same broad tradition, focused on individual mind as the proper unit of observation for social research. I want to review some of the consequences of the tradition shaped by Descartes, Locke, Hume, and Kant. I shall refer to this variegated tradition as "the received view."[2]

Before offering a brief review of the wreckage produced by the received view, one caveat is in order. I want to be clear that this essay is not another exercise in enlightenment bashing. Postmodern critics of the enlightenment challenge its tendency to treat selfhood and social order as a unified machine, and then critique the enlightenment as though it were a singular system rather than a diverse social movement. Mouffe (1996, p. 5.) shares "Rorty's conviction that it is high time to 'peel apart Enlightenment liberalism from Enlightenment rationalism'." By way of example, the interiorized sense of self evolved as an important part of the enlightenment and was invaluable in carving out a realm for independent creative thought. However, it is possible to have a different conception of selfhood and still affirm the importance of independent creative thought. The ancient Greeks began the tradition of western philosophy with a different conception of self than the modern western one. People from other cultures have participated, even reveled, in western freedom and attention to individual creativity without adopting the Cartesian model of the individual. Similarly, enlightenment notions of pluralism and democracy (however imperfectly practiced) may be valued without having to return to Newtonian science. Indeed, physical science has carried on quite brilliantly without Newtonian concepts.[3]

The psychology project replaced the classical rhetorical focus on public action with a strong tendency toward the interiorization of life. The solution to social problems came to be sought at the level of individual "mind." In this received view the coherence of life, and the coherence of any theory about life, became problematic. This came

---

[1]The interested reader should see: Cronen, 1994; Cronen and Pearce, 1991–1992; Dewey, 1929; Geertz, 1973; Harree, 1984; Rorty, 1979; Sampson, 1983; Taylor, 1985.

[2]While I identify the psychology project as the target of my criticism, I want to be clear that this is not an indictment of all work being done in departments of psychology or all those who call themselves psychologists. A growing number of psychologists have come to reject the traditional psychology project, and some of them have come to see communication as the best way to study *psyche*. Scholars such as Howard Giles and John Shotter have moved to communication departments from psychology. However, many communication departments still pride themselves on being a kind of psychology and even offer positions to psychologists of the most traditional stamp.

[3]MacIntyre (1981) has written about the failure of this tradition for our contemporary needs, but I have little sympathy for his ultra-conservative resolution (MacIntyre, 1988). As Stout (1988) has cogently argued, MacIntyre's conclusions are based on a failure to understand the possibilities of social interaction and on adoption of the very psychological ideas that MacIntyre criticizes.

into focus in what came to be known in communication as the "great paradigm debate" of the 1970s (see Cushman & Whiting, 1972; Pearce, 1973; Cushman & Pearce, 1977; Cronen & Davis, 1978). One point of agreement we shared was that, in addition to generality, any good theory has to provide some account of "necessity," or how events and observations are connected. We also agreed with the arguments of Harre and Madden (1975) that traditional psychology rested on Hume's famous skeptical argument that necessity can never be observed. Hume's position was based on accepting Locke's view of mind as a passive receptor for sensory impressions. Associated impressions he called "ideas." Hume, like Locke, thought that each stimulus left its impression on the mind at a unique point in time. This meant that each was a bounded unique event. Building upon these ideas, Hume extended Locke's position by saying the fundamental way by which sense impressions become associated was simple contingency. Notions such as cause or similarity were abstractions themselves. Harre and Madden argued that this skeptical position on the ability of science to observe causal connections opened the door for the use of statistics many years later. If all we can know is contingency, what more rigorous way to understand it than by statistics and experimental design? The result was that statistics became the surrogates for a real account of necessity. Thus, the coherence of social life and theories about it became problematic in two ways: First, the connections between ideas or observations were put beyond the reach of scientific observation; and second, the relationship between what people do and what they think became impossible to study because mind was a different substance from the material world of acting and making.[4]

---

[4]It might be objected that contemporary cognitive psychology does not share Locke's or Hume's view of mind and is in the contrasting tradition of Kant. This has made little difference, because the connections asserted to exist in the cognitive machine are, for methodological purposes, claimed on the basis of statistical associations and the individual remains the primary unit of observation.

As John Dewey (1929/1960) observed, the basic mind-body dualism (inner vs. outer) was elaborated into a whole set of additional ones that followed from it. These included individual vs. society, knowledge vs. conduct, empirical vs. rational, and intellectual vs. practical. It is because of this dualistic mode of thinking, in which thought is separated from action, that the coherence of thought became interiorized and hidden from view in the domain of mind. Dewey also observed that the mechanistic model of Newtonian thought led to dualisms within the interior domain including intellect vs. emotion, intention vs. knowledge, and perceptions vs. conceptions.

The success of the Newtonian conception had special consequences for the social disciplines because that success led to rejection of Aristotle's claims for the special character of the arts of *praxis*. In those arts the goal of study was wisdom, the ability to act and advise wisely in particular circumstances of situated action (*phronesis*). Instead, social theorists adopted what Dewey (1929/1960) referred to as the "quest for certainty" through theories that would have the universal form and generality of Newtonian physics. Adopting this quest necessitated the idea that the researcher must take, or at least strive to take, an objective or third-person position. In the social disciplines the results have so far been less than illuminating. Where are the universal laws of behavior we have been promised? What we have been given is a naive view of research in which the research situation is not understood as a real situated set of communication episodes. Of course, psychologists belatedly came to understand what they called "demand characteristics" and set about blinding and double-blinding experiments. A full communication view would require understanding that nothing removes the researcher's influence from the experiment. One can only change one's position and understand what is happening in light of the way particular methods embody positions for the researcher and subject.[5]

---

[5]There is a clear parallel to contemporary physics, particularly quantum mechanics, here.

The wedding of Newtonian mechanics to the statistical view had dramatic effects on our notion of data. Statistical analyses require data points that are mutually exclusive. This reduction of perceptions to unique data points was entirely consistent with the Lockean and even Kantian view of sensory input. The ideas of human subjects are reduced to either simple associations of data points, or the result of the mind's imposition on sensory data of Kantian categories, personal constructs, or some such in a wholly internal process. From there on it is all quite familiar. Individuals acting in isolation and out of the normal social context (human subjects) are asked to re-present their internal ideas in a way that allows researchers to measure responses as unique "variables." Variables, like Newtonian corpuscles, can be individually measured, correlated, and in some treatments, even their velocity assessed. But, however sophisticated the analysis, there remains the assumption that the data analyzed are independent.

Challenging this approach Howard Gadlin (1977) presented a study of "privacy." In that study he argued that "privacy" is not a variable in the individual mind that can be measured on a scale of more or less and/or divided into factorial dimensions. Indeed, there seemed to be no place for anything like the contemporary western conception of privacy in places like colonial Jamestown. The word was in use, but it had a different, not lesser, place in the lives of those people. It was a place that cannot be understood outside their grammars of identity, community, politics, and moral responsibility. Independent of those uses in situated action, "privacy" has no meaning at all.

Communication has little significant place in the received view. It does not seem to be clearly mind or body. If it is "body" or material (the best candidate of the two) then it is of less importance than mind. It is of use only as a medium for sending thought. By contrast, our rhetorical heritage focused on what persons do together, not on the individual alone. Our rhetorical heritage directs us to ever changing adjustments between people rather than to the pronouncement of timeless prin-

ciples. It also places the supposedly internal psychological processes within the unified social activity of living together. For example, memory was, in that older heritage, internal to the practical art of rhetoric and not a psychological precondition. The received view has little place for us. If I am right about what follows, that's good.

INTELLECTUAL WRECKAGE

The following examples show how the received view denies theorists and practitioners the intellectual tools needed to make socially useful contributions. It does the following kinds of damage to intellectual activity in the social disciplines.

It makes "meaning" itself opaque. I need not repeat here in any detail the brilliant criticisms of the symbol model and Fregian grammar offered by Stewart (1995) and by Baker and Hacker (1980; 1984) respectively. I will, however, venture a bit of summary: The Newtonian perspective produces a focus on objects so that their weight, volume, velocity etc., can be measured. This results in a tendency to treat utterances as "messages," made up of little corpuscles about which we can ask questions such as, "How abstract is that symbol?" "Does his message match her message?" "What valence does the message have?" "What act does the message perform?" "How many messages of this type are produced per minute?" These are all good Newtonian questions. Add a little Locke or Kant and we can ask, "What internal idea is represented by the message?"

Notice how the questions above transform situated conjoint doings into abstracted "things." Context usually disappears, and if it appears at all, it does so as another "thing."[6] It is treated in the received psychological view as a "frame" that can be similarly counted and measured. None of the Newtonian questions ring true to situated experience. What we say is not strictly individual and it

---

[6]The Latin origin of our word "context" is a *verb* that means "to weave together."

is formed as we act into the activities of others (Wittgenstein, 1953; Shotter, 1984; Cronen & Pearce, 1991–1992). Think about responding to an original question by a student in a class, or to an interesting response by a loved one. We may respond with a very original utterance, shaped in part by the way the other put the question. Notice also that the meaning of what is said is not finished at the moment of utterance. The significance an utterance will have depends on the affordances created by the utterance for a specific person, and the way you and others conjointly act into these emerg*ing* affordances and constraints.[7]

The received view is static, divorced of even Galileo's notion of instantaneous velocity. In the received view time is treated as a separate dimension and all we have to ask is when the finished message appeared. If time counts at all, the past counts exclusively (Dewey, 1925/1958). For the past, in the received view, creates the present, and since the future has not yet occurred it cannot be consequential for analysis. This has important consequences for the notion of meaning. As any good systemic therapist knows, the significance of an utterance is never fully finished (Shotter, 1984). Thought is substantialized at a moment of utterance, but meaning is realized as the conversation continues (Cronen, 1995a; Cronen & Lang, 1994).

The psychological view assumes a representational model of language.[8] But how can an utterance represent something having prior existence in the "mind," if its substantialization continuing realization happens within a conjoint process (Cronen, 1995a)? The resulting muddle looks like a serious philosophical issue. However, we do not need to think long and hard about ways to resolve such muddles. As Wittgenstein (1953) argued, what we need to straighten out the muddles over the "meaning of meaning" is not resolution, but

therapy to get over thinking philosophically and psychologically about meaning.

It obscures the coherence of everyday life. Some interpersonal communication texts seem to have been written for Commander Data of Star Trek.[9] They say little about emotion as a coherent aspect of communication. They usually say little or nothing about the emergence or disappearance of emotion in the history or culture and thus ignore the way emotion is constituted in communicative practices (Cronen, 1995a). As to the aesthetics of everyday life they are usually silent. However, without the ability to create moments that are beautiful, thrilling, and awe inspiring, life is empty. This holds for institutional life and public life as well as for intimate relationships. In such communication texts we see a reflection of the old psychological dualism of thinking and feeling accompanied by a clear preference for the rational side of the dualism. However, there is ample evidence that particular emotions are *coherent* features of relational and cultural life (Averill, 1980; Winegar, 1995; Josephs, 1995). When a client reports feelings that he or she cannot account for in personal, relational, episodic, and cultural terms, the sophisticated systemic clinician does not conclude that there is a pure feeling with which to deal and which needs only be named. Rather, the sophisticated clinician identifies this as a disorder precisely because the feeling cannot be constituted by the client as a coherent and identifiable aspect of situated action (Averill, 1980).

The received view also disconnects attention, perception, and recall from the process of communication. They become internal components operating prior to thought and communication. How did this happen? In the Newtonian model, processes like these should be studied each in its own right, like the subassembly of a car or clock. These subassemblies are conceived as "on-line" opera-

---

[7]In CMM theory affordances and constraints are elaborated as the operators of its deontic logic.

[8]This is clearly evident in semiotic perspectives based on Saussaure.

[9]The character "Data" is an android who does not have emotions.

tions prior to conjoint action, or as internal subassemblies that converge on a causal outcome. They are stripped from the particular character of real lived experience. I have even had psychologists tell me that the reason we have to study emotion, intellect, attention, etc., as separate subassemblies is so that we can apply regression equations and assess the contribution of each subassembly to an outcome. I suppose their motto is, "Damn the multicolinearity, full speed ahead!"

Chopping up of coherent action into discrete subassemblies makes it very hard to grasp the coordination and coherence of practices. In the received view, a person must attend to stimuli, *then* hold them in short-term memory, *then* process them into ideas, and finally, "encode" them into language. However, we have to learn how and to what we ought to attend for situated activity. We do not randomly attend to this or that. Learning to play basketball well, for example, crucially involves learning particular ways of focusing attention in patterns of coordinated action. There is no point in attending in a certain way except to deal with circumstances in the process of joint creation. Just as two basketball players learn to "read" each other such that moves are anticipated, conversational partners can learn how to attend to the other in anticipation of how an episode will go on. We do not attend first and then act. We attend as part of coordinated patterns of practice (Dewey, 1925/1958; Gibson, 1966, 1979). The same holds for recall (Shotter, 1990; Middleton & Edwards, 1990).

John Dewey (1896) discussed the absurdity of the received view. He suggested that we think about a lioness stalking her prey. Could it really be that she attends, observes, and then responds? The way she attends and observes is relevant to the kind of embodiment she has and the activity in which she is engaged. When she chases she does not mechanically observe a shift of her prey to the right, then change direction, then observe an obstruction, and then change direction in a set of little jerks. Instead, like a good basketball player, she *projects* a pattern anticipating future possibilities, modifying anticipations as events unfold.

What counts as a significant antecedent, *how* it counts, and *how to* attend to objects and events are informed by her behavioral abilities within a projected pattern. As Dewey (1896) put it, the response informs the stimulus.

It obscures the interactive making of social problems.   When we study problems in society we are typically interested in matters such as how families come into conflict, how people from different cultures encounter difficulties working together, how employees and managers deal with each other, or how nurses and older persons interact to produce patient helplessness or noncooperation. Unfortunately, the received view focuses on individual beliefs and ways of thinking that precede the communication event. This is obstructive on three counts: First, *the way we act is informed by the action of the other as well as the abilities we bring to the situation.* Once, when I was in the hospital for a procedure, the head nurse of the unit said in a *very* sweet voice, "Now, Vernon, are we ready for our procedure? They are all ready for us." To which I responded, "Oooo, his and hers procedures! Sounds a little kinky, but I'm for it if you are." At that point I began to usher her down the hall with me. The nurse quickly moved away from me. She first looked away, then shook her head, smiled and said, "No, Mr. Cronen, it's just for you this morning." The grammatical abilities I brought to the situation included a story about being treated as an adult even though I have reached, as novelist Colin Dexter put it "The cemetery side of the semicentury." The nurse brought a traditional story about how to treat gray haired folks and a story about how to conduct such episodes. I would bet, however, that if you gave the two of us a test of attitudes and beliefs, the test would not have predicted the episode that ensued.

The second point I want to make about that episode is that the way the nurse and I "made sense" of our perceptions was not by some wholly interior process in each of our heads. Rather, *we made sense of our perceptions as part of an active, conjoint process in that situation.* I did not come to the interaction with any contingency plans for what to do if treated in that way and neither did she. The way the nurse used her stories as grammatical abilities opened for me the affordance of making the response I did. I also knew some cultural stories about how to create a form of critical humor by taking her comment literally (an old Groucho Marx technique).

The third point involved here is that *pattern, in this discursive sense, is a very different matter than the statistical notion of redundancy against a background of randomness* (Jacobs, 1990). Frequency is only a rough (though sometimes very useful) clue to what is significant in social interaction. In the episode I had with the nurse there was only one instance of her talking to me as she would to a child. However, there is no way to understand how we got into the episode we did or how conversation between us developed later that day without reference to the affordances and obligations that were created at our first moments of interaction. Many scholars who have studied real communication episodes produced by persons seriously trying to find better ways to live have come to the same conclusion about the importance of pattern over redundancy (see Watzlawick, 1976). My experience working for many years with the therapy side of KCC International, London, has taught me that if we are to understand more seriously problematic episodes such as family violence, we need to look at how persons coordinate their actions in coordinated communication process (see also Harris, *et al.* 1984; Mason, 1993; Boscolo, *et al.* 1987).

It creates a distorted view of data participants provide.   The received view places great value on positioning the researcher as an external observer. This may be very problematic because the way participants and researcher act into the situation influences *how data are conjointly created.* The data we obtain is different depending on whether participants are positioned as objects of interest to an authority, as persons with ongoing responsibilities to each other, as clients of a helping professional, or in some other relationship.

The received view not only casts the researcher in a third person observer role, but also casts the subjects of research in the position of third person observers of their own or others' actions. It is assumed that the observers' position provides the best, if not the only, useful information. Consider the case of "scenario research." The assumption is that the subject, acting as a third person observer, thinks, observes, feels, and recalls when reading a scenario the same way he or she does when responding to persons present with whom they might also have ongoing relationships. In the abstract world of research and observation the first question to ask about action is usually "why?", but in the real world of situated action the first question is usually, "what do I do now?"—that is, if one does any reflecting at all. The consistent preference for third person positions, thus, twists the data, destroying the field validity of observations.

SOCIAL AND PERSONAL WRECKAGE

The worst wreckage is that wrought on persons beyond the walls of the academe. In my judgment the received psychological approach to social life does the following.

It threatens the individuality it values.   One of the great achievements of the enlightenment was to encourage the celebration of individual creative action. As an internal, natural potential, individuality of expression was given a set of legal protections for its expression. However, by assuming that individuality is a natural property of persons, we may be blinded to the need for developing institutions and practices that *constitute* it (Dewey, 1929–1930/1988). 1 have often told the story of the freshman student in one of my classes who was disturbed by my claim that individuality is socially constituted in situated practices. He said:

> *I know I like the same videos my friends do, I wear the same kind of clothes, I listen to the same music they do, and I like to do the same things*

they do. But, no one makes me do any of this. It's my choice. So, I'm an individual, just like everyone else!

How sad. The cultural story that we are naturally individuals leads him to think that intentionality is purely internal and that loss of freedom is identical with external force. Consider the list of similarities he identified and about which he is somewhat defensive: Videos, clothes, popular music. What institutional practices are at play that select out such matters for attention in situated action? Simply blaming the mass media will not do. The major problem with critical cultural media studies is that they typically fail to touch ground in real social action. Such research does not ask the critical questions about how elements of media presentations enter into the coherence of everyday life as people make forms of life together in such a way as to produce the mismatch between claims to individuality and the alarming banality of experience that our students so frequently bring to the university.

It encourages destructive or at least silly searches for communality and inner truth. The treatment of meaning as an individual representation makes it seem a mystery that any person can coordinate action with another. Strange terms are invented such as "intersubjectivity" to make the obvious seem possible. These new terms solve nothing. They leave in place the pseudo problem of how one mind can know another. That "problem" is created by assuming understanding is individual and prior to joint action. When problems occur we look to see which individual is responsible or competent. Because meaning is taken to be internal, and because one can never get "inside the head" of another person, confused action seems natural to the human condition. Even more frightening is the tendency for people to give up on joint action, and to focus on self. The consequences of such self-absorption have been discussed by others. In my own work (Cronen, 1991) I have described it as a paradoxical loop in which inner

freedom loses any criteria for assessing the worth of its own enactment.

When we recognize that things are going wrong we are supposed to enact a very strange kind of reflective episode. We should, according to the psychology project, think about what we "really mean" in the vain hope that we can clarify our ideas and compare them to those of others. Silly searches for our "true inner selves" or the "child within" are undertaken to fix the individual by getting at some hidden reality. Ignored is what is available for exploration: The interactive patterns through which persons create selfhood, ways of thinking, and relationships.

When the received view attempts to include processes of socialization, such processes are described as generalized social norms that create certain kinds of individuals. Those individuals then are supposed to solve the problem of how to act with others who are socialized differently. Deborah Tannen's (1991) work is exemplary. While her work is commendable in many ways, she consistently treats interaction as a problem to solve, rather than the place where ways of living together are created conjointly. Perhaps we should just get along without interaction between men and women. Indeed, some radical feminists have suggested just that. In some silly treatments of gender issues men and women are described as coming from different planets! Here is the mechanical, goodness of fit model run wild. Utterly ignored is the messy possibility that what we have to give to each other are our differences (Arendt, 1958). Cultural notions of male and female interaction are created in a world in which men and women create ways of living together in communication. Analyzing the ways these differences are brought together in patterns of action is useful. However, the real challenge is not simply to identify mutual understandings and misunderstandings. Mutual understanding can lead to repeated patterns that are frustrating, while misunderstandings can sometimes open possibilities for creative actions (Pearce and Cronen, 1980).

The traditional psychological view looks at an instance of interaction and assesses how well the gears mesh based on comparison of the individuals. As persons continue to enact strangely contexted episodes of "looking within," they will continue to "find" differences. Here is a sure way to destroy any relationship! The more differences a couple "finds," the more impossible satisfying conjoint action appears to be.

It inhibits useful political and institutional change. The psychology project bids us to look for the solution to most every problem inside individuals' minds. If the organization of working life makes it impossible to manage, we seek "solutions" by offering stress management programs. The political consequences are clear and have been insightfully discussed by Sampson (1983) and Lannamann (1991). If our arrangements for working life create difficulties for persons and their families, give employees therapy in one form or another. Teach them time management skills, stress management skills, and perhaps as Dogbert (1996) suggests, parenting by computer.

If we do set out to change the institutions, the psychology project abstracts interactive abilities and goals from real organizational life. It offers "team building" exercises. These are typically ways to "fix" the psyches of individuals by giving them "trust" or some such inner thing. These exercises are usually abstracted from the situated actions of particular institutions. Leadership is taught as a set of universal skills. Leadership workshops are usually organized as if leadership is the same thing in all contexts and in all cultures, and as if leadership could have any meaning outside of interaction.

It renders cultural differences either intractable or trivial. By treating meaning as individuals' command of a cultural code, the received view impairs our ability to deal constructively with cultural differences. From the received view our choice seems to be one of these alternatives: 1. Treat another culture as having little to say to us, but deserving respect; or 2. Treat cultural differ-

ences as merely surface features of universal, underlying variables.

Richard Rorty (1986), claiming to follow Wittgenstein, took the first alternative. He said that if the limits of our language are the limits of our world, we can only offer incommensurable cultural systems our distant respect. This is virtually the same as MacIntyre's (1988) position on moral systems. Geertz (1986) called Rorty's approach, "making the world safe for condescension." The difficulty with Rorty's understanding of Wittgenstein lies in his missing Wittgenstein's interactive orientation. Meaning, and thus the limits of one's world, evolves as one interacts with another, making their way with partial and even "misunderstanding." We use the rich resources of culture to make multiple comparisons. We think, "What the other does is somewhat like this, somewhat like that." Then we use these partial comparisons in continuing episodes of communication (Bernstein, 1985).

The second alternative assumes that notions such as "individuality," "sociality," and "face" are universal variables. There are large-scale projects based on this assumption (for example, see Gudykunst & Ting-Toomey, 1988). However, work in ethnography of communication (Carbaugh, 1996), cultural anthropology (Geertz, 1973), and CMM (Cronen, Chen, & Pearce, 1988) strongly challenges this view. For example, what are we to make of the continuum "Individualism-Collectivism" that Hofstede (1980, 1984) claims is a universal dimension along which cultures vary? According to the received view the most meaningful things to know about culture should be regularities behind appearances such as this universal dimension of cultural variation.[10] However, to believe it is universal we have to think that

---

[10]Searching for the reality behind appearances is easily traced back to Aristotle's doctrine of "substances," Plato's notion of "forms," and before them to Thalas and Pythagoras (see Reale, 1987). A more contemporary reflection of this view is the periodic table of elements which were once thought to be the most elemental substances behind the appearances of things.

"individualism" and "collectivism" are culturally neutral terms and not parts of cultural grammars. The Chinese think that they are highly individualistic, each having a very unique place in a web of responsibilities and informed by kinship roles, political order, work relationships, and one's unique abilities. The term "collective," as we use it, does not grasp the position of the Chinese individual in family episodes. The same argument can be made about the terms "reticence" and "face." To understand them we have to know how such terms are used in particular episodes of cultural practice.

If we want to do something helpful about intercultural understanding, we have to place less emphasis on preaching tolerance to the converted. We also have to recognize the limits of teaching others *about* another culture. We will need the kind of theory that will help us create circumstances in which people come together in joint action as first and second person participants. When doing so we will have to engage persons from other cultures in a way that respects their grammars as more than surface manifestations of a deeper commonality.

It obfuscates responsibility.   In the cognitive view, as in the older behavioral one, necessity is treated as a hidden force, dimly seen through the smoky lens of statistical probability. The result is to remove from human action any significant sense of moral order, and replace it with mechanical group tendency. Where value and virtue enter at all, they are reduced to corpuscular beliefs of a particular kind, exerting and undergoing force like any other. It is no wonder that the emergence of the received psychological view coevolved with the separation of social disciplines from the study of ethics. Only recently have there been moves to rectify this. If the way we act is the result of mechanical processes, then, moral questions have little place in the social disciplines of academe. How can we contribute to understanding the moral dimension of human life so long as human doings are the products of hidden mechanical forces or individual preferences?

It disconnects the practitioner from lived experience.   As I have argued above, the psychology project takes the primary reality to be hidden behind the doings of everyday life. This makes what people do interesting only to the extent that these doings provide a peephole into the realities behind them. The actions of real persons become mere symptoms. Therefore, in the received view, an eating disorder is treated as symptomatic of an underlying "mental disorder." Problematic ways of relating to others become symptoms of unresolved Oedipus or Elektra complexes. Difficulties in dealing with complex problems of life are symptoms of some mismatch between an individual's thought and what a well-ordered cognitive schema should include. In critical cultural studies we hear echoes of this same received view. In that tradition the practitioner or social activist thinks in terms of institutional-ideological forces acting upon the individual. What real people do in the rich details of their lived experience is again a mere symptom of the ideological reality.[11]

The result of this search for what is hidden is the disconnection of practitioners from the experience of those they seek to help. Intervention becomes irrelevant to the real situated doings of people. The consequence is that it becomes very difficult to join with people to produce change. Traditional psychologists do not understand clients' abilities. The data they get separate "meaning" from situated conjoint action. There is little training in traditional psychology and consultation in how to act into and explore the grammars of clients by exploring the situated details of life as lived. Because traditional therapists and consultants detach understanding from patterns of joint action and focus on clients' interpretations, efforts to join with clients so as to produce new possibilities for ways of living are undermined (Cronen & Lang, 1994). When a client at a subsequent session reports that things are worse, the traditional thera-

---

[11]It is no accident that Marxists and others in the critical cultural tradition appeal to Freud in their efforts to bridge the macro-micro gap created by their sort of theorizing.

pist wants to go deeper "inside" the client's "mind." What they do not do is examine in detail the episodes of practice in which the client used what was learned in the prior session, and how that new learning was elaborated, changed, or found impossible to use in action. Without a concern for conjoint action, traditional practitioners do not consider how any new learning of the client created affordances and constraints for those with whom the client communicates.

Traditional therapists and consultants with an individualistic and mentalistic way of working also fail to understand ideas, feelings, and stories as aspects of conjoint practices. Consider a consultation to a manager who says that his or her subordinates resist efforts at department reorganization. The consultant wants to "reframe" the situation so that the manager can entertain different understandings of what subordinates do in order to create new possibilities for everyone. The manager, however, is not going to consider a different story about subordinates unless he or she can figure out how to act usefully into a different kind of episode. To facilitate this the consultant must have skills for joining with the grammar of the manager *and* the subordinates in a way that will open the possibility of new practices. The psychology project persists in treating meaning as prior to action instead of as an aspect of interactive ability.

It makes relational problems worse.   Forms of consultation and therapy based on the received view can make problems much more intractable precisely because traditional practitioners think of the person as a container of beliefs rather than a locus of emerging abilities in conjoint action. My colleague Peter Lang (1994) frequently warns his trainees not to "interview into the pathology." He observes that clients in therapy often help the clinician by trying to answer clinicians' "why" questions. Suppose a client comes with fragmented and diverse stories about his or her situation. The clinician with traditional training goes for the pathology inside the head. The client is asked more and

more about how they feel and why they think they feel that way. Soon the client, with the help of the clinician, is putting together a detailed and coherent story within which their problems have a secure and sensible place. Now the problem is more detailed, complete, coherent, and, of course, more intractable. The clinician thinks the problem is now "out" and can be understood! The same holds in organizational and community work.

Therapy based on the received view can "clientize" persons such that it is only in therapy that life makes sense. Clientizing is a danger in any kind of consultation or therapy, but it is a particular danger in the received view. Freudians, for example, want to discover what is behind experience and are concerned primarily with past action. They have to teach clients a Freudian vocabulary before therapy can make any connections. That will further elaborate the individualized view of life with all of the problems I have described above. Moreover, therapy becomes the one place where the client, armed with the Freudian grammar, can coherently discuss problems. Consultants for organizations often run workshops in which they ignore the grammar of particular organizational practices and teach a grammar of "trust," "team building," and "support." The usual result is that participants enjoy the workshop and would like to have another. However, real organizational practices are unchanged. What has changed is that there is a new and highly unrealistic yardstick against which to compare the everyday practices of the organization, and a desire to have more workshops.[12]

---

[12]Once more the same problem that holds for the received view also holds for social activism in the critical cultural studies tradition. It is my guess that this accounts for why so many young activists who are converted to this tradition spend most of their time holding rallies of the faithful and making strident "demands" of those outside the movement. What can you do but make strident demands when you have no means of entering into the detailed grammars of practice that are alive in the situated, conjoint practices of persons? Of course, moments of excitement and joy can only come from inside the movement.

It can turn clients into ideological fodder. I have argued above that the container view of individual clients can make intervention more difficult. An additional problem can arise when the practitioner brings an ideological commitment to their practice.[13] Consider this situation: A woman comes to a therapist and says that she does not know what she is really feeling about her partner. She says she is confused and needs to "sort things out." The therapist thinks that the problem is to find out what emotion the woman is "really" feeling inside. If the therapist has a particular ideology, be that some form of radical feminism,[14] religious orthodoxy, or something else, the therapist may, without any conscious effort to do so, use one of these ideological templates to make sense of what the client is feeling so that therapy can go on. I know of many therapists who say they can identify for the client their "real" emotion. They may say, "You are angry and need to express it," or, "You need to express your grief." Such interpretations are powerful because the clients have before them a professional and a shared cultural idea that there is a preexisting internal reality that needs to be found and expressed.

If emotions are situated roles that are learned in cultural, relational, and personal contexts of interaction (Averill, 1980, 1988), then a different possibility arises. Let's suppose that persons who report confusion are really confused, but not about the match between an inner reality and a verbal label. Rather, they are likely confused in somewhat the same way a student is who cannot make sense of a mathematical problem set by a teacher. Following this later supposition, we would say that the client does not know how to construct a coherent identifiable emotional role in the course of important episodes (Averill, 1988). In that case, the responsibility of the therapist should be to assist the client in constructing identifiable emotional roles in the course of creating new episodes. What the ideological therapist is doing is not identifying the "real emotion," but rather guiding the client into the practitioner's own preferred politics.

WHAT KIND OF THEORY DO WE WANT FOR THE TWENTY-FIRST CENTURY?

Because this paper is part of a panel about taking the helm in communication theory, it is a bit embarrassing to say we should get over the need for theory. Of course, I mean the kind of theory sought by the psychology project. A communication oriented systemic therapist might begin helping us get over this craving for traditional theory by asking, "What was going on when people in communication got the idea that they needed theory?" We could begin to answer by referring to J. A. Winans (1915a, 1915b) in the first two issues of what was then called *The Quarterly Journal of Public Speaking.* The research agenda originally outlined by Winans was a call for scientific, experimental work. It was very much in keeping with the behavioral revolution going on in psychology and thus responsive to the legitimacy in the academy.[15] As we know, Winans's agenda was replaced for many years with figure studies of important rhetoricians outside the sophistic tradition and criticism based on historical models. Winans's agenda, however, returned in force in the 1960s. It returned as part of a revolt inside the discipline against the idea that our job was only to pass on received wisdom, and in part because of the seeming success of the psychology project.

---

[13]This idea has strong roots in Freud's view of the unconscious and is echoed in later psychological writings. For a review and critique see Jacques Bouveresse (1995), especially pages 22–42.

[14]This is not a general indictment of feminist therapy. It is only an indictment of forms of therapy that substitute ideology for an exploration of the unique situation of the client.

---

[15]Hunt (1915, 1916) responded by advocating a form of education close to the ideas of Cicero in *De Oratore.* Hunt's position lives on in many public speaking courses, but his is not the position I am taking here. Hunt was not advocating the careful development of principles from data so as to form a coherent conception of the communication process.

In order to consider an alternative to Winans's agenda, it is useful to examine the etymology of the words "theory," "art," and "practice." The word theory comes from the same Greek root as our English word "theater" and refers to spectator knowledge. That is not the kind of knowledge I think we should seek. In the politics of the contemporary academy it is risky to say that the communication is a "practical art," but permit me to continue this brief etymological exercise. In Aristotle's and Plato's writings an "art" is an activity organized by principle as opposed to simply trial and error learning. In Latin, an art is concerned with fitting, and putting together. Finally, in Scottish law, commanding an art refers to, "Skill in contriving and *active participation*" (*Oxford Etymological Dictionary,* 1966, p. 52) [emphasis added]. "Practice," from the Greek *praktikos,* refers to either "habitual or continuous performance" (*Oxford Etymological Dictionary,* 1966, p. 702). Because of the cultural and political situation of American universities, I can live with the phrase "practical theory," a phrase that Robert Craig has also advanced, but I do so with the full knowledge that what follows here is not "theory" by traditional definitions. In what follows I am proposing a pursuit that deliberately blurs the old distinction between the practical and the theoretical. It is not a call for limiting our discipline to the role of preserving the work of rhetoricians past, or offering alternative "readings" of texts. I am surely not calling for a retreat from rigorous scholarship or speculation without data. The enemy of theory is not practice but hack-work. To take the helm in communication theory for the twenty-first century I propose that we seriously develop "practical theory" by proceeding along these lines.

Communication should be treated as the "Ur" form of human experience.   The practical theories that we develop should look to communication as the primary form of experience *within* which are created ways of thinking, cultures, institutions, relationships, forms of selfhood, feelings, technologies, and specific communication epi-

sodes. If we make that commitment, then we would recognize new forms of communication that arise within the primary process such as performance with audience, writing, radio, television, and the new interactive technologies as much more than new vehicles for ideas. Instead, we would attempt to understand them as aspects of the very formation of our ways of thinking/acting (Ong, 1989). We would begin to study mass communication as an extension of the prehistoric ritual enactment with an audience and try to understand how this form retains aspects of the basic form of conjoint conversation while altering aspects of the communication process. We would also study mass communication as a set of episodes *within* the processes of everyday living. Both of the directions of research suggested above would focus on the differences and connections between forms of thinking, acting, observing, etc. However interesting such research might be, it will have little future if we continue the sharp institutional divisions among rhetoric, interpersonal, and mass communication.

The end for the sake of which we develop theory should be practical wisdom.   Let us end the quest for certainty. We should seek rigorous, principled systems to guide practice. Such systems must be internally coherent and consistent with existing data. However, their value should be assessed by the extent to which their use in real social situations guides practitioners *and* participants to wise understandings and actions. This kind of knowledge the ancient Greeks called *phronesis.*

CMM, for example, offers a set of places to look (very roughly akin to *topoi* in classical rhetoric). Those "places" (hierarchies of stories, moral operators, logical forces, person positions, etc.) guide the researcher and practitioner in the collection and organization of data, as well as in decisions about intervention. The reader will, of course, be aware that acceptance of this kind of theory entails rejecting the sharp division between theory and practice. Practical theory of the sort I advocate should evolve with practice. The consistency that a practical theory exhibits over time should be observable to an outsider as an evolving tradition.

The units of observation should be situated conjoint action. Human beings are born to coordinate their actions from the first weeks of life (Tronik, 1982). If we want to learn how people come to think/act as they do, we ought to try the radical communication approach. People learn to think as part of "forming coordinations" (Dewey's phrase) in which they act into the activities of others (Shotter, 1993; Cronen, 1995a).[16]

This kind of approach would not assume ways of thinking, culture, or selfhood to be external or internal givens. Nor would we treat them as variables in a regression equation with weighted summative effects. Instead, we would study how they are constructed and sustained in moments of situated practice. Individuality, like relationships and institutions, would be viewed as interactional achievements. From that perspective we would attend carefully to the way they are developed in communication practices.

The unit of analysis should be the episode. Episodic analysis avoids treating communication as the exchange of bounded messages. It preserves the vital temporal aspect of communication by treating every utterance as a moment having a past, a presence, and a projection into the future. Treating the episode as the unit of analysis is thus crucial to getting us beyond the symbol model (see Stewart, 1995) and the ties the symbol model has to traditional mechanism.

The episodic unit also provides a way to avoid stereotyping in intercultural work. It would direct us to the very different kinds of episodes in which persons participate. When we might observe Korean women behaving with what we call "reticence" in particular academic episodes, we would not wrongly assume they could not be more assertive than North Americans when bargaining at a marketplace or advising their husbands at home.

Meaning in practical theory should be treated as the ability to "go on." As communication scholars we should think about "meaning" in a way that is informed by the work of the latter Wittgenstein (1953), Dewey (1925/1958), and James (cited in Gunn, 1992). In Wittgenstein's (1953) often cited phrase, we know the meaning of something when we know how to "go on." Communication then moves to the central place. Meaning emerges within communication practices. We should examine the emergence and change of meaning within social action rather than trying to "fix" meanings to analyze an exchange.

The notion of meaning as use would also allow us to escape the dilemma of treating cultural differences as trivial or insurmountable. If meaning is made in an unfinished process of acting, "into the activities of others,"[17] then incommensurability does not constitute an impenetrable barrier. As Bernstein (1985) observed, the richness of culture provides resources of creating partial comparisons sufficient for us to muddle along in the process of creating meaningful intercultural interaction.

The mode of necessity in practical theory should be "rules" in Wittgenstein's sense. The "necessity" in human communication is made, altered, and dissolved in the process of com-

---

[16]There has been a movement in contemporary social theory to replace embodied persons with texts. This approach once again freezes the action at a moment in time and fixes the researcher in an observer's position. Doing so obviates one's ability to research persons' activities and abilities in different positions. Moreover, the unfinished character of communication is lost. The textual view, of course, ignores the way embodiment is part of our knowing, feeling, and acting. The mind-body split is simply replaced by a text-world split.

---

[17]I am indebted to my colleague John Shotter for this most felicitous phrase.

munication. Thus, there is no space between the rule and the utterance. Rules do not emerge as abstractions waiting to be "stuffed" with particular contents. A person grasps a rule by learning the affordances that come after this or that is done. Of course, learning to use rules is not simply learning a set of them. One learns how to learn rules and how to create modifications of them for new situations. We should treat learning to use rules with an eye to how learning to do simpler math problems enhances a child's ability to learn more complex problems.[18] With such an approach we would maintain a distinction between knowing a rule and using a rule (Wittgenstein, 1953). This distinction would change our ways of gathering data on communication abilities, deemphasizing self-reports with subjects in third person positions.[19] The emphasis would shift to communication abilities for doing specific things in specific episodes. When studying communication competence we would seriously maintain an interactional focus to include the way conjoint action transforms what a person substantializes as utterance, into the continuous realization of meaning (Cronen, 1995a).

With a rules approach we do not have to invoke some mystical kind of necessity lurking behind statistical associations.[20] We can set aside the old philosophical problem of accounting for cause at a distance and instead study the way persons work into each other's activities so as to produce episodes of communication. Within such episodes we can study the observable process of how persons "grasp" rules as they conjointly create them.

Understanding rules within an episodic focus would direct our efforts to finding out how rules connect to form the grammars of episodes. For example, we might explore what episodes exist in an organization within which persons can realize the excitement of achievement, and who can participate in those episodes. We would then direct organizational studies in the direction of exploring how situations for learning are afforded and to whom they are afforded.

In addition to dissolving the cause at a distance muddle, this rules-based approach to necessity would allow communication theorists in the twenty-first century to put aside two other pseudoproblems: One is the micro-macro gap. The second, derived from the first, is the sociality-idiosyncrasy gap. Obviously, people do not learn to communicate and then learn relationships and culture. Patterns of interaction in which persons learn ways of attending, thinking, talking, feeling, and moving are not divided into cultural, relational, and personal episodes. All experience has a cultural dimension. This extends even to ways that children hold the hands of caregivers. All experience must also bear the marks of particular relationships and situations, for experience can only be had in specific material circumstances. Cultural understandings will likely interpenetrate the grammars of our relational, episodic, and other stories, and lived experience will reflect back upon those stories. However, the issue is not how an external "force" such as culture can affect at a distance the internal process of thinking or the immediate interactive process of communication. If we regard culture as a description of widely interpretable and widely used grammatical abilities,[21] we set aside an unprofitable theoretical problem of how culture "affects" behavior in favor of a richer approach to research.[22] In that research we

---

[18]This is similar to Bateson's (1972) notion of learning how to learn, but with the difference that all learning has the potential to change a person's abilities so that he or she becomes a different learner. Such changes are not always for the better.

[19]My position is not that we should avoid all third person reports, only that we should regard these as a form of data among others.

[20]There is nothing wrong with stating a general rule to summarize a set of practices as ethnographers often do. However, they ought not to think they have "discovered" underlying rules, but rather that they have written some rule formulations useful to the ethnographer and others for particular purposes. The rules people use are always more complex and nuanced than any rule formulation could be.

[21]The rules composing such grammars are not limited in function to providing connections among utterances and behaviors, but also include the coherent integration of feelings, ways of attending, ways of recalling, and ways of behaving.

[22]Although not identical to his, this view of culture bears an important debt to the work of my colleague Donal Carbaugh.

would examine the grammatical abilities of persons and the circular relationship between grammatical abilities and situated action.

The approach I advocate would also erase the relevance of the individuality-sociality gap. The individuality-sociality gap is often reformulated as the "other minds" problem, or, "how can one mind know another mind?" If we treat communication as the fundamental form of human experience, there can be no meaning, no way of thinking, that is *exclusively* individual. Similarly, the conception of necessity based on emergent rules in conjoint action denies that ways of thinking/acting can be *exclusively* social. No two persons can occupy exactly the same position in a conversation at the same moment, thus a degree of idiosyncrasy will be present in all learning. Whether particular idiosyncrasies are identified and selected for elaboration in patterns of communication will strongly influence the kind of individuality that emerges. Notice, however, that in this approach, individual distinctions are social achievements.

Practical theories should be based on continuity, not dualism.   Useful practical theory for the twenty-first century should treat attention, perception, thought, feeling, action, and reflection as aspects of an integrated communication process. For example, instead of contrasting emotion with intellect, or trying to define how many basic emotions there are, we would explore how, in conjoint practice, feelings come to have rational, identifiable places. Similarly, we would explore how patterns of attention are created and integrated within the conjoint action.

The continuity of action perspective also makes a "great escape" from the mind-body gap problem. It does so much like the way biologists overcame "vitalism." The study of evolution has shown biologists that the movement from inanimate to living matter is a chemical process and therefore no appeal to a miracle for bridging the gap is needed. To make the same kind of move we need to get rid of the noun "mind." I prefer James Edwards's (1985) idea that persons are mindless,

but certainly not thoughtless. Of course thinking is important. Thinking (a neurological process) is an aspect of action, continuous with utterance, perception, movement, and feelings, within conjoint action.[23]

The dualistic heritage leads us to think that learning is uniquely a product of the brain or the mind. By contrast, consider Dewey's (1916/1966) example of a carpenter at work. His or her motor behaviors are adjusted to the state of affairs indicated by sensory organs. That motor response shapes the next bit of sensory experience. The way the brain is changing—learning—is shaped by the body and the materials on which the carpenter works. In conversation a person acts into a situation. Just as the carpenter's understanding is shaped by the resistance and feel of the wood, a conversant's understandings/feelings are shaped by embodiment and the affordances and constraints of others' actions. The brain changes as we act and as we make sense of the world and others' actions. That embodied continuity of change is what we call learning.

Walter Ong (1989) has extended the idea of continuity by arguing persuasively that our technologies are continuous with ways of thinking, feeling, and acting. They, too, are part of the continuous reflexive process, not simply conduits with different capacities. If we take seriously the continuity of technology, thought, feeling, and action, there will be serious matters of disciplinary organization to consider. Most immediately, this view would further question dividing into separate departments or divisions of mass and interpersonal communication. I hope we will evolve a view of our subspecialties that subordinates medium to process. A Ph.D. candidate in the twenty-first century might declare his or her specialty to be the learning of emotional abilities, drawing data from

---

[23]This position is consistent with contemporary neurology. Learning is doing. Brains do not store anything. To learn is to have a chemical change in the brain. Neurophysiologists are starting to understand just how changes in brain structure are materially connected to utterances, movements, and thinking (Harre & Gillett, 1984)

the organization of communication experiences in everyday life including interactive technologies, television, and face-to-face interaction.

Practical theory should treat the logic of social action as a moral logic.   One of the few cultural universals I know is that all cultures have a sense of what can be done, what must be done, what is prohibited, and what is ambiguous as to its acceptability. Cultures also develop ideas about what behaviors are those for which we ought not be held to account. The coherence of life depends on these fundamental ideas about what we can and cannot do with each other. This is consistent with Aristotle's argument that the arts of *praxis* have an intrinsic moral dimension.

The moral dimension of experience is a primary communication concern that cannot be glossed with the simplistic notion that it is good to keep the conversation going. As any spouse or parent knows, there are times when it is good to talk and times to shut up. The approach I am sketching here leads to the idea that morality is intrinsic to the primary human process of creating affordances and constraints in communication.[24] It also suggests that the special quality of human conjoint action is its potential for elaboration and transformation, and that this quality depends on the use of difference, incompleteness, and sometimes sheer muddling through.

What I am advocating would move our conversations about moral order away from abstract discussions of rights and justice, and toward a discussion of responsibility within conjoint action. It would also mean that any discussion of morality would have to begin with some serious consideration of the process of human communication.[25]

---

[24]In the late 1970s I first proposed a conception of rules for CMM theory in which rules are fundamentally moral matters. I expected that this would be one of the most controversial aspects of CMM theory. While our critics have been vocal about many features of CMM, little critical discussion has centered around this claim.

[25]The reader interested in my effort to develop a communication-based view of ethics should consult my essay on communication and post-enlightenment ethics (Cronen, 1991).

Practical theory should provide guidance for practitioners in assisting the transformation of communication practices.   Practical theories in the twenty-first century should include, but not be limited to, exploration and critique. They should provide ways of *acting into the practices of others so as to create new affordances and constraints.* In other words, they should offer a grammar of practice that the professional uses to join with others in order to create new abilities and new forms of action (Cronen, 1995b; Cronen & Lang, 1994). Indeed, a good practical theory should provide the practitioner with grammatical abilities for the conjoint creation of new contexts within which old problems have no place and new affordances may arise. This means that training must include skills for avoiding the temptation to interview into a problem as I discussed earlier in this paper.

I did not say that a sound practical theory creates the "correct" affordances. The approach I propose rejects the quest for ideal communication situations such as Habermas proposes. That is just another form of the quest for certainty. After all, how can one understand patterns of interaction, if we do not explore in action the ways power works in patterns of interaction? Reconstructing episodes requires bringing into the conversation precisely those persons and actions that would, in Habermas's (1979) view, "distort" communication.

Practical theory should regard all research as real communication events.   I have discussed earlier how the failure to treat research as real instances of communication is problematic. We should get beyond reports of research that reflect the old source message receiver model. Instead of reporting what the researcher/practitioner did and then how the participants responded, we should aim to report how the activities of inquiry create affordances and constraints for participants and how participant actions influence inquiry. This is much different than eliminating "bias." Every form of inquiry creates constraints and affordances. I am suggesting that the report of the research in the twenty-first century should look more like the analysis of communication episodes (see Fruggeri, Castellucci, & Marzafi, 1991).[26]

Practical theory should reverse the emphasis on qualitative and quantitative methods. I am not calling for the end of quantitative research, but I am calling for a change in emphasis. Quantitative research keeps the researcher in a fixed, third person position. It works best on static, finished products rather than on that which is unfinished and in process. That is precisely the problem with variable analysis. The variables must stay the same and be independent of each other. They can change only in quantity and in strength of correlation. The independence assumption of statistical tests and the assumption of a fixed set of meaningful variables are hard to reconcile with the conception of meaning as realized in communication (Wittgenstein, 1953).

Statistics can be of help in the preliminary stages of research for making rough and ready identification of social problems and their scope. They can be of good use in demonstrating that some patterns of action are so fixed and habituated that they are amenable to statistical treatment. However, when we need to explore the coherence of action through which problems are created, or how moments of beauty and ugliness are achieved, we will need finely honed qualitative techniques to study the details of practice and develop interventions.

CONCLUSION

Twenty years ago the five of us on this panel, along with my longtime colleague Barnett Pearce, were engaged in what has come to be called the "Great Paradigm Debate" in communication. Some have said that it has all been a waste of time. They say we should return to the field or laboratory and collect data. Surely, what I have argued for here is an empirical approach, but not an objectivist approach. I do not think that there can be data independent of

human thought. We do not constitute the world by our thinking and writing, but we do constitute the objects of knowledge. If so, it is important that we periodically examine what we have been doing and how we might proceed. When one says we ought to go and collect data on how persons send and interpret messages, they have not made a theory neutral statement. To paraphrase Wittgenstein, there is a cloud of theory in a drop of grammar. In this paper I have tried to raise questions about whether the grammar of words like "message," "sending," "theory," and "interpreting" serve us well in directing communication inquiry.

Perhaps the most controversial aspect of this paper is my claim that we should give up the quest for certainty. Some scholars may think that my desire to make communication a practical art amounts to a failure of nerve. To those people I say what I want is a Herring kind of theory. Allow me one last story to explain:

A small, nonviolent man from a village in the pale of settlement was drafted into the Czar's army. In battle he was so frightened that he fought with the energy of 10 men. After the battle the victorious Czar, celebrating with much vodka, lined up those who had fought with the most gallantry. He said he would grant any request to his heroes. As he passed down the line he received requests for gold, horses, castles, and land. To each he responded, "Yes, you shall have it!" When his turn came the little man said, "I would like a nice pickled Herring." "That's all?" asked the Czar, "No gold, no estates?" "No, your majesty, just a pickled Herring, but a nice one." The Czar turned to the quartermaster and said, "Get this fool his herring." The soldier next to the little hero turned to him when the Czar was well passed and said, "What is the matter, you love fish so much? You could have asked for anything." The little soldier responded, "Tomorrow the Czar will sober up. He will have forgotten all about the gold and estates. None of that is real, but a nice pickled herring, that I'm really going to get."

REFERENCES

Arendt, H. (1958). *The human condition*. Chicago: University of Chicago Press.

---

[26]We are now doing this in practical CMM casework by including the interviewer as part of the conversation using our analytic models.

Averill, J. (1980). A constructivist view of emotion. In R. Pluchik & H. Kellerman (Eds.), *Theories of emotion* (pp. 305–339). New York: Academic Press.

Averill, J. (1988) Disorders of emotion. *Journal of Social and Clinical Psychology, 6,* 247–268.

Baker, G. P. & Hacker, P. M. S. (1980). *Wittgenstein, meaning and understanding: Essays on the philosophical investigations* (Vol. 1). Oxford: Basil Blackwell.

Baker, G. P. & Hacker, P. M. S. (1984). *Language, sense & nonsense.* Oxford: Basil Blackwell.

Bernstein, R. J. (1985). *Beyond objectivism and relativism: Science, hermeneutics, and praxis.* Philadelphia: University of Pennsylvania Press.

Boscolo, L., Cecchin, G., Hoffman, L., & Penn, P. (1987). *Milan systemic family therapy.* New York: Basic Books.

Bouveresse, J. (1995) *Wittgenstein reads Freud: The myth of the unconscious.* Trans. C. Cosman. Princeton, NJ: Princeton University Press.

Carbaugh, D. (1996). *Situating selves: The communication of social identities in American scenes.* Albany, NY: State University of New York Press.

Cronen, V. E. (1991). Coordinated management of meaning theory and post enlightenment ethics. In K. G. Greenberg (Ed.), *Conversations on communication ethics* (pp. 21–53). Norwood, NJ: Ablex.

Cronen, V. E. (1994). Coordinated management of meaning: Practical theory for the complexities and contradictions of everyday life. In J. Sigfried (Ed.), *The status of common sense in psychology* (pp. 183–207). Norwood, NJ: Ablex.

Cronen, V. E. (1995a). Coordinated management of meaning: The consequentiality of communication and the recapturing of experience. In S. Sigman (Ed.), *The consequentiality of communication* (pp. 17–65). Hillsdale, NJ: Lawrence Erlbaum Associates.

Cronen, V. E. (1995b). Practical theory and the tasks ahead for social approaches to communication. In W. Leeds-Hurwitz (Ed.), *Social approaches to communication.* New York: Guilford.

Cronen, V. E., Chen, V., & Pearce, W. B. (1988). Coordinated management of meaning: critical theory. In Y. Y. Kim & W. Gudykunst (Eds.), *International intercultural annual: Vol. 12.: Theories of intercultural communication* (pp. 66–98). Beverly Hills, CA: Sage.

Cronen, V. E. & Davis, L. K. (1978). Alternative approaches for the communication theorist: Problems in the rules-laws-systems trichotomy. *Human Communication Research, 4,* 120–218.

Cronen, V. E. & Lang, P. (1994). Language and action: Wittgenstein and Dewey in the practice of therapy and consultation. *Human Systems, 5,* 5–43.

Cronen, V. E. & Pearce, W. B. (1991–1992). Grammars of identity and their implications for discursive practices in and out of academe: A comparison of Davies and Harre's view to coordinated management of meaning theory. *Research on Language and Social Interaction, 25,* 37–66.

Cushman, D. & Pearce, W. B. (1977). Generality and necessity in three types of theories, with special attention to rules theory. *Human Communication Research, 3,* 344–353.

Cushman, D. & Whiting, G. C. (1972). An approach to communication theory: Toward consensus on rules. *Journal of Communication, 22,* 217–238.

Dewey, J. (1896). The reflex arc concept in psychology. *Psychological Review, 3,* 357–370.

Dewey, J. (1934a). *Art as experience.* New York: Minton, Balch & Company.

Dewey, J. (1934b). *A common faith.* New Haven, CT: Yale University Press.

Dewey, J. (1950). *Human nature and conduct.* New York. Henry Holt. (Original published in 1922.)

Dewey, J. (1958). *Experience and nature.* New York: Dover. (Original published in 1925.)

Dewey, J. (1960). *The quest for certainty.* New York: Putnam. (Original published in 1929.)

Dewey, J. (1960a). *Theory of the moral life.* New York: Irvington Press. (Original published in 1908.)

Dewey, J. (1966). *Democracy and education.* New York: The Free Press. (Original published in 1916.)

Dewey, J. (1988). Individualism old and new. In J. A. Boydston (Ed.), *John Dewey. vol. 5: 1929–1930.* (pp. 41–125) Carbondale, IL.: Southern Illinois University Press. (Original published 1929–1930.)

Dogbert. (1996). *Dogbert's top secret management handbook.* New York: HarperBusiness. (As told to Scott Adams).

Edwards, J. C. (1985). *Ethics without philosophy: Wittgenstein and the moral life.* Tampa, FL: The University Presses of Florida.

Fruggeri, L., Castellucci, A., & Marzafi, M. (1991). When differences become a resource: Considerations on the therapeutic role of a rehabilitation service. In L. Gruggeri, U. Telfner, A. Castellucci, M. Marzari, & M. Matteini (Eds.), *New ideas from the Italian mental health movement* (pp. 63–76). London: Karnac.

Gadlin, H. (1977). Private lives and public order: A critical view of the history of intimate relations in the United States. In G. Levinger & H. L. Raush (Eds.), *Close relationships: Perspectives on intimacy.* Amherst, MA: University of Massachusetts Press.

Geertz, C. (1973). *The interpretation of culture.* New York: Basic Books.

Geertz, C. (1986). The uses of diversity. *Michigan Quarterly Review, 25,* 111.

Gibson, J. J. (1966). *The senses considered as perceptual systems.* Boston: Houghton Mifflin.

Gibson, J. J. (1979). *The ecological approach to visual perception.* London: Houghton Mifflin.

Gudykunst, W. & Ting-Toomey, S. (1988). *Interpersonal communication.* Newbury Park, CA: Sage.

Gunn, G. (1992). *Thinking across the American grain.* Chicago: University of Chicago Press.

Habermas, J. (1979). *Communication and the evolution of society.* Boston: Beacon.

Harre, R. (1984). *Personal being.* Cambridge, MA: Harvard University Press.

Harre, R. & Gillett, G. (1984). *The discursive mind.* Beverly Hills, CA: Sage.

Harre, R. & Madden, E. H. (1975). *Causal powers.* Oxford: Basil Blackwell.

Harris, L., Alexander, A., McNamee, S., Stanback, M., & Kang, K-W. (1984). Forced cooperation: Violence as a communicative act. In S. Thomas (Ed.), *Communication theory and interpersonal relations Vol. 2.* (pp. 20–32). Norwood, NJ: Ablex.

Hofstede, G. (1980). *Culture's consequences: International differences in work-related values.* Beverly Hills, CA: Sage.

Hofstede, G. (1984). Hofstede's culture dimensions: An independent validation using Rokeach's value survey. *Journal of Cross-Cultural Psychology, 15,* 417–433.

Hunt, E. L. (1915). The scientific spirit in public speaking. *The Quarterly Journal of Public Speaking, 1,* 185–193.

Hunt, E. L. (1916). General specialists. *The Quarterly Journal of Public Speaking, 2,* 253–263.

Jacobs, S. (1990). On the especially nice fit between qualitative analysis and the known properties of conversation. *Communication Monographs, 57,* 241–249.

Josephs, I. E. (1995). The problem of emotions from the perspective of psychological semantics. *Culture and Psychology, 1,* 279–288.

Lang, P. (1994). On systemic principles. Lecture given at the Kensington Summer Advanced Workshop on Systemic Therapy. Oxford, UK.

Lannamann, J. W. (1991). Interpersonal communication as ideology. *Communication Theory, 3,* 179–203.

MacIntyre, A. (1981). *After virtue.* Notre Dame, IN: University of Notre Dame Press.

MacIntrye, A. (1988). *Whose justice? Which rationality?* Notre Dame, IN: University of Notre Dame Press.

Mason, M. (1993). Shame: Reservoir of family secrets. In E. Imber-Black (Ed.), *Secrets in families and family therapy* (pp. 29–43). New York: W. W. Norton.

Middleton, D. & Edwards, D. (Eds.). (1990). *Collective remembering.* Beverly Hills, CA: Sage.

Mouffe, C. (1996). *Deconstruction and pragmatism.* London: Routledge.

Ong, W. J. (1989). *Orality and literacy: The technologizing of the word.* London: Routledge & Kegan Paul.

Pearce, W. B. (1973). Consensual rules in interpersonal communication: A reply to Cushman and Whiting. *Journal of Communication, 23,* 160–168.

Pearce, W. B. & Cronen, V. E. (1980). *Communication, action, and meaning: The creation of social realities.* New York: Praeger.

Reale, G. (1987). *From the origins to Socrates.* (J. R. Catan, Trans.) Albany, NY: State University of New York Press.

Rorty, R. (1979). *Philosophy and the mirror of nature.* Princeton, NJ: Princeton University Press.

Rorty, R. (1986). On ethnocentrism: A reply to Clifford Geertz. *Michigan Quarterly Review, 25,* 634.

Sampson, E. E. (1983). *Justice and the critique of pure psychology.* New York: Plenum.

Shotter, J. (1984). *Social accountability and selfhood.* Oxford: Basil Blackwell.

Shotter, J. (1990). *Knowing of the third kind.* Utrecht, Netherlands: Utrecht University Press.

Shotter, J. (1993). *Conversational realities.* London: Sage.

Stewart, J. (1995). *Language as articulate contact.* Albany, NY: State University Press of New York.

Stout, J. (1988). *Ethics after babel: The languages of morals and their discontents.* Boston, MA: Beacon.

Tannen, D. (1991). *Conversational style: Analyzing talk among friends.* Norwood, NJ: Ablex.

Taylor, C. (1985). *Philosophy and the human sciences: Philosophical papers (Vol. 2).* Cambridge: Cambridge University Press.

Tomm, K. (1984). One perspective on the Milan systematic approach. Part 1. Overview of development, theory, and practice. *Journal of Marital and Family Therapy, 10,* 113–125.

Tronick, E. (1982). *Social interchange in infancy.* Baltimore, MD: University Park Press.

Watzlawick, P. (1976). *How real is real?* New York: Random House.

Winans, J. A. (1915a). The need for research. *The Quarterly Journal of Public Speaking, 1,* 17–32.

Winans, J. A. (1915b). Should we worry? *The Quarterly Journal of Public Speaking, 1,* 197–201.

Winegar, L. T. (1995). Moving toward culture-inclusive theories of emotion. *Culture and Psychology, 1,* 269–277.

Wittgenstein, L. (1953). *Philosophical investigations.* New York: Macmillan.

Zimmerman, D. H. & D. Boden, (1991). Structure in action: An introduction. In D. Boden, & D. H. Zimmerman, (Eds.), *Talk and structure* (pp. 3–21). Berkeley, CA: University of California Press.

CHAPTER 2.

AT THE HELM IN INTERPERSONAL COMMUNICATION: RELATIONAL COMMUNICATION

Introduction

Teresa Sabourin
University of Cincinnati

It is an honor to be here today to introduce four out-standing relational communication scholars. Their work has been pivotal in creating and advancing both theory and research in the areas of marriage and family, friendship and romantic relationship development, and nonverbal communication and deception. The quality of their work is evidenced by the numerous awards and honors they have received; the quantity of their work is proven by publication of more than 200 journal articles, 135 book chapters, and 50 books over the last two decades. Our four speakers today, Dr. Mary Anne Fitzpatrick, Dr. Steven Duck, Dr. Judee Burgoon, and Dr. Leslie Baxter, are indeed the movers and shakers in relational communication.

Mary Anne Fitzpatrick, our first presenter, completed her Ph.D. in the Speech Department of Temple University in 1976. Her work as a relational scholar has focused upon marriage and family relationships; most notably, she has developed the typological approach to marital interaction. Dr. Fitzpatrick has been on the faculty of the University of Wisconsin, Madison, in the Department of Communication Arts, since 1978. She has been Chair of that department since 1993. Her work on family interaction appears in a book recently published by Sage, titled *Explaining Fam-*

ily Interactions (1995). The paper that she is going to present today is called "Interpersonal Communication on the Starship Enterprise: Resilience, Stability, and Change in Relationships in the Twenty-First Century."

The second presenter, Professor Steven Duck, received his doctorate from the University of Sheffield, Department of Psychology, in 1971. His work over the last 25 years has been devoted to the study of social and personal relationships. His recent work examines the meaning making process in social relationships, with an emphasis on everyday talk. Steven Duck has been on the faculty of the Department of Communication Studies at the University of Iowa since 1986, where he is the Daniel and Amy Starch Research Professor and the Chair of the department. The paper that he is going to present today is "Helms and Bridges: Relational Communication as Conceptual and Personal Linkage."

The next presenter is Dr. Judee Burgoon, who earned her Ed.D. from West Virginia University, in Communication and Educational Psychology, in 1974. Dr. Burgoon's work has been instrumental in advancing investigation of nonverbal communication and deception. Since 1984, Dr. Burgoon has been on the faculty and served as graduate director in the Department of Communication at the University of Arizona. She is going to present a paper called "It Takes Two to Tango: Interpersonal Adaptation and Implications for Relational Communication."

The final presenter on this distinguished panel is Dr. Leslie Baxter. Dr. Baxter completed her Ph.D. in the Department of Speech Communication at the University of Oregon in 1975. Her innovative work focuses upon interpersonal relationship development. She has made a significant contribution to this area through her explication and application of a dialectical perspective. She is currently on the faculty at the University of Iowa in the Department of Communication Studies. The paper she is going to present is on "Locating the Social in Interpersonal Communication."

Interpersonal Communication on the Starship Enterprise: Resilience, Stability, and Change in Relationships in the Twenty-First Century

Mary Anne Fitzpatrick
University of Wisconsin, Madison

INTRODUCTION

Researchers and theorists who study the family generally agree that the values, social constraints, and behaviors that affect family structures have changed a great deal over the past decades. The ability of families to survive in the face of such changes suggests that families are flexible. But what is it about family members that allows for this flexibility? Many scholars have turned to family communication as a means to answer this question. Whether it be in response to events external to the family or events that occur within the family context, family communication influences how members adapt and function. In this essay, I would like to discuss the research that I have conducted on family communication in the past 20 years and make some predictions based on that research about the nature of relationships between men and women and within families in the next century.

COMMUNICATION IN MARRIAGE AND THE FAMILY

Within any sample of couples or families, there are a limited number of marital or family types that can be isolated. A decade of research by Fitzpatrick (1976, 1977, 1981, 1984, 1988) has established empirically a typology for characterizing married couples. (For a comprehensive discussion of the typology's development and validation, see Fitzpatrick, 1988, *Between Husbands and Wives*). Briefly, the procedures followed by Fitzpatrick in the development of the typology were: (a) identifying significant conceptual areas in marital and family life, (b) developing measures that delineated

dimensions of marital life, and (c) comparing spouses' relational definitions to determine couple types.

The Relational Dimension Instrument (RDI) identified three dimensions of married life: ideology (e.g., relational beliefs, values, and standards), interdependence (e.g., degree of connectedness), and conflict (e.g., behaviors of avoidance engagement). By comparing spouses' responses to the RDI, couple types were characterized as Traditional, Independent, Separate, or Mixed. If both spouses agree independently on their relational definition, they are categorized as pure types (i.e., Traditional, Independent, or Separate), whereas husbands and wives who diverge in their perspectives of marriage are classified as Mixed couple types.

Traditional couples hold conventional ideological values about relationships (e.g., wives change their last names, infidelity is unacceptable), demonstrate interdependence (e.g., share time, space, companionship), and describe their communication as nonassertive but engage in rather than avoid marital conflicts. By contrast, Independents espouse nonconventional values about relational and family life (e.g., relationships should not constrain individual freedom), exhibit a high degree of sharing and companionship that qualitatively differs from Traditional couples in that Independents maintain separate physical space (e.g., bathrooms, offices), do not keep regular time schedules, yet tend to engage in rather than avoid conflict. Finally, couples who define themselves as Separates are conventional on marital and family issues yet at the same time uphold the value of individual freedom over relational maintenance, have significantly less companionship and sharing (e.g., maintain psychological distance, reflect autonomy in use of space), and describe their communication as persuasive and assertive, but avoid open marital conflict. Mixed couple types include spouses who define marital life differently on the dimensions of ideology, interdependence, and communication. Approximately 40% of couples surveyed fall into one of the mixed types and no one mixed type predominates numerically (Fitzpatrick, 1988).

The delineation of a typology of marriage through the use of a carefully constructed and thoroughly tested self-report device that questions spouses about important dimensions of relationships would scarcely be worthy of notice without the variety of methods that have been employed to explore its ramifications. Specifically, direct observations have been made of conflict, control, and disclosure processes within marriages of the various couple types. Expectations about marriage reflected in the typology can help to describe the communication behaviors of the Traditional, Independent, Separate, and Mixed couple types during conflict. The following representation of the various couple types emerges from the research on conflict interactions.

Traditionals tend to avoid conflict more than they realize but, in general, are cooperative and conciliatory. For these couples, conflicts are somewhat easier to resolve because traditionals tend to argue about content rather than relational issues. Traditionals value parenting, spending time with each other in close proximity, and place marriage (duality) over independence. Of particular note is that although the husband in this marriage exhibits many stereotypical masculine interpersonal behaviors, this husband is able to self-disclose to his wife.

Independents are constantly renegotiating relational roles and each spouse resents a partner's attempt to avoid conflict by withdrawing. Independents value their careers, co-workers, and/or friends outside the relationship, and need their own personal space. These couples can disclose

both positive and negative feelings to their spouses. The downside for Independents is that because of their high expressivity, they often experience serious conflicts with each other.

Separates touch base with partners regularly, but maintain both psychological and spatial distance. Most Separates seek emotional support/reinforcement outside the relationship. Overall Separates experience little direct conflict in their marriage for two reasons. First, because Separate couples agree with one another on a number of basic family issues, they have less potential for disagreements. Second, Separates appear unable to coordinate their interaction effectively to engage in a direct open discussion of disagreements. A Separate spouse may display outright hostility but quickly retreat if a partner disagrees. In other words, Separates rarely discuss conflict issues and withdraw immediately when spouses introduce stressful topics.

The conflict patterns of Mixed couple types depend on the specific combination of relational definitions under scrutiny. For example, Separate/Traditionals rarely argue but when they do argue, the burden of initiating a discussion of difficult issues falls to the wife. In the Traditional/Independent pairing, the wife is more likely to be conciliatory and prone to compromise.

As we see in the next section, couple types not only predict the patterns of communication between husbands and wives but also predict the family communication environment more generally.

Dimensions of Communication

Two fundamental dimensions of communicative behavior are conformity orientation and conversation orientation (Ritchie & Fitzpatrick, 1990; Fitzpatrick & Ritchie, 1994). *Conformity orientation* refers to the degree to which families create a climate that stresses homogeneity of attitudes, values, and beliefs. Families on the high end of this dimension are characterized by uniformity of beliefs and attitudes and interactions that focus on harmony and often obedience to the parents. Families on the low end of this dimension are characterized by heterogeneous attitudes and beliefs, a greater individuality of family members, and by interactions that focus on the uniqueness of the family members and their independence from their families.

Conversation orientation is defined as the degree to which families create a climate where all family members are encouraged to participate freely in interaction about a wide array of topics. In families on the high end of this dimension, family members freely, frequently, and spontaneously interact with each other without many limitations in regard to time spent and topics discussed. In families on the low end of this dimension, family members interact less frequently with each other and there are only a few topics that are openly discussed with all family members.

Fitzpatrick and Ritchie (1994) analyzed a random sample of 169 families and found a clear relationship between Fitzpatrick's typology and family communication environments defined along the dimensions of conformity and conversation (McLeod & Chaffee, 1972).

Families that are high on both conversation and conformity orientation are labeled *consensual*. Their communication is characterized by pressure toward agreement and by an interest in new ideas without disturbing the existing power structure within the family. Children in these families may either adopt their parents' views or escape into fantasies. These families are most likely to be headed by parents that fall into Fitzpatrick's Traditional category.

Families high in conversation orientation but low in conformity orientation are labeled *pluralistic* families. Communication in these families is characterized by open, unconstrained discussions that involve all family members, which foster communication competence and independent ideas in children of such families. Parents heading pluralistic families are likely to be of Fitzpatrick's Independent type.

Families low on conversation orientation but high on conformity orientation are labeled *protective* families. Communication in these families is characterized by emphasis on obedience and little

concern with conceptual matters. Children in these families are easily influenced and persuaded by outside authorities. Parents heading protective families are likely to be of Fitzpatrick's Separate type.

Families low on conversation and conformity orientation are labeled *laissez-faire* families. Their communication is characterized by little and uninvolved interactions among family members about a limited number of topics. Most members are emotionally divorced from their families. Children of these families are more likely to be influenced by external social groups. Parents heading these families are likely to be Separate/Independent or of another Mixed type of Fitzpatrick's typology.

Linking these two approaches to communication, we argue that family members have internal working models of family communication and relationships. We view these family communication environments as *schemata*. These schemata are knowledge structures that represent the internal world of the family and provide a basis for interpreting what family members say and do. Each schemata has its own set of beliefs, attitudes, and philosophies about family life and each is characterized by very specific communication behaviors. Family communication schemata influence attention and perception, memory for messages, inferences communicators draw from behaviors, and psychosocial outcomes (Fitzpatrick & Ritchie, 1994).

Families with a Traditional-Consensual schema encourage children to discuss issues and express opinions, although they are expected to agree ultimately with the parents. Although the climate in these families is lively, warm, and interesting, the hierarchy in the family remains largely unchallenged. Families with an Independent-Pluralistic schema emphasize communication and the expression of ideas and opinions but place little pressure on children to conform to parental viewpoints. Children in these families are encouraged to develop their own interests, to express needs and desires openly, and to strive to attain personal goals. Families with a Separate-Protective schema place a strong emphasis on child conformity but downplay interaction, maintaining an appearance of family peace and harmony by prohibiting dissent. Families with an Independent/Separate or Laissez-Faire schema similarly downplay interaction and exert little pressure on children to conform. Parents and children in these families tend to pursue individual goals with little concern as to the need and desires of other family members, fostering individuality and personal freedom by accident rather than through open and affirming interaction.

RESILIENCE, STABILITY, AND CHANGE IN RELATIONSHIPS

What does this 20-year program of research say about resilience, stability, and change in relationships? The answers to this question have implications for the future of families and for future studies of family communication. Twenty years ago, I began this program of research with attention to the ideologies that underlie the formation and maintenance of personal relationships. Indeed, one major side of the conceptual triangle of the typology was the couple's level of agreement with a *traditional* orientation, which views love and marriage as providing people with stable, committed relationships that tie them to a larger society, versus a more *therapeutic* orientation, which views love and marriage primarily in regard to the psychological gratifications given to the individuals. These ideological conceptions of relationships include a concern for gender role attitudes, although they are far more encompassing than the typical discussions that rely only on gender roles or gender specializations to differentiate marriages.

Over the course of this research, we have seen a move across all types toward more egalitarian notions of male and female roles. Whereas the general ranking of the types remains the same (i.e., Independents are more egalitarian than others), the overall supportive attitudes toward liberalization have increased. Unfortunately, although many men give lip service to equality, it appears that most do not approve of its concrete application. Even when they work outside the home, women still do most of the housework and childcare. Over time, men have increased their contribution to childcare but this increase must be measured in minutes a day (Goode, 1992). Severe discrepancies between attitudes and behaviors lead inevitably to conflicts. We should expect to see even greater family conflict as the society moves toward equality.

The second major implication of this perspective for the future of personal relationships concerns the functionality of these various family forms. We began 20 years ago with the assumption that one style of communication was not satisfying for all. In other words, there were many paths to a happy and fulfilling family life. In *What Predicts Divorce,* John Gottman (1994) finds strong support for the existence and stability of the three major couple types: his validating style is Traditional; his volatile style is Independent; and his conflict avoidant style is Separate. The parallelism in the work is strong and as he states (p. 137), "Independent replication and corroboration is one of the rare joys of scientific work."

Both programs of research agree that Mixed/Laissez-Faire families experience many negative outcomes and may be dysfunctional. Indeed, the inability to coordinate on three basic concepts of relational life relates to many negative psychosocial outcomes (Fitzpatrick & Koerner, in press). The issue of the functional Separate family is still an open one. In future research, we may find two subgroups of Separates. The first type are the regulated and functional Separates who are happy with their definition of the relationship and manage relational tension, when it exists, by avoidance. The second type of Separate family views this pattern as a deviation from the ideal form of the Traditional family. The deviation from the ideal leaves Separates depressed, sad, and dejected (Higgins, 1987). In partial support of this idea, Segrin and Fitzpatrick (1992) found wives in Separate marriages are significantly more likely than other wives to be depressed.

A final implication of this program of research for the future of the family as well as its scientific scrutiny is nature of the long-term personal investment that individuals make in the collectivity of the family. In 1988, I (Fitzpatrick, 1988) argued that the Independent relationship with its commitment to personal gratification in relationships was the vanguard of the future. In other words, individuals in this type of relationship are committed to their relationships only as long as they are personally satisfying. It appears that I was more right than I knew. In analyzing world changes in divorce patterns, the eminent family sociologist William J. Goode (1993) argues that there is a worldwide increase in divorce rates and cohabitation with a concomitant decrease in remarriage rates. These rates signal the decreased investment of people in the collectivity of the family.

How long the steady weakening of the family can continue is an open question. Clearly counterforces and opposing pressures will be brought to bear because as Goode (1993) reminds us the economy and the society as a whole cannot function reasonably well without the family. For communication researchers, it seems clear that we need to broaden our studies of the family in two ways. First, we need to study the many forms of modern family life and employ definitions of the family that depend on how families define themselves rather than definitions based on genetic or sociological criteria (Fitzpatrick & Vangelisti, 1995). Second, we need to explore the connection among commitment, communication, and the collectivity of the family. By documenting both of these areas, we will be poised to comment on communication in personal and family relationships in the next century.

CONCLUSION

The picture I have painted is a fairly bleak one. It is based on the empirical evidence. It brings up for me a question that we need to pose to ourselves as we think about studying relationships in the next century. In this program of research, the orientation to conversation seems to predict, and be very related to, many good outcomes for family life. If

an open communication environment seems to be protective of our relational health, why is it so difficult for us to form relationships based on openness and expressivity?

We may be evolutionarily prewired not to engage in open communication because to be open is to display vulnerability. For a number of years, many in the discipline proselytized for more open communication and self-disclosure. That work was often proscriptive. Our efforts now need to be directed toward conceptualizing openness and why expressivity appears to be such a difficult goal in personal relationships.

REFERENCES

Fitzpatrick, M. A. (1977). A typological examination of communication of relationships. In R. B. Rubin (Ed.), *Communication yearbook, 1* (pp. 263–275). New Brunswick, NJ: Transaction Books.

Fitzpatrick, M. A. (1981). Children as audience to the parental relationship. *Journal of Comparative Family Studies, 11,* 81–94.

Fitzpatrick, M. A. (1984). Marital interaction: Recent theory and research. In L. Berkowitz (Ed.), *Advances in experimental social psychology* (pp. 1–47). New York: Academic Press.

Fitzpatrick, M. A. (1988). *Between husbands and wives: Communication in marriage.* Newbury Park, CA: Sage.

Fitzpatrick, M. A., & Best, P. (1979). Dyadic adjustment in relational types: An examination of consensus, cohesion, affectional expression and satisfaction in enduring relationships. *Communication Monographs, 46,* 167–178.

Fitzpatrick, M. A., & Koerner, A. (1996). Family communication schemata and social functions of communication. Paper presented at the International Research Colloquium on Communication Research. Moscow, July 1996.

Fitzpatrick, M. A., & Koerner, A. (in press). Family communication schemata and children's resilience. In H. McCubbin (Ed.), *Resiliency in families.* Madison: University of Wisconsin Press.

Fitzpatrick, M. A., Marshall, L. J., Leutwiler, T. J., & Krcmar, M. (1996). The effect of family communication environments in children's social behavior during middle childhood. *Communication Research, 43,* 279–406.

Fitzpatrick, M. A., & Ritchie, L. D. (1994). Communication schemata within the family. *Human Communication Research, 20,* 275–309.

Fitzpatrick, M. A., & Vangelisti, A. (1995). Extending family boundaries. In M. A. Fitzpatrick & A. Vangelisti (Eds.), *Explaining family interaction* (pp. 253–256). Newbury Park, CA: Sage.

Goode, W. J. (1992). Why men resist? In B. Thorne & M. Yalom (Eds.), *Rethinking the family: Some feminist questions* (pp. 287–310). Boston: Northwestern University Press.

Goode, W. J. (1993). *World changes in divorce patterns.* New Haven: Yale.

Higgins, E. T. (1987). Self-discrepancy: A theory relating self and affect. *Psychological Review, 94,* 319–312.

Helms and Bridges: Relational Communication as Conceptual and Personal Linkage

Steve Duck
University of Iowa

I am fearful that we will see many nautical metaphors in this series and that by the end of the convention we will have been through stormy waters, charted new oceans, sought safe havens, and navigated many obstacles as we set sail to new horizons, rather too often to avoid us becoming (sea)sick of them. Part of my message, however, is that such everyday forms of thinking—metaphorical ways of thinking—are guiding not only our conference papers (and the themes in them) but also our research and our thinking as relating human beings. My point will ultimately be that the coalescence or joint acceptance of such styles of thought is the essence of both relating and research on relating. It is also the aspect of the enterprise so clearly overlooked by those who are unfamiliar with the interpersonal communicational approach to relationship research (a word that has the "sea" in it).

From my point of view in the crow's nest, communication scholars have more to contribute to the conceptualization of relationship than has previously been recognized and I was pleasantly surprised recently to see this recognized by an eminent social psychologist (Berscheid, 1996). Less recognizable, however, is the representation of interpersonal communication that is contained in the model of "Communication" offered in the recent *Handbook of Social Psychology*. We certainly have our work cut out in sharing the theoretical and conceptual contributions that communication studies can make to relationship research even though the trend towards interdisciplinary research rather than disciplinary imperialism seems to be one of the strongest recent developments (Acitelli, 1995).

Three interwoven strategic threads form the basis for addressing the question of how communication studies can become a John Paul Jones on the relational research seas. A strength that I see in communication studies is the dedication to representation of real-life relationships rather than only to the abstractions of them reflected in some researchers' theories and terminologies of relationships in different disciplines. Secondly, I believe that colleagues in this discipline—my own colleague Leslie Baxter being one of the most vigorous and distinguished—have done more serious thinking than most about the nature of the "person" reflected in research practices, theories, and presumptions. Thirdly, communication studies has a tradition—admittedly regarded as a weakness by some (Berger, 1991) of respecting, drawing from, and ultimately in my view improving and synthesizing existing research from different disciplines (based, as each always is, on somewhat different underlying presumptions and patterns of thought).

Recognizing perhaps that most ancient sailors spent more time swabbing the decks and mending nets than navigating new territories (of which there were fewer and fewer as time went by even though the decks still needed to be cleaned each day), those piloting the communicational seas seem to me to have recognized the importance of the mundane. We take the lead in charting and studying personal relationships in lived experience as distinct from unusual, atypical, and unrepresentative forms and actions of personal relationships found in research carried out in the labs of those who carry Likert sextants in every pocket. To lose sight of everyday lived experience is to lose sight of the purpose of research on personal relationships and to overlook the importance of "context" in modifying and influencing the ways in which relat*ing* is carried out (Duck, 1993; 1994a). As Duck, West, and Acitelli (1997) have noted, "A weak view of 'context' is that it is the momentary backdrop against which actions are carried out (such as place, environment, or situation; Argyle, Furnham, & Graham, 1981)—rather like a scenic backdrop in a stage play or as a black back-cloth can give a portrait photograph a different "feel" from a white one. A stronger view is that place, time, ritual, ceremony, celebration, and other temporal contexts render different the experiences of relaters on those occasions or in those places (Werner, Altman, Brown, & Ginat, 1993). The strongest view is that context is like the water in which fishes swim, and which covers everything that is done there, such that relationships are steeped in such cultural attitudinal, societal, normative, conversational, and dialectical contexts (Allan, 1993; Baxter & Montgomery, 1996).

Context is very powerful, and the most powerful and extensive contexts are the ones that we pilot every day. Recall that Delia (1980) urged nearly 20 years ago that we should note the fact that most personal relationships are not busily and steadily increasing in intimacy in the ways that are implied in most theories of close relationships. Instead, they are fluctuating and are being managed, somewhat like a sailing ship whose interaction with different forces needs to be handled and controlled in order for *any* course to be sustained. This is true of relationships with neighbors and workmates, but even also true of those with parents and children, and for the most part, with friends too. Relationships are established at some sort of equilibrial level and held there by everyday process and everyday work and management, and are not restlessly edging forward to an Ultimately Unreachable Intensity that represents the ever receding horizon. We're swabbing the decks of these relationships most of the time just to keep them operative; or we are trimming sails and tightening ropes. Only rarely do we lash ourselves to the helm to steer them strenuously through multitudinous seas. We just keep them working and they keep on sailing ahead, going somewhere or other we know not where.

Let me put this another way: the context for most experience of relationships is daily life and daily life is a messy business, not a steady state. We need to take account of the tides and waves of relationships, not just the rocks on the charts through which such surging change rushes and recedes. When we do research, the thing we tend to use is the chart of the fixed reference points, but real sailors attend to the tides and stars and winds, too. Whatever messy parts of real life and social context are stripped away or ignored on charts so that we provide realism in experiments or conceptual clarity for theory must later be consciously and explicitly reconnected to the explanation of the stripped-down processes, of course (Acitelli, 1995), but they must also be related to other seething and constantly *changing* forces.

Such observations matter because the paradigmatic "close relationship" in research (too often focused on openly conducted romantic relationships between able-bodied heterosexuals in their twenties, as everyone always says and does little to correct) is essentially context-free. As my colleague Leslie Baxter discusses more fully in her paper—and I agree with her—"relationships" are also misleadingly treated as the product or sum of two pre-formed contained minds. Consequently there is not enough attention paid to the very real tidal influence of public forces on apparently private and individual behavior; and therefore there is too little depiction of the effects of oceanic social context as a tidal process in relationships. Thus another value that I see in the interpersonal communication approach to relationships is that it highlights, and can offer theory to elucidate, the value of regarding participants, researchers, and scholars in other disciplines as swimmers in the cultural sea that also breaks over everything we do.

Historically, relationship research sought to focus on deterministic predictability, explanation, and control—and this is presented as a primary purpose of much research even today (Aronson, Wilson, & Akert, 1994; Berscheid, 1986, 1996).

By contrast, I have always found relational life to be characteristically uncertain, nonetheless. Like the tide, some of the actions can be predicted in broad terms and like navigation with tide tables, human beings (both research participants and research conductors) prefer prediction and control to reduce the sensation of chaos that is otherwise ubiquitous in relational life. One pervasive human characteristic is to develop categories and labels that create such a sense of repetition or stasis (Duck, 1994a). However, much about the tide is unpredictable and interacts with other elements like wind and season. Likewise, the fluid and uncertain quality of relationships is absent from much theory, and indeed it is the (real or imagined) theoretical certainties and continuities that have become the agreed bedrock of scholarly thinking about relationships. But, I argue, such is also the case with relaters who compare their charts with one another in search of agreements. People whose charts pick out the same features find their interactions more rewarding and more valuable, partly because they make an uncertainty at least consensual.

I have no problem with such apparent certainties as long as we recall their human origins. They are *created* or *imagined* by scholars or relaters as a result of selections made from the phenomenal pool of uncertainty; continuities are retrospectively *made into* predictable patterns from the many different sequences possible from a given starting point—whether by relaters or by researchers (Duck, 1994a). As Duck et al. (1997) indicate, "The kinds of predictabilities and certainties chosen by everyday relaters on the one hand and researchers on the other are determined by the different projects, needs, and audiences for whom each set of persons creates those categories at a given moment. In the case of social scientists, their method encourages researchers to isolate particular aspects of relationships from others in order to study them more effectively, and the consequence is that certain occurrences in relationships are given priority by such methods. The nature of everyday relationships, with all their tedium and repetitive boredom, has been allowed

to be represented by researchers' local and focused enthusiasms. These enthusiasms essentially lead to the endorsement of the caricature that relationships are composed of all (and only) those exciting and dramatic things to which researchers have so far given their attention—as if everyday life were like the news headlines—or that they *are* *essentially* orderly." Likewise, tide and winds come and go but are rather important elements in the daily lives of sailors, even if they do not show up on the progress charts that plot the ultimate movement from home to destination.

Like navigation, relationships have a constant balance of forces whose management creates the ultimate direction of progress. It is the *management* of the forces rather than the forces themselves that determines the direction of movement. Winds and tides—or relational darkness and light—are always there in some degree. Communication researchers have taken the lead in showing that the manner of steering between these forces, rocks, or storms is the key to ultimate happy landing or shipwreck. Communication scholars are also I believe prominent in their recognition of the fact "that relational experiences can be described in different ways from different vantage points" (Duck & Sants, 1983; Surra & Ridley, 1991) and that relational "facts" are actually someone's interpretations instead. For instance, as the passage of time adds a new vantage point, so a seeming negative aspect of a relationship can be transformed into a positive or neutral feature (e.g., the case where something negative like a conflict can be resolved in ways that advance the relationship) (Cate & Lloyd, 1985; Wood, Dendy, Dordek, Germany, & Varallo, 1994), or a seeming positive feature can be reconstrued as a negative one (e.g., when a trait like "reliability" can be reconstrued as "boringness") (Felmlee, 1995), depending on the reporter's present state of mind. Yet very little research indeed assumes that both the good and bad are present simultaneously in the same relationship or are defined as such at a particular moment or circumstance (Duck, 1994a, b; Duck & Wood, 1995) and that relationships offer opportunities and challenges for partners to manage the tension between these fluid aspects of human engagement (Duck et al., 1997). In short, the continuous ebb and flow of relationships cannot be ignored any longer and for one important reason that renders even more important the contribution of communication studies as a whole.

As we look to the work of our colleagues in rhetorical studies, so we see an equally important element of the shoreline. In real life, particular parts of relationships and relationship roles are variably foregrounded from time to time, and a relationship is not one consistent experience all the time. Indeed it is our research strategies that make clouds on the horizon appear to be land. Thus people in life and in research studies tend to choose particular roles or aspects of the relationship as foci on different occasions. In real life, though, it is far more important to notice that particular circumstances are used to *warrant* different psychological reconstructions of the relationship between people at different moments. For instance, a sudden disaster warrants and evokes different facets of relational obligations and duties from those regarded as "normal" at other times. Whereas friends are normally applauded for performing prototypical actions such as confiding in one another, disclosing, talking, having fun together, and showing intimacy, the occurrence of a disaster will warrant a switch from disclosure to actual support, from entertaining fun to emotional assistance, and from personal disclosure to self-sacrifice and perhaps physical effort. In the mundane squalls of everyday life, such choices are clearly a common experience: friends do not sit and confide intensely all day long, day after day any more than sailors spend all day hauling up anchors. In brief, sailors prototypically swab decks, but can also prototypically haul sails, weigh anchors, or splice a mainbrace as the occasion warrants.

To recognize the rhetorical significance of such momentary changes in warrants is to recognize a fundamental aspect of relational navigation. Relationships are multiplex, variable, subject to re-characterization, describable in many ways simultaneously open-ended, to some extent contentious, and certainly the kind of conceptual entity that can be the subject of disputes about their "true nature" on occasion. Much relating is the response to changing perceptions of warrants and to tensions of rhetorical exigency. Much daily discourse in relationships is responsive to such change since partners have choices about the language in which to characterize a relational act at a given point in time whether to partners or to researchers. Indeed, they even have choices about which relational act is the focus of attention. But to do so, they probably decontextualize it from other processes that swarmed around it at the time. Any person's selection of a description for features of a relationship at a particular time is a rhetorical act, not a simple descriptive one: it is done from the standpoint of a particular world-view and purpose, on a particular occasion, for a particular audience, or in a particular context (Duck, Pond, & Leatham, 1994). This is equally true for relational sailors as for research navigators. It is therefore important if we are to describe relationships usefully—let alone explain them—that researchers keep reminding themselves to return that which they took away in order to create a better experiment or a more focused study for a particular purpose on a particular occasion (Duck et al., 1997).

This is particularly important when one acknowledges that relationships are depicted in research at the moment of measurement. This risks depicting relationship processes themselves in a form generalized from a particular moment so that relationships are then discussed as entities characterized totally by that measurement, as Leslie Baxter argues in her paper. Yet in treating relationships only as landmarks on a chart, researchers may overlook the *simultaneous* presence and intersection of a number of forces and options or the pressures of real alternatives to the path actually taken. For example, "turning points" are *choices* between actual alternative options: to understand the choice one has to understand the psychological and social context of alternatives in which it was made (Duck, 1994a; Dixson & Duck, 1993). It is also necessary to portray the rhetorical context in which the choice was described and to depict not only the outcome but the processes and dynamics surrounding it (Duck et al., 1997).

I think we miss this point because the rhetorical choices made by researchers are usually concealed in the discourse of objective description (Bazerman, 1987) rather as the shifting sands may nonetheless be represented as fixed in any chart, we all—relaters and researchers alike—make choices about what to notice and how to describe it, what to treat as fixed and what to fudge, what to ignore and what to exclude from our charts and representations. People—in relationships and in research—have choices about the words used to convey information or to describe their relationship as well as about the slant to be given to information selected from the pool of all that could be said. In exercising such choices people do relational work as much as they do it with messages themselves (see, for example, Hopper, 1993, on the rhetoric of the divorce process). While a navigational aid can supply a sailor with a guide, it does not preordain action because the *use* made of the guide is not a part of its essence.

This is a problem only when researchers forget that prototypes of relationships originally contained "fuzziness" and we disregard its essential importance—again focusing on mapped coastline and not on the tides within it. I believe that research places too little emphasis on the change, variabilities, struggles, and tensions in relationships as lived experiences. The central tidal element of relationships is that they constantly present people with change, but also with interpersonal dilemmas and choices, even with choices in descriptions of those events (Duck, 1994a; Duck & Wood, 1995; Stein, 1993; Wood, 1994).

Finally, persons can take different tacks in the same breeze, can see partners as *simultaneously* "good" and "bad," or reflect negatively on each other without actually leaving the relationship as a consequence. In addition, partners can feel good about a relationship sometimes and not at other times, can quarrel and make up (i.e., cycle through different feelings and characterizations of "the same" relationship), or can have good days and bad days *in the same relationship* (Barbee, 1990;

Duck & Wood, 1995; Felmlee, 1995). We do not, however, dismiss the sea because it ebbs and flows, but there would be consequences if we treated it as being as motionless as it is on charts.

In the future, captains of research need to look at the tidal charts within individual relationships on several occasions in order to depict patterns, rather than presume a fixed pattern of experience in the relationship on the basis of charted landmarks of measurement, as is presently implicit in many of our methods. Where Hinde (1981) called for more description of relationships, I would call for more careful work on their currents, such as the contradictions and uncertainties with which partners must cope (Baxter & Montgomery, 1996; Duck, 1994b; Duck & Wood, 1995), variations in expectations about the relationship (Miell, 1987), and the changing or varied patterns of talk in and about relationships (Acitelli, 1988, 1993; Duck et al., 1991).

As relationship researchers we should ask ourselves what our research designs would look like if we were to investigate *relating* rather than *relationships,* attending to tide tables as much as to the coastal navigation charts. **BOTH.** In short we need to combine different aspects of the whole activity and pay only as much attention to the charts as we do to sailing itself, to the act and consequences of taking the helm rather than to the helm as a wooden object.

REFERENCES

Acitelli, L. K. (1988). When spouses talk to each other about their relationship. *Journal of Social and Personal Relationships, 5,* 185–199.

Acitelli, L. K. (1993). You, me, and us: Perspectives on relationship awareness. In S. W. Duck (Ed.), *Understanding relationship processes 1: Individuals in relationships* (pp. 144–174). Newbury Park: Sage.

Acitelli, L. K. (1995). Disciplines at parallel play. *Journal of Social and Personal Relationships, 12,* 589–596.

Allan, G. A. (1993). Social structure and relationships. In S. W. Duck (Ed.), *Understanding relationship processes 3: Social contexts of relationships* (pp. 1–25). Newbury Park: Sage.

Argyle, M., Furnham A., & Graham, J. (1981). *Social situations.* Cambridge : Cambridge University Press.

Aronson, E., Wilson, T. D., & Akert, R. M. (1994). *Social psychology: The heart and the mind.* New York: Harper Collins.

Barbee, A. P. (1990). Interactive coping: The cheering up process in close relationships. In S. W. Duck (Ed. with R. Cohen Silver), *Personal relationships and social support.* London: Sage.

Baxter, L. A., & Montgomery, B. M. (1996). *Relating: Dialogues and dialects.* New York: Guilford Press.

Bazerman, C. (1987). Codifying the social scientific style: The APA publications manual as a behaviorist rhetoric. In J. S. Nelson, A. Megill, & D. N. McCloskey (Eds.), *The rhetoric of the human sciences: Language and argument in scholarship and public affairs* (pp. 125–144). Madison: University of Wisconsin Press.

Berger, C. (1991). Communication theories and other curios. *Communication Monographs, 58,* 101–113.

Berscheid, E. (1986). Mea culpas and lamentations: Sir Francis, Sir Isaac and the "slow progress of soft psychology." In R. Gilmour & S. W. Duck (Eds.), *The emerging field of personal relationships* (pp. 267–286). Hillsdale, NJ: Lea.

Berscheid, E. (1996). From Madison to Banff: Much ground traveled but still some way to go. Paper to ICPR conference. Banff, Canada. August.

Cate, R. M., & Lloyd, S. A. (1985). The developmental course of conflict in dissolution of premarital relationships. *Journal of Social and Personal Relationships, 2,* 179–194.

Delia, J. G. (1980). Some tentative thoughts concerning the study of interpersonal relationships and their development. *Western Journal of Speech Communication, 44,* 97–103.

Dixson, M., & Duck, S. W. (1993). Understanding relationship processes: Uncovering the human search for meaning. In S. W. Duck (Ed.), *Understanding relationship processes 1: Individuals in relationships* (pp. 175–206). Newbury Park: Sage.

Duck, S. W. (1993). Preface on social context. In S. W. Duck (Ed.), *Social contexts of relationships [Understanding relationship processes 3]* (pp. ix–xiv). Newbury Park: Sage.

Duck, S. W., Pond, K., & Leatham, G. B. (1994). Loneliness and the evaluation of relational events. *Journal of Social and Personal Relationships, 11,* 235–260.

Duck, S. W., Rutt, D. J., Hurst, M., & Strejc, H. (1991). Some evident truths about communication in everyday relationships: All communication is not created equal. *Human Communication Research, 18,* 228–267.

Duck, S. W., & Sants, H. K. A. (1983). On the origin of the specious: Are personal relationships really interpersonal states? *Journal of Social and Clinical Psychology, 1,* 27–41.

Duck, S. W., West, L., & Acitelli, L. K. (1997). Sewing the field: The tapestry of research on personal relationships. In S. W. Duck (Ed. with K. Dindia, W. Ickes, R. M. Milardo, R. S. L. Mills, & B. Sarason), *Handbook of personal relationships,* 2nd ed. Chichester, UK: Wiley.

Felmlee, D. H. (1995). Fatal attractions: Affection and disaffection in intimate relationships. *Journal of Social and Personal Relationships, 12,* 295–311.

Hinde, R. A. (1981). The bases of a science of interpersonal relationships. In S. W. Duck & R. Gilmour (Eds.), *Personal relationships 1: Studying personal relationships* (pp. 1–22). London, New York, San Francisco: Academic Press.

Hopper, J. (1993). The rhetoric of motives in divorce. *Journal of Marriage and the Family, 55,* 801–813.

Miell, D. E. (1987). Remembering relationship development: Constructing a context for interactions. In R. Burnett, P. McGhee, & D. Clarke (Eds.), *Accounting for relationships* (pp. 60–73). London: Methuen.

Stein, C. H. (1993). Felt obligation in adult family relationships. In S. W. Duck (Ed.), *Understanding relationship processes 3: Social contexts of relationships* (pp. 78–99). Thousand Oaks: Sage.

Surra, C. A., & Ridley, C. (1991). Multiple perspectives on interaction: Participants, peers and observers. In B. M. Montgomery & S. W. Duck (Eds.), *Studying interpersonal interaction* (pp. 35–55). New York: Guilford.

Werner, C., Altman, I., Brown, B., & Ginat, J. (1993). Celebrations in personal relationships: A transactional/dialectical perspective. In S. W. Duck (Ed.), *Understanding relationship processes 3: Social contexts of relationships* (pp. 109–138). Thousand Oaks: Sage.

Wood, J. T. (1994). *Who cares? Women, care, and culture.* Carbondale, IL: Southern Illinois University Press.

Wood, J. T., Dendy, L. L., Dordek, E., Germany, M., & Varallo, S. M. (1994). Dialectic of difference: A thematic analysis of intimates' meanings for difference. In K. Carter & M. Presnell (Eds.), *Interpretive approaches to interpersonal communication.* New York: SUNY.

It Takes Two to Tango: Interpersonal Adaptation and Implications for Relational Communication

Judee K. Burgoon

University of Arizona

Imagine for a moment two dancers, swaying in perfect rhythm to the sensuous syncopation of a tango, their bodies in perfect harmony with the music and with one another as they dip and twirl and glide across the floor, each dancer's movement seeming to anticipate that of the partner, to respond to it and to mesh perfectly with it. Now transfer this visual and aural image to conversation and you have the touchstone of interpersonal communication—the full coordination of one person's communication with another's—in short, that which is both the subject and object of interpersonal adaptation.

Although perhaps oversimplified and idealized, this image conjures up one of the great mysteries of human communication—how is it that we as humans are able to negotiate with such apparent ease what is in reality as highly complex and intricate an activity as interpersonal communication? Can we trace our capacity to coordinate and adapt our communication to one another to an inborn trait, to a selective talent passed on through the vagaries of genetic diversity, or to a proclivity acquired in the earliest weeks of life and honed through a lifetime of trial and error? How rooted in biology or sociology are the motivations to approach or avoid others? Does our physiology dictate our interpersonal communication patterns? Is the capacity to adapt and coordinate communication a constant linked to individual personality and communication style or a variable amenable to intervention and modification? And how does it relate to the different trajectories that interpersonal interactions and personal relationships follow? Such questions interpenetrate the very essence of the enterprise we call human communication and the capacities attributable to human communicators.

Big questions seldom lend themselves to ready answers, and, this topic being no different, I am certainly unequipped to offer quick and satisfying answers to them here. However, my own quest to confront these provocative issues has fueled a series of investigations on dyadic interaction patterns and relational communication that have reshaped my thinking and brought me closer to some answers. Today I would like to share with you a few of our more tantalizing discoveries and the implications they hold for charting a course for future research on relational communication.

Relational communication to me has always meant the communication processes that define and maintain interpersonal relationships. It has centered on the constellation of verbal and nonverbal messages by which social actors express their beliefs, expectations, understandings, attitudes, and feelings about the nature of the relationship and one another within the context of relationship. As well, it has included how parties to a relationship discern and construe each other's actions as relational messages. In the context of this Helm series, the net has been cast somewhat more broadly to include a variety of interpersonal processes that may impinge upon, as well as define, interpersonal relationships. Interaction adaptation is one such process that may not only precondition the meaningful exchange of relational messages but may also *be* the relational messages. Thus, our mission, if we choose to accept it—acquiring a deeper understanding of relational communication—may inevitably draw us into the swirling eddies of interpersonal adaptation processes.

TO RECIPROCATE OR NOT
TO RECIPROCATE: THAT IS THE QUESTION

The first major conclusion we have come to is that *reciprocity is the order of the day*. It may even be the order of the species.

Reciprocity refers to a dyadic interaction pattern in which one person's verbal or nonverbal communication style is met with the same or similar style by another—such as responding to an affectionate hug with an affectionate kiss. By contrast, compensation occurs when an interactant responds to another's style with a highly dissimilar or opposite behavior pattern—such as responding to increased eye gaze with decreased gaze.

Our findings, and those from several other investigations, repeatedly indicate that under widely varying circumstances, many of which were actually designed to provoke compensation, reciprocity emerges as the most prevalent pattern (e.g., Burgoon, Buller, Dillman, & Walther, 1995; Burgoon, Ebesu, White, Kikuchi, Alvar, & Koch, in press; Burgoon, Le Poire, Stern, & Payne, 1993; Burgoon, Olney, & Coker, 1987; Guerrero & Burgoon, 1996; Manusov, 1995; White, 1996). Displays of interest and involvement are returned in kind; intimate disclosures beget intimate disclosures; a person's increased shows of affection are matched by those of a partner; so are acts of hostility and violence. In short, reciprocity and matching of others' communication patterns can be regarded as the default condition for human interaction.

Why might this be, that so often one person's communication is met with like behavior, and that acts of aggression as well as acts of affection are reciprocated rather than rebuffed? In *Interpersonal Adaptation,* Lesa Sern, Leesa Dillman, and I theorize that it is the confluence of biological, social, and communicological factors that have forged such a resilient and persistent interaction pattern. Among the factors we consider are: an apparent biologically based predisposition for conspecifics to synchronize and entrain their biological rhythms to one another, perhaps as a means of achieving a social order and securing survival; physiologically based needs to adapt to cohabitants and co-interactants so as to regulate one's own arousal and comfort; socially based norms and prescriptions for cooperation, reciprocity, and politeness that facilitate coordination at a societal level; a communicationally based necessity for some degree of mutual other-orientation between participants as a prerequisite to achieving comprehension and understanding; and, particularly relevant here, the possibility that embedded in these ritualized interaction patterns are relational meanings that are validated and fortified by their repetitiveness.

Ethologists and biologists tell us that many forms of social interaction have, through an evolutionary history spanning perhaps 150 million years, become specialized as ritualized communication signals. Ploog (1995) explains:

> *…in the beginning, the most basic modes of social behavior were nothing but approach and avoidance among members of the species. The outcome of such encounters was always unpredictable and depended upon each partner's actions and reactions.… Because communication between partners was advantageous, social signals evolved—as the theory goes—to permit more flexibility in encounters and a greater degree of information about the outcome. (p. 27)*

Speculatively, then, reciprocal adaptation patterns, like many dominance and submission cues, may have originated as primitive reflexes and instinctive signals that functioned to enhance security and reproduction. Through the course of human development, they may have been selectively retained and refined as means of expressing such essential relational messages as identification with one's conspecifics (what we now term homophily or similarity), availability and receptivity to approach, nonaggressiveness and nondominance, nonarousal, and attraction. Put differently, many of the fundamental topoi of relational communication—intimacy, with its subthemes of affection, immediacy, receptivity, trust, and depth; similarity; dominance or equality; composure and arousal (Burgoon & Hale, 1984)—may all be traceable to to our biological heritage (see, e.g., Burgoon, Buller, & Woodall, 1996; Liska, 1993).

Take relational messages of empathy and rapport, for example, which are typically expressed through such cues as mutual facing, open postures that mirror those of the partner, synchronized gestural and vocal rhythms, attentive listening, and smooth turn-exchanges. It seems reasonable to assume that such displays by early ancestors not only would have offered vivid visual and auditory reinforcement of perceived similarities as species-mates but also would have presented a nonthreatening demeanor that further signaled availability and invited approach. In this manner, reciprocal behavioral displays would have enabled the all-important identification of a conspecific as friend or foe and would have instigated approach rather than fight or flight. Interactional synchrony would have further facilitated the social coordination necessary for verbal communication and comprehension to take place. Over time, these interaction patterns may have become more specialized as shows of empathy, rapport, and affection.

A particularly important implication of this speculation is that we need not consciously learn elemental relational message forms nor labor to mimic the displays of co-interactants because such interaction patterns come naturally; they are an inherited and inherent part of humans' relational communication repertoire. From this it also follows that these relational message expressions can be meaningful without operating at a highly conscious level. As Cindy White and I contend in an upcoming volume on message production,

> ...adjustment of interactants to one another may, in itself, come to be part of the social signaling system and thus take on symbolic meaning (Ploog, 1995).... This is important because the nonverbal and verbal communication patterns that manifest adaptation can be viewed not merely as a reflection of underlying individual processes but as a potentially rich repertoire for creating shared understanding. (Burgoon & White, in press)

A sensible inference to be drawn, to rephrase the old saw, is that meanings are in interactions. More specifically, they reside in the conjointly created, often ritualized interaction patterns that habitually emerge when people communicate. And because they do so, and because such interaction patterns are highly routinized and regular, the meanings associated with them take on a high degree of stability. That is, contrary to assertions that meanings are totally context-dependent and must be studied at a molecular and localized level, the greater import of many interactions may lie in molar interaction patterns that are sustained throughout longer periods of discourse and, indeed, in the absence of discourse. To use a familiar analogy, they become the forest against which utterance-by-utterance and within-utterance discourse analyses are the trees. A crucial methodological implication is that highly localized, moment-to-moment analyses may miss the significance of the larger discursive pattern and/or detect "noise" rather than meaningful activity.

DISABLING THE DEFAULT

The claim that reciprocity is the default condition for interpersonal communication is not to say that all interactions will exhibit reciprocity nor that achieving a reciprocal and synchronized interaction pattern will always be effortless and automatic. Evidence from our research program and a related one on interpersonal deception reveals that a variety of factors, including individual social skills, can moderate and attenuate these patterns (Buller & Burgoon, 1996; Burgoon et al., 1995). Moreover, individuals can and do behave strategically, adopting compensatory or nonadaptive patterns to achieve their desired ends (Burgoon & Buller, 1994; Burgoon, Buller, Afifi, White, & Buslig, 1996; Burgoon et al., 1987; Ickes, Patterson, Rajecki, & Tanford, 1982). Thus, a second major conclusion is that *the default pattern can be, and often is, disrupted or disabled.* This of course becomes the challenge for theorizing in this area—to account for when, how, and why nonaccommodative or compensatory patterns arise. Let me elaborate on two ways in which we believe compensation may occur.

One concerns the role of arousal. The vast majority of theories related to interpersonal adaptation have made arousal a centerpiece of their explanatory calculus. Theories such as affiliative conflict theory (Argyle & Dean, 1965), the arousal-labeling model (Patterson, 1976), discrepancy-arousal theory (Cappella & Greene, 1982), the sequential-functional model (Patterson, 1983), expectancy violations theory (Burgoon, 1978), and cognitive valence theory (Andersen, 1989) all view arousal change as a key instigator of reciprocal or compensatory interaction patterns. Most predict that during interpersonal interaction, a substantial change in one person's communication will actuate a large increase in the other's level of arousal. This arousal change is predicted to be aversive and to prompt a compensatory interaction pattern. So, for instance, if you are subjected to a prolonged stare, you may react by breaking eye contact, setting up barriers with your arms or personal possessions, increasing the physical distance between you and the starer, or eventually taking flight. A relational message of too much immediacy or intimacy, too soon, may provoke, not a reciprocal escalation of intimacy, but instead a rapid withdrawal, presumably because of the excessive arousal that it engenders. An assertion of dominance may evoke a submissive response for the same reasons.

The theory we have been developing, interaction adaptation theory (IAT for short; Burgoon et al., 1995), specifies that one of the exceptions to the predominance of reciprocity is the case of people experiencing high-arousal states such as discomfort, anxiety, or fear. Consistent with other interaction adaptation theories, IAT predicts that under these conditions, interactants may exhibit a compensatory response. However, IAT restricts such compensation to nonverbal behaviors, such as immediacy cues and threat stares, that are themselves indicators or elicitors of arousal. Moreover, IAT posits that these patterns of compensation may arise on only a few individual behaviors amidst a larger behavior pattern of reciprocity.

Additionally, IAT takes a more refined approach to the concept of arousal. Rather than embracing the popular view of arousal as unidimensional, it recognizes that arousal varies along two dimensions—intensity and valence—and so may take the form of intensely positive as well as intensely negative arousal (see Burgoon, Kelley, Newton, & Keeley-Dyreson, 1989). The relevance for relational communication is that these two different forms of arousal are likely to generate, accompany, and/or convey different relational messages. Our distinction between positive and negative arousal aligns with Pribram's (1984) differentiation between physiological arousal and physiological activation. In his rubric, *arousal* refers to neurochemical and cortical systems that interrupt and immobilize behavior, whereas *activation* refers to alerting and energizing states of the organism that mobilize behavior. What Pribram is calling arousal is therefore typically associated with unpleasant or unfamiliar circumstances, making it consonant with our notion of negatively valenced high arousal, and so should lead to avoidant responses or inactivity. By contrast, activation is more commonly associated with pleasant and nonaversive circumstances and so fits our notion of positively valenced arousal. It should result in approach behaviors and/or intensified actions.

If future theorizing continues to cast arousal in a central role, it must differentiate between that which immobilizes and that which mobilizes, because what we in communication and psychology have been accustomed to calling arousal can have either effect. One implication for relational communication is that interaction conditions which foster greater attentiveness and behavioral readiness may be preconditions for expressing relational messages of interest, involvement, and receptivity—all of which are variants of approach—and for energized and dynamic behavioral displays. Interaction conditions that instead are aversive or distracting and trigger arousal (in Pribram's sense) may inhibit expressions of interest, involvement, and the like. In other words, the arousal or activation state of interactants may predetermine which relational messages are possible and likely.

Another implication is that overt manifestations of arousal or activation may be mistaken as relational messages—in the former case, as messages of disinterest, detachment, or dislike; in the latter case, as messages of engagement, enthusiasm, or attraction. What are merely avoidant reactions to an environmental stimulus or physical symptoms of an individual's internal state (what we in the nonverbal area call indicative behavior) may be falsely read as nonverbal relational messages about the state of the relationship. Because nonverbal and verbal cues are polysemous, the same nonverbal or verbal act may sometimes signal a relational definition and other times have quite independent meaning. Conversely, different behaviors may convey the same functional meaning. Confusions are therefore bound to be common. Here again, if individual and microscopic behaviors are examined within a larger gestalt, ambiguities may be mitigated. Profiling substitutable, complementary, and contingent relational message forms therefore becomes a worthy research objective.

I have identified elevations in arousal as one mediating factor that can produce a compensatory interaction pattern. In actuality, compensation can take two forms—a flight or avoidance response to discomfort, fear, threat, etc., i.e., the kind of reactive pattern just described—or a more strategic or deliberate and sometimes preemptive act in response to actual or anticipated goal frustration. This latter kind of compensation is neither a reaction to, nor a means of allaying, arousal but rather a deliberate effort to exert influence on another's behavior. It is intended to achieve one's own interaction goals or to prevent them from being subverted by another's communication style. It constitutes a second condition under which IAT predicts compensatory interaction patterns.

Although it has far-reaching implications for strategic communication that extend beyond relational messages, one important implication that is in keeping with the discussion of arousal is that not all interpersonal behavior constitutes a relational message. Contrary to the mythic axiom that one cannot not communicate all interaction behavior is *not* communication or even relational communication. Some of it is purely instrumental and is designed to model a desired interaction style in hopes of eliciting the same from another. For instance, if you anticipate talking with someone who is known to be irascible and unpleasant, you may open the conversation by being particularly solicitous, in hopes of prompting that person to adopt a civil and pleasant tone with you. Your pleasantries are not a relational message of affection and admiration for the other; they are just a means to a desired end—namely, a noncontentious interaction. This mundane example illustrates that it is essential to disentangle what actions during communication *are* communication from those that are influences on it. In the relational communication arena, this is an especially difficult charge because relational messages are swirling within a cauldron of verbal and nonverbal actions that are directed toward a multitude of purposes, only one of which is defining the interpersonal relationship.

BEWARE FALSE DICHOTOMIES

Yet another important conclusion we have drawn from this research is that *much of the theorizing about adaptation patterns has fallen victim to false dichotomies.* It is not the case that one account is right and the rest are wrong, that interaction is characterized by either reciprocity *or* compensation, or that interaction patterns and associated relational messages are attributable to either arousal *or* expectancy violations *or* some other unitary factor. Interactions can be reciprocal and compensatory at the same time, reciprocal in the sense, perhaps, of general levels of matched involvement and pleasantness, but compensatory in terms of particular cues, such as a forward lean in response to a backward lean, that may qualify or attenuate the overall pattern. In the same way, interaction patterns may simultaneously express both dominance *and* submissiveness, dominance, perhaps, in the use of an expressive and forceful voice and assertive language but submissive in the use of questions that solicit a partner's opinion and backchanneling behaviors that assure them the conversational floor (see Tannen, 1994 for other examples).

It should come as no revelation that relational communication is far more multilayered and complex than most current theoretical accounts imply, especially if we look at it "up close." But it is not so complex as to defy prediction and explanation, especially if we step back and begin to view it macroscopically, using the relational topoi as a schematic. In other words, we may make significant strides in predictive and explanatory power by linking interaction patterns to general relational message themes. Thus, if a relationship is a close, harmonious one of equality and trust, we should expect to see, for example, reciprocity of verbal self-disclosure and nonverbal receptivity cues and symmetrical rather than asymmetrical patterns of relational control. Within the overall profile, various cues may be substitutable for one another and may vary in their presence or absence and intensity over time but will emerge as more likely when trust and equality are the relational messages being exchanged than when distrust or inequality is being communicated.

INTERACTIONAL BEHAVIOR TRUMPS PREINTERACTIONAL COGNITIONS

A final important observation from our research is that *what happens during interaction often overwhelms what preceded it.* For someone who has built a career examining cognitions in the form of expectancies, it is no small admission to arrive at this revelation. But this is indeed the conclusion we are coming to, based on the merger of two programs of research, one on expectancy confirmation and violations and one on interaction adaptation. What we are finding is that a partner's communicative style during interaction often exerts far more influence on an individual's own communication style than that same individual's own cognitions prior to interaction (see, e.g., Burgoon, Le Poire, & Rosenthal, 1995; Manusov, Winchatz, & Manning, in press). The same is true for observers placing more weight on witnessed interaction behavior than induced expectancies (e.g., Forgas, 1978). For

example, recent investigations by Smith (1995) showed that when observers were faced with conflicting information between what they had been led to expect about a couple's level of intimacy and what they actually observed, they were far more influenced by the nonverbal intimacies they actually saw. The important implication is that the emergent and dynamic exchange of relational messages during interaction transcends prior expectancies and cognitions in guiding the interpretations and outcomes of interpersonal episodes.

CONCLUSIONS

We are accustomed to thinking that "at the helm" refers to the people who will guide our intellectual endeavors. I have suggested today that we also put certain ideas at the helm and that these lead us into our next epoch of relational communication research. Our progress toward understanding relational communication will be advanced immeasurably if we invest more of our intellectual capital in studying fundamental communication processes such as interaction adaptation and the ways in which such adaptations predispose and convey various relational messages. With dyadically defined communication processes at the helm of our research enterprise, the shores of greater insight may loom just beyond the horizon.

REFERENCES

Andersen, P. A. (1989, May). *A cognitive valence theory of intimate communication.* Paper presented to the biannual conference of the Iowa Network on Personal Relationships, Iowa City, IA.

Argyle, M., & Dean, J. (1965). Eye-contact, distance, and affiliation. *Sociometry, 28,* 289–304.

Buller, D. B., & Burgoon, J. K. (1996). Interpersonal deception theory. *Communication Theory, 6,* 243–267.

Burgoon, J. K. (1978). A communication model of personal space violations: Explication and an initial test. *Human Communication Research, 4,* 129–142.

Burgoon, J. K., & Buller, D. B. (1994). Interpersonal deception: III. Effects of deceit on perceived communication and nonverbal behavior dynamics. *Journal of Nonverbal Behavior, 18,* 155–184.

Burgoon, J. K., Buller, D. B., Afifi, W., White, C. H., & Buslig, A. L. S. (1996, May). *The role of immediacy in deceptive interpersonal interactions.* Paper presented to the annual meeting of the International Communication Association, Chicago.

Burgoon, J. K., Buller, D. B., Dillman, L., & Walther, J. B. (1995). Interpersonal deception: IV. Effects of suspicion on perceived communication and nonverbal behavior dynamics. *Human Communication Research, 22,* 163–196.

Burgoon, J. K., Buller, D. B., & Woodall, W. G. (1996). *Nonverbal communication: The unspoken dialogue.* New York: McGraw-Hill

Burgoon, J. K., Ebesu, A. S., White, C. H., Kikuchi, T., Alvaro, E., & Koch, P. (in press). The many faces of interpersonal adaptation. In M. T. Palmer (Ed.), *Progress in communication sciences.* Norwood, NJ: Ablex.

Burgoon, J. K., & Hale, J. L. (1984). The fundamental topoi of relational communication. *Communication Monographs, 51,* 193–214.

Burgoon, J. K., Kelley, D. L., Newton, D. A., & Keeley-Dyreson, M. P. (1989). The nature of arousal and nonverbal indices. *Human Communication Research, 16,* 217–255.

Burgoon, J. K., Le Poire, B. A., & Rosenthal, R. (1995). Effects of preinteraction expectancies and target communication on perceiver reciprocity and compensation in dyadic interaction. *Journal of Experimental Social Psychology, 31,* 287–321.

Burgoon, J. K., Le Poire, B. A., Stern, L. A., & Payne, M. (1993, May). *The quest for adaptation patterns in dyadic interaction.* Paper presented to the annual meeting of the International Communication Association, Miami.

Burgoon, J. K., Olney, C. A., & Coker, R. A. (1987). The effects of communicator characteristics on patterns of reciprocity and compensation. *Journal of Nonverbal Behavior, 11,* 146–165.

Burgoon, J. K., Stern, L. A., & Dillman, L. (1995). *Interpersonal adaptation: Dyadic interaction patterns.* New York: Cambridge University Press.

Burgoon, J. K., & White, C. H. (in press). Researching nonverbal message production: A view from interaction adaptation theory. In J. O. Greene (Ed.), *Message production: Advances in communication theory.* Mahweh, NJ: Lawrence Erlbaum.

Cappella, J. N., & Greene, J. O. (1982). A discrepancy-arousal explanation of mutual influence in expressive behavior for adult and infant-adult interaction. *Communication Monographs, 49,* 89–114.

Forgas, J. P. (1978). The effects of behavioural and cultural expectation cues on the perception of social episodes. *European Journal of Social Psychology, 8,* 203–213.

Guerrero, L. K., & Burgoon, J. K. (1996). Attachment styles and reactions to nonverbal involvement change in romantic dyads: Patterns of reciprocity and compensation. *Human Communication Research, 22,* 335–370.

Ickes, W., Patterson, M. L., Rajecki, D. W., & Tanford, S. (1982). Behavioral and cognitive consequences of reciprocal versus compensatory responses to pre-interaction expectancies. *Social Cognition, 1,* 160–190.

Liska, J. (1993). Signs of the apes, songs of the whales: Comparing signs across species. *European Journal of Cognitive Systems, 3/4,* 381–397.

Manusov, V. (1995). Reacting to changes in nonverbal behaviors: Relational satisfaction and adaptation patterns in romantic dyads. *Human Communication Research, 21,* 456–477.

Manusov, V., Winchatz, M. R., & Manning, L. M. (in press). Acting out our minds: Incorporating behavior into models of stereotype-based expectancies for cross-cultural interactions. *Communication Monographs.*

Patterson, M. L. (1976). An arousal model of interpersonal intimacy. *Psychological Review, 83,* 235–245.

Patterson, M. L. (1983). *Nonverbal behavior: A functional perspective.* New York: Springer-Verlag.

Ploog, D. W. (1995). Mutuality and dialogue in nonhuman primate communication. In I. Marková, C. Graumann, & K. Foppa (Eds.), *Mutualities in dialogue* (pp. 27–57). Cambridge: Cambridge University Press.

Pribram, K. H. (1984). Emotion: A neurobehavioral basis. In K. R. Scherer & P. Ekman (Eds.), *Approaches to emotion* (pp. 13–38). Hillsdale, NJ: Erlbaum.

Smith, S. W. (1995). Perceptual processing of nonverbal-relational messages. In D. E. Hewes (Ed.), *The cognitive bases of interpersonal communication* (pp. 87–112). Hillsdale, NJ: Lawrence Erlbaum.

Tannen, D. (1994). *Gender and discourse.* New York: Oxford University Press, Inc.

White, C. H. (1996). *Adaptation and communicative design: Patterns of interaction in deceptive and truthful interchanges.* Unpublished doctoral dissertation, University of Arizona.

Locating the Social in Interpersonal Communication

Leslie A. Baxter
University of Iowa

Gertrude Stein once observed about her hometown of Oakland, California, that when one went "there," there was no "there" there. If we went on a quest today to locate the "social" in the intellectual landscape of interpersonal communication scholarship, I think we would, like Stein, conclude that there is no "there" there. During the last couple of decades, interpersonal communication has evolved into a site of knowledge claims about the communicative behaviors of abstracted, contained selves who float in a cognitive world presumably unfettered by the sociality of their lived experience. I say this in spite of substantial research and theory on the topic of communication in personal relationships and believe that personal relationships research is no less devoid of the social than other research and theory domains within interpersonal communication.

Do not misunderstand my position: I am not arguing for the abandonment of the cognitive/social psychological approach to the study of interpersonal communication in general and the study of communication in personal relationships in particular, nor am I arguing against research and theory that examine the production and reception of face-to-face messages of individuals. What I *am* arguing against is the hegemonic status that such psychologically oriented research and theory occupies in the study of interpersonal communication, including the study of communication in personal relationships. Like any hegemonic force, the assumptions of the psychological approach are the taken-for-granted currency of the realm. We do not problematize what is privileged, and the quality of our theorizing suffers when we fail to make our presumptions "open to [scholarly] suspicion" (Gergen, 1994, p. 62). To paraphrase the Russian social theorist Mikhail Bakhtin (1986, p. 7), thinking only reveals its depths once it has encountered and come into contact with other, foreign assumptions. In the absence of dialogue across different communities of intelligibility, the criteria for valid research and theorizing within the dominant intelligibility will always be self-sealing and thus doomed to a vacuous self-appraisal in which assumptions are frozen (Gergen, 1994).

When I look to the future of interpersonal communication, therefore, I hope to hear not the monologue of the status quo but a cacophony of voices from different intelligibilities, all engaged in dialogue in which foundational assumptions are open to scholarly suspicion. Minimally, I hope that we will legitimate intellectual perspectives that challenge three core taken-for-granted assumptions that dominate current research and theory in interpersonal communication and the study of personal relationships, assumptions that flow directly from ignoring the social relatedness of interpersonal life:

- first, the assumption that interpersonal communication is centered in intersubjective understanding;
- second, the assumption that interpersonal communication is centered exclusively in our relational havens of intimacy, far removed from the arena of societal discourse; and
- third, the assumption that interpersonal life will be experienced as consensual, orderly, and stripped of its "bumps and warts" if communication is effective.

1. The assumption that interpersonal communication is centered in intersubjective understanding.

One of our taken-for-granteds is that meaning originates in the individual's mind, gains expression in his or her communicative actions, and is deciphered in the mind of an Other. This assumption of intersubjective understanding lies at the heart of interpersonal communication as we research, theorize, and teach it. From this perspective, "communication" is quickly reduced to a mere conduit for essentialized, psychological characteristics (Reddy, 1979). Ignored is the constitutive function of communication, in which communication creates, reproduces, and transforms (Duck, 1994; Duck & Pond, 1989).

There is an entirely different way to conceive of the interpersonal communicative enterprise, one that does not have the individual, sovereign mind as its starting point. From this alternative perspective, a social perspective, it is common participation in a system of significations and relations that enables meaning and understanding. From this alternative stance, says Gergen (1994, p. 263), "it is not the individual who preexists the relationship and initiates the process of communication, but the conventions of relationship that enable understanding to be achieved." It is human sociality that gives language its capacity to mean. It is the relation between interlocutors where meaning is realized. Or, as Voloshinov/Bakhtin (1973, p. 93) expressed it, "The organizing center . . . is not within but outside—in the social milieu surrounding the individual being."

What are the implications of this alternative perspective on the ways we view intersubjective understanding? First, I would assert that the concept of "intersubjectivity" no longer makes sense as we have conceived it, because we do not have two contained subjectivities connected through the conduit of communication. What we have instead is *social understanding* that emerges out of the relating between persons. Second, if meanings do not reside in individual minds, or in a language system,

but instead in the relation between interlocutors—what Shotter (1993) terms the "joint actions" of social life—then we can no longer feel satisfied with the individual as our unit of analysis or accountability. Concepts that we take for granted as located in the individual mind—including goals and intentions—become the stuff of joint action between relating persons (Stamp & Knapp, 1990).

Certainly, the dominant view of interpersonal communication as the process of intersubjective understanding feels comfortable to our individualistic senses of ourselves as autonomous agents who act on the world. I would argue that this sense of a stable and core self is absolutely essential to understand how we organize and anchor the indeterminate, continuous flow of our experiences with others. We have built our lives as members of a highly individualistic society around these notions because they make for good stories; they give us a vocabulary in our "accounts of personhood" as we interact with others (Shotter, 1984, p. 184). As Sampson (1993, p. 112) explains, "[If] we begin with the assumption of an ever-shifting multiplicity [of identities], [then] unity and continuity [are] a particular social accomplishment. If we experience a core self, then, this is not because we have a core, but rather because we function in a society in which that formulation has become a dominant belief that is usually reaffirmed by everyday social institutions and cultural practices."

Describing the self as a social phenomenon does not deny the importance of biological, chemical, or physiological conditions. However, as Baxter and Montgomery (1996, p. 181) note, it does require a distinction on our part between understanding the mechanics of a thing and understanding the use to which the thing is put. For instance, to attempt to understand the concept of "driving a car" by gathering information only about combustion engines is to overlook the essentially social quality of what happens when people actually drive. To understand the process as it unfolds, one must be attentive to the rules of the road, spontaneous negotiations at stop signs, gambits of rush-hour drives, and the like. What is required is the recognition of the inherently social foundations of the phenomenon in question. So, too, must we acknowledge and incorporate into our study of interpersonal communication the social foundations of the individual's mind, self, and identities.

The hegemonic assumption of interpersonal communication, including the study of communication in personal relationships, is that we are in the business of understanding *personal* communication, e.g., communication that originates within the sovereign individual. When we turn this assumption on its head and focus instead on how the *person originates in communication,* a different intelligibility is brought into the scholarly conversation. A "personal relationship," thus, can be reconceptualized as a process of co-participation in constructing one another's selves instead of a site for revealing preformed and intact identities (Baxter & Montgomery, 1996).

2. The assumption that interpersonal communication is removed from the arena of societal discourse and centered exclusively in relational havens of intimacy.

Over 20 years ago, Miller and Steinberg (1975) gave us the distinction between "interpersonal" communication and "noninterpersonal" communication. In failing to problematize this taken-for-granted distinction, we too easily have accepted that the border between "interpersonal" and "noninterpersonal" is fixed, stable, and impermeable. The distinction allows us to focus our intellectual gaze on intimate worlds as if these were somehow isolated from the discursive world of the broader society. It gives us license to ignore such macro-level issues as power, ideology, and marginalizations of a variety of kinds of peoples, values, and beliefs, as we retreat instead to the comfortable research havens of love, egalitarianism, and therapeutic ego-gratification that we believe to characterize intimate life (a naïve belief, I would note). It absents researchers and theorists of interpersonal communication from the broader scholarly conversation about the role of informal, everyday talk in so-called public life.

If I were to ask "what is at stake in the study of interpersonal communication and the study of personal relationships?" our research and theory to date would likely lead us to respond "individual well-being in private life." Although certainly this is an important stake, it is limiting. In addition, I would urge us to legitimate the view that society and the social order are at stake in the study of interpersonal communication and personal relationships.

It is difficult to eavesdrop on intellectual debates currently raging throughout the human sciences without realizing that the old dualisms of private-public, individual-social, and micro-macro have collapsed. Instead, the intellectual landscape that surrounds interpersonal communication is probing how society and the social order are produced and reproduced in everyday life. Social praxis has become the new currency of this multidisciplinary realm, as scholars from sociology, revisionist social psychology, cultural anthropology, social history, textual criticism, and postmodern philosophy position the everyday as the site where society *becomes*—the site where "society," "culture," "the social order," and other macro-level abstractions are reproduced in the moment and/or transformed anew. As Bakhtin (Todorov, 1984, p. 30) has noted, social order begins "with the appearance of the second person." It is born and lived in the moment, and yet is a product of the past and an anticipated future. It is stable to the point of being institutionalized while constantly in flux both locally and historically.

Perhaps most importantly, " it" is not singular at all. "Everyday life," "society," and "culture" are cross-currents of dilemmatic, contradictory, and multivocal exigencies, demands, values, traditions, and standpoints. The interpersonal communication of everyday life, thus, is a deeply contested discursive terrain. It is contested as parties determine which histories will be privileged and which forgotten. It is contested as parties determine which traditions and values will be legitimated and which not. It is contested as parties negotiate which identities in the moment will be accepted and which not. It is contested as parties determine whose futures are at stake and whose are subjugated. It is contested as parties enter the conversation of the moment with the realization that they hold different social resources that position them with unequal voices.

3. The assumption that "effective communication" is an elixir that will cure the "ills" of disorder, division, and difference.

If we take sociality seriously, we will be unable to ignore its fundamental messiness; the lived experience is one of indeterminacy in which order and disorder, division and unity, and sameness and difference are in ongoing and dynamic tension (Bakhtin, 1981). Despite growing evidence to support this dialogic view of interpersonal life (for an extensive review, see Baxter & Montgomery, 1996), interpersonal communication scholarship still aspires to the monologic view that disorder, division, and difference are social blemishes that could be alleviated if we only understood how to communicate more effectively. We persist in privileging as criteria for individual competence such skills as interactional control and openness and clarity of expression (see, e.g., Montgomery, 1988; Parks, 1994). Positive science still occupies the privileged high ground of our methodological landscape.

If we are to embrace the contingent messiness of the social world, we need a more sophisticated conception of what communication competence entails and how to study it. In particular, our conception of effective interpersonal communication, and our views about effective ways to study interpersonal communication, will need to become more dialogic in nature (Baxter & Montgomery, 1996). Effective communication under conditions of indeterminate sociality embraces contradictions, instead of seeking their extinction through legitimation of only one dialectical pole of competence (e.g., openness over closedness or clarity over equivocation). It displays respect for multiple realities rather than extinguishing difference under the relational banners of similarity and consensus. It is "jointly owned" by those interacting and thus cannot be attributed to individuals alone.

The ways in which we study interpersonal communication will need to become more dialogic, as well. In the face of ontological, epistemological, and methodological differences in how to study interpersonal communication, most interpersonal communication scholars can be categorized into one of these three positions: an ethnocentric view ("My approach is OK, but yours isn't"); a view of hollow pluralism ("My approach is OK and so is yours, but we have nothing to say to each other"); and a totalizing view ("You're OK because you're like me once superficial differences are stripped away") (Baxter & West, 1996). None of these positions embraces what Krippendorff (1980) refers to as the ethical imperative for dialogic inquiry, that is, acceptance and respect for the viability of other perspectives and a commitment to the active coordination of multiple, incommensurate views.

CONCLUSION

I have adopted a tone of scholarly suspicion in this address in order to question three taken-for-granted assumptions about interpersonal communication. These assumptions cohere around a conception of interpersonal communication that fundamentally ignores the social relatedness of everyday lived experience.

If you are thinking to yourself, "just more of that trendy postmodern stuff," you are partly correct. The issues I am raising here are among those embraced by several theorists who are defined as "postmodern" (for recent discussions of the implications of postmodernist thinking for interpersonal communication, see Stewart, 1991). But I think we are deluding ourselves if we think that such notions are mere fads that will disappear as our intellectual enterprise gets on with its business-as-usual. What is at stake in such issues as the self-in-relation, the micro-macro collapse, and the contested terrain of everyday interaction is a different way of conceiving the human experience than what is found in traditional interpersonal communication research and theory. As Bakhtin (1984, p. 287) has observed, it is a perspective that embraces "the highest degree of sociality."

REFERENCES

Bakhtin, M. M. (1981). *The dialogic imagination: Four essays by M. M. Bakhtin* (M. Holquist, Ed.; C. Emerson & M. Holquist, Trans.). Austin: University of Texas Press.

Bakhtin, M. M. (1984). *Problems of Dostoevsky's poetics* (C. Emerson, Ed. and Trans.). Minneapolis: University of Minnesota Press. (Original work published 1929)

Bakhtin, M. M. (1986). *Speech genres and other late essays* (C. Emerson & M. Holquist, Eds.; V. McGee, Trans.). Austin: University of Texas Press.

Baxter, L. A., & Montgomery, B. M. (1996). *Relating: Dialogues & dialectics.* New York: The Guilford Press.

Baxter, L. A., & West, L. (1996). On "Whistler's Mother" and discourse of the fourth kind. *Western Journal of Communication, 60,* 92–100.

Duck, S. (1994). *Meaningful relationships: Talking, sense, and relating.* Thousand Oaks, CA: Sage.

Duck, S., & Pond, K. (1989). Friends, Romans, countrymen, lend me your retrospective data: Rhetoric and reality in personal relationships. In C. Hendrick (Ed.), *Close relationships* (pp. 3–27). Newbury Park, CA: Sage.

Gergen, K. (1994). *Realities and relationships: Soundings in social construction.* Cambridge, MA: Harvard University Press.

Krippendorff, K. (1980). On the ethics of constructing communication. In B. Dervin, L. Grossberg, B. O'Keefe, & E. Wartella (Eds.), *Rethinking communication: Volume 1. Paradigm issues* (pp. 66–96). Newbury Park, CA: Sage.

Miller, G. R., & Steinberg, M. (1975). *Between people: A new analysis of interpersonal communication.* Palo Alto, CA: Science Research Associates.

Montgomery, B. M. (1988). Quality communication in personal relationships. In S. Duck (Ed.), *Handbook of personal relationships* (pp. 343–359). New York: Wiley.

Parks, M. R. (1994). Communicative competence and interpersonal control. In M. L. Knapp & G. R. Miller (Eds.), *Handbook of interpersonal communication* (2nd ed.) (pp. 589–620). Thousand Oaks, CA: Sage.

Reddy, M. J. (1979). The conduit metaphor: A case of frame conflict in our language about language. In A. Ortony (Ed.), *Metaphor and thought* (pp. 284–324). Cambridge: Cambridge University Press.

Sampson, E. E. (1993). *Celebrating the other: A dialogic account of human nature.* San Francisco, CA: Westview Press.

Shotter, J. (1984). *Social accountability and selfhood.* Oxford: Blackwell.

Shotter, J. (1993). *Conversational realities.* London: Sage.

Stamp, G. H., & Knapp, M. L. (1990). The construct of intent in interpersonal communication. *Quarterly Journal of Speech, 76,* 282–299.

Stewart, J. (1991). A postmodern look at traditional communication postulates. *Western Journal of Communication, 55,* 354–379.

Todorov, T. (1984). *Mikhail Bakhtin: The dialogical principle* (W. Godzich, Trans.). Minneapolis: University of Minnesota Press. (Original work published 1981)

Voloshinov, V. N./Bakhtin, M. M. (1973). *Marxism and the philosophy of language* (L. Matejks & I. R. Titunik, Trans.). Cambridge: Harvard University Press.

CHAPTER 3

AT THE HELM IN INTERPERSONAL COMMUNICATION: SOCIAL COGNITIVE APPROACHES

Introduction

Paul A. Mongeau
Miami University

When I teach the introductory interpersonal communication class at Miami, students sometimes lament having to spend an *entire semester* on such a topic. Their complaints center upon two specific and related points. First, since everybody communicates every day, interpersonal communication cannot be terribly complex or difficult to understand. Second, interpersonal communication is "only common sense." Of course, students only make these claims early in the semester. As the class develops, students realize that effective interpersonal communication does not follow a small number of simple, culturally developed, and widely shared rules of conduct (no matter what the plethora of popular self-help books and infomercials claim). Over the course of the semester, students realize that interpersonal communication is indeed a complex enterprise.

Work described by the three chapters in this section are examples of the challenging nature of interpersonal communication. As this section's title makes clear, these theorists' chapters center upon social cognitive perspectives on interpersonal communication. According to these perspectives, interpersonal communication involves an interplay of thought and action. According to

these theorists, cognitive work and cognitive structures play an important role in the production and interpretation of messages as well as in the relationships that these messages create.

The three papers in this section focus on varying aspects of the interplay between social cognition and interpersonal communication. First, cognitions influence both the production and the interpretation of messages produced in an interaction. Consistent with this focus, Roloff discusses messages and cognitions during conflict interactions in a variety of interpersonal settings. Second, an important component in many social cognitive approaches is the concept of self. Consistent with this focus, Burleson focuses on how similarity in cognitive structures and functions (both actual and perceived) influence relational satisfaction. Finally, Greene's work forces us to reconsider and expand our view of the self in social interaction and interpersonal communication.

It is in this complex interplay between thought and action where neophyte students of interpersonal communication miss the boat. Students' complaints about studying interpersonal communication reflect an assumption that one can mindlessly sail through interpersonal communication and not put a lot of thought in on what he or she is doing. Students and scholars of interpersonal communication gain considerable speed (i.e., understanding and competency) by considering the interplay between thought and action. It is these three scholars who have taken the helm in the study of this interesting and important set of issues in interpersonal communication.

How People Make Sense of Everyday, Interpersonal Events: Examining the Perceived Connection among Conflict Episodes

Michael E. Roloff
Northwestern University

Most individuals interact with others on an everyday basis. At first blush, such encounters seem quite ordinary, and therefore, inconsequential. However, such a judgment is woefully inaccurate. Although routine, the nature of everyday interactions can profoundly affect a person's sense of well-being. When most encounters are supportive, individuals enjoy higher self-esteem, and are more likely to believe that they can control their fate than when such encounters are rare (Lakey, Tardiff, & Drew, 1994). Conversely, when most of their daily interactions are negative, individuals suffer distress (Lakey, Tardiff, & Drew, 1994), and the frequency of such aversive encounters can have greater impact on a person's well-being than does the occurrence of supportive ones (Schuster, Kessler, & Aseltine, 1990). Ironically, those persons toward whom individuals feel most intimate are often sources of both supportive and negative encounters (Argyle & Furnham, 1983; Schuster et al., 1990; Vinokur & van Ryn, 1993). Not surprisingly, such daily intimate negative interactions can aversively affect relational satisfaction (Wills, Weiss, & Patterson, 1974), and stability (McGonagle, Kessler, & Gotlib, 1993). Clearly, the ordinary can be consequential.

Although most scholars recognize that conflict has the potential to serve a variety of positive functions (Folger, Poole, & Stutman, 1993), individuals frequently characterize their everyday conflicts as negative events (McCorkler & Mills, 1992). Accordingly, individuals try to identify the causes of their conflicts, the circumstances under which they occur, the nature of the negative consequences associated with them, and possible solutions (Witteman, 1988). Appropriately, communication researchers have taken up the challenge of identifying how individuals can effectively manage these commonplace threats to their psychological and relational well-being (e.g., Alberts, 1988; Canary & Spitzberg, 1989; Sillars, Pike, Jones, & Redmon, 1983; Ting-Toomey, 1983; Williamson & Fitzpatrick, 1985; Witteman, 1992). Although providing many useful insights, the utility afforded by extant research is limited by our approaches to studying relational problems.

For the most part, we have studied relational discord in one of two ways. First, we have examined the conflict management behaviors that are enacted within a given episode. To create such encounters, couples are instructed to discuss a real or hypothetical problem for some period of time selected by the researcher. Although during the study, individuals may be asked to discuss more than one issue, each issue is the focus of a separate episode. The content of their recorded discussion is then coded for any number of different communication behaviors. Second, other researchers have asked individuals to report how frequently they have engaged in certain behaviors during their discussions of actual relational problems over some recent period of time. This approach frequently ignores the issues about which couples are reporting in favor of summarizing their behavior across all such encounters.

Although each of the aforementioned approaches can be usefully employed to answer certain research questions, they both provide a distinct, but perhaps unintended, impression of what everyday conflict management is like. The former approach implies that "snippets" of conflict encounters provide complete, or at least representative, pictures of how individuals deal with a particular dispute. In a sense, the behavior enacted during the contrived encounter is assumed to provide the essential information for understanding interpersonal problem-solving. Similarly, the second approach assumes that the nature of a particular conflict is irrelevant. In effect, it implies that one can gain the best insight into relational problem-solving by focusing on patterns of behavior apparent across relational problems.

Both methodological approaches ignore the sense-making activities of the individuals experiencing conflict. Rarely are respondents asked about their impressions of the prior history of the dispute, or asked why they try to manage the disagreement in a particular fashion. Research on everyday conflict management suggests that our current approaches may not provide a complete account for how relational problem-solving is conducted. Although the methods employed to assess everyday conflict processes have their own inherent biases, they yield a somewhat different and more complex picture of relational problem-solving than has been afforded by our traditional methodological approaches. In this presentation, I will examine several insights emerging from this research.

First, the process of relational conflict management frequently starts well in advance of a confrontation between relational partners. I have always preferred Deutsch's (1973) definition of conflict because it separates conflict from arguing about an issue. He defines conflict as the existence of incompatible activity where incompatible means that one action prevents, interferes with, or makes another one less effective. Such interference can occur in the absence of a confrontation, and research on everyday conflict management suggests that it does.

Often, there is a delay between the point at which an individual perceives a relational problem, and when he or she confronts the partner about it (Lee, 1984). Even individuals who have been angered frequently do not disclose their frustration to their partners until there have been multiple provocations (Baumeister, Stillwell, & Wotman, 1990). During this time, the provocative partner may be completely unaware that there is a problem, or may misunderstand the depth of the individual's anger (Baumeister et al., 1990). However, this does not mean that conflict management is dormant.

Prior to confronting a partner, an individual may try to make sense of the problem, cope with it, and failing that, prepare for the initial confrontation. During this period, there may be substantial communication, albeit not with the partner, and frequently of a covert nature. Individuals may be mulling about the seriousness of the problem, and trying to identify its cause (Cloven & Roloff, 1991). To the extent that it is perceived to be unimportant, individuals may choose to withhold their complaint from their partner (Cloven & Roloff, 1994). Should the problem be sufficiently urgent, individuals may decide to engage the partner (Newell & Stutman, 1991). In preparation to do so, they may privately rehearse what they intend to say (Stutman & Newell, 1990), and may even construct an imagined confrontation in which the partner responds (Edwards, Honeycutt, & Zagacki, 1988). As a result of this preparation, they may reduce their anxiety and bolster their self-confidence (Stutman & Newell, 1990). On the other hand, they may become more self-critical (Cloven & Roloff, 1993b), or they may anticipate coercive reactions from their partner (Cloven & Roloff, 1993a) and choose to remain silent.

Clearly, there are important processes that occur prior to an encounter that are missed when we focus exclusively on a confrontational episode. Although some confrontations may begin impulsively (Trapp & Hoff, 1985), many may be the next step in a deliberative sequence.

Second, when a confrontation is initiated, conflict does not always ensue, and when it does, conflict episodes tend to be brief, and often end with no resolution. For a confrontation to become a conflict, the target must understand that a complaint has been made, and then respond in a manner that signals disagreement with the complaint.

In some cases, they may not recognize the initiation to be a complaint, or may not wish to take up the challenge (Newell & Stutman, 1989/90). Regardless of the reason, they avoid making an oppositional move. For example, when studying quarrels at the family dinner table, Vuchinich (1987) found a "1/3 avoid-2/3 fight" pattern. Across 114 confrontational initiations, the target of an initiation responded in a nonoppositional way (e.g., changed the topic, ignored the complaint) in 36 percent of the cases. In these cases, the target let the complaint pass without comment, and avoided conflict.

Furthermore, when the challenge is taken up, the episode is often relatively short. Vuchinich (1987) found that family quarrels ranged from 2 to 12 speaking turns and averaged about 5. College students who keep diaries of their daily arguments report that they average about 3 minutes in length (Benoit & Benoit, 1987). That does not mean that conflicts seem brief to their participants. When college students are asked to estimate the length of their typical daily argument, the average is 15 rather than 3 minutes (Benoit & Benoit, 1987).

Thus, individuals typically "get in and out" of their conflicts rather quickly. However, they often leave the issue unresolved. Vuchinich (1987) found that 65 percent of family quarrels ended with the parties changing the topic, refusing to discuss the matter any further, or leaving the room without resolving the issue at hand. About 40 percent of daily arguments among college students (Benoit & Benoit, 1987), and 48 percent of arguments between dating partners end in a similar fashion (Lloyd, 1987). The aforementioned patterns forecast another insight into the features of everyday conflicts.

Third, given that many conflict episodes end with no apparent resolution, it is not surprising that disputes sometimes reoccur. When describing their typical arguments, 45 percent of a sample of college students report that a given argument reoccurs fairly often with the same person, and an additional 50 percent indicate that it occasionally resurfaces with the same person (Benoit & Benoit, 1987). Furthermore, some intimates report that

their current arguments can be traced far back into their relational history (Hale, Tighe, Ficara, & Lyttle, 1995). Trapp and Hoff (1985) refer to such extended sequences as serial arguments. Instead of viewing a conflict as a single, time-bounded encounter, this perspective conceives of conflict as a series of distinct, but interrelated, episodes.

Treating conflict as a serial phenomena raises a number of interesting issues. One of the most important ones concerns the activity that occurs between argumentative episodes. Trapp and Hoff (1985) speculate that serial arguments go through a "flare up, cool off, try again" pattern. When encountering resistance, arguments can become heated, and individuals frequently disengage (e.g., change the topic, or even leave the situation) so as to prevent further escalation. After calming down, they may choose to re-engage.

The aforementioned pattern suggests that such "time outs" may enhance the ability to manage the dispute. However, the success of such disengagement may depend upon what individuals think about while they are apart. Some individuals may respond to their heated exchange by replaying the argument in their imaginations (Zagacki, Edwards, Honeycutt, 1992). When doing so, they may think about what they should have said, or plan what they will say in the next encounter (Honeycutt, Zagacki, & Edwards, 1990). Regardless, dwelling on negative interactions can increase one's hostility toward the partner (Sadler & Tesser, 1973).

A second issue concerns that manner in which the content of serial arguments might change over time. Unfortunately, extant research has not explicitly addressed this issue. However, research on formal negotiations indicates that across sessions, the arguments raised by the various parties shift in focus and proposals are modified (Putnam, Wilson, & Turner, 1990). Although everyday relational conflicts differ in obvious ways from formal negotiations, it is possible that the issues contained therein may also evolve. Issues may be added and others may be unlinked. Solutions may be proposed, modified, and abandoned. Regardless of the particular changes that are made, the key factor may be that the individuals involved in the dispute feel that they are making progress toward settling the issue . When the positions and statements become predictable, the partners may doubt that the conflict can be resolved, and the relationship is put in jeopardy (Johnson & Roloff, 1995).

The final issue is focused on why a particular argument becomes serial. Clearly, some issues are resolved in a single encounter. Why then do others become a permanent feature of the relational terrain? Although conflict researchers do not like to admit such, there may be some issues that are inherently beyond the control of individuals. For example, when a relational partner is discovered to have committed a relational transgression (Metts, 1994; Roloff & Cloven, 1994), the transgressive act cannot be changed. The transgressor might apologize, make restitution, and promise never to repeat the act. The victim might even be forgiving, but the act itself cannot be rescinded. It occurred and remains an event in relational history. As a result, it may become a reoccurring topic of argument, or may play an explicit or implicit role in other disputes.

The *last* insight afforded by research on everyday conflicts is that individuals often find ways to cope with them. Relational partners may not be able to solve their problems, but may be able to control or minimize their negative impact. In some cases, a relational topic may become taboo, rarely, if ever, to be discussed again (Baxter & Wilmot, 1985). In other cases, individuals may effectively cope with their relational problems by focusing on how their relationship is improving, or is better than that of their peers (Meneghan, 1982). In yet other cases, they may try to repair the damage done to their relationship (Courtright, Millar, Rogers, & Bagarozzi, 1990). Thus, relational partners may enact strategies aimed at resolving the issue and controlling any damage arising from it.

In my view, research on everyday conflict has yielded important insights into the lives of individuals. There is an element of realism and complexity inherent within the findings. That is not to

say that prior research has produced unrealistic, simplistic results. Indeed, interaction-based research is an important tool for understanding conflict management, and its use should be continued. However, we should not assume that it captures the entirety of everyday conflict management. To do that, we will need to employ a wide variety of methods.

I realize that the study of everyday conflicts may require methodologies that have their own set of contestable assumptions. For the most part, it will be difficult to gather data about ongoing disputes without relying upon either self-reports or behavioral assessments of small samples. The former are subject to a variety of documented distortions, and the latter will suffer from low statistical power. Furthermore, it will be virtually impossible to follow the "life" of an ongoing dispute. It is difficult to know when they begin, and their endpoint may be equally unpredictable. As a result, our approach to studying them will require us to examine short segments of an ongoing conflict which may yield pieces of the puzzle that do not fit together well. Hence, the conclusions that we draw from such inquiry, including those cited in this paper, must be treated with appropriate caution.

Yet, methodological problems are not new, and should not discourage us. Professor Gerald R. Miller once told me that the demanding methodological standards we enforce on ourselves discourage some scholars from pursing important research questions. After all, if you cannot do it right, why do it at all? Gerry did not advocate reduced standards, but instead noted that our demanding ones should motivate us to develop new and better methods, or to find ways of compensating for the inherent weaknesses in the traditional ones. Such should be the case for those interested in researching everyday conflicts.

I also acknowledge that the study of everyday conflicts may require us to explore phenomena that some scholars may not judge to be appropriate subject matter for communication researchers. Increasingly, research in interpersonal communication has focused on interaction. Certainly, everyday conflict includes such conversational processes, but it also involves covert, sense-making processes that take place before, during, and after confrontational episodes. The latter may not seem like "communication" to some scholars. However, research on intrapersonal communication has grown over the last few years, and it is an accepted part of communication inquiry. In my view, it can be studied without losing our distinct professional identities.

Although this presentation has focused on my own research specialization, I think (hope) that it provides insights for scholars working in other areas. Not all everyday interactions are focused on conflicts between relational partners. Some conversations are of a supportive nature as individuals work together to deal with extra-relational threats or challenges (e.g., unemployment, illness) to their well-being. It is possible that many of the same processes that are associated with making sense of everyday conflict may also be observed in these domains.

Thus, as I noted at the beginning of the paper, I believe that the ordinary can be consequential. Although dramatic events will and must draw our scholarly attention, the everyday is equally important and should not be overlooked.

REFERENCES

Alberts, J. K. (1988). An analysis of couples' conversational complaints. *Communication Monographs, 55,* 184–196.

Argyle, M., & Furnham, A. (1983). Sources of satisfaction and conflict in long-term relationships. *Journal of Marriage and the Family, 45,* 481–493.

Baumeister, R. F., Stillwell, A., & Wotman, S. R. (1990). Victim and perpetrator accounts of interpersonal conflict: Autobiographical narratives about anger. *Journal of Personality and Social Psychology, 59,* 994–1005.

Baxter, L. A., & Wilmot, W. W. (1985). Taboo topics in close relationships. *Journal of Social and Personal Relationships, 2,* 253–269.

Benoit, W. J., & Benoit, P. J. (1987). Everyday argument practices of naive social actors. In J. W. Wentzel (Ed.), *Argument and critical practices* (pp. 465–473). Annandale, VA: Speech Communication Association.

Canary, D. J., & Spitzberg, B. H. (1989). A model of perceived competence of conflict strategies. *Human Communication Research, 15,* 630–649.

Cloven, D. H., & Roloff, M. E. (1991). Sense-making activities and interpersonal conflict: Communicative cures for the mulling blues. *Western Journal of Speech Communication, 55,* 134–158.

Cloven, D. H., & Roloff, M. E. (1993a). The chilling effect of aggressive potential on the expression of complaints in intimate relationships. *Communication Monographs, 60,* 199–219.

Cloven, D. H., & Roloff, M. E. (1993b). Sense-making activities and interpersonal conflict, II: The effects of communicative intentions on internal dialogue. *Western Journal of Communication, 57,* 309–329.

Cloven, D. H., & Roloff, M. E. (1994). A developmental model of decisions to withhold relational irritations in romantic relationships. *Personal Relationships, 1,* 143–164.

Courtright, J. A., Millar, F. E., Rogers, L. E., & Bagarozzi, D. (1990). Interaction dynamics of relational negotiation: Reconciliation versus termination of distressed relationships. *Western Journal of Speech Communication, 54,* 429–453.

Deutsch, M. (1973). *The resolution of conflict: Constructive and destructive processes.* New Haven, CT: Yale University Press.

Edwards, R., Honeycutt, J. M., & Zagacki, K. S. (1988). Imagined interaction as an element of social cognition. *Western Journal of Speech Communication, 52,* 23–45.

Folger, J. P., Poole, M. S., & Stutman, R. K. (1993). *Working through conflict: Strategies for relationships. groups, and organizations* (2nd ed.). New York: Harper Collins College Publishers.

Hale, J. L., Tighe, R., Ficara, L., & Lyttle, M. (1995, November). *Accounts and attributions of serial arguments in personal relationships.* Paper presented at the Annual Convention of the Speech Communication Association, San Antonio, TX.

Honeycutt, J. M., Zagacki, K. S., & Edwards, R. (1990). Imagined interaction and interpersonal communication. *Communication Reports, 3,* 1–8.

Johnson, K. L., & Roloff, M. E. (1995, November). *The nature and effects of serial arguments in dating relationships.* Paper presented at the Annual

Convention of the Speech Communication Association, San Antonio, TX.

Lakey, B., Tardiff, T. A., & Drew, J. B. (1994). Negative social interactions: Assessment and relations to social support, cognition, and psychological distress. *Journal of Social and Clinical Psychology, 13,* 42–62.

Lee, L. (1984). Sequences in separation: A framework for investigating endings of the personal (romantic) relationship. *Journal of Social and Personal Relationships, 1,* 49–73.

Lloyd, S. (1987). Conflict in premarital relationships: Differential perceptions of males and females. *Family Relations, 36,* 290–294.

McCorkler, S., & Mills, J. L. (1992). Rowboat in a hurricane: Metaphors of interpersonal conflict management. *Communication Reports, 5,* 57–64.

McGonagle, K. A., Kessler, R. C., & Gotlib, I. H. (1993). The effects of marital disagreement style, frequency, and outcome on marital disruption. *Journal of Social and Personal Relationships, 10,* 385–404.

Meneghan, E. (1982). Measuring coping effectiveness: A panel analysis of marital problems and coping efforts. *Journal of Health and Social Behavior, 23,* 220–234.

Metts, S. (1994). Relational Transgressions. In W. R. Cupach & B. H. Spitzberg (Eds.), *The dark side of interpersonal communication* (pp. 217–239). Hillsdale, NJ: Erlbaum.

Newell, S. E., & Stutman, R. K. (1989/90). Negotiating confrontation: The problematic nature of initiation and response. *Research on Language and Social Interaction, 23,* 139–162.

Newell, S. E., & Stutman, R. K. (1991). The episodic nature of social confrontation. In Anderson, J. A. (Ed.), *Communication yearbook* (Vol. 14, pp. 359–392). Thousand Oaks, CA: Sage.

Okun, M. A., Melichar, J. F., & Hills, M. D. (1990). Negative daily events, positive and negative social ties, and psychological distress among older adults. *The Gerontologist, 30,* 193–199.

Putnam, L. L., Wilson, S. R., & Turner, D. B. (1990). The evolution of policy arguments in teachers' negotiations. *Argumentation, 4,* 129–152.

Roloff, M. E., & Cloven, D. H. (1994). When partners transgress: Maintaining violated relationships. In D. J. Canary & L. Stafford (Eds.), *Communication and relational maintenance* (pp. 23–44). San Diego: Academic Press.

Sadler, O., & Tesser, A. (1973). Some effects of salience and time upon interpersonal hostility and attraction during social isolation. *Sociometry, 36,* 99–112.

Schuster, T. L., Kessler, R. C., & Aseltine, R. H. (1990). Supportive interactions, negative interactions, and depressed mood. *American Journal of Community Psychology, 18,* 423–438.

Sillars, A. L., Pike, G. R., Jones, T. S., & Redmon, K. (1983). Communication and conflict in marriage. In R. Bostrom (Ed.), *Communication yearbook* (Vol. 7, pp. 414–429). Thousand Oaks, CA: Sage.

Stutman, R. K., & Newell, S. E. (1990). Rehearsing for confrontation. *Argumentation, 4,* 185–198.

Ting-Toomey, S. (1983). An analysis of verbal communication patterns in high and low marital adjustment groups. *Human Communication Research, 9,* 306–319.

Trapp, R., & Hoff, N. (1985). A model of serial argument in interpersonal relationships. *Journal of the American Forensic Association, 22,* 1–11.

Williamson, R. N., & Fitzpatrick, M. A. (1985). Two approaches to marital interaction: Relational control patterns in marital types. *Communication Monographs, 52,* 236–252.

Wills, T. A., Weiss, R. L., & Patterson, G. R. (1974). A behavioral analysis of the determinants of marital satisfaction. *Journal of Consulting and Clinical Psychology, 42,* 802–811.

Witteman, H. (1988). Interpersonal problem solving: Problem conceptualization and communication use. *Communication Monographs, 55,* 336–359.

Witteman, H. (1992). Analyzing interpersonal conflict: Nature of awareness, type of initiating event, situational perceptions, and management styles. *Western Journal of Communication, 56,* 248–280.

Vinokur, A. D., & van Ryn, M. (1993). Social support and undermining in close relationships: Their independent effects on the mental health of unemployed persons. *Journal of Personality and Social Psychology, 65,* 350–359.

Vuchinich, S. (1987). Starting and stopping spontaneous family conflicts. *Journal of Marriage and the Family, 49,* 591–601.

Zagacki, K. S., Edwards, R., & Honeycutt, J. M. (1992). The role of mental imagery and emotion in imagined interaction. *Communication Quarterly, 40,* 56–68.

The Dawning of a New Conception of the Social Actor

John O. Greene
Purdue University

All approaches to the study of human behavior, scientific or otherwise, can be seen to reflect some root metaphor concerning the fundamental nature of human beings. Although typically implicit, such metaphors play a powerful role in legitimating specific theoretical perspectives and research questions. With respect to social cognitive approaches to human behavior, Fiske and Taylor (1991) have identified a series of these metaphors that have characterized the assumptive foundation of researchers at one time or another. My primary purpose here is to sketch a new conceptual framework concerning the nature of the social actor. This view represents a rather radical departure from prevailing perspectives, both inside and outside cognitive science, but I believe that it expresses a conception of human beings that will become increasingly prominent in cognitive research and theory in the coming decades.

COMMUNICATION'S PLACE
IN THE DISCIPLINARY MATRIX
OF COGNITIVE SCIENCE

Before turning to exposition of the view of the social actor I have in mind, it is important to note that scholars in the field of communication, particularly those pursuing scientific approaches to the study of human behavior, have a considerable stake in such issues. Two points can be seen to support this claim. First, cognitive science is no less a legitimate part of communication than it is of any other academic discipline. Beyond this, it is important to realize that a very large number of people in disciplines other than communication are bringing the theories and methods of cognitive science to bear in exploring issues of message production and

processing that fall squarely within the realm of what we in the field of communication would take to be "our own" (see Greene, 1995).

With respect to the first of these points, communication scholars need to keep in mind that cognitive science is not co-extensive with the field of psychology (or any other traditional academic field for that matter); rather, it is an interdisciplinary enterprise that stands at the confluence of a number of scholarly disciplines including artificial intelligence, linguistics, neuroscience, philosophy, and anthropology, as well as psychology (see Gardner, 1985). Moreover, I have argued elsewhere (Greene, 1995) that the intellectual traditions of our field place communication researchers in a position not simply to be legitimate players in the cognitive revolution, but to make a unique contribution to the broader fabric of cognitive science.

On the second point, the study of communication processes from a cognitive perspective by scholars in other fields is a thriving intellectual enterprise. If we are to hold our own at a time when the very existence of communication departments at universities around the country is being called into question, then we need to be actively engaged in the discussion of issues such as that under examination here.

COGNITIVE SCIENCE AND THE STUDY
OF HUMAN BEHAVIOR

As might be expected for such a widespread, interdisciplinary movement, the practitioners of cognitive science can be seen to hold a range of distinct philosophical, theoretical, and methodological commitments. Nevertheless, it is possible to articulate a set of general features that, while not applicable for every individual and research tradition, does characterize the mainstream of cognitivism as an approach to the study of human behavior. Among these characteristics are the positions of cognitive science with respect to three interrelated metatheoretical issues or problems: (1) locus of explanation, (2) explanatory stance, and (3) prominence of non-mental constructs (see Greene, 1994).

The locus of explanation problem concerns whether the causal mechanisms governing human action are located within or outside the individual. Virtually all cognitive scientists would readily acknowledge the impact of extra-individual influences on human behavior, but the individual is identified as the locus of the mechanisms underlying behavioral production, and external factors are seen to exert their influence only via the operation of more causally proximal internal events (see Greene, 1984).

To locate the causal mechanisms for human action within the individual leaves us confronting the problem of explanatory stance, i.e., what sort of terms are appropriate for characterizing the intra-individual mechanisms that give rise to behavior. In his seminal essay, Dennett (1971) distinguishes three general approaches to characterizing intra-individual constructs: (1) the physical stance, in which the behavior of a system is explained via recourse to the physical composition of that system, (2) the design stance, where explanation involves specifying the system's functional architecture, and (3) the intentional stance, where explanation is given by the goals and information ascribed to the system in question. Of these three approaches, cognitive science is dominated by intentional and design-stance models (see Flanagan, 1984).

Finally, there is the issue of the role accorded non-mental constructs. More specifically, how does cognitivism treat physiological factors, on one hand, and social influences on the other? While there are certainly exceptions, the general thrust of cognitive science has been to minimize the prominence of both of these sorts of factors. As Gardner (1985, p. 6) has noted, cognitive sci-

ence tends to de-emphasize the physiological and social, and instead pursues "a level of analysis wholly separate from the biological or neurological, on one hand, and the sociological or cultural, on the other."

Again, I do not mean to suggest that cognitivism's stance with respect to these three metatheoretical problems exhausts the definitive characteristics of the approach or that all of the theoretical and empirical work being conducted under the rubric of cognitivism reflects a consensus on these issues. Still, the bulk of the work on human behavior from a cognitive perspective involves attempts to advance explanatory accounts by recourse to intra-individual constructs cast either in intentional (e.g., beliefs, goals, attitudes) or functional (e.g., semantic networks, scripts, production systems) terms. And, while most cognitivists would readily acknowledge that social and physiological factors play a role in human behavior, these influences are typically accorded a relatively minor role.

A NEW CONCEPTION
OF THE SOCIAL ACTOR

At the very foundation of the perspective I want to develop here is an observation that is at once straightforward and yet laden with implications for how we think about people and for the nature of the theories we construct to explain their behavior. This observation is simply that human behavior is the result of the joint interplay of social, psychological, and physiological influences. I suspect that very few of those engaged in the study of human behavior would take issue with such a claim. At the same time, there is a disjunction between this observation and the way we typically talk and theorize about human behavior. The prevailing approach among social and behavioral scientists is to come at the study of some behavioral phenomenon from the perspective of one (or in some cases, some amalgam of two) of these three domains. Thus, in the realm of emotion, for example, there are those who emphasize the role of social forces in emotional responses, others who accord prominence to psychological factors, and still others who apprehend emotions primarily in terms of physiological mechanisms.

In contrast to such parochial approaches, the conception of the social actor I want to advance here emphasizes that people are *not* social beings; neither are they psychological beings, nor physiological beings. Rather, they are more appropriately viewed as being simultaneously *all* of these things.

Now the real point here is not simply to pay lip service to the idea that human behavior is the product of the joint interplay of social, psychological, and physiological influences. Instead, if behavior is, indeed, the result of such a tripartite system, then we need to be engaged in the task of developing theories about the nature of the mechanisms by which the elements of this system interact in the production of behavior. Elsewhere (Greene, 1994) I have suggested that the situation is analogous to the development of person-by-situation interactionism in psychology (see Magnusson & Endler, 1977). In that case, there was some value in explicit recognition that both person and situation factors play a role in human behavior. The real promise of interactionism, however, lies in developing theories about the nature of person factors, situational factors, and the mechanisms governing their functional interplay in behavior. In much the same way, the tripartite-system view suggests the need for theories of human behavior that address the phenomena within their purview by recourse to specification of the mechanisms governing the interaction of social, psychological, and physiological factors.

TOWARD A NEW COGNITIVE SCIENCE

The implications of viewing human beings and their behavior in terms of the tripartite system extend beyond theoretical concerns with developing models that capture the operation of all three components of the system. At a metatheoretical level, this view suggests an alternative conception of the project of cognitive science. To illustrate, consider again the three metatheoretical problems outlined

above in light of a commitment to the notion that human behavior arises from the interplay of social, psychological, and physiological influences.

With respect to the problem of locus of explanation, it is important to note that acceptance of the tripartite-system view does not necessitate rejection of an internal locus for the explanatory mechanisms that give rise to human behavior. That is, it may be possible to incorporate social influences by recourse to intra-individual mechanisms (see Greene, 1984, 1994).

At the same time, while it is *possible* to retain an intra-individual approach in light of a commitment to the tripartite-system perspective, the tripartite system suggests at least three possible variations on cognitivism's traditional treatment of the locus of explanation problem, and these can be arrayed along a continuum of increasing departure from the prevailing approach. One possibility is simply to focus greater attention on the social-to-individual processes that govern the ways in which extra-individual factors, via the operation of internal mechanisms, come to play a role in a person's behavior. A second possibility is to explore models which treat external and internal mechanisms on an equal footing in attempting to specify the mechanisms that govern the interplay across the person-environment partition. Finally, it may be possible to reformulate the locus of explanation problem by doing away with internal versus external constructs altogether in favor of alternative perspectives that posit theoretical systems whose constructs are located neither within nor outside the individual.

On the question of explanatory stance, the implications of the tripartite-system perspective are clear. While cognitive science has been dominated by intentional and design-stance models, accepting the notion that social, psychological, and physiological factors act conjointly in the production of behavior suggests that hybrid models that incorporate physical-stance terms as well as elements of either the design- or intentional-stance (or both) are in order.

Finally, perhaps the most immediate implication of the tripartite-system view concerns its implications for the role accorded non-mental constructs. As I noted above, cognitive science has tended to de-emphasize the social and physiological, and, instead, has focused on psychological factors. Accepting the notion of the tripartite system suggests the need for a re-orientation that gives greater prominence to social and physiological constructs.

CONCLUSION

As an approach toward the study of human behavior, including those behaviors associated with message making and processing, cognitive science has proven to be an enormously productive enterprise. The cognitive revolution has resulted in a much better understanding of social attention processes, inference making, processing of nonverbal cues of emotion produced by others, reading, memory for social information, processing of persuasive messages, interpretation of indirect speech acts, production of verbal strings, slips of the tongue and other speech errors, and acquisition of social skill, to name just a few of the many areas that have been illuminated via the application of the theories and methods of cognitivism.

At the same time, I suspect that the approaching millennium will be accompanied by a gradual shift in the nature of work conducted under the rubric of cognitive science. At the foundation of this shift is recognition of the fact that human behavior is the result of the interplay of social, psychological, and physiological factors. At the level of our root conception of human beings, the implication of this fact is to emphasize that rather than viewing people as social beings, or psychological beings, or physiological beings, we are more appropriately

seen to be simultaneously all of these things. With respect to the development of theories of human behavior, the task is to develop theories that explicate the mechanisms of interaction between the three domains of the tripartite system. Finally, at a metatheoretical level, recognition of the role of this tripartite system in human behavior suggests an alternative characterization of the nature of cognitive science. Exploring these implications of the tripartite-system view should have the effect of further enhancing the already impressive list of insights about human behavior gleaned from research and theory in the cognitive tradition.

REFERENCES

Fiske, S. T., & Taylor, S. E. (1991). *Social cognition* (2nd ed.). New York: McGraw-Hill.

Flanagan, O. J., Jr. (1984). *The science of the mind.* Cambridge, MA: MIT Press.

Gardner, H. (1985). *The mind's new science: A history of the cognitive revolution.* New York: Basic Books.

Greene, J. O. (1984). Evaluating cognitive explanations of communicative phenomena. *Quarterly Journal of Speech, 70,* 241–254.

Greene, J. O. (1994). What sort of terms ought theories of human action incorporate? *Communication Studies, 45,* 187–211.

Greene, J. O. (1995, November). *Does the field have a future in the study of communication processes?* Paper presented at the annual meeting of the Speech Communication Association, San Antonio, TX.

Magnusson, D., & Endler, N. S. (Eds.). (1977). *Personality at the crossroads: Current issues in interactional psychology.* Hillsdale, NJ: Lawrence Erlbaum.

Similarities in Social Skills, Interpersonal Attraction, and the Development of Personal Relationships

Brant R. Burleson
Purdue University

Several of the classic questions in the social sciences concern the origins and outcomes of close personal relationships: Why are people attracted to certain others? And why do some relationships develop successfully while others do not? Scholars in different disciplines often provide distinct answers to these questions. For example, communication researchers view social-cognitive abilities and communication skills as major influences on interpersonal attraction and relationship development (see Burleson & Samter, 1994; Spitzberg & Cupach, 1989). In contrast, social psychologists have often seen interpersonal attraction as a product of similarity, especially similarities in attitudes, values, and personality traits (see Berscheid, 1985; Hendrick & Hendrick, 1992).

Recently, my colleagues and I have carried out a series of studies combining elements of both communication-based and social-psychological approaches to the origins and growth of close relationships. In our studies, we have focused on how similarities in social-cognitive and communication skills promote interpersonal attraction and the development of mutually satisfying relationships. In this brief article, I provide an overview of the rationale guiding these studies, summarize the results obtained in them, and consider several possible explanations for our findings—findings which, though predicted, have several unexpected implications.

SKILL SIMILARITY
AND INTERPERSONAL ATTRACTION

The notion that similarity promotes attraction and relational harmony is one of the oldest and most venerated ideas in the social sciences. The similarity-attraction thesis is at least as old as Aristotle's Nichomachean Ethics. Moreover, the assumption that similarity promotes attraction is an item of popular faith, as well as scientific hypothesis. After all, everyone knows that "birds of a feather flock together."

In psychology, research exploring the similarity-attraction thesis has largely focused on how similarities in attitudes, values, and personality traits affect interpersonal attraction and relationship development. Much of this research has been heavily influenced by the important theoretical and empirical work of Byrne and his associates (e.g., Byrne, 1971). Byrne was chiefly concerned with how similarities in internal psychological states such as attitudes influenced attraction, especially in initial interactions. In addition, Byrne's research primarily focused on the extent to which *perceived* similarities, rather than *actual* similarities, promoted attraction. In recent years, numerous features of Byrne's program have been criticized by both psychologists (e.g., Berscheid, 1985) and communication scholars (e.g., Sunnafrank, 1991). These critiques have led to alternative analyses of how similarity affects interpersonal attraction.

One intriguing alternative to Byrne's approach has become known as the *rewards of interaction* model (e.g., Berscheid, 1985; Davis, 1981). In the communication discipline, this model has been developed by my colleagues and me in research examining how similarities in social skills influence relationship growth and development (see Burleson, 1995; Burleson & Samter, 1994). In particular, we have focused on how similarities in social-cognitive skills (such as cognitive complexity and social perspective-taking ability) and functional communication skills (such as comforting skill, ego support skill, and conflict management skill) affect interpersonal attraction and relationship satisfaction. We chose to examine these skills because of the substantial research by both communication scholars and other social scientists showing that they serve important functions in initiating, maintaining, and managing close personal relationships (see the reviews by Burleson & Samter, 1994; Riggio & Zimmermann, 1991; Spitzberg & Cupach, 1989).

Our research has focused on how *actual* similarities, rather than *perceived* similarities, in social skills promote attraction and relationship satisfaction. In this research, we have assumed that similarities in social skills enhance attraction by *facilitating more enjoyable social interactions* (researchers expressing assumptions similar to ours include Duck, 1973; and Dweck, 1981). More specifically, our research has rested on two key postulates. First, we have assumed that people are attracted to others with whom they have *enjoyable interactions*. In other words, the engine driving relationship development is assumed to be enjoyable interactions. If people enjoy interacting with someone they will want to interact more with that person, with additional interaction leading to deepening intimacy, involvement, pleasure, and commitment to further interaction.

Our second core assumption—and the one central to our approach—is that *similarities in certain social and cognitive skills promote enjoyable interactions*. Specifically, we have reasoned that people with similar conceptions of social relationships, similar levels of social-cognitive development, similar communication skills—in short, similar levels of social skills—are more likely to: define social situations in the same way, see similar features of social situations as interactionally salient, view the duties and obligations of relationships similarly, want the same things from their relationships, enjoy talking about the same things, and so forth. Similarity in these areas is believed to contribute to mutually enjoyable interactions.

The conjunction of our two key assumptions has led to two basic predictions: First, we have hypothesized that people with more similar relationship conceptions, social-cognitive abilities, and communication skills will be more attracted to each other. Second, we have expected that persons having similar levels of social skills will form more satisfying relationships with each other.

RESEARCH EXAMINING HOW SIMILARITIES IN SOCIAL SKILLS AFFECT RELATIONSHIP FORMATION AND DEVELOPMENT

Colleagues and I have recently conducted a series of studies examining how similarities in social skills affect relationship formation and development (Burleson, 1994; Burleson & Denton, 1992; Burleson, Kunkel, & Birch, 1994; Burleson, Kunkel, & Szolwinski, in press; Burleson & Samter, 1996; Burleson, Samter, & Lucchetti, 1992). Each of these studies has addressed one or more of the following questions:

1. Do people who are attracted to each other have similar levels of social skills?
2. Are partners with similar levels of social skills happier or more satisfied with their relationships than partners who have dissimilar levels of skills?
3. Does level of relationship satisfaction vary with the social skill levels of partners, or is relationship satisfaction constant across level of social skill?

Do Those Who Are Attracted to Each Other Have Similar Skill Levels?

In our studies examining whether relationship partners have similar skills, participants have completed batteries of tasks assessing varied social-cognitive abilities, communication skills, and communication values. For example, Burleson (1994) had a sample of elementary school children complete measures of four different social-cognitive abilities (cognitive complexity, construct abstractness, social perspective-taking skill, affective perspective-taking skill) and five different communication skills (comforting skill, listener-adapted skill, persuasion skill, and two types of referential skill). Patterns of friendship and interpersonal attraction were assessed in each of the children's classrooms through sociometric procedures. As predicted, children were attracted to peers who had levels of social skills similar to their own. In addition, friends—pairs of children who expressed a high degree of reciprocal liking for each other—had similar levels of social skills, especially those skills used in the detection and management of emotional states.

The same research paradigm has been employed in studies examining several other relationships. Results comparable to those observed in our sample of children have been obtained with adult friends (Burleson & Samter, 1996; Burleson et al., 1992) and married couples (Burleson & Denton, 1992), though not with dating partners (Burleson et al., 1994; Burleson et al., in press, Study 2). Our results with children, adult friends, and married couples are consistent with the findings of other correlational research examining the role of social skill similarities in the relationships of children (Kurdek & Krile, 1982; Rubin, Lynch, Coplan, Rose-Krasnor, & Booth, 1994) and adult friends (Duck, 1972; G. Neimeyer & Neimeyer, 1981, 1986; R. Neimeyer & Mitchell, 1988; R. Neimeyer & Neimeyer, 1983; see the review by R. Neimeyer, Brooks, & Baker, 1995).

Although the results obtained in correlational studies are important, they do not establish that similarities in social skills directly enhance interpersonal attraction. Thus, Burleson et al. (in press, Study 1) conducted an experiment examining the effect of similarity in social-cognitive ability on diverse forms of interpersonal attraction. In this study, participants read interpersonal impressions putatively authored by a college student; these impressions were actually constructed by the researchers to reflect either a low or high level of interpersonal cognitive complexity. After reading these impressions, participants indicated their degrees of social, task, and intellectual attraction to the putative author. Participants' levels of cogni-

tive complexity were also assessed. As predicted, the cognitively complex author was perceived as more attractive by highly complex than less complex participants, while the cognitively simple author was perceived as more attractive by less complex than highly complex participants. These results, along with those of other experimental investigations (e.g., Johnston & Centers, 1973; Powers, Jordan, Gurley, & Lindstrom, 1986), support the claim that similarity in level of social-cognitive development is tied causally to increases in interpersonal attraction.

In sum, considerable support has been found for the notions that partners in close relationships have similar levels of social skills and that skill similarity enhances interpersonal attraction. Moreover, several studies (e.g., Burleson & Denton, 1992; Burleson et al., 1994; Burleson et al., in press; Burleson et al., 1992) have found that length of relationship does not moderate the degree of association in partners' skill levels. This latter finding suggests that the similarities in partners' skills cannot be attributed to *convergence* (the tendency to become increasingly alike over time). Rather, it appears that similarities in skills antedate the onset of the relationship, and thus may contribute to the attraction partners initially feel toward each other.

Are Similar Partners Happier?

Are partners who have similar levels of skills happier and more satisfied with their relationships than partners who have dissimilar skill levels? This is the second major question addressed in our research. If similarities in social skills facilitate more enjoyable social interactions, then relationship partners who have similar levels of skills should be more satisfied with their relationships than partners who have dissimilar skill levels.

We have addressed this research question in several studies. For example, in one study of dating partners (Burleson et al., in press, Study 2), we examined whether partners with similar levels of social perception skill (cognitive complexity) would be more attracted to each other than partners with dissimilar levels of cognitive complexity. An index of similarity in partners' levels of complexity was created by computing for each couple a discrepancy score for the difference in their complexity levels; a median split was then used to distinguish couples having low and high levels of similarity. To create couple-based indices of mutual attraction, partners' scores were summed for each of three different measures of attraction: social attraction, task attraction, and intellectual attraction. As expected, partners with similar levels of cognitive complexity expressed greater intellectual attraction to one another than partners with dissimilar levels of complexity. High-similarity partners also expressed greater social attraction and task attraction for each other than low-similarity partners, but these differences were not significant. In a related study (Burleson et al., 1994), correlational procedures showed that dating partners having similar communication values were both more attracted to each other and more satisfied with their relationship than partners having dissimilar communication values.

These findings are quite helpful in clarifying other results obtained with our sample of dating partners. When simply correlating partners' scores on measures of social cognition and communication values, few significant similarities were detected. However, further analyses revealed that the dating partners *who were similar* were more attracted to each other and more satisfied with their relationship. Thus, similarities in social-cognitive abilities and communication values may not effectively predict *who* people will date, but they are useful in predicting *how happy* partners will be in their dating relationships.

Similar procedures have been used in our studies of adult friends (Burleson & Samter, 1996) and married couples (Burleson & Denton, 1992) to determine whether partners having comparable skill levels are happier and more satisfied than partners having dissimilar skill levels. In general, the results of these studies were as expected, with partners who exhibited high levels of similarity in social-cognitive and communication skills report-

ing higher levels of happiness and satisfaction than partners who had low levels of similarity. Moreover, other researchers (e.g., G. Neimeyer, 1984) have also found that marital partners with similar levels of social-cognitive ability are more satisfied with their relationship than those having a dissimilar level of ability. In sum, it appears that partners with similar levels of social skills are happier with each other and have more satisfying relationships than partners who have dissimilar levels of skills.

Are Low-Skill Couples as Happy as High-Skill Couples?

The third major question pursued in our studies represents an effort to explain why people with similar skill levels chose each other as partners. It's easy enough to understand why high-skilled people end up with each other: They choose each other. But why do low-skilled people end up with each other? Is it because they are the only ones that will have each other? That is, are low-skilled options all that is left after the highly skilled pair off with each other? Or, do low-skilled people actively seek each other out? Are low-skilled people more attracted to similarly low-skilled individuals than they are to high-skilled persons? If low-skilled people end up with each other as the result of some residual selection process they should be less happy with each other and their relationship than high-skilled couples. On the other hand, if low-skilled people actively choose each other as partners, then they should be just as happy and satisfied with their relationships as high-skilled couples. Thus, we have sought to determine whether pairs of low-skilled partners are as happy with their relationships as pairs of high-skilled partners.

For example, in our study of married couples (Burleson & Denton, 1992), we identified couples where both partners had comparatively low levels of social-cognitive and communication skills as well as couples where both partners had high skills. We then compared the low-skilled and high-skilled couples on measures of marital satisfaction and liking for one's spouse. No differences were found between the low-skilled and high-skilled couples. Thus, low-skilled couples were just as happy with each other and just as satisfied with their marriages as high-skilled couples.

In our study of young adult friends (Burleson & Samter, 1996), we examined whether pairs of friends in which both partners had low levels of communication skills were less satisfied with their relationship (i.e., more lonely) than friend pairs in which both partners had high skill levels. Low-skilled dyads were no less satisfied (no less lonely) than high-skilled dyads. And in our study of dating couples (Burleson et al., in press), we examined whether dyads in which both partners had high levels of cognitive complexity were more attracted to one another and more satisfied with their relationship than couples in which both partners had low levels of complexity. Again, we found no differences between the low-skilled and high-skilled couples in their reported levels of interpersonal attraction and relationship satisfaction. In sum, we consistently have found that low-skilled dyads are no less happy or satisfied with their relationships than high-skilled dyads.

Finding that high-skilled couples are no more satisfied with their relationships than low-skilled couples is surprising and carries some disturbing implications for our ideas about social skill. These results clearly follow from the notion that skill similarity enhances the enjoyability of interactions. But although predicted by theory, these results are, in a very real sense, unexpected. They certainly are counter-intuitive to those who regularly preach (and teach!) that highly developed communication skills are necessary components of good, satisfying relationships. If good communication skills are essential to relationship success, then dyads where both partners are highly skilled should be very successful. And, in contrast, dyads where both partners have relatively low skill levels should be much less "successful"—the relationships of low-skill dyads should be less satisfying for their participants. But our results show that is not the case. In my remaining

space, I consider some potential explanations for these surprising findings.

WHY LOW-SKILLED COUPLES ARE JUST AS HAPPY AS HIGH-SKILLED COUPLES: SOME POTENTIAL EXPLANATIONS

I see four possible explanations for the finding that low-skilled couples are just as satisfied with their relationships as high-skilled couples. I will refer to these explanations as the *differential importance account,* the *ignorance is bliss account,* the *sour grapes account,* and the *skill-level-as-culture account.* To date, none of these accounts have been subject to direct test, although existing findings can be interpreted as supporting (and challenging) all four accounts. Thus, these accounts are presented as hypotheses that future research should seek to evaluate.

The *differential importance account* suggests that communication may not be that frequent or important an activity for some people, specifically the low skilled. If this assumption is true, then the low skill levels of one's partners shouldn't have much effect on relationship satisfaction because low-skill partners don't spend a lot of their time communicating. This explanation may seem like heresy to communication researchers, but we need to acknowledge that just because communication is important to us doesn't mean that it is necessarily important to everyone! Activities other than communication may be much more central in the relationships of the low skilled. Perhaps they *do* things rather than talk about them. Consistent with this view, critics such as Parks (1981) have argued that social scientists tend to overstate—and over-rate—the importance of communication in the personal relationships of many people. Supporting these critics, there is evidence that persons differ systematically in the importance they attach to communication skills in the context of personal relationships (e.g., Burleson & Samter, 1990). Research on gender differences in the communication of friends is also consistent with the view that communication plays a bigger role in the personal relationships of some people than others (see Aries, 1996).

The *ignorance is bliss account* suggests that people are satisfied with the relationships they have because they are unaware of better alternatives. In particular, the low skilled may be satisfied with their comparably low-skilled partners because they are unaware of alternatives. If the low skilled rarely encounter potential partners with high skills, they may remain unaware that there are "better" relationship alternatives. Levels of social skills tend to be relatively homogeneous within family, ethnic, and socioeconomic groupings (see Applegate, 1990). Because the field of potential relationship partners is often circumscribed by ethnic and socioeconomic factors, it is at least plausible to suggest that people can remain unaware that there are others who have substantially different levels of communication skills.

The *sour grapes account* suggests that persons with less developed social skills probably *are* aware that there are relationship alternatives more desirable than those they have. But, these better alternatives remain beyond the grasp of the low skilled. Hence, they rationalize their plight and reduce their dissonance by viewing the relationships they have as good—as good as it gets. They may even come to devalue the things they really want in relationships, but rarely receive (e.g., emotional support, intimacy). The sour grapes account thus retains the idea that the low skilled end up with each other as a function of a residual selection process. Highly skilled persons choose other highly skilled individuals as relationship partners, leaving the low skilled for each other. However, the sour grapes account invokes a dissonance reduction process on the part of the low skilled to explain the finding that low- and high-skilled couples do not differ in reported degree of relationship satisfaction. There is, of course, plentiful research showing that when people experience cognitive dissonance, they attempt to reduce it through just such rationalizations.

The final account, the *skill-level-as-culture account,* is the most radical explanation and carries some serious ramifications for our ideas regarding social skills and personal relationships. This account is premised on the assumption that most social scientific ideas about what's needed for a "good" relationship are elitist, biased, narrow, and flawed. The account further suggests that what we call differently skilled groups—the low skilled and the high skilled—are really different cultures (or co-cultures), each with its own ideas about the important skills in social relationships, and each with its own conceptions of what constitutes "skilled behavior." Indeed, there is some evidence showing that what we call the "low skilled" and "high skilled" have different implicit theories of communication (see the findings summarized by Burleson & Denton, 1992).

Viewing the "low skilled" and "high skilled" as different cultural groups has profound implications for how researchers should conceptualize and assess social skills. Most centrally, it entails recognizing that ideas about what constitutes "skill" are *arbitrary,* and necessarily must *remain* arbitrary. On this view, what counts as skill is solely a matter of cultural convention. Behavior isn't skilled because of some intrinsic feature or structure it exhibits; there is nothing in a behavior *per se* that makes it more or less skilled. Rather, it is social convention that determines some behavior to be more skilled than other behavior. And conventions will, naturally, be different for different groups. Hence, to make judgments about social skills, it is necessary to examine the values, practices, and standards of each group and extract the implicit theories of relationship development and communication held by those groups. Note that this account preserves the integrity of our subjects of study—researchers don't challenge participants' notions about what constitutes a good and satisfying close relationship. But this account does provide a radical challenge to contemporary ideas about what constitutes social skill and how social skills should be conceptualized and assessed.

CONCLUSION

The finding that low-skill couples are as satisfied with their relationships as high-skill couples, although predicted by theory, is inconsistent with many popular assumptions about the role of social skills in relationships. I have sketched four possible explanations for this surprising finding. Presently, there is not sufficient data to warrant choosing among these alternatives. However, the issues raised by these explanations certainly establish an agenda for future research. In particular, the "skill-level-as-culture" account suggests that researchers need to examine whether their conceptualizations and operationalizations of social skills are culturally variable or culturally invariant.

My guess is that most of our current conceptions of social skills contain elements that are both culturally variable and invariant. Obviously, though, this hunch is not very informative: We need to know the *particular* aspects of *specific* skills that are variable and invariant. Or, we need to discover the ways in which invariant aspects of skill are manifested in culturally variable ways. Carrying out the needed research on these issues will not be easy. But such research should contribute substantially to our understanding of personal relationships, the meaning of these relationships for their participants, and the roles played by social skills in the constitution and maintenance of these relationships.

REFERENCES

Applegate, J. L. (1990). Constructs and communication: A pragmatic integration. In G. Neimeyer (Ed.), *Advances in personal construct psychology* (Vol. 1, pp. 203–230). Greenwich, CT: JAI Press.

Aries, E. (1996). *Men and women in interaction: Reconsidering the differences.* New York: Oxford University Press.

Berscheid, E. (1985). Interpersonal attraction. In G. Lindzey & E. Aronson (Eds.), *Handbook of social psychology* (3rd ed., Vol. 2, pp. 413–484). New York: Random House.

Burleson, B. R. (1994). Friendship and similarities in social-cognitive and communication abilities: Social skill bases of interpersonal attraction in childhood. *Personal Relationships, 1,* 371–389.

Burleson, B. R. (1995). Personal relationships as a skilled accomplishment. *Journal of Social and Personal Relationships, 12,* 575–581.

Burleson, B. R., & Denton, W. H. (1992). A new look at similarity and attraction in marriage: Similarities in social-cognitive and communication skills as predictors of attraction and satisfaction. *Communication Monographs, 59,* 268–287.

Burleson, B. R., Kunkel, A. W., & Birch, J. D. (1994). Thoughts about talk in romantic relationships: Similarity makes for attraction (and happiness, too). *Communication Quarterly, 42,* 259–273.

Burleson, B. R., Kunkel, A. W., & Szolwinski, J. B. (in press). Similarities in cognitive complexity and attraction to friends and lovers: Experimental and correlational studies. *Journal of Constructivist Psychology.*

Burleson, B. R., & Samter, W. (1990). Effects of cognitive complexity on the perceived importance of communication skills in friends. *Communication Research, 17,* 165–182.

Burleson, B. R., & Samter, W. (1994). A social skills approach to relationship maintenance: How individual differences in communication skills affect the achievement of relationship functions. In D. J. Canary & L. Stafford (Eds.), *Communication and relational maintenance* (pp. 61–90). Orlando, FL: Academic Press.

Burleson, B. R., & Samter, W. (1996). Similarity in the communication skills of young adults: Foundations of attraction, friendship, and relationship satisfaction. *Communication Reports, 9,* 125–139.

Burleson, B. R., Samter, W., & Lucchetti, A. E. (1992). Similarity in communication values as a predictor of friendship choices: Studies of friends and best friends. *Southern Communication Journal, 57,* 260–276.

Byrne, D. (1971). *The attraction paradigm.* New York: Academic Press.

Davis, D. (1981). Implications for interaction versus effectance as mediators of the similarity-attraction relationship. *Journal of Experimental Research in Social Psychology, 17,* 96–116.

Duck, S. W. (1972). Friendship, similarity, and the reptest. *Psychological Reports, 31,* 231–234.

Duck, S. W. (1973). *Personal relationships and personal constructs: A study of formation.* London: Wiley.

Dweck, C. S. (1981). Social-cognitive processes in children's friendships. In S. R. Asher & J. M.

Gottman (Eds.), *The development of children's friendships* (pp. 322–333). New York: Cambridge University Press.

Hendrick, S. S., & Hendrick, C. (1992). *Liking, loving, and relating* (2nd ed.). Belmont, CA: Brooks/Cole.

Johnston, S., & Centers, R. (1973). Cognitive systemization and interpersonal attraction. *Journal of Social Psychology, 90,* 95–103.

Kurdek, L. A., & Krile, D. (1982). A developmental analysis of the relations between peer acceptance and both interpersonal understanding and perceived social self-competence. *Child Development, 53,* 1485–1491.

Neimeyer, G. J. (1984). Cognitive complexity and marital satisfaction. *Journal of Social and Clinical Psychology, 2,* 258–263.

Neimeyer, G. J., & Neimeyer, R. A. (1981). Functional similarity and interpersonal attraction. *Journal of Research in Personality, 15,* 427–435.

Neimeyer, G. J., & Neimeyer, R. A. (1986). Personal constructs in relationship deterioration: A longitudinal study. *Social Behavior and Personality, 14,* 253–257.

Neimeyer, R. A., Brooks, D. L., & Baker, K. D. (1995). Personal epistemologies and personal relationships: Consensual validation and impression formation in the acquaintance process. In D. Kalekin-Fishman & B. M. Walker (Eds.), *The construction of group realities* (pp. 127–159). Malabar, FL: Krieger.

Neimeyer, R. A., & Mitchell, K. A. (1988). Similarity and attraction: A longitudinal study. *Journal of Social and Personal Relationships, 5,* 131–148.

Neimeyer, R. A., & Neimeyer, G. J. (1983). Structural similarity and the acquaintance process. *Journal of Social and Clinical Psychology, 1,* 146–154.

Parks, M. L. (1981). Ideology in interpersonal communication: Off the couch and into the world. In M. Burgoon (Ed.), *Communication yearbook 5* (pp. 79–107), New Brunswick, NJ: Transaction Press.

Powers, W. G., Jordan, W. J., Gurley, K., & Lindstrom, E. (1986). Attributions toward cognitively complex sources based upon message samples. *Communication Research Reports, 3,* 110–114.

Riggio, R. E., & Zimmermann, J. (1991). Social skills and interpersonal relationships: Influences on social support and support seeking. In W. H. Jones & D. Perlman (Eds.), *Advances in personal relationships* (Vol. 2, pp. 133–155). London: Jessica Kingsley.

Rubin, K. H., Lynch, D., Coplan, R., Rose-Krasnor, L., & Booth, C. L. (1994). "Birds of a feather...": Behavioral concordances and preferential personal attraction in children. *Child Development, 65,* 1778–1785.

Spitzberg, B. H., & Cupach, W. R. (1989). *Handbook of interpersonal competence research.* New York: Springer-Verlag.

Sunnafrank, M. (1991). Interpersonal attraction and attitude similarity: A communication-based assessment. In J. A. Anderson (Ed.), *Communication yearbook 14* (pp. 451–483). Newbury Park, CA: Sage.

CHAPTER 4

AT THE HELM IN SOCIAL INFLUENCE AND GROUPS

Introduction

Paul E. Nelson
Ohio University

This "At the Helm" program, sponsored by NCA's First Vice President, Dr. Judith S. Trent, brings together the foremost scholars in social influence and small groups.

My name is Paul Nelson currently on sabbatical leave for 1 year after serving for 15 years as Dean of the College of Communication at Ohio University. My experience in social influence was not in the area of scholarship but in advancing teaching, research, and service in a college that was very highly regarded in the university. The small groups I lived with every day were college promotion and tenure committees, five-year planning committees, and the college executive committee. My role today is to introduce you to four of the finest scholars our discipline has produced, to get them on and off stage in an efficient manner, and to answer your questions.

I begin with Dr. Michael Burgoon, a Michigan State Ph.D. who comes to us from the University of Arizona. He is a Professor of Communication, Director of Communication Research in the Community Medicine section of the College of Medicine, and Research Professor in the Behavioral Sciences section of the Arizona Cancer Center in Tucson. A lecturer at a number of universities here and abroad, he is perhaps the only scholar in our field who is a board-appointed Visiting Distinguished Scholar in Psychology at Harvard. His most recent appoint-

ment is Senior Executive at Large reporting to the CEO of USA Today/Gannett Co., Inc., where for 18 months he will do research in new communication technologies, product development, and organizational change.

Dr. Burgoon is author of over 200 published articles and manuscripts, and editor or author of 38 chapters and 15 books. The winner of eight national or international awards for research excellence, he has published in many academic disciplines including communication, medicine, public health, psychology, management, education, and mass media studies.

Dr. Burgoon is a Fellow of the International Communication Association and an elected member of the Society for Experimental Social Psychology.

Dr. Burgoon has probably surpassed everyone in our discipline at garnering outside support from federal agencies, foundations, and corporations. Currently an investigator on three projects funded by the National Institutes of Health with budgets in excess of $4 million, he studies cancer prevention protocols, the impact of message strategies to promote sun safety, and HIV/AIDS education and prevention. His research on incorporating changing communication technologies is supported by the Gannett Company, the Gannett Foundation, and Assymetrix Software.

He did the original research that resulted in the design and launch of *USA Today*.

This morning, Dr. Burgoon's presentation is entitled "Social Influence Research at the Helm, on the Edge, or over the Abyss? *Quod enim malvut homo verum est id potius credit.*"

Our second paper this morning will be presented by Dr. Marshall S. Poole, a University of Wisconsin Ph.D. who is a Professor at Texas A&M University. Dr. Poole moved quickly through all three ranks at the University of Minnesota with earlier experience at the University of Illinois, the University of Michigan, and Michigan State University.

Dr. Poole has earned many prestigious awards since graduating Phi Beta Kappa from the University of Wisconsin. He earned the Dissertation of the Year Award from NCA in 1980. He wrote top-ranked papers five times for the International Communication Association in the Information Systems Division, the Interpersonal and Small Group Communication Division, and the Human Communication Technology Interest group. He won NCA's Golden Anniversary Monograph Award for his article on group decision making, and he won NCA's Organizational Communication Division Research Award.

Two of Dr. Poole's books have won honorable mention from professional organizations outside the field of communication, and he won the Best Paper Award in the Collaboration Technology Track at the International Conference on System Sciences. Still another paper was a finalist for the Outstanding Achievement Award of The Institute of Management Sciences. The co-author or editor of 6 books, Dr. Poole also contributed 30 articles, many book chapters, and numerous proceedings to our body of scholarship.

Dr. Poole has found funding 14 times for his research including a couple of National Science Foundation studies for $210,000 and $432,000. Many groups have turned to him as a consultant.

Finally, students at both the University of Illinois and at the University of Michigan rated him many times as a top teacher at those very large Research institutions.

This morning, Dr. Poole will talk with us on the topic "The Small Group Should Be the Fundamental Unit of Communication Research."

Our next presenter is Dr. Dennis S. Gouran, a Ph.D. from the University of Iowa and currently Professor of Speech Communication and Head of the Department of Speech Communication at Pennsylvania State University. Dr. Gouran was an Assistant, Associate, and Full Professor at the University of Indiana before moving to Penn State as Department Head.

Dr. Gouran has spent his professional life studying communication theory with a specialization in group decision making. In the process, he has earned an abundance of honors starting with the Central States Outstanding Young Teacher Award and ending with NCA's Distinguished Service Award. In the 20 years between those two honors, he earned NCA's Robert J. Kibler Award for Professional Excellence, NCA's Distinguished Scholar Award, and Penn State's University Faculty Scholar's Medal for the Social and Behavioral Sciences.

The advisor for over 40 Ph.D. students, Dr. Gouran has authored or edited ten books, monographs or edited collections; 34 book chapters or articles in published works; 37 published articles; 3 pages of book reviews; and more convention papers and appearances than I could count. In addition he has been associate editor of many of our most important publications and held enough professional offices in our national and regional associations to stagger the imagination.

This morning Dr. Gouran will speak on "The Signs of Cognitive, Affiliative, and Egocentric Constraints in Patterns of Interaction in Decision-Making and Problem-Solving Groups and Their Potential Effects on Outcomes." I present you with Dr. Dennis Gouran.

Our fourth speaker this morning is Dr. Robert Bostrom, a Ph.D. from the University of Iowa and Professor in the Department of Communication at the University of Kentucky. An army veteran, he taught previously at Sacramento State, Western Illinois University, and Ohio University before moving to the University of Kentucky where he also served as Chair of the Department.

Dr. Bostrom has written six books and edited three others. He has also published 10 book chapters and 32 articles, and delivered 50 convention papers. He has had seven grants. He has been dissertation advisor for 15 Ph.D. students and thesis advisor for another 48 students. The Young Scholar Award given annually by the Southern Speech Association is named after him, and he is the only person in this program to display talent. He played the lead in *Fiddler on the Roof,* served

as Artistic Director for the Lexington Musical Theatre for three years, and directed five musical theatre productions. I dare say that he can sing better than anyone on display here today.

Among his many professional and consulting activities, Dr. Bostrom has served as editor of the *Journal of the International Listening Association,* paper referee for nine journals, and President of the Southern Speech Communication Association.

This morning Dr. Bostrom will speak with us on the topic of "'Put the Helm Over!' and Steer a New Heading: Communication and 'Social Influence.'" I present you with Dr. Bostrom.

Social Influence Research: At the Helm, on the Edge, or over the Abyss?

Quod enim malvut homo verum est id potius credit

Michael Burgoon
University of Arizona

This is not the first occasion on which I have been asked to comment on the "state of the discipline," most usually but not limited to some area of social influence (cf. Burgoon, in press; Burgoon & Bailey, 1992; Burgoon & Miller, 1990; Miller & Burgoon, 1978). Obviously, one who has been asked *or* allowed to editorialize and/or pontificate (depending on your views of the comments) in so many venues, for this length of time, must be well past his intellectual prime. That being the case, it is quite likely that I will end my career being more well known for my political leanings and "editorials" than for the years I spent attempting to do decent science and advance knowledge in my area of keen interest, social influence. But so be it, for I am off on another such editorial journey in the Helms series sponsored by this organization.

As I approached this task, I decided not to forecast the future direction of events, either specifically in the study of social influence or the discipline of communication in general. It has been my observation with the self-censorship brought on by a bit too much self-importance, humor does not work well with academics. Rather, I am going to talk about the past in some detail, and then offer an assessment of present scholarly activity in the realm of the scientific study of social influence processes.

IN THE BEGINNING: A DYNASTY EMERGES

It is perhaps appropriate to begin a discussion of the history of the study of persuasion (later to become known as social influence processes for reasons I will deal with later in this essay) by writing of a scholarly culture that emerged in the middle to late Pleistocene Age. Little is known today of this culture, as we have little except oral histories and the archaeological efforts of social constructionists and historical revisionists. Part of this lack of knowledge surely stems from the fact that this culture existed in a place that is barely inhabitable by human beings because of its long nine months of winter and darkness that are its climate. This culture developed in the lower part of Michigan in a place called East Lansing. We know that this civilization was ruled for a long period of time by a man-god named Berlo. His injunctions to his followers have been unearthed in a tractate titled *The Process of Communication*[1], which proclaimed that "all communication was persuasive in nature." Thus, the study of communication (which of course was only persuasion) reached its zenith during this age.

The tools used in this scholarly community were primitive by modern standards. Through our archaeological efforts, there has been uncovered 80-column cards with seemingly randomly punched holes in them. Some people today collect (or save) these cards in the same way that my daughter collects sports cards. It is also known that these cards were continually fed into a machine called a counter-sorter, well into the night and early morning hours for months on end. All of these efforts tended to result in nicely constructed

---

[1]It appears to me that the present-day critical theorists and cultural studies folks were given everything that they have had to say in their pages and pages of sometimes impenetrable writing when Berlo said "meanings are in people."

2 × 2 data tables that were immediately shipped off to journals (usually not by the ruler but by his protégés and their progeny) for immediate publication. Few variables escaped the interest of these persuasion researchers, especially if they were some easily measured individual personality differences. What has left many historians of science puzzled are reports of the Ancient Ones of the seemingly morbid fascination of this group with nuclear bomb shelters and civil defense. We know that huge sums of money and lots of hours of effort were spent researching the presumed elimination of the species by nuclear holocaust, but little of this was ever published.

While the tools of these scientists might have been primitive, the capacity for developing intelligence networks that allowed them to penetrate the world of the more established discipline of Social Psychology was quite sophisticated. In fact, few could discern the difference between the creative work of the famous social psychologists of the time, and the efforts of these upstart scientists in what Berlo had proudly proclaimed as a new discipline called "Communication" (which, if you are following, was really just the scientific study of persuasion, or what I think should have been called the empirical study of persuasive public address).

The halcyon years of this dynasty were marked with frequent publication, political clout in this professional association in the form of the Behavioral Sciences Interest Group (the home of all good empirical persuasion researchers at the time), and tribal warfare with the dreaded "Rhetoricians" who were seen as blood-enemies then. But as all things good must end, the era was soon to be over. The exclusive lock that persuasion scientists had on the discipline was replaced with the more glamorous study of interpersonal communication by a new generation of more methodologically sophisticated scientists. As if afraid of our own success in truly carving out an area of important study of interpersonal communication that was a unique contribution by this discipline, there was an almost immediate emergence of leftist political ideologues who brought us critical/cultural studies under various names and formats. In this essay, I will detail how I think political ideology impacted the study of social influence processes in a most negative way.

ON BEING HOMELESS: THE YEARS IN EXILE

There are some existing differences of opinion on what actually happened to the remaining members of this once-thriving breed of persuasion scholars. My friend Bob Bostrom, a contributor to this series also on social influence, was the first (at least that I know of) to point out the amount of knowledge about persuasion and attitude change that was generated by the late Gerald R. Miller, his students, and the students of his students. Professor Bostrom offered this comment as what I thought was a deserved, sincere tribute to Miller, the culture from East Lansing, and the knowledge that had been generated by a relatively small number of scholars interested in a common problem area.

Others did not see things quite the same way. The prolific data collector, Daniel O'Keefe, while still just a young assistant professor, had the insight to declare all of logical positivism dead. Hearing our own obituary, as we persuasion researchers are inextricably intertwined with some derivation of positivistic notions, was obviously disconcerting and drove some "underground." At about the same time, the eminent theorist James McCroskey declared that we who were interested in attitude change "had never let a correlation coefficient get in the way of our ANOVA-based research endeavors," and criticism from McCroskey should have been the death knell for any area of empirical research. But others remain unconvinced that we persuasion researchers are harmless relics from the past. For example, the ever-rational Phil Wander, in a recent guest-edited volume of the *Journal of the Western Communication Association,* seems to believe that the descendants of this previously discussed culture have collected in three separate areas and taken hegemonic control of the major journals in the discipline.

Whatever the reality of the situation (and the intellectual nihilists in critical studies have told us that there is no reality anyway), it is the case that interest in persuasion and attitude change experienced a rapid decline in the last part of the 1970s that continued until the end of the 1980s. I think part, but only part, of that decline was due to the rise of interpersonal communication as an important area of research in communication. Unfortunately, from my point of view, the study of interpersonal communication became almost isomorphic with the study of "relational" communication and criterion measures such as persuasion or attitude change were replaced with questions about dyadic "feelings." In effect, persuasion researchers had neither Division 2 (interpersonal communication) or the Interpersonal/Small Group Division of NCA to any longer call home. It was simply not debatable that a different paradigm was in vogue in these divisions and it did not look much like what was going on in the study of social influence processes.

I also believe that the meta-theoretical discussions brought to us with terms like "constructivism," "rules," and "systems theory" took far too much attention and journal space and left more than a few persuasion researchers feeling adrift in this strange land of what I think was third-rate writing about "philosophy of science" that was just wrong and wrong-headed. That opening foray of people like Delia, Cushman, Pearce, and Monge left open the door for others to come in and do some good old science bashing under the guise of eliminating privilege, co-constructing reality, and what I have called the seeking of uniform mediocrity in our society. Obviously, persuasion research in such a political climate became somewhat of a "devil-word." After all, we have always sought ways to privilege certain voices in that we have been interested in ways that people can alter the beliefs, attitudes, and behaviors of others. In the views of some (perhaps many), those doing scientific persuasion research were the ultimate in Eurocentric, male-dominated, oppressors. I am not sure we placated any of those people by dropping the control-implying word "persuasion" and replacing it with the seemingly more acceptable phrase "social influence processes."

Unlike philosophers of communication, critical theorists, and cultural studies people, it is difficult, if not impossible, for a person doing empirical science to publish the same thing over and over again. With the shift in a great deal of effort and much good scientific inquiry to relational communication, and the influx of various political treatises in our convention halls and in the pages of our journals, there is no doubt that it was considerably more difficult to publish and present sound research in persuasion in any known place in our discipline. We were also not assisted by methodological criticisms, ignored by social influence researchers in all disciplines except communication, that called into question any and all research that did not use an ungodly number of message replications. I also think the coming of age of meta-analysis was just plain boring, and there were a huge number of mistakes made in the presentation of said analyses. When we engaged others in theoretical debates over theoretical issues like the burgeoning interest in cognitive/social theories of attitude change in Social Psychology, we did not fare very well (in my estimation) in those exchanges. So many external (to active persuasion researchers) forces combined to make it seem as if we might have lost our centrality, if not our home, in this particular discipline.

While I mentioned many external forces, I would be the first to admit that there was a bit of weariness developing in the persuasion research camp that had absolutely nothing to do with what has been discussed above. Clearly, many people who had been frequent contributors to the persuasion literature became less enthralled with laboratory studies using college students, and some variation of variable-analytic research. I, for one, remain amazed that Social Psychology operates much the same as it was 30 years ago in terms of the way it goes about the business of doing and reporting research. I do not know how they can stay interested in the kinds of questions they ask! I could (and have) said the same thing about the fascination of interpersonal communication people with criterion measures like "satisfaction" and "warmth," but attitude researchers in psychology are in a class by themselves in dealing with micro-issues, one study at a time, one after the other.

Those of us interested in persuasion research have not done ourselves a great deal of good by avoiding the difficult task of developing formal theories or of extending our interests from strictly the one-to-many context to rigorous study of influence in face-to-face interactions. Some would argue that the empirical study of persuasion and attitude change has added only a modicum of knowledge of theoretical import of practical relevance. While I do not agree with the harshest critics of our accumulated knowledge to date, the way we have presented our results is part of the puzzle in the title of this paper (*Quod enim malvut homo verum est id potius credit*—man more readily believes what he already believes). I concede that the best reading of our variable-analytic approach has clearly demonstrated that pretest attitudes are the *very best* predictor of posttest attitudes, but it is my contention that we have a great deal more theoretical explanations and predictive ability about human communication than this one universal would suggest. Others might not concede that point.

THE RETURN: RELEVANCE, RESPECTABILITY, AND REVENUE ($$$$$)

Somewhat like the Wandering Tribes of Israel, persuasion and attitude researchers have cast about and searched for new homes, sometimes in the discipline of communication and sometimes not (e.g., political communication, media studies, public health and medicine). It now appears to me that several forces are emerging that are bringing social influence research back to the fore. Gerry Miller and I argued (Burgoon & Miller, 1992) that there are dialectical tensions in any discipline that "push out" programs of research for a time and that an almost pendulum-like motion brings what was made unfashionable for a time back to center stage over time. While I think that has happened with social influence research, I do not envision the pendulum

swinging so far that laboratory research using college students and simple message manipulations will ever again be a dominant research paradigm in this discipline.

But as I said, there are several forces that will make the study of and research in social influence more central, rather than less, in the near future. One of those external forces happens to be the change in the nature of university administrators in the past decade or so. We have gone from a long era of being managed by academics to a new era of bean counters and itinerant managerial class that are attempting to emulate corporate America with an emphasis on graduates having "job skills" and preparation for the world of work. Certainly persuasion and attitude/behavior change skills that we can "sell" to our new corporate-like administrators as critical skills for college graduates. While I am annoyed at this skill-oriented, please-corporate-America approach that has been embraced by many university administrators, it is a reality of our time.

There is also a crisis in many of the applied disciplines (for example, public health and medicine) in that huge sums of money are being spent in attitude/behavior change campaigns and the results of such labor-intensive, expensive efforts are disappointing to say the least. I have argued elsewhere (Burgoon, in press) that extant theories of persuasion are supported mostly by data from highly controlled laboratory experiments. Simply stated, extant theories of persuasion do a remarkably poor job of explaining and/or predicting the behavior of people in disease prevention and control. I believe that efforts in this discipline are clearly superior to much of the social influence research being conducted in this venue, and that this line of inquiry will allow us to stake out our territory as leaders, rather than accept our role as followers of intellectual trends. While it may seem to some that a return to our roots as a practical, problem-oriented discipline will rob us of our intellectual integrity and inhibit the development of communication theory, I see no reason why there should not be high-quality, theory-driven research done in problem-oriented contexts in the "real world."

With this concern for social problems, there is a tremendous opportunity for social influence researchers to attract significant amounts of extramural funding. I see that as a clear positive for the discipline, although not everyone agrees with my position on the necessity of first-line communication scholars seeking and *getting* grants and contracts funded. It is a form of external validation that others understand. It also might well be the future of some doctoral programs in this discipline, given the continuing decline in state support of higher education.

The emergence of affordable technology that will allow researchers to develop high-quality computer-mediated messages for research purposes will afford us the opportunity to do kinds of research that were simply impossible in the recent past.[2] Clearly, the days of handing out mimeographed messages or written messages of most any kind is past. Moreover, we do not have to rely on off-air taping of commercials or settle for less than broadcast quality video in creating persuasive messages. It is my hope that new technology will allow researchers to produce persuasive messages that are more veridical with the kinds of influence attempts that barrage the populace on a daily basis. With such technological ability, it should follow that research programs will be better able to explain and predict in a variety of contexts.

Perhaps it would be appropriate to close this brief treatise with a return to my earlier comments about the archaeological efforts in mid-Michigan and comment on the notion of who is really at the "helm" (as used in the title of this program series) in the study of social influence. The Ancient Ones in East Lansing begot a generation of scholars who pursued a variety of interests, including social influence. While those descendants were not the only "players" in the game, for a number of years they made their mark in the study of persuasion and attitude/behavior change.

But one has to look at the history of this particular discipline and conclude that it is the exception, not the rule, for empirical scientists in the discipline of communication to remain productive and prolific data generators in the later years of their careers. While I argued that the lack of senior scholars, still productively doing scientific research, is an anomaly of the field of communication, it appears to me that for whatever reason we pass the research torch to a younger generation at a relatively early point in our careers. I know not if that is "good" or "bad"; it just *is*. So, it should be noted that those "at the helm" in the study of social influence are at least twice-removed from the ancient civilizations previously discussed.

One source of immense pride for me is that I have had the good fortune to work with a number of very bright students over the years who are quite capable of taking social influence to the next step. For example, my colleague and friend David Buller has established an admirable program of research in cancer prevention and control. Michael Pfau continues to do excellent theory-driven research in political communication. Michael Miller and Renee Klingle are extending the boundaries of knowledge in health communication. My friend and former student, James Price Dillard, is an exemplar of a young scholar blending his interest in social influence processes and interpersonal communication research. While I have mentioned but a few (and all closely associated with me), I am quite confident that we have a new generation of scholars (from several venues) who are now "at the helm" and will revitalize inquiry in social influence.

While paying a rare public tribute to my intellectual progeny, I am not quite ready to "hang it up" myself just quite yet. I have managed to keep busy for these nearly three decades and will leave it to others to judge my contribution to the study of social influence. But being no more than a simple boy from Kansas, I have always believed that one "should dance with the one what brung them" and

---

[2] I am fortunate and grateful to the Office of the Provost for recently providing funds to me for the purpose of developing a state-of-the-art multi-media laboratory. Without this funding from the University of Arizona, it would be impossible to do the kind of social influence research that we desire to produce.

the study of attitudes brought me to this discipline and has held my intellectual interest for a very long time. I guess I will just go out when the time is right in the same way I came in: curious about why people do or do not respond to messages aimed at changing beliefs, attitudes, and behaviors.

REFERENCES

Burgoon, M. (in press). (Non) Compliance with disease prevention and control messages: Communication correlates and psychological predictors. *Journal of Health Psychology.*

Burgoon, M. & Bailey, W. (1992). PC at last, PC at last, thank God almighty, PC at last! *Journal of Communication, 42,* 95–104.

Burgoon, M. & Miller, G. R. (1990). Paths. *Communication Monographs, 57,* 152–160.

Miller, G. R. & Burgoon, M. (1978). Persuasion research: Review and commentary. In B. Ruben (Ed.), *Communication yearbook II,* pp. 29–47. New Brunswick, NJ: Transaction Books.

The Small Group Should Be
the Fundamental Unit of Communication Research

Marshall Scott Poole
Texas A&M University

The study of group communication has always attracted the interest of a relatively small set of communication scholars. The number who focus on this topic has fluctuated over the years, with the peaks coming in the late 40s, the late 60s and early 70s, and now again in the early 90s. The fluctuation seems to be highly correlated with the concern for groups in society as a whole, as Steiner (1974) noted. In periods that emphasize individualism and social stability, such as the early 80s, the area does not fare well, while in times that emphasize collectivism and social change, such as the 60s, the area tends to enjoy relative prosperity. With the current emphasis on teamwork, quality, social responsibility, and empowerment in societal discourse, the area is currently experiencing an upswing.

"Experiencing an upswing" is, of course, a relative statement. Generally the number of active group communication researchers (those who produce at least 1 relevant article or convention paper per year) seems to peak at about 30, with maybe 100 others producing the occasional piece.

I have argued elsewhere (Poole, 1996) that the field of group studies is actually rather large, if we consider the entire group of interested scholars scattered across fields like communication, psychology, political science, management, and social work. If these scholars could form a more closely knit research community, the area would no longer be peripheral. This possibility notwithstanding, in this essay I would like to focus on the issue of why group communication is not more central in our field.

Here I want to argue that the group should be **THE** basic unit of analysis in communication research. Despite the fact that most influential theories of communication focus on the individual or on larger social units, I believe there is a more appropriate nexus of analytic interests. The small group, composed of 3 to 10 members, is the minimal unit of analysis in which the social context of communication comes into play, yet the individuality of the actors can be discerned. Hence, it seems natural to take the small group as the basic experimental and analytical unit for communication research.

This idea seemed obvious to social scientists working before 1950. Mead, Cooley, Newcomb, Lewin, Gordon Allport, and Hadley Cantril took as given the notion that the individual can be understood only as part of a larger system. They analyzed subjects such as attitude formation and change, cognition, and action—subjects which most in our field treat as individual-level phenomena—in the context of social groups such as the family, a circle of friends, a neighborhood, or a community. For these seminal thinkers, individual behavior could not be divorced from its surround, and the small group was a critical part of this surround. The small group was the locus for the construction of social reality, with its associated ways of thinking, evaluating, and acting. Socialization occurred through small groups, especially the family, but also through church groups and classrooms. While some of these same scholars, especially Lewin, laid the groundwork for the individually oriented psychological research which predominated in the 1950s and after, always in the background of their work was the small group as the locus of individual and interpersonal processes. Unfortunately, as studies emphasizing the individual moved to the forefront, their group foundations were forgotten. As this work influenced communication inquiry, it transmitted a presumption toward the individual.

This was reinforced by early models of communication that drew on Shannon's formulation of mediated communication, which linked a single source and a single receiver. Originally directed to the problem of designing electronic communication systems, the Shannon model focused on a single source sending to a single receiver. Because human communication processes were not the impetus for Shannon's model, there was no need to factor in the social situation that surrounded human communication. Other influences on communication, such as the social influence of the group context or other group members, were lumped together and defined as noise, which interfered with the fidelity of transmission. This approach implicitly deemphasized other communicators or complex nets of communicators in communication theory. This valorization of the individual and the dyadic linkage was further reinforced by the transformation of Shannon into the SMCR model. With its affinities to the rhetorical tradition (S = rhetor, R = audience, etc.) this model further solidified attention on individual senders and receivers. Even later complexifications of this model, which tried to take into account other people and contextual factors that influenced communication, left primary emphasis on two folks, the individual sender and receiver.

This perspective was further reinforced by the dominant cultural assumptions of U.S. society. The assumption that the group is the basic building block of society runs counter to one of the cherished values of U.S. culture, individualism. As a result of the widespread emphasis on individualism, most people value the individual over the group and attribute more "reality" and impact to individuals than to groups. They may even regard groups as a hindrance to decisive action, which is seen as depending on individual initiative or on supraindividual entities, such as organizations.

It is, of course, impossible to deny that groups matter if we consider the family, the peer group,

the classroom, the work group. However, I believe that the general tendency to ignore and devalorize groups per se is reflected in the diaspora of research on specific types of groups across numerous sectors of our field. Families are studied in interpersonal or relational communication, work groups in organizational communication, and interest and legislative groups in political communication. Propp and Kreps (1996) review many of these lines of research and call for more interchange among them. However, it seems unlikely to me that such interchange will elevate the group from its secondary status.

Entertain for a moment the possibility that the individual is not the basic building block of communication theory. To do so is to take seriously the arguments of various postmodernists, who argued for a "decentering" and denial of the unitary subject; of R. D. Laing, who analyzed the fragmented self; of George Herbert Mead, who saw the self as changing from situation to situation; and of Erving Goffman, who theorized the construction of selves. If not the individual, what should be the basic building block of communication theory?

A number of alternatives have been presented. Many media researchers would argue for whole societies; organizational researchers would advance entire organizations; and theorists of many types would advocate "discursive formations" of various types. While all of these are worthwhile candidates, I believe that most studies of these entities have in common the following flaw: Each of these large units is so complex in itself that a theoretical analysis is driven to treat them as though they were individuals. So societies are most often treated as individual entities; if their subdivisions or classes are recognized these are most often treated as entities in their own right, and studied in isolation, rather than as a group of components that influence each other in any meaningful sense. In the same vein, organizations tend to be treated either as unities or decomposed into components which are approached as isolated unities. While much is made of tracing "fractures" in discursive formations, by far the largest part of scholarship on such formations treats them as individual unities. In short, most scholarly analyses of organizations, societies, or discursive formations in communication treat them as giant individuals, much as more micro theories focus on individual human organisms. The problem here is that, again, the influence of other giant individuals on the central subject is omitted from most of these theories. These macro level theories are like the micro level theories which valorize the individual writ large.

Theories which take organizations, societies, or discursive formations as their basic unit have another problem. They omit (or at least relegate to the background) the role of the organic human being in communication. Focusing on larger units downplays the role of the human as efficient and final cause of communication. While theories at the macro level will always be important to communication, they must ultimately be grounded in human action.

There are only two units of analysis which facilitate the detailed study of human communicative exchanges in context, the dyad and the small group. Both units promise insights into the nature of interaction because they enable researchers to witness message production and reception processes. Both are simple enough to enable study of individual cognitive and affective processes which influence and are influenced by communication. And both mediate the influence of context and the larger organization and society on individuals and the communicative process.

However, I believe the group is superior to the dyad in one important respect: the group includes multiple others. The dyad provides a useful and realistic model for communication because it includes *an* other. Including only one other, however, does not adequately capture the complex nature of social situations. Multiple others, up to the number that a communicator can take into account as individuals, should be included in the basic unit. The German sociologist Georg Simmel understood this at the turn of the century. His incisive analysis of the role of numbers in social interaction indicated that the dyad was a very unusual unit, lacking the characteristics of more numerous groups. Unlike dyads, groups of three or more have a future even if one member departs (the more members they have the more secure their future); because of their future, they have a degree of social reality for the subject that the dyad does not. Because the group captures the full "bite" of the social situation and confronts the communicator with several others, it offers the richest base for developing communication theory and research.

Cognitive studies indicate that humans can attend to more than 1 person at a time, but there are limits to human processing capacity which suggest that 5 to 10 others should be the maximum who can be considered as individuals at any one time. This suggests that relatively small groups are the maximum size necessary to invoke the social situation as transmitted by individuals.

Focusing on the group requires us to address several problems which have not received much attention by those plying individual-centered or society-centered models. First, there is the *problem of intersubjectivity:* fully realized groups are emergents, with properties which are more than a combination of the beliefs and attitudes of the individuals who make them up. Certain properties of groups (and societies for that matter) are not located in any individual, but are intersubjective in that they are maintained by the interaction system of the group (or society). How do emergents arise and how are intersubjective constructs created and maintained? These are very slippery issues, issues not often dealt with in individual- or dyad-based theory and research; unfortunately societal- or organizational-based theories have largely ignored this question. Turning our attention to the group forces us to confront this central problem which is directly connected to issues such as the creation of social reality, the nature of meaning, and the relation of action and structure.

Second, there is the *boundary problem.* As Linda Putnam and Cynthia Stohl have argued, groups are constantly having to reestablish and renegotiate their boundaries. Group boundaries are permeable, due to communication between groups, overlapping membership with other groups, relationships among group members in other contexts, and fluctuations in membership. Being able to maintain boundaries that preserve their identities as groups while at the same time managing and profiting from their permeability is a key issue not only for groups but also for all communication relationships. The nature of boundaries determines the character of the context for communication, and hence the influences that come to bear on the communicator.

These are thorny problems, but ones that an adequate theory of communication should grapple with. They supplement traditional issues that have arisen in communication studies which take the dyad as the central unit. These issues are just as relevant for larger units such as organizations and societies as they are for groups, but they are posed in manageable terms when groups are studied.

Despite the potential benefits of moving to the group as the unit of analysis, there is a price to be paid. Studying multiple interactors requires more time and effort (for the data yielded) than studying individuals or dyads or survey research in large social formations. The time-consuming and difficult task of coding, and then making sense of complex group data in quantitative group studies, is only one of the difficulties that would confront researchers. The problem inherent in trying to ensure large samples of even three-person groups is another. The complicated theories and methods required to represent and explain interaction among multiple actors is yet another.

These difficulties, combined with the general predilection toward the individual, suggest that adherents will not flock to my position. However, theoretical gains almost always come at the price of complexity. I suggest it is a price worth paying.

REFERENCES

Poole, M. S. (1996). Breaking the isolation of small group communication studies. *Communication Studies, 45,* 20–28.

Propp, K. M., & Kreps, G. L. (1996). A rose by any other name: The vitality of small group communication research. *Communication Studies, 45,* 7–19.

Putnam, L. L., & Stohl, C. (1996). Bona fide groups: An alternative perspective for communication and small group decision making. In R. Y. Hirokawa & M. S. Poole (Eds.), *Communication and group decision-making* (pp. 147–178). Newbury Park, CA: Sage.

Steiner, I. D. (1974). Whatever happened to the group in social psychology? *Journal of Experimental Social Psychology, 10,* 94–108.

The Signs of Cognitive, Affiliative, and Egocentric Constraints in Patterns of Interaction in Decision-Making and Problem-Solving Groups and Their Potential Effects on Outcomes

Dennis S. Gouran
Pennsylvania State University

For most of the nearly 30 years I have been involved in the study of groups, my focus has been on decision-making, problem-solving, and the role that communication plays in determining the appropriateness of choices members make relative to what they seek to accomplish. In the process, what has emerged is the view that appropriateness varies directly with the extent to which the exchanges in which the members of groups engage function to ensure that specifiable requirements of the tasks they perform are satisfactorily fulfilled (Gouran, 1988). This view entails certain assumptions about the qualifications of the participants, their attitudes, their motives, the information to which they have access, and, notably, their ability to make warranted inferences from that information (see Gouran & Hirokawa, 1996; Gouran, Hirokawa, Julian, & Leatham, 1993).

Under conditions in which these assumptions pertain, it appears that groups are most likely to make appropriate choices when their members' interaction serves to help them

1. make clear their interest in arriving at the best possible decision;
2. identify the resources necessary for making such a decision;
3. recognize obstacles to be confronted;
4. specify the procedures to be followed;
5. establish ground rules for interaction;
6. attempt to satisfy fundamental task requirements by

a. showing correct understanding of the issue to be resolved;
b. determining the minimal characteristics any alternative, to be acceptable, must possess;
c. identifying a relevant and realistic set of alternatives;
d. examining carefully the alternatives in relationship to each previously agreed-upon characteristic of an acceptable choice; and
e. selecting the alternative that analysis reveals to be the most likely to have the desired characteristics;
7. employ appropriate interventions for overcoming cognitive, affiliative, and egocentric constraints that are interfering with the satisfaction of [other] fundamental task requirements; and
8. review the process by which the group comes to a decision and, if indicated, reconsider judgments reached (even to the point of starting over) (Gouran & Hirokawa, 1996, pp. 76–77).

Much of the empirical foundation for this perspective has been laid largely through the efforts of Randy Hirokawa and his associates (see Littlejohn, 1996, pp. 284–286), and many of the fundamental presuppositions have been further reinforced in Habermas's (1996) new book *Between Facts and Norms: Contributions to a Discourse Theory of Law and Democracy*. Most problematic with the perspective at this point is Proposition #7.

It does not enjoy the same level of support as the others, largely because it has not been subjected to scholarly inquiry and scrutiny. If the functional perspective in its present state of development is to achieve viability, inattention to the communicative aspects of cognitive, affiliative, and egocentric constraints cannot persist. My hope is that the thoughts developed herein will provide a stimulus for moving in desired directions and, thereby, contribute to ensuring the longer-range promise of the perspective.

Although Janis (1989) has shown how the three categories of constraints of interest can adversely affect the performance of decision-making and problem-solving groups, unfortunately, he failed to illuminate their connections to patterns of interaction. Because the signs that cognitive, affiliative, and egocentric constraints are operative have not been well explicated, theorists and researchers interested in choice-making have not had much basis for determining suitable interventions when any or all three of the types of constraints Janis has identified take hold.

Identifying such interventions and testing their effectiveness would appear to require reasonable grounds for inferring the presence of these constraints and recognizing the conditions under which they are exerting negative influence on satisfaction of the other task requirements summarized above. In what follows, I speculate about some of the manifestations of cognitive, affiliative, and egocentric constraints in interaction and what relevant signs may reveal concerning the likelihood that a group will make appropriate choices.

SIGNS AND CONSEQUENCES OF COGNITIVE, AFFILIATIVE, AND EGOCENTRIC CONSTRAINTS IN DECISION-MAKING AND PROBLEM-SOLVING GROUPS

Cognitive Constraints

Cognitive constraints arise when at least one member of a group feels that the time available for making a choice is inadequate, relevant information is not readily available, or the complexity of the issue(s) to be resolved is unusually high. Whether accurate or not, if such perceptions exist, group members may deal with their attendant anxiety and feelings of frustration by becoming what Janis and Mann (1977) refer to as "defensively avoidant" or "hypervigilant" and rely on such heuristics, or mental shortcuts, as analogizing, satisficing, and following standard operating procedures rather than attend to the requirements their tasks impose. At the very least, they may fail to utilize such interpretive, analytical, evaluative, and communication skills as they may possess to maximum effect.

Although cognitive constraints often originate in conditions external to a group, as with other constraints, they initially and typically are operative at an internal, covert level and, hence, may have influence on interaction without the conscious awareness of the parties to it. Such awareness comes about as a result of one's capacity for recognizing and accurately assessing telltale signs. Some signs are fairly conspicuous; others may be subtle. In either case, a failure to discern them can result in interaction's going adrift, with the concomitant consequence that group members will inadequately satisfy essential task requirements.

When any of the cognitive constraints mentioned is, or is in the process of becoming, dominant, one may see evidence of its presence in direct and indirect—sometimes even cynical— acknowledgments of the condition or conditions to which it applies; for instance, "How can they expect us to have something on this by next week?" (suggests a constraint posed by time pressures), "If you are looking for someone with a little knowledge on this subject, I have as little as anyone I know" (suggests a constraint posed by a felt inadequacy of information), and "What do they think we are, a bunch of Einsteins?" (suggests a constraint posed by perceived complexity of the task).

In other instances, a cognitive constraint may remain beneath the surface, and one can infer its presence only from other sorts of verbal and nonverbal signs, for example, apparent impatience on the part of one or more members, frequent reminders of the need to press forward, mention of how similar matters have been approached in the past, and demonstrable irritation with those who appear to be overly methodical or concerned with procedure. Such signs, of course, are not always unequivocal evidence of a cognitive constraint's having become dominant. To assume automatically that they are not, however, would be a mistake.

The actual or possible presence of a cognitive constraint in itself is not undesirable. What occurs in response is the object of concern here. Comments and behavior of the kind noted above invite further such input, and before too long, reasons for why a group sees itself as limited in its ability to fulfill substantive requirements can easily become the focus of discussion. When cognitive constraints remain covert, moreover, inadequate attention to task requirements is even more likely, in that group members are reacting to feelings, the sources of which may not even be apparent to them, and eliminating the discomfort they create becomes more important than making the best possible, that is, most appropriate, choice.

Affiliative Constraints

An affiliative constraint may emerge when relationships among the members of a group are of concern and one or more of them either fear rejection and other sorts of sanctions or attach greater importance to preservation of the group than to the issues under consideration. These conditions are often sufficient to induce tendencies to pressure deviant members to conform (Andrews, 1996) and increase the likelihood that others will display compliance even when, in fact, they are not being so pressured (Harvey, 1974; Schanck, 1932).

As in the case of cognitive constraints, affiliative constraints may not be apparent to those on whom they are exerting influence. In some instances, they can, almost ironically, be least apparent to group members on whom they are having the greatest impact. Signs that affiliative constraints are at work may include an uneven distribution of participation, continuous promotion of cohesive-

ness, and excessive efforts to placate disgruntled participants (Courtright, 1978; Gouran, 1996).

When the surface features of group interaction are fraught with such signs, one can be reasonably confident that at least one of the members of the group has resorted to a reliance on one or more of several heuristics Janis (1989) has identified. Specifically, "Avoid Punishment" (p. 46), "Follow the Party Line" (p. 54), "Exercise One-Upsmanship" (p. 54), "Rig Meetings to Suppress the Opposition" (p. 54), and "Preserve Group Harmony" (p. 56).

Even though the origins of affiliative constraints and the heuristics on which individuals who fall prey to their influence draw differ from those associated with cognitive constraints, and even though their effects on interaction similarly vary in content and form, the consequences of this class of constraints, when dominant, are the same. Group members are either diverted from requirements of the task or fail to fulfill them in a way that provides reasonable assurance of their making appropriate choices. Interaction instead promotes consensus and unity as the principal goals of the group, with the attendant cost that potentially valuable thoughts and points of view are excluded (Phillips, 1996).

Egocentric Constraints

The third type of constraint in Janis's (1989) taxonomy is the one he refers to as egocentric. In Schutz's (1958) terminology, egocentric constraints relate to group members' needs for control. Those who are susceptible to their influence are apt to adopt a win–lose orientation (Folger, Poole, & Stutman, 1993) and to be satisfied only if the alternative or solution to a problem they personally favor is the one the group as a whole comes to endorse. Such individuals tend to be happy winners and sore losers.

When egocentric constraints are driving group interaction, one can expect to observe certain imbalances in how those coming under their influence examine information and react to positions on issues. They are likely to be relatively uncritical of information that is supportive of their thinking and preferred positions and overly critical of information that is not supportive. They also are inclined to react similarly to the views and contributions of other group members.

Even when acknowledging that a competing view may have merit, such individuals display a certain degree of disingenuousness and persist in bolstering their own views and preferences (Janis & Mann, 1977). When pushed, moreover, egocentrically motivated participants may display a high degree of defensiveness (Gibb, 1961). The communicative behavior of this type of group member also frequently conveys implied threats to those who disagree, or a more general tone of vindictiveness, as when President Johnson began referring to his Press Secretary, Bill Moyers, as "Mr. Stop-the-Bombing" because of his opposition to United States involvement in Vietnam (Janis, 1982, p. 115).

Heuristics that come into play when egocentric constraints take strong hold in the decision-making or problem-solving process, according to Janis (1989), are captured by such catch phrases as "Rely-on-Gut-Feelings," "Retaliate!," and "Can Do!" (p. 71). Resorting to such heuristics, as in the case of those associated with cognitive and affiliative constraints, does little to brighten the prospects of a group's making informed, defensible choices. On the contrary, under these circumstances, it is likely that a group will makes choices that are ill-informed at best and possibly injurious.

Despite a recently published critique focusing on the adequacy of Janis's (1989) notions concerning groupthink (see Mohamed & Wiebe, 1996), his case studies of foreign policy debacles and disasters, if nothing else, rather clearly have established that groups in which an authority figure and others are subservient to the influence of egocentric constraints are prone to exercise poor judgment in situations involving highly consequential choices. Those who are insensitive to the signs that such constraints are operative have little hope of avoiding their potentially negative influence and even less hope of counteracting it.

CONCLUDING THOUGHTS

In this brief overview, I have attempted to address a significant deficiency in the functional perspective on communication in decision-making and problem-solving groups. Although that perspective enjoys an increasingly growing base of empirical support (albeit not altogether consistent), at present, little of that support relates to one of the key propositions embraced by the theory. An important reason for this deficiency is the fact that scholars working in the area have not focused on the signs that would enable participants in groups to know when, or at least be reasonably certain that, various types of constraints are dominating the choice-making process. Without such understanding, assuming that groups can overcome the problems posed by cognitive, affiliative, and egocentric constraints and that they will know what counteractive strategies are most effective, or best suited to the contingencies of the situation, is unrealistic.

Without such knowledge, it is unlikely that participants in decision-making and problem-solving groups can consistently satisfy other task requirements. I hope that the ideas I have introduced will contribute to research along these two lines and that, as a result, functional theory will not only receive added support and, if necessary, undergo some needed refinements, but that the practitioner will, in the long run, be the ultimate beneficiary.

REFERENCES

Andrews, P. H. (1996). Group conformity. In R. S. Cathcart, L. A. Samovar, & L. D. Henman (Eds.), *Small group communication: Theory & practice* (7th ed., pp. 184–192). Madison, WI: Brown & Benchmark.

Courtright, J. A. (1978). A laboratory investigation of groupthink. *Communication Monographs, 45,* 229–246.

Folger, J. P., Poole, M. S., & Stutman, R K. (1993). *Working through conflict* (2nd ed.). New York: HarperCollins.

Gibb, J. R. (1961). Defensive communication. *Journal of Communication, 11,* 141–148.

Gouran, D. S. (1988). Group decision making: An integrative approach to research. In C. H. Tardy (Ed.), *A handbook for the study of human communication* (pp. 247–268). Norwood, NJ: Ablex.

Gouran, D. S. (1996). Principles of counteractive influence in decision-making and problem-solving groups. In R. S. Cathcart, L. A. Samovar, & L. D. Henman (Eds.), *Small group communication: Theory & practice* (7th ed., pp. 120–133). Madison, WI: Brown & Benchmark.

Gouran, D. S., & Hirokawa, R. Y. (1996). Functional theory and communication in decision-making and problem-solving groups: An expanded view. In R. Y. Hirokawa & M. S. Poole (Eds.), *Communication and group decision-making* (2nd ed., pp. 55–80). Thousand Oaks, CA: Sage.

Gouran, D. S., Hirokawa, R. Y., Julian, K. M., & Leatham, G. B. (1993). The evolution and current status of the functional perspective on communication in decision-making and problem-solving groups. In S. A. Deetz (Ed.), *Communication yearbook 16* (pp. 573–600). Newbury Park, CA: Sage.

Habermas, J. (1996). *Between facts and norms: Contributions to a discourse theory of law and democracy* (W. Rehg, Trans.). Cambridge, MA: MIT Press.

Harvey, J. B. (1974). The Abilene paradox: The management of agreement. *Organizational Dynamics, 3,* 63–80.

Janis, I. L. (1982). *GroupThink* (2nd ed.). Boston: Houghton Mifflin.

Janis, I. L. (1989). *Crucial decisions: Leadership in policymaking and crisis management.* New York: Free Press.

Janis, I. L., & Mann, L. (1977). *Decision making: A psychological analysis of conflict, choice, and commitment.* New York: Free Press.

Littlejohn, S. W. (1996). *Theories of human communication* (5th ed.). Belmont, CA: Wadsworth.

Mohamed, A. A., & Wiebe, F. A. (1996). Toward a process theory of groupthink. *Small Group Research, 27,* 416–430.

Phillips, K. R. (1996). The spaces of public dissension: Reconsidering the public sphere. *Communication Monographs, 63,* 231–247.

Schanck, R. L. (1932). A study of a community and its groups and institutions conceived of as behaviors of individuals. *Psychological Monographs, 43,* No. 2 (Whole No. 195).

Schutz, W. C. (1958). FIRO: *A three dimensional theory of interpersonal behavior.* New York: Holt, Rinehart and Winston.

"Put the Helm Over!" and Steer a New Heading: Communication and "Social Influence"

Robert N. Bostrom
University of Kentucky

It would be hard to imagine a definition of communication that doesn't include social influence. Yet today we see that the primary mission of NCA has been characterized as the study of "messages." In fact, in many instances, the primary object of study has been the cognitive aspect of these messages, and little else. Research focusing on "conversational analysis" (Pomerantz, 1990), "attitudes" (Dillard, 1991), "listening," (Bostrom, 1990), and "compliance-gaining" (Dillard, 1988) are some of the many instances of research in which the study of messages has been seen as the center of human activity. Some of us have taken an even more extreme view—subscribing to "symbolic interactionism," a viewpoint in which words are considered to represent "reality" (Eisenberg & Goodall, 1993). Studies of language are interesting, and are a central concern for all of us in communication. But what has been missing is study of the relationship between messages and subsequent behavior which may be caused by these messages. I would like to suggest that in focusing on messages *only* we have allowed ourselves to be "blown off course." Perhaps it is time to "put the helm over, trim our sails, and steer" ourselves back to our original heading: the *interaction* of messages with behavior.

Indeed, we might redefine "messages" to include the *effect* that messages may or may not have. I would propose that if verbalization has no effect on *instrumental* behavior, then we have no business calling it a message. You will recognize fairly old issues here—"cognitivism," "behaviorism," and the like—but the issues are important ones, and will apparently not go away. But I believe that our current emphasis on cognitive activity has led us away from the vital links between messages and behavior, with the result being that communication, as a field of study, is still a long way from its potential as a force for the improvement of our society and being a central force in solving important problems.[1]

It is difficult to pinpoint exactly when interest in communication shifted away from producing significant change in the behavior of individuals to become the search for "meaning" and the reconstruction of "reality." These seem like unproductive searches to me. I would like to see us turn our attention to three main issues: the development of a typological scheme concerning language and behavior, more intense research into the causes of behavior and the way that language intersects with them, and the decision process itself. Research in these three areas would enable us to examine the role of communication in changing real behavior. This position seems so obviously generational[2] that a heavy burden falls on one who makes it. I am confident, however, that close examination of my position—that the most obvious corrective is to rethink the relationships among sources, messages, and behavior—will speak for itself. But the largest question is: what kind of behavior?

Originally changes of "social significance" were considered the most important aspect of communication activity, and since most definitions of "attitudes" centered on behavioral changes of social significance (Doob, 1947; Hovland, Janis, & Kelley, 1956), it is easy to see why the study of communication and social influence emphasized the attitude construct. While all conceded that attitudes had cognitive and affective components as well as the behavioral ones (Rosenberg & Hovland, 1960), communication research was justified on the basis of an assumed strong connection between attitudes and actions. This was a good assumption (Kim & Hunter, 1993), but today most would agree with Dillard (1993) who has redefined attitudes as "object appraisals." But people really do change their behavior, and sometimes in dramatic ways.

MESSAGES AND BEHAVIOR

I feel strongly that our discipline, which has so much to offer the world, has actually given it very little. A good deal of the problem lies in our acceptance of a "messages" paradigm in which language alone serves as a justification for inquiry. A significant change would be the expansion of the "message" paradigm to include the *effects* of messages in bringing about social change. We can approach the problem in a number of ways. I am not contending that we should abandon the study of messages—far from it. But I would like to see us look for the ways in which messages help people stop smoking, use less fossil fuels, and support the arts. How can we do this? First would be the development of a typology of the links between language and behavior[3], and the role of communication in bringing them together. If we do this, and discover the many truly practical aspects of communication study, we can then stop some of the self-justification that currently masquerades as "communication theory."

The early promise of "behaviorism" was eroded by a number of factors, including Skinner's contention that linguistic behavior was little different than other kinds of responses (Skinner, 1968). It is certainly true that verbal behavior can be changed through responses and rewards, but it is also true that the bulk of language and cognition are formed in other ways. Skinner's error was treated as a foundational flaw in behavioristic thinking, rather than the simple mistake it was. Another was the assumption that responses to attitude tests actually were behavior of a sort, and

could therefore be classified as "behaviorist" research. But probably of greater importance has been a suspicion that behaviorists strive for manipulation and control, and individualistic and personalized responses represent individual freedom and self-expression. The stringent assumptions of objectivity and control were therefore seen as artifacts of mistaken thinking and less rigorous methods of research were therefore given a legitimacy they certainly didn't deserve.

Even though "symbolic interactionism" asserts that our social life is constructed of words, few of us believe that using "politically correct" language is the same as working for meaningful changes for the role of women and minorities in our institutions. Our folklore is riddled with aphorisms about words and deeds. Indeed, the assumption that thoughts (a form of language) and plans (a form of schemas) affect our behavior is often referred to as "folk" psychology (O'Keefe, 1992).

This is not to say that linguistic responses are inconsequential. For example, when General Colin Powell used the words "Fellow Republicans," at the national Republican convention in August, the phrase was more than a ritual salutation. Words *may be* responses of consequence, and communicative activities that aim at alterations of verbal behavior can be truly important ones. But the connection, if any, between words and deeds is seldom explored. In addition, it is clear that verbal and instrumental behaviors follow different rules and different methods for alteration, and differ substantially in amount of effort involved.

The usual rationale for focusing on verbal behavior is the assumption that words present a reliable picture of our "real" self. Even though we know that the "inner reality" of other persons is a convenient fiction to explain their external behavior, we typically make the assumption that these fictions explain a number of important communication concepts. We conveniently disregard any evidence that inner perceptions and the outer behaviors may be at odds with one another. We certainly can think of times in which our own pre-communicative cognitive activity has been wildly at odds with what we say or do. For example, reports of behavior in questionnaires are heavily influenced by the role of memory and self-image (Bradburn, Rips, & Shevell, 1987). Realistically, we must recognize that statements about "cognitive" activity are necessarily grounded in observations of behavior, and therefore include an inferential step in their formulation.

The problem of assessing internal cognition is a large one, and readers should examine Waldron and Cegala's (1992) explication of "conversational cognition" and the related methodological issues involved in assessing it. Waldron and Cegala ask the question "how do we figure out what people are thinking when they talk?" But we should also ask, as does O'Keefe (1992), whether it really matters what they "think." O'Keefe takes the position that undue concern with cognitive events is an excellent example of "folk psychology."

There are two important questions that should be helpful in exploring relationships between words and actions. The first question might be, "Are there situations in which we don't care what people say—we only care what they do?" The second question is its opposite: "Are there situations where we don't care what people do, we only care what they say?" The answers are yes to both. In addition, there are countless situations in which both words and actions are valued in more or less degree. In other words, there are gradations in between each of these extremes. Let's look at some examples:

I. *Situations where language is irrelevant*
   A. Altering health-related habits (smoking, drinking, overeating)
   B. Manipulating environment (work activities, locomotion, etc.)
   C. Sports (hitting a ball, etc.)
   D. Minor social acts (passing the salt, cashing a check)
II. *Situations where language mediates behavior strongly*
   A. Legal matters (contracts, etc.)
   B. Ceremonies (weddings, etc.)
   C. Conforming to external systems (speed limits, street signs, etc.)
   D. Computer interaction
III. *Situations where language mediates behavior only weakly*
   A. Social and political attitudes
   B. Human relationships
   C. Organizational behavior
   D. Religion
IV. *Situations where behavior is irrelevant*
   A. Poetry
   B. Music
   C. Mathematics

The equivalence of words and acts is far overstated. In short, *changes in language alone are not always sufficient to accomplish what is needed in many situations, and in fact are sometimes totally irrelevant to what is called for.* In many aspects of communication study, then, we ought to focus on *situations in which communication can be observed to have a strong connection with behavior rather than situations in which communication has strong connections with language.*

Two more examples are worth describing in detail—the work of Erwin Goffman and the systems proposed by Searle. Both write as if they are describing behavior, and do so in an extremely persuasive fashion. Close analysis, on the other hand, yields an entirely different view. Erwin Goffman is well known for the concept of "face." Goffman assumes that everyone has concern for "face," and in approximately the same amounts; and that everyone has concern for others' face, and in approximately the same amounts (Goffman, 1959). He also assumes that the social situations create these concerns. There is no doubt that in many social situations, Goffman's assertions probably describe a portion of the internal states of the participants. But years of research in the many manifestations of personality, such as self-esteem, locus of control, gender, and especially argumentativeness, ought to convince us that Goffman's hypotheses have only a tenuous connection with the actual behavior employed by real people. The power of the theory is in the persuasiveness of the word chosen—*face*. In other words, this is a word-oriented theory, not a people-oriented theory.

Searle's classification of "speech acts" is much the same. For example, he proposes a language act called a "commissive" in which individuals refer to future action (Searle, 1990). "I promise to pay you" is an example of Searle's "commissive" form. Searle goes on to assert that "I pledge allegiance to the flag" is also a "commissive," because they have the same form. The fact that one sentence has a behavioral referent and the other does not is irrelevant to Searle. The *form* is the same. "Reasoning" like this is certainly not helpful.

In short, we have accepted the unsupported assertions of both Goffman and Searle that words and behavior are one and the same. Why have we been so uncritical of these assertions and allowed them to remain essentially untested? They may well be true. On the other hand, they may also be false. What is probably correct is that they are manifestations of particular cultures and are subject to alteration. To discover how such alteration might be brought about would be a major breakthrough in making communication a significant element in our daily lives and well-being.

WHY DO PEOPLE DO WHAT THEY DO? AND WHAT DOES COMMUNICATION HAVE TO DO WITH IT?

One major difficulty in proposing causal models of communication arises from the fact that human behavior is not generally "caused" by any one type of activity or another. Probably one of the best overviews of the causes of human behavior is that proposed by Peter Anderson (1989). He analyzed some of the "forces" which produce "regularities" in human behavior, and suggests that the question of "why do people do what they do" will be highly varied. Anderson grouped these "regularities" in behavior (and their accompanying theoretical statements) into five separate categories: (1) Natural forces (such as physiology or physics), (2) cultural rules (customs or taboos), (3) personal traits, (4) relational patterns (such as an organizational position, or a marriage), and (5) intentional, goal-oriented behavior. Clearly no one behavioral influence is "pure" in that sometimes an individual can be influenced by several of these at once.

At the same time, we are accustomed to classifying communication into broad general categories, ranging from mass to interpersonal (Miller, 1990). Putting these two elements together would result in a table with some very interesting categories (see Table 1).

There is no doubt that often changes in behavior do follow changes in symbol systems. But at the same time, there is abundant evidence to indicate that changes in behavior occur through coercion, social pressure, physiological and chemical changes, and sometimes random events. These changes, often termed "mindless" ones, are then "justified" by subsequent explanations by the participant. An individual who bows to social pressure in making a group decision then "rationalizes" the event by constructing evidence and

TABLE 1   Classifying Communication into Categories

	NATURAL FORCES	CULTURAL RULES	PERSONAL TRAITS	RELATIONAL PATTERNS	INTENTIONAL BEHAVIOR
Interpersonal					
Small Group					
Organizational					
Mass					

logical processes. When this occurs, then it is the case that language follows behavior, rather than the other way around. While individuals certainly can make use of symbols as mediating phenomena, it is definitely not essential.

ACTUALLY MAKING A DECISION

Even though communication may establish new frames of reference, alter our existing attitude, or change our entire worldview, it is still no guarantee that any real behavioral change will result. For example, here are four instances of real change in the lives of four people. The cases range from major to minor changes:

CASE ONE: Sarah, a successful and highly regarded choral director at a major Midwestern university, approaches age 50 with trepidation and boredom. While clearly an enormous success at her job, the need for a different life seems critical. She applies for early retirement and enters a program in nursing education. After four years, she graduates with distinction and takes a job in the emergency room of a large hospital.

CASE TWO: Charles, a professor of theater in a small southern school in a large city, has been a practicing homosexual for all of his adult life, but has kept this activity a secret. His sexual contacts have been furtive and transient. Given the way that gay men have become more open, Charles decides to "come out of the closet" and live more openly, and especially seek a longer-range emotional partner. He joins a "gay rights" group and takes visible positions on gay issues.

CASE THREE: Raleigh has been an inveterate cigar smoker for 20 years, subjecting his family and coworkers to a fairly pungent inundation of secondhand smoke. Usually he consumed four or five of these cigars per day. One day he simply decides to quit, to the great relief of those who work with him and those who live with him.

CASE FOUR: Fern has a lovely bicycle and lives less than a mile from her workplace. However, she usually drives her car to work, even in the pleasant weather. One day she simply decides "today, I try it," and takes the bike to work.

Each of these instances of behavioral change may have been "mediated" by attitudes, and those attitudes could have been "changed" by communication. When questioned, Sarah reported an admiring attitude for the nursing profession; Charles admitted feeling that society should be more tolerant of gays; Raleigh, like many smokers, always felt tobacco was a bad habit; and Fern had long believed that bicycles are more environmentally responsible than automobiles. So what, if anything, pushed each of the changers to change? Each had no idea when a formal "decision" was reached, and none could remember a specific communicative experience that resulted in the new behavior. Are these instances typical? If so, does this mean that communication is good at getting us ready to act, but is of little use in actually instituting action? If so, problems in ethnic and gender discrimination, continued degradation of the environment, government's lack of fiscal responsibility, spouse and child abuse, AIDS, and political correctness are beyond the reach of communication and bureaucrats are justified in calling for coercive methods. I feel that some focus on the decision process itself would be a better way of eliciting good information about why people decide to act. In this regard, the "functionalistic" approach to group behavior shows much promise (Gouran, Hirokawa, Julian, & Leatham, 1993).

In brief, communication research has been seriously compromised by subscribing to a worldview that is essentially symbolic. Recentering theoretical and research interest on behavior would provide a beginning for such usefulness. Redefining "messages" as linguistic events with strong causal connections to subsequent instrumental acts would be an important first step. Then a more careful view of the actual causes of behavior as they interact in communicative settings would be possible; these steps, together with more intensive study of the decision processes, would all be helpful. This could be the new compass heading for those "at the helm" to use to bring our vessel to a more interesting, productive, and significant course.

NOTES

1. This generalization, as with all generalizations, is obviously only partly true. We see strong movements now in "health" communication in which connections between messages and patient behavior are receiving intensive study. The strongest new movement in small group communication has a focus on group functions, not interactions per se (Gouran, Hirokawa, Julian, & Leatham, 1993). But at the same time, there are those who assert the value-oriented critical study of communication is practical just because they think it is (Craig & Tracy, 1995; Rorty, 1994, 1996).

2. I am sure that Franklin Knower thought I was an idiot (even though he was unfailingly courteous), and I am even more sure that Howard Gilkinson secretly thought Jim McCroskey was seriously misguided.

3. One artifact of the sixties was the assumption that words were "behavior" in the same way that more instrumental responses are. In this paper, I will use "behavior" to mean instrumental responses, i.e., goal-oriented, visible movements.

REFERENCES

Bostrom, R. N. (1990). *Listening behavior.* New York: Guilford.

Bradburn, N. M., Rips, L. J., & Shevell, S. K. (1987). Answering autobiographical questions: The impact of memory and inference on surveys. *Science, 236 (10 April),* 157–161.

Craig, R. T. & Tracy, K. (1995). Grounded practical theory: The case of intellectual discussion. *Communication Theory, 5,* 248–272.

Dillard, J. (1988). Compliance-gaining message selection: What is our dependent variable? *Communication Monographs, 55,* 162–181.

Dillard, J. P. (1993). Persuasion past and present: Attitudes aren't what they used to be. *Communication Monographs, 60,* 90–97.

Doob, L. W. (1947). The behavior of attitudes. *Psychological Review, 54,* 135–156.

Eisenberg, E. W. & Goodall, H. L., Jr. (1993). *Organizational communication: Balancing creativity and constraint.* New York: St. Martin's Press.

Goffman, E. (1959). *The presentation of self in everyday life.* New York: Doubleday.

Gouran, D. S., Hirokawa, R. Y., Julian, K. M., & Leatham, G. B. (1993). The evolution and current status of the functional perspective in decision-making and problem-solving groups. In S. Deetz (Ed), *Communication yearbook* (Vol. 16, pp. 573–600). Newbery Park, CA: Sage.

Hovland, C. I., Janis, I. L., & Kelley, H. H. (1956). *Communication and persuasion.* New Haven, CT: Yale University Press.

Kreps, G. L., Frey, L. R., & O'Hair, D. (1991). Applied communication research: Scholarship that can make a difference. *Journal of Applied Communication Research, 19,* 71–83.

Miller, G. R. (1990). Interpersonal communication. In Dahnke, G. L. & Clatterbuck, G. W. (Eds.), *Human communication: Theory and research* (pp. 91–122). Belmont, CA: Wadsworth.

Motley, M. T. (1992). Mindfulness in solving communicators' dilemmas. Communication: Inherently strategic and primarily automatic. *Communication Monographs, 59,* 306–314.

O'Keefe, B. J. (1992). Developing and testing rational models of message design. *Human Communication Research, 18,* 637–650.

Pomerantz, A. (1990). Conversation analytic claims. *Communication Monographs, 57,* 231–236.

Rice, R. E. (1996, January). *Making a place for the new American scholar.* Paper presented at the American Association for Higher Education Conference of Faculty Roles and Rewards, Atlanta, GA.

Rorty, R. (1987). Science as solidarity. In Nelson, J. et al. (Eds.), *The rhetoric of the human sciences* (pp. 38–52). Madison, WI: University of Wisconsin Press.

Rorty, R. (1994). Does academic freedom have philosophical presuppositions? *Academe, 80,* 52–63.

Rorty, R. (1996, Winter). Remembering John Dewey and Sidney Hook. *Free Inquiry, 16 (1),* 40–43.

Rosenberg, M. & Hovland, C. (1960). Cognitive, affective, and behavioral components of attitudes. In Rosenberg, M. (Ed.), *Attitude organization and change.* New Haven, CT: Yale University Press.

Russell, B. (1945). *A history of western philosophy.* New York: Simon & Schuster.

Searle, J. (1990). A classification of illocutionary acts. In D. Carbaugh (Ed.), *Cultural communication and intercultural contact* (pp. 349–372). New York: Erlbaum.

Skinner, B. F. (1968). *Verbal behavior.* New York: Appleton-Century-Crofts.

Skinner, B. F. (1986). What is wrong with daily life in the western world? *American Psychologist, 41,* 568–574.

Smith, M. J. (1982). Cognitive schema theory and the perseverance and attenuation of unwarranted empirical beliefs. *Communication Monographs, 42,* 116–126.

Waldron, V. R. & Cegala, D. J. (1992). Assessing conversational cognition: Levels of cognitive theory and associated methodological requirements. *Human Communication Research, 18,* 599–622.

CHAPTER 5

AT THE HELM
IN POLITICAL COMMUNICATION

Introduction

Kathleen E. Kendall
University of Albany SUNY

My name is Kathy Kendall, of the Department of Communication, University at Albany, SUNY. I am pleased to introduce this distinguished panel on "At the Helm in Political Communication." The language of the title, "At the Helm," is appropriate because these scholars in political communication have studied the people who are at the helm of the ship of state, those who aspire to be at the helm of the ship of state, and the furies encountered by that ship.

The field of political communication is growing rapidly, with political communication divisions now in the NCA, ICA, and APSA, as well as regional organizations, and articles published not only in the NCA national and regional journals, but in two new journals focusing specifically on political communication: *Political Communication,* jointly sponsored by the Political Communication divisions of the ICA and APSA, and *The Harvard International Journal of Press/Politics,* published at the Joan Shorenstein Center on the Press, Politics and Public Policy at the Kennedy School of Government, Harvard University.

These four scholars, Roderick P. Hart, Lynda Lee Kaid, L. Patrick Devlin, and Robert V. Friedenberg, have contributed directly to this surge of interest and research with their original ideas, publications, organizing leadership, oral presenta-

tions, and through their excellent training of undergraduate and graduate students.

Roderick P. Hart is the F. A. Liddell Professor of Communication and Professor of Government at The University of Texas at Austin. He received his B.A. degree from the University of Massachusetts, and his M.A. and Ph.D. degrees from the Pennsylvania State University. Between 1970 and 1979, Hart served as Assistant and Associate Professor of Communication at Purdue University.

His area of special interest is politics and the mass media, and he is the author of *Public Communication* (Harper & Row, 1975, 1983), *The Political Pulpit* (Purdue University Press, 1977), *Verbal Style and the Presidency* (Academic Press, 1984), *The Sound of Leadership* (University of Chicago Press, 1987), *Modern Rhetorical Criticism* (Harper, 1990), and *Seducing America: How Television Charms the Modern Voter* (Oxford, 1994). In addition, he has published numerous journal articles.

As a teacher, he was chosen as the 1991 Professor of the Year for the State of Texas from the Carnegie/C.A.S.E. Foundation. He has received many awards from the NCA for his research, and in 1993 he was named a Research Fellow of the ICA and a Distinguished Scholar by the NCA. He has also served as Chair of the Research and Finance boards for the NCA, Vice President of the ICA, and Division Chair for the APSA.

Most recently, he has been the Co-Director of the Campaign Mapping Project, funded by the Carnegie Corporation and Ford Foundation, using computer software to track word patterns in political discourse throughout Campaign 1996.

Professor Hart's topic today is "Hope and American Politics."

Lynda Lee Kaid is Professor of Communication and George Lynn Cross Research Professor at the University of Oklahoma, where she also serves as the Director of the Political Communication Center and supervises the Political Commercial Archive. She received her Ph.D. degree from Southern Illinois University.

Her research specialties include political advertising and news coverage of political events. A Fulbright Scholar, she has also done work on political television in several Western European countries. She is the author or editor of 12 books, including *Political Campaign Communication: A Bibliography and Guide to the Literature* (Scarecrow Press, 1985), *New Perspectives on Political Advertising* (Southern Illinois Press, 1986), *Mediated Politics in Two Cultures* (Praeger, 1991), and *Political Advertising in Western Democracies* (Sage, 1995). She has also written numerous journal articles and book chapters on various aspects of political communication. She has received over $1 million in external grant funds for her research efforts, including support from the U.S. Department of Commerce, the U.S. Department of Education, the National Endowment for the Humanities, and the National Science Foundation.

Dr. Kaid is a former Chair of the Political Communication Division of the ICA, and has served in leadership roles in the NCA and the APSA.

Her topic today is "Research Trends in Political Campaign Communication."

L. Patrick Devlin is Professor of Communication Studies at the University of Rhode Island. He chaired the Department of Speech Communication there from 1980–1986. He received his B.A. from William Paterson College, his M.A. from Columbia University, and his Ph.D. from Wayne State University.

His research specialties are political campaign commercials, and political persuasion in presidential campaigns. He has published two books, *Contemporary Public Speaking* (Wadsworth, 1971), and *Political Persuasion in Presidential Campaigns* (Transaction Books, 1987). He has published in many scholarly journals, including *Political Communication, American Behavioral Scientist, Quarterly Journal of Speech,* and *Communication Quarterly,* as well as contributing chapters to books. His two most recent chapters, one on political commercials and one on the 1992 Gore-Quayle-Stockdale vice presidential debate, were published in books edited by two of our other panelists, Professors Kaid and Friedenberg.

In addition to being an active participant in academic panels at the NCA and ICA, Professor Devlin has organized and appeared on panels with experienced professional campaign consultants, such as Presidents Ford's and Carter's media creators, President Reagan's and Vice President Mondale's pollsters, and Washington lobbyists.

His topic today is, "Trends in Political Television Advertising."

Robert V. Friedenberg is Professor of Communication at Miami University. He received his B.S. from Towson State College, and his M.A. and Ph.D. from Temple University. From 1980 to 1987 he served as Director of the Humanities Division at Miami University, Hamilton Campus, and in 1977–1978 he was the Executive Director of the Coro Foundation for Graduate Training in Public Affairs, St. Louis. He has been a political campaign consultant in over 70 campaigns ranging from state senate races to presidential campaigns.

His research specialties are political campaign communication, political debates, and the history of American Jewish preaching. He has published four books: *Hear O' Israel: The History of American Jewish Preaching 1654–1970* (University of Alabama Press, 1989); *Theodore Roosevelt and the Rhetoric of Militant Decency* (Greenwood Press, 1991); *Rhetorical Studies of National*

Political Debates: 1960–1992 (Praeger, 1994); and *Political Campaign Communication* (with Judith Trent) (Praeger, 1995). He has published in scholarly journals including *Speaker and Gavel, Journal of Communication and Religion,* and *The Journal of the American Forensic Association,* and written many book chapters. Harvard University recently awarded him a Goldsmith grant in support of his research.

Dr. Friedenberg has been a regular contributor to panels at the NCA, and has served as President of the Religious Speech Communication Association.

His topic today is, "Narrowcast Media and Political Campaigns: Trends and Implications."

Rhetoric, Hope, and American Politics

Roderick P. Hart
University of Texas at Austin

There is something deep inside us that rejects politics. When asked to explain such feelings, people often respond with a language of instances—Cambodia, Watergate, Iran-Contra, Proposition 187, Whitewater. Without prompting, they can also recite a litany of political sinners—Richard Nixon, most famously, but also Jim Wright, Gary Hart, Roger Ailes, Clarence Thomas, Anita Hill, Oliver North, Jim Guy Tucker. People hate the particularities of politics but they hate its generalities too. Some hate its mindless pluralism, others its numbing orthodoxies. Most hate the crucibles within which legislation is fashioned, the odious compromises and deal-making politics requires. All hate the PAC money and the sound-bites and the payoffs and the cronyism and the 15-second ads. Not everyone hates the sexism and racism in politics but, those who do not, hate its political correctness instead. In the United States of America, on the eve of the twenty-first century, the American people are bound together by their antipathies for the governance they collectively manage.

The mass media aid and abet such attitudes. Cultural critics who analyze depictions of politicians on television and in the movies find unanimously negative portrayals (Prince, 1992; Savage and Nimmo, 1990). Scholars examining news coverage report that politics is described as a troubled, bureaucratic nightmare and they find such negative portrayals increasing steadily over time (Hart, et al., 1996). Other researchers use polling data to document increasing political cynicism in the land, as well as declining senses of political efficacy, plummeting turnout rates, and appalling levels of political knowledge (Delli Carpini and Keeter, 1996; Teixeira, 1987; Rosenstone and Hansen, 1993). Given these portrayals, the American people have ample reason to quit the political scene entirely. Why don't they?

Why do half of the eligible voters in the United States still vote? Why do pollsters report *cyclical* trends in political optimism rather than a single, linear plunge into Hades? Why did television's *Murphy Brown* trim her sails when confronted by the erstwhile Daniel Quayle in 1988? How can Eagle Scouts and astronauts, Gulf War generals and Olympic gymnasts, still inspire feelings of nationalism in the hard-bitten '90s? What makes Americans respond chauvinistically at times to global economic pressures and why do professional cynics like Dennis Miller age so poorly? Why do Chelsea Clinton jokes, or Reagan/Alzheimer jokes, have a comparatively short shelf-life, and why do older Americans know more, and care more, about politics than do their grandchildren? Why do we feel a twinge of loss when catching a glimpse of Gerald Ford or Lady Bird Johnson these days? Why did people cry, not laugh, when watching the funeral of Richard Nixon and why did people laugh, not cry, when Rush Limbaugh's television show fizzled out? How could George Bush, a person of modest rhetorical talents, galvanize a nation over night to do battle in the Middle East and why did the nation's media cooperate with him in that regard? And speaking of media personnel, why do we hate them more than we hate politicians?

These are oddly juxtaposed questions. Perhaps they suggest a manic state. But they also direct us toward a single, common answer: Somehow, in an age of massive political cynicism, hope remains. But how? And why?

I do not know the answer to the latter question. Perhaps the American people are addle-brained or perhaps they are caught up in the postmodern vortex where everything is true and false at the same time. Perhaps they are resigned to living with their indeterminacies and actually enjoy their languid waltz in the vestibule of hell. More optimistically, perhaps hope flies in on the wings of American pragmatism, or Puritan resolve, or neo-classical traditions, or the Enlightenment Continued. These are all possibilities but I, for one, cannot tell you why hope abides…when it abides.

But I may be able to shed light on *how* it abides because I am a rhetorical critic and hence an expert on How. The How I offer here is not elaborate. Indeed, it is altogether pedestrian for I arrived at my determinations by counting words. The data to be sketched out here were gathered by using a piece of software called DICTION 4.0, a dictionary-based language protocol employing a 10,000-word search corpus to search a text for forty-six distinct semantic features. DICTION is a lexically based program; that is, it only calculates the relative use of a given set of words, thereby ignoring what many of us think of as verbal "context." It ignores context for a reason. Actually, for six reasons: (1) given the limitations on human memory, the context of a text evaporates virtually the moment it is created; (2) there is no reason to believe that a speaker's "context" has a necessary relationship to a listener's "context" (or else why do we so often hear the phrase "but that's not what I meant"); (3) context is never as important to an in-the-moment audience as it is to an after-the-fact critic; (4) only an accountant with a magnifying glass (and without an understanding of deconstruction) could find a context after a text has flitted about in the minds of a large collectivity; (5) yesterday's presumably settled contexts becomes today's eminently debatable texts, as the Rodney King videos eternally remind us; (6) the most important kind of context is produced *after* the fact of communication, not during it.

Because I believe these things—fabulous though they are—I harbor neither guilt nor shame when counting words. I ward off guilt and shame by insuring that DICTION counts a great many words quickly (the program processes 30,000 words in one minute) and by comparing each text processed to a data bank of 15,000 previously analyzed passages. In other words, my research technique empirically engages the notion of a *community of discourse*. It assumes that no text is understandable apart from the rhetorical world from which it was drawn and it assumes, further, that all critics are mathematicians of a sort because they base their insights on an (explicit or implicit) sense of correspondence and proportionality. Because this is so, DICTION uses the same comparative logic critics always already use. That, at least, is my reasoning.

What do these ruminations-on-method have to do with political hope? The intersection lies in the Campaign Mapping Project, a research endeavor funded by the Ford and Carnegie Foundations and directed by me and Kathleen Hall Jamieson of the University of Pennsylvania. The purpose of the Project is to understand how political discourse has changed, if it has changed, during the last fifty years. To arrive at such understandings, we have collected a large database of campaign speeches, political ads and debates, press reports (from both the print and broadcast media), and a large selection of letters-to-the-editor from ten small city newspapers (to represent the voice of the people). All of these materials were produced during general election campaigns from 1948 to the present.

For the Project, Kathleen is studying political argument and I political style. She wants to know if the nation's leaders are more inclined, or less inclined, to engage political issues in a meaningful fashion and if campaign levels of factual accountability and argumentative completeness have risen or fallen in the age of television. I, in turn, am interested in language and political culture. I want to know how the three voices of democracy—politicians, the press, and the people—have operated in the post-war period and what can be said about the nation's political trajectory as a result.

For me, some of the most important political trends are best revealed at the lexical level. This is so for several reasons: (1) by and large, people do not choose their words carefully; (2) people could not choose their words carefully even if they tried to choose them carefully; (3) this is as true for professional communicators as it is for non-professionals; (4) word-choice reflects raw epistemic stance better than any other human modality; (5) this is as true in a visual age as it was in a pre-visual age; (6) because culture is epistemology writ large and because political culture is epistemology writ specifically, language behavior sheds light on some of the most delicious aspects of political affairs.

I do not have the time today to defend these propositions although I would dearly love to do so. To defend them I would have to take on an unholy assemblage of literary aestheticians, survey researchers, poststructural philosophers, and media determinists. Rather than defending my assumptions theoretically, however, I will attempt to redeem them with data from the Campaign Mapping Project. In this paper, I will argue that American politicians are largely responsible for the nation's reservoir of political hope and that that can best be seen by examining their micro-stylistic choices. Heretofore, it has been chic to dismiss politicians' sweet nothings. I think it is unwise to do so and I shall try to explain why.

Harold Zullow (1994, p. 218) reports a fact that will not be surprising to most readers (see Figure 1): Optimism for the nation's economy has generally declined among the American people between 1950 and 1990, with the 1970s being a time of special disenchantment. But here is a curious fact: Zullow shows that there has been a predictable rise every four years in economic optimism, a momentary spike in an otherwise steady slide southward. More curiously, these optimistic up-ticks are most reliably found during presidential campaign years. More curiously still, they occur whether the overall economic mood is positive or negative. For some odd reason, political campaigns make us smile a bit more.

But why? Some as-yet-undiscovered economic principle? An almost anthropological need to renew the tribal spirit on a quadrennial basis? Or does the explanation lie in lunar regularities, Pavlovian habituation, or Vician philosophical cycles? Perhaps rhetoric does it.

Figure 2 reports data from the Campaign Mapping Project that show a rather dramatic difference in verbal optimism between the nation's political leaders and (1) press coverage during the campaign and (2) a large selection of letters written by citizens to their local newspapers between 1948 and 1992. Figure 3 shows that even the highly conten-

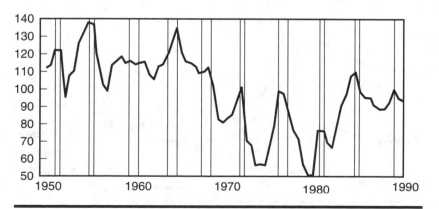

FIGURE 1 Economic Optimism over Time
Copyright © 1994 by Westview Press. Reprinted by permission of Westview Press.

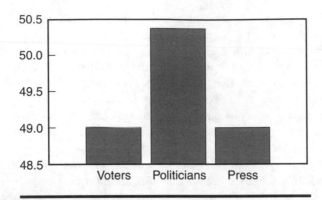

FIGURE 2   Optimism Scores by Political Voice

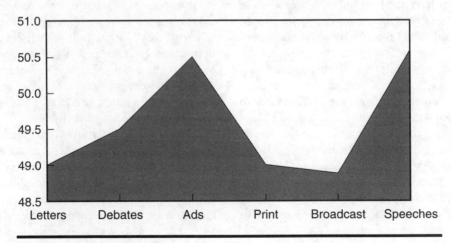

FIGURE 3   Optimism Scores for Campaign Discourse

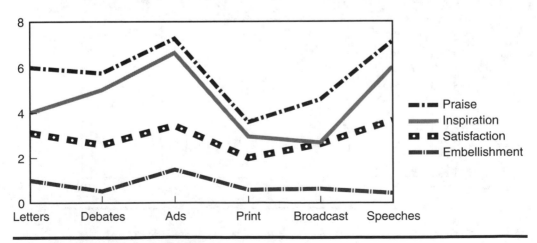

FIGURE 4   Defining Features of Political Ads

tious genre of political debating has more verbal optimism than media reports, and Figure 4 indicates that the much reviled political advertisement loads highest on four different optimistic measures. In addition, politicians use their speeches, particularly, to lionize communal ties (see Figure 5) and they are especially likely to draw upon the nation's civil religion (see Figure 6).

From many vantage points, then, political hope is most predictably nurtured by the nation's politicians. Given the diversity of political leaders in my sample (18 in all), given the panorama of time being studied (almost fifty years), and given

the vicissitudes that have beset the nation's leaders during this time period (the Korean and Vietnam conflicts, continuing threats from the Soviet Union, sustained periods of economic distress, and a volatile Middle East), the magnitude of the differences just reported is all the more remarkable. Despite the nation's difficulties, and despite the disappointments that governance inflicts on people, political discourse serves as a compensatory source of hope (or so it seems at this stage of my research).

This is either surprising or it is not. Some pundits, for example, would decry such happy-talk as a

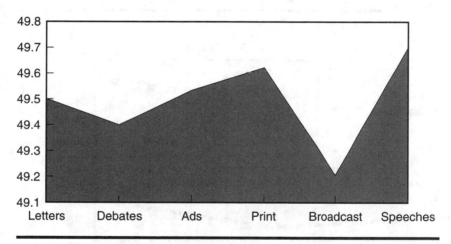

FIGURE 5 Commonality Scores in Campaign Discourse

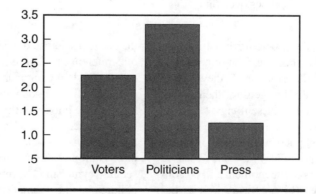

FIGURE 6 Use of Patriotic Language by Political Voice

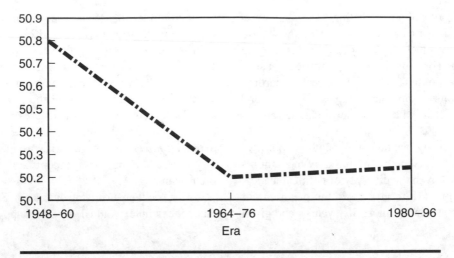

FIGURE 7 Optimism Scores Across Time

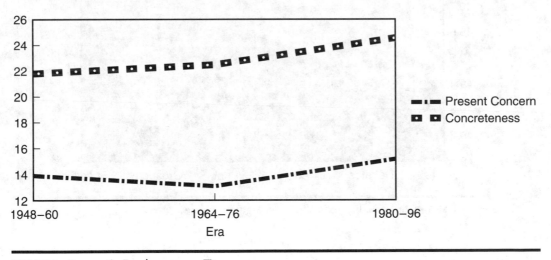

FIGURE 8 Pragmatic Emphases over Time

cosmic deferral of the problems besetting the American people. "We need less sweetness-and-light and more real-life solutions," they would claim. They appear to be getting their wish. Figures 7 through 10 tell us these things: (1) while politicians are still more optimistic than the press or the people, they have slipped in that regard in recent years (Figure 7); (2) politicians have also focused increasingly on matters of the moment and on concrete, empirical issues (Figure 8), as well as becoming more technocratic (Figure 9); (3) finally,

they have participated in an overall decline in patriotic references (Figure 10). Increasingly, that is, people like Bill Clinton and Bob Dole are hunched over the nation's hood with candidate Perot, tinkering with the quotidian things to be found there.

In a recent book (Hart, 1994), I argue that the age of television—and the medium of television—have equipped the American people with a self-sealing cynicism. Evermore, it would seem, we children of the moment are taught how to think about politics by the media products we consume.

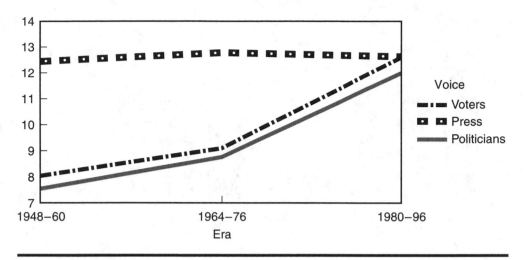

FIGURE 9   Use of Numerical Terms over Time

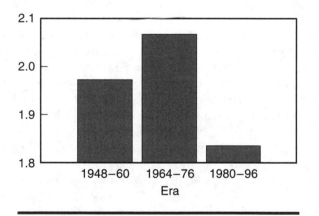

FIGURE 10   Patriotic References over Time

The lessons they teach—trust psychology, not policies; stay inert, not active; nurture cynicism endlessly—have produced in us a kind of postmodern swagger, a way of feeling good about feeling bad about politics. We now place little faith in hope and we decry the hopeful among us as simple-minded, manipulated, or worse.

More ominously, *the American people may be in danger of losing a distinctive language of political engagement.* That is, the Voice of Media seems to be becoming dangerously determinative, as tele-

vision tells us which aspects of politics to discuss and how to apply its template of cynicism to each political exigence we face. These media-based attitudes bully us, making it impossible for us to say in polite company that we respect our national leaders, that we feel blessed to live in a participatory democracy, or that we are uncertain how to address a complex political issue. Who among us, who in this room, could admit to such sentiments?

Consider my last figure, Figure 11. It reproduces the Optimism scores for presidents and

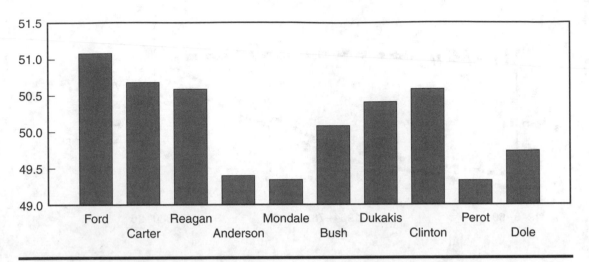

FIGURE 11 Optimism Scores since 1976

presidential candidates since 1976. Among the highest stands Jimmy Carter, that pestilence of a former president, that scared-of-the-Ayatollah, stand-in-gas-lines, beat-up-a-rabbit former president. There stands Jimmy Carter, telling us that the United States is a great and good place, that it has had its excesses but even greater strengths, that political work can be the work of the Lord, that there is glory in citizenship.

What arrant nonsense this seems to a media-savvy people. The Jimmy Carter of the still-remembered malaise speech is more our cup of tea. And the media's cup of tea. For it was the American mass media that turned the malaise speech into a synecdoche for Jimmy Carter and the Carter presidency into a synecdoche for abject political failure. It was as if the media—and the American people—had found a storyline ideally suited to their ill-tempered, gas-guzzling mood. So the Carter speech became an unrepresentative anecdote and the electorate was encouraged once again to think its darkest thoughts. It seemed to make little difference to them that Carter spent most of his time in the speech expressing confidence that the American people could work themselves out of their national funk.

The data I have collected here suggest, then, that in remembering the Carter presidency as a

negative one we misremember it. Mr. Carter was, for example, every bit as optimistic as his much vaunted successor in office and that fact discomfits us. Hence the Campaign Mapping Project. Its purpose is to arrange facts in the proper order, to test half-perceptions against full-perceptions. The tools I use in this study are not everyone's tools, but it does not take a very large brain to distinguish happy words from sad words and then to count them. My counting tells me that the inspirational side of American politics is part of an untold story and that in strange, elliptical ways, politicians nurse the national psyche. Perhaps the American people half-sense this, and half-depend on it, which allows them to be as crotchety as they want to be.

Larry Rosenfield (1977, p. 89) suggested something of this phenomenology some years ago when noting that the accumulation of political discourse we hear each day has a strange capacity to comfort us. For Rosenfield, it is not what is said in politics but the regularity of the saying that steadies us. If the politicians are yapping and the media folks are carping, we seem to reason, all must be right with the world. In this model, the tintinnabulation of politics comes to resemble the ocean rhythms—slowly, steadily, gently, firmly, primordially sustaining us, Perhaps that is how it is with political optimism. Perhaps it, too, becomes a felt-but-unseen cultural backdrop. Perhaps only political silence could send us all screaming into the night.

I return to the place I began: What gives the American people the heart to continue as citizens? My answer: their leaders. In one sense this finding should not surprise us for we have long known that governance is linked in complicated ways with matters of the spirit. But we contemporaries often act as if the soft side of leadership were an embarrassment. Especially during an election year, we act as if tax cuts, and open-housing legislation, and space travel, and international trade, and military conquest are all that matter. At the behest of the press, we look past the heart, the soul, the psyche. But in doing so we look past the human condition as well. Thus my scholarly summons: to study political hope anew and to examine how the language of leadership interacts with public opinion, media practices, and economic conditions to give citizens the courage to stay connected in some measure. It has been my experience that even those who study rhetoric can underestimate its power. This is a tendency we can resist. This is a tendency we must resist.

REFERENCES

Delli Carpini, M. and S. Keeter. (1996). *What Americans know about politics and why it matters.* New Haven: Yale University Press.

Hart, R. (1994). *Seducing America: How television charms the modern voter.* New York: Oxford.

Hart, R., et al. (1996). News, psychology, and presidential politics. In A. Crigler (Ed.), *The psychology of political communication* (pp. 37–64). Ann Arbor: University of Michigan Press.

Prince, S. (1992). *Visions of empire: political imagery in contemporary American film.* New York: Praeger.

Rosenfield, L. (1977). The terms of commonwealth: Response to Arnold. *Central States Speech Journal, 28,* 86–95.

Rosenstone, S. and J. Hansen (1993). *Mobilization, participation, and democracy in America.* New York: Macmillian.

Savage, R. and D. Nimmo (1990). *Politics in familiar contexts: Projecting politics through popular media.* Norwood, NJ: Ablex.

Teixeira, R. (1987). *Why Americans don't vote: Turnout decline in the United States.* New York: Greenwood.

Zullow, H. (1994). American exceptionalism and the quadrennial peak in optimism. in A. Miller and B. Gronbeck (Eds.) *Presidential campaigns and American self-images.* (pp. 214–230). Boulder: Westview.

Research Trends in Political Campaign Communication

Lynda Lee Kaid

University of Oklahoma

Although political communication can trace its roots to the earliest studies of classical rhetoric, Nimmo and Sanders (1981) in the *Handbook of Political Communication* suggest that political communication began to emerge as a substantive field in the 1950s (pp. 12–13). Also like Nimmo and Sanders, I prefer to negotiate the mine field of definitional matters somewhat cautiously, lest the discipline be prematurely and injudiciously narrowed. Perhaps the best definition of political communication may, therefore, be Steve Chaffee's 1975 offering: "the role of communication in the political process" (Chaffee, 1975, p. 15). In discussing the trends in political campaign communication, this presentation will concentrate on the directions political campaign communication research has taken over the past few decades and will provide an assessment of what some of the future directions may be.

DOMINANT AREAS OF STUDY

The study of political communication has in the last few decades been dominated by the study of campaign communication. The earliest and most popular textbook in the area, Dan Nimmo's *The Political Persuaders,* focused on the growing significance of modern communication techniques and political consultants in political campaigns (Nimmo, 1970), and the most popular current textbook is Trent and Friedenberg's *Political Campaign Communication* (Trent & Friedenberg, 1995).

Bibliographic resources also provide some indication of the growth and trends in a field. The earliest attempt at a comprehensive bibliography was undertaken by Kaid, Sanders, and Hirsch (1974), who used the definition "communication as it oper-

ates in a political campaign or similar context in the U.S...." (p. 3) to compile a bibliography of over 1500 articles and books from 1950 through 1972. The most frequently-occurring topics during these early years of the discipline's growth were television and politics, debates, image, issues, presidential campaigns, polling, rhetoric and public speaking, and professional campaign consultants.

Ten years later in 1985, Kaid and Wadsworth published a sequel to this volume covering the period from 1973 through 1982. This bibliography contained 2,461 items in a ten year period, substantially more entries than in the entire 23 years covered in the earlier volume. While categories like television and politics remained dominant and studies of television news burgeoned, many new topics emerged as significant in this second volume. For instance, agenda setting and uses and gratifications deserved their own categories at this point. Some categories, such as "Watergate," could not even have existed before. The category for "Women and Politics" had only two entries in the first bibliography but had grown to 26 entries in 1985.

Unfortunately, no similar effort has followed these works to provide an update for scholars. Noteworthy, however, is an unpublished bibliography compiled by Mary Lynn Hanily (1993) and covering a period from 1977 through 1992. Although it uses a somewhat different definition and an overlapping time period, it provides a useful indication of the continuing growth of the field. This bibliography of over 1,100 entries does not provide an index, but divides the entries into topics. Topics like "Media," "Audiences," "Source," and "Campaign Communication-general" dominate subject matter in this bibliography.

Another important way of keeping up with the directions in a developing field is the publication of overviews or bibliographic essays on particular topics. In the first several volumes of the International Communication Association's *Communication Yearbook* series, regular overviews of political communication were included (Jackson-Beeck & Kraus, 1980; Larson & Wiegele, 1979; Mansfield & Weaver, 1982; Nimmo, 1977; Sanders & Kaid, 1978), and these still provide a useful guide to political communication trends. The most recent similar overview was done by Anne Johnston (1990) who reviewed more than 600 articles that appeared after the publication of the *Handbook of Political Communication.* This analysis characterizes the study of political communication in the 1980s as still dominated by campaign studies: "Although the focus remains on communication from candidates to voters, there has been increased interest in looking at communication among voters about candidates" (p. 330).

Finally, one can use citation analysis as a way of tracking the developing of a field or discipline. I have been working with Yang Lin (1996) at the University of Oklahoma to apply the methods of co-citation analysis (White, 1990) to the study of political communication. For this analysis, using the *ComIndex* which indexes 71 journals, 51 political communication scholars who had published six or more articles were identified and subjected to a co-citation analysis in the DIALOG database. The data in the resulting correlation matrices were subjected to multi-dimensional scaling with three resulting dimensions representing the **topics** of research, the **centrality** of the research, and the **methodological approach** of the research.

The placement of scholars in the field on these dimensions helps one understand the structure and trends in the field of political communication. Looking at Figure 1, which graphs the topics dimension by the centrality dimension, scholars on the far left, such as Hart and Bormann, concentrate their work on political discourse or rhetoric of media. Such researchers look at the effects of political messages with emphasis on message content. On the far right are scholars who look at message ef-

fects emphasizing channels of the messages, typified by researchers like Charles Atkin and Lee Becker. In the center or mainstream are researchers who reflect a balanced emphasis on content, channels, and effects. Examples are Hellweg's work on political debates and Kaid's work on political advertising. The study of political communication, in the campaign setting, or political campaign communication, represents the mainstream or centrality of the field in this analysis. The dimension of **approach** is also interesting, indicating that the majority of scholars in political communication use quantitative methods. This finding is in line with that of Jackson-Beeck and Kraus (1980) who found that the prevailing methods of study in political communication were content analysis and survey research.

CURRENT AND FUTURE DIRECTIONS

Given this summary of the trends our field has taken, a concentration on political campaign communication, on messages and their effects, using quantitative methods, it may be helpful to try to assess the current theoretical perspectives and to suggest topics that may emerge or become more important as we near the next millenium. A first concern is the overall approaches or theoretical perspectives prominent in the field. Kaid (1996) has outlined four basic perspectives that typify political communication research: (1) rhetorical, critical, and interpretive approaches, (2) effects research, (3) agenda-setting theory, and (4) the uses and gratifications approach. Of these, agenda-setting is well established. It remains a mainstay of our research tradition and is advancing from the study of issue agendas to agendas of candidate attributes. The uses and gratifications approach has been difficult to substantiate, and its research tradition has not moved forward in recent years. Rhetorical/critical/interpretative approaches remain central to our field, but it is probably research in the effects area that is advancing the most at the current time. A few decades ago, of course, so enamored were we of the "limited effects" model that it was considered naive to suggest that communi-

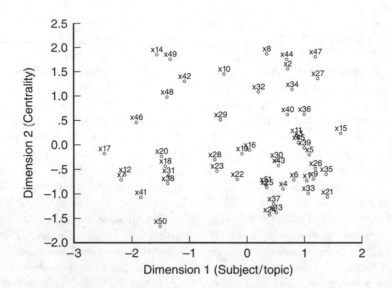

Selected Author Pool

Atkin, Charles (x1) Atwater, Tony (x2) Atwood, L. Erwin (x3) Beasley, Maurine (x4)
Becker, Lee B. (x5) Blumler, Jay G. (x6) Bormann, Ernest G. (x7)
Brosius, Hans-Bernd (x8) Chaffee, Steve (x9) Chang, Tsan-Kuo (x10)
Dennis, Everette E. (x11) Devlin, L. Patrick (x12) Fitzpatrick, Mary Anne (x13)
Fortner, Robert S. (x14) Gaziano, Cecilie (x15) Graber, Doris A. (x16)
Hart, Roderick P. (x17) Hellweg, Susan (x18) Hofstetter, C. Richard (x19)
Jamieson, Kathleen (20) Jeffres, Leo W. (x21) Jenson, Klaus Bruhn (x22)
Kaid, Lynda Lee (x23) Krippendorff, Klaus (x24) McChesney, Robert W. (x25)
McLeod, Jack M. (x26) Meyer, Phil (x27) Nimmo, Dan (x28) Paletz, David L. (x29)
Perry, David K. (x30) Pfau, Michael (x31) Reese, Steve (x32) Rubin, Alan (x33)
Shoemaker, Pamela (x34) Stamm, Keith R. (x35) Stevenson, Robert L. (x36)
Swanson, David (x37) Trent, Judith (x38) Weaver, David H. (x39)
Whitney, D. Charles (x 40) Zarefsky, David (x41) Smith, Craig Allen (x42)
McCain, Thomas A. (x43) Wanta, Wayne (x44) Thomas, Sari (x45)
Wilkins, Lee (x46) Zhu, Jian-Hua (x47) Synder, Leslie (x48) Foote, Joe (x49)
Biocca, Frank (x50) Caspi, Dan (x51)

FIGURE 1   Political Communication Scholars: Subject (Topic)
by Centrality
Source: Yang, 1996

cation had strong effects on the political system. However, the large body of research on political advertising, political debates, and news coverage of political campaigns is advancing the belief that there are identifiable effects of communication in the political system.

Finally, turning to new research trends, the following areas seem to be the most important current topics:

1. Political Advertising Research.   Research on political advertising, particularly television

spots, is one of the most robust areas in our field. From a handful of studies in the early decades of the discipline, this area has mushroomed into a theoretically rich, methodologically diverse, and pragmatically-relevant area. We now know that political advertising has effects on voter attitudes, cognitions, and behaviors, and we can especially pinpoint many of the conditions under which negative advertising is likely to be effective (Kaid, 1981; 1996).

2. News Coverage of Campaigns.   News coverage studies, particularly, those concentrating on newspapers and television, remain an important area of study. More research is done on this topic than any other. The news about news coverage, however, is that content analysis studies are finding more identifiable bias in television news coverage than ever before (Lichter & Noyes, 1996).

3. New Technologies and New Media. It is entirely possible that when political campaign communication is assessed in the next millenium, maybe only ten years from now, the entire communication process by which we now define political campaigning will be completely different. Our field is only just beginning to give attention to these changes, but scholars are studying new formats for communication, ranging from television and radio talk shows to the WWW/Internet. As our televisions and our computers mesh and as traditional news channels lose more and more of their dominance, in the next few years, even by 2000, national presidential campaigns may look somewhat different from today. Scholars in our discipline are ready for these changes and are already working on projects that will be in the forefront of identifying the effects of new technologies and new communication formats on the electorate.

4. International and Cross-Cultural Research. One of the most exciting developments for researchers in political campaign communication has been the chance to apply our research perspectives and methods to campaigning and politics in other countries. From such research scholars are not only learning about the applicability of American-style politics to other countries, but they are learning about the cultural variables that determine the effects of communication on voters around the world.

CONCLUSION

I'd like to make two final points about the status of political campaign communication research. First, our discipline has always been and continues to be truly cross-disciplinary and multi-disciplinary in the most genuine sense of the terms.

While many universities in general and other disciplines in particular are crying out for more cross-fertilization among scholars and perspectives, political communication scholars have always known and practiced the value of working with ideas and colleagues from many points of view. One exciting new development that points up this commitment among our colleagues is the newly formed Media Content Consortium that is interfacing with the National Election Studies (NES) at Michigan. As a part of this group, I am pleased to say that, after years of just talking and promising, the National Election Studies are beginning to take the role of communication in voting behavior much more seriously. Not only were more communication questions included on the 1996 NES surveys, but for the first time ever media content data generated by the Media Content Consortium will become part of the NES data sets to be distributed in conjunction with the survey data. This will provide scholars for the first time with a way to explore more fully the integration of media content with effects from voting behavior surveys. The Political Communication Center at the University of Oklahoma will provide the political television commercial analyses for this project.

Finally, I am also proud to be one of the researchers at the helm of political communication research because our discipline has never lost its concern with applied and policy-oriented research. Our discipline has continued to harbor not only deeply committed theoreticians but also those with a dedication to the pragmatics of communication in political campaigns. We continue our research in this vein because, as scholars, we truly care about the outcomes as well as the processes of campaign communication.

REFERENCES

Hanily, M. L. (1993). *Bibliography on political communication.* Unpublished bibliography, University of Georgia, Athens, GA.

Jackson-Beeck, M., & Kraus, S. (1980). Political communication theory and research: An overview

1978–1979. In D. Nimmo (Ed.), *Communication yearbook 4* (pp. 449–465). New Brunswick, NJ: Transaction Books.

Johnston, A. (1990). Trends in political communication: A selective review of research in the 1980s. In D. L. Swanson & D. Nimmo (Eds.), *New directions in political communication* (pp. 329–362). Newbury Park, CA: Sage Publications.

Kaid, L. L. (1981). Political advertising. In D. Nimmo & K. R. Sanders (Eds.), *Handbook of political communication* (pp. 249–271). Beverly Hills, CA: Sage Publications.

Kaid, L. L. (1996). Political communication. In M. Salwen & D. Stacks (Eds.), *An integrated approach to communication theory and research.* (pp. 443–457). Hillsdale, NJ: Erlbaum.

Kaid, L. L. (1996, October). *The effects of advertising in election campaigns.* Paper presented at the International Colloquium on the Effects of Election Campaigns, University of Montreal, Montreal, Canada.

Kaid, L. L., & Wadsworth, A. (1985). *Political campaign communication: A bibliography and guide to the literature, 1973–1982.* Metuchen, NJ: Scarecrow Press.

Kaid, L. L., Sanders, K. R., & Hirsch, R. O. (1974). *Political campaign communication: A bibliography and guide to the literature.* Metuchen, NJ: Scarecrow Press.

Larson, C. U., & Wiegele, T. C. (1979). Political communication theory and research: An overview. In D. Nimmo (Ed.), *Communication yearbook 3* (pp. 457–473). New Brunswick, NJ: Transaction Books.

Lichter, S. R., & Noyes, R. (1996). *Campaign '96: The media and the candidates.* First Report to the Markle Foundation. Washington, D.C.: Center for Media and Public Affairs.

Lin, Y. (1996). *A co-citation author analysis of the intellectual structure of political communication scholars: Theoretical perspectives, research foci, and research methods.* Unpublished paper, Political Communication Center, University of Oklahoma, Norman, OK.

Mansfield, M. W., & Weaver, R. A. (1982). Political communication theory and research: An overview. In M. Burgoon (Ed.), *Communication yearbook 5* (pp. 605–625). New Brunswick, NJ: Transaction Books.

Nimmo, D. (1970). *The political persuaders.* Englewood Cliffs, NJ: Prentice Hall.

Nimmo, D. (1977). Political communication theory and research: An overview. In B. Ruben (Ed.), *Communication yearbook 1* (pp. 441–452). New Brunswick, NJ: Transaction Books.

Nimmo, D., & Sanders, K. R., (1981). Introduction: The emergence of political communication as a field. In D. Nimmo and K. R. Sanders (Eds.), *Handbook of political communication* (pp. 11–36). Beverly Hills, CA: Sage Publications.

Nimmo, D., & Swanson, D. L. (1990). The field of political communication: Beyond the voter persuasion paradigm. In D. L. Swanson & D. Nimmo (Eds.), *New directions in political communication* (pp. 7–47). Newbury Park, CA: Sage Publications.

Sanders, K. R., & Kaid, L. L. (1978). Political communication theory and research: An overview 1976–1977. In B. Ruben (Ed.), *Communication yearbook 2* (pp. 375–389). New Brunswick, NJ: Transaction Books.

Trent, J. S., & Friedenberg, R. V. (1995). *Political campaign communication* (3rd. ed). Westport, CT: Praeger.

White, H. D. (1990). Author co-citation analysis: overview and defense. In C. Borgman (Ed.), *Scholarly communication and bibliometrics* (pp. 84–105). Newbury Park, CA: Sage.

Trends in Political Television Advertising

L. Patrick Devlin
University of Rhode Island

Because this analysis had to be completed before a September deadline I thought it wise to focus on ad trends that occurred during the primary campaigns rather than the just completed general election. You'll have to await my quadrennial article to read about general election ad trends.

Some trends that manifested themselves during the primaries, such as a heavier use of party ads or negative ads that used the words of candidates caught on camera against them continued into the general election. Not only was there a heavier use of party ads during the pre-primary and primary period, but in the period after the party nominees had been chosen leading up to the conventions, the Democratic National Committee sponsored 29,500 spots versus only 1,600 Clinton/Gore primary campaign ads (Ad Detector, 3/27/96 to 7/31/96). Never before had so many party ads been used in selected markets using mostly negative ads to soften up the opposing candidate before his convention.

The big story about political ads during the primary campaign was that they were relied on more in 1996. Let me give you some quantification of this judgment from my analysis of the ads used during the 1996 New Hampshire presidential primary campaign.

New Hampshire is a good place to track primary campaign trends for several reasons. First, it is a state with one major television station acting as its most important news and ad viewing outlet. Second, New Hampshireites see the most ads by the most candidates over the longest period of time. It is true that some candidates target ads for states that are never shown in New Hampshire, e.g., in 1996 Buchanan made single ads for Alaska and Louisiana and Lugar and Dole used several unique Iowa ads. Candidates also make new ads that are shown in primaries coming after New Hampshire. However, these subsequent ads are usually fewer than the total number of ads shown in New Hampshire. In 1996 the four highest vote getters, Alexander, Buchanan, Dole, and Forbes aired the following: Alexander twenty New Hampshire ads, six after New Hampshire; Buchanan twelve New Hampshire ads, three after New Hampshire; Dole twenty-four New Hampshire ads, five after New Hampshire; Forbes sixty New Hampshire ads, fifteen after New Hampshire. So whether candidates used a few ads before or after New Hampshire, all candidates used over 75 percent of all their primary ads during the New Hampshire primary.

What are the trends that emerge from the analysis of the 1996 New Hampshire primary ads?

1. Ads were on earlier in 1996.

Alexander started his ads in New Hampshire in June, 1995—five months earlier than Tsongas used ads in 1992. Alexander even advertised his town meetings with New Hampshire voters in February and March, 1995, almost a year before the primary vote. Even President Clinton went on the air in selected markets in June, 1995 with an ad sponsored by the Democratic National Committee focusing on the Republicans seeking to repeal the ban on assault weapons.

2. Candidates used more ads in 1996.

In 1992 I collected 69 ads used during the New Hampshire primary campaign. During 1996, 183 primary campaign ads were collected. That is a

265 percent increase in the number of candidate ads. In 1992 during the New Hampshire campaign, Clinton aired the highest number of ads (17), while Bush aired but 4, and all seven candidates used an average of 10 ads per campaign. In 1996, the eight Republican candidates who used ads averaged 22 ads per candidate.

But averages may be deceiving because one candidate in 1996 was an ad story in himself. The Steve Forbes campaign aired 60 of its 75 total ads in New Hampshire. Nothing in my twenty-four years of ad research matches the Forbes campaign in the number of ads used. Another candidate, Morry Taylor, who achieved but 1.4 percent of the New Hampshire vote, made 30 ads and showed most of them in New Hampshire. But taking out Forbes and Taylor from the mix, all other candidates who stayed in the race until the end—Buchanan with 12, Dole with 24, Alexander with 20, and Lugar with 12,—made and used more ads. So even these campaigns, without the aberrations of Forbes and Taylor, still used more ads averaging 17 ads in 1996. Jim McKay, Lugar's New Hampshire coordinator admitted, "It was a real surprise to us that we would have to use as many different ads as we did" (McKay, 1996).

3. More was spent on advertising in 1996.

Examining the exact spending comparisons from the most important single ad spending outlet in New Hampshire—WMUR, Manchester, is revealing. Years ago it was a little-watched station with a weak signal somewhere north of Boston. Now it is a prominent ABC affiliate that put on three televised debates where all candidates showed up. Its 6:00 p.m. local news program is watched by 111,000 New Hampshire adults. This is more news viewers than all three Boston stations combined, whose New Hampshire adult viewing audience is but 69,000.

In 1992 all candidates spent $851,000 advertising just on WMUR. In 1996 all candidates spent $2,696,480 on WMUR. This was a 317 percent increase in advertising spending and there wasn't

even a race or ads on the Democratic side. Candidates spent the following on WMUR:

Forbes	$852,350
Alexander	494,840
Dole	344,770
Gramm	281,475
Taylor	265,905
Buchanan	231,900
Lugar	153,025
Wilson	72,215
	$2,696,480

Forbes's total spending alone was more than all seven candidates spent together in 1992. Bob Kerry was the biggest spender on WMUR in 1992, spending $177,000. In 1996, all candidates except Lugar and Wilson spent in excess of the 1992 big spender.

One perspective on 1996 television ad spending needs to be made. In 1992 Buchanan was the top spender in New Hampshire with $1.4 million spent on New England outlets. In 1996 Buchanan spent only $750,000 on New England outlets. His $231,000 spent on WMUR made him the sixth biggest spender. Buchanan spent half as much on television ads in 1996 as he did in 1992, and in 1996, he won.

Buchanan in 1996 emphasized late television buys during the last six weeks because as his ad maker admitted "We didn't go on there early because we didn't have the money to do it" (Townsend, 1996). Instead Buchanan emphasized paid radio—$250,000 in total buys—and countless free interviews narrow casted on talk radio to reach his voters and keep "his profile up" (Melby, 1996). Buchanan's time buyer proudly proclaimed "Our strategy was...we didn't want to spend one dime we didn't have to.... Our media buys were targeted to our potential voter.... The Gramm people told us we did brilliant buying" (Melby, 1996). Dole's media maker put Buchanan's buying in perspective. "Buchanan's spots never mattered because Buchanan was a spot.... He would have gotten the same percentage if he didn't run a single ad" (Stevens, 1996).

Much more was spent on television advertising in New Hampshire, but the candidate who won spent comparatively less, and the top spender, Forbes, achieved but 12 percent of the vote. So New Hampshire demonstrated you could not spend your way to victory, and the victorious candidate was a modest television spender.

4. More negative advertising was used in 1996.

If I were to tell you that half of Forbes's ads were negative, that wouldn't be much of a surprise. But, if I tell you that in New Hampshire Forbes used thirty-one negative ads, that number should floor you. In 1992, Harkin used but one negative ad and Buchanan used ten negative ads. In 1996, all candidates used 71 straight negative or comparative negative ads. This was a 645 percent increase in negative advertising. The 71 negative ads outnumbered all ads aired in 1992. So even though there were gigantic increases of 317 percent in spending and 265 percent in total ads, the 645 percent increase in negative ads is astonishing. New Hampshireites could say "ouch" at being exposed to so many negative ads. Even though Forbes used the highest number of negative ads (31), Dole used the highest percentage of negative ads (67 percent).

Dole used 6 positive ads, 12 negative attack ads, and 6 negative comparison ads which blended both positive and negative appeals—yet the overwhelming impression after seeing these blend ads was negative. Comparison ads are really strong negative ads although ad makers don't like to admit it. Forbes, the candidate who used the most negative comparative ads, had his ad maker argue, "I don't believe we had very many that were negative.... Saying Bob Dole voted for this and saying he's a Washington politician is not very negative" (Sanderson, 1996).

But comparison ads emphasize through unequal time, unequal graphics, or complementary versus less complementary candidate pictures the negatives of the other candidate more. A Dole comparison blend ad titled "Crossfire" exemplified comparison ads. This ad attacked Buchanan for a statement he made about women "as simply

not endowed by nature…with…the will to succeed" and a statement he made about "arming South Korea, Japan, and Taiwan with nuclear weapons." Rather than stating where Dole stood on women or nuclear weapons the ad concluded in its final seconds simply by highlighting Dole's agenda of a balanced budget, appointing conservative judges, and workfare, not welfare. This and other comparison ads are usually unequal comparisons. It is fair to say Dole had six positive ads and eighteen negative ads. The irony of this negative emphasis, his ad creator argued, was "The reason Dole lost New Hampshire is he didn't do enough positives" (Stevens, 1996).

The 645 percent increase in negative advertising was the biggest story of trends in the 1996 primary ads. Three important individual ad stories emerged from the primary campaign and all three were negative. Alex Castellanos, Gramm's ad creator, posed this insight. "There were only three ad stories that mattered and unfortunately we weren't involved in any of them—the Forbes ads against Dole, the Dole ads against Forbes, and the Dole ads against Alexander" (Castellanos, 1996). Negative television ads did make a difference in these three campaigns. "Forbes nearly decimated Bob Dole.... Forbes ads did work" (Castellanos, 1996). However, Castellanos observed that when Dole counterattacked in mid January and went after Forbes, "He couldn't take a hit because they hadn't created a candidacy....They were trying to play football with just offense. So when the other team's offense got on the field they ran right down for a touchdown" (Castellanos, 1996).

Although Forbes made almost an equal number of positive (29 ads) and negative (31 ads) the impression from his time buying was that his ads were overwhelmingly negative. Dole's ad maker concluded, "It wasn't just the 31 negative Forbes ads, it was the air time that they bought" (Stevens, 1996). Forbes' ad maker admitted, "My mom lives in Vermont and she would call and say 'why are you playing those negatives over and over and over?' And they [Carter Wrenn & Co.] would say, 'See, that means it's working'" (Sanderson, 1996). Susan Tindle, ad producer for the Lugar campaign—a campaign that didn't use negative ads—summed up her feelings after watching a compilation reel of opponent ads, "I immediately threw myself against the wall and said 'wow, no wonder people say they are undecided'—this is horrible" (Tindle, 1996).

Even before the first Dole ad went on the air, Forbes spent $364,000 on WMUR ads that were characterized as a "mega bulk buy" (Capasano, 1996) by his ad buyer and characterized as a "we'll buy any time slots available" (Capasano, 1996) by Julie Capasano, program director at WMUR who canceled her Christmas vacation due to so much candidate time buying.

Forbes's early ads touted his flat tax but his next and subsequent flights of ads went after Dole. Forbes's ad maker disclosed

> Anybody who started when we did with almost no name recognition would have to have done it the way we did. One of the things we did right off the bat was compare ourself to Dole because he was number one.... Comparing with him helped us both to bring up Dole's negatives and bring us up. We put out so many it was hard to answer. That was part of the strategy.... It wasn't the nature of the ads. It was that we played them so many times.

Forbes used almost an ad a day strategy where others may have used an ad a week in the past. He had many positive ads but an equal number of more heavily played negative ads, 75 percent of which were directed at the front-runner Dole.

This heavy October through December buying by Forbes canceled out Alexander's early buy strategy. Alexander's "buys were totally washed away by Forbes" (Stevens, 1996). Alexander stayed in single digits while Forbes went from single to double digits by mid October. By early February, after months of heavy advertising, Forbes surged ahead in New Hampshire. Forbes went from almost 20 points behind (37% to 18%) in early January to four points in front (29% to 25%) in a February 5, 1996 poll (WMUR—Dartmouth College Primary Poll, 1996). More importantly, Forbes gained supporters directly from Dole, con-

firming that his negative campaign ads helped him and hurt Dole. "Dole Lost Supporters To Forbes" proclaimed the WMUR/Dartmouth poll showing that "23% of those who now say they will vote for Forbes were supporting Dole in October" (WMUR—Dartmouth Poll, 2/6/96).

As I watched the sheer number of Forbes ads and saw his rise in the polls, first to challenge and then lead Dole, I remember thinking—"Wow, this guy is going to win just on advertising." In the 1996 primaries Forbes was the biggest story for an advertising analyst because of his unprecedented spending of $400 per vote in Iowa, $40 per vote in Arizona, and his $35 per vote just on Manchester, New Hampshire television.

The power of television ads both helped to create a Forbes candidacy and ultimately did him in. His ad maker made these confirming insights about the effectiveness of the Forbes ads and the effectiveness of the Dole ads used against Forbes:

> Our campaign proves the power of video. Ads put us there because that's all we had.... Our negative ads—that was not what got us.... It was their negative ads that got us. It was like fighting by the sword and dying by the sword. Our biggest weakness was we had no staying power. We had a glass jaw. When we got hit we couldn't bounce back. So ad campaigns do work (Sanderson, 1996).

Dole's ad maker confirmed that Dole's negative ads "worked as a blunt instrument" (Stevens, 1996). Initially he wanted to use humorous ads with the tag line "President Steve Forbes—what a joke," using an ad asking what tough decisions has Steve Forbes faced—then picturing him sitting in a restaurant trying to decide whether to order red or white wine (Stevens, 1996). However, "the campaign wouldn't do that....The campaign focus grouped when it got in a panic about attacking Forbes...they found these people loved Forbes so they decided we can't make fun of him, he's gotten too big" (Stevens, 1996). Instead the Dole campaign, under the direction of Bill Lacey, made heavy-handed ads that "put up their poll questions as spots.... They just took copy points like 'untested' or 'too risky' and put them up there" (Stevens, 1996). No matter that Dole's 10 negative ads against Forbes were heavy-handed. They worked. Just as the negative Forbes ads had capitulated him to the status of poll equal or front-runner, now Dole's attack ads brought Forbes down.

The last ad campaign from the primary that made a difference was the three late Dole ads against Alexander. In 1988 Dole was hurt during the last weekend in New Hampshire by the unanswered Bush "Senator Straddle" ad. In 1996, the anti-Alexander ads became the Senator Straddle ads and will now work their way into the folklore of media myth.

Dole used three ads—one with the popular governor Merrill stating on camera in the snow that Alexander was "too liberal" for New Hampshire. In two final ads aired during the last week of the primary, Alexander was hit in a Dole ad titled "Great Pretender" by the tag line "He's not what he pretends to be," and in an ad titled "Lamar's Income Tax" he was labeled as a "tax and spend liberal" who once proposed an income tax for Tennessee. "Tax" and "liberal" proved as powerful as the words "untested" and "too risky" had earlier in New Hampshire.

Alexander didn't answer these Dole ads and stayed with his positive closing advertising. Dole's ad maker observed, "They made a crucial mistake running all that early media. In the final week they had about 200 ads versus our over 1,000 ads.... How come they didn't answer? ...Had he had the resources at the end, he could have gotten second place. Had he gotten second place that might have secured him the nomination. Buchanan was never going to get the nomination" (Stevens, 1996).

Buchanan's ad maker confirmed the wiseness of the ending anti-Alexander ad strategy. "One of the most brilliant moves was Dole's decision to go after Alexander. He solved a problem for us because my fear was that Alexander would surge past both of us. If Alexander would have finished ahead of Dole and us, you would have had an entirely different race because had Dole finished third in New Hampshire, the establishment would

have thrown their money to Alexander and pronounced Dole dead.... If Lamar wins New Hampshire, Lamar would have surged through. He becomes everybody's favorite because he is not Dole or not Pat. He's clean and he won't embarrass us" (Townsend, 1996).

Had Alexander won or placed even second, Dole may have been mortally wounded and withdrew as Bob Woodward asserts in his book *The Choice.* Tom Rath, New Hampshire policy advisor for the Alexander campaign, confirmed that after Iowa "the Alexander campaign was growing at a pace of one to one and one half points per day—on a trajectory that would have put us at 27 points by election day. Unfortunately, the trend did not continue because of the two ads that Dole used in the final week against us" (Rath, 1996).

Several ad makers—Buchanan's and Gramm's—confirmed the power of Dole's ad against Alexander. "The only guy in that field who could have beaten Bob Dole was Lamar Alexander. Bob Dole strategically did the right thing. He took out the only guy left who could beat him. That was the other instance where advertising proved decisive and settled the nomination" (Castellanos, 1996).

A few percentage points—Buchanan 27 percent, Dole 26 percent, Alexander 22 percent—made all the difference in New Hampshire between the stories of winner, strong finisher, and also-ran in 1996. With Forbes achieving but 12, percent his candidacy was crushed.

The Dole campaign "made a decision to play for second in New Hampshire. It was a conscious decision thinking a third would threaten the survivability of his candidacy" (Stevens, 1996). Dole achieved second place, survived, and went on to take out Buchanan in later primaries as he had taken out Alexander and Forbes in New Hampshire. Dole won the nomination and his ads against his rivals helped him achieve victory.

Surely there were other persuasive phenomena at work in the 1996 primaries aside from ads. Dole's use of push-pull polling—thousands of calls made to prospective voters pushing them away from rivals due to negative information and toward Dole with positive information—was also instrumental to his victory. Forbes's use of absentee ballots in Arizona while his popularity was still high was instrumental to his victory there. And Dole's use of governors and party endorsements in places like South Carolina helped build a fire wall that hurt rivals unable to gain those endorsements and party workers. However, advertising, especially negative advertising, was a big story and an important trend that emerged from the 1996 presidential primary campaign.

REFERENCES

Ad Detector (1996, March 27 to July 31). National Media, Alexandria, VA.

Capasano, J. (1996, January 14). Interview with Julie Capasano, Program Director, WMUR-TV, Manchester, NH.

Castellanos, A. (1996, May 23). Interview with Alex Castellanos, Media Producer, Gramm for President Campaign, Alexandria, VA.

McKay, J. (1996, February 17). Interview with James McKay, New Hampshire Director, Lugar for President Campaign, Manchester, NH.

Melby, C. (1996, April 22). Interview with Caroline Melby, Time Buyer, Buchanan for President Campaign, Maryland.

Rath, T. (1996, March 15). Interview with Thomas Rath, Policy Director, Alexander for President Campaign, New Hampshire.

Sanderson, P. (1996, April 9). Interview with Paul Sanderson, Media Producer, Forbes for President Campaign, New York, NY.

Stevens, S. (1996, July 17). Interview with Stewart Stevens, Media Producer, Dole for President Campaign, New York, NY.

Tindle, S. (1996, May 24). Interview with Susan Tindle, Media Producer, Lugar for President Campaign, Maryland.

Townsend, J. (1996, April 29). Interview with Jay Townsend, Executive Producer, Buchanan for President Campaign, New Jersey.

WMUR–Dartmouth College Primary Poll (1996, February 6). Dartmouth News, Hanover, NH.

Narrowcast Media and Political Campaigns: Trends and Implications

Robert V. Friedenberg
Miami University

A few days after the March 1996 Ohio primary and local elections, the *Cincinnati Enquirer* headlined its letters to the editor column "Are Voting Booths Secret Any More?" Under that rather provocative headline, the Enquirer printed a letter that illustrates the growing influence of narrowcast media in even the most local of campaigns.

To the Editor: On election day, after a day in the office and a stop at the polls I came home to an answering machine message. A woman asked specifically for me, and proceeded to point out that:

- *As of 3 P. M. I had not yet voted.*
- *It was imperative I vote before 6:30 P. M.*
- *The success of the Milford School Levy depended on my "yes" vote…*

Will someone please enlighten me when the secret of the voting booth ceased to be sacrosanct? While I understand releasing lists of eligible voters, and perhaps even lists of those who actually voted, I think it outrageous to allow the election days' proceedings to be perused by special interest groups. For all I know, these same groups may have found a way to be privy to the choices made as well…The secret ballot is at the very core of America's greatness…I suggest that our boards of election be reminded again that the secret ballot remains one of our most precious freedoms. (Signed) Karen N. Cain. (Cain, 1996)

Let me ask you to focus your attention on two of Ms. Cain's observations. First, a woman asked specifically, "for her." The caller did not ask for any other possible voters living in her household. Second, and most importantly, that woman evidently felt that if she voted, it was highly likely that Ms. Cain would vote "yes." There would have been no point to this woman calling if she did not believe she knew how Ms. Cain would vote. Is it any wonder that Karen Cain felt that the secrecy of the voting booth might well have been violated?

The techniques of narrowcast campaigning, apparent in the Milford, Ohio School Levy effort described by Ms. Cain arc based on an intimate knowledge of the voter. Indeed, that knowledge is so intimate, that though the campaign cannot be absolutely certain what the voter will do in the voting booth, it has, as the Milford School Levy group evidently did with Karen Cain, a very, very, very, good idea.

It might not dismay Ms. Cain to learn that political campaigns have ready access to information identifying the Congressional district in which she lives, or even the state legislative districts in which she lives, the precinct in which she votes, the school district, park district, sewer district, zoo district, and similar political subdivisions in which she lives and votes. But it might begin to disturb Ms. Cain to learn that political campaigns also know her mailing address, even if it differs from her home address. Indeed, probably unlike Ms. Cain herself, they know the full nine digits of her zip code and her carrier route. And of course, as she found out, they also know her phone number.

It might prove yet more disturbing to Ms. Cain to learn that political campaigns know whether she has voted in the last three primaries and the last three general elections. Moreover, those campaigns are aware of what federal candidates, and in many instances state candidates, to whom she has made financial contributions. Additionally, they are aware of the size of that contribution.

Upsetting as this information might be to Ms. Cain, you can imagine her concern to learn that any interested campaign could likely determine, with relative accuracy, her income level, her ethnic heritage, her religious preference, and of course her party affiliation. Though Ms. Cain's relatives might wonder, an industrious campaign might even determine her age. Perhaps Karen Cain was called by the Milford School Levy advocates because they were aware of the presence of school-age children in her home, or her status as a homeowner, for this information too, could have been available to them. Regardless, of what particular information ultimately generated that call to Karen Cain, the incredible growth in the availability of a broad spectrum of demographic information that can be readily manipulated through the use of computers, is one of the two primary reasons for the rapid growth of narrowcast media in political campaigns (Harmon, 1996).

Narrowcast media, in contrast to broadcast media, derive their usefulness in contemporary campaigns from the ability of data handlers to segment the population. Karen Cain was no doubt segmented by the Milford School Levy campaign into a group of prospective supporters. For whatever the reasons, unlike others who might even live at her address, the levy campaign had segmented her from among thousands of voters, and sent a very specific message tailored explicitly to her.

Karen Cain received her message by phone, on election day. Though narrowcast media such as the phone are used heavily on election day for get-out-the-vote efforts such as the one involving Ms. Cain, it is likely that in most major campaigns narrowcast media play an equally if not more important role prior to election day. Those media, most noticeably, direct mail, customized mailed video cassettes, and phone messages, facilitate both voter persuasion, and fundraising, in a "high interest, low backlash," fashion. That is, by targeting to a narrow spectrum of the public, campaigns can develop a very precise and personalized message,

touching the "hot buttons" of the receiver and presumably motivating them to support a candidate. In so doing, the narrowcast messages do not generate any backlash from members of the public who are uninterested in these issues, or disagree with the candidate's position on those issues. Those individuals might well also be contacted by the same campaign using narrowcast media, but the message would be different and appropriate to them as members of a different constituent group.

The growth of narrowcast media in contemporary campaigns is a function of several factors. First, as I have already indicated, computer technology has allowed campaigns to manipulate vast amounts of data in such a fashion as to facilitate precise targeting. The second major factor giving rise to the growth of narrowcast media in political campaigns are the campaign finance reforms of the early 1970s. Passed largely as a consequence of the financial abuses of the Watergate era, those federal laws, which were widely emulated at the state level, placed ceilings on the size of campaign contributions, presumably thus outlawing the abuses of the Watergate era.

The birth of direct mail fundraising as we know it today can be traced to the work of Richard Viguerie. In 1965, Viguerie hired two employees and the three of them transcribed by hand, because the law prevented the use of photocopy machines, the names and addresses of the 12,500 donors who had contributed $50 or more to the preceding year's Goldwater campaign. This became the initial direct mail conservative contributor list and was first used in 1966 to help Senator Robert Griffin of Michigan (Viguerie, 1980).

In that same year another Senator asked Richard Viguerie for help. Viguerie claims that he quickly perceived that this Senator had a greater appreciation for the fundraising possibilities of direct mail than virtually anyone in public life at that time. But, Viguerie felt uncomfortable with the Senator's liberal beliefs and declined to work for him. Rather, Viguerie suggested that he contact liberal consultants, and attempt to develop his own mailing lists. Senator George McGovern followed Viguerie's advice, contacted Morris Dees and Tom Collins, spent four years developing a mailing list of 250,000 supporters of liberal causes, and largely financed his 1972 presidential race from that list (Viguerie, 1980). The Watergate-inspired campaign finance reforms placed low ceilings on the amounts of money that a single individual could give to a campaign. Those reforms encouraged candidates to seek small contributions from hundreds of thousands of contributors, as had Nixon's opponent, Senator George McGovern. By so doing, the finance reforms gave great impetus to the use of narrowcast media. By preventing massive contributions from a few wealthy individuals, those reforms placed a premium on obtaining small contributions from large numbers of individuals. This focus on limited contributions from unlimited numbers of people, has greatly stimulated the rapid growth of direct mail fundraising since the mid-1970s (Sabato, 1981). Thus, by placing a premium on raising small amounts from large numbers of people, campaign financial reforms are a second principle cause of the growth of narrowcast media such as direct mailpieces, video cassette mailers, and the use of phones, all of which facilitate a highly personal fundraising appeal.

Though there has been a growing trend towards increased use of narrowcast media in political campaigns, several implications of that growth are potentially disturbing. First, narrowcast media may encourage candidates to treat campaigning much as merchandisers might treat niche marketing. That is, candidates might seek to appeal strongly to 5%, 10%, or 20% of the citizenry. In the past, candidates with such a limited appeal might not choose to run. Or, if they did choose to run, at some point such candidates would either broaden their appeal, often by moving to the center of the political spectrum, or lose the ability to have a serious impact on public affairs.

However, I fear that the very success that some candidates achieve through the use of narrowcast media may cause them to linger on the political fringes, often serving as divisive figures, rather than unifying ones. Analogous to the product manufacturer who carves out a small niche of the market, and makes a comfortable living for years by maintaining that limited market share, narrowcasting allows candidates to carve out a small niche of the political market and may encourage them to remain focused on that niche. Hal Malchow, a principle in the Democratic direct mail fundraising firm of Malchow, Adams, and Hussey, observes that "as a general rule, candidates who are more liberal and conservative do better in direct mail fundraising" (Raising Big Bucks, 1996.) Is it a coincidence that some of the most polarizing figures in American politics (George McGovern, Ted Kennedy, Pat Buchanan, and Oliver North come immediately to mind), have relied heavily on narrowcast media, particularly for fundraising?

Second, the growth of technological advances facilitating the retrieval of information, and the quest for specific information to impress a host of narrowcast media audiences, provides more and more material that can be used in all negative campaigning, including narrowcast campaigning. This year the Democratic National Committee used optical scanners to better access the millions of pages of Congressional documents extending back 35 years to the start of Robert Dole's congressional career. It is not an accident that the request for this equipment came from Director of Opposition Research at the DNC, Eric Berman (Fineman and Hosenball, 1996).

Evidence of technological advances facilitating the retrieval of information in use was common during the 1996 campaign. For example, on October 6, Jill Zuckerman of *The Boston Globe* reported that as Bob Dole spoke at Elizabethtown College in Hershey, Pennsylvania, Clinton supporters distributed handouts indicating that 30 years earlier Dole had voted against a bill which included a rider to provide $300,000 in federal money to roof a building on the Elizabethtown campus (Zuckerman, 1996).

Third, might the narrowcast media encourage candidates to take extreme positions and thus contribute to the general shrillness of American political rhetoric? I question whether it is entirely accidental that the same period that has been marked by the growth of narrowcast media in political campaigns has also been marked by the growth of negative advertising. Certainly, the use of narrowcast media might well foster a climate that creates a greater propensity for this type of rhetoric. By enabling the message to be precisely targeted to a limited audience, narrowcast media may well encourage the use of extreme positions which polarize our society, rather than unify it.

We hear much of negative advertising on radio and television. However, the very fact that it is narrowcast, rather than broadcast, makes narrowcast media highly inviting for campaigners seeking to send negative messages. Though it's ready visibility causes the public to focus on negative advertising in the broadcast media, it was slanderous and misleading phone calls made on behalf of Governor Lawton Chiles in the 1994 Florida gubernatorial race that may have in fact have decided that race, and ultimately caused the governor to apologize for the way his campaign was conducted (Faucheux, 1996).

Often overlooked in this year's Republican primaries, while the press and public focus was on negative TV commercials, the Dole campaign spent nearly one million dollars planting negative information about Dole's primary rivals through the use of what his campaign called "suppression phone banks," operated by Campaign Tel. Ltd. of New York City. It was this negative phone operation that enabled the Dole campaign, during the critical primary month of March, to contact approximately 1,400,000 voters in key primary states (Morris, 1996). During the pivotal primary month of March that saw Dole break from the pack and wrap up the nomination, the Dole campaign spent more money on its phone operation, $877,000, than on his media campaign, which cost him $871,000 during that month (Morris, 1996). It was Dole's negative phone operation during the decisive March primaries, not his advertisements, that Pat Buchanan, no stranger to hardball politics, characterized as "over the line"(Fineman, 1996).

Clearly narrowcast media are here to stay. Not only has modern technology facilitated the precise targeting of narrowcast media, but technology has improved the very media itself. For example, according to Tom Edmonds, former President of the American Association of Political Consultants and the founder of Political Video Duplicators, since 1990, technology has brought the cost of producing and mailing a persuasive ten minute video cassette to under two dollars (Edmonds, 1997). The use of such cassettes brings a precisely targeted message into the viewer's living room at a cost that makes it competitive with other media.

Moreover, one can scarcely think of a more perfect media for highly targeted messages than the Internet. Though technological problems currently make narrowcasting through the Internet difficult, no doubt technology is likely to improve in the near future. Currently, a visitor might leave an E-mail address on a web site and then be contacted by those who operate the web site. Doug Thompson, one of the political consultants most responsible for the growing use of the Internet by political campaigns, claims that in 1996, there were approximately 25,000 candidates, among the 110,000 candidates for public office, who had home pages on the World Wide Web (Thompson, 1997). Many utilized interactive features where a visitor might leave an E-mail address, enabling the campaign to subsequently contact that visitor. But, unless the voter provides the campaign with an address, current technology makes it difficult for a campaign to send a message to a specific voter over the Internet. Yet one can envision a day in the not too distant future when campaigns can use the Internet to contact voters with narrowcast messages, much as the mail is currently used. Moreover, though currently Jim Robinson of the Democratic fundraising firm of Robinson and Muenster is no doubt correct in observing that, given security problems on the Internet, it is unlikely to be used extensively for fundraising purposes in the near future (Raising Big Bucks, 1996), it is hard to imagine that technological improvements will not conquer these problems in the future.

Given the rapid evolvement of this technology, it is not difficult to imagine the potential of the Internet as a political narrowcast media. Political parties are already examining patterns of Internet usage. The Republican National Committee was recently astonished to learn that according to a survey it commissioned, fully 20% of all Republican voters get information from the Internet (Fineman and Hosenball, 1996). Republican media consultant Alex Castallanos claims that it will not be long before lists of primary voters will be contacted by campaigns through E-mail (Castallanos, 1996). Political consultants such as Doug Thompson are the first to acknowledge that it would be impossible to draw a causal relationship, but by the same token, he and many others are intrigued by studies of the 1996 elections which show that 69% of open seat and challenger candidates with web sites won, while 77% of open seat and challenger candidates without web sites lost (Thompson, 1997).

While Karen Cain's concern for the secrecy of the voting booth may have been somewhat exaggerated, it is clear that political campaigns are growing more and more sophisticated in their analysis of voters and their attempts to communicate with voters. As campaigns slice and dice the electorate, narrowcasting messages into ever smaller groups, perhaps our field should grow a bit concerned. At the least we should recognize that campaigns are changing, and with changes come new opportunities, both for good and for bad.

REFERENCES

Cain, Karen. (1996, March 26). Are Voting Booths Secret Any More? *The Cincinnati Enquirer*, p. A12.

Castallanos, Alex. (1996, June 7). *Campaigns and Elections Consultants Roundtable*. Washington D.C.: C-Span Network.

Edmonds, Tom. (1997, January 8). Interview with the author.

Faucheux, Ron. (1996, April). Unfair Ads, Push Polls. *Campaigns and Elections*, 5–6.

Fineman, Howard. (1996, March 18). Hunting the Angry Voter. *Newsweek*, 26.

Fineman, Howard and Hosenball, Mark. (1996, May 20). Dishing Dirt. *Newsweek*, 27–28.

Harmon, Shawn. (1996, Summer). Telephone interviews and personal correspondence between Shawn Harmon, Sales Manager of Aristotle Industries, and the author throughout the summer of 1996. Available from the author.

Morris, Dwight. (1996, May 3). The Big Black Hole *ElectionLine*. Available at http://www.electionline.com/HTEL/ymorris050396/page1.cgi.

Raising Big Bucks. (1996, May). *Campaigns and Elections*, 45–47.

Sabato, Larry. (1981). *The Rise of Political Consultants*. New York: Basic Books.

Thompson, Doug. (1997, January 8). Interview with the author.

Viguerie, Richard. (1980). *The New Right: We're Ready To Lead*. Falls Church: The Viguerie Company.

Zuckerman, Jill. (1996, October 6). *Road to the White House*. Washington D.C.: C-Span Network.

CHAPTER 6

AT THE HELM
IN ORGANIZATIONAL
COMMUNICATION

Introduction

Dennis K. Mumby
Purdue University

Over the last 15 years the field of organizational communication has undergone—to push the nautical metaphor to its breaking point—a "seachange" in its approaches to the study of organizing. The 1980s and 1990s have seen the emergence of new systems—rhetorical, interpretive, critical, postmodern, and feminist studies that have transformed the field both theoretically and empirically. Each of the four scholars featured here has been integral to this paradigm revolution.

Phil Tompkins is Professor of Communication and a member of the Comparative Literature Faculty at the University of Colorado. He received his Ph.D. in 1962 from Purdue University, where he studied with Charles Redding. Phil is a past President and Fellow of the International Communication Association, and the 1990 recipient of SCA's Robert Kibler Memorial Award. Through his scholarship, Phil has played a pivotal and defining role in the emergence of rhetorical approaches to organizational communication. His books include *Organizational Communication Imperatives: Lessons of the Space Program* (Roxbury, 1993), and *Organizational Communication: Traditional Themes and New Directions* (edited with McPhee), (Sage, 1985). More than anything else, Tompkins has helped to shape our self-

understanding as a field, and to draw important and far-reaching connections amongst two areas of study that, before his intervention, seemed largely irreconcilable.

Linda Putnam is Professor and Head of the Department of Speech Communication at Texas A&M University. She received her Ph.D. in 1977 from the University of Minnesota, and from 1977 to 1993 was on the Communication faculty at Purdue University. In 1995 she was elected Fellow of the ICA. Linda is that rare scholar who is able to move effortlessly amongst different academic constituencies. Long recognized internationally for her research on bargaining and negotiation, she was also, in the early 1980s, a key player in the development of the interpretive approach to the study of organizations, editing (with Mike Pacanowsky) *Communication and Organizations: An Interpretive Approach*. In addition, Linda has contributed to the emergence of feminist and critical approaches to organization communication. As the co-editor of two organizational communication handbooks, she continues to be instrumental in helping our field define itself.

Stan Deetz received his Ph.D. in 1973 from Ohio University. He has held appointments at Bridgewater College and Southern Illinois University, and is currently Professor of Communication at Rutgers University. In 1994 he was a Fulbright Senior Scholar at Göteborgs Universitet in Sweden. He is the current President of ICA. Stan's 1992 book, *Democracy in an Age of Corporate Colonization* (SUNY Press) set the standard for the development of critically based, communication conceptions of organizational life. His work continues to articulate important connections amongst the continental philosophical tradition, communication theory, and issues of identity formation and democracy in the workplace.

Dave Seibold received his Ph.D. from Michigan State University in 1975. Prior to his current appointment at University of California, Santa Barbara, he held positions at Purdue University, University of Illinois, and University of Southern California. Dave is an internationally renowned scholar in the areas of organizational change and small group decision making. With Scott Poole and Bob McPhee he has been instrumental in the development and application of a structuralizational approach to the study of small group communication. This research has generated fresh insight into the dynamics of group decision-making. Dave is also a widely respected organizational change management consultant, and is one of a handful of scholars in our field able to successfully reconcile the rigors of academia and the demands of the corporate world.

Together, these four scholars represent the best of our field, and demonstrate that organizational communication studies has developed a maturity and richness that bode well for our future.

International Developments in Theory: Conversations, Networks, Texts, Solidarity, and Virtual Organizations

Phillip K. Tompkins
University of Colorado, Boulder

It is, of course, a great honor to deliver one of the four "At the Helm" lectures in organizational communication. It is also a temptation to extend the nautical metaphor, but instead let me explain my intentions in terms of dry land and firm footing. I intend to use this occasion to call attention to, if not dig into, the theoretical work of four persons in scattered locales, so scattered that I could use the word "international" in my title with a clear conscience. These four people have made recent theoretical contributions to the foundations of organizational communication that will change the way we think and talk about organizational communication, not to mention how we will "do" it in the future. Let me create suspense for a few moments by identifying now only each place of residence for the four scholars: (1) West Lafayette, Indiana USA; (2) Montreal, Canada; (3) Helsinki, Finland; and (4) Boulder, Colorado USA.

I

These four contributions do not create the field anew; they are emerging out of old traditions in the field of organizational communication—and in my conclusion I will show how their contributions add up to *collective* insights. We start with a faculty member at that red brick campus on the west bank of the Wabash River, Purdue University—Professor Cynthia Stohl. Stohl's recent contribution was made in her (1995) book, *Organizational Communication: Connectedness in Action.*

Stohl's topic—network analysis—is nothing new to organizational communication (as indicated by the discussion of network research conducted in other fields in the first state-of-the-art publication in the field, Tompkins, 1967). Her treatment, however, is refreshingly new. Network analysis in our field began as an empirical, data-driven approach to organizational communication. It was a positivistic, objective approach—we could just as well call it modernism—subject to the standard tests of reliability and validity.

For some doing case studies at the time, network analysis seemed a project of bloodless reification. People, for example, were called "nodes." For this and other reasons, network analysis was the mostly unidentified target of the epithet, "functionalist" organizational communication. A more serious complaint about network analysis was that it was atheoretical and unconnected from standard organizational concepts (Tompkins, 1984) as well as the kind of communication theory W. Charles Redding (1972) believed we should integrate into our empirical work.

Stohl acknowledges that the network approach is a metaphor, a perspective on organizations rather than a representation of objective reality itself. Having effected this move she can afford to use the term "functions" (e.g., p. 67 and p. 123) as something other than a dirty word. In addition Stohl (1995) argues that networks are *"constituted and reconstituted through interpersonal communication"* (p. 19, emphasis in the original).

The well-known work by Stohl and Redding (1987) summarizing all knowledge of *messages* in organizational communication is condensed by Stohl in the third chapter to serve as the foundation for the *meaning* of network experience. The category system includes ostensive vs. internally-experienced messages, verbal vs. nonverbal, intentional vs. unintentional. Thus, Stohl rescues network analysis from its atheoretical quicksand and from its epistemological origins in logical positivism.

In a chapter on relationships Stohl attempts the long overdue task of integrating organizational and interpersonal concepts. As a particularly important example, under the heading of relational symmetry in networks, Stohl introduces the interpersonal work of Watzlawick, Beavin, and Jackson (1967). Organizational concepts are integrated into network theory as well, for example "concertive control" (Tompkins & Cheney, 1985) is discussed in the network nomenclature. The implications of Redding's work on the ethics of organizational communication are also considered from the network-analytic perspective.

In developing a network perspective on organization, Stohl could not avoid taking up the timeless concept of hierarchy. The result is a somewhat indecisive stance. At times she seems to quote approvingly the futurists' predictions that networks will one day, perhaps soon, replace the formal organization and its hierarchical manifestation. For much of her analysis, hierarchy is set up by Stohl as a foil or dialectical opposition for her development of the new network analysis. She seems in the end to conclude, however, that hierarchy is inevitable, the "prototypical relational pattern" of organization (p. 108).

II

The second thinker we visit is James R. Taylor of the University of Montreal. His project, as advanced in *Rethinking the Theory of Organizational Communication: How to Read an Organization* (1993), is a bit more ambitious than Stohl's. He intended to accomplish nothing less than a paradigm shift in organizational studies in general and organizational communication in specific. This can be seen in the section titles of his book: "Part I: Paradigms Lost: Deconstructing the Office Automation View of Organization" and "Part II: Paradigms Regained: Reconstructing a Communication Theory of Organization."

Taylor reports his own studies of government agencies in Canada, studies measuring the effects of the adoption of the technology of office automation in the agencies: *"There were no very important effects at all!"* (Taylor, 1993, p. 3, emphasis in original). No effects. And yet there was an indirect consequence—"creeping overhead" (p. 27). Taylor suggests that part of the explanation for a slow economy in North America is the "prolonged buying binge" (p. 31) in which Canadian and U.S. firms and government agencies mortgaged themselves for technology that has not improved organizational efficiency.

Taylor is no Luddite; he harbors no religious fears of technology, nor does he share Heidegger's mystical fear of planetary technicity. He spent part of his career as a producer for the mass media before beginning his doctoral studies in the Annenberg School at Pennsylvania. He simply reports his results: office automation has proved to be a fiasco. The rest of his book is an attempt to answer why this is the case. The answer comes only after his rigorous rethinking of organizational theory.

Taylor's boldest stroke is to posit two basic orientations, or *worldviews,* in regard to organization. Borrowing from the language of software design, Taylor describes the two worldviews as *particle* and *activity.* A particle perspective concentrates on the path of the entities processed by the organization; an activity perspective concentrates on the units doing the processing to the entities. A particle perspective is more or less equal to "a *product* or *service* or *customer orientation*" (Taylor, 1993, p. 35, emphasis in the original); an activity perspective would concentrate on productivity measures, such as time-and-motion studies.

The point is that one can neither simulate nor analyze organizations from both perspectives or worldviews simultaneously. (This principle is analogous to the Uncertainty Principle in Physics; i.e., one can measure the location of a particle and the velocity of a particle, but not simultaneously.) Different cultures and perhaps different ages and eras tend to have a bias toward one or the other.

The Japanese have concentrated on a particle orientation—quality from the point of view of the consumer—while the traces of Taylorism in North America encouraged the other perspective.

Taylor analyzes the dysfunctional consequences of an exclusively activity-based worldview (Taylor, 1995, p. 41). In the Canadian agency studied by Taylor, the activity worldview took priority over the particle. This seems to be a general problem with office automation; managers start to count pages of productivity to the exclusion of a particle-oriented concern for satisfied customers.

Taylor even implies that traditional organizational theory—not just organizational communication discourse—is biased in the direction of activity. An organization chart depicts mainly what people *do*. Management is an activity. The "dead hand of accounting" is absorbed if not obsessed with "the bottom line," the results of transactions. And although Taylor did not make the point in this context, he did need later to develop that communication is action, a form of activity. The cultural approach to organizational communication oriented toward performance has little or no concern for the particle worldview.

All of this sets the stage for a rigorous series of theoretical moves. Taylor rethinks Chomsky, Austin, conversation analysis, and the text metaphor; he marches through Mead, Schutz, Malinowski, Ashby, Whorf, and others. He replicates Stohl's attempt to introduce relationship theory into conventional network analysis.

Having developed his root metaphors, a comparison of life to dialogue, or conversation, and a first draft, or text (see also Cheney & Tompkins, 1988, for an elaboration of the textual metaphor). Taylor returns to the opening question, what is information? He argues that computers and information do not in any sense create a conversation, nor a meaningful text. To condense the argument, information is not about communication; office automation is thereby conceptually flawed.

We confront now the complete argument: Conversations are the stuff of organizations; conversations lead to narratives or texts meaningful to the conversationalists. From this conclusion Taylor proved the validity of his theory by generating seven principles of artful managerial conversation. He discussed in a down-to-earth way the characteristics of good management, all the while maintaining that organization is a communication system—"an ecology of conversation" (p. 244).

III

The next international contributor to organizational communication theory is Antero Kiianmaa of the Helsinki University of Technology in Finland. Kiianmaa is a Social Psychologist and Psychoanalyst who studied organizational communication for 18 months (1991–2) at the University of Colorado at Boulder. His book (in press), *Moderni Totemismi: Tutkimuksia Solidaarisuudesta ja Sosiaalisista Verkostoista Suomessa* (*Modern Totemism: Studies in Solidarity and Social Networks in Finland*), reports the results of Kiianmaa's own studies in Finland. The book is much more than that, however, in that it integrates theoretical insights and empirical data across cultures and time periods. For example, the concept of solidarity, the Finnish word which is recognizable to English readers in the book's title, is similar to what is called identification and commitment in the U.S.

Solidarity becomes the integrating concept of empirical network studies in Finland and the U.S. In addition, Kiianmaa integrates forgotten passages in Durkheim, Freud, and Weber that provide the verbal scaffolding for viewing networks, organizational and otherwise, as providing in the modern world that social cohesion or solidarity first identified by Durkheim as originating in early religious organizations. An English translation of this work is expected in December of 1996.

IV

Finally, I mention a work in progress in the Department of Communication at the University of Colorado at Boulder. David Noller (in press) is completing a doctoral dissertation on the "virtual organization," a phenomenon discussed more in trade journals than academic ones. Noller has been a participant observer for 18 months in a video production company that survives from contract to contract; each job is different from the last one, requiring fewer or more people. Despite a surprising degree of stability and continuity, one can almost say that a new organization is created for each contract. And the contract is usually with another organization, creating what Noller began to see as networking, with a particular applicability of the concept of *multiplexity.*

Noller also began to see in both the trade literature and the limited academic work on "virtual" organizations a theoretical confounding of two factors that needed to be separated for analytical purposes. And, as if to maintain a sense of continuity for this paper, Noller was inspired by Taylor's work to see what those factors were. He calls the first the structural factor, the second the technological one. Most assume that some sort of technology, e.g., telecommunication and computer-mediated communication gadgetry, is a defining characteristic of the virtual organization. Not so. Noller advances a compelling redefinition of the virtual organization as a kind of network with a limited temporal existence that reaches across traditional boundaries. Unlike Stohl, Noller sees hierarchy in the virtual organization. But technology may or may not be a means of achieving such an organization.

Apart from helping us achieve clear thinking about the ballyhooed virtual organization, Noller also advances the theme of networks and networking and theorizes, with Taylor, that communication is *both the figure and the ground* of organization, both the canvass and the paint. Notice that the work of all four is having the effect of revitalizing network studies, primarily by integrating communication theory and network analysis (cf. Charles Redding's [1972] little-known attempt to ground organizational study in the communication theory of his day). Notice also that Stohl's work on *multiplexity* is reflected in Noller's empirical work; Taylor also inspired Noller to separate analytically the structural from the technological. And a neat irony exists in the fact that all four of these scholars are breaking down the wall between interpersonal and organizational

communication at the same time that they are conceptualizing networks as interorganizational in nature—i.e., breaking down boundaries between and among organizations.

Finally, organizational communication for much of its existence was a parochial enterprise, very much made in the USA; today we have featured work by persons in Helsinki and Montreal as well as West Lafayette and Boulder. We welcome and encourage this internationalization of our field. We can also be grateful that these thinkers have provided us with a thicker, richer nomenclature than ever by which to select and reflect reality for analysis. We are now on solid theoretical ground.

REFERENCES

Cheney, G., & Tompkins, P. (1988). On the facts of the text as the basis of human communication research. In J. Anderson (Ed.), *Communication Yearbook/11,* 455–481. Newbury Park, CA: Sage.

Kiianmaa, A. (in press). *Moderni totemismi: Tutkimuksia solidaarisuudesta ja sosiaalisista verkostoista Suomessa.* Helsinki: Hanki ja Ja.

Noller, D. (in progress). *Communication and Virtual Organization.* Unpublished Ph.D. dissertation, University of Colorado at Boulder.

Redding, W. C. (1972). *Communication within the organization: An interpretive review of theory and research.* New York: Industrial Communication Council.

Stohl, C. (1995). *Organizational communication: Connectedness in action.* Thousand Oaks, CA: Sage.

Stohl, C., & Redding, W. C. (1987). Messages and message exchange processes. In F. Jablin, L. Putnam, K. Roberts, & L. Porter (Eds.), *Handbook of organizational communication: An interdisciplinary approach* (pp. 451–502). Newbury Park, CA: Sage.

Taylor, J. (1993). *Rethinking the theory of organizational communication: How to read an organization.* Norwood, NJ: Ablex.

Taylor, J. (1995). Shifting from a heteronomous to an autonomous worldview of organizational communication: Communication theory on the cusp. *Communication Theory, 5,* 1–35.

Taylor, J., Cooren F., Giroux, N., & Robichard, D. (1996). The communicational basis of organization: Between the conversation and the text. *Communication Theory, 6,* 1–39.

Tompkins, P. K. (1967). Organizational communication: A state-of-the-art review. In G. Richetto (Ed.), *Conference on Organizational Communication.* Huntsville, AL: NASA.

Tompkins, P. K. (1984). The functions of communication in organizations. In C. Arnold & J. Bowers (Eds.), *Handbook of Rhetorical and Communication Theory* (pp. 659–719). New York: Allyn & Bacon.

Tompkins, P. K., & Cheney, G. (1985). Communication and unobtrusive control in contemporary organizations. In R. D. McPhee & P. K. Tompkins (Eds.), *Organizational communication: Traditional themes and new directions* (pp. 179–210). Newbury Park, CA: Sage.

Watzlawick, P., Beavin, J., & Jackson, D. (1967). *Pragmatics of human communication.* New York: Norton.

Metaphors of Communication and Organization

Linda L. Putnam
Texas A&M University

Organizational communication scholarship grew out of concerns for the ways that communication can contribute to organizational effectiveness. Communication was a skill that made individuals more effective communicators on the job or a factor that contributed to systemwide effectiveness or ineffectiveness (Redding & Tompkins, 1988). Even when scholars entered the arenas of organizational culture, symbols, and meaning, the dominant thrust of this work centers on the effective use of communication. This paper draws upon metaphor as a theory-building construct to track the dominant images of communication in the organizational literature. This paper contends that organization communication scholars both inside and outside the field are shifting toward discourse perspectives rather than relying on conduit conceptions of communication. This discourse perspective, I contend, is consistent with the changes that are occurring in organizations and with the challenges that organizational communication scholars will face in the next century.

METAPHORS AND IMAGES OF ORGANIZATIONS

Metaphor has become a common topic in organizational studies. In particular, metaphor as a system of beliefs about figure-ground relationships facilitates theory building by examining images at multiple levels of analysis. In organizational theory, metaphor analysis aids 1) in articulating ontological assumptions of alternative perspectives on organizations (Morgan, 1986) and 2) in revealing the assumptive ground of such organizational constructs as images and socialization (Alvesson, 1993; Smith & Turner, 1995). Organizational

members also use metaphors to depict the nature of their particular organizations—casting them as zoos, military structures, tribes, or games (Koch & Deetz, 1981).

This chapter calls into question the traditional metaphors used to depict organizations by taking communication as figure and organization as ground. Most analyses of organizational metaphors do the reverse and develop universal metaphors that have become cornerstones of organizational theory—for example, organizations as machines or as organisms. This paper challenges the centrality, rigidity, and salience of these traditional metaphors by introducing a new way of looking at organizations through the lens of the communication-organization relationships. Seven metaphors emerge from analysis of research programs in organizational communication: conduit, lens, linkage, performance, symbol, voice, and discourse. This paper summarizes the central features of these metaphors, illustrates how they are employed in recent communication studies, and explores how they recast the nature of organizational communication.

Dominant Metaphors in Organizational Communication

Four dominant perspectives in organizational communication have governed research and thinking in the past. The four perspectives include: conduit, lens, linkage, and symbol. Even though each perspective differs in ontological and epistemological roots of organizations, they embrace a common orientation to communication in the literature.

The *conduit* perspectives (Axley, 1984) of communication cast organizations as containers in which messages are transmitted throughout the organization. Words that signal the use of a conduit metaphor are *send, exchange, relay,* and *convey.* The conduit metaphor treats transmission as figure and message and sender/receiver as ground. The conduit metaphor evokes an image of communication as easy, effortless, and linear. A vast majority of the current research that centers on adoption and use of communication technologies, improving performance feedback, and fostering organizational change is driven by not only conduit assumptions of message flow but conceptualizations of communication as a tool. A tool is an instrument, device, or a means of accomplishing some goal. Communication is a channel, a technology, or a task that organizational members must do. Communication media are effective if the technologies aid in reaching organizational goals.

The *lens* perspective of organizational communication treats communication as a filter that centers on the searching, retrieving, and routing of information. The lens metaphor also relies on transmission, but unlike the conduit metaphor, senders and receivers are active agents. Distortion and filtering occur naturally through message flow. Reception plays a significant role in the lens metaphor whereas sending is the critical element in the conduit perspective. Research on information flow and decision making, superior-subordinate communication, perceived environmental uncertainty, performance feedback, media richness, and communication technology adopt a lens perspective by treating organizations as sensors, brains, and information processing organisms.

Studies of information sources, perceptions of ambiguity, accessibility and decision making, and consequences of information seeking employ themes drawn from the lens metaphor (Stohl & Redding, 1987). Research on strategic management and public relations that focus on how organizations monitor their environments and manage information flows to the public also embrace the tenets of the lens metaphor (Eisenhardt, 1989; Grunig & Grunig, 1992). Although this perspective adopts many assumptions of a containment view of communication, it also treats organizations as communication through the information

processing modality that governs much of this work. Organizations, then, are not simply containers for communication; rather they are information processing systems.

Another perspective of communication that surfaces in the literature is *linkage* or connector. In this metaphor, communication produces organizations as networks of interconnected relationships. In the linkage metaphor, organizations are not containers with fixed structures and boundaries. Interactants are intertwined through dyadic processes that reside within relationships rather than perceptual systems as in the lens metaphor.

The literature on network roles and structures, however, tends to adopt a stance that organizations produce linkages while work on emergent networks places communication as the producer of organizations. Linkage, as Taylor (1993) points out, is a variation of linear models of communication, returning to the conduit and transmission views of communication. Specifically, the degree of participation or inclusion in networks that stem from the presence or absence of a link, the amount of communication exchanged, the directionality of messages, and the type of content discussed force-fit the linkage or connection metaphor into a conduit model. Recent work on semantic networks departs from this tradition (Stohl, 1995).

For research that treats networks as emergent from communication linkages, organizations consist of multiple, overlapping connections among people with permeable boundaries. Communication becomes the building block that connects individual, group, organizational, and interorganizational levels. Linkages promote coordinated action, constellations of task activities, and extend webs of social influence (McPhee & Corman, 1995; Stohl, 1995). The linkage metaphor challenges traditional notions of organizations as static boundaries, unidimensional functions, and immobile structures.

Finally, the *symbol* perspective shifts the foci to communication as the creation, maintenance, and transformation of meaning (Bantz, 1993). A symbol is something that stands for or represents something else through association or convention.

Communication in this metaphor is interpretation through making sense of the nature of symbols. Rooted in the links between symbols and culture, the relationship between communication and organization varies in this literature.

Some studies illustrate how communication produces culture while other literature presumes the existence of culture and examines the role of meaning as contained within organizations or as the way that organizations produce sensemaking. The organization within this metaphor becomes a complex collection of interpretations that define a symbolic milieu. Organizations are novels or literary texts that members inscribe as they interpret the symbols in their organizational landscape.

Studies that focus on the construction and maintenance of organizational cultures (Bantz, 1993; Goodall, 1989); on organizational commitment (Tompkins & Cheney, 1985); on organizational folklore (Bell & Forbes, 1994) and on such symbolic forms as narratives, rites, rituals, and metaphors illustrate the way communication acts as interpretation in making sense of organizational symbols. The metaphor of symbol provides a direct link between representation and interpretation. Hence, the relationship between communication and organization is one of production, with symbols producing texts.

Emergent Perspectives in Research Domains

Three emergent perspectives offer the potential to change the fundamental relationship between communication and organization. These emergent perspectives are: performance, voice, and discourse. In the *performance* perspective, social interaction becomes the focal point for organizational communication research. Performance refers to process and activity, rather than to an organizations productivity or output. In this metaphor, communication consists of interconnected exchanges, for example, message-feedback-response, action-reaction-adjustment, symbolic action-interpretation-reflection, and action-sensemaking. Social interaction is rooted in the sequences, patterns, and meanings that stem from exchanging verbal and nonverbal messages.

In the performance perspective, organizations emerge as coordinated actions, that is, both communicating and organizing are the enacting of rules, structures, and environments through social interaction. Performance, however, serves as an umbrella for three schools or clusters of research: enactment (Weick, 1979); co-production (Eisenberg, 1990); and storytelling (Boje, 1991, 1995). Social interaction is both behavioral and symbolic, with a simultaneous emphasis on action and sensemaking. In the *enactment* school, organizational environments are constructions. Organizations enact their environments which they, in turn, rediscover and use to constrain or to enable future actions.

Co-productions are collaborative performances that stem from the way participants produce social practices and coordinating local agreements. For example, improvisations or jazz performances are worked out through mutual responsiveness, complex verbal and nonverbal cues, shared focus and attention, and altercasting (Bastien & Hostager, 1988, 1992). In like manner, jamming is a co-production in which participants experience a transcendence through suspending self-consciousness, co-orienting to each other, and surrendering to the experience (Eisenberg, 1990). As the metaphor of performance suggests, jamming and improvisation treat communication and organizations as co-constructing each other—communication produces organizations while organizations produce communication.

Another way in which organizational members co-construct performances is through *storytelling*. Storytelling is how members dramatize organizational life and transform mundane events into passions and zeal (Pacanowsky & O'Donnell-Trujillo, 1983). This approach focuses on the way organizational members introduce stories in conversations; how listeners co-produce them through prompting the teller; how stories unravel through subsequent performances of sharing them (Boje, 1991). Thus, storytellers and listeners serve as co-authors to simultaneous construct and make sense of their interactions. Researchers act as organizational detectives who engage in storytelling through constructing plots based on organizational talk (Goodall, 1989) and through writing and staging organizations as theatrical productions (Mangham & Overington, 1987). Stories, then, are not simply cultural artifacts or monologues; rather they emerge as performances that are never complete.

A second emerging perspective for studying organizational communication is the notion of *voice* which centers on who can speak, when, and in what way. To have a voice is to be able to speak in the context of the organization; organizations, then, exist as a *chorus* of member voices. The idea of communication as voice clusters into categories of distorted voices, voices of domination, different voices, and access to voice. In *distorted voices,* members are able to speak, but not in ways that represent their interests (Alvesson, 1993; Deetz, 1992). Such ideological aspects of communication draw attention to the role that meaning plays in the service of power and unobtrusive control (Fairclough, 1992; Tompkins & Cheney, 1985). Power and meaning join together to distort voices so that even though voices may be heard, they echo the sentiments of the elite (Clair, 1993a; 1993b).

In the *voice of domination,* speaking becomes hegemonic in that patterns of activity and institutional arrangements culminate in common sense, thus concealing the choices and interests of the dominant group (Deetz, 1992; Deetz & Mumby, 1990). Hegemony exists in everyday activities and influences the way dominant coalitions control organizations through political, cultural, and economic actions.

The voice perspective finds its most direct and common usage in feminist organizational studies (e.g., Bullis, 1993; Buzzanell, 1994; Fine, 1993; Marshall, 1993). This work highlights the fact that some people need to speak *in a different voice.* Because their voices are unique, they are often ignored, silenced, or misunderstood. These studies question the role of communication in constructing gendered organizations and the need for research to move away from treating gender as

a variable to conceiving of it as a fundamental organizing principle (Marshall, 1993).

Another school in the cluster of voice is *access to voice.* In traditional, hierarchical organizations, voice typically refers to the degree of organizational participation. While most research that studies access to voice targets traditional bureaucratic organizations, other work focuses on alternative organizational forms such as democratic institutions (Cheney, 1995; Deetz, 1992; Harrison, 1994). These organizations take specific steps to provide members with access to voice. Alternative organizational forms demonstrate how communication develops interdependence and provides a balanced understanding of institutions.

Voice as a perspective on organizational communication brings together different orientations to the issues of speaking, hearing, and making a difference in organizations. Communication functions simultaneously to express and suppress voice; that is, voices may be heard but they are distorted or dominated; new voices may be added to change existing asymmetries, but they result in merely echoing them. The organization constitutes a chorus of diverse and often muted voices; the tune they sing is not always clear.

The *discourse* metaphor surfaces as the third emerging perspective in organizational communication. Discourse refers to language, grammars, and discursive acts that form the foundation of both performance and voice. In the discourse metaphors, communication is a *conversation* in that it focuses on both process and structure, on collective action as joint accomplishment, on dialogue among partners, on features of the context, and on micro and macro processes (Taylor, 1993). Conversation becomes a simile for organizations. In fact, Bergquist (1993) contends that conversations are both the essence and the product of organizations in that conversations lay the groundwork for community. Discourse foregrounds language as the nexus for untangling relationships among meaning, context, and praxis. In the discourse perspective, communication casts organizations as *texts* (Barthes, 1981). Texts are sets of structured events or ritualized patterns of interaction that transcend immediate conversations (Taylor, 1993).

The study of organizational communication as *discursive practices,* subsumes research on language as emotional expressions, as genres, as paradox, and as dialogue. Discourse, in this orientation, is the way that organizational understanding is produced and reproduced. Labels such as "ideal patient" and "health care provider" are not simply terms that classify occupational groups; rather they define expectations, forms of knowledge, and task activities for organizational groups.

Emotion expressions as discursive acts center on the way that members produce organizational knowledge through regulation and control (Fineman, 1993; Waldron, 1994). Regulation occurs through display rules that translate discourse and emotions into acceptable organizational forms (Hochschild, 1983). Emotional expression is intertwined with dichotomies that privilege a rational view of work and marginalize the private, feminine, and informal side of organizational life (Mumby & Putnam, 1992). Both the display and the interpretation of emotion hinge on the way that feelings are legitimated and the social costs for displaying emotions (Conrad & Witte, 1994).

The study of **communication genres** as discursive practices centers on the form, audience, and socio-historical situation (Yates & Orlikowski, 1992). Developed from structuration theory, genres are recurring patterns of communicative practices that form types of interaction, for example, reports, memos, meetings, and email. Organizational members enact genres for particular purposes; hence, they become institutional templates for social interaction. Orlikowski and Yates (1994) show how the presence and the absence of genres such as memos, reference manuals, and dialogue establish an organization's identity as temporary, accountable to a professional community, and flexible in work processes.

Paradoxes and ironies as discursive practices focus on relationships among discourse, meaning, and praxis. Paradoxes are statements and actions that are self-contradictory, but seemingly true (Putnam, 1986) while irony arises when intended meanings contradict customary interpretations (Brown, 1977). Paradoxical goals can lead to enacting reward structures and operating procedures that violate the overall mission of the organization.

Paradoxes are evident in double-loop learning and organizational changes (O'Connor, 1995); incongruities between individual and group goals (Smith & Berg, 1987); dialectical tensions rooted in the "deep structures" of organization life (Benson, 1977); and double bind messages in superior-subordinate communication (Putnam, 1986; Tompkins & Cheney, 1983). They appear in the interwoven but oppositional forces that evoke organizational change, namely through struggles between action and structure, internal and external, and stability and instability (Van de Ven & Poole, 1988). Ironic remarks and ironic humor acknowledge the contradictory and paradoxical nature of organizing by disrupting historical frames through reversals in meanings. Irony transforms organizational experiences by providing members with an opportunity to confront new versions of social reality and grasp unthinkable propositions. In a postmodern world characterized by rapid changes and fragmentation, the management of ironies and paradoxes becomes particularly vital. Understanding and accepting paradoxes as discursive practices becomes a way of navigating in a world defined by junctures (Smith & Berg, 1987).

Another discursive practice, **dialogue,** also stems from assumptions about postmodern organizations. Participants who engage in dialogue suspend defensive exchange, share and learn from experiences, foster deeper inquiry, and resist synthesis or compromise (Eisenberg & Goodall, 1993). Dialogue can transform action and promote organizational learning through developing synergy, empathy, and authentic deliberation among individuals (Evered & Tannenbaum, 1992). Dialogue legitimates each person's experience from connecting with others to determine what counts as knowledge and how it is valued. Self-recognition and transformation arise from the additive nature in which each person's experience contributes to the whole (Eisenberg, 1994).

Treating organizational communication as a discursive practice clarifies the relationship between discourse and texts. A text is the structured sets of events that comprise the organization. These events, created and reconstituted through discourse, have symbolic meaning to participants. A text as symbolic meaning substitutes for treating organizations as objects or entities. Texts are the gestalt meanings aligned with the underlying frames of discursive practices (Strine, 1988). They are symbolic forms, open to multiple and unlimited readings, frequently ruptured displays, reflexivity between authors and texts, and concerns for transcendence and transformation (Strine, 1988). Researchers serve as authors who produce both the texts and the readings of the texts as they engage in organizational studies (Cheney & Tompkins, 1988).

DISCUSSION AND CONCLUSIONS

This chapter notes changes in research domains through reviewing different metaphors that appear in our literature over the past 15 years. In general, recent perspectives in organizational communication are moving toward the linguistic turn in social sciences. The growth of research domains that embrace emotional expression, communication genres, paradox, and dialogue attest to this movement in the field. Performance and voice, as precursors to discourse metaphors, also embody assumptions about communication that differ from the tool perspectives evident in the conduit, lens, or linkage metaphors.

The relationship between communication and organization is fundamental to understanding emerging perspectives in the field. Basically, the dominant metaphors treat communication as a means to organizational ends. Research on uses of communication technology, strategies and functions of communication in conflict management, boundary role spanning, and information processing exemplifies this view. The tool conception of the communication-organization relationship is not simply casting communication as a skill or a system within organizations; rather it represents an ontological stance about organizational communication.

More recent approaches to the study of organizational communication challenge the nature of communication and organization. In the performance perspective, communication is connected to organizing through process-action rather than means-end. In the voice metaphor, communication becomes defined as expression or suppression. Finally, in the discourse perspectives, communication is equated with discursive acts that not only constitute organizations but also become the organizing process. Dialogue is community, paradox is fragmentation and ambiguity, and conversations and genres are texts. Thus, new domains of organizational communication reconceptualize the communication-organization relationship.

REFERENCES

Alvesson, M. (1993). *Cultural perspectives on organizations.* Cambridge: Cambridge University Press.

Axley, S. (1984). Managerial and organizational communication in terms of the conduit metaphor. *Academy of Management Review, 9,* 428–437.

Bantz, C. R. (1993). *Understanding organizations: Interpreting organizational communication cultures.* Columbia, South Carolina: University of South Carolina Press.

Barthes, R. (1981). Theory of the text. In R. Young (Ed.), *Untying the text: A poststructuralist reader* (pp. 31–47). Boston: Routledge & Kegan Paul.

Bastien, D. T., & Hostager, T. J. (1988). Jazz as a process of organizational innovation. *Communication Research, 15,* 582–602.

Bastien, D. T., & Hostager, T. J. (1992). Cooperation as communicative accomplishment: A symbolic interaction analysis of an improvised jazz concert. *Communication Studies, 43,* 92–104.

Bell, E., & Forbes, L. C. (1994). Office folklore in the academic paperwork empire: The interstitial space of gendered (con) texts. *Text and Performance Quarterly, 14,* 181–196.

Benson, J. K. (1977). Organizations: A dialectical view. *Administrative Science Quarterly, 22,* 1–26.

Bergquist, W. (1993). *The postmodern organization: Mastering the art of irreversible change.* San Francisco, CA: Jossey-Bass.

Boje, D. M. (1991). The storytelling organization: A study of story performance in an office-supply firm. *Administrative Science Quarterly, 36,* 106–126.

Boje, D. M. (1995). Stories of the storytelling organization: A postmortem analysis of Disney as "Tamara-Land". *Academy of Management Journal, 38,* 997–1035.

Brown, R. H. (1977). *A poetic for sociology.* Cambridge: Cambridge University Press.

Bullis, C. (1993). At least it is a start. In S. A. Deetz (Ed.), *Communication yearbook/16* (pp. 145–154). Newbury Park, CA: Sage.

Buzzanell, P. (1994). Gaining a voice: Feminist organizational communication theorizing. *Management Communication Quarterly, 7,* 339–383.

Cheney, G. (1995). Democracy in the workplace: Theory and practice from the communication perspective. *Journal of Applied Communication Research, 23,* 167–200.

Cheney, G., & Tompkins, P. K. (1988). On the facts of the text as the basis of human communication research. In J. A. Anderson (Ed.), *Communication yearbook/11* (pp. 455–481). Newbury Park, CA: Sage.

Clair, R. (1993a). The use of framing devices to sequester organizational narratives: Hegemony and harassment. *Communication Monographs, 60,* 113–136.

Clair, R. (1993b). The bureaucratization, commodification, and privatization of sexual harassment through institutional discourse. *Management Communication Quarterly, 7,* 123–157.

Conrad, C. and Witte, K. (1994). Is emotional expression repression oppression? Myths of organizational affective regulation. In S. A. Deetz (Ed.), *Communication yearbook/17* (pp. 417–428). Thousand Oaks, CA: Sage.

Deetz, S. A. (1992). *Democracy in an age of corporate colonization.* Albany, NY: State University of New York Press.

Deetz, S. A., & Mumby, D. K. (1990). Power, discourse, and the workplace: Reclaiming the critical tradition. In J. A. Anderson (Ed.), *Communication*

yearbook/13 (pp. 18–47). Newbury Park, CA: Sage.

Eisenberg, E. M. (1990). Jamming: Transcendence through organizing. *Communication Research, 17,* 139–164.

Eisenberg, E. M. (1994). Dialogue as democratic discourse: Affirming Harrison. *Communication yearbook/17* (pp. 275–284). Thousand Oaks, CA: Sage.

Eisenberg, E. M., & Goodall, H. L., Jr. (1993). *Organizational Communication: Balancing creativity and constraint.* New York: St. Martin's Press.

Eisenhardt, K. M. (1989). Making fast strategic decisions in high velocity environments. *Academy of Management Journal, 32,* 543–576.

Evered, R., & Tannenbaum, R. (1992). A dialog on dialog. *Journal of Management Inquiry, 1,* 43–55.

Fairclough, N. (1992). *Discourse and social change.* Cambridge: Polity Press.

Fine, M. (1993). New voices in organizational communication: A feminist commentary and critique. In S. P. Bowen & N. Wyatt (Eds.), *Transforming visions: Feminist critiques in communication studies* (pp. 125–166). Cresskill, NJ: Hampton Press.

Fineman, S. (1993). Organizations as emotional arenas. In S. Fineman (Ed.), *Emotion in organizations* (pp. 9–35). London: Sage.

Goodall, H. L., Jr. (1989). *Casing a promised land: The autobiography of an organizational detective as cultural ethnographer.* Carbondale, Ill.: Southern Illinois University Press.

Grunig, J. E., & Grunig, L. A. (1992). Models of public relations and communication. In J. E. Grunig (Ed.), *Excellence in public relations and communication management* (pp. 285–325). Hillsdale, NJ: Erlbaum.

Hanison, T. M. (1994). Communication and interdependence in democratic organizations. In S. A. Deetz (Ed.), *Communication yearbook/17* (pp. 246–274). Thousand Oaks, CA: Sage.

Hochschild, A. (1983). *The managed heart: Commercialization of human feeling.* Berkeley: University of California Press.

Koch, S., & Deetz, S. A. (1981). Metaphor analysis of social reality in organizations. *Journal of Applied Communication Research, 9,* 1–15.

Mangham, I. L., & Overington, M. A. (1987). *Organizations as theatre: A social psychology of dramatic appearances.* New York: Wiley.

Marshall, J. (1993). Viewing organizational communication from a feminist perspective: A critique and some offerings. In S. A. Deetz (Ed.), *Communication yearbook/16* (pp. 122–143). Newbury Park, CA: Sage.

McPhee, R. D., & Corman, S. R. (1995). An activity-based theory of communication networks in organizations applied to the case of a local church. *Communication Monographs, 62,* 132–151.

Morgan, G. (1986). *Images of organizations.* Beverly Hills, CA: Sage.

Mumby, D. K., & Putnam, L. L. (1992). The politics of emotion: A feminist reading of bounded rationality. *Academy of Management Review, 17,* 465–486.

O'Connor, E. S. (1995). Paradoxes of participation: A textual analysis of case studies on organizational change. *Organization Studies, 16,* 769–803.

Orlikowski, W. J., & Yates, J. (1994). Genre repertoire: The structuring of communicative practices in organizations. *Administrative Science Quarterly, 39,* 541–574.

Pacanowsky, M. E., & O'Donnell-Trujillo, N. (1983). Organizational communication as cultural performance. *Communication Monographs, 50,* 126–147.

Putnam, L. L. (1986). Contradictions and paradoxes in organizations. In L. Thayer (Ed.), *Organization—communication: Emerging perspectives I* (pp. 151–167). Norwood, NJ: Ablex.

Redding, W. C., & Tompkins, P. K. (1988). Organizational communication—past and present tenses. In G. M. Goldhaber and G. A. Barnett (Eds.), *Handbook of organizational communication* (pp. 5–33). Norwood, NJ: Ablex.

Rice, R. E. (1993). Media appropriateness: Using social presence to compare traditional and new organizational media. *Human Communication Research, 19,* 451–484.

Smith, K. K., & Berg, D. N. (1987). *Paradoxes of group life.* San Francisco: Jossey-Bass.

Smith, R. C., & Turner, P. (1995). A social constructionist reconfiguration of metaphor analysis: An application of "SCMA" to organizational socialization theorizing. *Communication Monographs, 62,* 152–181.

Stohl, C. (1995). *Organizational communication: Connectedness in action.* Thousand Oaks, CA: Sage.

Stohl, C., & Redding, W. C. (1987). Messages and message exchange processes. In F. M. Jablin, L. L. Putnam, & K. H. Porter (Eds.), *Handbook of organizational communication* (pp. 451–502). Beverly Hills, CA: Sage.

Strine, M. S. (1988). Constructing "texts" and making inferences: Some reflections on textual reality in human communication research. In J. A. Anderson (Ed.), *Communication yearbook/11* (pp. 494–500). Newbury Park, CA: Sage.

Taylor, J. R. (1993). *Rethinking the theory of organizational communication: How to read an organization.* Norwood, NJ: Ablex.

Tompkins, P. K., & Cheney, G. (1983). Account analysis of organizations: Decision making and identification. In L. L. Putnam & M. E. Pacanowsky (Eds.), *Communication and organizations: An interpretive approach* (pp. 123–146). Beverly Hills, CA: Sage.

Tompkins, P. K., & Cheney, G. (1985). Communication and unobtrusive control in contemporary organizations. In R. D. McPhee & P. K. Tompkins (Eds.), *Organization communication: Traditional themes and new directions* (pp. 179–210). Beverly Hills, CA: Sage.

Van de Ven, A. H., & Poole, M. S. (1988). Paradoxical requirements for a theory of organizational change. In R. E. Quinn & K. S. Cameron (Eds.), *Paradox and transformation: Toward a theory of change in organization and management* (pp. 19–64). Cambridge, Mass.: Ballinger.

Waldron, V. R. (1994). Once more, with feeling: Reconsidering the role of emotion in work. In S. A. Deetz (Ed.), *Communication yearbook/17* (pp. 388–416). Thousand Oaks, CA: Sage.

Weick, K. E. (1979). *The social psychology of organizing* (2nd ed.). Reading, Mass.: Addison-Wesley.

Yates, J., & Orlikowski, W. (1992). Genres of organizational communication: An approach to studying communication media. *Academy of Management Review, 17,* 299–326.

Stakeholders and Negotiating the New Social Contracts: A Communication Theory Perspective

Stanley A. Deetz
Rutgers University

The relations between organizations and their employees, various constituent groups, and host societies are undergoing significant transformations. A flat and bland statement like this, of course, misses the anxiety, uncertainty, and often blatant opportunism that is its life world manifestation. The re-occurring media headlines of the past year announcing/decrying white collar layoffs, the rise of temporary work, and declining benefits packages, as well as abstract expert descriptions, are simply late and often rather superficial accounts of fundamental and often frightening changes taking place in the workplace during the past two decades (for example, see *The New York Times* series March 3–9, 1996). Some speak of coldheartedness and betrayal and others of reality and competitiveness, but most seem to agree that times have changed.

Perhaps some of the most recent outcries can be mocked to some extent. Sympathy for middle managers grows thin when one considers that they are simply now experiencing what they have imposed since the beginning of the industrial revolution on workers subject to their charge (but then again, it's not yet my job). The white collar layoffs are important, however, in the way that they have brought forth a public discussion of what has been taken for granted or tacitly implied in the old work contract. The explicit work contract may only have specified the exchange of work effort for money and benefits but it carried with it a social contract that exchanged personal life decisions, loyalty and subordination for growth and advancement opportunities and, often, lifetime employment (see Heckscher, 1995).

This brief essay reviews the interrelated implicit social contracts centered on the workplace as a way of discussing what is needed in the teaching and study of organization communication research as we move into the future. I will show first that the "parentalism" in the passing work contract has been also present in the relations among work organizations and different groups in society and is being replaced with at least a rhetoric of "partnering." Second, I suggest that a "stakeholder/multiple interest" model of organizations, rather than a "stockholder/economic" model, can lead us further in advancing economic, productivity, and social interests. Finally, I argue that the full development of such a model requires a conception of communication that focuses on postmodern dialogic interactions and creative negotiations rather than liberal democratic conception of freedom, advocacy, and "open" information exchanges. Throughout I hope to make clear that communication professionals have a moral responsibility to promote fuller participation in workplace decisions because of shared values in a democratic society, and because it works.

FROM PARENTING TO PARTNERING

While many may now lament the passing of the old social contract, it carried with it a heavy downside, producing a society of parents and children, stifling dissent and creativity in the workplace, and leading many to never seriously examine what they wanted to be or do when they grew up. As the shock of betrayal and economic uncertainty passes, many laid-off managers begin to discover the heavy price they were paying. The passing of the old contract may initially benefit upper managers and stockholders (or fulfill their image of what will benefit them or the "company"), but ultimately it may provide the space for negotiating a better deal for all. The economic question (What is a good deal?) becomes a communication question (How do we establish the times, places, and processes for developing and working under a new contract?). The development of a new implied work contract is important, especially if it can be developed with a fuller account of the variety of needs and interests of employees and companies. But some simply want some version of the old contract back, managers who want to be parents without responsibilities, and employees who want to be children without costs. Negotiation versus paternalism poses two models of work relations and two possible models of organizational communication—one connected to the past and one to the future.

But this is not the only or even most central contract issue we face as we move into the future. The current salience of the implied work contract issue often hides the other social contracts surrounding work organizations that have or are undergoing similar transformation with similar uncertainties and opportunities. Historically the dominant model of the relation of upper managers of organizations to all members of society has been that of parents and children as if these managers were more rational, tough-minded, future-thinking, and universal in responsibility than other institutional leaders and people in general. Certainly there have been questions raised about managers' responsibility and stewardship. These have been clearest in cases of monopoly, environmental damage, health and safety standards, and ethical principles. Regarding most of these issues the society has substituted governmental parentalism for corporate parentalism. Even in regard to the harder to discuss issues of responsibility (for example, the economic efficacy of upper management decisions, maintenance of control-centered work processes with resultant loss of quality and productivity, the waste of natural re-

sources, inequitable income distributions, and the advocacy of consumer life-styles), most appear more to question the quality of the parenting than the parental model. Business leaders appear to still be the groups turned to when there are problems in government, education, or even the church. To be run more like a business is a common euphemism for to be run more like upper managers think and thus failing to recognize the many ways the parental model of business has failed (see Deetz, 1995a; Korten, 1995; and Estes, 1996 for reviews).

Further, to a large extent the commercial corporate organization has colonized other potentially competing social institutions. As I have shown in other places, while corporations have always had great influence in "company towns" and on state political processes, the effects have become both more subtle and pervasive as the degree of social interdependence has increased (see Deetz, 1992). Corporations have come to overshadow the state, the civil community, and the moral community in making decisions directing personal lives and general social development. Corporate organizations make most proactive decisions regarding technology development, utilization of natural resources, product development, working relations among people, and distribution of income. Most of these decisions are based primarily on social values of corporate leaders rather than simple market and other economic conditions. Furthermore, corporate values and practices extend into life outside of work, providing personal identities, structuring time, constraining child rearing practices, influencing education and knowledge production, directing entertainment and news production, rewarding personality types, influencing availability of the arts, and defining and preferencing consumption-based life-styles. While economic reasons are often given for corporate choices, they have clear political motives and consequences. As the impact of such organizations is broader and deeper, the quality of parenting, and even more so the model of parent, is of great social concern. The various contracts commercial organizations (via their leaders) have with other groups in society is important.

Clearly the parental model is being questioned in regard to a variety of social contracts as well as that surrounding the work contract itself. For numerous social, historical, and economic reasons, many have discussed the change from a model of parenting to one of partnering, the so-called "new social contract" (e.g., Chilton and Weidenbaum, 1994). Partnering with suppliers, customers, work groups and unions, educational institutions, and governments has been much promoted during the past few years. This along with team and worker participation arrangements provide the possibility of a radically different way that commercial organizations could be run (see Iannello, 1993; Cheney, 1995). I believe whether by new economic and social pressures or by the decision that these entail better ways of working, that such conceptions will be core to the way organizations work in the future. Whether these become kinder, gentler, and more open forms of parenting or a radically different way of doing business among mutually respecting adults rests on the choices we make. These choices arise in three areas: (1) Who will be allowed to participate? (2) How or by what process will decisions be made? (3) What is open to mutual decision making?

For those who study communication, however, the primary concerns do not principally regard technical issues of effective communication. Rather, communication concerns go deep into the models of social relations and decision making. The parenting/partnering difference draws on deep longer-term communication model differences between the didactic and dialectic, strategic interaction and dialogue, adversarial and participatory communication. Conceptually changing the model of management or the implied social contract without changing the model of communication performs a pseudo change where the parenting becomes more insidious. This is perhaps clearest in many cases where upper management has implemented team and worker participation programs. These are often directed at the start as a strategic management attempt imposed on workers to increase commitment, quality, and productivity. The strategic implementation creates distrust on the part of workers and retains for management a sense of superiority when what appears to be the case is that workers when left to their own devices are committed, productive, and produce high quality goods and services. Only in managerially controlled bureaucracies do those things decline. This reproduced superiority is used to justify the restriction of the range of decisions and to shift traditional managerial functions, but not pay, to lower levels.

A STAKEHOLDER MODEL OF WORK ORGANIZATIONS

The dominance of the economic/stockholder model of work organizations has been a central feature of the maintenance of organizational parentalism. In this model the sole investment of concern is the money which comes in at the top. The management group as a result of fiscal responsibility is left to control all other groups, resources, and work processes to maximize return on investment (see Deetz, 1995a). Other social values are either treated as secondary (nice if you can) or recast instrumentally, focusing on their indirect impact on profits. Of course this model has always been a fiction in that organizational decisions are usually heavily value-laden and made in conditions of uncertainty, and clearly managers manage stockholders as well as others. Market forces are hardly neutral and external; they contrive interests and values in particular ways (Schmookler, 1992) and large units are able to "externalize" their costs to individuals, communities, and other groups and thus distort market forces. The effect of the economic logic is to enable a universalization of upper managerial interests by making their interests the "company's" interest and the company's interests appear to be in everyone's interest.

But if we consider the public effects of workplaces, the full variety of types of investments people make in them and their value-laden nature, work organizations are clearly better understood as complex political sites than as economic ones (see Deetz, 1995b). The modern corporation has a variety of "stakeholders" with competing interests within and between each of them which could be more equably and productively resolved in internal workplace decisions (see Osigweh, 1994). Political conceptions can recognize the way partners talk out differences in needs and values rather than how parents rule by holding the purse strings. *Work organizations could be positive social institutions providing a forum for the articulation and resolution of important social conflicts regarding the use of natural resources, the production of meaningful goods and services, and the development of individuals.* These political processes are often closed, however, owing to a variety of practices which produce and privilege certain interests—principally managerial—in both corporate decision making and in the production of the type of person that exists in modern organizations and society.

Traditionally, stakeholders were considered external to the company and management groups attempted to strategically control them for the sake of "company" (though most often managerial) objectives (see Freeman, 1984; Carroll, 1989). The standard approach of management is based on narrow values and strategic control processes. The key element of transformation is for management to consider stakeholders as legitimate parts of the company. The management role then becomes the coordination of the various stakeholder needs and objectives. With a concept of service to all, "good" management attempts to facilitate creative decisions which meet what otherwise might appear to be incompatible objectives. Evidence supports this as a wise as well as appropriate change. The presence of diverse goals, rather than creating costly conflicts and impasse, creates the conditions whereby limited decisional frames are broken and the company *learns*. In the process the faulty bases of reoccurring conflicts are exposed and synergistic energy is created.

In sum, with the parental model, management groups have dominated the construction of stakeholders, each stakeholder's interest, and the means of interest representation. And further, they have manufactured consent to these through systems of definition and distorted value and information pro-

duction. Thus high degrees of control rather than coordination are evident in many corporations with relatively predictable production inefficiencies and inequalities in meeting stakeholder interests. The attempt to translate all interests into an economic codes creates additional distortions in communication and representational deficiencies. Communication teachers and scholars should be especially concerned with the gradual replacement of discussion with calculation in contemporary society whether it be with voting rather than deliberation, market economy rather than public sphere, or opinion polls rather than the pursuit of joint commitment. A low regard for discussion is professionally costly as well as destructive to the invention of mutually satisfying decisions and mutual commitment. The stakeholder model focusing on partnering reclaims the political nature of decision making and communication replaces monetary calculation as the primary decisional process. Communication processes have the potential to be (though are not necessarily) more representative and creative.

THE DIALOGIC RESPONSE: REPLACING ADVOCACY WITH NEGOTIATION

In stockholder models, social values entered into corporation decisions in four ways: through consumer value representation in purchasing choices, through governmental tax guidance and regulation, through manager's voluntary commitment to social values, and through investment choices of workers and capital holders in employment and stock purchase. Each of these is a weak form of representation because of structural limitations and recent social changes (investors want short-terms payoffs, managers have removed themselves from community). And none of them foster the type of social interaction that leads to innovative solutions to conflicting stakeholder values and objectives.

The stakeholder model draws attention to the potential opportunities for wide-spread representation. But actualizing the potential in the model requires a conception of communication that focuses on postmodern dialogic interactions and creative negotiations rather than liberal democratic conception of freedom, advocacy, rational negotiation, and "open" information exchanges. If the stakeholder conception is linked to liberal democratic conceptions of an autonomous individual engaging in self-interest advocacy, parenting and managerial control systems will continue in more subtle forms, a gridlock of special interest politics is likely even where they do not, and creativity is unlikely. Democracy becomes linked to endless meetings and voting rather than productive discussions and creative decision making.

Overcoming subtle control process and fostering productive mutual decisions requires changing the way we think about human communication (see Mumby, 1993). A dialogic view of communication offers possibilities not present expressionist/ information/adversarial view that dominates contemporary society. Influence-centered, informational views of communication which focused on meaning transmission as if meanings were value-neutral led us to overlook processes in the formation of social meanings that can be merely reproductive or genuinely transformational. A dialogic communication conception shifts our attention from choices within politically defined contexts with fixed decisional alternatives to concern with the constitution of political contexts and the alternatives. Concern with effective use of language changes to questions of whose language it is, its social/historical partialities, and means of reclaiming alternative voices.

As I have developed at length elsewhere, the differences between using liberal democratic and dialogic models are greatest in consequence in times and places of social heterogeneity and rapid change (see Deetz, 1995a, chapter 5). These are sites where productive, rather than reproductive, possibilities in communication are clearest. The stakeholder approach to workplace organizations both reclaims and advances heterogeneity. In doing so it advances the potential in communication descriptions and explanations that are hidden by economic, sociological, and psychological accounts (see Deetz, 1994).

Within the workplace most partnering, unfortunately, has developed with liberal democratic conceptions of communication. As such they have provided new *forums* where stakeholders could be represented. While these new forums are significant, most of these have been contrived in ways that reduce the actual value representation—they lack an opportunity for *voice*. Both forums and voice must be considered in assessing representation.

Inventing Forums for Discussion

In many companies the opportunities for employee participation in decision making are much greater today. The customer focus of many companies provides contexts for direct consumer representation in ways that have been missing for some time. Many companies have partnering arrangements with suppliers and large customers. The growth of communication and information technologies allow for more frequent, sustained, and interactive contact among groups.

But each of these have been limited in important ways. For example, employee involvement plans have often been developed more to increase compliance, commitment, and loyalty than to broaden value debate and increase innovation. Most often the involvement is limited to application decisions and do not include representation in company-wide planning and social goal formation. Research on teams and participation programs have consistently demonstrated process of ideological, disciplinary, unobtrusive, or concertive control and high degrees of employee consent to arrangements that are not to their own or company benefit (see Knights & Willmott, 1989; Bullis & Tompkins, 1989; Bullis, 1991; Barley & Kunda, 1992; Barker, 1993; Barker & Cheney, 1994). Similarly, customer focus groups often function more to solicit information on tastes and pricing to aid sales rather than to determine what consumers really want. And rarely are social values solicited at all except again as they might affect sales. The new technologies are being developed in most cases to extend the corporate influence outward rather than to provide the public with better information upon which to make their decisions or to enable the public to participate in corporate decision making. *In short, most representation forums are used by management to suppress or diffuse conflict arising from stakeholder groups rather than foster genuine conflict and debate for the sake of company improvement.* Still, with concerted effort these mechanisms can be transformed and utilized for quite different ends. A first step to increasing stakeholder representation is the expansion of these means.

Increasing Voice

But the current problem is not only the lack of sufficient opportunity for stakeholder representation. Often the interaction itself is systematically distorted. The stakeholder can speak but, owing to contrived and flawed understandings, the representation is skewed. There are several ways this happens. In general a prior social construction (a predetermination or prejudice) stands in the place of the indeterminate character and open negotiative possibilities of actual people and events in actual situations. Such constructions contain embedded values which are not disclosed. Since the construction is treated as the reality it is not open to discussion nor are alternative value premises and means of construction/reconstruction considered. Many standard forms of discursive closure become common (see Deetz, 1992, chapter 7). Generally, managerial values and perspectives become implicitly universalized and neutralized rather than understood and contestable. Hence conflict is suppressed and decisions are routinized rather than actively discussed with the possibility of mutuality and creativity. Most of my attention has been directed to how this happens to employees, especially in professional (knowledge-intensive) workplaces, but a similar analysis would follow for other stakeholders (see Deetz, in press a & b).

Four types of social constructions can limit voice. Each of these social constructions *could* be the result of open interaction, held temporarily and continuously revised in ongoing micro negotiations. They limit voice, however, when they become fixed and taken for granted, hence closed to negotiation. Often the stakeholder unknowingly consents to these constructions. Stakeholders then enact values which are not their own in what often appear to be free acts of self-representation and thus they demonstrate complicity in their own disregard. The four areas of social constructions regard identities, social order, knowledge, and values. Having voice means these are open to determination in an open interaction process, communication is about them. The absence of voice indicates that these constructions are taken for granted as a basis for interaction. Voice is hampered through reduction of personal complexity, frozen social orders, contrived knowledge and information, reduction of value debate through "neutral" efficiency, and performativity standards. Much of what is considered stable in work organizations is the result of social constructions, constructions accomplished under conditions of unequal power.

First, voice is reduced through the fixing of roles and the reduction of personal complexity. An individual has many identities and conflicting aspirations arising from identities like being a parent, citizen, and softball player, as well as being an employee. Corporations tend to sequester these other identities or elicit their support on behalf of managerial objectives. Thus if considerations arise for the employee as a parent or citizen they are to be suppressed in favor of the employee identity. This suppression is not only costly to the individual but also steals from the company the richer set of values that might guide corporate practices to social benefit. A wide range of forms of thinking, emotions, moral principles, and values are thus set aside. The employee stakeholder in these cases speaks as a "partial" person reducing representation and value debate.

Second, despite the moves to decentralization and attacks on bureaucracy, most companies still have rather fixed structures, especially when it comes to major decisions. Workplaces that have shared authority have shown impressive gains even on most standard productivity measures. The ability to continuously renegotiate authority relations based on shifting needs and points of expertise is critical in changing environments. Voice is always limited if discussions happen within rules and authority relations rather than being about them. If stakeholders are to be partners in meeting the needs of all, it cannot be a partnership of unequals. Compliance, consent, and loss of voice are characteristic of all fixed social relations.

Third, voice requires that stakeholders are informed. In most cases the information available to stakeholders is manufactured by management groups and is both limited and skewed. Even if management does not intentionally distort stakeholder understandings, most options and data reported were produced from the same limited set of values and assumptions that more generally drive management decision making. If stakeholders are to overcome managerial limitations, they must challenge the values embedded in company information and knowledge. If this is understood, communication is no longer seen as the transfer of information or decision making with information (the standard views in most companies). Communication must be about the processes by which information is produced—an in-formational politics. The temptation is to let measurable outcomes substitute for important discussions of what is measured and what is lost in measurement. Efficiency and productivity measurements cannot replace discussions of values and alternative interests. Accounting theorists and groups working with social accounting principles are becoming much clearer about the values embedded in standard accounting practices and the consequences of letting measurement substitute for discussion (see Power, 1994). But all information is fundamentally value-laden (see Harding, 1991). The choice of linguistic distinctions producing categories of people (e.g., secretaries and administrative assistants), the euphemism for what things are called (business expenses or indirect salaries), the forms that are used for reports (including what is collected and what not, as well as the categorical divisions), and the creation of spurious casual relations are only the more obvious aspects of information creation (see Bourdieu, 1991). When people use information they consent to the values on which it is based and

voice is usually lost if these are not their values. Opening information production activities to stakeholder discussion is a critical element of overcoming consent and gaining voice. Widespread sharing of information does not open discussion if the activities of information construction are left closed and invisible.

Finally, voice is hampered by discussions that focus on the means rather than the ends. The interests of different stakeholders are often considered fixed rather than focusing on the values and goals giving rise to them. Many modern organizations have developed a logic that emphasizes efficiency or effectiveness based on measurable indices which hide even further the values and goals themselves (see Wilkinson & Willmott, 1995). The means of goal attainment often become goals in themselves. And people often become treated as mere means of goal attainment rather than as ends themselves. Unfortunately in doing so the actual outcome goals become increasingly fixed and invisible. One becomes fixed on increasing performance measures without asking what is sought, its value, or alternative ways of accomplishment. The company operates like people who treat earning more money as an end without asking whether they are actually getting what the money is to give them or whether there are better ways of goal accomplishment that require less money. The processes of goal and indices creation in most companies is not an open process and does not represent the full set of stakeholder goals well. Further, the debate over preferred means of goal attainment reduces the possibility of finding ways that the goals of various different groups can be simultaneously attained.

THE FUTURE

Creating corporations that are economically and socially sound begins with a mutual commitment to the whole, to the entire set of stakeholders. To organizational communication teachers and scholars this requires both a commitment to a stakeholder model of work organizations and to a communication concept capable of providing voice to relevant groups and individuals. The pursuit of self-interest whether expressed in the name of profits, particular stakeholders, or one's own strategic advantage works against any genuine attempt at communication or productive joint decision making and presents deep moral difficulties (see Habermas, 1984). To the extent that managers or any stakeholder can personally internalize the needs of others, they grow, they free themselves from routines and habitual positions, and begin to reclaim suppressed needs and conflicts. Having conflicting needs and goals is a reality of being human at the individual and organizational level. Positive communication practices provide creativity in meeting what appear to be conflicting needs and goals rather than in preferencing some and suppressing others. A dialogic response would aim to recover those things that are feared and excluded from rational actor models or organizational and negotiation—emotions, the body, the feminine, and pleasure. In conflict we can begin to see a potential path that may otherwise be hidden by our everyday routines and "taken for granted" ways of understanding the world. This framework suggests that responsibility does not rest in agreement or consensus but in the avoidance of the suppression of alternative conceptions and possibilities.

The stakeholder model of corporations complemented by adequate conceptions of communication and micro-practices of negotiation can enable responsible daily practices in work organizations. Development in three areas of organizational communication research appear most important:

1. Continued work on the relation between communication practices and various forms of unobtrusive control in workplaces is very important. Communication researchers can do their part by demonstrating and critiquing forms of domination, asymmetry, and distorted communication showing where and how reality can become obscured and misrecognized. Of special concern are forms of false consciousness, consent, systematically distorted communication, routines, and normaliza-

tions which produce partial interests and keep people from genuinely understanding or acting on their own interests.

2. Further work on decision making in groups is pressing. Despite much of our experience and research many remain naive about the training and effort necessary for effective democratic decision making. Members of the workplace appear to share with others in society a belief in "instant" democracy—if you give people a place to talk they will make creative and representative decision together. The concept of democracy itself is often reduced to "free speech" and meetings. The liberal democracy tradition with its inadequate conception of communication continues to hamper the contribution of our field and work in organizations. We often, thus, have endless unproductive meetings which in many ways undermine the possibility of genuine participation. Better research and training are both needed.

3. Finally, we must rethink the role of conflict and the nature of communication in conflict situations. Studies of conflict resolution and conflict management have often retained conceptions of fixed interests, rationality, and linear communication. New conceptions focusing on suppressed conflicts, emergent and complex interests, and creativity in discussion offer possibilities that will be indispensable to stakeholder-based organizations of the future.

The field of communication studies is uniquely situated to provide leadership in these important areas of study and in developing a productive new social contract. Such insights from our research can help produce forums where the conflicts can be reclaimed and voice so that they are openly discussed and resolved with fairness and justice. The central goal of organizational communication studies can be to create a society and workplaces which are free from domination and where all members can contribute equally to produce systems which meet human needs and lead to the progressive development of all or it can continue as a handmaiden of special interests hiding under a pretense of neutrality and instrumental efficiency.

REFERENCES

Barker, J. (1993). Tightening the iron cage—Concertive control in self-managing teams. *Administrative Science Quarterly, 38,* 408–37.

Barker, J. & Cheney, G. (1994). The concept and the practice of discipline in contemporary organizational life. *Communication Monographs, 61,* 19–43.

Barley, S. & Kunda, G. (1992). Design and devotion: Surges of rational and normative ideologies of control in managerial discourse. *Administrative Science Quarterly, 37,* 363–99.

Bourdieu, P. (1991). *Language and symbolic power.* Cambridge: Harvard University Press.

Bullis, C. (1991). Communication practices as unobtrusive control: An observational study. *Communication Studies, 42,* 254–71.

Bullis, C. & Tompkins, P. (1989). The forest ranger revisited: A study of control processes and identification. *Communication Monographs, 56,* 287–306.

Carroll, A. (1989). *Business and society: Ethics and stakeholder management.* Cincinnati: South-Western.

Cheney, G. (1995). Democracy in the workplace: Theory and practice from the perspective of communication. *Journal of Applied Communication Research, 23,* 167–200.

Chilton, K. & Weidenbaum, M. (1994). *A new social contract for the American workplace: From paternalism to partnering.* Policy Study Number 123. St. Louis: Center for the Study of American Business.

Deetz, S. (1992) *Democracy in the age of corporate colonization: Developments in communication and the politics of everyday life.* Albany: State University of New York Press.

Deetz, S. (1994). The future of the discipline: The challenges, the research, and the social contribution. In S. Deetz (ed.), *Communication yearbook 17* (pp. 565–600). Thousand Oaks, CA: Sage.

Deetz, S. (1995a). *Transforming communication, transforming business: Building responsive and responsible workplaces.* Cresskill, NJ: Hampton Press.

Deetz, S. (1995b). Transforming communication, transforming business: Stimulating value negotiation for more responsive and responsible workplaces.

International Journal of Value-Based Management, 8, 255–78.

Deetz, S. (in press a). Discursive formations, strategized subordination, and self-surveillance: An empirical case. In A. McKinlay & K. Starkey (eds.), *Managing Foucault: A Reader.* London: Sage.

Deetz, S. (in press b). The business concept, discursive power, and managerial control in a knowledge-intensive company: A case study. In B. Sypher (ed.), *Case studies in organizational communication,* 2nd edition. New York: Guilford Press.

Estes, R. (1996). *Tyranny of the bottom line: Why corporations make good people do bad things.* San Francisco: Berrett-Koehler Publishers.

Freeman, R. E. (1984). *Strategic management: A stakeholder approach.* Boston, MA: Pitman.

Habermas, J. (1984). *The theory of communicative action, volume 1: Reason and the rationalization of society.* Trans. T. McCarthy. Boston: Beacon.

Harding, S. (1991). *Whose science? Whose knowledge?* Ithaca, NY: Cornell University Press.

Heckscher, C. (1995). *White-collar blues: Management loyalties in an age of corporate restructuring.* New York: Basic Books.

Iannello, K. (1993). *Decisions without hierarchy: Feminist interventions in organizational theory and practice.* London: Routledge.

Knights, D. & Willmott, H. (1989). Power and subjectivity at work: From degradation to subjugation in social relations. *Sociology, 23,* 535–58.

Korten, D. (1995). *When corporations rule the world.* San Francisco: Berrett-Koehler.

Mumby, D. (1993). Critical organizational communication studies: The next ten years. *Communication Monographs, 60,* 18–25.

The New York Times (March 3–9, 1996). *The downsizing of America.* Seven part series.

Osigweh, C. (1994). A stakeholder perspective of employee responsibilities and rights. *Employee Responsibilities and Rights Journal, 7,* 279–95

Power, M. (1994). The audit society. In A. Hopwood and P. Miller (Eds.), *Accounting as social and institutional practice* (pp. 299–316). Cambridge: Cambridge University Press.

Schmookler, A. (1992). *The illusion of choice: How the market economy shapes our destiny.* Albany: State University of New York Press.

Wilkinson, A. & Willmott, H. (Eds.) (1995). *Making quality critical.* London: Routledge.

Groups and Organizations: Premises and Perspectives

David R. Seibold
University of California, Santa Barbara

Group behaviors, including symbolic interactions, have long been a focus of study in a variety of academic disciplines (Hare, Blumberg, Davies, & Kent, 1994). Within the past decade alone, major reviews of group research have appeared in industrial psychology (Bramel & Friend, 1987), management (Bettenhausen, 1991), sociology (Couch, Katovich, & Miller, 1987), social psychology (Levine & Moreland, 1990; McGrath & Gruenfeld, 1993; Moreland, Hogg, & Hains, 1994), organizational behavior (Mowday & Sutton, 1993; O'Reilly, 1991), and anthropology (Schwartzman, 1986) among others. The study of group interaction similarly has enjoyed a long tradition in communication (Frey, 1996), although it also has been characterized by excoriating self-critique for the past 25 years (see a summary at the outset of Frey, 1994). Indeed, scholars in our field continue to vacillate between calls for the need to "revitalize" the area (Frey, 1994) and counterclaims that small group communication is quite vital and growing more so (Gouran, 1994; Poole, 1994; Propp & Krepps, 1994; Seibold, 1994).

More central to my aim in this essay, I also wish to underscore that the study of groups and group communication has proceeded, for the most part, *independent* of the study of organizations and organizational communication. In our discipline, for example, even a cursory glance at major reviews that have appeared in the last decade concerning the state of organizational communication (e.g., Redding & Tompkins, 1987; Redding, 1985; Mumby & Stohl, 1996) reveals that—other than perfunctory acknowledgment of the potentially powerful, even transformative, effects of group membership and identifications on individuals' actions—there is almost no discussion of the interface between group communication and organizational communication. Nor is there examination of the role of groups' interactions in creating and recreating organizational structures. Similarly, perusal of the Jablin et al. (1987) *Handbook of Organizational Communication* reveals no treatment of groups and organizations. Ironically, students of same must turn to the Knapp and Miller (1994) *Handbook of Interpersonal Communication* in order to find a systematic review of work group communication (see the chapter by Jablin & Krone, 1994).

Why is the communication discipline beset with this bifurcation of group and organizational communication? On one hand, factors endemic to *organizational* scholarship may have fostered its separation from group communication. First, there has been a long-standing reification of organizations as self-contain(er)ed entities, rather than a conceptualization of them as systems of groups loosely or tightly coupled vis-a-vis overlapping tasks, shared or interdependent goals, frequent interactions, and the like. Second, there has been a similar historical orientation toward organizations as bureaucracies of vertical dyads organized in scalar fashion and relying upon chains of command, rather than as horizontally integrated units of members and stakeholders. Third, organizational communication research has evidenced a reductionistic bent toward the individual level of analysis, notably in functionalists' apparent presumption that aggregating analyses of individuals' behaviors can serve as an indication of "the organization" along some dimension or in terms of some variable—but also in interpretivist researchers' treatments of (selected) individuals' discursive practices as representations of "organi-

162

zation". Fourth, perhaps the fact that prominent scholars (e.g., Lull, Zelko, Redding, as well as Tompkins, Farace, and Thayer), in what was then the nascent organizational communication field, had relatively little affiliation with group communication scholarship may have contributed to a course charted away from the work of group communication scholars. Indeed, it seems to have been the students of early organizational communication scholars who have integrated group perspectives into their organizational scholarship, notably Fred Jablin, Dave Johnson, and Cynthia Stohl among others. Fifth, to the extent that research on organizational communication has been influenced by scholarship in other disciplines, it is not surprising to find a schism between group and organizational research given the "macro" organizational perspectives and theories in political science, sociology, higher education administration, and management (e.g., resource dependency theory, institutional theory, natural adaptation, and population ecology perspectives). Finally, in light of these factors *and* the relatively small number of publishing organizational communication researchers, it also is not surprising that a small fraction of published organizational communication studies reflect a group perspective. For example, in their review of 889 organizational communication studies appearing between 1980 and 1991, Allen, Gotcher, and Seibert (1992) identified only 41 (.046) as group-related.

At the same time, factors endemic to *group* communication studies also may have contributed to the bifurcation of group and organizational communication. First, there seems to have been a belief among many group researchers that groups are sufficiently interesting and complex in their own right (Ellis & Fisher, 1994), and a concomitant unwillingness to further complexity matters by dealing with practices and structures reflective of intergroup interactions. Second, the traditional laboratory orientation that precluded study of naturalistic groups beyond controlled and artificial confines (e.g., Cragan & Wright, 1990 found that only 16% of the empirical studies of group communication published by speech communication

scholars during the 1980s used natural groups) also precluded concern with the permeable boundaries of embedded groups and qualities of context that impact group interactions (Ancona & Caldwell, 1992). Third, the research of many prominent group communication scholars (e.g., Fisher, Gouran, Bormann, and Scheidel) reflected little concern with organizational matters. Just as with the protèges of early organizational scholars, it has been the students and young colleagues of these group researchers who have forged conceptual and empirical links to organizations in their own writings (see especially the work of Linda Putnam, Scott Poole, and Randy Hirokawa). Fourth, the separation of group and organizational scholarship also may be an artifact of the administrative structure of the National Communication Association, in which group scholarship has been nested within the Interpersonal and Small Group Interaction Division rather than as a part of the Organizational Communication Division or as a separate interest group or division. Finally, if Poole (1994) is correct in his assertion that there may be as few as thirty researchers who are actively publishing studies of small group communication, an estimate consistent with Frey's (1988) report that only 4.2% of the articles published in the communication journals he surveyed were focused on group communication, it also is not surprising to note the absence of a critical mass of scholarship focused on groups *and* organizations. Indeed, Cragan and Wright (1990) reviewed all 96 articles on group communication published by speech communication scholars during the 1980s. Only 9 (11%) of the 72 quantitative investigations studied groups in organizational settings.

All this has been unfortunate because the study of groups and organizations not only *can* be mutually informing but, as theorists have recently underscored (Ancona, 1987; Putnam, 1989; Putnam & Stohl, 1990, 1996; Poole, Seibold, & McPhee, 1996) study of each is so intertwined that they *should not* be separated. Indeed, my aim here is to enjoin organizational communication scholars to remember that the study of organizational groups and organizations *cannot* be separated other than analytically, and even that is not without perils. In the remainder of this essay I take up two tasks. First, I underscore *premises* integral to groups and organizations that underscore their mutuality. I then highlight recent theoretical *perspectives* that make clear this connection.

PREMISES

Organizational groups should be a core concern to *both* group and organizational theorists for theoretical, empirical, and practical reasons. From a *theoretical* standpoint, organizational groups are at the nexus of interaction and structure. They are the forum within which many systems we recognize (decision making, productivity, climate) are produced in organizational members' interactions. As such, organizational groups are the locus of causation where individuals—whether viewed as weak or strong causal agents—become enmeshed in collective activity that creates organizational structure. At the same time that organizational groups have pervasive effects that transform individual agency, groups also mediate organizational structures in ways that constrain and condition individuals. As Weick (1979, p. 236) observed, organizational groups are "eminently sensible as places to understand the major working of organizations."

There also is an *empirical* complexity endemic to organizational groups that could be untangled by group and organizational scholars working together. Although groups may display some processes that we have come to understand in dyads, most of the dynamics associated with increasing group size and multiple tasks create more complex empirical challenges for researchers. In the multiparty, mixed-motive interactions so characteristic of organizational activity, there arc increased information processing demands due to both overt and covert interests, goals, and strategies (Bazerman, 1982). Interpersonal relationships also typically are more intricate in groups since power structures, role differentiation, and the potential for coalitions are salient. Furthermore, the nature and quality of interactions in groups include different network configurations, differences in amount and depth of

feedback and in members' voice, meanings, and satisfaction with communication (Parks, 1985; Stohl, 1986, 1987, 1989; Stohl & Jennings, 1988). In no small part these are due to complexities involving task jurisdiction, resource allocation, temporal constraints on coordination, and multiple levels of operation across groups in organizations (Lammers & Krikorian, 1997).

Finally, *practical* realities impel group researchers and organizational researchers alike to consider groups in organizations, including cross-functional product teams, task forces, work units, project groups, perennial agenda committees, quality teams, executive/administrative committees, management teams, labor groups, and many others. As a consequence of a variety of forces—notably the extension of organizations' commitments to enhancing the quality of members' work-life (Cotton, 1993), a general turn to participative management philosophy and practices (Seibold, 1995; Seibold & Shea, in press), gains won by organizational employees' bargaining agents, organizations' adoption and implementation of technological innovations that have the potential to enhance collaboration (Poole, 1991; Poole & DeSanctis, 1990), and the mimetic force (Powell & DiMaggio, 1991) of international competitors' reliance on group-based structures and activities in the workplace such as self-directing and semi-autonomous teams (Wellins, Byham, & Wilson, 1991)—group meetings and work arrangements like those above are not merely prevalent, but they are becoming increasingly so. An independent study by Xerox Learning Systems in the 1980s revealed that its clients were spending 100% more time in meetings than they had ten years before (Seibold & Krikorian, 1997). Nor is this trend confined to business and industry. According to the U.S. President's 17th Annual Report on Federal Advisory Committees, during fiscal 1988 alone, 58 federal departments and agencies sponsored 1020 advisory committees, a 17.3 percent *increase* compared with the number of groups in existence during fiscal 1987 (Seibold & Krikorian, 1997). Furthermore, hierarchical position and time spent in meetings appear to be monotonically related. While first-level supervisors were found to spend 15% of their time in meetings, middle mangers spent 35%, and executives as much as 80% (Mosvick & Nelson, 1987).

PERSPECTIVES

Reviews (cf. Cragan & Wright, 1990; Frey, 1996) note the emergence of four distinct theoretical perspectives in small group communication research during the past two decades: Functional Theory (Gouran & Hirokawa, 1996), Symbolic Convergence Theory (Bormann, 1996), Structuration Theory (Poole, Seibold, & McPhee, 1996), and the Bona Fide Groups perspective (Putnam & Stohl, 1996). Given the scope of each, the latter two approaches arguably are the most suitable for interpreting a wide range of organizational group practices, although both the functional and symbolic convergence perspectives have offered insights into communication processes and outcomes in organizational groups (see Propp & Nelson, in press; and Lesch, 1994, respectively). Furthermore, although the structurational perspective has self-consciously sought to account for the interpenetration of organizational and group structures and to make a case for the centrality of group structuration in streams of organizational activity (see Poole et al., 1996), the bona fide groups perspective has made that integration more clearly and more compellingly (albeit without as much theoretical infrastructure at this time).

Beginning with the early position papers of Linda Putnam (Putnam, 1988, 1989), Putnam and Stohl (Putnam & Stohl, 1990, 1996; Stohl & Putnam, 1994) have elaborated a perspective that is central to understanding the articulation of groups and organizations, as their definition implies. Bona fide groups are "characterized by stable yet permeable boundaries and interdependence with context" (Putnam & Stohl, 1990, pp. 248). Key to their perspective is an emphasis on "boundary," including a sensitivity to dynamics endemic to organizational groups: stability, permeability, connectivity, overlapping memberships, relations with members in other contexts, and fluctuations in membership. Similarly, Putnam and Stohl underscore the embeddedness of groups' contexts, including multiple levels of operation, degree of coupling with other groups, task jurisdiction issues, resource dependency, and competing authority systems.

The work of Putnam and Stohl has been seminal and heuristic for those interested in groups and organizations. However, work by John Lammers and Dean Krikorian (1997) offers important advances to this perspective in two ways. First, in their analysis of surgical teams, Lammers and Krikorian develop clearer empirical *indicators* of all of the constructs in the bona fide groups perspective. For example, Lammers and Krikorian describe "resource dependency" in terms of buffering, bridging, diversifying, and merging. "Task jurisdiction" is reflected in terms of programmatic, instrumental, and funding decision rights. "Connectivity" is given similar precision by distinguishing among degree centrality, betweenness centrality, and closeness centrality. Second, Lammers and Krikorian *extend* the bona fide groups perspective in important ways. For example, rather than conceptualizing "boundary" strictly in terms of *membership* stability, overlap, and the like, the researchers reformulate the concept—correctly, to my mind—to include space, time, and activity. In their empirical examination of surgical teams, Lammers and Krikorian also find added aspects of bona fide groups that have direct relevance for the study of organizational groups in general: age, task duration, characteristic of the group's membership pool, and institutional history. Their research demonstrates that the study of bona fide groups without attention to their institutional context makes the concept artificial. Their work, taken together with that of Putnam and Stohl, proffers groups and organizational scholars "a greater understanding of how work groups accomplish their ends in an institutional context" (Lammers & Krikorian, 1997, p. 38). If further research bears out this promise, it will be a welcome solution to the lament voiced by Cragan and Wright (1990): "We appear to be developing two parallel, and potentially competing, explanations of small groups: one based on the study of autonomous groups, the other on the study of organizational groups...Presently we do not have a theory or body of research that satisfactorily integrated these two different strains of small group communication research" (p. 227).

REFERENCES

Allen, M. W., Gotcher, J. M., & Seibert, J. H. (1992). A decade of organizational communication research: Journal articles 1980–1991. In S. A. Deetz (Ed.), *Communication yearbook 16* (pp. 252–330). Newbury Park, CA: Sage.

Ancona, D. G. (1987). Groups in organizations: Extending laboratory models. In C. Hendrick (Ed.), *Annual review of personality and social psychology: Group and intergroup processes* (pp. 207–231). Newbury Park, CA: Sage.

Ancona, D. G., & Caldwell, D. F. (1992). Bridging the boundary: External activity and performance in organizational teams. *Administrative Science Quarterly, 31,* 634–665.

Bazerman, M. H. (1982, August). *The framing of organizational behavior.* Paper presented at the annual meeting of the Academy of Managment.

Bettenhausen, K. L. (1991). Five years of group research: What have we learned and what needs to be addressed? *Journal of Management, 17,* 345–381.

Bormann, E. (1996). Symbolic convergence theory and communication in group decision making. In R. Y. Hirokawa & M. S. Poole (Eds.), *Communication and group decision making* (2nd ed., pp. 81–113). Thousand Oaks, CA: Sage.

Bramel, D., & Friend, R. (1987). The work group and its vicissitudes in social and industrial psychology. *Journal of Applied Behavioral Science, 23*(2), 233–253.

Cotton, J. L. (1993). *Employee involvement: Methods for improving performance and work attitudes.* Newbury Park, CA: Sage.

Couch, C. J., Katovich, M. A., & Miller, D. (1987). The sorrowful tale of small groups research. *Studies in Symbolic Interaction, 8,* 159–180.

Cragan, J. F., & Wright, D. W. (1990). Small group communication research of the 1980s: A synthesis and critique. *Communication Studies, 41,* 212–236.

Ellis, D. G., & Fisher, B. A. (1994). *Small group decision making: Communication and the group process* (4th ed.). New York: McGraw-Hill.

Frey, L. R. (1988, November). *Meeting the challenges posed during the 70s: A critical review of small group communication research during the 80s.* Paper presented at the meeting of the Speech Communication Association, New Orleans, LA.

Frey, L. R. (1994). Introduction: Revitalizing the study of small group communication. *Communication Studies, 45,* 1–6.

Frey, L. R. (1996). Remembering and "re-membering": A history of theory and research on communication and group decision making. In R. Y. Hirokawa & M. S. Poole (Eds.), *Communication and group decision making* (2nd ed., pp. 19–51). Thousand Oaks, CA: Sage.

Gouran, D. S. (1994). The future of small group communication research: Revitalization or continued good health? *Communication Studies, 45,* 29–39.

Gouran, D. S., & Hirokawa, R. Y. (1996). Functional theory and communication in decision-making and problem-solving groups: An expanded view. In R. Y. Hirokawa & M. S. Poole (Eds.), *Communication and group decision making* (2nd ed., pp. 55–80). Thousand Oaks, CA: Sage.

Hare, A. P., Blumberg, H. H., Davies, M. F., & Kent, M. V. (1994). *Small group research: A handbook.* Norwood, NJ: Ablex.

Jablin, F. M., & Krone, K. J. (1994). Task/work relationships: A life-span perspective. In M. L. Knapp & G. R. Miller (Eds.), *Handbook of interpersonal communication* (2nd ed., pp. 621–675). Thousand Oaks, CA: Sage.

Jablin, F. M., Putnam, L. L., Roberts, K. H., & Porter, L. W. (Eds.) (1987). *Handbook of organizational communication: An interdisciplinary perspective.* Newbury Park, CA: Sage.

Knapp, M. L., & Miller, G. R. (Eds.) (1994). *Handbook of interpersonal communication* (2nd ed.). Thousand Oaks, CA: Sage.

Lammers, J. C., & Krikorian, D. H. (1997). Theoretical extension and operationalization of the bona fide group construct with an application to surgical teams. *Journal of Applied Communication Research, 25,* 18–41.

Lesch, C. L. (1994). Observing theory in practice: Sustaining consciousness in a coven. In L. R. Frey (Ed.) *Group communication in context: Studies of natural groups* (pp. 57–82). Hillsdale, NJ: Lawrence Erlbaum.

Levine, J. M., & Moreland, R. L. (1990). Progress in small group research. *Annual Review of Psychology, 41,* 585–634.

McGrath, J. E., & Gruenfeld, D. H. (1993). Toward a dynamic and systemic theory of groups: An integration of six temporally enriched perspectives. In M. Chemers & R. Ayman (Eds.), *Leadership theory and research: Perspectives and directions* (pp. 217–243). New York: Academic Press.

Moreland, R. L., Hogg, M. A., & Hains, S. C. (1994). Back to the future: Social psychological research on groups. *Journal of Experimental Social Psychology, 30,* 527–555.

Mowday, R. T., & Sutton, R. I. (1993). Organizational behavior: Linking individuals and groups to organizational contexts. *Annual Review of Psychology, 44,* 195–229.

Mumby, D. K., & Stohl, C. (1996). Disciplining organizational communication studies. *Management Communication Quarterly, 10,* 50–72.

O'Reilly, C. A. (1991). Organizational behavior: Where we've been, where we're going. *Annual Review of Psychology, 42,* 427–458.

Parks, M. R. (1985). Interpersonal communication and the quest for personal competence. In M. L. Knapp & G. R. Miller (Eds.), *Handbook of interpersonal communication* (pp. 171–201). Beverly Hills, CA: Sage.

Poole, M. S. (1991). Procedures for managing meetings: Social and technological innovation. In R. A. Swenson & B. O. Knapp (Eds.), *Innovative meeting management* (pp. 53–109). Austin, TX: 3M Meeting Management Institute.

Poole, M. S. (1994). Breaking the isolation of small group communication studies. *Communication Studies, 45,* 20–28.

Poole, M. S., & DeSanctis G. (1990). Understanding the use of group decision support systems: The theory of adaptive structuration. In C. Steinfield & J. Fulk (Eds.), *Organizations and communication technology* (pp. 175–195). Newbury Park, CA: Sage.

Poole, M. S., Seibold, D. R., & McPhee, R. D. (1996). The structuration of group decisions. In R. Y. Hirokawa & M. S. Poole (Eds.), *Communication and group decision making* (2nd ed., pp. 114–146). Thousand Oaks, CA: Sage.

Powell, W. W., & DiMaggio, P. J. (Eds.) (1991). *The new institutionalism in organizational analysis.* Chicago: University of Chicago Press.

Propp, K. M., & Kreps, G. L. (1994). A rose by any other name: The vitality of group communication research. *Communication Studies, 45,* 7–19.

Propp, K. M., & Nelson, D. (in press). Problem-solving performance in naturalistic groups: The ecological validity of the functional perspective. *Communication Studies.*

Putnam, L. L. (1988). Understanding the unique characteristics of groups within organizations. In R. S. Cathcart & L. A. Samovar (Eds.), *Small group communication: A reader* (5th ed., pp. 76–85). Dubuque, IA: Wm. C. Brown.

Putnam, L. L. (1989). Perspectives for research on group embeddedness in organizations. In S. S. King (Ed.), *Human communication as a field of study* (pp. 163–181). New York: State University of New York Press.

Putnam, L. L., & Stohl, C. (1990). Bona fide groups: A reconceptualization of groups in context. *Communication Studies, 41,* 248–265.

Putnam, L. L., & Stohl, C. (1996). Bona fide groups: An alternative perspective for communication and small group decision making. In R. Y. Hirokawa & M. S. Poole (Eds.), *Communication and group decision making* (2nd ed., pp. 147–178). Thousand Oaks, CA: Sage.

Redding, W. C. (1985). Stumbling toward identity: The emergence of organizational communication as a field of study. In R. D. McPhee & P. K. Tompkins (Eds.), *Organizational communication: Traditional themes and new directions* (pp. 15–54). Beverly Hills, CA: Sage.

Redding, W. C., & Tompkins, P. K. (1987). Organizational communication: Past and present tenses. In G. Goldhaber & G. Barnett (Eds.), *Handbook of national communication* (pp. 5–34). Norwood, NJ: Ablex.

Schwartzman, H. B. (1986). Research on work group effectiveness: An anthropological critique. In P. Goodman & Assocs. (Eds.), *Designing effective work groups* (pp. 237–276). San Francisco: Jossey-Bass.

Seibold, D. R. (1994). More reflection or more research: To (re)vitalize small group communication research, let's "just do it". *Communication Studies, 45,* 103–110.

Seibold, D. R. (1995). Developing the "team" in a team-managed organization: Group facilitation in a new plant design. In L. R. Frey (Ed.), *Innovations in group facilitation techniques: Case studies of applications in naturalistic settings* (pp. 282–298). Cresskill, NJ: Hampton Press.

Seibold, D. R., & Krikorian, D. (1997). Planning and facilitating group meetings. In L. R. Frey & J. K. Barge (Eds.), *Managing group life: Communicating in decision-making groups* (pp. 272–305). Boston: Houghton Mifflin.

Seibold, D. R., & Shea, C. (in press). Participation and decision making. In F. M. Jablin & L. L. Putnam (Eds.), *The new handbook of organizational communication.* Thousand Oaks, CA: Sage Publications.

Stohl, C. (1986). Quality circles and changing patterns of communication. In M. McLaughlin (Ed.), *Communication yearbook 9* (pp. 511–531). Beverly Hills, CA: Sage.

Stohl, C. (1987). Bridging the parallel organization: A study of quality circle effectiveness. In M. L. McLaughlin (Ed.), *Communication yearbook 10* (pp. 416–430). Newbury Park, CA: Sage.

Stohl, C. (1989). Understanding quality circles: A communication network perspective. In B. Dervin, L. Grossberg, B. O'Keefe, & E. Wartella (Eds.), *Rethinking communication: Vol. 2. Paradigm exemplars* (pp. 346–360). Newbury Park, CA: Sage.

Stohl, C., & Jennings, K. (1988). Volunteerism and voice in quality circles. *Western Journal of Speech Communication, 52,* 238–251.

Stohl, C., & Putnam, L. L. (1994). Group communication in context: Implications for the study of bona fide groups. In L. R. Frey (Ed.) *Group communication in context: Studies of natural groups* (pp. 57–82). Hillsdale, NJ: Lawrence Erlbaum.

Weick, K. E. (1979). *The social psychology of organizing* (2nd ed.). Reading, MA: Addison-Wesley.

Wellins, R. S., Byham, W. C., & Wilson, J. M. (1991). *Empowered teams: Creating self-directed work groups that improve quality, productivity, and participation.* San Francisco: Jossey-Bass.

CHAPTER 7

AT THE HELM IN GENDER STUDIES IN COMMUNICATION

Introduction

Cynthia Berryman-Fink
University of Cincinnati

We are fortunate to have with us three most distinguished scholars in the area of gender and communication who will address paradigmatic and epistemological issues of studying gender communication. This session presents an opportunity for us to step back from specific topical research questions and concrete research results that are typical of the majority of conference presentations. Instead, we take time to examine larger questions—to hear insightful reflections from veteran scholars about the perspectives and world views from which research on gender and communication is embedded and the role of gender communication research in contributing to knowledge about human behavior.

Collectively, the three panelists represent 75 years of academic work in the speech communication discipline, including the publication of 30 books and several hundred articles, chapters, and conference papers. The quantity of their collective work, however, does not do justice to the role these individuals have played in creating and providing legitimacy for the area of gender studies in communication. They have forged new ground, brought gender-related issues to the public's attention, and made significant contributions to the gender communication literature.. It is my pleasure to introduce the individual panelists and to "woman" the helm of this vehicle for perspective-taking in gender and communication research.

Karlyn Kohrs Campbell, Professor of Speech Communication at the University of Minnesota, has received the Distinguished Scholar Award from the NCA, as well as the Ehninger Research Award, the Winans-Wichelns Book Award, and the Charles M. Woolbert Award for Scholarship. She is most recently known for her two volumes on *Women Public Speakers in the United States* and her two volumes of critical studies on early feminist rhetoric, *Man Cannot Speak for Her.* Additionally, she has published books and articles on presidential rhetoric, rhetorical criticism, feminist communication scholarship, and a wide range of women orators. As a neophyte scholar of communication in the mid-70s, I was introduced to her work via the 1973 *Quarterly Journal of Speech* article, "The Rhetoric of Women's Liberation: An Oxymoron." So insightful was that piece that it has since been reprinted in a 1990 volume on a twentieth-century perspective on *Methods of Rhetorical Criticism.* Dr. Campbell is truly a legendary figure in speech communication and in feminist rhetoric.

Celeste Condit, Professor of Speech Communication at the University of Georgia, has published books including *Decoding Abortion Rhetoric, The Anglo/African Word,* and *Women's Health Messages,* and has authored over 45 journal articles and book chapters in a short career of just 14 years since receiving the Ph.D. degree. Her research interests focus on the use of rhetorical analysis to explore the role of public address in processes of social change and stability, with emphasis on issues of human reproduction and the impact of genetic technologies. She is the 1994 recipient of NCA's Marie Hochmuth Nichols Award for Outstanding Scholarship in Public Address; she has received a $95,000 grant from the National Institutes of Health; and has been invited to give scholarly lectures at NIH, the University of Chicago, the University of Kansas, the University of Utah, the University of Iowa, and several other institutions.

Julia T. Wood is the Nelson Hairston Distinguished Professor of Communication Studies at the University of North Carolina at Chapel Hill. Her research interests focus on gender in personal relationships; feminist theory and research; and gender, communication, and culture. Her scholarship on gender and communication has been recognized by the National Communication Association's Francine Merritt Award, the Organization for the Study of Communication, Language, and Gender's Outstanding Book Award and Most Distinguished Scholarship Award, as well as Southern Speech Communication Association's Gender Studies Award. She has solely authored or collaborated on 17 books in a 14-year period, while publishing steadily in the major communication journals, serving as Editor of the *Journal of Applied Communication Research,* and earning several teaching awards.

Dr. Campbell will speak on, "Relationships Between Rhetorical and Critical/Cultural Studies of Discourse by and about Women." Dr. Condit will speak on "Gender Diversity: A Theory of Communication for the Postmodern Era." Dr. Wood's topic is "From Isolation to Integration: Gender's Place in the Core of Knowledge."

Relationships between Rhetorical and Critical/Cultural Studies of Discourse by and about Women

Karlyn Kohrs Campbell
University of Minnesota

Before I can address my topic, some background is needed. Since the Wingspread conference that produced *The Prospect of Rhetoric,* critics have acknowledged that objects suitable for criticism extend far beyond the texts of formal speeches delivered to immediate audiences (Bitzer and Black, 1971, esp. pp. 205–206). The people who were training future critics in the 1960s, however, had little or no training in criticism—almost none was available—and those of my generation learned whatever we learned about criticism in classes outside speech communication departments (in my case, English). Our aim was to bring the techniques of new criticism into our field so rhetorical criticism could mine the symbolic riches in public discourse, in addition to its historical and biographical contributions.

In regard to the discourse by women, the situation was even worse. Just as no women were invited to participate in the Wingspread conference (Nichols, 1972, p. 96), so women's discourse was not part of studies of U.S. public address. In that regard, work on women's discourse has had to retrace the steps that the field had taken years before. Doris Yoakam's fine essay on "Woman's Introduction to the American Platform" in the first volume of *History and Criticism of American Public Address* (1960, pp. 153–192) was not assigned, and Lillian O'Connor's earlier award-winning work, *Pioneer Women Orators* (1954), identified extant texts and provided a kind of neo-Aristotelian assessment of them. No women were included in the first two volumes of *A History and Criticism of American Public Address* (Brigance, 1943/1960) and only Susan B. Anthony was included in volume 3 (Hochmuth, 1955, pp. 97–132). Yes, we have come a long way, but even from a text-based critical perspective, there remains much to be done, and whatever our excitement over other kinds of rhetoric and other kinds of critical perspectives, that work should not be deprecated.

To address my topic directly, I begin with an example.

In 1977, at the height of the second wave of U.S. feminism, an essay by Gloria Steinem appeared in *Ms.* magazine. It asked:

What would happen … if suddenly, magically, men could menstruate and women could not?

The answer is clear—menstruation would become an enviable, boastworthy, masculine event:

Men would brag about how long and how much.…

Sanitary supplies would be federally funded and free. (Of course, some men would still pay for the prestige of commercial brands such as John Wayne Tampons, Muhammad Ali's Rope-a-dope Pads, Joe Namath Jock Shields—"For Those Light Bachelor Days," and Robert "Baretta" Blake Maxi-Pads.)

Military men, right-wing politicians, and religious fundamentalists would cite menstruation ("men-struation") as proof that only men could serve in the Army ("you have to give blood to take blood").…

Street guys would brag ("I'm a three-pad man") or answer praise from a buddy ("Man, you lookin' good!") by giving fives and saying, "Yeah, man, I'm on the rag!"…

In fact, if men could menstruate, the power justifications could probably go on forever.

If we let them.

Obviously, the essay from which these excerpts come is an example of humor in the service of feminism. In addition, it is a classic example of one of the richest and oldest sources of rhetorical invention—symbolic reversal. Reversal has great force as we know from the slogan "Black Power," the title "Bitch Manifesto," or the label "queer nation." In those cases, the reversal involves transforming a term of derision, an epithet, into a proud symbol of a newly-affirmed identity.

This case, however, is more complicated. What has often been called the "curse" is reversed by being imaginatively projected onto men in whose symbolic hands it is transformed into a badge of pride. The essay develops as a skillful parody of macho bragging, inviting our amused participation through its appropriation of cultural icons of masculinity, its playful use of language, and its imitation of the familiar hyperbole of advertising.

As it unfolds, the essay creates a space in which and from which a female voice or subjectivity can emerge. Its foundation is stereotype—women are imaginative (not rational), given to fancies—surely they must be allowed a bit of fantasy. The space enlarges through irony, the stance of the outsider who is particularly well situated to perceive incongruity. The hostility that might be aroused by the satiric overtones is mitigated by the author's manifest familiarity with cultural processes and events she describes and by a gentle amusement at these all-too-human foibles.

Note, however, that female space is carved out of highly resistant material—the degradation of females as unclean, as bodies (not minds) linked to nature (not civilization), and as powerless in the face of raging hormones—and the essay is something of a high-wire act because it flirts with taboo by publicly discussing that most unmentionable of women's physiological processes—menstruation.

In addition, the essay is reflexive; it achieves its purpose by showing not telling, by portraying the social construction of reality, in this case, a parodic reality in which menstrual blood is reconstructed as the ultimate sign of manliness, and by so doing it calls all such constructions into question. It is a fine example of women inventing spaces in which and platforms from which a female voice can emerge.

At the same time that it is an example of invention, it also illustrates similarities and tensions among cultural, rhetorical, and feminist criticism. The essay is a work of popular culture that relies on intertextuality, and its purpose is political and ideological. It is clearly rhetorical, but it is a text of little interest to traditional critics because it works indirectly and nondiscursively (try to recall a work that relies primarily on humor and is routinely studied in courses in U.S. public address). It is open to the charge of elitism because of its author, Gloria Steinem, and its outlet, *Ms.* magazine, and in my use of it, it becomes an example of the tendency of rhetorical critics to focus on single texts by single authors.

There isn't space to address all the issues raised by the topics in my title but the nature of the relationships among them is extremely important. Let us recognize the commonalities among rhetorical, critical/cultural, and feminist criticism: (1) All three are inherently interdisciplinary, with all the intellectual advantages and bureaucratic disadvantages we know so well. (2) All are ideological and political, although that stance is more controversial for rhetoricians than for women's or cultural/critical studies scholars. In that regard, I think the battle is being won by those of us who for years asserted that criticism had to be interpretative and evaluative and who argued that objectivity was a mask that hid critical biases (Campbell, 1971). (3) All are rhetorical, by which I mean they focus on discourse and try to understand how influence works, how rhetors and audiences make meaning out of discourse.

Let me recognize areas of tension and disagreement: 1) Cultural/critical studies has been extremely hospitable to studies of discourse by and about women; rhetoric has not. 2) Cultural/critical and women's studies have welcomed analyses of the discourse of non-elites, whether as social history or analyses of popular culture; rhetoric has not. 3) Cultural/critical and women studies have abandoned the assumptions of modernism and liberalism; most rhetorical critics have not. Accordingly, in rhetorical studies, there is still an overemphasis on reason and argument as modes of appeal, on treating texts as closed, and on a subject-centered view of authorship. Nowhere have the implications of these tensions been clearer than in the interchanges between Biesecker (1992; 1993) and me (1993) in *Philosophy and Rhetoric.*

I do not propose to revisit that controversy nor to make pronouncements about what other critics and scholars should do. Instead, I want to recall the meanings of two rather neglected concepts in rhetorical theory that might provide additional grounds for a rapprochement between rhetoricians and cultural/critical studies scholars. They are *techne* or art and its near relation, invention or artistic proofs.

Our concepts of rhetoric as an art are overlaid with the notions that developed about individual authorship because of the printing press and with Enlightenment concepts of the individual. When cultural/critical studies scholars appropriate the Derridean idea that it is language that speaks or the Foucauldian notion that it is the discursive formation that speaks, they are adopting notions that bear many similarities to Aristotle's understanding of an art. Gerald Else, the premier interpreter of Aristotle's *Poetics,* comments on our difficulty in understanding the Aristotelian conception. He writes: "[W]e in the Anglo-Saxon tradition are on the whole too far gone in individualism to think of 'poetry' as actually *made* by an Art of poetry. Yet that is what Aristotle, if honestly read, requires us to do" (1967, p. 4). He explains the Aristotelian notion of an art this way:

> The artist does not produce qua man [sic], *person, individual, but* qua *artist; or as Aristotle says, with his special brand of vividness, 'it is accidental to the sculptor that he is Polyclitus'* (Phys. 2.3.195a 34). *Although the artist is the proximate*

> *efficient cause of the productive process, the ulterior or true efficient cause is the art (the art in him). (p. 5)*

Else elaborates, writing that in the *Poetics, dynamis* refers to "the 'power' or 'capability' of the art, what it can do ... when put in operation" (p. 8). Later, he adds, "The point of view, then, under which we approach the subject is *art as cause*" (p. 10). Following Burke, we tend to associate rhetorical action with individual character, whereas the Aristotelian view suggests that communicative *praxis* is rooted in patterns, forms, schemata, and genres that belong to the art. One becomes an artist by mastering technique, the rules and principles, the patterns and forms, of the art, and it is through them that one is enabled to speak. Without them, no artistic production is possible; no meaning can be negotiated either by artist or audience.

As Carolyn Miller (1984) points out, form enables us to understand content; it provides instruction about how to perceive and interpret. These schemata are what Northrop Frye (1957, pp. 95–105) calls communicable units, the conventions through which encoding and decoding become possible, whether what we encounter is fragmentary or an apparent whole. Becoming skilled in the use of artistic proofs or invention requires familiarity with and practice in the use of the forms, patterns, genres, strategies, topics, tropes, and, I would add, practices that constitute the art but must be selected based on function or purpose and adapted to a historically and socially situated audience. In my experience and that of my students, cultural studies critics know very little about artistic proofs, and it seems to me no accident that those who have talked about how forms in popular culture engage audiences and prompt them to participate in and accept messages often have been English scholars trained in textual analysis, e.g., Horace Newcomb (1974) and John Cawelti (1976). Ironically, only a few rhetorical critics have been interested in these kinds of patterns and forms, but they are the means through which meanings are made, negotiated, and resisted. We need to master the forms and patterns of plot, genre, and journalistic practices through which public issues are deliberated in soaps, prime-time programming, and local newscasts, among others.

Aristotle's idea of the role of art in artistic production and Miller's insightful comments on the relationships between form and content are echoed in the opening pages of *The Power of Genre* (1985) in which Adena Rosmarin argues that genres do not exist in nature; they are socially constructed, a reaffirmation of Aristotle's view of art. In particular, however, she argues that genres are critics' tools, the means through which critics are able to understand and explain how meanings are made and, in turn, interpreted. In setting out her argument she turns to visual representation, the area in which we are least able to recognize the techniques through which the illusion of realistic representation is created. She writes:

> The convincing illusion... is an achievement not of nature but of technique.... The history of art teaches...that visual representation is like all other suasive enterprises in that it begins with a schema or premise that the painter modifies to meet the demands of his [sic] purpose and audience. (1985, pp. 10–11)

Two things are important in her statement. One is the reaffirmation of the role of schemata, genres, forms, conventions, and the like in convincing and effective artistic production—and here I include all the popular arts, of which rhetoric is one.

The other comment of importance is her statement that the artist modifies these schemata to meet the demands of her purpose and her audience. The history of women's invention is a history of appropriating and subverting available forms to feminist ends. There are almost endless examples, such as Christine de Pizan's fifteenth-century reworking of the materials of such misogynists as Boccaccio in *Book of the City of Ladies* (1982), Queen Elizabeth I's strategic use of familial terms in order to protect her monarchical power (Orlin, 1995), novelist Marietta Holley's use of humor to adapt domestic fiction to the service of women's rights and women's suffrage, e.g. in *Sweet Cicely* (1885; see Warren, 1984), and, of course, the example of Steinem's essay. Given what I know about the discourse of women and discourse by and about women, the central critical issue we need address is how such forms limit and constrain invention by and about women and, thus, work to limit and distort feminism, and how the inevitable residues of past *praxis* confound and contradict efforts for social change. In other words, we need to understand the circumstances under which forms can be subverted, what audiences need to be familiar with in order to negotiate meanings and produce oppositional readings. Celeste Condit's work on abortion in popular discourse (1990) and her essay on the limits of polysemy (1989) have been important contributions, but they are only a beginning.

Our understandings of invention, the artistic proofs, need to be enlarged to incorporate ideas associated with postmodernism. In a very provocative article about the effects of past *praxis* on invention, Stephen Glynn quotes a passage from Jacques Derrida's *Writing and Difference* (1978): "[W]e can pronounce not a single destructive proposition which has not already had to slip into the form, the logic, the implicit postulations of precisely what it seeks to contest" (in Glynn, 1986, p. 137). In other words, those who seek feminist social change are burdened with forms saturated with the residues of patriarchy. As such a formulation makes apparent, contradiction is inevitable, and contradiction, which I linked to the oxymoron (1973), is a key term in understanding and analyzing discourse by feminists and about feminism. Contradictions open up possibilities for negotiated and oppositional readings, yes, but they also offer fractures that can be exploited to facilitate cooptation or to reinscribe dominant ideas, as vividly illustrated in advertising and television programming targeted at women.

The type of focus on invention that I am describing resembles studies of intertextuality because it emphasizes links between bodies of discourse—discourse arises out of prior discourse; rhetoric arises out of prior rhetoric. Accordingly, it requires a synthetic approach to text and context and a treatment of related discourse as a vital context. Audiences are trained through discursive practice to read discourse (including fragments) in certain ways, to expect certain patterns, to enjoy and find satisfaction in certain forms, and to make certain kinds of inferences. We will not be able to explain how public discourse works to enable oppositional readings and to subvert dominant ideas or to engage audience members in ways that make them collaborators in their own oppression unless we understand the artistic elements through which these processes occur, the historical and social processes in which they are learned, or the historical, economic, and social circumstances that prompt audiences to attend to and participate in discourse and to draw some inferences and not others.

Although my pleasure in reading the works of such feminist cultural critics as Susan Douglas (1994) and Andrea Press (1991) is great, I remain an unreconstructed rhetorical critic who still is convinced that unless we understand the *techne* through which encoding and decoding occur, we cannot explain the meanings made by rhetors, whether individuals or groups, or by their audiences. Historians and cultural studies scholars are equally able to study and analyze the situated circumstances of those who engage in rhetorical transactions, but the expertise that we bring to that process, an expertise they do not share, is our knowledge of the artistic processes through which we come to understand how to interpret content. Ask yourselves, which is more important in understanding Steinem's essay, the cultural allusions, the situation of the audience then or now, or the use of symbolic reversal and enactment? The answer, of course, is that *all* are essential (see, for example, Dow, 1996, 1997).

I am so often struck by the ways in which we squander our inheritance, in large part, because we do not seem to realize that it is ours. We are the inheritors of a tradition that makes us uniquely suited to understand how language, how discursive formations, how artistic forms and proofs are able to speak to and engage audiences, to prompt collaboration.[1] Make no mistake about it, advocating close readings of texts is not to be confused with treating texts as closed. A commitment to our tradition is not a rejection of cultural studies; rather, it is a recognition of its inadequacies and of rhetorical studies' strengths.

REFERENCES

Arnold, C. C. (1974). *Criticism of oral argument.* Columbus, Ohio: Charles E. Merrill.

Biesecker, B. (1992). Coming to terms with recent efforts to write women into the history of rhetoric. *Philosophy and Rhetoric* 25:140-161.

Biesecker, B. (1993). Negotiating with our tradition: Reflecting again (without apologies) on the feminization of rhetoric. *Philosophy and Rhetoric* 26: 236–241.

Bitzer, L. and E. Black. (Eds.) (1971). *The prospect of rhetoric: Report of the national developmental project on rhetoric.* Englewood Cliffs, N.J.: Prentice-Hall.

Brigance, W. N. (Ed.) (1943/1960). *A history and criticism of American public address.* (vols. 1 and 2.) New York: Russell & Russell.

Campbell, K. K. (1971). The rhetoric of black nationalism: A case study in self-conscious criticism. *Central States Speech Journal* 22 (Fall): 151–160.

Campbell, K. K. (1973). The rhetoric of women's liberation: An oxymoron. *Quarterly Journal of Speech* 59: 74–86.

Campbell, K. K. (1993). Biesecker cannot speak for her either. *Philosophy and Rhetoric* 26:153–159.

Cawelti, J. G. (1976). *Adventure, mystery and romance: Formula stories as art and popular culture.* University of Chicago Press.

Condit. C. (1989). The rhetorical limits of polysemy. *Critical Studies in Mass Communication* 6:103–122.

Condit, C. (1990). Decoding abortion rhetoric: Communicating social change. Urbana: University of Illinois Press.

de Pizan, C. (1982). *The book of the city of ladies.* (E. J. Richards, Trans.) New York: Persea Books.

Derrida. J. (1978). *Writing and difference.* Trans. Alan Bass. University of Chicago Press.

Douglas, S. (1994). *Where the girls are: Growing up female with the mass media.* New York: Times Books.

Dow, B. J. (1996). *Prime-time feminism.* Philadelphia: University of Pennsylvania Press.

Dow, B. J. (1997). Feminism, cultural studies, and rhetorical studies. *Quarterly Journal of Speech* 83 (February), forthcoming lead book review.

Else, G. (1967). *Aristotle's* Poetics: *The argument.* Cambridge, Mass.: Harvard University Press.

Frye, N. (1957). *Anatomy of criticism.* Princeton, N.J.: Princeton University Press.

Glynn, S. (1986). Beyond the symbol: Deconstructing social reality. *Southern Speech Communication Journal* 51 (Winter): 125–141.

Hochmuth, M. K. (Ed.) (1955). *A history and criticism of American public address.* (vol. 3.) New York: Longmans, Green.

Miller, C. (1984). Genre as social action. *Quarterly Journal of Speech* 70: 159–160.

Newcomb, H. (1974). *TV: The most popular art.* Garden City, N.Y: Anchor Books.

Nichols, M. H. (1972). Two windows on *The prospect of Rhetoric. Quarterly Journal of Speech* 58:92–96.

O'Connor, L. (1954). *Pioneer women orators: Rhetoric in the ante-bellum reform movement.* New York: Vantage Press.

Orlin, L. C. (1995). The fictional families of Elizabeth I. (pp. 85–110). *Political rhetoric, power, and Renaissance women.* (Eds.) Carole Levin and Patricia A. Sullivan. Albany: State University of New York Press.

Press, A. (1991). *Women watching television: Gender, class, and generation in the American television experience.* Philadelphia: University of Pennsylvania Press.

Rosmarin, A. (1985). *The power of genre.* Minneapolis: University of Minnesota Press.

Steinem, G. (1977). If men could menstruate: A political fantasy by Gloria Steinem. *Ms.* 7 (October): 110.

Warren, H. (1984). Marietta Holley and the nineteenth-century domestic novel: Feminist subversion of an anti-feminism form. Unpublished paper presented at the Speech Communication Association Convention.

NOTE

1. As one example, see the brilliant but neglected "Special Rhetorical Meanings of Verbal Forms" in which Carroll Arnold (1974, pp. 197–215) describes and illustrates the ways in which verbal devices can argue through repeating, comparing, associating, constraining, and contrasting meanings.

Gender Diversity: A Theory of Communication for the Postmodern Era

Celeste M. Condit
University of Georgia

Feminism is one of the most important intellectual and social movements in the history of the human species. It is not, moreover, a movement that has yet run its course. Women still suffer oppression, primarily at the hands of men, simply because of their sex. Like every human intellectual movement, however, feminism has its limitations. Feminists have been engaged in debates about the limitations of their respective versions of feminism throughout the movement's history, but feminisms of many sorts have tended to share a series of blind spots and errant tendencies with regard to their references to men. Because feminism was built as a response to patriarchy, and because feminism is for women, it has exhibited strong tendencies to be largely unconcerned with the interests of men and sometimes even to indict men and treat them with hostility. In doing so, it has tended to polarize and dichotomize human sex in ways that are ultimately counterproductive for producing a world that is maximally just and decent for all people.

It is time, therefore, to shift the lens of feminism slightly, to overcome our history, which was one inevitably and appropriately (for its time) based in opposition, and to try to formulate a feminist view that focuses not just on the interests of women but on the interests of gendered people. I call this position gender diversity. It is a project on which a variety of scholars have recently been working. Today I hope to outline the application of this position in communication studies and show how it might be desirable.

The gender diversity perspective advocates a respect and care for persons of all genders and gender types (as long as those types do not di-rectly harm others or infringe on the human rights of others). It urges us to stop seeing sex in the simple dichotomies of male and female, encouraging us instead to explore the variability of both human sex and gender. The gender diversity perspective builds from the work done by theorists who are sometimes called gender deconstructionists or postmodern feminists. A host of theorists, including Judith Butler (1990), Toril Moi (1985), and Bonnie Dow (1995) have made substantial arguments for breaking up the classical dichotomy of male/female that has dominated both traditional societies and many feminist perspectives. They have emphasized that our identities are not neatly and uniformly formed around the sole factor of some essential and uniformly shared sex/gender characteristics. They have denied even that these identities are stable, universal parts of our lives. They point out that we perform our genders and that these performances vary by context. This is a liberating version of feminism for women who do not fit the traditional molds of femininity—for black women, chicanas, and lesbians, but also for those of us who are white, straight, middle-class, but uppity nonetheless.

The gender diversity perspective that I am urging you to consider applies these insights to both male and female. It assumes that gender is a combination of temporally and locationally specific interactions among biological, social, and individual components, but that all of these categories themselves admit diversity. At the biological level, gender diversity is evident. It is true that the need for reproduction has produced two sexes with different reproductive apparatus. However, in our species, as in other species such as ants, reproductive fitness is not an individual phenomenon, but a collective one. Hence, homosexuality and a range of other sexual variations may effectively serve reproductive ends in various environmental and cultural niches. As a consequence of the fact that different reproductive strategies may be effective, our species is only mildly dimorphic, and within each biological sex there is an enormous range of sexual characteristics. These variations in sexual characteristics may distribute themselves on a bell curve, creating the illusion of shared "typical" characteristics, but the diversity is real and the persons at any point of the curve are *normal,* that is, part of the normal diversity of human biology. In addition, because biology is inherently unstable, there are individuals who fit neatly neither sex set.

In eras when maintaining a level of reproduction sufficient to sustain or expand species or community survival was a struggle, cultural devices to channel biological diversity into reproductive efficiency may have been appropriate. Individual variation could be more efficiently sacrificed to mass production, as it were. Hence, many cultures developed ideological sets that dramatically simplified and dichotomized sex into two simple genders, even though this violated the biological configurations of many persons. The human race is obviously no longer in that position, and it is also now capable of more reasonable assignment of responsibilities for species survival, so that there is no need to heighten heterosexual attraction and to dichotomize child-raising responsibilities according to gender. Cultural fixation on heightening and maintaining heterosexual sex drives may receive some "bottom up" reinforcement from the evolved biological drives of those at some points of the sexual spectrum, but intellectually and logically, based on species needs, this is an obsolete practice. Moreover, for those who believe that the world is over-populated with humans relative to the needs of other species, it is probably a counter-productive emphasis as well. Refocusing our attention on the possible ranges of human gendering is therefore not only

practicable, but perhaps also desirable for the health of the planet. Expanding our vision of gender possibilities might also enrich human experience for this talking animal, capable as it is of artistic and intellectual evolution, creativity, and play.

It is difficult to get people to give up their sense that "men and women are different, damn it." So it is worth spending a bit more time exploring biological diversity. This is especially important given that the news media have of late been on a sex-dichotomy extravaganza, promoting every possible study that might be taken as demonstrating sexual dichotomy, especially with regard to "brain sex." All of these studies are grossly misleading, however, because even in the most basic of traits, the human species does not simply come in the forms of male and female. At the chromosomal level, variability exists. Some persons with XY chromosomes appear to be physically female, and variants from the XX or XY patterns, such as XXY, XYY, XXX, or XO exist, along with various mosaics of these, and various forms of hermaphroditism. Not only is there variation at the gross chromosomal level, but at the level of the gene itself there is vast variation. As a consequence of this genetic variation, no two women are alike. Gender dichotomy positions are built on the false assumption that women share some essential characteristics, when at the most basic biological level, no two women share all the same characteristics, and there is almost certainly not a single invariant allele of any gene shared by all women. Along the X chromosome itself, a symphony of different options play.

In the contemporary era, biological studies of sex have attempted to override this biological diversity through the choice of a single statistical measure that is designed to efface diversity—the use of means. Studies of biological sex almost invariably measure mean differences, and some report "statistically significant differences" based on these means. These researchers then conflate these statistically generated groupings with *essential* differences belonging to individual human beings, whereas in virtually all cases with which I am familiar, there is actually more overlap between male and female populations than there is difference. In other words, for almost all females on any given measure, there are males who have the same score, and vice versa (see Figure 1; for a concrete example, see Gur et. al, 1995, Figure 3). Difference in means may exist, but it is created by a few outliers on either end of the distribution (a very few men for whom there are no females with the same score, and vice versa) and by the relative numbers of men and women at a given score. Average differences are not reflective of essentially disparate biologies in men and women. When most women have the same score on any biological measure as some men, it can hardly be said that this measure is an indication of an essential, dichotomous variation between the sexes. Instead, the overwhelming overlap suggests that those few "outliers" who are not matched by members of the other sex are the truly unusual cases, rather than cases that ought to be treated as ideal gender representations. Perversely, however, our culture treats the extreme caricatures of masculinity and femininity as ideals. In addition, we should not forget both that the differences in averages that are found are usually on the order of 5% or less, and that variables in which statistically significant variations between sexes can be measured are also themselves extremely rare. In most ways men and women are indistinguishable. If an intelligent monosexed creature from another planet were to visit us, they would probably find perplexing our insistence that men and women were essentially different.

This same treatment—emphasizing biological ranges rather than means or averages—can be given to any other biological variable. Not all women menstruate or give birth. To date we have chosen to characterize such women as "abnormal," just as we portray men who enjoy childcare as abnormal (i.e. "effeminate"). That characterization is a cultural choice, and not one that is particularly well-founded. A woman who gives birth to five children and stays out of the paid labor force is as statistically anomalous today as the woman who has a career but no children, but the former woman (though perhaps open to some

forms of critique) is not likely to be stigmatized as gender-atypical, while the latter woman still is subject to challenges to her sexual normalcy and acceptability. Similarly, with an average life-span of 77 years, women now spend about as much of their life in the menstrual phase as out of it. Menstruation is therefore a poor candidate for a defining characteristic of female experience.

If biology manifests diversity, we can hardly expect culture to be neatly dimorphic, and indeed some preliminary social scientific work also reveals the diversity hidden in the averages produced by social scientific studies of gender (Condit & Williams, 1994/1995). In both culture and biology, then, the few, minor differences between averages of men and women are heavily outweighed by the rich variations in gender across the human scale. Our scholarship should accelerate the exploration of that diversity. The scholarship of women of color has already guided us in such a direction (Flores, 1996; Houston, 1985, 1992) as they have insistently encouraged us to attend to the cultural differences among female experiences across race, class, religion, region, and other aspects of identity. Re-orienting the understanding of gender we employ in our research from dichotomy to diversity, as these pioneering scholars have modeled for us, will offer three types of benefit. First, it will be better for many women. Second, it will be better for most men. Finally, it offers an approach that is strategically advantageous.

Many women will benefit from a gender diversity perspective because it will allow us to stop feeling like failures in the "ideal woman" game. Much feminist work in our field has, in the past, traded heavily on the dichotomy between men and women. The most prominent version of feminism in our field in the last decade emphasizes the merits of femaleness and thereby obviously makes a great deal of the presumed oppositeness of the characteristics of persons born/raised male and female, assuming that all women have fundamental common interests and that these are opposite from, or at least substantially different from, those of men (who are also reduced to a homogeneous group). According to these accounts women are more nurturing than men, more prone to cooperation, more appropriately identified with sewing, cooking, childcare, and if identified with careers, more appropriately identified with artistic careers such as architecture or writing (Foss & Foss, 1991). While there are attractive features of such positions, they ultimately are too constraining for women. They deny the identity of women who are ambitious, career-oriented, or who like physical action (repudiating these women as "male identified"). They ignore not only racial diversity, but class and regional diversity, as well as personal idiosyncrasy.

Those emphasizing gender dichotomy reply that postmodern versions of feminism have their own weakness—they loosen the bonds of political identity that make for political action. It is argued that if we don't all identify tightly and uniformly with a single signifier—WOMAN—then we won't

achieve effective political action. At one time, I myself made that argument. I have come to see that position, however, as an argument which insists that some women's Being be taken as the paradigm case by all women so that the dominant women's interests and agendas can be effectively served. That argument doesn't work anymore. You can force women to identify with a false stereotype, but probably not easily and forever, and you do psychological violence by trying to do so. Political action that seeks to reduce oppression has to find other means to effect its goals. It can do so because this older vision of political action was itself formed on some faulty (patriarchal) understandings of social change processes.

Because feminism was formed in opposition to patriarchy, it set itself in opposition to men and the practices authorized by the public rule of men.

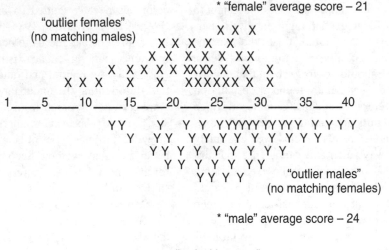

FIGURE 1 *Summary Model of Typical Sex Dichotomous Biological Data.* For comparison, see Gur et al. (1995, Table 3). *Categories of "male" and "female" are usually assigned by subject self assessment or researcher cursory visual judgment; chromosome tests are not usually performed. The magnitude of difference here is exaggerated; most studies show 5% difference in means or less, and usually only one or two variables out of 20 or more show any statistically significant difference at all; furthermore, characteristics of outliers have never been assessed; are male outliers linebackers or physicists?

That was a natural and necessary step in the evolution of human consciousness. Dichotomizing may be initially necessary for breaking away from an older ideology. However, the dichotomy relies on an agonistic approach to public processes, drawing deeply if subtly on the image of war. The "battle of the sexes" is not a feminist's metaphor, but it accurately reflects tendencies in feminist rhetorics. The promotion of the term "radical" as the god-term of feminism is indicative of the ways in which being as far as possible from men (the enemy) has become central to the identity of many feminists. But feminism itself (along with a broader sense of linguistic reflexivity sponsored by persons as diverse as Burke, Weaver, and Derrida; summarized in Condit, 1995) has provided a trenchant critique of such dichotomizing and agonistic worldviews. It is time for feminism to give up the simplistic and inappropriate image of "men the enemy." We need to begin envisioning the change that we seek not primarily as the destruction of patriarchy, not as "winning" something away from men, but rather as creating (or birthing) something new that is good for all people. As gender diversificationists we can re-envision ourselves by replacing the metaphor of radical oppositional revolution with metaphors for "raising change," as we would raise a garden or a child. These more gender inclusive metaphors also more aptly characterize the indeterminacy and long-term investment required for successful and meaningful social change.

This less agonistic and less dichotomizing approach is desirable because it is just and caring (see Hall, 1996, for an exploration of the justice/care matrix). The potential of a gender diversity perspective to increase care and justice for men as well as women can be suggested by exploring the ways in which patriarchy does violence to most men, as well as women. I do not deny that men profit at women's expense in patriarchy, but I do deny that it is the best way for men to live (even in their own self-interest). Many men have come to recognize the ways in which traditional patriarchy sets for them devastating and destructive identities. They are required to shut down their emotions, to spend their efforts chasing empty status markers, to retreat from human contact and communication that is meaningful, and to batter their bodies. Few men that I know really want to be Rocky or the Godfather, but that is what patriarchy requires of them if they are to be "dominant." Most men suffer many forms of psychic, and even physical and economic, damage at the hands of patriarchy. Men may be better off than women (in some significant ways) within patriarchy, but that does not mean that patriarchy is good for most men.

Why then does it seem that men defend patriarchy so vociferously? First, it is often highly advantaged men who are in the position to speak, and they of course have a great deal to gain by protecting patriarchy—for they reap the benefits of the pain of most women *and* men. However, even less advantaged men defend patriarchy. I believe that this occurs in large measure because the feminist attack on patriarchy has been launched in the name of women, in the interests of women, and with disregard for men. We have told men that they are the oppressors, and so they deny it. We tell men that we are out to strip away the advantages that they gain from patriarchy, and so they defend those advantages—for these advantages are all that patriarchy has left them, and at considerable cost. As feminists, we may have occasionally added a few phrases about how feminism will help men get in touch with their feminine sides—but these are shallow gushes, and if we put ourselves in men's shoes, we would notice the extent to which this is an offensive band-aid to offer. If we wish men to recognize that patriarchy is bad for all people, we need to espouse an ideology which, throughout its substance, recognizes the value of the diversity of people, including people who are sexed as male. We need to stop portraying men as our opposite. We need to emphasize whole spectrums of human gender diversity and give up our dichotomous boxes.

For some, this approach may smack of humanism, and feminists have appropriately discredited humanism on the grounds that it presumed a monoform human (and one that was implicitly white and male). Gender diversity, however, accepts humanism's goals of valuing all humans, but understands far more deeply that such valuation entails recognizing and accounting for diversity, rather than ignoring it. A gender diversity perspective explicitly recognizes gender as a significant component of human life, action, and identity, just as it introduces race, class, sexual orientation, age, handicap, and other facets of diversity—each one a factor that disrupts the simplicity of gender (and vice versa, each factor interacting with the others) producing plurality rather than dichotomy.

I hope that what I have said indicates the philosophical and ideological value of adopting a theory of gender diversity. This approach to human sex and gender also has strategic value. Diversity perspectives may reduce the simplicity of "woman" as a rallying term, but they increase the number of people who can be rallied to the cause. Consider the issue of rape, for example. This is an issue that has been strongly polarized between men and women. Some feminist theorists have even argued that men are by nature rapists (chillingly echoing the claims of the conservative sociobiologists). The strategic consequence of such a stance should be obvious. If all men see themselves as rapists, they are unlikely to support strict and effective punishment for rape. It is far better to encourage men to see rape as a deviation from human action, and to see themselves as potential victims of rape (whether homosexual or heterosexual). When most men understand rape as alien to their nature and are able to imagine themselves as victims of the act, they are far more likely to participate actively in reducing this scourge.

Focusing on a diversely gendered human population is also of value because it encourages us to extend the lenses of our research. I will concentrate on rhetoric here, since I am a rhetorician, but I suspect examples would be similar in other subfields of communication. Traditional research, sponsored by patriarchal sources, focused heavily on issues of war and the presidency. Feminism responded by valorizing different issues—women's rights, abortion, rape, wife abuse, etc. But many issues escape central attention in both the patriarchal and feminist visions. We have not attended sufficiently to issues

of labor, the environment, and health in the last two decades in part because these issues are central neither to feminism nor to patriarchy. They are, however, central human issues and a gender diversity perspective should help open up these issues as pressing research concerns.

Even when an issue can be fit into the patriarchal or feminist perspective, gender diversity perspectives help draw attention to a wider range of concerns about the issue. The issue of health provides an excellent example. Feminists have treated women's health in the past two decades, and there has been a small contingent of feminist rhetoricians involved in this work. Much of that work, focused exclusively on women, has been enormously productive. I believe my own small contributions to the area have been well worth doing (Parrott & Condit, 1996). However, the lens of feminism has also created gaps and errors in our health research. Dichotomizing women and men has encouraged us to assume that men get good treatment in the health care system, when this is not particularly true. Men avoid the health care system far more assiduously than do women, sometimes at great detriment to their health. Men live shorter life spans than women, and while there are biological and historical contingencies that account for some of this difference, there are also issues of gender framing at work here. Men avoid doctors (even though physicians are still predominately male) because of the gender casting of masculinity and the gender casting of the role of patient conflict. Understanding these practices in terms of gender will help women (as has traditional feminist work), but it will also help men. It also puts the power of men behind the reform.

Adopting as our purpose the effort to understand the impact of gender diversity on our communication practices also might open up richer avenues of research even in the most traditional topics to which we have attended. With some notable exceptions (Biesecker, 1990; Sells, 1995) published feminist criticism in communication studies is threatening to develop a tedious predictability, offering us two basic findings: women talk differently from men and all existing discourse is patriarchal. The gender diversity perspective opens up new territory for feminist criticism and analyses. Instead of trying to describe how men and women speak differently, we can begin to explore the range of gendered options available to people. Instead of merely repeating the apt insight that women's gender limits their speaking, and then rotely applying that insight to endless case studies, we can begin to explore the ways in which successful women like Barbara Boxer, Carol Mosely-Braun, and Elizabeth Cady Stanton have constructed genderings that allowed them to speak effectively for their audiences. Parallel explorations are available in other areas of communication studies if we begin to ask the question "what are the range of genderings available to people in their personal, group, and organizational communication and what impacts do these have?" instead of asking simply, and misleadingly, "how do men and women communicate differently?"

Feminism has produced both many important insights and many important social changes, and it should not be discarded. Feminism should, however, evolve into a broader framework that attends to all human genders with both justice and care. The gender diversity perspective asks us to take seriously the issue of gender in communication, but to do so with respect to the impact of gender on all persons, in all their variety, There is a lively debate about whether men can be feminists. There is no reason to doubt that men can be gender diversificationists. Opening up our visions of gender should produce advantage for men at the same time that it improves the conditions of life for women on the small and fragile planet that we share.

REFERENCES

Biesecker, S. (1990). Feminist criticism of classical rhetorical texts: A case study of Gorgias' *Helen*. In V. Vitanza & M. Ballif (Eds.), *Realms of Rhetoric: Phonic, Graphic, Electronic* (pp. 67–82). Arlington, TX: Rhetoric Society of America.

Butler, J. (1990). *Gender trouble: Feminism and the subversion of identity*. London and New York: Routledge.

Condit, C. M. (1995). Kenneth Burke and linguistic reflexivity: Reflections on the scene of the philosophy of communication in the twentieth century. In B. L. Brock (ed.), *Kenneth Burke and contemporary European thought*. Tuscaloosa: University of Alabama Press, pp. 207–262.

Condit, C. M. & Williams, M. (1994/1995). Gender differences and argumentation: A positional account of the reception of genetics arguments. *Speaker and Gavel, 32,* 1–12.

Dow, B. J. (1995). Feminism, difference(s), and rhetorical studies. *Communication Studies, 46,* 106–117.

Flores, L. A. (1996). Creating discursive space through a rhetoric of difference: Chicana feminists craft a homeland. *Quarterly Journal of Speech, 82,* 142–156.

Foss, K. A., & Foss, S. K. (1991). *Women speak: The eloquence of women's lives*. Prospect Heights, IL: Waveland Press.

Gur, R. C., Mozley, L. H., Mozley, P. D., Resnick, S. M., Karp, J. S., Alavi, A., Arnold, S. E. & Gur, R. E. (1995). Sex differences in regional cerebral glucose metabolism during a resting state. *Science, 267,* 528–31.

Hall, M. W. (1996). The personal was political: Toward a feminist reconstruction of the boundaries between public and private. Unpublished master's thesis, Duquesne University, Pittsburgh.

Houston, M. (1985). Language and black women's place: Evidence from the black middle class. In P. Treichler, C. Kramerae, & B. Stafford (Eds.), *For alma mater: Theory and practice in feminist scholarship* (pp. 177–193). Urbana: University of Illinois Press.

Houston, M. (1992). The politics of difference: Race, class and women's communication. In L. F. Rakow (Ed.), *Women making meaning: New feminist directions in communication* (pp. 45–59). New York: Routledge.

Moi, T. (1985). *Sexual/textual politics*. New York and London: Routledge.

Parrott, R. L. & Condit, C. M. (1996). *Evaluating women's health messages: A resource book*. Thousand Oaks, CA: Sage.

Sells, L. (1995). Where do the mermaids stand?: Voice and body in the *Little Mermaid*. In E. Bell, L. Haas, and L. Sells (Eds.), *From Mouse to Mermaid: the Politics of Film, Gender, and Culture*, (pp. 175–192). Bloomington: Indiana University Press.

From Isolation to Integration:
Gender's Place in the Core of Communication Knowledge

Julia T. Wood
University of North Carolina, Chapel Hill

Between 1972 and 1975, I pursued masters and doctoral studies. Then there were no courses in gender and communication, much less ones in feminist theory and research. Yet, there was a gender curriculum—one that implicitly defined male speakers and speech as normative and that assumed traditional and masculine ways of conducting and reporting research were the only appropriate forms of scholarship (Keller, 1985). By implication, women's speech and modes of research were either absent in research and teaching or were depicted as inferior to masculine forms.

Much has changed in the 21 years since I received my Ph.D. Women rhetors who were invisible during my graduate studies have gained a measure of visibility. Feminine and feminist lines of inquiry and ways of conducting research have earned a measure of prominence in many quarters, including some in the field of communication.

Although gender and feminist studies have won some recognition and respect, they remain marginal in our field, as well as many others. In my talk, I will suggest that gender should be accorded a more central place in the study and teaching of communication. I'll begin by discussing and criticizing the current position of gender studies in the field of communication. Next, I will identify two areas that I consider especially important for future research and teaching. I will close by emphasizing the special role of the university in generating knowledge that accurately represents rich diversity of the human community.

THE POSITION OF GENDER AND FEMINIST STUDIES

Not long ago I was working on a book on personal relationships. As is customary, my publisher asked several faculty members to review my draft manuscript. One reviewer took me to task for discussing gender in a book on interpersonal communication. As the reviewer said—and I'm quoting directly since I saved this review—"Material on gender and gender differences should be reserved for courses in gender and communication. It does not belong in a book on interpersonal relationships."

That comment perplexed me. Neither then nor now can I understand why gender is anything but directly relevant to the study of communication in personal relationships. What I have inferred from similar responses to other book and article manuscripts that I and others have written is that some people in our field regard gender and communication as a marginal area of study and teaching that has no bearing on what they define as the core of the field. In contrast, I believe that gender and communication should be woven into the basic fabric of our field.

Although gender may not be the single most important influence on communication, it is so basic that it affects interaction in varied contexts. Motives, expectations, interpretations, and communication styles have been shown to differ systematically, though not dramatically or universally, between women and men. These differences are germane to public speaking, group communication and leadership, personal relationships, organizational communication, performance of literature, political communication, mass communication, interaction via electronic means, and intercultural communication. There is no intellectually sound reason to sequester gender studies into a distinct corner that is unconnected to the range of communication forms and contexts.

Consider how research findings about gendered communication styles might apply to specific areas in our discipline. Karlyn Campbell's (1989a, b; 1991; 1993; 1995a, b) ongoing program of research has recovered the long-silenced voices of American women rhetors in the nineteenth and twentieth centuries. Her work demonstrates forms and goals of rhetoric that were not visible when only male speakers were studied. Bonnie Dow and Marie Tonn (1993) have identified distinctive qualities of the speech of women politicians. The findings of Campbell and Dow and Tonn should be incorporated into the core knowledge base of rhetoric and public address.

As a second example, consider how findings from research on gender and communication pertain to interaction in personal relationships. Recent work by Teresa Sabourin (1995) and Glenn Stamp and Teresa Sabourin (1995) reveals gendered dynamics embedded in sexual violence between intimates. It is directly relevant to interpersonal communication to understand how women and men, in general, perceive and justify violence in their relationships. Other scholars in communication (West, 1995; Wood, 1997), as well as scholars outside of our field (Gottman & Carrére, 1994; Tannen, 1990), have identified gendered patterns of dealing with relationship conflict. If masculine and feminine orientations and responses to conflict differ in general ways, then scholars and teachers of interpersonal communication should recognize this and incorporate it into their classrooms and research.

Consider a third area in our field to which gender and communication research can contribute. Work by Elizabeth Natalle (1996), Shereen Bingham (1996), and Bren Murphy and Ted Zorn (1996) illuminates generalizable differences in how women and men interact in professional settings. There are definable gender-linked patterns of expectation, interpretation, and action that affect what happens in the workplace and what it is understood to mean. This kind of knowledge should be woven into research and teaching about organizational communication. The areas I've discussed illustrate, but do not exhaust, the ways in which knowledge of gender and communication pertains to traditional areas of research and teaching (see, Blair, Brown, & Baxter, 1994).

MAJOR FOCI FOR FUTURE RESEARCH AND TEACHING

Of the many topics that invite our attention in the years ahead, I regard two as especially significant.

Intersections among Gender, Class, Ethnicity, & Sexual Orientation

Gender cannot be understood accurately in isolation. Instead, it is one of several interlinked dimensions of selfhood and social life. An urgency for communication scholars is to discern how gender intersects with other basic aspects of identity and social structure, such as ethnicity, sexual orientation, and class.

As Sandra Harding (1991) noted, "it is simply not true that gender relations create a set of human experiences that are more important than those created by such other inequalities as race and class" (p. 213). To identify and explore intersections among interlinked dimensions of individual identities and cultural ideology we must move beyond distinct theories about sex, race, class, and so forth. To replace them, we need to develop a theory that fosters insight into the multiple, overlapping, and highly complex social organizations that result in different experiences, opportunities, and knowledges for different groups of people.

To illustrate the importance of this line of inquiry, let me offer a few examples of how gender interacts with other aspects of identity and social structure. Textbooks on gender and communication routinely advance the claim that women are less assertive than men. They also regularly assert that males are the privileged members of Western society. Yet, both of these claims should be tempered by recognition of the impact of race on assertion and privilege. African American women, for example, tend to be more assertive, independent, and self-confident than European American women. African American men do not routinely benefit from the so-called "male privilege" enjoyed by many European American men; African American males, in fact, often have less social status than African American women. Consider a third example: Both scholarly and popular publications note the emphasis on thinness for women and its possible relation to eating disorders. Yet, when I discuss this topic in my classes, the African American students are puzzled. For the most part, they aren't obsessed with being thin, and eating disorders are relatively rare among African American women, whereas they seem to be epidemic among European American women. These examples illustrate how gender is inflected by race. It is also inflected by class and sexual orientation, connections I do not have time to illustrate here.

In the years ahead, I hope we will develop more layered, nuanced, accurate understandings of how multiple aspects of identity and social structure interact in particular eras and societies.

Claiming a Public Voice to Criticize Popular Psychology's Misrepresentations of Gender Communication and Feminism

The second urgency I see is for scholars of gender and communication to take a public voice in the life of our culture. Popular psychology books are being published in record numbers. They are also being read and, too often, swallowed unreflectively by millions of women and men.

Many of my students quote John Gray to me as if he had written a sacred scripture instead of an un-

derresearched bestseller. They are astounded when I tell them that the only person from Mars is John Gray himself. His books, like many written for the popular market, are filled with half-truths, egregious overgeneralizations, and distortions about differences between women and men. Meanwhile, Katie Roiphe, Christina Hoff Sommers, and Naomi Wolf disparage feminism without any informed understanding of the movement's history or current character (see Wood, 1996).

Scholars of gender and communication should assume a public voice to respond to the misrepresentations and excesses of popular books. Without response from those of us who base knowledge claims on research, pretenders to knowledge, such as John Gray and Katie Roiphe, will continue to shape public understandings of women, men, and feminism.

The university is an institution that should be at the vanguard of social change. Historically, universities have had a special identity as breeding grounds for knowledge and social progress. The university's power to provoke fundamental change in life is most easily seen in the contributions of the hard sciences. For example, geneticist Barbara McClintock earlier in this century was the first to discover that genes jump or reorganize themselves, rather than being controlled by a master molecule as had been previously assumed. This discovery dramatically altered our understanding of genetic organization and change and of life itself. And Ruth Hubbard's groundbreaking biological research earned her a Nobel Prize only a few years ago.

The contributions of the humanities and social sciences are sometimes less dramatic, but certainly no less important than those of the hard sciences. For instance, historian Gerder Lerner has made us aware of conspicuous absences and misrepresentations of women's contributions to social life (1972). Social critic Nancy Fraser (1989) has incisively analyzed gender biases in existing and proposed social policies. Psychoanalysts such as Nancy Chodorow (1978, 1989) and Janet Surrey (1983) have opened our eyes to the gendered dynamics of family life and the ways in which these dynamics reproduce restrictive identities for women and men.

And critical theorists in the field of communication such as Mary Strine (1992) have enlarged our understanding of communicative practices that legitimize and normalize sexual harassment in everyday life. Each of these insights changes how we see ourselves, each other, and the communities we collaboratively create and inhabit.

No less than historically, an important mission of the university today is to spark critical reflection on society and to foment constructive social change. Our mission is not to paddle along in the wake of changes wrought by legal rulings, shifting demographics, and evolutions—or devolutions—in social attitudes and activities. Instead, we should lead the way by insisting on knowledge that is as accurate, as comprehensive as is possible.

CLOSING

I have spoken about feminist theorizing and research on gender and communication. At a more basic level I've been speaking about what we shall define as the knowledge of our field. In recent years scholars have increasingly recognized that what we call knowledge is intimately shaped by knowers. Knowledge never exists apart from some knower; it always, inevitably reflects the identities, experiences, ways of knowing, and learned perspectives of particular human beings who exist in distinct material, symbolic, social, and historical circumstances (Haraway, 1988; Keller, 1985; Wood & Cox, 1993; Wood & Duck, 1995). For this reason, the university's traditional mission of discovering and sharing knowledge requires us to inquire into the different kinds of knowledge that arise from diverse social standpoints.

The university and those of us who work there are not minor players in the cultural drama. By virtue of its traditions and its special protections of free thought, the university should be an especially preeminent player. I believe we can and should assume an active role in shaping the ideal and the reality of our culture as a richly textured mosaic in which differences among us are not disparaged, forced into false congruity, or resisted.

Our ability to represent the intricate mosaic of human communication will depend, in no small measure, on the character of what we teach and study. When research, teaching, and daily practices at universities recognize and respect the experiences of different groups, then gender will no longer be relegated to marginal status in what we define as disciplinary knowledge. As a result, we will be able to create a more holistic and accurate portrait of humans and their communication practices. This is the challenge of generating knowledge in a pluralistic world, and is a challenge and an ideal worthy of the energy and commitment required to achieve it.

REFERENCES

Bingham, S. (1996). Sexual harassment on the job, on the campus. In J. T. Wood (Ed.), *Gendered relationships* (pp. 233–252). Mountain View, CA: Mayfield.

Blair, C., Brown, J., & Baxter, L. (1994). Disciplining the feminine. *Quarterly Journal of Speech, 80,* 383–409.

Campbell, K. K. (1989a). *Man cannot speak for her I: A critical study of early feminist speakers.* Westport, CT: Praeger.

Campbell, K. K. (1989b). *Man cannot speak for her II: Key texts of the early feminists.* New York: Greenwood Press.

Campbell, K. K. (1991). Hearing women's voices. *Communication Education, 40,* 33–48.

Campbell, K. K. (1993). *Women public speakers in the United States: A bio-critical sourcebook.* Westport, CT: Greenwood Press.

Campbell, K. K. (1995a). Gender and genre: Loci of invention and contradiction in the earliest speeches by U. S. women. *Quarterly Journal of Speech, 81,* 479–495.

Campbell, K. K. (1995b). In silence we oppress. In J. T. Wood & R. B. Gregg (Eds.), *Toward the 21st century: The future of speech communication* (pp. 137–149). Cresskill, NJ: Hampton Press.

Chodorow, N. (1978). *The reproduction of mothering: Psychoanalysis and the sociology of gender.* Berkeley, CA: University of California Press.

Chodorow, N. (1989). *Feminism and psychoanalytic theory.* New Haven, CT: Yale University Press.

Dow, B., & Tonn, M. (1993). Feminine style and political judgment in the rhetoric of Ann Richards. *Quarterly Journal of Speech, 79,* 286–302.

Fraser, N. (1989). *Unruly practices: Power, discourse, and gender in contemporary social theory.* Minneapolis: University of Minnesota Press.

Gottman, J., & Carrére, S. (1994). Why can't men and women get along? Developmental roots and marital inequities. In D. Canary & L. Stafford (Eds.), *Communication and relational maintenance* (pp. 203–229). New York: Academic Press.

Haraway, D. (1988). Situated knowledges: The science question in feminism and the privilege of partial perspective. *Signs, 14,* 575–599.

Harding, S. (1991). *Whose science? Whose knowledge? Thinking from women's lives.* Ithaca: Cornell University Press.

Keller, E. F. (1985). *Reflections on gender and science.* New Haven, CT: Yale University Press.

Lerner, G. (Ed.). (1972). *Black women in white America: A documentary history.* New York: Pantheon.

Murphy, B. O., & Zorn, T. E. (1996). Gendered interaction in professional relationships. In J. T. Wood (Ed.), *Gendered relationships* (pp. 213–232). Mountain View, CA: Mayfield.

Natalle, E. (1996). Gendered issues in the workplace. In J. T. Wood (Ed.), *Gendered relationships* (pp. 253–274). Mountain View, CA: Mayfield.

Sabourin, T. (1995). The role of negative reciprocity in spouse abuse: A relational control analysis. *Journal of Applied Communication Research, 23,* 271–283.

Stamp, T., & Sabourin, T. (1995). Accounting for violence: An analysis of male spousal abuse narratives. *Journal of Applied Communication Research, 23,* 284–307.

Strine, M. S. (1992). Understanding how things work: Sexual harassment and academic culture. *Journal of Applied Communication Research, 10,* 391–400.

Surrey, J. L. (1983). The relational self in women: Clinical implications. In J. V. Jordan, J. L. Surrey, A. G. Kaplan (Speakers), *Women and empathy: Implications for psychological development and Psychotherapy* (pp. 6–11). Wellesley, MA: Stone Center for Developmental Services and Studies.

Tannen, D. (1990). *You just don't understand: Women and men in conversation.* New York: William Morrow.

West, J. T. (1995). Understanding how dynamics of ideology influence violence between intimates. In S. Duck & J. T. Wood (Eds.), *Understanding relationship processes, 5: Confronting relationship challenges* (pp. 129–139). Thousand Oaks, CA: Sage.

Wood, J. T. (1996). Dominant and muted discourses in popular representations of feminism. *Quarterly Journal of Speech, 82,* 171–185.

Wood, J. T. (1997). *Gendered lives: Communication, gender and culture,* 2nd ed. Belmont, CA: Wadsworth.

Wood, J. T., & Cox, J. R. (1993). Rethinking critical voice: Materiality and situated knowledges. *Western Journal of Communication, 57,* 278–287.

Wood, J. T., & Duck, S. (1995). Off the beaten track: New frontiers in relationship research. In J. T. Wood & S. Duck (Eds.), *Understanding relationship processes, 6: Off the beaten track: Understudied relationships.* Thousand Oaks, CA: Sage.

CHAPTER 8

AT THE HELM
IN COMMUNICATION EDUCATION

Introduction

Rebecca B. Rubin
Kent State University

The ship, Communication Education, is a four-master, one of those tall square-rigger ships. Each mast represents a facet of discipline, and the sails represent the scholarship that propels the ship in the channel. At the bow is our most recent mast, training and development; sailors trim this sail by studying how we can best train others to do specific jobs. In the center is the tallest mast, teacher preparation; seamen trim this sail by training new teachers how to be best prepared to teach communication classes. The third mast is the strongest of all, instructional communication; seamen trimming this sail study teacher characteristics and classroom behaviors and how these affect student learning. At the stern is the basic course mast; we all trim this sail when we study how students new to the discipline can best be taught, and what information they should receive in their first speech course. The tall ship, Communication Education, is about to get underway. Listen to its crew. Four scholars have been chosen to guide its journey.

Our first scholar at the helm, James McCroskey, leads the field in Instructional Communication. Part of his research program, within the last decade, has focused on how teachers can function best in the classroom. Jim and his shipmates have identified behavior alteration techniques teachers can use with their students to bring about learning. He has also investigated immediacy and affective

social styles and how they influence affective and cognitive learning. An even larger part of his research has focused on students in instructional settings and how apprehension, willingness to communicate, and other related constructs affect their lives; his scholarship has helped teachers identify and reduce student apprehension. Thus, our course today is set by our navigator, Captain James McCroskey. Jim has read the stars and will speak on "The Future of Communication Education: Communication as a Content Discipline."

Our second scholar at the helm, Jo Sprague, trims the ship's Teacher Training mast. Although her shipboard duties require her to perform many different jobs, what stands out most is her work preparing teachers of tomorrow to teach and how teaching works. The word "Pedagogy" appears in most of her articles and is central to her work with new apprentice seamen, such as new TAs, women, high school students, and at-risk students. Aboard ship, she too reads the stars, and navigates us towards the year 2000. Thus, our second sail is tended by Captain Jo Sprague. Jo will speak "On Nets, Webs, Scaffolds, and Tightropes: Changing Conceptions of Instructional Communication in the Post-Information Age."

Our third scholar at the helm, Douglas Trank, tends the ship's Basic Course mast. Actually, you have seen his name on the masthead of *Communi-*

cation Education journal for the last three years. But what is most apparent from his log is his scholarship on how to best teach the basic course in both high school and college. Doug has been concerned with alternative approaches to the basic course, directing multiple sections of it, evaluating it, surveying it, choosing textbooks for it, using standardized tests in it, developing graduate instructors for it, measuring the effects of it, using student feedback in it, and preserving the integrity of it. Thus, our third sail is tended by Captain Doug Trank. Doug will speak on "Communication Education's Integrative Role: Providing an Intersection for Multiple Constituencies."

Our fourth scholar at the helm, John Daly, once a deck hand of Captain McCroskey, has risen in rank and now tends the ship's Training and Development mast. John's connections to business and management, both professionally and academically, have resulted in consulting at over 75 companies, including that of our Commander and Chief, as well as scholarship in organizational and instructional communication. John studies communication traits and basic skills—listening, vocal activity, self-esteem, social relaxation, affinity, sensitivity, writing—and shows how training in these can reduce maladies—such as anxiety, disengagement, loneliness, and narcissism—in both business and social worlds. Thus, our helmsman today is Captain John Daly. His topic is "If Communication Matters So Much, Why Don't We Get the Attention We Deserve?"

The Future of Communication Education: Communication as a Content Discipline

James C. McCroskey
West Virginia University

I came to the field of Communication by way of the field of Speech. I was an undergraduate debater who also participated in contests in discussion, extemporaneous speaking, and after-dinner speaking. I also acted in many high school and college plays. I directed drama at the high school level. I coached high school debate and taught junior and senior high school public speaking classes for three years. I coached debate at the college level for three years and judged college debate extensively for another nine years. I taught public speaking at the college level for nine years. I have a book on public speaking which Allyn and Bacon is releasing in its seventh edition which is entering its thirtieth year in print. I have published many articles in journals relating to effective oral communication performance.

I do not begin my remarks with all of this self-description to boast about my past. Rather, I do so to establish that I am not an enemy of the traditional field of speech but rather a product of it. It is a background of which I am proud, not one of which I am ashamed or wish to hide. While the views I will express in these remarks will in some ways echo views expressed in *Communication Education* in 1989 by my friend, Michael Burgoon, I do not call for our field of Communication to divorce "Dame Speech" as he did. I do, however, find myself in full agreement with Dr. Burgoon when he states that extant "theory and research in communication have far outstripped what presently is being taught in Speech" (p. 303). Although seven years have passed since I heard him deliver those remarks on a panel at the Central States Communication Association,

his comments are as accurate today as they were then.

As Dr. Burgoon has suggested, what we teach most of our students has little to do with what our scholarship has made available to teach our students. It is not an exaggeration to say that most of our scholarship is wasted effort. We teach public speaking much like it was taught at the beginning of the twentieth century. The *absence* of research to indicate that what we do is effective is overwhelming. In the process we ignore the rest of the field of communication. It is critical that we teach the next generation of communication scholars and professionals what is known about communication rather than simply "how to do it." The "how-to-do-its" rather consistently are not based in solid scholarship and the bad information is pushing out the good.

For most of us who currently see ourselves as members of a discipline we choose to call "Communication" or some similar title, the field of Speech is not our intellectual spouse, from whom we can effect a divorce. Rather, the field of Speech is our grandparent, someone from whom we have learned and who has helped us grow to where we are today. We are different from our grandparent. What our grandparent built should continue to be respected, maybe even revered, but it cannot be expected to be fully adaptable in today's realities. To understand where we are today, it is vital that we understand from whence we came.

Our ancestors who formed the National Association of Teachers of Public Speaking parted company with our friends in the field of English in

191

large part because of their primary concern with public speaking as an art—an applied art. They saw effective public speaking as the foundation for successful participation in the professions and as the entry to the seats of power in the society. They were carrying forth the noble cause of the rhetoric of Aristotle in the grand tradition of the Judeo-Christian, Greco-Roman culture. We were taught that through effective public speaking we would all achieve "freedom," "liberty," and "equality."

Unfortunately, too few of us appear to be aware that what these words meant throughout most of the last 2,500 years is not what we take them to mean today. Recognize that the people who were able to participate in the rhetoric of Athenian society of 300 or so B.C. (or most anywhere else in Europe, Africa, or the Middle East) were a very small proportion of the people of the society. They were virtually all male, non-slaves who owned considerable property, and were fairly well-educated. Much of the population was constituted of slaves, and of course over half of the non-slaves were women, people who had virtually no rights at all. The rhetorical system was designed for the elite few males who could participate in the governmental and economic systems of the culture.

The same basic pattern survived in the Judeo-Christian, Greco-Roman cultures of Western societies, including the United States, until very recently. Slavery was not abolished until the nineteenth century in the U.S. But even after that, neither former slaves nor their descendants were allowed to vote or fully participate in most of the aspects of everyday economic life or political life. Although women were finally given the right to vote in the 1920s, neither women nor the descendents of former slaves were granted the legal status of equality until the 1960s in the U.S., and they still do not have that status in most other countries. It should not be surprising, therefore, that few non-white or female scholars had an opportunity to make meaningful contributions to the study of rhetoric and public speaking until recent years. It simply was "not appropriate."

In the middle 1960s in the U.S., education as a whole, and particularly our own field of speech, began going through enormous change. Women, minorities, and white males of the middle and lower classes flowed into schools in enormous numbers. The interests of these individuals were not fully consistent with those of the former occupants of higher education, those representing the economic and cultural elite. This led to a revolution in the study of human communication which drew increasing attention to that communication which exists outside the infrastructure dominated by the cultural elite. The study of communication became open to those who had never had an opportunity to study it, and the questions these new students asked often were very different than those who went before them. They filed into our required public speaking classes and started asking why they had to study something as foreign to them as this strange behavior.

With the growth in student enrollments in colleges and universities, course requirements mandated massive numbers of faculty and/or graduate students for some offerings. With many freshman classes numbering between 5,000 and 10,000 students (and some even more) came a realization on the part of many university administrators that offering 200 to 400 (or more) 25-person sections of public speaking classes each year made no economic sense. People in our field were forced to re-evaluate the nature of the basic course, and many courses were changed to "fundamentals" courses rather than pure public speaking. Since some of the skills being taught in these "fundies" classes did not require individualized presentations, enrollments could be increased to keep administrators happy.

As a function of extended interactions with many of the "new" students in our environment, many of us in Speech began to reluctantly admit that what we were teaching might not be what the modern student needed. At the same time, our research brought into question the usefulness of our skills courses in accomplishing one of two primary goals which they professed to meet—to reduce students' fear of speaking with others. Other research indicated that in the new economic world the importance of public speaking was greatly reduced in the society, and people had new needs for understanding such things as interpersonal communication, organizational communication, political communication, mass communication, nonverbal communication, health communication, and intercultural communication—none of which had much to do with public speaking.

Our scholars responded to these needs, and continue to do so. But our pedagogy did not follow our scholarship. To this day, in most of our institutions the way students gain access to the content of the discipline is by passing through prerequisite—and sometimes required—basic courses which focus on oral performance skills. While the analogy is not perfect, this is something like Psychology requiring a performance course in therapeutic techniques prior to being introduced to the content of psychology—or the medical profession requiring a performance course in surgical techniques prior to being introduced to basic human anatomy.

It should not be a surprise to learn, as we do from several surveys that have been reported in our field, that the *only* course taken in our field by the overwhelming majority of students in most of our colleges and universities is a basic course in public speaking or an oral performance fundamentals course. This is the only picture of our field these students have, they find it of minimal value to them (or strongly aversive if they are communication apprehensives), and they want no more of it—ever. They can't get to the "good stuff" because they must take the performance course first, and/or they don't even find out that there is "good stuff" to be had in other courses.

Teaching performance courses to the cultural elite served us well as a field for the more than the first half of this century. We should continue to make such courses available to those students who want them and can benefit from them. But if we are to compete in the academic marketplace and attain and maintain a position of centrality in our colleges and universities, we must move these courses to the margin and bring the solid content of our discipline to central prominence. Instead of

requiring a public speaking course prior to allowing the student to study basic rhetorical theory and/or the social scientific data related to persuasion, we need to turn that system around. We need to require that the student obtain a basic understanding of rhetorical and/or communication theory before being allowed to enroll in a performance course in public speaking.

My argument for Communication as a Content Discipline rests in part on my belief that becoming an effective communicator in today's society is far more dependent on what one understands about how and why effective communication occurs than on specific oral presentational skills. I am convinced that the only reason many of us cling to presentation as a core is because we were born with certain talents in this area and our academic self-esteem is riding on the alleged value of what we happen to be good at! But let's face it, the mind is far more important to effective communication than the larynx—although both are of importance in the larger scheme of things.

Beyond that, the goal of the entire instructional program in communication does not necessarily need to be directed toward making students more effective communicators. *Understanding* communication, like understanding history, psychology, or chemistry, does not necessarily have to lead to *doing* communication (or history, psychology, chemistry). This is a problematic orientation that we have inherited from grandparent Speech. The speech field has always claimed to be most concerned with *application.* There is absolutely nothing wrong with teaching students how to apply the knowledge about communication which we share with them. Unfortunately, the narrow and extremely limited application of our field's knowledge to the marginalized context of public speaking cannot be at the cutting edge of a discipline. The generation of knowledge must take that position. Producing students who have a solid understanding of what is known about communication and are challenged by the questions remaining to be pursued is the proper central focus of communication education. This is not accomplished in oral performance classes.

In addition, and at least equally as important, to be known for our performance classes is to be known as "skill providers." In today's systems of higher education, such a reputation will place us at a third-rate level in the system—one which is not seen as particularly important and certainly not central to the intellectual functioning of a quality institution of higher learning.

If we do not move the content of our discipline to the center of communication education, our discipline will be considered increasingly marginal in an area of shrinking budgets. The question of what content should be included, of course, is a difficult one. Not all of us necessarily would agree on everything to include, and that issue is an important one which goes beyond the scope of my remarks today. My suggestions would probably be obvious to those who have read my papers and books over the years, but I hardly expect that everyone hearing (or reading) these remarks would be in agreement with me. It is not immediately essential that we settle on one narrow definition of communication content and all teach that content as our basic course, although that is a direction toward which I think we should move with due haste.

It is time that our professional associations work to achieve disciplinary consensus on the nature of a content course (or courses) which can gradually supplant oral performance courses as the entree for students to our field. We must resist those both from within and without who sing the siren's song of public speaking or oral fundamentals as the foundational course in our field. Oral performance courses are the "Model T" of courses in communication. It was a fine car for its day, but hardly what we need for the twenty-first century! We have a very large Lexus hiding in our garage. It is time to polish it up and drive it with pride!

On Nets, Webs, Scaffolds, and Tightropes: Changing Conceptions of Instructional Communication in the Postinformation Age

Jo Sprague
San Jose State University

The language we speak is inherently and profoundly metaphorical. There are some metaphors people choose quite consciously and rhetorically. In selecting "Taking the Helm" as the theme for this convention, Judith Trent offered NCA members a template to think about the ways they can seize initiative and move forward toward their goals. She also, of course, unleashed the tidal wave of nautical terms that flood the convention program. My title is loaded with metaphors which I chose to help me make certain points. There are other less conscious kinds of metaphors, more deeply embedded in our speech and perhaps more revealing of one's taken-for-granted cultural assumptions. What startled me as I developed this presentation was the root metaphor that began to emerge. I, who so often bemoan the colonization of business into every aspect of life, seemed to be developing an argument based on a notion from marketing: namely that those of us committed to the study of instructional communication need to define and publicize our area's distinctive niche!

In its approximately quarter century of existence our subdiscipline has not fully differentiated *instructional* communication from all other kinds of communication. Nor have we really explained how instructional *communication* differs from all other aspects of instruction. Figuring, quite reasonably for the most part, that teachers and students are persons, researchers have drawn variables out of interpersonal communication theory to make up the corpus of instructional communication research. Textbooks on communication in the classroom similarly borrow the best advice from interpersonal communication and public speaking and small group communication and offer applications for teachers. At the same time, rather than being fully communication based, we have tended toward rather diffuse thinking about good teaching in general, pulling in principles from educational psychology or instructional design. If we can tease out the insights from the best of our research and practice so far and relate those to the challenges of a postinformation age, we will make important contributions to both education and communication. To develop this thesis I will explain what I mean by a postinformation age and then assess four possible metaphors for instructional communication in a time of such radical social and intellectual change.

EDUCATION IN A POSTINFORMATION AGE

I use the term postinformation to stress a couple of important distinctions. First, there is no defensible way to argue that we are now coming into the information age. We have been in the information age for nearly half a century. The term first appeared, as far as I have been able to determine, in the late fifties. Economically, some date our move to being an information society, in contrast to earlier agrarian, industrial, and service societies, to about 1968 at which point more than half of the GNP was generated, not by the movement of goods and services, but by the exchange and transfer of symbolic data, either words or numbers. In our narrower academic history, Shannon and Weaver's classic work came out in 1949 and by the 60s our theories featured concepts like encoding, decoding, transmission, reception, noise, fidelity, and channel overload that persist in popular usage and in many of our textbooks. If we accept the classic definition of information as reduction of uncertainty, then the mere presence of faster and wider access to data does not mean that we have more information. We may actually have less. The glut of data available and the speed with which it can be retrieved solves some problems and creates others. The challenges of the postinformation age center on issues that are not new to us—issues of how best to select, organize, interpret, evaluate, and use all the data now available.

I also choose the term postinformation to refer to a broader transformation of academic communication studies that is described by Deetz (1995). What he calls an information perspective on communication is one in which "people on the street as well as researchers think about human interaction in terms of message transmission and expression" (p. 101). In both instances the reified message is assumed to be pre-formed, stable, existing in one communicator and needing to be gotten across to another. The information approach is also control oriented, seeking out strategic ways for some communicators to use information to gain or hold control over others. Deetz contrasts the informational perspective to a communication perspective that treats knowledge as constitutive of reality rather than reflective of it and strives toward the codetermination of decisions through negotiation and consensus. This conceptualization addresses the two central topics raised by communication theory in recent decades: issues of meaning and issues of power. In a postinformation age, meaning is seen as socially created, emergent, contextual, and highly contestable. Power is now understood as symbolically produced and reproduced in an ongoing struggle over meaning.

Four Metaphors for Instructional Communication

The various metaphors we use in talking about our interest in instructional communication reveal the tensions between what I have outlined as an information perspective and a postinformation or com-

munication perspective. They also offer images that differ in their ability to capture the uniqueness of instructional communication.

Nets, an information transmission perspective. When instructional communication stresses the information transmission dimensions of education, we hearken back to the early days of network analysis that tallied who talked to whom, how often, about what general topics. In educational terms, teaching entails sending information through a conduit. This sort of thinking might, for instance, celebrate distance learning primarily on the grounds of how many linkages are established so that students can "get information" from a teacher. I heard a professor who had started to utilize e-mail as a course supplement enthusiastically report that communication with students increased by 150%. It turned out, of course, that this had been calculated comparing the number of e-mail contacts to previous office hour visits. There was no qualitative sense of the content of the increased contacts, but upon questioning, this professor admitted than many of them dealt with simple "informational" questions like: "will chapter 7 be on the test?," or "what day is our next paper due?" Now, my point here is not to deny the value of these informational supplements to instruction, but to note that our word "communication" is being used in the most static and simplistic sense of a contact.

If we get into the game of being the quickest or most entertaining or most current source of information transmission, we will lose that game. That is no longer our market niche. In the ancient and medieval world universities were, truly, the depositories of knowledge. Scholars gathered there to conduct their studies and scribes spent lifetimes copying manuscripts. Long after the invention of printing, universities remained the generators of a great deal of knowledge and schools transmitted that knowledge to students. Even then, nearly every educational philosopher minimized the informational aspect of education. They, along with students themselves, placed the power of education less in what was learned than in the transformations that occurred.

These pragmatic reminders of the limits of an information transmission metaphor of instructional communication coincide with the intellectual trends already referred to: 1) the move from an epistemological to an ontological view of language, 2) the shift from psychological/individualistic to social/communal understandings of communication, 3) the redefinition of knowledge as reproductive of social power relations rather than reflective of reality, and thus 4) a rejection of information as ethically and politically neutral and a critical stance toward information as partial and interest-laden.

We need to be vigilant in keeping the net metaphors in check and resist the common usage of information as synonym for knowledge, wisdom, and meaning. I also advocate keeping our sense of perspective about just what the new multimedia and information technologies really do and do not make possible. We have had televised teaching and individualized programmed learning for decades, and we know something about their strengths and weaknesses as they now expand to more attractive and accessible forms. First, let us not use the word *interactive* to describe any form of instructional activity that merely lets learners choose from a menu or cycle back through options to relearn. With whom is a student interacting? Some anonymous programmer or instructional designer from another time and place? Why then is not a textbook interactive?

In assessing educational technologies, which we should certainly embrace and use in many cases, we also need to be alert to what I call the Stone Soup phenomenon in educational technology. Remember the fable about the visitor who came to town with the magic stone and promised the townspeople that he would make the most delicious soup they had ever tasted? He assembled them around the pot of water, added the magic stone, and then began to ask: Does anyone have a few carrots? Could you bring me some onions? Is there a little meat we could add to the pot? Who has some seasonings? The story ends with everyone enjoying a wonderful meal as the well-fed visitor surreptitiously slips the stone out of the soup and leaves town. When I read about many of the successes of distance education and digital classrooms, I learn that teachers first had to reconceptualize their classes from teacher-centered to student-centered learning, to build in roles for team teachers and tutors, to write engaging study questions, to discover how to use cooperative learning activities and out-of-class study groups, to make themselves much more accessible to students for interaction (Allen, 1996). These are wonderful changes, many of them based in sound principles of instructional communication, but like the stone in the soup, the technology is extraneous to the outcomes for which it somehow is receiving credit. If technology is a catalyst to innovate, or at least to try well-tested ideas that have been previously resisted, then it is valuable. But we can keep our own heads and vocabularies clear about what aspects of instruction really generate the value.

Webs, a relational perspective.   Another prominent metaphor for instructional communication foregrounds relationship bonds rather than information links. In this view as it is often played out, learning occurs not by getting information but by contact with others who form a web of interpersonal relationships. Like the information model, this metaphor taps into some important dimensions of education. People do learn from being with teachers and peers. My concern again is that we have not developed this approach in a way that differentiates instructional communication sufficiently from enlightened human relations in general. We have attempted to isolate certain qualities teachers have that are helpful to student learning. If I am a warm approachable person or if I typically do certain relationship-building things like standing close to students or using self-disclosure then this will either lead to compliance from students or feelings of affinity toward me and my subject matter or perhaps even enhanced learning. The difficulty with this relational web metaphor is that education is conceptualized as a series of dyadic bonds that are either present or absent. Instructional communication does not really enter into it except as attributional behavior on the part of a receiver or image management on the part of a sender. All of this research and teacher training work still falls within the definition Deetz used for an informational approach. That is, one person tries to express certain qualities (for example warmth) which if perceived as hoped, have the strategic effect of eliciting a certain response in the learner.

Here in California when our governor decided to reduce class size by hiring thousands of teachers, uncredentialed if necessary, he targeted retired military personnel as potential teachers. Their qualification was their presumed ability to maintain order and discipline in the classroom. At another extreme, those of us who work with elementary teacher candidates know of the all-too-common answer to the question "why do you want be a teacher?": "I just love children." Now both loving students and being able to maintain classroom control are important relational elements of education. But are they central to instructional communication? Does our field's most significant educational contribution really lie in teaching teachers how to love children (or appear to) or even how to maintain order? It seems that these are more general tasks of education. There are fine educational studies on the traits and characteristics of good teachers and there is work in psychology dealing with teacher temperament and personality. Our distinctive perspective, it seems to me, attends to the actual communication in real time and in context that occurs once a teacher has established a pleasant relationship with students and order in the classroom. When the intellectual work of teaching begins, what kind of talk occurs?

Scaffolds, an assisted performance perspective. The metaphor of the scaffold, drawn from the work of Vygotsky (1986/1962), calls forth some important characteristics of instructional communication. Scaffolds themselves are supportive, functional, and temporary. They are put up hastily, almost improvisationally, and dismantled as soon as they have done their job. Scaffold building is cumulative and incremental. Vygotsky and his followers define teaching as assisting learning and maintain that teaching is useless unless it occurs

in a Zone of Proximal Development. At any given point, there is a range of tasks that a person can perform with assistance but cannot perform without assistance. Within that range, a teacher or an advanced peer constructs props that allow for successful achievement of the task and then gradually removes the scaffolding. The essence of the teaching–learning encounter is in joint performance. The teacher literally *acts with* the learner in artfully calibrated ways. Instructional assistance generally takes the form of communication. While listening closely to identify what learners can and cannot do alone, teachers ask leading and focusing questions, pose alternatives and give verbal cues to help students achieve more than they could without help. Talk is central to this approach because the learning process itself is explained in terms of the movement from external to inner speech. The voice of the teacher is internalized and later becomes part of the learner's thought process.

This metaphor offers a view of instructional communication that differentiates instructional talk from other kinds of talk and from other instructional activities teachers engage in such as classroom management, relationship building, or thinking about instructional design. Notice that this view of instruction makes teaching an active intellectual process that is created and performed in each unique situation. The teacher is not providing information or displaying personality but is focusing intensely and analytically on each learner and making thoughtful decisions from moment to moment. This kind of de-centered attention is the second greatest gift we have to give others.

Tightropes, a dialogic perspective. The final metaphor I offer for instructional communication is meant to draw forth those elements of communication that are most artful and risky. Stepping onto a tightrope is making an existential commitment. It requires trust, courage, and minute rebalancings from second to second. I feel somewhat breathless thinking about those moments when teachers leave certainty and strategy back on the platform and step out on that wire. The greatest gift teachers have to give is themselves.

When a teacher enters into genuine learning dialogues this goes beyond just transmitting, relating, or even helping. If instructional communication is defined as a form of dialogue, it contrasts radically to the informational perspective outlined by Deetz. Education so conceived makes knowledge itself problematic. This allows the unfolding communication to shape the events and the participants, and thus power is inherently codetermined. Dialogic education offers the most promising definitive niche for instructional communication work I believe, not because most of the theory has been written by our scholars; it has not. It is our special domain because dialogue at heart is not only a communicative act, but a contextual, contingent, performed, embodied, and oral act. And though we have sometimes rejected some of these aspects of our discipline, the combination of them is still what distinguishes us.

It is particularly important that we in instructional communication reclaim the spoken word. There may be good reasons for deleting Speech from our association's name, but there is absolutely no justification for denying orality in our intellectual heritage. We really need to hear the scholars in and out of our field who are telling us that the aural/oral mode has developed our humanness and our consciousness and that face-to-face groups present to each other in time and space have allowed us to sustain civil societies. Unless we come to terms with the role of orality in our development as a species, we will continue to underestimate the role of orality in the development of children and youth. Once a culture has been established to a point through spoken language, it can go on to design alphabets and computers. But as Frank Dance (1995) has been telling us for years, spoken language is the staging area for all other forms of communication. Writing and electronic media are not just co-equal forms of communication; they are thoroughly permeated with the residue of orality.

A model of dialogue rather than information exchange requires physical presence and interactive talk to ensure accountability of the participants. There are deep cultural and social reasons that we form communities with continuity of time and place. Without accountability to each other how can ethical and civil relationships be practiced and learned? Again, while always acknowledging that textbooks, and study groups, and tutors, and distance learning, and interactive computer programs, and e-mail chat rooms all have interesting roles to play in education, we can say without reservation that the heart of educational experience should remain in the face-to-face learning community where students can experience dialogue with a skilled teacher and with each other.

I have argued that we are now in a postinformation age that demands new ways of thinking about communication and a crisper articulation of the uniqueness of instructional communication. *Instructional* communication is unique among types of communication because of it is a kind of talk that features active intellectual co-performance in an authentic dialogic between teachers and learners. Instructional *communication* is unique among approaches to instruction because the pivotal issues of meaning and power are dealt with in ways that reflect the socially co-constructed and contested nature of the knowledge on which schools are based. Metaphorically, we have become ensnared in nets and webs when we might better be building scaffolds and daring to venture out on tightropes.

REFERENCES

Allen, L. R. (1996, March/April). *An instructional epiphany. Change,* 49–54.

Dance, F. E. (1995, November). *The Digital Noetic.* Paper presented at the annual meeting of the Speech Communication Association, San Antonio.

Deetz, S. (1995). *Transforming communication, Transforming business.* Cresskill, NJ: Hampton Press.

Vygotsky, L. (1986). *Thought and language.* A. Kozulin (Trans.), Cambridge, The MIT Press. (Original work published in 1962).

Communication Education's Integrative Role: Providing an Intersection for Multiple Constituencies

Douglas M. Trank
University of Iowa

Part of the intrigue of participating in this "At the Helm" series of presentations is to discover the perspectives from which our colleagues approach this opportunity. I have no doubt that many will seize this invitation to identify their perceptions of our destination and to provide the directions for a safe and profitable journey. Others will skirt the responsibility and dream of what might be, giving only hints of our destination or our route. Others, like me, will be more skeptical of attempting such a journey, skeptical of either forecasting our destiny or prescribing the navigational decisions for such a diverse group of scholars and teachers.

In this brief personal essay, I want to look at a few relevant aspects of our relatively short history as a professional organization, glance at similar questions and concerns in other professional organizations, and ask some questions about what we might profitably do as a discipline. Finally, I will offer my suggestion concerning what we might consider while "at the helm," one which may well be out of step with other essays in this collection. But, given the opportunity to be "at the helm in communication education," I cannot resist the challenge.

Concern for the centrality, direction, and purpose for our discipline has generated an on-going discussion since the modern beginning of our professional history. Communication education has, in the past, provided a locus for our discipline. A small group of individuals formed *The National Association of Teachers of Speech* 80 years ago in an attempt to establish a professional organization for those who were interested in teaching and researching issues more directly related to oral communication. We left our previous professional

affiliation because we did not want to be simply thought of or referred to as English teachers or teachers of literature. We thought we had much more to offer our students and the academic world. Merely leaving the "English" identification and forming a new organization did not, however, answer all our questions nor identify us adequately for ourselves or for our colleagues in other disciplines. We have spent these past eight decades searching for common ground. Thus far, that search has failed to provide answers that adequately plot our destination, our purpose, our identity, or our common goals. The controversy over our quest for the *raison d'être* and the central core of our discipline began at the first convention and has continued nearly unabated since that time.

In a rather prophetic statement at the first national convention of *The National Association of Teachers of Speech,* President J. M. O'Neill (1915) noted that "I feel confident that we shall be spared the blight of unanimity of opinion for some time to come." He most certainly was not wrong. A primary issue for annual discussion in the Forum in the early issues of the *Quarterly Journal of Speech* concerned who we were and what our focus ought to be. This discussion took on added importance during the decade of the 1950s as the organization debated and finally adopted the *Speech Association of America* as its official new name.

At one of the national conventions during this period of time, a panel of distinguished colleagues attempted to define "speech." A. Craig Baird claimed it was rhetoric. Wayland Parrish, suspicious of that word "communication," claimed that we needed to go back to the "elocution movement" to find our center. Henry Eubank pleaded the fifth amendment and refused to participate in the discussion. It seems that we have been searching for that center that defines us for the entirety of our professional existence. We have changed the name of our national organization three times and have plans to do so again.* Similar heated discussions and debates took place as we changed our association's name to the *Speech Communication Association.* Interestingly, the current debate concerning yet another name change no longer centers on whether we can define "speech," but rather on whether "speech" even belongs in our title. As we once again search for a name that unites us, Gaudino (1996) notes that "previous [recent] efforts to change our name may have failed not because of a desire to keep the present name but because there is disagreement concerning what the new name should be" (p. 3). Could it be that although we cannot agree on who we want to be, we do know who we do not want to be? As other members of this panel have mentioned, we suffer from an "identity crisis" as a professional organization. Ironically, the strategic plan for our organization adopted at the November 1996 convention fails to define "speech," "communication," or "speech communication."

This constant search for common ground has often found its way into our convention themes. In 1977, Jane Blankenship gave us "Anatomy of Purpose: A Center Which Holds" as a convention theme because of her "concern with our lack of a commonly agreed upon central focus or perhaps even central foci." One of her purposes for that convention was to "define and articulate that center." A number of conventions since that time have had themes that urged us to define a national view of communication, to provide a focus, and locate our common ground. To a certain extent, this year's theme is asking the same questions. "Taking the Helm" implies that we have some sort of destination, that we have the ability to steer the organization toward that goal, and that we have individuals capable of guiding us to our agreed upon destination.

Lest we become too critical of our professional search for an identity, we should note that other disciplines continually face similar problems. A comprehensive worldwide examination of math and science teaching recently concluded, "There is no one at the helm of U.S. mathematics and science education. In truth, there is no one helm." It goes on to claim that "no single coherent vision of how to educate today's children dominates U.S. educational practice" and that instruction in our schools is "a mile wide and an inch deep" (*Los Angeles Times,* October 21, 1996). I mention this report not only because the word "helm" fits so well into this convention theme, but to emphasize that this search for a focus or center is not unique to our discipline. As disciplines expand to respond to the knowledge explosion common to all of us, as scholars narrow their research programs and interests in order to achieve "expert" status for promotion and tenure, and as more cross-disciplinary material finds it way into our journals, the more difficult locating and articulating that "center" becomes. This phenomenon is clearly not unique to our discipline.

Within our discipline, it is certainly not unique to the *National Communication Association.* Ellen Wartella made three claims about our discipline in her 1994 *International Communication Association* presidential address:

> First, as communication researchers we lack a clear vision about who we are, which is manifested in a fractured set of subfields that not only know little about each other but whose practitioners seem more intent on the internal debates of our field than our public responsibility as scholars of an increasingly important topic. Second, we have little visible presence as public intellectuals and have done little to enhance that presence. Third, we offer an inchoate curriculum for communication study, particularly on the undergraduate level. This lack of coherence also contributes to our lack of public presence (p. 55).

This particular part of the "helm series" and my assignment focus on *communication education.* Those of us interested in this "part of the world" have not been immune from these discussions and the confusion over names and identities. We changed the name of *The Speech Teacher* to

Communication Education. The official audience for the journal changed from elementary and high school teachers to college and university teachers. In fact, issues that deal with suggestions for classroom teachers are no longer welcome in the journal, but are referred to the *Speech Communication Teacher.*

More than any other subfield within the speech communication discipline, however, this area may be able to provide a central focus for teaching/learning regardless of the specific area of interest. This is where our discipline began. Nearly every article in the earliest issues of the *Quarterly Journal of Speech* dealt with teaching some aspect of our discipline. Even when *The Speech Teacher* was added as the third journal for NCA in 1950, the emphasis on "teachers" remained for our other two journals. The minutes of the executive committee at the 1950 convention stated that *The Speech Teacher* was "designed primarily for elementary and secondary school teachers of Speech." "*QJS* and *SM* are understood to reach college and university teachers of undergraduate and graduate Speech courses." (Forum, p. 61.) All three journals have obviously evolved considerably in the past 35 years. In addition, NCA has added several other journals to service the emerging scholarly interests of our colleagues.

As public interest intensifies from projects like "A Nation at Risk" and "Goals 2000," we may be forced to return to a significant focus on our collective interests with curriculum and the results of our instruction. Our public wants to know what we are teaching, why we are teaching it, how it fits into a liberal education, and how we know that we are accomplishing our goals. This public criticism may, in fact, force an increased interest in education and instruction across our discipline. Perhaps it is here that we might find one of the "helms." The journals of our discipline (or any discipline) provide the mirrors by which we see ourselves, by which we identify ourselves, and by which the broader academic community identifies us. We have seen *Communication Education* move toward a broader inclusion of issues within our discipline as well as into the arena of instructional communication across all disciplines. In recent issues, feminist education, performance studies, the information highway, and a variety of other topics have received attention.

It is this approach and these interests, more than any other, that may allow communication education to provide some leadership within the broader discipline. As Goals 2000 and other state and federal programs become more of a reality within our institutions, we will be required to respond to repeated calls for accountability for our curriculum and for the outcomes of our instruction, our programs, and for the overall quality of the undergraduate education we provide. All colleagues across our discipline will be faced with the same issues, regardless of their scholarly and teaching interests. By providing a forum for discussion and leadership concerning issues related to curriculum and instruction, communication education may be in a position to provide leadership at the helm of our discipline.

As I indicated in the introduction to this essay, however, I am a bit skeptical about assuming the helm—or in allowing anyone else to assume it if we are all on the same ship. Like psychology, I think we are not a single discipline. I believe we are many disciplines. Even if the flood comes, I do not believe we should all get on the same ship. I do not want to do scholarship or teach in film theory or theater or single parent communication relationships or communication apprehension or any number of other areas of this discipline that I find interesting but not personally rewarding in terms of my own work. Most of my colleagues have not set foot inside a public school since they graduated and have no plans to do so—certainly not as a place for teaching or scholarship. We have an enormously broad spectrum of scholarly and academic interests.

Perhaps our discipline's lifelong search for a "center that holds," for a "central focus," for a definition that unites us, for a name that includes all of us equally and excludes none of us, for a vision that provides a mutually acceptable "national view of communication" is essentially a waste of our time. Certainly, hundreds of former and current colleagues have wrestled with these issues for years without successful resolution. Perhaps, in keeping with the metaphor for this convention, it is better to view ourselves as members of an armada. We have many ships representing the discipline. Like any armada, those ships have a wide variety of functions, goals, and objectives. They move at different speeds, are of many different sizes, and have different strengths and weaknesses. Over the years, the ships evolve to become stronger and more efficient at what they have been designed to accomplish. Different individuals take the helm of each ship, sometimes steering a straight course, other times veering off in both interesting and sometimes dangerous courses.

We are not a single discipline and there is not a single ship. We are many disciplines and there are several ships and several helms. Many of us choose different ships and different disciplines during our careers. Perhaps the most important thing we can do is to chart a general course—such as the better understanding of human communication—and discover if everyone wants to follow that course. Many former colleagues, notably in speech pathology and audiology and theater, have chosen completely different courses. For me,

then, the ultimate goal of all persons at the helms of these many ships is to avoid running into and sinking each other. Sinking another ship most often results in damage to both vessels. It is a big ocean with much we do not yet know or understand. As I hope most of us would agree, it is an exciting voyage and one I do not want to miss.

REFERENCES

American math and science instruction called superficial. (1996, October 21). *Los Angeles Times,* p. C2.

Blankenship, J. (1977). Anatomy of purpose: A center which holds. *1977 Convention Program.* Speech Communication Association.

Forum. (1955). *Quarterly Journal of Speech,* XLI, 61.

Gaudino, J.L. (1996, September). SCA looks toward new strategic plan, internet services, name change, and convention. *Spectra, 32,* 3.

Wartella E. (1994). Challenge to the profession. *Communication Education, 43,* pp. 54–62.

EDITOR'S NOTE:

In March 1997, the membership of the Speech Communication Association voted to change the organization's name to the National Communication Association.

If Communication Matters So Much, Why Don't We Get the Attention We Deserve?

John A. Daly
University of Texas

We are a diverse discipline—our professional interests are broad and our concerns are many. Yet one belief we all hold in common is that communication is central to people's lives. Communication counts! We know the importance of communication. And knowing how important communication is makes us want to teach it to others. The critical centrality of what we teach and study underlies why we entered this discipline and why we stay in it.

Yet all too often we find people outside our field do not share this view. When you mention the discipline some still say "What's that?" Others, after politely asking about what we do, begin to glaze over as we explain our interests more deeply. Most people, in their minds, if not aloud, wonder why we study something so "obvious." While they seldom disagree openly and directly with the proposition that communication is important, they often fail to really "buy" the idea that what we address is fundamental. The unwillingness of people to truly value what we do is reflected in the decisions of policy-makers when it comes to communication. We often fail to garner the attention and respect we deserve from decision-makers as they determine where to put money (in funding agencies), what to emphasize (in workplace settings as well as in education), and what to count as substantive (in our academic worlds).

In this brief chapter I suggest first that what we study and teach is critically important. Then I discuss some reasons I think communication is not often considered central to many educational, organizational, or policy agendas.[1]

DOES COMMUNICATION MATTER?

There is no question that empirically, communication matters. In reviewing the literature on the importance of communication to every person and every organization one can place hundreds of studies in three major categories: (1) impressionistic studies of the value of communication, (2) empirical studies of communication skills and requirements, and (3) projects that link communication to important outcomes. All three clusters offer resounding support for the notion that communication matters.

Impressionistic studies of the importance of communication

In this category you find scholars answering the question "how important do people think communication is in their life and in the lives of others?" Open any popular magazine that focuses on relationships, business success, or individual skills and you will find the answer. Communication is seen as vital. These anecdotal descriptions are buttressed by a host of empirical studies that highlight the people's judgments of the importance of communication.

In a review I conducted a few years ago (Daly, 1994) I examined many studies that rank order the importance of communication. In some of these studies, communication was ranked along with a variety of others skills or issues. For instance, Curtis, Winsor, and Stephans (1989) asked more than 400 personnel managers to indicate the relative importance of various skills in obtaining a position and successfully performing in that position. Not surprisingly, communication skills were at the top of the list. In the mid-seventies, a national survey research group, The Bruskin Associates, found that public speaking anxiety was the biggest fear of the American population. Most recently, in a survey published in *USA Today* (Nov. 21, 1996) during our national convention, interpersonal communication skills were listed as one of the top five training initiatives of corporate America. These are only three of many studies to confirm that when people identify the critical competencies required in today's competitive world, communication appears, if not as the most important, then as one of the most important. Besides investigations that compare communication to other important job tasks (e.g., time management, task-focus), many other studies probe the relative importance of various communication skills (e.g., contrasting listening to presentations). These include projects that ask business executives, teachers, and "everyday" citizens what sorts of social or communicative skills are critical for people to exhibit.

Empirical measures of communication skills and requirements

In this category you find investigators focusing on the question "How much and how well do people communicate?" One strand of research on this topic examines just how much time individuals spend communicating. Early projects by Rankin (1928), Klemmer and Synder (1972), and others consistently offered empirical validation for the presumption that people spend a good portion of their daily lives communicating. Luthens, Hodgetts, and Rosenkrantz (1988) found that effective managers spend much of their workday speaking and listening. And the economist, D. McCloskey, in her many writings (e.g., 1994) has taken the role of communication in our society to an even broader level suggesting that a substantial portion of our economy is dependent upon communication.

In addition to studies highlighting communication's central role in our lives, our jobs, and our nation, there are a number of investigations under the broad rubric of DACUM[2] (Englebert & Wynn, 1995) that have identified very specific communication requirements for a variety of jobs. In these projects, workers such as secretaries, nurses, architects, and educators describe, in-depth, the specific behaviors required for the successful execution of key tasks in their occupations. Across a wide variety of jobs, communication skills are found to be paramount.

Given its centrality to individuals' lives, you would expect that people do well at communicating. Yet the little empirical evidence we have suggests this is a poor assumption [note a recent book by Shachtman (1995)]. Vangelist and Daly (1989), using national survey data drawn from Americans aged 18 to 24, discovered that many, many participants failed to accomplish even the most basic of communication tasks. For example, upwards of 25% were incapable of giving clear and accurate directions to a fire department about how to get to their homes. Similarly, when studies ask people what bothers them in various settings, poor communication is often at the top of the list. A recent study by the American Hospital Association (*Wall Street Journal,* January 28, 1997), found that communication-related problems (e.g., emotional support, information, and education) topped Americans' concerns about hospital care—far exceeding, by the way, physical comfort.

Communication affects important social and personal outcomes

In this cluster you have projects scrutinizing the relationship of communication to important outcomes. The underlying proposition is that people who are poor at communication fare less well in work, at home, and in school than others more skilled in communication.

Much empirical research conducted by communication scholars in the last few decades supports this proposition. The list of correlates is far too extensive for this brief chapter so let me offer just a few strands of research:

Communication apprehension. Literally hundreds of studies link people's anxieties about communication to a wide assortment of variables. For example, greater anxiety about communicating is tied to less success in school, less interpersonal effectiveness in groups, and less advancement into many prestigious organizational positions.

Communication-related personality variables. Extensive work on communication-related personality variables such as argumentativeness, rhetorical sensitivity, cognitive complexity, communicator style, loneliness, interaction involvement, conversational sensitivity, and many others shows that people's predispositions about various sorts of communication activities have significant personal, social, and organizational consequences.

Conflict. Communication scholarship demonstrates that the ways people engage in verbal conflict directly affect individuals' satisfaction and stability in marriages, the quality of their workplaces, the political and legal environments they live within, and the climate of their families.

Classroom performance. Numerous studies of teacher immediacy, classroom questioning patterns, compliance gaining by teachers, and other related topics tie communication to important educational outcomes such as learning by students.

Interpersonal relations. Investigations of topics such as effective criticism, comforting skills, self-disclosure, affinity seeking and maintenance behaviors, listening, social support, defensiveness, nonverbal communication, assertiveness, and deception all suggest that communication plays a central role in creating and maintaining positive interpersonal relationships.

Influence and persuasion. We have clear evidence that there are more and less successful means for persuading others in public settings, meetings, and interpersonal encounters. In applying various theories of persuasion, recommending

different methods for compliance gaining, or suggesting specific influence tactics (e.g., evidence, fear appeals, credibility), our research clearly proves the relevance of communication scholarship to that most ancient of skills—persuading others.

Organizational contexts. Projects that examine topics such as interviewing success, upward and downward influence in organizations, small group performance, communication receptivity, negotiation effectiveness, and both informal and formal networks point to the critical role of communication in work settings.

WHY DON'T WE GET THE ATTENTION WE DESERVE?

The evidence is clear: Communication matters. So why don't we get the attention from policymakers, campus leaders, and the public that this importance merits? Let me offer a few hypotheses.

We are too obvious

Perhaps communication is too obvious to people. Like the proverbial fish never knowing it is in water until pulled out, people are seldom aware of their communication milieu. Traveling overseas teaches us that even when we think we know another language, we actually know far less than we thought. Communication surrounds us. As a consequence, unless we are pulled out of our comfortable communication world, we may not appreciate how important it is to us. Think of times when you have said something you wish you had not said; when you were at a loss for words to express a deep-felt emotion. In those cases, the importance of communication becomes apparent. This may be why so many students choose to study in our discipline after experiencing their first communication course. That course often makes them aware, for the first time, how central communication is to their lives and how inadequate their skills are when faced with tough communication challenges.

We are poor at marketing our discipline

For experts who are interested in communication we have not the best job communicating, to our various publics, how central we are. Academic disciplines today must take a proactive role in making their case to the world. We cannot assume that people automatically know and appreciate what we do. How do academic units do this? Often, they use the "great person" approach. Consider the field of astronomy and the genius of Carl Sagan in opening the discipline to so many others; consider the place of Stephen Gould in evolutionary biology; consider the value of Steven Hawking for certain realms of physics, or Warren Bennis or Michael Porter for business, or E. D. Hirsch in English. Our discipline needs more public scholars.

We are unwilling to sacrifice complexity for clarity

One of the toughest dilemmas faced in any academic field is that as scholarly knowledge of a topic become greater, with concomitantly greater complexity, the ability to clearly explain the topic to people not deeply conversant with the discipline becomes ever more difficult. Interest wanes quickly when we answer any question with a preface of "Well, it depends…" We need to be willing to take risks, simplifying complexities in ways that impart key information while leaving tangential material for more scholarly exchange. Think of the field of economics where public economists in government and business are daily forced to make forecasts and offer opinions in one or two sentences. Underlying those brief comments are vast complexities left to their academic journals.

We also need to value our expertise more. There are many people with far less expertise than ours preaching to the public about communication. We need to be more willing to take risks with our knowledge. Experts, because of their background and wisdom, should be willing to proffer informed opinions about topics related to their discipline even when there is little or no existing research on those topics. To always say, "That's a good question…We do not really have any research on that topic…" lets people less intellectually sophisticated about the topic take the public leadership role. Consider the vast amount of research we have on gender and communication. Scholars like Mulac, Wood, and others have spent years toiling to discover important relationships. Yet John Gray triumphs (with a close second going to scholar Tannen). Never underestimate the importance of being able to instantly and skillfully produce a pithy "sound-bite."

We have not yet discovered enough "interesting" phenomena

Murray Davis, a well-known sociologist, many years ago wrote a fascinating article entitled "That's interesting." In this article he probed what it is that makes a few investigations "interesting" in a reader's mind and most studies mundane and uninteresting. His conclusion was that "interesting" pieces were those that made or proved a counterintuitive claim. Most of our scholarship shows effects that are intuitively appealing. They validate people's "naive" beliefs. One way we might enhance of "marketability" is discovering and presenting some non-intuitive findings. For instance, might we make arguments that sometimes conflict is healthy, that often the best thing to do is be quiet, that listening is not always an important activity?

We have not had a crisis of communication

Many years ago, sociologist (and later Senator) Daniel Moynihan raised America's consciousness about poverty by creating a crisis mentality—if we don't do something about poverty, we will be haunted by it. Similarly, the publication of *A Nation at Risk* portrayed a country quickly moving toward an educational disaster. Efforts at educational reform proliferated soon after.

Most academic areas that develop a public reputation, to some degree, have gained that reputation because of a perceived crisis. Infectious medicine, to take one example, was a relatively underappreciated medical speciality for many years. The emergence of AIDS and other viral infections prompted a fresh interest in that discipline. In the last year, Americans have perceived a crisis in the quality of television children are watching. What a lucky break for one part of our discipline where scholars like Donnerstein and Wartella now hold forth in public media. I suspect not a day goes by where many, many people in America wonder about what is "known" about television and its effects. Every four years we enjoy (or suffer) a Presidential election. Scholars such as Jamieson interested in political communication have their day (or year) in the sun because of the perception, by the media, that expertise is needed.

We are not outcome-focused in our research

In much of our research and teaching the "so what" is missing. We, as scholars and instructors, rightfully emphasize the critical place of understanding processural elements involved in communication phenomena. But perhaps we fail too often to show how those elements lead to important personal or societal outcomes. As a consumer, I really care very little about the inner workings of a car engine. What I care about is that the car gets me there safely, quickly, and enjoyably. Car owners know their "so what" questions. Consumers of communication probably have similar "so what" concerns. Are we answering those "so what" questions? Do we even know what those questions are?

We lack a consensus on our "core"

If we had to sit down, as a discipline, and identify our core courses, our core knowledge claims, or core questions, what would they be? I suspect that each person reading this would come up with a somewhat different list. This heterogeneity of ideas is intellectually exciting but practically troublesome. If we, as teachers and scholars in the field, cannot lay claim to a core, how can we expect our various publics to understand what we profess? Try this exercise out—have ten people, each well established in the discipline, name five

key principles of human communication that they think every member of the public ought to know and understand. What do you think you would get? Unanimity? Not based on a small field exercise I completed. Indeed, the lack of overlap was striking. Certainly, you might say, that is the nature of a field as broad as ours. Then try narrowing this question to your individual area of study. I will bet you get the same results.

What this tells me is that we have some professional homework to do before we even opt for a greater public awareness of our discipline. We may have to agree on some basic principles, findings, questions, and the like. We may need to insist that students, no matter what school they attend, know some key concepts, understand some critical theories, and be able to engage in some desired behaviors.

This leads to a conversation I recently had with a friend of mine who is also a distinguished professor of mathematics. His daughter was majoring in our Department and he was at a loss when looking over her anticipated course work. His confusion lay in discovering that while students in mathematics experience a clear hierarchy of courses, students in communication seldom are faced with any hierarchy. In mathematics you take classes in sequence knowing that to be able to understand courses at an advanced level you will need to have taken the basic courses. In our discipline this is not an accepted practice. What is our hierarchy? And, if we cannot answer that question, what does that say about our field? Perhaps everything is equally difficult? Perhaps we are so gifted a group of teachers that we are able to explain any concept to any group of students. Or perhaps, we haven't done the hard work of thinking through our discipline.

We underestimate the value of the skills we teach

In many ways, our discipline blossomed in the world of the land-grant college. These colleges were founded with a focused mission: to teach average citizens ideas and skills that would allow them to succeed in a highly competitive world. And one critical skill that was identified, early on, as vitally important for success was the ability to communicate well. What was meant by communication was, in today's world, a relatively narrow collection of skill—making oral presentations. But while narrow, it is still important.

I worry sometimes that many of us have forgotten that a foundational element of our discipline is our capacity to teach people to speak clearly and effectively. It is the one thing we do that no other academic field even attempts to lay claim to in the intellectual marketplace. Yet we, as a discipline, spend relatively little time studying that most basic of skills. Look at our undergraduate texts in public speaking. If public speaking is a core foundational element of this discipline, you would expect to see those texts littered with research citations about presentations. But that isn't so. More broadly, we seem to pay little attention to the actual development of any communication skill. That may be a mistake.

Let's summarize. We have strong evidence that communication is vitally important. We also know that many people are not very good at communication. So why don't people pay as much attention as they should to what we study and teach? In this brief essay I suggest a variety of reasons and some potential ways of enhancing our reputation. What I am proposing is that our field might profit from a sustained marketing campaign. We are the discipline that studies that most central of human tasks—communication. In so many ways it is what makes us human. It provides our greatest happinesses and often our greatest sadnesses. It allows civilized society. It is something that should be valued more.

NOTES

1. In this chapter I focus primarily on non-mass communication related skills. This is not because mass communication is unimportant—for certainly, it is a major part of our society today—but because, compared with person-to-person communication, mass communication has already been accepted as societally very important.

2. DACUM stands for *Developing A CurriculUM*. It originated in Canada and has been used throughout the U.S. for many years. Its purpose is to identify the critical tasks and responsibilities performed by individuals in a particular job.

REFERENCES

Curtis, D., Winsor, J. & Stephens, R. (1989). National preferences in business and communication education. *Communication Education, 38,* 6–14.

Daly, J. (1994). Assessing speaking and listening: Preliminary considerations for a national assessment. In A. Greenwood (Ed.), *The national assessment of college student learning: Identification of the skills to be taught, learned, and assessed.* Washington D.C.: U.S. Department of Education.

Davis, M. (1971). That's interesting: Towards a phenomenology of sociology and a sociology of phenomenology. *Philosophy of Social Science, 1,* 309–344.

Englebert, I. & Wynn, D. (1995) DACUM: A national database justifying the study of speech communication. *Journal of the Association of Communication Administrators, 1,* 28–38.

Klemmer, E. & Synder, F. (1972). Measurement of time spent communicating. *Journal of Communication, 20,* 142–158.

Luthens, F., Hodgetts, R., & Rosenkrantz, S. (1988). *Real managers.* Cambridge: Ballinger.

McCloskey, D. (1994). *Knowledge and persuasion in economics.* Cambridge: Cambridge University Press.

Rankin, P. (1928). The importance of listening ability. *English Journal, 17,* 623–630.

Shachtman, T. (1995). *The inarticulate society.* NY: Free Press.

Vangelist, A. & Daly, J. (1989). Correlates of speaking skills in the United States: A national assessment. *Communication Education, 38,* 132–143.

CHAPTER 9

AT THE HELM
IN HEALTH COMMUNICATION

Introduction

Scott C. Ratzan
*Emerson College and
Tufts University School of Medicine*

A recent $1.1 million settlement reminds women who have had breast implants that they must decide by December 1996 to file a lawsuit individually or join thousands of others throughout the country who might be eligible to receive a part of the $4.25 billion class action settlement agreed to by manufacturers of the implants.

The settlement provides $1.2 billion for women claiming current implant-related illness and over $2 billion for apparently healthy women who might become ill in the next 30 years. The remaining $1 billion is earmarked for lawyers.

In the first case (in Massachusetts), a 66-year-old woman contended that silicone gel from the implants leaked out and caused her a host of illnesses ranging from fatigue and ringing ears to memory loss and chest pain. While this woman's symptoms are real and undeniable, many who have no implants also share similar ailments. The jury's "judgment" is among many nationwide based on weak scientific proof that implants can cause debilitating illnesses.

The challenge to seek justice and truth in courts of law is uniquely determined by a jury system in the United States. In other countries the decisions of who is to "blame" are done by a judge who hopefully makes the decision based on careful deliberation of scientific fact, valid evidence, and reasoned arguments. In civil cases in the United States—whether it is O. J. Simpson or breast implants—a jury renders a decision that is often based on emotion rather than reason. This leads to what Dr. Marcia Angell, Executive Editor of the *New England Journal of Medicine,* terms a "'never mind the facts' sympathy verdict for an appealing plaintiff who is taking on a rich corporation."

Dr. Angell's research on breast implants is highlighted in her book *Science on Trial.* She reminds us of well-documented studies at Harvard Medical School, the Mayo Clinic, and the University of Michigan, all of which concluded there was no increased risk with implants. Some of these studies included 90,000 nurses and eight years of monitoring.

However, scientific evidence did not stop lawyers who claimed their clients had been harmed by the implants as they filed over 20,000 cases.

This is not the first incident dealing with a misunderstanding of health issues—many other cases have great consequence. The Dalkon Shield, mad cow disease, electromagnetic fields, radon, and others have been based on real or alleged health hazards. Many studies on fat substitutes, beef, or heart medications are promoted just because they have made good stories to cover.

Unfortunately, information instantly becomes "factual" as many of us in turn repeat what we have heard or read.

However, it is difficult for most of us to find out more about **health.** Although there has been a fourfold increase in medically related news in the *New York Times* during the past two decades, we are all limited on where to find the best and most accurate information. We all do not read or have access to the 25,000 scientific/medical journals published throughout the world, nor do our health care providers. The result is that tabloid television, talk shows, and other forms of infotainment fill the knowledge gap with their own kind of substance abuse. What gets lost is the public's right to know the facts, prior to acceptance of fallacious claims that grab attention but fail to meet the test of sound logic.

The breast implant controversy is but one example of the challenges we face in health communication. The three professors joining this panel in health communication—Drs. R. Lewis Donohew, Teresa L. Thompson, and Barbara Sharf—bring a unique perspective to ways we communicate health issues to publics. Their individual achievements are exemplified in Donohew's work in health campaigns, Thompson's applications of interpersonal communication in the health environment, and Sharf's focus on the patient and women's issues.

As a proponent of the multidisciplinary nature of health communication—a burgeoning field with now over 500 division members in NCA—we must tackle the large issues of health in a time when perception is of the greatest importance. Perhaps we can look at a new definition of the *patient** and serve as true doctors—from *docere* (a teacher)—objectively and ethically communicating optimal health.

If those of us in academia do not get involved and motivate the government, media, or private sector to think of the consequences of the current approach to communicating health, the breast implant case is only an example of the dilemmas we are certain to face in the future.

***Patients Advocating Their Interests Effectively Negotiating Treatment**

Awareness, Attention, and the Tug of our Primal Past: Rethinking Our Target Audiences for Design of Health Messages

Lewis Donohew
University of Kentucky

I am honored to be among those invited to present a paper in the Helm series and to offer perspectives on our field based on research on the communication process carried out over a long career. I have had the good fortune to have—especially in the 80s and 90s—substantial federal funding for my research and bright and responsible people as colleagues and research assistants, not only in communication but also in other disciplines, particularly in physiological and social psychology and sociology. This has greatly broadened my perspective on human behavior and led me to a far greater appreciation of the role of our biological roots in what we do.

When we design health interventions, such as media and school-based campaigns, we make implicit assumptions about the nature of the human attention and persuasion processes. It seems to me that the designers of most interventions have an exaggerated view of how humans operate in their day-to-day existence and this may be why most interventions fail. Except in special circumstances when a stimulus is powerful enough to grab our attention, we don't behave like the alert, thinking creatures we envision ourselves to be. In this paper, I will propose that much of our behavior is carried out at a low level of awareness which may be driven primarily by biologically-based needs. This, of course, requires considerable rethinking of the whole intervention process but it does offer hope for greater success.

It is easy to forget that the human being is only a higher level of primate, born savage and made more civilized—or sometimes more savage—by the environment in which it is born and raised, yet humans are treated by most of our colleagues in the social and behavioral sciences as if they were something far greater, endowed with qualities of awareness and thoughtfulness for which there is little evidence. Their research implicitly assumes humans to be constantly aware and largely rational in the way they respond to the ongoing swirl of stimuli that define their lives. In truth, most humans merely muddle through each day, responding—often dimly—to what is thrown at them probably more on the basis of their biologically-based needs than on rational decision processes.

When you *ask* them why they did things, they will give you answers, but often they haven't the slightest notion why they did them, and sometimes they weren't even aware they *were* doing them. If in real life human beings *were* the aware, logical creatures implicit in the cognitive theories of our field, there would be no need for those of us in health communication to seek ways to attract their attention and persuade them to live more healthful lives.

There would not even be a need to teach them to "just say no." They would be going out and getting information and doing it without our prompting.

In fact, however, human beings are probably *not* the noble creatures we in communication—and particularly *health* communication—seem to envision. One characteristic of these imperfectly evolved creatures is a need for novelty, left over from an ancient past when detection of novel stimuli was a fundamental survival behavior (Bardo, Donohew, & Harrington, in press). This need for novelty is associated with a number of other genetically-based characteristics, and the range of these characteristics in humans leads to differences in what attracts and holds attention and what leads to impulsive decisions about whether to go on or turn away. Human beings might be better described as going through life more frequently tuned to these needs than to creating a higher order. A good deal of the time, the guidance of their systems may be left to overlearned and familiar routines which provide a sort of automatic pilot while they are being influenced in their behaviors by forces of which they are not aware.

Occasionally, in the process of negotiating that environment while operating at a low level of awareness of doing so, such as driving home from work, a siren or the flashing light of an emergency vehicle intrudes and brings the human to focus its attention processes on the larger world around it. It is at *that* point that humans probably behave the way we have assumed they behave all the time.

If any of you doubt that this is the real world for those of us who study communication, I invite you to carefully study the research of those who implicitly assume humans are aware logical creatures and those who assume more primitive biological forces at work.

Why, then, do we continue to use theories which assume that people operate at a much higher level of awareness than they do and that they are persuasible by rational appeals alone?

In criticizing one of the major rational models used in our field, the Health Belief Model, Vicki Freimuth (1992) states that in explaining risk-taking behavior related to HIV infection and to predict change in HIV-preventive behaviors, "the results have been disappointing." She adds that the problem is that the Health Belief Model is a "rational-cognitive model and assumes a 'rational' decision-maker." She contends that "most adolescents, and many adults, do not seem to approach the AIDS issue from such a logical perspective."

Vicki's views are echoed by many others in the field of prevention research, among them Brown, DiClemente, and Reynolds (1991), who state that rational models may not offer sufficient explanation for adolescent risk-taking behaviors. Michal-

Johnson and Bowen (1992), also note that other theories based on reasoned action may be ineffective because areas of behavior such as those related to AIDS are heavily influenced by emotions.

All of the foregoing is said as background to what I feel is a more realistic and hopeful approach to improving the health of our fellow creatures by causing them to engage in behaviors with more positive health outcomes. The problem has not been that they are not *capable* of intelligent behavior. Our gloomy preface here is not intended to be *that* negative.

It is simply that we need to learn more about the biological tugs and constraints Mother Nature has placed upon us and to find ways to use them to our advantage or get past them so that we may attract and hold the attention of our intended audiences and ultimately persuade them to engage in more positive behaviors.

If that sounds like *1984*-speak or *Brave New World,* it isn't. The human being is still the best ultimate judge of what is best for him or her. The fundamental process I am referring to here is not different from fundamental processes and assumptions underlying all communication processes.

AN ILLUSTRATION

In the time remaining to me here, I'm going to try to illustrate some of what I have said by talking about one approach which takes some of these more biologically-based assumptions into account and how it deals with them in the process of development of prevention campaigns.

A fundamental assumption underlying some of these approaches is that an alerting or arousal response has evolved as a survival behavior (Zuckerman, 1990) and there is growing evidence that individual differences in responses to novelty are biologically-based (Bardo & Mueller, 1991; Bardo, Neiswander, & Pierce, 1988). The most recent evidence for this is the finding by teams in the United States and Israel that novelty seeking is connected with the D4 dopamine receptor gene (Benjamin, et al., 1996; Cloninger, Adolfson, & Svrakic, 1996; Ebstein, et al., 1996).

This phenomenon has also been described by psychological theories of personality, most notably Zuckerman's theory of sensation seeking (Zuckerman, 1979, 1984, 1988, 1994). The latter theory holds that individuals on the upper end of the sensation seeking continuum seek out situations and experiences which provide an escape from repetition, constancy, and over-familiarity and are willing to take physical and social risks for the sake of these experiences (Berlyne, 1971; Zuckerman, 1994).

A substantial number of studies have shown that individuals exhibiting traits described in these theories are at greater risk for early onset of drug use, for continued drug use (e.g., Andrucci, et al., 1989; Bates, Labouvier, & White, 1986; Newcomb & McGee, 1989; Donohew, et al., 1990), and for involvement in risky sexual behaviors (Zimmerman & Donohew, 1996). Under established procedures for determining levels of need for sensation, approximately one-third to one-half of various age groups (e.g., adolescents) are classified into this higher-risk category.

All of this has considerable implications for those of us doing research in those aspects of health communication which involve media, interpersonal, or school-based instructional prevention programs for two reasons. One is it tells us who should be the prime target audience on health behaviors involving novelty and risk-taking, and a second is it gives us some clues on how to attract and hold attention long enough for persuasive messages to get through. It even gives us some clues on what not to do in the persuasion messages.

In a recent review of this research, its theoretical bases, and its implications for health campaigns, we wrote (Donohew, Palmgreen, & Lorch, 1994):

> It is our belief that research in health communication, involving mass media campaigns and human persuasion processes, must take into account fundamental human attention processes and their biological basis. In the area of application to which we have addressed ourselves, this biological basis has profound implications both for identifying prime target audiences most at risk for drug use

> and for the design of messages to reach those audiences. (p. 311)

Over the past 12 years, my associates and I have been carrying out research in which we have sought to identify the characteristics of messages and strategies which are successful with these difficult-to-reach individuals. In a series of laboratory and field experiments starting in 1985, we have learned a great deal about the characteristics of health-related messages which attract and hold attention, which motivate members of this prime target audience to call a hotline, and which have a desired effect on their health behaviors.

We currently are carrying out two studies. One involves *media campaigns* in two matched cities, with a replication in one of them, and measuring the effects with a large-scale time series analysis involving 6,400 subjects. Our principal objective is to trace and identify the processes of attitude and behavior change and the role of the media messages and other factors in that process.

In a second study in two other cities, we have drawn upon our findings about what attracts and holds the attention of our prime target audience to redesign an HIV and alcohol prevention *curriculum* to make it more appealing and effective with sensation seekers and impulsive decision makers. We know from previous studies that messages which reach these people will also be attended by the other members of the audience, but this is not true when it's the other way around.

Our research is primarily guided by an attention and activation theory of information exposure (Donohew, Palmgreen, & Duncan, 1980) which treats arousal value of a message as a prime motivator for attending it, rather than assuming some higher motivation. It also relies on elementary and primal sources of motivation (such as "it's available now, and it's enjoyable") to persuade.

Although prevention campaigns often are guided by learning models, frequently little attention is paid to a vital prerequisite: how to reach key target audiences with persuasive messages and hold their attention long enough for the messages to be processed. In this paper, I will describe the research—almost all of it carried out in a health communication context—guided by a theory of attention to information (Donohew et al., 1980) some of its psychological and biological antecedents, and applications of the theory to interventions aimed at HIV and drug abuse prevention.

Drawing upon a notational scheme offered by Hempel (1965), I have attempted to more formally express this theory as follows:

CHARACTERISTICS

C_1 Individuals vary in their levels of need for stimulation as a function of their inherited drives and learned needs based on rewarded and non-rewarded experiences.

C_2 In messages, stimulation is provided by: (a) formal features, including (1) fast action, (2) novelty, (3) color, (4) intensity, (5) complexity, and others, and by (b) the verbal content.

LAWS (THEORETICAL STATEMENTS)

L_1 Individuals seek to achieve or maintain a level of activation at which they feel most comfortable.

L_2 Attention to a message is a function of (a) individual level of need for stimulation, and (2) level of stimulation provided by a stimulus source (such as a message).

DEDUCED PROPOSITIONS

L_3 Individuals will turn away from messages that fail to generate enough arousal to meet their needs for activation in order to seek more exciting stimuli.

L_4 Individuals will turn away from messages which generate too much arousal in order to seek less exciting stimuli.

L_5 Individuals will attend to messages which fulfill their needs for activation.

A fundamental assumption of the theory is that human beings have individual levels of need

for activation or arousal at which they are most comfortable, and which are largely biologically based. It follows then that attention is a function primarily of an individual's level of need for stimulation and the level of stimulation provided by a stimulus source. Cognitive needs probably come in there somewhere, but we're doing rather well at predicting exposure to information with just these two basic elements, given demographically and ethnically appropriate content in our messages. We can further deduce that if individuals do not achieve or maintain this state upon exposure to a message, that is, if activation falls below or exceeds the desired level, individuals will turn away from the message and seek a source of stimulation—which might be another message—that helps them achieve the desired state. If activation remains within some acceptable range, however, individuals will continue to expose themselves to the information. All of this switching or staying usually is carried out, we believe, with the individual being either totally or at best dimly aware it is happening.

We have tested these propositions of the theory in a number of situations, including laboratory experiments on audience responses to drug abuse prevention messages across varying conditions and in field experiments. Because high sensation or novelty seekers are attracted to dramatic and novel stimuli, the model relies on manipulation of message novelty and sensation value to attract and hold the attention of high-risk audiences long enough for persuasive messages—also designed to contain appeals likely to be more effective with higher sensation and novelty seekers—to achieve a maximum effect.

This approach has been supported in our research program (e.g., Donohew, Palmgreen, & Duncan, 1980; Donohew, Finn, & Christ, 1988; Donohew et al., 1990; Donohew, Palmgreen, & Lorch, 1994; Everett & Palmgreen, 1995; Lorch et al., 1994; Palmgreen et al., 1991, 1994) and has been found to be a successful way of surmounting cognitive and attitudinal barriers to prevention messages raised by those engaged in or more likely to become engaged in drug use.

There also is growing evidence to support a biological basis for individual differences in need for stimulation which are at the heart of the theory. As noted earlier, these were posited a long time ago by Zuckerman and associates, who found relationships among sensation seeking, the level of monoamine oxidase—an enzyme that regulates the levels of monoamine transmitters in brain neurons—and testosterone level. My colleague, Mike Bardo, has found that novelty seeking behavior in animals (and presumably in humans as well, may involve the mesolimbic dopamine system in the brain which also is connected to drug seeking behavior (Bardo & Mueller, 1991). As reported earlier in this paper, more recently teams in Israel and the United States have discovered a relationship between the D4 dopamine receptor gene and novelty seeking.

Need for stimulation may be measured in a number of ways, such as through Zuckerman's sensation seeking scale or Cloninger's novelty seeking scale, or through blood sample measures of testosterone or monoamine oxidase (MAO). Another measure we have recently added is impulsive decision-making, measured with a scale developed by Langer, Zimmerman, Warheit, and Duncan (1993). This scale provides a better measure of that element of impulsivity most relevant for our work on prevention of risky sex in the HIV study.

Individuals predicted by some or all of these measures to be seekers of higher sensation and greater novelty and who are impulsive decision makers are highly likely to become drug users and to practice risky sex. These differences have been demonstrated in both adolescent and adult populations.

This approach employs substantial formative research, using both surveys and focus groups to identify issues, channels, or forms of instruction likely to be watched or listened to, and to pre-test messages. These messages may be for distribution through the mass media (such as paid or unpaid advertisements or PSAs) or for presentation in the classroom (such as instructional materials and procedures). The messages and instructional materials found to be most effective with the target audiences are those which are (1) novel, creative, or unusual; (2) complex; (3) intense (auditory and visual); physically arousing (exciting, stimulating); emotionally strong; (4) graphic or explicit; (5) ambiguous; (6) unconventional; (7) fast-paced; or (8) suspenseful.

The approach currently being employed in the classroom program to increase the arousal value of the instruction involves introduction wherever possible of greater novelty, complexity, and a faster pace to the instruction, such as through inclusion of more audiovisual materials, such as short "trigger" films, and increasing student participation in the instructional process, such as through creation of more realistic role-plays, or a wide range of other techniques.

REFERENCES

Andrucci, G. L., Archer, R. P., Pancoast, D. L., & Gordon, R. A. (1989). The relationship of MMPI and sensation seeking scales to adolescent drug use. *Journal of Personality Assessment, 53* (2), 253–266.

Bardo, M. T., Donohew, L., & Harrington, N. G. (In press). Psychobiology of novelty seeking and drug use. *Behavioural Brain Research, 77*, 23–43.

Bardo, M. T., Neiswander, J., & Pierce, R. (1988). Effects of opiate and dopaminergic drugs on novelty preference behavior. *Society for Neuroscience Abstracts, 14*, 683–689.

Bardo, M. T., & Mueller, C. W. (1991). Sensation seeking and drug abuse prevention from a biological perspective. In L. Donohew, H. Sypher, & W. Bukoski (Eds.), *Persuasive communication and drug abuse prevention*, (pp. 195–207). Hillsdale, NJ: Erlbaum.

Bates, M. E., Labouvier, E. W., & White, H. R. (1986). *The effect of sensation seeking needs on alcohol and marijuana use in adolescence.* Unpublished Manuscript, Rutgers University, Center of Alcohol Studies, New Brunswick, NJ.

Benjamin, J., Li, L., Patterson, C., Greenberg, B., Murphy, D., & Hamer, D. (1996). Population and familial association between the D4 dopamine receptor gene and measures of novelty seeking. *Nature Genetics, 12*, 81–84.

Berlyne, D. E. (1971). *Aesthetics and Psychobiology.* New York: Appleton-Century-Crofts.

Cloninger, C. R., Adolfson, R., & Svrakic, N. M. (1996). Mapping genes for human personality. *Nature Genetics, 12* (3,4).

Donohew, L. (1990). Public health campaigns: Individual message strategies and a model. In L. Donohew & E. B. Ray (Eds.), *Communication and health: Systems and applications,* 3–8.

Donohew, L., Finn, S., & Christ, W. (1988). The nature of news revisited: The roles of affect, schemas, and cognition. In L. Donohew, H. Sypher, and E. T. Higgins (Eds.), *Communication, social cognition, and affect.* Hillsdale, NJ: Erlbaum.

Donohew, L., Helm, D., Lawrence, P., & Shatzer, M. J. (1990). Sensation seeking, marijuana use, and responses to drug abuse prevention messages. In R. Watson (Ed.), *Prevention and treatment of drug and alcohol abuse* (pp. 73–93). Camden, NJ: Humana Press.

Donohew, L., Palmgreen, P., & Lorch, E. P. (1994). Attention, sensation seeking, and public health campaigns. *American Behavioral Scientist, 38* (2), 310–322.

Ebstein, R., Novick, O., Umansky, R., Priel, B., Osher, Y., Blaine, D., Bennett, E., Nemanov, L., Katz, M., & Belmaker, R. (1996). Dopamine D4 receptor (*D4DR*) exon III polymorphism associated with the human personality trait of novelty seeking. *Nature Genetics, 12,* 78–80.

Everett, M., & Palmgreen, P. (1995). Influences of sensation seeking, message sensation value, and program context on effectiveness of anti-cocaine public service announcements. *Health Communication 7,* (3), 225–248.

Hempel, C. (1965). *Aspects of scientific explanation.* New York: The Free Press.

Langer, L., Zimmerman, R., Warheit, G. J., & Duncan, R. C. (1993). An examination of the relationship between adolescent decision-making orientation and AIDS-related knowledge, attitudes, beliefs, behaviors, and skills. *Health Psychology 12,* 3, 227–234.

Lorch, E. P., Palmgreen, P., Donohew, L., Helm, D., Baer, S., and Dsilva, M. (1994). Program context, sensation seeking, and attention to televised anti-drug public service announcements. *Human Communication Research, 20,* 390–412.

Newcomb, M. D., & McGee, L. (1989). Adolescent alcohol use and other delinquent behaviors: A one-year longitudinal analysis controlling for sensation seeking. *Criminal Justice and Behavior, 16*(3), 345–369.

Palmgreen, P., Lorch, E. P., Donohew, L., Rogus, M., Helm, D., & Grant, N. (1991). Sensation seeking, message sensation value, and drug use as mediators of PSA effectiveness. *Health Communication, 20,*(4) 217–234.

Palmgreen, P., Lorch, E. P., & Donohew, L. (1991). Sensation seeking and targeting of televised anti-drug PSAs. In L. Donohew, H. Sypher, & W. Bukoski (Eds.), *Persuasive communication and drug abuse prevention* (pp. 209–226). Hillsdale, NJ: Erlbaum.

Palmgreen, P., Lorch, E. P., Donohew, L., Harrington, N. G., Dsilva, M., & Helm, D. (1994). Reaching at-risk populations in a mass media drug abuse prevention campaign: Sensation seeking as a targeting variable. *Drugs and Society, 8* (¾), 29–45.

Zimmerman, R., & Donohew, L. (1996). *Sexual risk-taking, alcohol, and HIV prevention in youth.* Paper presented at American Public Health Association, New York, November, 1996.

Zuckerman, M. (1979). *Sensation seeking: Beyond the optimal level of arousal.* Hillsdale, NJ: Erlbaum.

Zuckerman, M. (1984). Sensation seeking: A comparative approach to a human trait. *Behavioral and Brain Sciences, 7,* 413–471.

Zuckerman, M. (1988). Behavior and biology: Research on sensation seeking and reactions to the media. In L. Donohew, H. E. Sypher, & E. T. Higgins (Eds.), *Communication, Social Cognition, and Affect* (pp. 173–194). Hillsdale, NJ: Erlbaum.

Zuckerman, M. (1994). *Behavioral expressions and biosocial bases of sensation seeking.* Cambridge: Cambridge University Press.

Health Communication as the "Invisible Helping Hand": Just How Much Do We "Help"?

Teresa L. Thompson
Univesity of Dayton

I'm not quite sure when I moved from "young Turk" to "old buffalo," but somehow it happened. I think you have to be an "old buffalo" to be asked to share your thoughts about an area of study in this type of forum. Nonetheless, I am happy to be asked to do so. My comments today envelop both my historical perspective on the area of health communication, especially as it has been reflected in and affected by the journal I edit, *Health Communication,* and my thoughts on the usefulness or helpfulness of health communication research.

HISTORICAL PERSPECTIVE

It was 10 years ago this NCA that I first began discussions with Lawrence Erlbaum Publishers about a journal reporting research in health communication. The discussions did not begin at my initiation; I was rather surprised to be contacted by them. Erlbaum was at that time busily expanding their offerings within the field of communication and was particularly interested in including within those offerings a new scholarly journal. Discussions with their editorial consultants and some early marketing research had indicated to them a need for a journal focusing specifically on health communication. Someone (I think Jennings Bryant) had recommended that they talk to me about possibly editing it, so we met at NCA in 1986. Following my discussions with them, I began talking with various other health communication researchers to garner their perceptions about the fruitfulness of such an endeavor. Although many enthusiastically endorsed the idea, feeling that there was both a market for the journal and an abundance of research being conducted that could be published in it, a couple of "old buffaloes" (even older than me!) thoughtfully indicated that they believed, "with the launching of...there wasn't really a need for a health communication journal or enough research being conducted to fill it."

Fortunately, their concerns were unwarranted. After preparing a proposal for Erlbaum and going through another series of discussions with them, I began reviewing submissions for the journal in the Fall of 1987. Slowed down just a little by the loss of a couple of submissions when our building at the University of Dayton burned down in December of 1987, the journal has been going great guns since that time. I just recently sent Vol. 9, issue #3 to the publisher.

The quality of those early submissions to the journal was not, however, always what I would have hoped. Although some of this can be attributed to "new editor syndrome," some of it must be blamed on the mediocre nature of the research being conducted by many people with a sincere interest in the study of communication problems in the health care context but without either: (1) a sophisticated understanding of communication theory; (2) a thorough knowledge of the medical context; or (3) much knowledge of the previous research on the phenomena in question. Much of the interest was prompted by personal experiences of the researchers, either due to their own health problems or related to health problems experienced by a family member. Fortunately, almost hidden among the hundreds of mediocre submissions were enough very good submissions to fill the first few issues of the journal. I recall with joy one submission by

Kathleen Reardon and Ross Buck (1989) which caused a very demanding reviewer to write "BRAVO!" across the "comments to the editor" portion of the reviewer reporting form.

Over the years, however, I am pleased to say that I have observed a great many such submissions, demonstrating astounding improvement in the quality of the research received by the journal. It has been many, *many* years since I cringed while reading the proofs of an issue or gave my students a piece from the journal to critique, certain that they would be able to find problems with it. That never happened much, but there were a couple of pieces....

My problem now is how to fit in the plethora of fine pieces of research that I receive in my capacity as editor of the journal. While the pieces still exhibit the same sincere concern about communicative phenomena in the health care context found in the early submissions, they are now typically well-grounded in communication theory, methodologically strong, and built upon past research. Much of the research is now being conducted by people who have been trained by those who are established experts in the area of health communication, rather than being conducted by those of us who were more "self-taught," in that we brought to our research a background in either health *or* communication and had to make the links on our own.

Although in the early years of editing the journal I received the final versions of articles accepted for an issue just in time to send that issue to press, I am now consistently several issues ahead in acceptances. I have been able to become very rigorous in my criteria for acceptance. Indeed, the large amount of high quality work being done in this area is indicated by the launching last year of yet another health communication journal, focusing more specifically on social marketing concerns.

In addition to significant improvement in the quality of the work in the area of health communication, the last 10 years have also seen some changes in the focus of that research. Most of the early submissions to the journal focused on provider-patient interaction and less on mediated

communication or health campaigns. This emphasis was so strong that early perceptions of the journal were that interpersonal issues were our only focus. That was never the case—the fact that early issues included mostly pieces focusing on provider-patient interaction was merely a reflection of the inclinations of most researchers at that time. Since those days, more and more researchers have moved to the investigation of mass-mediated health communication or public health concerns. You see these developments reflected in the articles published in the journal.

Another notable change in the journal over the years has been its internationalization. After the first few years of publication, I was pleased to note that I was receiving many acceptable submissions from Great Britain, the Scandinavian countries, Australia and New Zealand, Canada, Germany, and several African countries. Just as different fields develop different criteria, so do different academic cultures, so international submissions do not always fulfill the same rigorous criteria to which my reviewers are accustomed. But over the years the reader of the journal will note a substantial increase in the breadth of nationalities and traditions represented by the authors.

The same trend has emerged in terms of academic fields of study represented by the researchers publishing in the journal. Although it was always intended that the journal would be interdisciplinary both in terms of readers and authors, most early submissions came from people trained in speech communication. It's been many years, however, since that preponderance existed. We now publish articles from researchers trained in nursing, medicine, psychology, sociology, public health, political science, anthropology, and on and on and on as well as those trained in communication.

It is evident to me that much change and improvement has occurred in the research that has been conducted within the area of health communication over the last 10 years. In my capacity as editor of the journal, I have enjoyed observing and participating in this change. However, I still have some dissatisfaction with much of the research in the area—and some of the dissatisfaction has not changed much since I first began familiarizing myself with the area of health communication.

A HELPING HAND?

As is the case with many researchers, my entree into health communication was indirect. My early research focused on interpersonal aspects of communication between those who are physically disabled and those who are not. It was other people, most notably the late Gerry Phillips, who saw the link between my research and the new area which was variously labeled "medical communication" and "health communication." In his capacity as editor of *Communication Quarterly,* Gerry had published a couple of my earlier pieces and, I think, ornery as he was, liked the way I had fought back at a particularly nasty reviewer. While editing a special issue of *CQ* in honor of an ECA anniversary, Gerry asked me to write a review piece on communication research in the health and social service professions. That piece was titled, "The invisible helping hand: The role of communication in the health and social service professions." Gerry had first told the authors of the solicited review pieces that he was thinking about putting the articles in a book, so we were free to write as much as we wanted. My initial draft was 100 pages long. When it was decided to put the pieces in an issue of *CQ,* it had to be cut to 20 pages. After this editing, of course, most of the review was gone, and only the critique was left (Thompson, 1984). The goal of the remainder of this essay is to measure the current health communication research against the criticisms of that early piece and to assess how well, in my opinion, things have changed and health communication researchers currently really offer a "helping hand" to others through our work.

Former vice-president and noted liberal Hubert Humphrey is reported by Bill Moyers to have said, "The moral test of a society is how well it helps people in the dawn of life—children, the twilight of life—the elderly, and the shadows of life—the poor, the sick, and the handicapped." Many have applied the same criteria to the social sciences, arguing that the most valuable research is that which is socially significant and of value to people. How much, then, does health communication research help people?

Overall, I think that health communication research is perhaps more *helpful* to people than is the case with most other communication research. Most health communication research is not esoteric, but is *problem-oriented*—it is geared towards direct examination of problems experienced by many people. The focus of health communication research is on improving people's health. There is a great deal of evidence that communication has both direct and indirect impacts on health outcomes. Unfortunately, most health communication research, although it examines the communication characterizing health care interaction, does not make the leap to actual health outcomes. The potential for doing so is, I think, the great strength of the area of health communication. But such data are difficult to gather, and typically necessitate correlational field studies which are frequently not easy to publish—causality is not clear. Ethically, of course, it is difficult to *manipulate* communicative or noncommunicative variables that the researcher has reason to believe may positively or not-so-positively impact a patient's health. Thus, experimental studies are not common in this area.

Some studies, of course, have made the leap to actual health outcomes, and have provided important insights for care providers. More frequently, however, outcome variables focus on issues relating to patient satisfaction—a highly criticized dependent variable. Although some have argued that patient satisfaction is at least important in cases of chronic or terminal illness where improved health is less likely to be an appropriate measure, there is evidence even among persons with AIDS that communication is related to longevity of life. Why not, then, include longevity as an outcome variable? I would not argue, as have some, that health outcomes are the only appropriate dependent variables, but a focus on health-related outcome variables would likely increase the helpfulness of health communication research.

The helpfulness of our research could also be improved by a continued move to a more dyadic-rather than provider-oriented unit of analysis in our research. A notable development at the 1995 SCA meeting was a mini-conference focusing on the role of the *patient* in health communication research. The first issue of Volume 9 of *Health Communication* reports the results of this conference. The mini-conference and the special issue of *HC* are notable and exciting because of the *lack* of such research in the past. This may seem ludicrous in light of the oft-argued dyadic nature of the communication process, but much research still at least *implies* that the blame for communication problems in the health care context lies with the care provider or that the care provider is the key determinant of the communication that occurs. Just the day before first drafting this essay, I reviewed a grant proposal that essentially argued that a key interactional role of the physician is keeping the patient conversationally on track and preventing tangents. Although such a perspective is consistent with that which would be advocated by many physicians, this research proposal, which was good in most other ways, was written by respected social scientists. A perspective such as the one implicit in that proposal ignores the fact that important diagnostic information may be "tangentially" communicated by patients and assumes that the physician's superior understanding should guide the course of the interaction.

Although health communication research has focused on a variety of different target populations, not enough research has yet included children as part of the interactional dyad. Perhaps this is because most communicologists lack the requisite expertise in developmental issues to competently study children. There are, however, many health communication issues of relevance to children that have yet to be investigated.

Other concerns about the focus of current health communication research relate to the narrow nature of that research. Work still focuses on interpersonal aspects of physician-patient communication, ignoring all the other messages that impact our health behavior. Similarly, the focus on *physical* health has been narrow. It has ignored quality of life issues and broader health concerns. Recent attempts to broaden this scope, however, can be seen in Eileen Berlin Ray's (1996a, b) books on communication issues related to disenfranchised populations, which address concerns identified as problematic in that early *CQ* piece to which I referred above. Similar broadening of the scope of health communication is found in Marsha Vanderford and David Smith's (1996) new book on the breast implant controversy and Athena Du Pre's (1997) book on humor and the healing arts.

Apart from the concerns mentioned above, there is much positive that can be said about the helpfulness of research done in the area of health communication. Much of it is interdisciplinary rather than being arbitrarily constrained to a particular perspective. As mentioned earlier, it is problem-oriented. Although health communication research is now published in a variety of forums, unlike 10 years ago, when it was difficult to find publication outlets for much health communication work, the most focused research outlet during the last 10 years has been the journal *Health Communication*. A perusal of the articles published in the journal over the years indicates that, although a few are more esoteric, most address important social and health concerns. They focus on such topics as patient understanding of medical terminology, patient metaphors on which care providers can pick up to assess patient coping, organizational communication issues of interest to health care administrators, issues related to home care givers, suggestions for communication in dentistry including improving utilization of dental services, social support for the elderly, how to suggest condom use to a sexual partner, coping with cancer, cancer prevention, lifestyle changes in cancer patients, communicating about medications, smoking cessation, drug and alcohol abuse prevention, increasing mammography use, heart disease, weight control, accuracy of science news and the consequences of inaccuracy, medical compliance/cooperation issues, organ donation strategies, family planning, health care provider burnout, bone marrow testing, communication with the terminally ill, well-care, and multitudinous others. The research includes very specific suggestions for health campaigns, down to such details as how to convince gatekeepers to air health messages directed to teens. It also includes very specific implications for provider-patient interaction, including such details as the influence of a companion or increasing patient participation in health care. As I read the proofs for each issue of the journal, I am convinced that there is a lot of very helpful information available in the health communication literature.

Just because information is helpful, however, does not mean that it is actually helping people. Although campaign designers who work for the CDCs are familiar with the literature, many health messages are designed by local care providers who have never heard of an area called "health communication." When a local pediatric hospital becomes alarmed at the numbers of babies dying in the emergency room because they've been shaken, hospital personnel design their own local campaign. Rarely does it work, because rarely does it take into account what we know about effective message design. The same thing happens when a local hospital puts together a display at the mall for Breast Cancer Awareness Month, or when the local chapter of the dietetics association attempts a campaign designed to lower cholesterol. Most are wasted efforts.

Similarly, does the average care provider become aware of the findings from research on provider-patient interaction? Such findings are interesting enough that they could and should receive media coverage, but usually do not. Most academics are quite good at conducting research, and quite bad at disseminating those findings to anything outside of scholarly forums. Most universities have very active PR offices, but many scholarly findings do not get reported to these offices. At the University of Dayton, we have a wonderful University Communications Office staffed by experienced PR and journalism professionals who not only know how to write a great press release, but also have contacts within the media throughout the country. They check with various academic units on an annual basis, usually scheduling meetings with departments in the summer, and keep informed on the research that faculty are

conducting. Various staff members note on their calendars dates when projects are expected to move to completion, and phone faculty at the appropriate time. The faculty member passes a copy of the paper on to the PR professional, who later interviews the faculty member for more information. A press release is written and then revised with input from the researcher. It is sent out along with researcher contact phone numbers. Public Relations staff then follow-up with personal contacts to various local and national media.

This process has, over the years, led to coverage of my research, especially that conducted with graduate students, on the front page of the *Wall Street Journal,* on CNN, on the radio and in papers all across the country, and in magazines such as *Glamour* and *Mademoiselle.* I've received calls from Entertainment Tonight, and this research has been mentioned by Jay Leno in his monologue on the Tonight Show. My colleagues at the University have had their work discussed in *USA Today, Time,* and *Newsweek.* Our work has resulted in hundreds of interviews with local and national media outlets. Unfortunately, most of the research that has been covered has not been work in health communication—it's been on sexier topics, such as gender or the three stooges. But some of that has been due to packaging, and I am convinced that, with a bit of effort, health information can be packaged to be more successfully marketed. Both *Glamour* and *Mademoiselle* have, for instance, discussed some of my health communication research.

Most universities have such PR offices, even if they are not as aggressive as that at the University of Dayton. You may have to seek them out rather than being sought out by them. You may have to take the initiative. We have seen some success with similar efforts through Bill Eadie's work with NCA and the Health Comm. Division's press conferences and releases at NCA and ICA meetings. We shouldn't rely on these national efforts, however—there's too much work to be done to put all the responsibility on them. We all need to take the initiative at the local level—at your own university. Maybe you can't write a press release, but they can. Take advantage of them.

Many academics are reluctant to popularize their research for fear of distorting it or looking unprofessional. One is reminded a bit of physicians who see a concern with bedside manner as a concession to salesmanship, as Barbara Korsch long ago asserted. I believe, however, that we're just treading water—just running in place—if we conduct research without passing it on to the people who can be helped by it. There is indeed a very real potential for distortion in such a process, but much of that can be controlled by researcher input and participation. I have, of course, received phone calls from smart-aleck disc jockeys intending to make fun of scholarly research, but that's been minimal compared to the opportunity to discuss legitimate research findings in an interesting manner and reach people who need the information.

Media dissemination of research findings is not, of course, the only method of passing information on to people. Back in the days when I used to have time for such things, I did training in health care organizations that involved passing on the findings of my work and that of other researchers. That, too, is an important outlet. But media dissemination of findings also makes them available to other people who do full time training and encourages broader knowledge of your research.

CONCLUSION

My concerns about the state of health communication research, then, focus not so much on the research being conducted and published, although I'd like to see some refocusing onto dyadic concerns and health outcomes, as on the lack of dissemination of the findings to the people who could be helped by them. Our research provides helpful information—let's make sure that people can really be helped by it.

REFERENCES

Du Pre, A. (1997). *Humor and the healing arts.* Mahwah, NJ: Lawrence Erlbaum Associates.

Ray, E. B. (1996a). *Communication and disenfranchisement.* Mahwah, NJ: Lawrence Erlbaum Associates.

Ray, E. B. (1996b). *Case studies in communication and the disenfranchised.* Mahwah, NJ: Lawrence Erlbaum Associates.

Reardon, K. K., & Buck, R. (1989). Emotion, reason, and communication in coping with cancer. *Health Communication, 1,* 41–54.

Thompson, T. L. (1984). The invisible healing hand: The role of communication in the health and social service professions. *Communication Quarterly, 32,* 148–163.

Vanderford, M., & Smith, D. (1996). *The silicone breast implant story.* Mahwah, NJ: Lawrence Erlbaum Associates.

Reframing Health Care Agendas:
Voices of Activist-Survivors as a Focus of Study

Barbara F. Sharf[1]
Univesity of Illinois at Chicago

If we are to translate the silence surrounding breast cancer into language and action, then the first step is that women with mastectomies must become visible to each other, for silence and invisibility go hand in hand with powerlessness.

Audre Lorde, *The Cancer Journals*
(1980, p. 61)

Although health communication as a field of study has evolved to include a broad working definition of what constitutes health, our scholarship has tended to coalesce around the study of interaction between providers and patients in clinical settings, and of health promotion messages occurring within a variety of formats and contexts. Significantly less attention has been paid to the multiple functions communication plays in the formulation of national health policy and the social construction of health care issues. If we are to take seriously Ellen Wartella's (1994) challenge that the profession of communication intellectually address the very important questions pertaining to communication on the public agenda, a fundamental part of our work should include examination of the big picture: how and why certain health-related themes rise to public prominence, which constituencies are affected, and with what results.

In the moribund drama of health care reform that took place within the U.S. government nearly three years ago, political in-fighting resulted in a near stalemate of major legislative initiatives.[2] Nonetheless, at the corporate/professional level, the evolutionary preeminence of managed care is, in fact, irreversibly transforming the economics, modes of access, and expectations for participants in the American health care system. That is top-down change. Lupton (1994) argues that health communication research needs to address the ideological and structural impediments to effective communication in health contexts. This line of reasoning eventually points attention to practices of advocacy as a way of examining change from the bottom up. The increasingly powerful voices of citizen-activists, many of whom are themselves survivors of the health problems for which they are advocating, are having a major impact on agenda setting for health policy. The thesis of this essay is that health communication scholars must pay careful attention to that body of discourse being generated though health activism if we wish to contribute to an understanding, or influence the direction, of social change in health care and promotion.

Political activism, of course, is hardly a new phenomenon; in this country, the Boston Tea Party provides evidence of a long historical tradition. And advocacy is not always a bottom-up activity—

[1]The author wishes to acknowledge a grant from the Susan G. Komen Breast Cancer Foundation which helped to enable research on breast cancer activism presented in this essay.

[2]The exception being the bi-partisan Kassebaum-Kennedy compromise legislation signed into law during summer, 1996 which protects the rights of citizens to maintain health insurance in the face of changing or losing jobs, sets limits on pre-existing conditions restrictions, and offers some protection against discrimination on the basis of genetic information.

we have only to look at corporate and institutional lobbyists as prime examples of the powerful acting to maintain their hierarchical status. What is interesting about the recent development of health care activism is not only that citizen groups formed at a grassroots level are taking on the traditionally authoritative medical and scientific bodies, but also that patients are demonstrating that people who have undergone devastating illness can still speak out, and use hard-earned wisdom based on experience and independent judgment to formulate new approaches to problems constructed upon old assumptions. Such behaviors run counter to conventional notions of patienthood as a vulnerable, dependent state.

In a recent issue of *Health Communication* (Sharf & Street, 1997), the currently touted notion of patient-centeredness is both explored and critiqued. At its heart, the philosophy of patient-centered care asserts that the concerns, values, and preferences of actively engaged patients will be taken into account so as to guide the clinical actions of professionals and to better assess health-related outcomes. In the alternate role of health advocates, patients (as well as other concerned individuals) emphasize their prerogatives as citizens in the public arena to seek a seat at the table in policy deliberation and whose voices are reflected in the final results. Recent advocacy activities for such health issues as AIDS and physical disabilities provide excellent case studies for analyses of the impact of grassroots rhetoric on health care issues.[3] By targeting the American public, the President, members of Congress, the medical and scientific communities, and major corporations, these movements have had significant effects. Among these are the rise of overall public consciousness and information, increases in governmental and private funding, new citizen rights legislation, and changes in the drug approval process.

---

[3]For example, these issues were represented by survivors featured as speakers at both the 1996 Republic and Democratic conventions.

THE CONTEXT FOR BREAST CANCER ACTIVISM

Because my own research for the past few years has focused on the public communication of breast cancer, I am going to use the breast cancer advocacy movement to illustrate the importance of health citizen activism and the scholarly opportunities it affords as a locus for health communication studies.

As recently as the late seventies, despite the public admission of First Lady Betty Ford in 1974 about her diagnosis and subsequent mastectomy, breast cancer was a topic that continued to prompt shame and secrecy. Poet Audre Lorde, whose cancer was diagnosed in 1978, wrote of her feelings of isolation and wondered prophetically, "What would happen if an army of one-breasted women descended upon Congress?" (Lorde, 1980, p. 16).

During the eighties, women with this disease began to identify themselves in order to talk with one another, discovering the benefits of sharing information and mutual support, through organized networks such as the Y-Me National Breast Cancer Organization, which was the first when it was started in 1978 and has grown to be the largest group of its kind. As the decade proceeded, hundreds of other national, regional, and local organizations formed to provide education, services, psychosocial support, and in some cases, to raise money for research. Along with increased visibility, reported incidence of the disease was rapidly escalating (ironically, probably in part due to enhanced quality of and better access to mammographic screening), while survival rates remained static. By 1990, two decades had passed since the Nixon Administration had issued its War on Cancer, infusing large amounts of funding into the National Cancer Institute, but women concerned about breast cancer did not perceive that their situation had improved.

Up to this point in time, little organized advocacy on behalf of breast cancer had occurred, though a few individuals made extraordinary, lasting contributions, exemplifying that activism can take many forms. Although the focus of this paper is on political advocacy, breast cancer advocates have raced for the cure; led mountain-climbing expeditions; painted, sculpted, and photographed; written autobiographies, poetry, and fiction; and have otherwise communicated their concerns in multiple, varied forms. The foremost prototype for political activism, by all accounts, was Rose Kushner, an investigative reporter who had a mastectomy in 1974 and remained a vital force for reform until her death from the disease in 1990. She single-handedly pressed for change in the standard medical procedure of performing a one-step biopsy and mastectomy on anesthetized women, who would wake up to find a confirmed diagnosis of cancer and their breast gone in one fell swoop. Far ahead of her time, she also brought to the surface such still-current breast cancer issues as environmental toxins, dangers of irradiation, unnecessarily mutilating surgery, overstimulation of estrogen production, and the severe limitations of mammography as the major method for early detection (Kushner, 1975). Another prominent activist is Nancy Brinker, founder of the Susan G. Komen Breast Cancer Foundation in 1982, who was the earliest woman to raise large sums of money for breast cancer research and services, as well as to attract bi-partisan political interest in this cause (Brinker & Harris, 1990).[4]

THE RHETORIC OF ADVOCACY

By the time of Kushner's death, public awareness of the increase in breast cancer diagnoses was heightened. Campaigns to encourage women to have mammographies and perform breast self-examination were widespread, another First Lady and a Supreme Court Justice had been diagnosed, and popular attention had been given to the availability of choice between lumpectomy and mastectomy. Demographics had also shifted. Women in their forties who were now being diagnosed (and

even many who were not, but felt that they were entering the threshold of being highly at risk) were baby-boomers who had come of age during the sixties, been part of protest demonstrations, participated in the burgeoning women's rights and women's health movements, and witnessed the AIDS activism of the eighties. Unlike the generations who had come before them, many had developed political and persuasive skills, and they were not intimidated about speaking out on this topic, including saying words like "breast" and "cancer" aloud. They did not perceive that medical research was paying a good deal of specific attention to identifying the causes of breast cancer, advances in its treatment, or a cure. As the prevalence statistics increased from 1 in 11 women in the mid-eighties to one in nine[5] within a few years, the prospects for themselves and for the daughters who would follow appeared bleak. It was in this social climate that the National Breast Cancer Coalition (NBCC) was formed in 1991.

Comprised of more than 270 preexisting groups, all of whom have a stake in improving the breast cancer situation even if that issue is not their primary objective, the NBCC is an umbrella organization whose mission is "to eradicate breast cancer through advocacy, action, and change by involving…women with breast cancer and their supporters" (Visco, 1994). The formation of this coalition was no small feat since members encompass a broad spectrum, including groups whose primary interests are very targeted, such as women's rights, religious beliefs, women of color, and lesbians, as well as major hospitals and cancer centers. Likewise, operational styles and political leanings range from the conservative American Cancer Society (who many consider to be part of the "cancer establishment") to the progressive Na-

---

[4]My intent in this section has been to sketch an historical context for the analysis of current activist rhetoric. For an exhaustive history of breast cancer activism, see Batt (1994).

[5]Despite the fact that conditions such as heart disease and diabetes affect much greater numbers, the perceived morbidity, potential mortality, and suffering that is attached to breast cancer makes it one of the most feared afflictions for women. Many advocates, including the National Breast Cancer Coalition, dispute the current rate, citing instead a one-in-eight statistic.

tional Women's Health Network. Nonetheless, this varied assortment of organizations have been willing to subordinate their differences in order to work together to achieve the common goals of: 1) increasing funding for breast cancer research which is appropriately focused; 2) ensuring access for all women to high quality screenings, treatment, and care; and 3) increasing the influence of women with breast cancer in the decision-making that impacts their lives. Certainly, strength in numbers is crucial to making the efforts of the NBCC successful, but is insufficient by itself. Further attention also must be paid to choice of themes and strategies.

The rhetorical tasks faced by breast cancer advocates differ somewhat from those of other groups. In the area of women's health, Condit (1990) explicates the evolution of various discourses on abortion and reproduction that eventuated in the polarized world views that still frame this dilemma. AIDS activists had to battle the perception that this is a disease of marginal peoples and, thus, not a threat to mainstream America.[6] Unlike abortion and AIDS, once breast cancer had become a topic of open discussion, there were no visible antagonists. To be opposed to helping those with breast cancer was literally to oppose the health of one's mother, sister, or wife. The more subtle issue was to convince the public that the need to do something about breast cancer was both urgent and great. Thus, mass mailings from the Coalition labeled the disease an epidemic: "Striking another American woman every 3 minutes. Somehow, it will touch *your* life." In fact, people are acquainted with someone who has had the disease. It is, at least in part, for this reason that many members of Congress and people associated with the Executive Branch, such as Marilyn Quayle and Bill Clinton, have a deep-seated interest in this issue. In 1993, an initial petition drive aimed at obtaining 175,000 signatures to represent the number of women who would be diagnosed that year culminated in 600,000 signatures; interestingly, signers were asked to include, not only their endorsement of a request for infusion of research monies, but also the people they knew who had been affected and how they would like to see additional funds used. Such tactics helped to put a personal face on this problem, stressed its proximity, enlisted the active involvement of large numbers of the public, in addition to survivors themselves, and helped to define breast cancer as a disease that devastates whole networks of family and friends, not only individuals.

As one activist noted, a key rhetorical strategy of the NBCC is to convey the message that "The glass is half empty, rather than half full" (Borwhat, 1996). For example, while the rising incidence rate is repeated over and over in fund-raising letters, the fact that mortality has dropped slightly in the past two years is not noted. Such tactics run the risk of back-firing. The NBCC's photographic exhibit, entitled "The Faces of Breast Cancer," builds on the personalization theme by showing portraits and brief written biographies of women from every state who have died from the disease. This exhibit travels around the country and is often shown in public places, such as shopping malls, where people—including women with breast cancer—may inadvertently wander through. Some spectators have reported reactions of negativity and despair, as opposed to motivation and resolve, after having seen the photographs.

Another key word for the NBCC is "action." Their newsletter is entitled *Call to Action* and, following the petition drive (delivered and received personally at the White House), the Coalition asked the government for the creation of a National Action Plan. Under the auspices of Secretary for Health and Human Services Donna Shalala, delegates from the NBCC met for the first time with an assembly of government officials, research scientists, representatives from the pharmaceutical industry, and other major players in December 1993. The resulting collaborative document, which the Coalition regards as a blueprint

---

[6]For an example of the kinds of rhetorical strategies used by AIDS activists to draw attention to their cause, see Christiansen and Hanson (1996).

for evaluating progress, details goals for health care, research, and policy along with specific action steps for implementation.

Through successful lobbying of the Congress and the President, the NBCC has been remarkably successful in "securing the first meaningful increase" in appropriations specifically allocated for breast cancer research (Zuckerman, 1992). Between 1991 and 1995, the monies increased from $90 million to $475 million a year. Although the Coalition had secured the advice and endorsement of renowned scientists in estimating how much money was needed and for what types of investigations, this success still has met with criticism from some scientists that earmarking monies for specific types of diseases is not a good way to direct research, insofar as an advance in one domain may, unintentionally, benefit several others. Fran Visco, President of the NBCC, sees the issue from a slightly different perspective: "There are many scientists out there who love the fact that we got more money, and are not happy about the fact that we got it for breast cancer. They want us to raise more money for medical research and let them decide what to do with it" (Visco, 1994). Others protest that diverting money to one deserving area necessarily means cutting another. The argument of the advocates has been that they do not wish to compete with the needs of other diseases, but rather new sources of funding should be found. In fact, with the help of Senator Harkin from Iowa, in 1992 a designation of $200 million for a new breast cancer research program was made with money from the Department of Defense, in addition to the regular budget of the National Cancer Institute.

Perhaps an even more contentious point of disagreement between the Coalition and the scientific community has been in fulfilling the goal of empowering survivors to have more say in decision-making that affects them. For several years, breast cancer activists have been critical of the potentially fruitful areas of study, such as environmental causes, behavioral implications, and educational interventions, that have been edged out of the competition for the comparatively small pot of money that existed. Following the lead of AIDS activists who gained representation on scientific advisory committees, the NBCC has gone a step further in pushing to include their representatives on the peer-review study sections that choose and prioritize which grant proposals are funded. This idea is already being enacted in the new Department of Defense research program, though the more traditional establishment of the NCI has resisted this degree of involvement by lay persons (Erikson, 1995). The gist of the tension was expressed by Visco in this way: "There's never enough to fund all of the research that should be funded, so decisions are made within the scientific community on acts and not why. And too often…those decisions were made at the expense of women's health…. And we're coming in and saying, 'You can't do that anymore'" (Visco, 1994).

To respond to this opposition and ensure credible representation, the Coalition has created Project LEAD, an intense four-day program of leadership education and advocacy development with carefully selected candidates in order to familiarize them with the language and concepts of basic and clinical science, and epidemiology, and other ways to present a strong presence on these committees. So far, there have been many more applicants than spaces available.

In addition to advocacy for governmental appropriations, breast cancer activists have also been successful in competing in the social marketing arena, enlisting the avid sponsorship and dollars of corporations (Belkin, 1996). Pink ribbons and other symbols of breast cancer support have been promoted by entities as diverse as cosmetics companies, women's apparel manufacturers, and national restaurant chains. While this sort of campaigning has translated into rapidly increased revenues and public awareness, critical observers also question if this kind of support is likely to be faddish and unsustained, as well as exploitive in terms of being used superficially to elevate corporate image.

IMPLICATIONS FOR HEALTH COMMUNICATION SCHOLARSHIP

Even in so brief analysis, it is clear that breast cancer advocacy has had a very significant impact in its short five-year history—enlisting some level of active support of thousands of citizens, sensitizing and winning allies among government and corporate officials, nearly quadrupling the funding base, and forging a new and powerful role in policy and research decisions for survivors. Though I have chosen to delve into the details of one grassroots disease-centered movement, the potential for generalization of knowledge based on such kinds of studies should be recognized for there is a good deal of mutual influence which occurs among health advocacy groups. The American Disabilities Act was prompted by cancer groups, as well as by advocates for the physically disabled. The breast cancer activists were inspired by and learned a tremendous amount from AIDS activists. Likewise, the fledgling male advocacy for prostate cancer is building on what has been achieved for breast cancer. Other constituencies that have so far lacked public visibility, such as those whose lives have been impaired by Alzheimer's disease or mental illness, are undergoing stages similar to the earlier work of breast cancer proponents.

What, then, is the role of communication research in regards to grassroots advocacy and its influence in changing the health care system? What do we have to offer, as well as to gain, in choosing the voices of activists as an important focal point in our studies of how matters of health are communicated?

A focus on health care activism is a rich ground for application of a variety of theoretical perspectives and research methodologies. It generates investigative questions about public persuasion through language and other symbolic forms of popular culture; political and organizational strategies; and the development of health-based coalitions and communities. Most important, at a broader level of conceptualization, it invites exploration of the relationship of political advocacy to scientific research, medical care, and public health at one end of the continuum and empowerment at a personal level at the other.

Up until now, when communication scholars have designed studies related to health in the public domain, the result has been an emphasis on specific health promotion campaigns. Typically, health promotion campaigns are the means of implementing policy decisions that already have been determined. For breast cancer in particular, there has been interest in assessing and improving programs aimed at encouraging women to have mammographies (e.g., Marshall, Smith, & McKeon, 1995). However, breast cancer advocacy has not only promoted wider use of the technology, but also has questioned its quality, safety, and efficacy, as well as pressured for improved, alternate modes of detection and emphasized the need for genuine prevention in lieu of early diagnosis. By widening our scope of studies to include activist rhetoric, we move toward consideration of questions of policy formation and reform, and the processes that are, at least in part, integral to how policy and funding decisions are made.

REFERENCES

Batt, S. (1994). *Patient no more: The politics of breast cancer.* Charlottetown, P.E.I., Canada: Gynergy Books.

Belkin, L. (1996, December 22). Charity begins at…the marketing meeting, the gala event, the product tie-in: How breast cancer became this year's cause. *The New York Times Magazine,* 40–46.

Borwhat, M. (1996, October 23). Panel presentation at Medical Center Hour, University of Virginia, Charlottesville, VA.

Brinker, N. & Harris, C. E. (1990). *The race is run one step at a time.* New York: Simon & Schuster.

Christiansen, A. E. & Hanson, J. J. (1996). Comedy as cure for tragedy: ACT UP and the rhetoric of AIDS. *Quarterly Journal of Speech, 82,* 157–170.

Condit, C. M. (1990). *Decoding abortion rhetoric: Communicating social change.* Urbana: University of Illinois Press.

Erikson, J. (1995). Breast cancer activists seek voice in research decisions. *Science, 269,* 1508–1509.

Kushner, R. (1975). *Breast cancer: A personal history and investigative report.* New York: Harcourt Brace Jovanovich.

Lorde, A. (1980). *The cancer journals.* Argyle, NY: Spinsters Ink.

Lupton, D. (1994). Toward the development of critical health communication praxis. *Health Communication, 6* (1), 55–68.

Marshall, A. A., Smith, S. W., & McKeon, J. K. (1995). Persuading low-income women to engage in mammography screening: Source, message, and channel preferences. *Health Communication, 7,* 283–300.

Sharf, B. F. & Street, R. L. (Eds.) (1997). The patient as a central construct in health communication research (special issue). *Health Communication, 9.*

Visco, F. (1994, February 7). Personal interview. Philadelphia, PA.

Wartella, E. (1994). Challenge to the profession. *Communication Education, 43,* 54–62.

Zuckerman, M. (1992, November 23). Battling breast cancer. *U.S. News & World Report,* 104.

CHAPTER 10.

AT THE HELM IN RHETORICAL ANALYSES OF PUBLIC DISCOURSE

Introduction

Dan F. Hahn
New York University

Welcome to "At the Helm in Rhetorical Analyses of Public Discourse." "At the helm"—what does that mean? I have, of course, no way of seeing into the head of the series originator, Vice President Judith Trent, so am not sanguine I know what she had in mind in selecting that title.

Perhaps she meant no more than that these are the leaders of the field. If so, the participants are well chosen, for this program features some of the most productive and insightful scholars in the field: the authors of 20 books and over 160 articles; the winners of 4 Winans-Wichelns awards; 3 Golden Anniversary Monograph awards; and a plethora of other "Best Article," "Distinguished Professor," and "Distinguished Scholar" awards. But they have not been hermetically sealed away, churning out scholarship, for on this panel we also find a Western States President, Central States President, NCA President, two QJS Editors, etc. These are, indeed, leaders in our field. They have been "at the helm."

And if I may be permitted a bit of "humanizing" of the panel, may I say that I have found each of them to be exceptionally social human beings. Without saying anything directly about any of *their* social habits, perhaps it will suffice to admit that in their company I have sometimes, in Thomas Hood's line, "took more port than was exactly portable." But I digress.

If, on the other hand, Vice President Trent meant "at the helm" to imply that these are the people who have "steered" or "governed" the area of rhetorical analysis of public discourse, her metaphor may be less apt, as the recent history of the field demonstrates.

As you know, for years and years rhetorical analysis was firmly moored at the neo-Aristotelian dock, and rhetorical analysis became not only sterile but puerile. Then in 1965 a recalcitrant captain, Ed Black, lifted the anchor with *Rhetorical Criticism: A Study in Method,* to be followed six years later by a whole raft (or boatload) of scholars who, in *The Prospect of Rhetoric,* held that rhetorical analysis need not be lashed to the mast of discrete speeches but could be cut loose to study all forms of symbolic communication.

Thus, in the last 30 years the field has not moved to order from chaos, but in the opposite direction, demonstrating the truthfulness of the Henry Adams line that "chaos often breeds life, when order brings habit." So today rhetorical analysis is not a "landed" occupation, traveling a narrow road. Rather, we are on the high seas, capable of going any direction the social winds and our own sailing expertise take us. We have become ungovernable.

And that is a good thing. While the neo-Aristotelian approach still can provide insight in the hands of a competent Aristotelian scholar like Forbes Hill, most of us are better off—and certainly the field is much improved—now that we are each sailing our own ships, following our own stars.

But we are not rudderless—we still have David Zarefsky, Walt Fisher, Dick Gregg, and Ed Black to investigate new routes, chart new courses, improve our sailing techniques, and captain the lead ships. We may not always follow in their wake, of course, but that in no way is a denial that they are in their rightful place "at the helm."

Taking the Helm? Rhetorical Analysis? Public Discourse?

David Zarefsky
Northwestern University

The question marks in my title are central. Each of the key terms is, if not confused, at least contested. The result is paradoxical. We are assured of a lively self-reflexive disciplinary discussion about some of our most basic premises and assumptions—surely a happy result for communication scholars who forego the easy appeal of the unexamined life. At the same time, however, we undercut our collective ability to make powerful and significant statements about the supposed objects of our study. We instead make statements about ourselves and what we are doing, and the reach of those statements is naturally limited. While not stifling our own sense of ferment, therefore, if we are to "take the helm" we must either resolve or, more likely, transcend these basic questions that so often shape our work.

Let me begin with the concept of "taking the helm" itself. Elaborating the nautical metaphor from the specific apparatus for steering a ship to the more general notion of "a position of control," I understand the issue before us to be: trying to determine how communication scholars can occupy such a controlling position in the rhetorical analysis of public discourse. I take it as a given that we think our work justifies such a position but that, outside the range of our own voices and the pages of our own journals, we do not occupy such a position now. With few but notable exceptions, rhetorical analysis of contemporary public discourse is the province of journalists; of earlier public discourse, the province of political scientists and historians. The point is not to demean the understanding or insight that any of them can provide. But they come by their rhetorical training secondarily, often on the job or even intuitively, whereas for us an understanding of rhetoric is the *raison d'etre*. Why are they and not we at the helm?

The problem of how to take the helm is at least twofold. In part it truly is a matter of institutional politics, disciplinary promotion, and public relations, and I shall have something to say about those. But before any of these things, it is an intellectual problem. We must have something to say that warrants the attention and respect of communities who implicitly determine whose voices shall have the controlling position. Beyond our own colleagues, these communities include scholars in other disciplines, journalists and other interpreters of public life, a variety of specialized groups, and what sometimes has been referred to as the active or engaged public. Simply put, these audiences tend not to be interested in such disciplinary issues as whether the text is made by the rhetor or by the audience, whether the critic's role is to emancipate or to dominate, whether an account of a rhetorical act can be made to fit the category system of any particular theorist, or whether we wish to consider ourselves as pre-, post-, or "just" modern. Beyond ourselves, I believe that potential users of our work need answers to some basic questions about public discourse (both in specific cases and in general): What's going on here? What about it? Why should I care?

The first of these questions asks about the rhetorical dynamics of public discourse. What can a sensitive analyst see beneath the surface that helps to explain how the discourse works? What are the patterns, the allusions, the ritual dramas, the strategies, the arguments, the themes? Beyond identifying them, what can we say about how they work in the discourse? The second question asks for significance, for the meaning to be given to these rhetorical dynamics. It is a check against not only the analyses we denigrate with the adjective "cookie cutter" but also the pedestrian or banal and the analysis which serves no purpose other than an intellectual exercise. And the third question is one of relevance. It asks why our work should warrant the attention and adherence of those to whom we wish to speak. Because of our own disciplinary identity, we often answer this question from a theory-building perspective: our analysis is important because it creates, supports, modifies, limits, challenges, or undermines rhetorical theory. This answer, though important, limits our relevance beyond those for whom rhetorical theory really matters. We need also to answer the question from a *culture*-building perspective: our analysis is important because it shows how discourse constitutes, reconstitutes, sustains, advances, redirects, undermines, or destroys a culture. The disciplinary orientation of our own journals inclines us to concentrate on the first kind of relevance question, but the desire to "take the helm" must incline us to equal sophistication in answering the second.

The first prerequisite to "taking the helm," then, is for us collectively to do better work. We need to become more sophisticated analysts of discourse, more able to see into, through, and beyond a text, more knowledgeable about context and culture, more adept at examining and explaining the relationship between text and context, and more committed to making our work accessible beyond the boundaries of our own discipline. I offer these admonitions not as indictments of what we are now doing but as challenges to ourselves. We will not take or keep the helm unless we are always dissatisfied, always pushing ourselves harder to take our work to the next level of significance in understanding the richness of human communication and drawing on that understanding to explain the making of society and culture.

That is the intellectual dimension of "taking the helm." But since even the most substantial work does not automatically gain interest and acclaim, we need also attend to matters of public relations. Here I offer some practical, probably obvious, suggestions. We should engage our colleagues in cognate disciplines, publishing in their journals and participating in their conventions and encouraging

them to do the same with ours. We should continue our efforts to publish scholarly books that reach an audience beyond disciplinary boundaries. We should write for general-interest publications as well, and we should make ourselves available for analyses in the broadcast media and on the Internet. We should work for the inclusion of our journals in the appropriate abstracts, bibliographies, and citation indexes of other fields. We should examine the experience of those of our scholars who have succeeded in attracting the attention of a broader audience, to see whether it offers insight or guidance for others. We should emphasize for our students the value of learning to "think rhetorically," in the hope that they will carry this skill into their careers and professions. And, through our institutions and our disciplinary associations, we should use the press release, the press conference, and other such techniques to bring the work that we do to the attention of opinion leaders.

But what is this work that we do? In talking about "taking the helm," I have treated "rhetorical analysis of public discourse" as if it were an unproblematic set of terms. As we know, and as the question marks in my title remind us, that is hardly the case. Indeed, these terms provide us with the contestations we must figure out how to settle or surmount.

I'd like now to focus on the term "rhetorical analysis," both words of which are somewhat problematic. In his seminal essay seventy years ago (Wichelns, 1925), Wichelns sought to mark out the function of rhetorical analysis by noting that, unlike literary or aesthetic criticism, it was concerned not with permanence or beauty but with effect. This statement was easy to misunderstand, however, because "effect" is an empirical term. A generation of analysts believed that their task was to report the effects of public discourse, and they went about it in the most mechanical way imaginable: by citing the editorial reactions of prominent newspapers or reporting the results of subsequent public opinion polls. The former, of course, was not truly a report of the discourse's effects, and the latter suffered from the *post hoc* fallacy because the environment could not be controlled nor extraneous variables neutralized. Both types of report were often clumsily or superficially done; not for nothing were they disparaged by later writers as "cookie cutter" studies. Even more troublesome, though, was that they were not *analytical.* They did not bring the insight, interpretive acuity, or judgment of the rhetorical scholar to bear on the discourse. In treating discourse primarily as an event that had consequences rather than as a richly layered text, they made statements little different from those that might be offered by a journalist, historian, or political scientist, yet without the benefit of their experience and expertise. With no significant value added by their work, it was hard for rhetorical scholars to take the helm.

More recent research has avoided this problem by treating the concern for effect differently. Rather than report on effects, scholars attempt to examine *how* discourse can have effects. Believing that discourse can shape the very frame of reference in which an issue is considered, they explore what in the text might invite, or facilitate, or encourage a particular response, and the response may be less a judgment about the speech than a way of thinking about its subject. To cite just a few examples: Michael Hogan's study of the Panama Canal treaties (Hogan, 1986) explores how a particular characterization of public opinion poll results might facilitate a judgment about the acceptability of the treaties. Garry Wills argues (Wills, 1992) that Lincoln's portrayal of the Declaration of Independence in his Gettysburg Address "remade America" by enabling nationalism to trump states' rights. My own study of Lyndon Johnson (Zarefsky, 1986) considered how the prevalence of a military metaphor could influence thought and action.

These and other scholars basically were *interpreting* possible effects, but their language sometimes slipped into *identification* of causes and effects much like the social scientist would do. Since these proclamations usually were unaccompanied by evidence of their alleged effects—that, after all, was not their true purpose—they could be called into question, as George Edwards has done in a trenchant critique (Edwards, 1996). If

rhetorical scholars asserted but could not prove that discourses had effects, then how could they possibly "take the helm" in the study of discourse? Indeed, critiques such as Edwards's could be misconstrued to support the prejudice that the word "rhetoric" *deserved* to be preceded by such adjectives as "mere," "shallow," or "empty."

These critiques need to be taken seriously. Unlike the "cookie cutter" accusations, though, I believe they will lead to clarification rather than abandonment of the rhetorical analyst's enterprise, to a sharper understanding of the difference between description and interpretation, between prediction and explanation, and hence to a clearer recognition of the special insight the rhetorical analyst can contribute.

Meanwhile, however, the word "analysis" also has been rendered troublesome. It suggests a distance between the analyst and the rhetor. In principle the analyst is neutral, standing back from the action and explaining what is taking place in another person's discourse. In recent years the goal of analytic neutrality has been attacked as both impossible and undesirable. Rhetorical analysis is itself public discourse and the analyst is also an advocate; it is false and deceptive to pretend otherwise. According to this view, rhetorical analysis does and should have a political purpose. And, perhaps, since rhetoric is so often a means to promote or extend institutional power, the analyst or critic should seek to limit or question power, to give voice to those silenced by it, and to empower those who have been marginalized. Something akin to this line of thinking has animated inquiry ranging from the controversy in our journals a generation ago about Richard Nixon's 1969 "silent majority" speech (Newman, 1970; Hill, 1972; Campbell, 1972) to the "critical rhetoric" project advanced in recent years by Ray McKerrow (1989) and others.

This line of inquiry does take rhetorical analysis in a different direction, and may position it for a leading role in critical studies asserting the significance of ideology. But, as I wondered 25 years ago, if one's goal is to stop the Vietnam war, is one more likely to "take the helm" by leading protest rallies, by influencing legislative opinion, or by writing essays for the *Quarterly Journal of Speech?* And, as I wonder now, if one's ideology largely predetermines the outcome of one's analysis, will the analysis "take the helm" in convincing those not already committed to the cause? My purpose is not to answer these questions; despite the probably loaded way in which I have framed them, there is a good case to be made on both sides. My point is only that in focusing so heavily on these questions we may render difficult the goals of "taking the helm" in the senses I have discussed it above.

One final difficulty deserves mention here. As the interpretive turn has marked the social sciences and humanities, as scholars in many disciplines have discovered rhetoric, and as the interdisciplinary field of cultural studies has been in the ascendant, some have found it pointless to mark out any territory for rhetorical analysis as distinct from any other kind. Rhetoric not only constitutes culture; it *is* culture. On this view, discourse indexes or reflects culture; it inscribes and reinscribes cultural narrative, ritual dramas, and hierarchies. Surely this perspective expands the significance of what the rhetorical analyst might say. But if everything is discourse, and every analysis is rhetorical, not only is there far too much ground to cover but also there is no special voice for the trained rhetorical analyst to add. That may make it difficult to "take the helm."

In sum, then, we collectively are uncertain about rhetorical analysis—what "analysis" means, whether that is what we wish to do, what makes analysis "rhetorical," and whether that is a distinction we wish to invoke. These certainly are fundamental questions. And equally deep concerns are raised by the term "public discourse."

Traditionally, we thought "discourse" meant "speeches." We studied the great orations of earlier eras and the closest approximations we could find in our own time. As our emphasis on orality diminished, we broadened our concerns to any use of language to inform or persuade, and we felt as much at home examining pamphlets, editorials, and letters as we did with speeches. Under the influence of television, we have focused increasingly on the visual and nonverbal modes of representation. Under the influence of the "performance paradigm," we have collapsed the distinction between action and representation, and have made all the world a discourse. One prominent sociologist (Brown, 1987) captures the expansiveness of this notion in the title of his book, *Society as Text.* If all of human action is discourse, then what can we say we are studying? On the other hand, distinctions among modes of discourse increasingly seem artificial when we realize that the processes of rhetorical construction and reconstruction, symbolic action, and influence can occur in virtually any form of discourse. Not only that, but such diverse objects and activities as the architecture of museums and monuments, the massing of bodies, and the conduct of war do have a significant rhetorical dimension: they convey messages and influence people. Studying nonverbal representations and even physical actions as texts foregrounds this dimension and makes it accessible for analysis. Rhetorical analysis, in fact, can offer a unique insight into these actions and objects by exposing them through a lens that no other analyst will use. There probably is no way ultimately to resolve the meaning of "discourse" and it may be best if the term remains essentially contested.

This claim is even more true of the term "public." Public discourse may be seen as discourse that is addressed to a public, or as discourse of public figures, or as discourse that is concerned with public issues, or as discourse that is situated in the public sphere. Each of these notions, in turn, raises problems.

Perhaps the simplest notion of public discourse is that it is addressed to a public. At minimum, this means that it is not a private matter such as an internal dialogue between one's self and soul or an informal conversation with another person, of which no record is kept. But beyond these fundamentals, difficult questions quickly intrude. Is a "public" any different from an audience? Typically the answer has been yes; we have imagined an audience as a specific instantiation of a broader public and have treated as public discourse that which is available to, or potentially important to, "secondary audiences" beyond the one immediately addressed. A speaker addressing a question of tax policy before a specific audience would still be speaking publicly because the subject of her remarks would be of interest to others. If the speech was transcribed, taped, or broadcast live, it also would be public because it would be available to others.

Another way to think of public discourse is to ask whether the participants are public figures, persons who are widely known and recognized. Whatever such a celebrity might say, in whatever circumstance, counts as public discourse. On this view, for instance, Richard Nixon's Oval Office conversations would have been considered public discourse, whether or not the tapes had been preserved, because of President Nixon's significance as a public figure. In contrast, the first view of the public would have excluded the discourse—it consisted, after all, of confidential conversations—were it not for the fact that the tapes preserved the interaction and made it accessible by others.

Yet a third way to conceive of "public discourse" is to focus on discourse concerned with public rather than private issues. Here it is the subject matter, not the formal properties of discourse, that determines whether it is public. Issues may be seen as public if they affect people collectively as well as individually, if they require cooperative action for their resolution, if the choice of action must be based on subjective judgment because it is impossible ever to have all the relevant evidence, and if—despite this last constraint—a decision nevertheless is required. *Phronesis,* or practical wisdom, is the goal of such decisions, and the central question on which public discourse is focused is "What should we do? "

This account privileges discourse concerned with matters of politics and governance, legislation, collective social choices, deliberations about policy, and the conduct of war and peace. These matters, of course, are similar to Aristotle's common topics and to his statement that rhetoric was an offshoot of politics and ethics. Questions of per-

sonal identity become public issues insofar as they focus on who is eligible to participate in the discussion (as in the Civil Rights movement of the 1950s and early 1960s, for example). But expressions of self-affirmation for their own sake, like matters of fad or fashion and some of the materials of popular culture, would not enjoy the same presumptive status as public issues. This whole view, of course, has been open to challenge, and probably the most fundamental challenge is to question whether the very distinction between public and private is meaningful, especially in an age in which "the personal is political" and in which popular culture often engages political or social issues.

Still another way to think of public discourse is as discourse situated in the public sphere. The literature on the public sphere is vast and multidisciplinary, and neither space nor time permits me to do it justice here. The concept of the public sphere has been contrasted usefully with the personal and technical spheres, each of which has different norms for the validation of claims (Goodnight, 1982). The public sphere engages people in their capacity as citizens rather than in their capacity as specialized experts, partisans, or committed ideologues. Moreover, neither power, nor force, nor money, nor any other variable except the force of the better argument is the standard for making judgments. Public discourse, then, is discourse that aims to be appraised according to these standards. This view often is put forth not as a description of actually existing discourse but as a norm to which discourse should aspire. The norms regulating discourse, then, rather than its subject matter or the demographics of the audience, determine whether it is regarded as "public."

This view also is controversial. Critics maintain that the public sphere as described here is an impossible ideal and hence an inappropriate norm; others claim that the public sphere actually exists, or at least that it has existed at defined places and times. Some of this second group believe that a sense of the public sphere can be reclaimed; others, that it has been eroded or lost as a result of changes in both society and communication technology. Yet other critics contest the notion that the public sphere stands apart from the personal and technical; they prefer to see it as yet another specialized sphere. And still other critics object to the very idea of the public sphere, arguing that it is inherently conservative and favors white men of power, social status, and wealth. The argument that the public sphere is defined in exclusionary terms is sometimes used to support its expansion and sometimes to call for the formation of what have been called "subaltern counterpublics" (Fraser, 1990) that function as publics for those traditionally marginalized and that challenge the dominant public sphere. These calls, in turn, raise the question of whether it makes sense to conceive of *a* public or only to conceive of *the* public. None of these issues, it is safe to say, is anywhere near resolution.

In sum, every one of the terms in my title is uncertain and subject to dispute. How can we possibly "take the helm" in rhetorical analysis of public discourse if we are this unsure about what we are doing?

Certainly I do not propose that we seek to settle these questions, either by resolving them in some ultimate sense or by stipulating answers for the discipline by fiat. The latter would stifle inquiry and we could not do the former if we tried. Besides, it is healthy for us to be reflexive and to grapple with such fundamental questions. But our danger is that our grappling with them can become obsessive, that an exclusive focus on matters of disciplinary identity and definition can eclipse our work with cases. We will not "take the helm" if we talk so much about what we are doing that we stop doing it. Along with these reflective inquiries, then, we need to keep doing rhetorical analysis of public discourse, hoping to make claims that are themselves significant and compelling, and addressing them to an audience wider than just ourselves.

We need, on the one hand, studies that press and extend and challenge the boundaries of rhetorical analysis of public discourse. These are studies that are innovative in their subjects, approaches, methods, or conclusions; studies that illumine in new ways both the objects of our analysis and the nature of our enterprise. On the

other hand, we also need more studies of the clear paradigm cases—the great speeches delivered by great speakers. We sometimes act as though this were a thoroughly explored canon. But it isn't. In fact, the paucity of serious scholarship on many of the landmarks in public discourse is astonishing. There is plenty still to be said about these canonical works, and as the reception of Garry Wills's book on the Gettysburg Address indicates, there is a receptive public audience for fresh and insightful scholarship. And this is as true of the texts of an earlier age as it is of the contemporary on which we sometimes lavish more attention.

One thing going for us as we try to take the helm is the centrality of our subject. Public discourse is everywhere; it both regulates and constitutes significant arenas of our life. But it does not automatically follow that our discipline, much less our subfield, will be recognized as central. The very ubiquitousness of public discourse makes it of interest to scholars in almost every discipline. Our ability to take the helm will depend on our skill at using rhetorical perspectives to make unique claims that are compelling to others. Even while we discuss among ourselves what is the nature of the beast, we must continue to get down to cases and let our significance be evident in our work.

REFERENCES

Brown, R. H. (1987). *Society as text.* Chicago: University of Chicago Press.

Campbell, K. K. (1972). *Critiques of contemporary rhetoric.* Belmont, CA: Wadsworth.

Edwards, G. C. (1996). Presidential rhetoric: What difference does it make? In M. J. Medhurst, (Ed.), *Beyond the rhetorical presidency.* College Station: Texas A & M University Press.

Fraser, N. (1990). Rethinking the public sphere. *Socialtext, 8–9,* 56–80.

Goodnight, G. T. (1982). The personal, technical, and public spheres of argument: A speculative inquiry into the art of public deliberation. *Journal of the American forensic association, 18,* 214–27.

Hill, F. I. (1972). Conventional wisdom—traditional form: The President's message of November 3, 1969. *Quarterly Journal of Speech, 48,* 373–86.

Hogan, J. M. (1986). *The Panama Canal in American politics: Domestic advocacy and the evolution of policy.* Carbondale: Southern Illinois University Press.

McKerrow, R. E. (1989). Critical rhetoric: Theory and praxis. *Communication Monographs, 56,* 91–111.

Newman, R. P. (1970). Under the veneer: Nixon's Vietnam speech of November 3, 1969. *Quarterly Journal of Speech, 46,* 168–78.

Wichelns, H. A. (1925). The literary criticism of oratory. In A. M. Drummond, (Ed.), *Studies in rhetoric and public speaking in honor of James Albert Winans.* New York: Century.

Wills, G. (1992). *Lincoln at Gettysburg: The words that remade America.* New York: Simon & Schuster.

Zarefsky, D. (1986). *President Johnson's war on poverty: Rhetoric and history.* Tuscaloosa: University of Alabama Press.

From Criticism to Critique to…

Walter R. Fisher
University of Southern California

If my title has caused you to wonder what I may have had in mind when I wrote it, you are not alone. I have wondered too. In fact, I have been wondering off and on since last March when Judith Trent insisted that I have a title for this presentation. The best that I have been able to come up with are some random thoughts and reflections. They all concern the ramifying movements in rhetorical criticism from its foundations in the writings of Herbert A. Wichelns, Ernest J. Wrage, and A. Craig Baird and Lester Thonssen to the ideas contained in theoretical pieces by Michael McGee, Raymie McKerrow, and Philip Wander.

What interests me in these movements are the shifts in positions regarding what sorts of knowledge, intellect, imagination, self-understanding, and disposition undergirds or should undergird the work of the rhetorical critic. In the beginning, as it were, the rhetorical critic was some sort of historian especially educated in rhetorical lore. For Wichelns, the critic was a cousin to the literary critic, an adept in the crossroads of literature and politics (Wichelns, 1962). For Wrage, the critic was an intellectual historian, an expert in how the public articulation of ideas advanced or enriched the nation's mind (Wrage, 1947). And for Baird and Thonssen, the critic was a cause and effect historian, a scholar armed with Aristotelian theory who assessed the immediate or long-range effects of public discourse (Baird & Thonssen, 1947). I am aware that there is no news in this Reader's Digest summary, but it is essential to what follows.

On rethinking these early works, it occurred to me that rhetorical criticism was not a monolithic, uniform intellectual enterprise. While Wichelns, Wrage, and Baird and Thonssen focused on the role of speeches in the constitution of the public mind, they thought of and assessed discourse in different ways: as political literature, as intellectual documents, and as agumentative catalysts for historic change. Yet, their similarities in presuppositions are striking, especially so in regard to what was to come. They were at one in stressing that speeches were instruments for the expansion of ideas. They shared Matthew Arnold's (1952) standard of excellence: "to know the best that is known and thought in the world, and by its turn making this known, to create a current of true and fresh ideas" (p. 458). They believed in "great men," authors, audiences, reason, and history. They were, in short, modernists. The rhetorical critic for them possessed "an appreciation of oratory," "familiarity with the background of rhetoric," "an inquiring mind," a disposition to "withhold judgment" until one's investigation was done, and "a dispassionate, objective attitude toward the object of investigation" (Thonssen & Baird, 1948, pp. 19–20).

Before considering our most recent writers on rhetorical criticism, I would like to note several more points about rhetorical criticism's beginnings: First, theory did not come into it until Baird and Thonssen wrote their classic text, *Speech Criticism.* Neither Wichelns nor Wrage was an adherent of any particular theoretical formulation. It was Baird and Thonssen who gave us neo-Aristotelianism. The fault in this was not, in my judgment, that they insisted on the critic knowing and using Aristotle's theory; it was the way in which their ideas were used—most often to name components of speeches rather than explain how they worked. The same can be said of much that passes for criticisms that employ Kenneth Burke's theories. Baird and Thonssen (1947), in the article they published in *QJS* announcing their approach to rhetorical criticism, specifically admonished the critic to "wisely refuse to succumb to the rigidities of any formula…" (p. 136).

My second observation here may seem trivial, but, for the record, I confess that I was educated as a neo-Aristotelian—with A. Craig Baird; I was not trained as one. Dogs and Marine Corps recruits are trained. Scholars are educated—to know, to think, to imagine, to be curious, to appreciate, and to honor the profession and those who inhabit it. These are, in any case, the sorts of things I learned from Baird and Thonssen, however imperfectly.

My third observation concerns the early stress on method. For Wichelns (1962), the necessary topics of criticism were "The man, his work, and his times.…" For Wrage (1947), the focus was on the speech rather than the speaker, and the critic was supposed to follow the paths set by such historians as Vernon L. Parrington, Merle Curti, and Ralph Gabriel. For Baird and Thonssen (1947), the critic was to analyze speakers and speeches following the rhetorical canons—not, however, as determinants of what necessarily should be written but as guides to insure thoroughness. The aura of method was not, then, so much a mandate of the founders of rhetorical criticism as it was a general propensity to emulate the historian, who wanted to emulate the natural scientist. Happily now, even natural scientists question the role of method in inquiry. Discovery and creative, critical thinking are stultified by rigorous adherence to method, if not completely denied by it.

In moving from the founders to the present era, I see two broad movements: reformation and reconstitution. Both movements involve reconstruction, and while those whom I would place in these movements are no more intelligent, talented, or wise than the founders, they are, on the whole, more sophisticated in their understanding of things rhetorical. And the world is not the same as it was—whether it is designated as neo-modernist or postmodernist. If one believes all one reads and hears about our time, we live in the midst of death and decline—of history, philosophy, nation-states, language, religion, and so on. Virtually all possible stable foundations of knowing, valuing, and acting are supposedly gone or going. Those whom I would place in the reconstitution movement generally adhere to these ideas; they include, as I have already suggested, Michael McGee, Raymie McKerrow, and Philip Wander. Those whom I would include in the reformation movement are such writers as Tom Farrell, Stephen Lucas, Edwin Black, Michael Leff, James Andrews, Robert Scott, and myself. There are no magic markers to distinguish these groups, as each person mentioned is as concerned with the future as any other. However, there are world views or presuppositions that separate them. My ruminations have led me to think as follows.

A focal point of resistance and difference between the groups concerns the concept of reason. If not totally committed to the notions of postmodernism, those who would reconstitute rhetorical criticism seem to endorse a line of thinking that began with Nietzsche, who despaired the will to power in enlightenment thought. Foucault added that knowledge, and thereby, reason was an historical construction of public and academic institutions. Derrida deconstructed the idea in order to subvert the will to truth he saw as its motivation. He wrote: "No truth, no war." For his part, Lyotard declared the end of metanarratives—the stories that have aspired to universal application and on which dreams of transcendental and local communities have depended. The twentieth-century death of metanarratives, I suspect, is yet another casualty of the death of God in the last century. It is interesting to me that in declaring the end of metanarratives, Lyotard implicitly affirms a new metanarrative. Rather than a story that accounts for one's being in an ongoing narrative that grounds one's identity in a continuous historical or transhistorical epic, the postmodern story asserts that progressive history is at an end; life is a short story marked by contingency, discontinuity, and accidents of birth, experience, and death; the only ground for one's identity is local circumstance, one's religion, ethnicity, nationality, economic or social class, sexual orientation, ideology, desire, and so on. The world is fragmented and at war, and rhetorical expression is a primary weapon in this war. If I were to construct an axiom for this view, it would be this: whoever controls the word or symbolic exchange, controls the world. The role of the critic, then, is to unmask the rhetorical dynamics of this war. His or her mode of analysis is critique. As McGee (1990) writes: "Every bit of discourse …invites its own critique" (p. 281).

But what is critique, and how does it relate to criticism? Both words have the same root and are often used interchangeably. However, I will suggest that there is a difference between assessment that is open and that which is closed, between that which begins with curiosity or a hunch and that which begins with an agenda and certainty, between appreciative appraisal and determined dismantling, and between conclusions that are subject to argument and those that are not. I do not want to be misunderstood here. I am suggesting differences, perhaps too strongly. I value revelations of the machinations of those who would oppress us, negatively define us, or inhibit humane practices. And I value the knowledge of the material conditions that shape and are shaped by rhetorical transactions and events. It is good to understand the role of ideology, desire, simulation, and indeterminacy in these experiences. All this is fair, given the nature of things rhetorical, whether conceived in terms of ideas, proofs, signs of consubstantiation, texts, contexts, discourse, fragments, or performance. The truth is that rhetorical things have been and can be interpreted in a myriad of ways. There is no discipline that has not in one or more of its manifestations studied communication, from the natural sciences to the social sciences, to the humanities. The question for the rhetorical critic, I think, is: What conceptualizations will enable a work that reveals what is remarkable about a given rhetorical transaction or event? The contribution of such a work is that it usefully informs those who care about things rhetorical. It may or may not change the world for the better, but, in one way or another, it should. On the other hand, I do not think that rhetorical criticism serves well when it reflects the practices it condemns—hegemonic intolerance, opposition to other ways of thinking and act-

ing—or professes a denial of reason or truth while insisting at the same time that it contains the truth about unreason and truth. On this, I agree with Gadamer (1981), who wrote: "the exigence of reason for unity remains inexorable" (p. 19). Reason does not have to be foundational in order to serve well, as the history of rhetorical reason has demonstrated. And as Blumenberg (1989) observed: "The axiom of all rhetoric is the principle of insufficient reason…" (p. 447).

So far, I have noted some similarities among writers in two movements, and some differences between those I have designated as the reformers and reconstituters. There are, of course, major differences among writers of the same movements. For instance, Tom Farrell's (1993) neo-Aristotelian, John Deweyian effort to restore a sense of rhetorical community stands in stark contrast to Michael Leff's neoclassical, close reading of texts to establish a mid-level theory of rhetorical analysis and a heightened appreciation of the rhetorician's art (Leff & Sachs, 1990). And there are important differences between Michael McGee's (1990) conception of fragments and Philip Wander's (1983) emphasis on ideology. But, with the reformers, it is clear that tradition strongly informs their reformation; and with the reconstituters, it is clear that new grounds are being plowed with the potential of radically altering that tradition.

However, there is one more world that I would like to outline, one that I think may not be denied by postmodernist but which definitely seems to be submerged; it is a view I think is shared by those who would reform rhetorical criticism. The world, as suggested by Martha Nussbaum (1992, pp. 216–222), is the world in which we live, we die; in it, we hunger and thirst; we need shelter; we experience sexual desire and pursue relationships; we try to avoid pain and seek pleasure; we prize an ability to use all of our senses and when any of them fail, we want remedies; we want love, or at least recognition and respect; and we want to live free from repression and oppression, and free enough to realize our own being. These attributes I hasten to say are functional, not metaphysical. With this view in mind, it is possible to conceive and recognize discourse that is not coercive or corrosive, that encourages the celebration of the human capacity for honor as well as hubris. It is a world in which both reformers and reconstituters can struggle together to enrich the knowledge and appreciation of things rhetorical.

In conclusion, if this presentation had a thesis, it would say essentially what T. S. Eliot (1952) once wrote about criticism in relation to poetry: "So our criticism, from age to age, will reflect the things that the age demands; and the criticism of no one man and of no one age can be expected to embrace the whole of poetry or exhaust all of its uses" (p. 545). So it is with rhetoric and rhetorical criticism. Just as our time is stressed by tensions and transition, so are our conceptions of rhetorical criticism. As for its future, all I can say for certainty is that the conversation should continue with all the good will participants can muster. For the time being, the issue is criticism or critique, and will remain so for some time. For sure, there will be transformations in each movement and between them.

REFERENCES

Arnold, M. (1952). The function of criticism at the present time. In W. J. Bate (Ed.), *Criticism: The major texts* (p. 458). New York: Harcourt, Brace and World.

Baird, A. C., & Thonssen, L. (1947). Methodology in the criticism of public address. *The Quarterly Journal of Speech, 33,* 134–138.

Blumenberg, H. (1989). Anthropological approach to the significance of rhetoric. In K. Baynes, J. Bohman, & T. McCarthy (Eds.), *After philosophy: End or transformation* (pp. 428–458). Cambridge, MA: MIT Press.

Eliot, T. S. (1952). The modern mind. In W. J. Bate (Ed.), *Criticism: The major texts* (pp. 538–545). New York: Harcourt, Brace, and World.

Farrell, T. B. (1993). *Norms of rhetorical culture.* New Haven, CT: Yale University Press.

Gadamer, H. (1981). *Reason in the Age of Science.* Cambridge, MA: MIT Press.

Leff, M., & Sachs, A. (1990). Words the most like things: Iconicity and the rhetorical text. *Western Journal of Communication, 54,* 252–273.

McGee, M. C. (1990). Text, context, and the fragmentation of contemporary culture. *Western Journal of Speech Communication, 54,* 274–290.

McKerrow, R. E. (1989). Critical rhetoric: Theory and praxis. *Communication Monographs, 56,* 91–111.

Nussbaum, M. (1992). Human functioning and social justice: In defense of Aristotelian essentialism. *Political Theory, 20,* 216–222.

Thonssen, L., & Baird, A. C. (1948). *Speech criticism: The development of standards for rhetorical appraisal.* New York: The Ronald Press Co.

Wander, P. (1983). The ideological turn in modern criticism. *Central States Speech Journal, 34,* 1–18.

Wichelns, H. A. (1962). The literary criticism of oratory. In A. M. Drummond (Ed.), *Studies in rhetoric and public speaking in honor of James Albert Winans* (pp. 181–216). New York: Russell & Russell.

Wrage, E. J. (1947). Public address: A study in social and intellectual history. *The Quarterly Journal of Speech, 33,* 451–457.

"The Mind's I," "The Mind's We," "The Mind's They": A Cognitive Approach to the Rhetorical Analysis of Public Discourse

Richard B. Gregg
Pennsylvania State University

There is general agreement among the observers of our age that we are in a time of transition. One of the phrases prominently employed characterizes ours as the "age of information." Other character-izations have referred to different developments that are equally pertinent, among them the realiza-tion of researchers in the cognitive sciences that, epistemologically speaking, we are in the age of the brain. In recent years, advances in the knowl-edge of how our brains work have been enormous. If we attend to those findings, we are being chal-lenged to reexamine our understanding of such fundamental behaviors as perceiving, knowing, feeling, valuing, and symbolizing. Whatever it is that we call rhetoric—however it is that we charac-terize rhetorical activity—it is one of the phenom-ena that takes shape in the theatres of the mind. Thus, the discoveries regarding how our brains work are relevant to our efforts. I suggest that a cognitive approach promises rewarding work for the future, for we will gain a more complete and accurate comprehension of rhetorical behaviors central to our being than we have managed up to now. I want to briefly outline the grounds upon which the cognitive sciences beckon us to stand, and to suggest the shape of the terrain beyond.

For some who espouse and emphasize hu-manistic perspectives, there will be deep-seated and longstanding feelings of aversion to such find-ings. Our Western intellectual tradition has as-sumed a separation of the intellectual and emotional "mindedness" of human beings from the material structures that house that mindedness. Part of the aversion may be the belief that neuro-physiological findings will reveal deterministic tendencies and constraints that foreclose human initiative and choice. Initiative and choice lie at the heart of values dear to students of rhetoric. But if we look closely at what is known about the nuts and bolts of brain function, our aversion will dis-appear.

Roughly put, each human brain has approxi-mately 100 billion neurons. Each individual neuron has the potential to respond variously to the same stimulus, and response can change in a twinkling, or over time. But neurons never fire alone; they are always activated in neuronal patterns located throughout the brain, which fire in conjunction with other patterns. All of this is made possible by some 100 trillion synaptic connections, which are modifiable, so that possible combinations become incalculable. Paul Churchland (1995) points out that "each individual human is a unique hand dealt from this monumental deck. It is at different points within this almost endless space of connective pos-sibilities that each individual human personality re-sides, that each distinct set of religious, moral, and scientific convictions resides, and that each distinct cultural orientation resides" (p. 5). But our expla-nation is not yet complete, for we must add to the mix the interaction of chemical systems that have only begun to be systematically studied, the "tides of neurochemicals seeping from many sites and ed-dying through the body, sending messages via re-ceptors on immune, nerve and organ cells." Gallagher (1996) goes on to point out that we are looking at something more akin to a squishy aquatic ecosystem than a computer, and notes that "this highly responsive web affects and is affected by the individual's characteristic style of self-regulation and handling challenge" (p. 115). With this in mind, Churchland concludes that *your physical brain is far too complex and mercurial for its behavior to be predicted in any but the broadest outlines or for any but the shortest distances into the future. Faced with the extraordinary dynamical feature of a functioning brain, no device constructible in this universe could ever predict your behavior, or your thoughts, with anything more than merely statistical success (p. 3).*

In sum, human cognitive development is epigenetic; it develops and changes through interaction with phenomena in our external environment, and intentions and purposes that lie within us. It does not partake of absolute necessity, nor is it susceptible to easy and sure prediction. At the same time our cognitive processes are conserving in nature, seeking to locate and secure those phenomena that nurture our well being and avoid those that threaten and endanger us. They provide stability because they are themselves stable in the principles of their operation. They are efficient in varying degrees as they iteratively settle on phenomena that prove to be efficacious and satisfying. Thus it is that we can study human behavior in general, and rhetorical behavior in particular.

My title for this presentation adumbrates several fundamental postulates for a cognitive orientation to the rhetorical study of public discourse. *The Mind's I* is the title of a book authored by Hofstadter and Dennett (1981). I steal it because it emphasizes that all human meaning begins and ends in the human mind. Meaning does not begin or end in any system of language; it does not begin or end in what we broadly or narrowly construe to be a text; it does not begin or end in those interactive factors we identify as context; it does not begin or end in those phenomena we refer to as culture. All of these phenomena have the potential to induce and influence our meanings. But in the fundamental sense, meaning begins and ends in the individual human brain. Put another way, the patterns, or structures, or schema that shape and express our perceptions, feelings, and purposes, emanate from the actions of our brain's architecture. Rhetorical behavior is deeply imbedded in the functioning of the human brain.

The Mind's We is the title of a book authored by Gillespie that discusses cognitive functioning in terms of interpersonal and social interaction. Such interaction begins as the neurological system of the birth mother monitors, constrains, and encourages the neurological system of the unborn. In this environment, sensory and rhythmic contact initiates perceptual structuring. The need for such contact continues after birth through personal interaction with care givers. Perceptions of self based on bodily images develop; displacement occurs, revealing a world of other selves and artifacts; a purposeful self in search of control emerges. All of this is enabled by the fact that we innately possess a unique ability to recognize and respond to human facial patterns. We read them from birth, get meanings from them, behave on the basis of them. As humans mature, it is partly through social interaction that we perceive and structure various units of meaning and their relationships in growing complexity. Commonalities and differences emerge, so we unify, divide, and engage in related actions of subspeciation. Rhetorical behavior is inherent in such actions.

The Mind's They should not require much explanation. If the student of public rhetoric wishes to comment beyond his/her own reactions, then knowledge of the general workings of the human mind/brain must be brought to bear on specific situations and contexts. As I noted earlier, certain stabilities of human cognition make the public perspective possible.

Over a decade ago, the findings of cognitive research revealed six principles of processing that were constant and generalizable (Gregg, 1984, p. 50). I reiterate them here, because research has continued to prove their stability:

1. Detecting and Forming Boundaries. Boundaries help establish units of meaning. This principle is so important that the mind/brain will complete discontinuous boundaries in perception and will construct borders or boundaries in perception where none exist.

2. Abstraction. The basic neurological act of perception is one that helps structure meaning by abstracting from the total environment. Abstraction achieves economy and efficiency, and by its nature can lead to distortion.

3. Association. The largest portion of the brain is engaged in the activity of forming associations, an action that involves comparing and contrasting. The enormous cognitive potential for formulating association is often central to rhetorical action.

4. Classification. Classification is an outcome of associative processes. The mind/brain classifies and groups all aspects of human meaning.

5. Hierarchy. The mind/brain, in structuring the patterns and schema that we call meaning, orders networks of association. We are quite capable of operating with schema that might be perceived to be inconsistent, and even contradictory.

6. Rhythm. Mind/brain activity is inherently rhythmic. The symbolic inducements of rhythm, while pervasive in all human symbolizing, have rarely received the attention from students of rhetoric they deserve.

All of these processes constituting major principles of mind/brain activity have the potential to induce consonant or dissonant responses. They are among the deep currents of cognitive constancy.

In the last decade, new methods of brain and cognitive research have allowed scholars to study the operations of normal brains in addition to drawing inferences from brain damaged cases. The results lead to profoundly different understandings of the workings of the mind/brain.

First, the monumental mistake of Descartes, passed on by Kant, that "reason" is essentially some kind of "spiritual" or "mindful" essence that occurs apart from our physical materiality must be cast aside. There is no separation of mind and body; they are inextricably joined. If we must establish an equational relationship we would do better to adopt the suggestion of Damasio (1994) that the mind is the attentive audience of the body. As he explains, every muscle, joint, and internal organ of the body sends signals to the brain through the peripheral nerves, and chemical substances generated by bodily activity influence brain operation through bloodstream transmis-

sion. Alternatively, the brain acts on all parts of the body through nerves, and manufactures and orders the release of chemicals to all parts of the body (p. 88). Damasio concludes that the body does not just provide support for brain activity, but acts as a kind of yardstick to provide topics for brain representations: "our minds would not be the way they are if it were not for the interplay of body and brain during evolution, during individual development, and at the current moment. The mind had to be first about the body, or it could not have been" (pp. xvi, xvii).

The interactive unit of the mind/brain acts in concert with the environment to form an inseparable ensemble, and is fundamental to social and cultural activity. As I noted earlier, one's self-image begins in infancy with the perceived schema of one's own body. Thus, at all levels of meaning, cognitive schema of the human body and its actions form the basis for intellectual comprehension and find their way into the manifestations of rhetorical suasion. One of the most comprehensive discussions of the interaction of the functions of the body with the articulations of the mind can be found in *The Body in the Mind* (1987) where Johnson discusses the way fundamental body schema such as "containment," "force," "balance," and "center-periphery" act as basic units for "understanding," proliferate radially into associational concepts, and find their way into the symbol systems we develop such as language and mathematics. By tracking this developmental path, we can sometimes account for the rhetorical force of public discourse. Thus, in another place, I argue that staunch pro-life advocates are motivated, in this time of rapid change, by threats to the personal boundaries of their selfhood, with bodily schema being central to the cloud of emotions and values stirred up in political debate. For the true believing pro-lifer, the issue of abortion will override all others in presidential and other political campaigns (1995).

Rejection of the mind/body dichotomy leads to rejection of the nature/nurture dichotomy, and brings the reason/emotion dichotomy into view. I must deal with it briefly, because it impacts directly on the study of rhetorical discourse.

The emotion/reason dichotomy draws heavily on the mind/body distinction; it depends on the assumption that what we have called "emotions" and "feelings" are phenomena of a lower order than the more intellectual processes of reason, and that we must strive to see to it that reason functions in a superior fashion to tutor the more "irrational" pangs of emotion. This relationship has been thoroughly refuted by contemporary research. Damasio (1994) explains that:

> there appears to be a collection of systems in the human brain consistently dedicated to the goal-oriented thinking process we call reasoning, and to the response selection we call decision making, with special emphasis on the person and social domain. This same collection of systems is also involved in emotion and feeling, and is partly dedicated to processing body signals. (p. 70)

He goes on to accord emotions and feelings a "truly privileged status":

> They are represented at many neural levels, including the neocortical, where they are the neuroanatomical and neurophysiological equals of whatever is appreciated by other sensory channels. But because of their inextricable ties to the body, they come first in development and retain a primacy that subtly pervades our mental life. Because the brain is the body's captive audience, feelings are winners among equals. And since what comes first constitutes a frame of reference for what comes after, feelings have a say on how the rest of the brain and cognition go about their business. Their influence is immense. (pp. 159, 160)

Reason, then, cannot tutor emotion—the reverse is the case; emotion functions to tutor reason!

What the conclusive results of research in the cognitive sciences show is that there is nothing in the world that corresponds with the mind/body, nature/nurture, and reason/emotion dichotomies. They exist only in our thoughts for reasons of discursive, expository convenience, the same reasons that have led us to focus on the processes of categorization and inference, rather than emotion and motivation (Tooby & Cosmides, 1995, p. 72).

While the cognitive perspective that I am outlining demands that we discard old dichotomies and understand new unities of human behavior, it also demands that we engage in conceptual separations. I mention one such case because it reveals one of our frequent easy assumptions of unity or near unity where none exists. Language and meaning are not the same. What we conventionally refer to as language is a narrow discursive representation of the larger patterns of meaning we operate from. There is no debate about the matter; language and meaning are simply not identical. Human intelligence without language is extremely powerful. "Among the uniquely human capacities found in the complete absence of language are a capacity for spontaneous gesture and mime…; toolmaking and praxis in general; emotional expression and social intelligence, including an ability to comprehend complex events and remember roles, customs, and appropriate behavior" (Donald, 1991, p. 93).

Evidence indicates that children understand certain grammatical and phrasing complexities, and certain scientific laws like the law of conservation before they can verbally articulate anything about them. Our ability to recognize and discriminate such sensory properties as taste and color far outstrips our ability to express the basis for such discriminations in words. In similar fashion, we discriminate human faces and human facial expression of emotions. "In fact, the cognitive priority of the preverbal over the verbal shows itself, upon examination, to be a feature of almost all of our cognitive categories" (Churchland, 1995, p. 144). Throughout his recent book, Churchland discusses the processes by which patterns recognized and structured in various parts of the brain come together to form what I have called schema, the meanings that we shape and act upon. He calls this activation pattern "vector coding," and he says it is now fairly clear that the basic unit of cognition is the activation vector, and that the basic cognitive process is vector to vector transformation. "None of these things have anything essential to do with sentences or propositions, or with inferential relations between them. Our traditional language-centered conception of cognition is now confronted with a very different brain-centered conception, one that assigns language no fundamental role at all" (pp. 322, 323).

I believe that language can function to facilitate thought processes; I think there is no question that language often acts to stabilize, or fix meanings. But evidence clearly shows that what we conventionally call language does not evoke or reveal all the layers and nuances of meanings that are a part of symbolic action. Casting thought and feelings into words often ignores or distorts the most telling aspects of cognition. But by broadening our gaze beyond the usual intellectual and grammatical meanings of inference and relationship to examine such phenomena as metaphorical and metonymic relations that are emotive and valuative, and by considering nonverbal units of meaning in relation to the verbal, analysts of public rhetoric may arrive at a more complete, albeit complex understanding of rhetorical events.

Let me illustrate briefly with an example that comes from the recent presidential campaign via the work of a foremost cognitive scholar, Lakoff (1996), who undertakes to examine certain values that comprise the world views of prototypical conservatives and liberals by analyzing the moral assumptions underlying the themes of family and family values. "Family," of course, becomes an easy metaphor for larger complexes of political and social relationships. It is also a significant metaphor, representing a fundamental unit of nurturing and relationship that goes far back in our evolutionary history. Drawing on knowledge gained from his very complex study of human cognition, Lakoff (1987) capsulizes the two metaphorical perspectives with the phrases, "strict father morality" and "nurturant parent morality," and argues for rejection of the "strict father" metaphor.

Following a cognitive orientation, we have reason to enlarge Lakoff's analysis concerning the potency and force of the family values issue. In this age of change when many individuals feel threatened by what seem to be impersonal forces bigger than any individual, and beyond our control, it is entirely human to become conservative in thought, and revert to conceptualizations that

were important and comforting earlier in our lives, and in the development of our species. In the personal experiences of many, the family is a unit where interactions could be personalized and some control over the environment could be exercised. Regardless of family background, the mythology of the family becomes a natural schema to employ in the face of environmental threat. But realities and notions of family are also in flux, and many would argue that old stereotypes of family should be discarded as misleading. Another term was heard with frequency during the recent campaign: "community." Of the two major candidates for the presidency, Clinton employed examples of "community" more often and more consistently than Dole. The schema of community is more encompassing and more flexible than that of "family," but still implies borders and boundaries that structure a space where individual impact and control might be experienced. My comments here argue that in this age when impersonal forces seem to be threatening on a large scale, personal nurturance and control can become an imperative goal, and issues clothed in the terms of family and community values reveal the felt need for personal control to be part of a larger cognitive and rhetorical effort to renegotiate our relationship with the environment in which we now find ourselves.

I close with a personal observation. In keeping with the way we tend to personalize the presidency and campaigns for that office, I call attention to the facial visages of Bob Dole and Bill Clinton who symbolize the fathers of Lakoff's mythical families. I remember that infants universally respond to facial characteristics of care givers as they begin to comprehend themselves and others. I recall that infants tend to determine the intentions and emotions of their care givers as revealed in their faces before attributing meanings to the sounds and words that are uttered. I further recall that anger and happiness are among the several emotions universally recognized by infants. Finally, I recall that during the 1988 presidential campaign, some of the press observed that they could accurately predict who was going to win the election between Bush and Dukakis by tracking answers to the question, "if your child was lying injured as the result of an automobile accident, which of the two candidates would you rather have looking down into your child's eyes, offering help?" Following the leads suggested by this observation, it might be that the most telling answers from the recent campaign may have come to questions like, "who would you most like to order your pizza toppings for you?" or "if you died, who would you most want to leave your children to?"

I suggest that the answers will reveal emotion tutoring reason and personal motives to be centrally involved, that the mind will check with the body for benchmarks, that a history of personal and social relationships will come to bear on an imagined interpersonal interaction, that attitudes and values regarding inclusion and exclusion, discipline and flexibility, punishment and reward, companionship and leadership will come into play. I further suggest that if pushed for explanation and justification, respondents will be unable to adequately convey their cognitive move from private to public meaning. Unpacking the intricacies of cognitive interaction, the rhetorical analyst may come to new understandings of the phrase, "the personal presidency," and to the realization that public meanings are laced with private feelings and purposes.

REFERENCES

Churchland, P. (1995). *The engine of reason, the seat of the soul.* Cambridge, Massachusetts: MIT Press.

Damasio, A. R. (1994). *Descartes' error: Emotion, reason, and the human brain.* New York: G. P. Putnam's Sons.

Donald, M. (1991). *Origins of the modern mind.* Cambridge, MA: Harvard University Press.

Gallagher, W. (1996). *I.D.: How heredity and experience make you who you are.* New York: Random House.

Gillespie, D. (1992). *The mind's we.* Carbondale: Southern Illinois University Press.

Gregg, R. (1984). *Symbolic inducement and knowing: A study in the foundations of rhetoric.* Columbia: University of South Carolina Press.

Gregg, R. (1995). Rhetorical strategies for a culture war: Abortion in the 1992 campaign. In K. Kendall (Ed.), *Presidential campaign discourse,* pp. 201–220. Albany: State University of New York Press.

Hofstadter, D., & Dennett, D. (1981). *The mind's I.* New York: Basic Books.

Johnson, M. (1987). *The body in the mind: The bodily basis of meaning, imagination, and reason.* Chicago: University of Chicago Press.

Lakoff, G. (1987). *Women, fire and dangerous things: What categories reveal about the mind.* Chicago: University of Chicago Press.

Lakoff, G. (1996). *Moral politics: What conservatives know that liberals don't.* Chicago: University of Chicago Press.

Tooby, J., & Cosmides, L. (1995). The psychological foundations of culture. In J. Barkow, L. Cosmides, & J. Tooby (Eds.), *The adapted mind.* Oxford, England: Oxford University Press.

Tacks in Rhetorical Analysis

Edwin Black

University of Wisconsin, Madison

As you know, a tack has to do with the direction of a ship with respect to the trim of its sails. When you are at the helm of a sailboat, there are only two tacks that you can take. One tack is starboard, and the other is port. But every sailor knows that within each tack, there are a thousand subtle adjustments that have to be made to the vagaries of wind and current and craft.

The maritime metaphor that guides this program—the helm—is a convenient frame for my remarks because in defining rhetorical analysis, as in sailing a vessel, there are two tacks available, and within them, uncountable adjustments that a good critic makes to the nuanced pressures of the critical object.

One way of interpreting the term "rhetorical analysis" is to hold that it is a generic procedure applied to certain kinds of objects. If you take this starboard tack, then you view analysis, simply and always, as the identification and examination of the constituents of an object. The analytic schema would be constant, regardless of what objects are being analyzed, in the same obstinate way that two plus two always equals four, regardless of what objects are being aggregated. "Rhetorical analysis," therefore, would be the identification and examination of the constituents of a rhetorical object; "literary analysis" would be the same general procedure applied to a novel or a poem; and if the object of analysis were an economic transaction, then the procedure would be "economic analysis." The procedure—analysis—would be stable, at least in its broad outlines. The subject of the procedure would determine its adjectival modifier. On this starboard tack, therefore, "rhetorical analysis" would be defined as the analysis of rhetorical objects, which would be

such objects as speeches, campaigns, persuasive movements, advertisements, and arguments. Because this view identifies rhetorical analysis by its object of inquiry, let us call it the "objectivist definition."

The other tack in construing the term "rhetorical analysis" is to hold that the term refers to a particular procedure or method—one that may be more useful with some subjects than with others, but one that may, at least in principle, be applied to any subject whatever. Thus, on this port tack, an analytic system derived from Aristotle's theory of rhetoric, for example, or from Kenneth Burke's pentad could be deployed to examine not only what we conventionally regard as persuasive discourses, but also objects that we don't ordinarily consider to be persuasive discourses: scientific reports, for example, or automotive designs or metaphysical treatises or landscape paintings, or even landscapes themselves. This tack on rhetorical analysis is also generic, and it is also applicable to an incalculably huge class of objects, but it would have such broad applicability not because it is analytic, but rather because it is rhetorical. Inasmuch as this direction of rhetorical analysis identifies it not as an analysis of certain kinds of objects, but instead as a certain kind of analysis, let us call it the "methodological definition."

Although the adherents to each of these tacks may not always admit it, and sometimes may not even be aware of it, each tack is predicated on a certain larger view of the world. The objectivist definition of rhetorical analysis rests on the conviction that there are objects in the world of which each has an innate and substantial character, and that those objects can, at least in principle, be discriminated from one another. In order to be coherent, the objectivist view has to postulate the existence of rhetorical objects that are distinguishable from literary or monological or other commensurate objects.

Both the objectivist and the methodological interpretations are primarily definitional rules. They work, often competitively, to shape the conduct of criticism by regulating the language of critics, especially critics' use of the noun "rhetoric" and the adjective "rhetorical."

Hoyt Hudson's essay of 1924, "Rhetoric and Poetry," was an early statement of the objectivist view, but its most influential articulation was published the following year in Herbert Wichelns's "The Literary Criticism of Oratory." Even though we can now see Wichelns's essay as transitional, opening the way, as it did, to a methodological conception of the discipline, the essay still associated rhetorical criticism with a certain class of discursive objects—"the work of the speaker, of the pamphleteer, of the writer of editorials, and of the sermon maker."

There is a problem with the application of the objectivist definition. It is not always a serious problem, but it is a persistent one. The problem is that the critic's decision about whether a subject is appropriate for rhetorical analysis is a decision that the critic has to make prior to the analysis and not as a result of the analysis. And consequently, the work of critics who adhere to the objectivist definition almost always reinforces, but seldom challenges, our conventional conceptions of what is rhetorical and what isn't. But of course, if you are a committed objectivist and believe that there are indeed phenomena that are essentially and distinctively rhetorical in character, then you will not see this as a problem.

By contrast, critics who sustain the methodological definition of rhetorical analysis presuppose that an enormous number of objects that we do not ordinarily identify as "rhetorical"—such as, for example, lyric poems or institutional budgets or cathedrals or athletic events or musical compositions or styles of dress—participate in the ceaseless process of shaping and reshaping human consciousness. In the methodologists' view, there is no identifiable class of objects that can be discriminated from other objects and called "rhetoric." Methodologists regard "rhetoric" not as the label for a class of phenomena, but rather as the name of a function—a function so pervasive that its limits cannot be fixed. Hence, they interpret rhetorical analysis as a methodological discipline, like arithmetic or grammar or logic. And just as arithmetic is applicable to anything at all that can be quantified, and grammar is applicable to anything at all that can be said, and logic is applicable to anything at all that can be reasoned, so, in this view, rhetorical analysis is applicable to anything at all that can exercise influence.

In 1971, Richard McKeon published a definition of rhetoric as "an art of structuring all principles and products of knowing, doing, and making." Arguably, McKeon's definition makes rhetoric coincident with the whole of human experience. In its extravagance, the definition is really a repudiation of identifying anything as peculiarly rhetorical, and for that very reason, it is the sort of all-inclusive definition that well serves the methodological interpretation of rhetorical analysis.

Whatever variety there may be among the methods of rhetorical analysis—Aristotle's or Burke's or whoever's—they have some uniformities that entitle them to the rubric, rhetorical analysis. One of their common characteristics is that, somehow or other, they are all concerned with influence, with persuasion, with relations of inducement in the formation or deformation of attitudes. I doubt that we would regard a method of analysis as rhetorical if it did not have those concerns.

Just as there is a recurrent problem of circularity in the application of the objectivist definition, so too there is a differently manifested, but similarly chronic problem of circularity in the application of the methodological definition. That problem takes the form of self-confirmation. When a methodological rhetorical analyst applies an apriori system to a phenomenon, the system always ends up affirming its own categories. Not even crack-pot methods of rhetorical analysis are inapplicable if their sponsors are intent on applying them. A priori critical systems seem always to fulfill themselves, no matter how insular or reductive or overdetermined. And so we have methodological rhetorical analysts whose range is oceanic, uninhibitedly voyaging, as they do, into such seemingly remote areas as theoretical physics or neurophysiology, happily discovering that the destinations they reach at the end of their journeys are the very ports from which they embarked. But of course, if you believe yourself to have a method capable of illuminating "all principles and products of knowing, doing, and making," then you won't regard that as a problem.

More, perhaps, than any writer of this century, Kenneth Burke has demonstrated how an adventurous explorer could lead us into a masterly possession of works that once would have seemed unlikely subjects for rhetorical analysis—works that range from Hesiod's "Works and Days" to "Hamlet" to Hitler's autobiography. And once the pioneering expeditions had been made, it was inevitable that others would be emboldened to steer toward yet other "unpath'd waters," applying one or another method of rhetorical analysis within regions so alien that they were not even identified on the maps of traditional rhetoric.

The debate between Burke and Wilbur Samuel Howell in the pages of *Quarterly Journal of Speech* in 1976 represented a lively and strikingly distilled expression of differences between the objectivist and methodological definitions. That debate was probably the last engagement in which the two definitions were in a condition of reasonable parity.

Whatever the merits of the two definitions, their relative popularity among critics has completely reversed in the course of this century. The objectivist definition of rhetorical analysis dominated the early years of our discipline; but now the methodological definition is everywhere triumphant. So much so that in American universities, whose departments are, by and large, constituted by their objects of study, the methods of rhetorical analysis are scarcely associated any longer with a particular academic discipline.

Still, the objectivist definition of rhetorical analysis, however passé and unfashionable its

current condition, has its utility. That is because the most interesting rhetorical analysis of an object is not always one that focuses on the object's rhetoricity.

Please indulge me while I briefly take for an example an occupational obsession of mine, the public discourse of Richard Nixon. The rhetorical career of Richard Nixon discharges a Niagara of intriguing questions, but the one in which I am immersed cannot be answered by any procedure that we would associate with methodological rhetorical criticism. The question is how to understand the tortuously personal character of much of Nixon's public discourse. The discourse invites the critic to a symptomatic interpretation. Such an interpretation may impinge on the relations between speeches and their audiences, but it is not centrally concerned with them. The raw material of the criticism is rhetorical discourse, by any definition; but the subject demands a critical approach that is concerned less with issues of persuasion than with issues of psychodiagnosis, perhaps even psychopathology. Of course, a dedicated methodologist could insist that such criticism is not really rhetorical analysis. Then let it be called something else. Whatever it may be called, any examination—even a diagnostic one—of public speeches obviously has something to do with "rhetoric," at least as the term has been used for a couple of millennia.

No matter how incompatible their advocates sometimes represent them to be, both the objectivist and the methodological construals of rhetorical analysis really are inextinguishable. They abide because each interpretation is capable of producing understanding; and they abide also because the tension between them can be liberating to critics. Insofar as these two views of rhetorical analysis are different from one another, their very polarity generates options for the critic—choices that a monistic conception of rhetorical analysis could never accommodate. The skillful critic is an explorer who seeks new discoveries. And that stipulation requires that the skillful critic not hold an arbitrary course, but navigate between object and method, adapting to the ever-changing eddies and currents of critical inquiry.

So, however enduring the ascendancy of the methodological definition, there will always be at least a few rhetorical analysts who persist in defining themselves by their attention to the deliberative, forensic, and epideictic flurries of squalling humanity, which is why the sailing metaphor suggested by this "helm" series is so felicitous in considering rhetorical analysis. Like many another, ours is a craft propelled by wind.

REFERENCES

Burke, K. (1976). The party line. *Quarterly Journal of Speech, 62,* 62–68.

Howell, W. S. (1976). The two-party line: A reply to Kenneth Burke. *Quarterly Journal of Speech, 62,* 69–77.

Hudson, H. H. (April, 1924). Rhetoric and poetry. *Quarterly Journal of Speech Education, 10,* 143–154.

McKeon, R. (1971). The uses of rhetoric in a technological age: Architectonic productive arts. In L. F. Bitzer & E. Black (Eds.), *The prospect of rhetoric.* Englewood Cliffs, NJ: Prentice-Hall.

Wichelns, H. A. (1962). The literary criticism of oratory. In A. M. Drummond (Ed.), *Studies in rhetoric and public speaking in honor of James Albert Winans.* New York: Russell & Russell.

CHAPTER 11.

AT THE HELM
IN MASS COMMUNICATION

Introduction

Nancy Signorielli
Univeristy of Delaware

Good Morning! I'm delighted to Chair the Mass Communication session of the "At the Helm" series. This series has a unique status at this year's convention—aside from this and four other "At the Helm" sessions, there are no other meetings to otherwise distract the membership. Even more important, the series is "designed to recognize and honor scholarship in communication." Clearly the panelists featured in "At the Helm in Mass Communication" are worthy of both recognition and honor.

Mass communication is certainly "at the helm" in our society. The mass media play a singularly important role in our lives. Practically everyone watches television for a few hours each day. In addition, many read newspapers, go to the movies, listen to music, and are otherwise involved with some type of media, even if just to talk about a favorite show, movie, or something they saw in the paper or a magazine. Our children become television viewers before they can walk or talk and are otherwise immersed in media at an early age. Increasingly, schools are becoming aware that our children must be literate media users. Media have also come to be regarded as one of the traditional agents of socialization in our society. Moreover, today we are becoming more and more concerned, from both a societal as well as individual perspective, with what our children learn from the media, particularly television. On

yet another level, the greying of the baby boomers necessitates that we now assess how media continue to socialize and resocialize as people move from one stage in the life cycle to another.

Everyday involvement with media also raises numerous questions. We wonder about the media—what we see, how it affects us, and its role in our lives. Schools often provide forums for parents to explore the role of the media in their families' lives. Books on media literacy, written for a general audience as well as the community of scholars, are becoming more prevalent and more widely available. Children's picture books, as well, examine the pitfalls of "too much television."

Lifetime involvement with media, and questioning its role in society, is reflected in our colleges and universities. Mass communication continues to be one of the most important and popular areas of study. Our programs do not lack for majors and often we find that our resources are stretched to the limit in our everyday dealings with students. Similarly, mass communication plays an important role in our national organizations. The Mass Communication Division, in both the ICA and NCA, attracts numerous scholars and members. In the NCA, in particular, the Mass Communication Division has more than 1,200 members and is now at the forefront of technology with our newly instituted Web page.

Today, four of our senior scholars—Alan Rubin, Jennings Bryant, Clifford Christians, and Ev Rogers—will explore what they believe is now "at the helm" in mass communication. I trust that you will find this a very thought provoking and stimulating discussion.

Our first speaker, Alan Rubin, is Professor and Director of Graduate Studies in the School of Communication Studies at Kent State University. Alan received his Ph.D. in Speech Communication from the University of Illinois at Urbana-Champaign in 1976, and his M.A. and B.A. from Queens College of the City University of New York.

Alan studies the uses and effects of the mass media, including television and radio news and entertainment, and the interface of personal and mediated communication. Most recently he has examined the effects of listening to talk radio, the coviewing of televised sports, and the effects of listening to popular music. Identified as one of the top 20 active publishing scholars in the field of communication, he has written more than 55 book chapters and journal articles.

Professor Rubin currently serves as Editor of the *Journal of Communication* and as Mass Communication Advisory Editor for Lawrence Erlbaum Associates. He is a past Editor of the *Journal of Broadcasting & Electronic Media* as well as an earlier Review and Criticism Editor for *JOBEM*. Active in our professional organizations, he is a past Chair of our Mass Communication Division and also served as Secretary of the Mass Communication Division of ICA. He has been on the editorial boards of eight different communication journals and an editorial consultant for over a dozen other scholarly publications, professional associations, and publishers.

Today Alan will talk about "Personal Involvement with the Media."

Our second speaker this morning is Jennings Bryant, Professor of Communication and holder of the Ronald Reagan endowed chair of Broadcasting and Director of the Institute for Communication Research at the University of Alabama. Jennings received his Ph.D. in 1974 from Indiana University and his B.A. from Davidson College.

Jennings has authored more than 50 articles in peer-reviewed journals, has written more than 30 chapters published in edited scholarly books, and has delivered more than 65 papers at conventions of national and international professional associations. Eighteen of his articles or papers have received awards. He has authored or edited 13 books including *Children's Understanding of Television, Media Effects: Advances in Theory and Research,* and *Reinventing Media.*

In addition to his own research and writing, Professor Bryant has been actively involved in editing and promoting the work of other scholars. He has served on the editorial boards of nine scholarly journals and currently holds editorial board appointments on seven scholarly journals. He also serves as an Editor or Co-Editor of several series of scholarly books published by Lawrence Erlbaum Associates. To date, more than 160 volumes have been published in the two LEA book series, many of which have won major awards.

Jennings has also been a Spencer Fellow at Children's Television Workshop, where he worked on *Sesame Street* and *The Electric Company.* He has founded and sold two companies that produce specialty television programs and has been a paid consultant to more than 40 major media companies.

Professor Bryant will talk today on "Trends in Mass Communication Theory and Research: Differences That Make a Difference."

Our third presentation this morning is by Clifford Christians, Research Professor of Communications and Director of the doctoral program at the University of Illinois, Urbana-Champaign. He holds joint appointments as Professor of Journalism and Professor of Media Studies. He has a B.A. in classical philosophy, a B.D. and Th.M. in theology and culture, an M.A. in sociolinguistics from the University of Southern California, and a Ph.D. in social communications from the University of Illinois. He has been a Visiting Scholar in philosophical ethics at Princeton University, in social ethics at the University of Chicago, and a PEW Fellow in ethics at Oxford University.

Professor Christians has published essays on various aspects of mass communication, including professional ethics, in numerous peer-reviewed journals and has lectured all over the world. He contributed the article "Media Ethics" to the *International Encyclopedia of Communications.* He has co-authored several books including *Good News: Social Ethics and the Press* (Oxford University Press, 1993), and *Media Ethics: Cases and Moral Reasoning* (Longman), now in its fourth edition. His most recent book, written with Michael Traber, is *Communication Ethics and Universal Values,* currently in press with Sage Publications.

He serves on the editorial boards of a dozen academic journals, and is the former Editor of *Critical Studies in Mass Communication.* On the faculty at Illinois since 1974, Christians has won four teaching awards. He currently teaches courses on media technology, communication theory, and journalism ethics.

Cliff will today talk on "Critical Issues in Communication Ethics."

Our last speaker, Ev Rogers, has been teaching and conducting research in communication for the past 41 years and almost needs no introduction. Ev received his doctorate from Iowa State University and is currently Professor and Chair in the Department of Communication and Journalism at the University of New Mexico. He has also served on the faculty of Ohio State University, Michigan State University, University of Michigan, Stanford University, and the University of Southern California.

Professor Rogers is particularly known for his book *Diffusion of Innovations,* now in its fourth edition. In 1983, he co-authored, with Judith Larsen, a best-selling book *Silicon Valley Fever.* He has recently authored or co-authored books on the history of communication study, organizational aspects of health communication campaigns, and media agenda-setting.

Professor Rogers presently conducts research on the effects of an entertainment-education radio soap opera about HIV/AIDS prevention and family planning in Tanzania, and on the effects of MADD's Victim Impact Panels on drunk drivers in New Mexico. He also directs research on technology transfer for government R&D institutes in New Mexico and Japan, and on the performance of university-based research centers.

Ev will speak to us today on "When the Mass Media Have Strong Effects: Intermedia Processes."

Personal Involvement with the Media

Alan M. Rubin
Kent State Univesity

Involvement is a critical factor when seeking to explain communication processes and effects. I will attempt to address: (a) how the role of involvement emerges from a framework of audience activity; (b) how involvement reflects an active, motivated state; and (c) how parasocial interaction highlights the role of interpersonal involvement in media effects.

INVOLVEMENT AND AUDIENCE ACTIVITY

Involvement is crucial to perspectives that speak to the role of active interactants in communication. By active, I am referring to people who are capable of: (a) exhibiting intent or purpose to communicate, (b) being selective or making choices among available alternatives when they communicate, and (c) thinking and processing information.

In extending this to the media context, I am not arguing that audiences are universally active. As Windahl (1981) observed, the media audience is not always "superrational and very selective" when acting with or reacting to media (p. 176). People, though, are capable of cognitive thought and reason, and of purposive and selective action. Although motivated behavior and involvement are central to an active audience, I would simply argue that behavior is motivated to meet people's interests, although sometimes to a lesser extent than at other times and often with different degrees of purpose. In other words, an audience is active to a greater or lesser degree.

This view is consistent with the evolution of uses and gratifications as an audience-centered perspective. With its roots in studies of media functions for people and societies, uses and gratifications evolved into a psychological communication perspective (Fisher, 1978; A. Rubin, 1993, 1994a).

Researchers have emphasized individual choice, cognitive processes, and social circumstances when seeking to explain the role and effects of the media. They have addressed how such elements as lifestyle, life position, personality, and loneliness influence media behavior (e.g., Finn & Gorr, 1988; A. Rubin, Perse, & Powell, 1985; A. Rubin & Rubin, 1982). They also have examined how individual differences and variations in exposure and motivation affect outcomes such as cultivation, parasocial interaction, communication satisfaction, and news recognition and elaboration (e.g., Carveth & Alexander, 1985; Perse, 1990a, 1990b, 1990c; R. Rubin & McHugh, 1987).

Activity, then, is a core uses and gratifications concept and a critical mediator of communication outcomes. It is evident in people's motivation to use and involvement with media content (Blumler, 1979).

Initially, the notion of an active audience emerged as a response to powerful effects models. Katz (1959), for example, argued that the media cannot affect those who have no use for messages they might encounter. And Bauer (1963) argued that we need to consider the initiative of the audience in "getting the information it wants and avoiding what it does not want" (p. 7). We see clues to such notions of audience initiative in the radio research of the 1940s, more developed arguments for audience activeness in the arguments of Klapper, Katz, and others in the 1950s and 1960s, and more integrated explanations by Katz, Blumler, Rosengren, and others in the 1970s. Although some have interpreted this idea to mean that media can have few effects on people, such a conclusion is akin to arguing from Klapper's (1960) writings that media can never alter attitudes or behavior.

Motivation and involvement are critical to explaining how variations in how active an audience might be influence the outcomes of media encounters (i.e., in media uses and effects models; see, e.g., A. Rubin, 1994a; Windahl, 1981). Variations in motivation and involvement are also important when seeking to explain how some activities might facilitate, whereas others might inhibit, communication effects (Kim & Rubin, 1994). Certain activities, such as avoidance, disinterest, and distractions, might render audience members obstinate (Bauer, 1964) or impervious to influence (Blumler, 1979) because they lessen involvement with media messages (Kim & Rubin, 1994). Distractions to attention decrease awareness and comprehension of messages, and lessen attitude change (McGuire, 1969).

Involvement, then, affects whether a message has the opportunity to influence cognitions, attitudes, or behavior. Based on their own interests and preferences, people exhibit different levels of attention and cognitive effort with messages (Kahneman, 1973). Over 40 years ago, Schramm (1954) reminded us that you first need to gain a person's attention and interest to have the opportunity to persuade him or her. Variations in selection, attention, and interest lead people to focus on different aspects of messages such as a plot (i.e., content) or characters (i.e., personalities) (Rouner, 1984), and encourage people to respond differently to messages. Involved consumers should be more susceptible to the influence of messages because they have selected, attended to, and acted upon a message.

INVOLVEMENT AS MOTIVATED ACTIVITY

Consumer Researchers

As a construct, involvement has been treated somewhat differently by researchers in several fields. For example, in consumer and advertising research, involvement has had four foci: (a) as a motivated state of consumers that affects how information is acquired; (b) as a situational state whereby involvement resides in the message rather than the consumer; (c) as a process that occurs in stages; and (d) as an enduring state of stable involvement with a product over time (Andrews, Durvasula, & Akhter, 1990). Andrews et al. defined involvement as "an individual, internal state of arousal with intensity, direction, and persistence properties" (p. 28). These properties lead to a motivational state that affects information processing.

The common feature of most definitions of involvement is an "activated motivational state" (Mittal, 1989). Involvement signifies interest, motivation, and arousal (Munson & McQuarrie, 1987). A common thread in treatments of involvement is in assessing involvement's role as a mediator of attitudes and responses to people, objects, or messages such as product advertising. Individual needs, communication sources, and situational factors affect the degree of involvement (Zaichkowsky, 1986).

Communication Researchers

Communication and other researchers have looked at the persuasive and participatory qualities of involvement. For example, ego-involvement is key to social judgment theory, which reflects involvement based on the "interest" of the participant. It recognizes that certain attitudes are more central to one's self-concept and, thus, more resistant to attempts at persuasion (Sherif, Sherif, & Nebergall, 1965). Others, however, have reasoned that involvement based on the relevance or "salience" of the message is more likely to lead to attitude change (Petty & Cacioppo, 1979). Consistent with both schools of persuasion thought, Salmon (1986) described involvement as being (a) an internal motivational state, (b) that is evoked by a stimulus, and (c) that influences subsequent information processing.

Others in communication have considered the participatory nature of involvement. Interaction involvement, for instance, reflects "the extent to which an individual partakes in a social environment" (Cegala, 1981, p. 112). An involved participant is engaged and focused on the other interactants. Greater interaction involvement means greater attentiveness, perceptiveness, and responsiveness to others (Cegala, Savage, Brunner, & Conrad, 1982), that is, interpersonal participation.

Involvement, then, is best seen as a motivated state of anticipation and engagement (Greenwald & Leavitt, 1984; Petty & Cacioppo, 1979; Zaichkowsky, 1986). It reflects participation in message processing (Williams, Rice, & Rogers, 1988), and mediates how we acquire, process, and share information (Salmon, 1986). Involvement signifies participation, attention, and emotion with messages (Krugman, 1966). It is a state of readiness to select, to interpret, and to respond to media and other messages.

Media Researchers

Media researchers often place involvement under the rubric of audience activity and have defined it as: (a) the degree of connection between the audience member and the media content, and (b) the degree with which the audience member psychologically interacts with the medium or message (e.g., Blumler, 1979; Levy & Windahl, 1985). Involvement is the cognitive, affective, and behavioral link between the individual and message. In addition, involvement should be evident before media exposure (e.g., planning), during exposure (e.g., attention), and after exposure (e.g., identification) (Levy & Windahl, 1984, 1985).

In our own research, involvement has been manifested and examined in several ways, primarily: sociopsychological circumstances, attitudes, and media orientations. These factors impact potential media effects. We have observed that the social context and potential for interaction influence the degree of media involvement. For instance, immobility leads to greater reliance on television (A. Rubin & Rubin, 1982, 1985), and loneliness leads to more reliance on electronic media than on interpersonal interaction and to more passive television viewing to occupy one's time (Perse & Rubin,

1990). Attitudes such as affinity, perceived realism, and credibility mediate responses.

Media orientations reflect differences in audience utility, initiative, and involvement (A. Rubin, 1984, 1994a). A ritualized or diversionary (i.e., to divert one's attention from another task) orientation is less active and more habitual use of a medium such as television mainly to occupy one's time. It signifies reduced involvement with media content. Time displacement is an effect of ritualized media use. An instrumental or cognitive utilitarian (i.e., to engage in cognitive processing) orientation, on the other hand, is more active use of the media to seek communication content for information and interaction purposes. It signifies increased involvement with media content and should enable more robust media effects such as learning and attitude change.

As illustrated in several studies, involvement is central to an instrumental media orientation. For example, researchers have found that: television viewers can be distinguished based on whether they orient themselves to content or the medium (Hearn, 1989); television viewers actively seek news to gain information, but do not actively seek diversion (Levy & Windahl, 1984); and surveillance and communicatory utility orientation to television news leads to news involvement (McDonald, 1990).

Involvement, then, reflects participation with relevant or salient media content. Media researchers have described involvement as: "the extent to which audience members attend to and reflect on content" (A. Rubin & Perse, 1987b, p. 59); "cognitive, affective, and behavioral participation during and because of media exposure" (A. Rubin & Perse, 1987a, p. 247); cognitive and emotional participation during message reception (Perse, 1990b, 1990c); and attention and depth of message processing (Roser, 1990).

These views reflect a cognitive, information-processing view of involvement. Being cognitively involved should mean being more aware of and knowledgeable about media characters, plots, and information such as election stories (Lemish,

1985; Shoemaker, Schooler, & Danielson, 1989). Perse (1990b), for example, found that greater attention to and elaboration of government and crime news produced more intense emotional reactions. We have also found that being more involved and selectively perceiving media content predicted greater cultivation effects (Kim & Rubin, 1994; A. Rubin, Perse, & Taylor, 1988). Being involved, then, should result in more robust media outcomes such as learning, modeling, attitude formation, priming, cultivation, and agenda setting.

INVOLVEMENT AS PARASOCIAL INTERACTION

Involvement also reflects an affective or emotional state. Being affectively or emotionally involved means being "caught up in the action of the drama" (Bryant & Comisky, 1978, p. 65), and identifying and parasocially interacting with media personalities (Rosengren & Windahl, 1972; A. Rubin & Perse, 1987a). We have found that a greater sense of parasocial interaction with soap opera characters follows from instrumental (i.e., information and social utility) motivation to watch and a more active (i.e., selective, attentive, and involved) orientation to viewing (Kim & Rubin, 1994).

Parasocial interaction has been a key affective involvement construct linking personal and mediated communication. Based on a person's affective ties with a media personality, parasocial interaction is a relationship of friendship or intimacy with a media "persona" (Horton & Wohl, 1956). It is media involvement that may be experienced in such forms as "seeking guidance from a media persona, seeing media personalities as friends, imagining being part of a favorite program's social world, and desiring to meet media performers" (A. Rubin et al., 1985, pp. 156–157).

Parasocial interaction is grounded in interpersonal notions of attraction, perceived similarity, and empathy. Horton and Wohl (1956) had suggested that such elements should remind us of face-to-face interaction. Media personae often anticipate audience responses and use informal gestures and a conversational style that mirror interpersonal communication and invite interaction (A. Rubin et al., 1985). Parasocial interaction, then, "parallels interpersonal interaction so that a sense of intimacy and self-disclosure should follow from increased and regular interaction" (A. Rubin, 1994b, p. 273).

Several studies support the interpersonal nature of parasocial interaction. In particular, in two studies R. Rubin and her colleagues found parasocial interaction to relate positively to: (a) perceived relationship importance, (b) the social and task dimensions of interpersonal attraction (R. Rubin & McHugh, 1987), (c) reducing uncertainty, and (d) the ability to predict the attitudes of the persona (Perse & Rubin, 1989).

Researchers have often treated parasocial interaction as an outcome of media behavior (e.g., Rosengren & Windahl, 1972). Levy (1979) stated that the causal direction is from media exposure to parasocial interaction. Parasocial interaction, though, has also been treated as an affective mediator of perceived relationship importance (R. Rubin & McHugh, 1987), and as an antecedent that affects media motivation, intention, and selection (Conway & Rubin, 1991).

Parasocial interaction is affective, interpersonal involvement that influences media uses and outcomes. It reflects purposive and involved media use which should accentuate potential effects. This is supported by the findings of several studies in which parasocial interaction had positive links to: (a) instrumental, information news viewing motivation; (b) perceived news realism and affinity (A. Rubin et al., 1985); and (c) cognitive and emotional involvement with television news (Perse, 1990c) and soap operas (A. Rubin & Perse, 1987a).

This potential impact of parasocial interaction on cognitions, attitudes, and behaviors is further illustrated by a recent study in which we looked at talk-radio listeners. We found that parasocially interacting with a talk-radio host predicted: (a) planned and frequent listening to that host, (b) treating the host as an important source of societal information, and (c) feeling that the host influenced how listeners felt about and acted upon societal issues (A. Rubin, Step, & Hofer, 1996).

CONCLUSION

Involvement is an active, yet variable, motivated state. It influences and mediates our communication choices, interactions, and outcomes. Consistent with Andrews and colleagues (1990), when studying involvement, we need to clarify its antecedents (e.g., need for cognition, relevance) and outcomes (e.g., recall, elaboration), and to focus on consumer actions and responses, not just message or product attributes. Involvement, especially the affective involvement witnessed in parasocial interaction, has been shown to influence how people think about, feel about, and plan to act upon information they receive.

A future media effects agenda must include a detailed examination of the role personal involvement plays in mediating influences on cognitions, attitudes, and behaviors. How active and involved an audience member might be, of course, depends on situational factors such as a desire for particular information or interpersonal and family interaction. It also depends on personality factors such as the need for cognition and aggressive tendencies (which have environmental and biological origins). A research agenda must include an examination of the variable influence of such situational and personality factors on motivation, involvement, and media outcomes. I would suggest that such situational and personality influences on and explanations for behavior are more crucial than the typical demographic indicators we have been prone to include in our research studies.

The research agenda must also recognize the changes that have occurred in societal structures and communication technologies. Family structure, for example, is different than it was two decades ago. In addition, communication technologies have greatly increased the rapidity and expansiveness of information and the multiplicity of choices that are readily available to many people. Such changes accentuate differences among groups in society and societies themselves. They will affect our motivation to seek out and our involvement with information.

REFERENCES

Andrews, J. C., Durvasula, S., & Akhter, S. H. (1990). A framework for conceptualizing and measuring the involvement construct in advertising research. *Journal of Advertising, 19,* 27–40.

Bauer, R. A. (1963). The initiative of the audience. *Journal of Advertising Research, 3,* 2–7.

Bauer, R. A. (1964). The obstinate audience: The influence process from the point of view of social communication. *American Psychologist, 19,* 319–328.

Blumler, J. G. (1979). The role of theory in uses and gratifications studies. *Communication Research, 6,* 9–36.

Bryant, J., & Comisky, P. W. (1978). The effect of positioning a message within differentially cognitively involving portions of a television segment on recall of the message. *Human Communication Research, 5,* 63–75.

Carveth, R., & Alexander, A. (1985). Soap opera viewing motivations and the cultivation process. *Journal of Broadcasting & Electronic Media, 29,* 259–273.

Cegala, D. J. (1981). Interaction involvement: A cognitive dimension of communication competence. *Communication Education, 30,* 109–121.

Cegala, D. J., Savage, G. T., Brunner, C. C., & Conrad, A. B. (1982). An elaboration of the meaning of interaction involvement. *Communication Monographs, 49,* 229–248.

Conway, J. C., & Rubin, A. M. (1991). Psychological predictors of television viewing motivation. *Communication Research, 18,* 443–464.

Finn, S., & Gorr, M. B. (1988). Social isolation and social support as correlates of television viewing motivations. *Communication Research, 15,* 135–158.

Fisher, B. A. (1978). *Perspectives on human communication.* New York: Macmillan.

Greenwald, A. G., & Leavitt, C. (1984). Audience involvement in advertising: Four levels. *Journal of Consumer Research, 11,* 581–592.

Hearn, G. (1989). Active and passive conceptions of the television audience: Effects of a change in a viewing routine. *Human Relations, 42,* 857–875.

Horton, D., & Wohl, R. R. (1956). Mass communication and para-social interaction: Observations on intimacy at a distance. *Psychiatry, 19,* 215–229.

Kahneman, D. (1973). *Attention and effort.* Englewood Cliffs, NJ: Prentice-Hall.

Katz, E. (1959). Mass communication research and the study of popular culture. *Studies in Public Communication, 2,* 1–6.

Kim, J., & Rubin, A. M. (1994, November). *Audience activity as a facilitator and an inhibitor of media effects*. Paper presented at the Speech Communication Association annual convention, New Orleans, LA.

Klapper, J. T. (1960). *The effects of mass communication*. New York: Free Press.

Krugman, H. E. (1966). The measurement of advertising involvement. *Public Opinion Quarterly, 30,* 583–596.

Lemish, D. (1985). Soap opera viewing in college: A naturalistic inquiry. *Journal of Broadcasting & Electronic Media, 29,* 275–293.

Levy, M. R. (1979). Watching TV news as para-social interaction. *Journal of Broadcasting, 23,* 69–80.

Levy, M. R., & Windahl, S. (1984). Audience activity and gratifications: A conceptual clarification and exploration. *Communication Research, 11,* 51–78.

Levy, M. R., & Windahl, S. (1985). The concept of audience activity. In K. Rosengren, L. Wenner, & P. Palmgreen (Eds.), *Media gratifications research: Current perspectives* (pp. 109–122). Beverly Hills: Sage.

McDonald, D. G. (1990). Media orientation and television news viewing. *Journalism Quarterly, 67,* 11–20.

McGuire, W. J. (1969). The nature of attitudes and attitude change. In G. Lindzey & E. Aronson (Eds.), *Handbook of social psychology* (2nd ed., Vol. 3, pp. 136–314). Reading, MA: Addison-Wesley.

Mittal, B. (1989). A theoretical analysis of two recent measures of involvement. *Advances in Consumer Research, 16,* 697–702.

Munson, J. M., & McQuarrie, E. F. (1987). The factorial and predictive validities of a revised measure of Zaichkowsky's Personal Involvement Inventory. *Educational and Psychological Measurement, 47,* 773–782.

Perse, E. M. (1990a). Cultivation and involvement with local television news. In N. Signorielli & M. Morgan (Eds.), *Cultivation analysis: New directions in media effects research* (pp. 51–69). Newbury Park, CA: Sage.

Perse, E. M. (1990b). Involvement with local television news: Cognitive and emotional dimensions. *Human Communication Research, 16,* 556–581.

Perse, E. M. (1990c). Media involvement and local news effects. *Journal of Broadcasting & Electronic Media, 34,* 17–36.

Perse, E. M., & Rubin, A. M. (1990). Chronic loneliness and television use. *Journal of Broadcasting & Electronic Media, 34,* 37–53.

Perse, E. M., & Rubin, R. B. (1989). Attribution in social and parasocial relationships. *Communication Research, 16,* 59–77.

Petty, R. E., & Cacioppo, J. T. (1979). Issue-involvement can increase or decrease persuasion by enhancing message-relevant cognitive responses. *Journal of Personality & Social Psychology, 37,* 1915–1926.

Rosengren, K. E., & Windahl, S. (1972). Mass media consumption as a functional alternative. In D. McQuail (Ed.), *Sociology of mass communications* (pp. 166–194). Harmondsworth, England: Penguin.

Roser, C. (1990). Involvement, attention, and perceptions of message relevance in response to persuasive appeals. *Communication Research, 17,* 571–600.

Rouner, D. (1984). Active television viewing and the cultivation hypothesis. *Journalism Quarterly, 61,* 168–174.

Rubin, A. M. (1984). Ritualized and instrumental television viewing. *Journal of Communication, 34*(3), 67–77.

Rubin, A. M. (1993). Audience activity and media use. *Communication Monographs, 60,* 98–105.

Rubin, A. M. (1994a). Media uses and effects: A uses-and-gratifications perspective. In J. Bryant & D. Zillmann (Eds.), *Media effects: Advances in theory and research* (pp. 417–436). Hillsdale, NJ: Erlbaum.

Rubin, A. M. (1994b). Parasocial interaction scale. In R. B. Rubin, P. Palmgreen, & H. E. Sypher (Eds.), *Communication research measures: A sourcebook* (pp. 273–277). New York: Guilford Press.

Rubin, A. M., & Perse, E. M. (1987a). Audience activity and soap opera involvement: A uses and effects investigation. *Human Communication Research, 14,* 246–268.

Rubin, A. M., & Perse, E. M. (1987b). Audience activity and television news gratifications. *Communication Research, 14,* 58–84.

Rubin, A. M., Perse, E. M., & Powell, R. A. (1985). Loneliness, parasocial interaction, and local television news viewing. *Human Communication Research, 12,* 155–180.

Rubin, A. M., Perse, E. M., & Taylor, D. S. (1988). A methodological examination of cultivation. *Communication Research, 15,* 107–134.

Rubin, A. M., & Rubin, R. B. (1982). Contextual age and television use. *Human Communication Research, 8,* 228–244.

Rubin, A. M., & Rubin, R. B. (1985). Interface of personal and mediated communication: A research agenda. *Critical Studies in Mass Communication, 2,* 36–53.

Rubin, A. M., Step, M. M., & Hofer, C. (1996, November). *Impact of motivation, attraction, and parasocial interaction on talk-radio listening effects.* Paper presented at the Speech Communication Association annual convention, San Diego, CA.

Rubin, R. B., & McHugh, M. P. (1987). Development of parasocial interaction relationships. *Journal of Broadcasting & Electronic Media, 31,* 279–292.

Salmon, C. T. (1986). Perspectives on involvement in consumer and communication research. In B. Dervin & M. J. Voigt (Eds.), *Progress in communication sciences* (Vol. 7, pp. 243–268). Norwood, NJ: Ablex.

Schramm, W. (1954). How communication works. In W. Schramm (Ed.), *Process and effects of mass communication* (pp. 3–26). Urbana: University of Illinois Press.

Sherif, C. W., Sherif, M., & Nebergall, R. E. (1965). *Attitude and attitude change: The social judgment-involvement approach.* Philadelphia: Saunders.

Shoemaker, P., Schooler, C., & Danielson, W. A. (1989). Involvement with the media: Recall versus recognition of election information. *Communication Research, 16,* 78–103.

Williams, F., Rice, R. E., & Rogers, E. M. (1988). *Research methods and the new media.* New York: Free Press.

Windahl, S. (1981). Uses and gratifications at the crossroads. *Mass Communication Review Yearbook, 2,* 174–185.

Zaichkowsky, J. L. (1986). Conceptualizing involvement. *Journal of Advertising, 15*(2), 4–14, 34.

Trends in Mass Communication Theory and Research: Differences that Make a Difference

Jennings Bryant
University of Alabama

Gregory Bateson, the noted anthropologist and communication theorist, often referred to "differences that make a difference" (e.g., Bateson, 1972). Life today is replete with so-called differences, because in the information age the only constant is change, and the rate of change is constantly changing (always increasing, of course). The communication discipline, as much as—if not more than—any other area of inquiry, has been bombarded by myriad changes wrought by the information age. But how many of these changes are "differences that make a difference?"

In order to help frame this examination of significant trends in mass communication theory and research, we began by resorting to a time-honored communication research ploy. A couple of doctoral students and I performed a rather systematic content analysis of published research in mass communication from 20 years ago (1976), 10 years ago (1986), and from this year (1996). Only a few peer-reviewed journals have consistently published mass communication research for 20 years or more, so we limited our scrutiny to three that have been stalwarts in the discipline for several decades: the *Journal of Communication,* the *Journal of Broadcasting and Electronic Media,* and *Journalism Quarterly.* It is amazing how much you can learn by spending a few hours with very dusty volumes of these repositories of so much of our intellectual history.

What one learns is determined by the questions that are asked, of course, and we began with a fairly straightforward question: Have the loci of our research interests shifted over time? To answer this question more systematically, we adopted a relatively conventional typology, presented in Table 1, and coded all of the mass communication research articles for each year accordingly.

A podium such as this is not the best forum for presenting the detailed outcomes of such a research project, but permit me to share with you a few figures that very selectively illustrate differences that may make a big difference for our discipline. The results are reported in percentages for two reasons: The absolute number of studies per journal volume varies greatly over time (e.g., today's journals report far fewer but much longer articles), plus this investigation was conducted late this summer, so obviously not all of the issues of the 1996 volumes of the three journals examined were available.

As you can see in Figure 1, the loci of our research appear to have shifted rather markedly over

TABLE 1 Typology of Journal Articles by Research Loci

Message System Analysis
   Systematic content analyses
   Other content studies (including programming)
Source Analysis
   Management Studies
   Institutional Research
   Other
Audience Research
   Processes
   Uses
   Impact
Opinion Pieces
Other
   Methodological Studies
   Law, Regulation, and Policy Research
   Economic Assessments

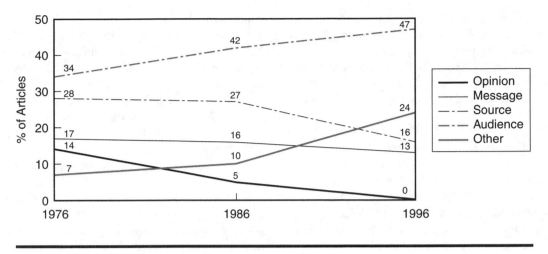

FIGURE 1   Proportion of Articles by Type of Article by Year

time. Our interest in message and source variables has apparently declined, whereas research attention increasingly has been paid to audience assessments and to that nebulous "other" category, which includes economic analyses—which typically tend to span source, channel, and audience dimensions—methodological research; and law, regulation, and policy studies. Moreover, opinion pieces in these journals seem to have disappeared, at least those masquerading as research articles have. Because we would need a lot more data points to make the case for significant trends, we should look at these "findings" as tentative "markers" calling for further investigations. Which of these markers suggest differences that may well prove to make a difference?

If subsequent research confirms that we are conducting less and less message and source research, this suggests that we may well be losing much of the original heart and soul of our discipline. Jim Bradac (1989) warned of the perils of forsaking message research in his edited volume entitled *Messages in Communication Science: Contemporary Approaches to the Study of Effects.* Moreover, with issues associated with concentration of ownership of media properties being accentuated by the Telecommunications Act of 1996, can

we afford to de-emphasize source factors, especially institutional studies?

Let's look more closely at audience studies, which now represent virtually one-half of the articles in the three major journals we examined. As someone who has conducted quite a bit of audience or user research over the years, I may have contributed to these "markers" somewhat, but some aspects of this apparent shift concern me. My primary concern is that we seem to be conducting more of the type of audience research for which our discipline has less primary ownership and, seemingly, less sophistication. For several years now, it has been my privilege to serve on various editorial boards in psychology as well as in communication. Reviewing at least a dozen manuscripts each year in both disciplines, I cannot help comparing and contrasting research in these two domains of inquiry. In doing this, my subjective perception is that some of our models of media users and some of the methods we use to scrutinize them are not always as sophisticated as they could be, especially when it comes to measuring issues like selectivity, uses, cognitive processes, and emotional behavior. When it comes to assessing media impact, it seems to me that we typically demonstrate more sophistication and insight than the typical psychologist, but I would be less than honest if I made that claim for other areas of audience-centered inquiry.

Which leads us to another graphic illustration. As can be seen in Figure 2, our interest in assessing the impact of media appears to have declined dramatically, whereas scholarly attention given to audience process research and to media usage investigations has increased markedly. We had noticed this shift earlier and have discussed it elsewhere (Black, Bryant, & Thompson, 1996). For example, at the 1996 convention of the International Communication Association, 15 or so papers were devoted to the perennially popular topic of media violence and children. However, only two of the presentations were concerned with media effects. The bulk of the papers addressed issues like the attraction of violence, the regulation of violence in children's television programs, or the processes via which children cope with media violence. "The times they are a'changin.'" So what? A recent comment about the primacy of media effects research in our discipline caught my attention. The lead sentence in a review essay in a 1996 issue of the *Journal of Communication* reads: "Understanding 'effects' remains the primary scientific as well as social justification for the field of mass communication research" (Jensen, 1996, p. 138). If that claim is true, then our "core" research area now ac-

counts for only 10 percent of the articles in those very journals that historically have reported the bulk of our investigations into the social, psychological, and cultural impact of mass media. A difference that makes a difference? Perhaps.

On the other hand, if you focus on positive aspects of the seeming growth in research examining our uses of media and the processes that underpin such research, the good news is that much of that research increasingly seems to be asking the difficult questions of "how" and "why" we use media, and, equally importantly, we seem to be asking those questions with more impressive research strategies and protocols. This leads to the next question we asked in our content analysis: How has the level of sophistication of our research emphases in mass communication shifted over time? (See Figure 3.)

I interpret this graphic as a very healthy report card for our discipline. As you can see, the "roarin' 70s" appear to have been largely a time of descriptive research in our discipline. Articles offering systematic analysis were occasionally present, but synthesis and prediction do not seem to have entered the picture very often. By the mid-80s, more than one-half of our articles focused on analysis, whereas our time serving as "visually challenged natives describing the elephant" had been dramatically reduced. And during the cur-

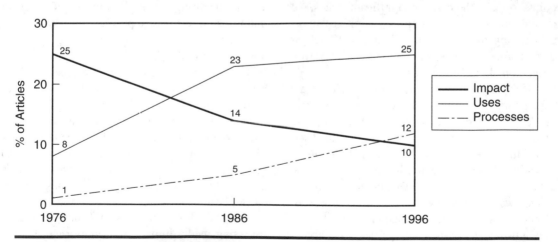

FIGURE 2 Proportion of Audience Article by Orientation by Year

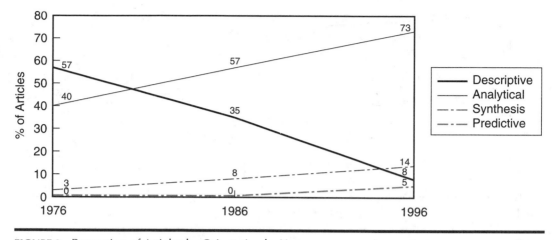

FIGURE 3   Proportion of Articles by Orientation by Year

rent year (1996), I was thrilled to see that more so-phisticated forms of critical thinking definitely have come of age in mass communication re-search. As we increasingly focus on analysis, syn-thesis, and prediction, I am confident that we will find differences that make a difference.

One final illustration from our content analy-sis: We also made several theoretical judgments—a difficult task, but one achieved with greater than 85 percent agreement between pairs of coders—only one of which will be reported here. We deter-mined whether each study better fit one of two dominant "meta-models" of our discipline: *trans-mission* models, those derived from stimulus-re-sponse psychology, or *interaction* models, which focus on the shared meaning created by co-partic-ipants in the communication process (Black & Bryant, 1995). Let me hasten to add that only 70% or so of the articles could be shoehorned into ei-ther category. Of those that did fit, an interesting pattern emerged (Figure 4).

As you can see, although transmission mod-els are still slightly more common in our disci-pline than interaction models are, a shift in emphasis appears to be occurring. This reorienta-tion to transaction rather than transmission un-doubtedly will be one of those differences that make a difference, as interaction models practi-cally mandate the inclusion of process features

into even the most blatantly "effects"-oriented re-search, motivating the sort of theoretical integra-tion that should give us a substantial boost in sophistication and veridicality.

Now, if I might, I would like to abandon the frame offered by our content analysis and turn briefly to three developments that seem to be mak-ing tremendous differences in our field. The first primarily applies to the media effects arena. Al-though a smaller portion of the published mass communication research today may be effects re-search, some very important developments seem to be taking place in the models we are applying to assess media impact. During the past month I have reviewed manuscripts reporting two seemingly ground-breaking studies that employed either ep-idemiological or risk-assessment models. Both authors (or sets of authors—these were blind re-views) had adapted these public health models beautifully and had skillfully integrated their very powerful findings into critical public policy dis-cussions in ways that were quite compelling. Last year I attended a policy conference in Washing-ton, DC, that included officers of several federal agencies and regulatory commissions. For the first time I saw presented a typology of research per-spectives that would be accepted with varying de-grees of authority by federal policy makers. Heading the list was longitudinal research utiliz-

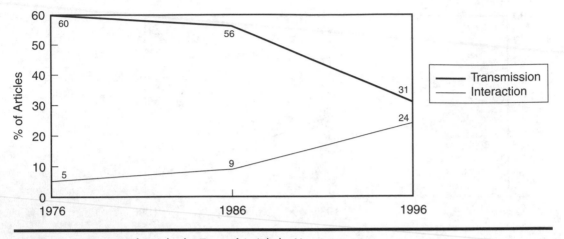

FIGURE 4   Proportion of Articles by Type of Article by Year

ing field experiments; in the middle of the list was meta-analyses, which are beginning to show up with some regularity in our journals; the type of one-shot, cross-sectional lab studies that have so often typified research in mass communication was near the bottom of the list, ahead of only "expert testimony." Hopefully we are beginning to see a shift in the sort of impact models and methods that will enable us to build theory with greater confidence at the same time as we meaningfully and progressively influence public policy regarding mass communication.

I just mentioned longitudinal research. When I was a graduate student, my teachers frequently bemoaned the lack of longitudinal research in mass communication, pointing out how much more we would know if our field were graced with such designs. We cannot make such complaints any longer. For example, for the 1997 convention of the Society for Research in Child Development, a symposium entitled "The Long-Term Effects of Television Viewing" is on the docket. Four presentations of longitudinal investigations of the consequences of early television viewing are scheduled that use a variety of designs and methodologies. Importantly, the results that are being uncovered via such designs are exceedingly different from those typically reported by cross-sectional studies.

This difference promises to make a real difference in our understanding of mass communication.

Final examples of a difference that make a difference are the adoption of multimethod approaches to mass communication research. My favorite example of this is a study on the effects of advertising on teenager smoking, published in the *Journal of Marketing* in April 1996. In tracing "The Epidemiology of Pediatric Nicotine Addiction," this study employed "strategic analysis, consumer research, econometric metanalyses, historical research, and corporate documents" (Pollay et al., 1996). We also have used a wide variety of qualitative and quantitative methods in a two-year evaluation of the effects and effectiveness of Nick Jr's curriculum-based television programs *Allegra's Window* and *Gullah Gullah Island*. By content analyzing every episode of both seasons of each program, by creating behavioral measures and caregiver assessment instruments to assess every curriculum goal, by observing a large sample of preschoolers in their homes, by creating a case study for each child participating in the investigation, by employing traditional measures of attention, viewing diaries, and the like, and by conducting these evaluation sessions repeatedly over the course of two years, we have been able to understand the nature of the relationship between media, message, and children in ways previously beyond our comprehension. This employment of multiple complementary methodologies in a longitudinal design has, for us, been the equivalent of breaking the four-minute mile, although in this instance it was breaking the knowledge barrier. It also makes it almost impossible to return to the old ways of doing business. I guess that's a difference that makes a difference.

REFERENCES

Bateson, G. (1972). *Steps to an ecology of mind.* New York: Ballentine.

Black, J., & Bryant, J. (1995). *Introduction to media communication* (4th ed.). Madison, WI: Brown & Benchmark.

Black, J., Bryant, J., & Thompson, S. (1996). *Reinventing media.* Madison, WI: Brown & Benchmark.

Bradac, J. J. (Ed.). (1989). Messages in communication science: Contemporary approaches to the study of effects. *Sage Annual Review of Communication Research* (Vol. 17). Newbury Park, CA: Sage.

Jensen, K. B. (1996). Media effects: Convergence within separate covers. *Journal of Communication, 46*(2), 138–144.

Pollay, R. W., Siddarth, S., Siegel, M., Haddix, A., Merritt, R. K., Giovini, G. A., & Eriksen, M. P. (1996). The last straw? Cigarette advertising and realized market shares among youths and adults, 1979–1993. *Journal of Marketing, 60,* 2–20.

Critical Issues in Communication Ethics

Clifford G. Christians

University of Illinois

Our theory and research in communications is highly moralistic these days—almost beyond belief. As a savage century comes to a close, we speak gingerly of v-chips in public, but curse media violence in our bull sessions with friends. Sexism and racism are stark in the Army and Texaco, but the immorality of media representations is obvious too. Privacy is in tatters; we can find nowhere to hide from the news, and computer giants barter profile bits among themselves to sell my composite for profit. Tele-evangelism, calling on heaven for unction, is offensive to high heaven in the process. Walt Disney sterilizes Pocahantas lore. Political ads have become nauseous to the core of our being. As we ply our trade, with William James we see the trail of the serpent.

The question is not the righteous few—Noah in the land of wickedness. A few do-gooders here and there are not very interesting conceptually. The profusion of moral language intrigues me instead—moralistic incantations from one end of our enterprise to the other. What sense do we make of it—the heavy moralism, that is, our lamentation and unceasing complaints? What does our value-laden language mean? What are the logic and rationale for moral knowledge at this critical juncture in communications scholarship?

When objectivity defined the field, moral values languished in the margins, footnotes, and appendix. Now with the fact–value dichotomy broken down, we seem to have an embarrassment of riches. But those of us in communications tend to situate moral agents discursively, and to my mind such a turn is counterproductive. I am willing to pay tribute to narrative ethics over against an ethics of rationalism. Locating the moral life close to the bone of everyday experience puts a hammerlock on abstract canons. The switch from principle to story invigorates our analysis.

But in the end a narrative foundation for ethics is no foundation at all. Our busy moralism does not amount to much intellectually. Discursiveness is friendly enough, in fact, benign, a patina for good will. But finally we cannot come to grips with technologically sophisticated mass communication systems through discursive context. Situating moral agents discursively is not as convincing as an ethics of being at the dawn of a new millenium. My argument denies the validity of rationalistic ethics, shows appropriate deference to contextual values, and then builds a case for an ontological ethics as an alternative to both.

ETHICAL RATIONALISM

Ethical rationalism has been the dominant paradigm in Western moral philosophy. Reason made the human species distinctive and only through rationality were moral canons legitimate. The truth of prescriptions could be settled by formal examination of their logical structure. In Descartes' version, reason was considered "the same for all thinking subjects, all nations, all epochs and all cultures" (Cassirer, 1951, p. 6).

> *Just as Western science has held there are universal truths about the world, discoverable through reason and accessible in principle to people of all times and places, so Western philosophers such as Plato, Aristotle, and Kant have held that there are timeless moral truths, arising out of human nature and independent of the conventions of particular societies (Paul et al., 1994, p. vii).*

The idea of a common morality known to all rational beings had its detractors, of course, from within the Western tradition itself. Giambattista Vico (1948), professor of rhetoric at the University of Naples (1699–1741), argued for imaginative universals born of *fantasia* rather than rooted in linear rationality. David Hume (1739, 1963) took seriously the multiplying discoveries of other cultures in the eighteenth century, recognizing within the framework of empirical philosophy that these diverse conceptions of the good life might turn out to have nothing in common. But such oppositional voices were of limited influence, until in the late twentieth century the paradigm of immutable and universal morality has been generally discredited. Though presumably based on shared features of human beings as a whole, it has been exposed as the "morality of a dominant gender and class" (Outka and Reeder, 1993, p. 4). Postulating an abstract good is no longer seen as beneficent, but rather as imperialistic control over the moral judgments of particular communities.

The idea of universal principles founded on rational consent has been pre-eminent in Europe and North America since the eighteenth century. But now the curtain is coming down on 300 years of Enlightenment modernity. The concept of norms themselves has eroded; the Western world legitimizes diverse values instead. The modernist project to establish reason and truth as everywhere and always the same has failed.

And societies feeding from the Enlightenment worldview face a crisis of validation. What still counts as legitimate knowledge for them? There are no widely accepted rational means for people committed to different beliefs to defend them constructively. Metaphysical certitude has been replaced by philosophical relativism; moral principles are presumed to have no objective application independently of the societies within which they are constituted. Nihilism (no moral truths exist) and skepticism (moral propositions cannot be justified) are prevalent responses as well.

For ethics to be meaningful in mass communications studies over the long term, we have to recover the very idea of moral universals itself. And this must be done without presuming first foundations, without the luxury of an objective transcendental reality from which to begin. The future of communication ethics, in Seyla Benhabib's (1992, p. 3) terms, depends on whether "a post Enlightenment defense of universalism, without metaphysical and historical props, is still viable." Obviously, as one period of history is left behind and another begins, our mandate is not a communication ethics of any sort under any conditions. The only legitimate option is an ethics that is culturally inclusive rather than biased toward Western hegemony. Nor does a minimalist, limpid, quandary ethics have any credibility as the global information society takes shape.

NARRATIVE ETHICS

Pragmatism and the symbolic interactionists turned the ethics of rationalism on its head. They contradicted the metaphysical foundations on which the Western canon was based. They worked from the inside out, from the backyard and the grass roots. Social constructions replaced formal law systems. Moral values were now situated in the cultural context rather than anchored by philosophical abstractions. The moral life developed through community formation and not in essentialist sanctums of isolated individuals. Contextual values replaced ethical absolutes.

For Dewey's *Human Nature and Conduct,* our task in ethics is understanding those problem-situations where we distinguish good conduct from bad. Conflict and a tangle of incompatible impulses prompt us to ask the question, "What is good?" These are the clues we need for a conception of values that is nonfoundational. Goodness and badness are not objective properties of things themselves. On the other hand, as Hume argued, values cannot be mere sentiment either. In our value judgments we say something that we believe is true about the world and not merely express subjective attitudes. Thus Dewey's contextualism challenges both metaphysics and emotivism as possible homes for values. He does not seek an ultimate normative standard, but investigates the social conditions under which we consider our assertions warranted. For Dewey, interpretation rather than pure reason or divine revelation is the only appropriate method.

In his *Contingency, Irony, and Solidarity,* Rorty concentrates on moral theory and language. For making life worth living he advocates the values of human fulfillment—creativity and freedom, community formation, shared rituals, inclusive language. He looks for those values that emerge when we clear the deck of normative ethics, Enlightenment epistemology, theology, and metaphysics. The narrative level—the vision of liberal irony as he calls it—constitutes our best shot for liberalism as a social myth to prosper and authoritarianism in all forms recede. In narrative we rehearse our common doubts, affirm our mutual contingencies, and push away fundamentalisms which purport to be the final answer (cf. Fackler, 1992).

Rorty abandons those moral problems which appeal to an order beyond time and change. Ironists have continuing doubts about their vocabulary. The discourse of others impresses them and they do not consider their own language closer to reality or superior. Ironists simply play the new off against the old (Rorty, 1989, p. 73), believing in the contingency and arbitrariness of language to make whatever truth there is. From this perspective, truth does not correspond to reality, but is what we come to believe "in the course of free and open encounters" (Rorty, 1989, p. 68).

Dewey and Rorty illustrate narrative ethics. They contend for an ethics closer to the ground where the moral life takes place. Clearly, for the communications enterprise, the shift from principle to story, from formal logic to community formation, is an attractive option. Stories are symbolic frameworks that organize human experience. For Walter Fisher (1987), we are narrative beings, aware of discursive coherence (whether or not a story hangs together) and of narrative fidelity (whether or not a story rings true). Through stories we constitute ways of living in common.

Narratives are linguistic forms through which we think, argue, persuade, display convictions, and establish our identity. They contain in a nutshell the meaning of our theories and beliefs. "Not only

men and women of affairs but also ordinary people tell themselves stories about who they are, what they care about, and how they hope to realize their aspirations" (Rosaldo, 1989, pp. 129–30). Storytelling "cuts through abstractions and other obscurities," enables us "to think creatively and imaginatively" about "the endless details of…a disorderly world," and in the process transforms "essentially private experience into a shared and therefore public reality" (Glasser, 1991, pp. 235–36). The stories of Nelson Mandela's twenty-six years in prison, Paul Revere's ride, the Selma march, the demolition of the Berlin Wall, and the "velvet revolution" in Czechoslovakia have been fodder for political revolutions. Cardinal Bernardin of Chicago told us how to face an accuser with integrity and death itself with dignity. Great storytellers probe deeply into our belief systems and shape the social landscape. Accordingly, the narrative turn in the human disciplines (cf. Cortazzi, 1993; Richter, 1996) has produced multiple strategies for reading stories in the "televisual societies of the twenty-first century" (Denzin, 1997, p. 250).

Hermeneutics has taught us that language is the matrix of the social order, and Rorty's great conversation, Hauerwas' social ethics, Gadamer's intersubjectivity, Pierce's semiology, and literary journalism's news as narrative are compatible with important trends toward symbolic theory in communications and interpretive studies in the social sciences (Denzin, 1997, chs. 5, 9). Taking ethics out of the ether and situating values contextually is a paradigm revolt of historic proportions. Narrative ethics stakes out its territory in radically different terms than ethical rationalism (cf. Ellos, 1994). But upon decentering rationality, it is coopted by the status quo. After providing a thick reading of how societies work in a natural setting, narrative ethics is mute in its own terms on which valuing to value. Whatever is identified experimentally cannot in itself yield normative guidelines. If phenomena situated in immediate space and present time are presumed to contain everything of consequence, the search for values outside immediacy and particularity is meaningless.

The narrative paradigm yields arbitrary definitions of goodness, as if to say, "This is good because I say it is good" or "This is good because most people in a social group identify it as good." From David Hume through G. E. Moore, we have recognized the fallacy of deriving ought statements from is statements. To assert prescriptive claims from an experiential base entails a contradiction (Christians, 1995, pp. 126–27).

ETHICS OF BEING

Cornel West's *The American Evasion of Philosophy* opens the door to another path—an ethics of being. Rorty requires no fundamental change in our cultural and political practices (West, 1989, p. 206). While celebrating Rorty's antirealism, West points instead to a morality of being at odds with both a rationalistic ethics and one of narrative. He represents an army of intellectuals not content with contextual values and the narrative ethics derived from it. And I join them in rejecting a narrative ethics of the empty center. A morality of collective values settles for the short-term goals of better education and socially responsible mass media as prerequisites for generating truth. It only allows us exhortation and busy maneuvering. Democratic institutions are viewed as a cooperative experiment, rolling along without an axle. But, in fact, its gaping hole in the middle leaves the integrity of the entire structure in doubt.

For Rorty (1988), the vacant center is a virtue. No agreed-upon cosmology is required to hold a free society together. He opts for a self that is historically contingent all the way through. Egalitarian democracy, he insists, should stay on the surface, and create a set of operations for democratic life distinct from matters of ultimate importance. But what if the context within which values are supposed to percolate is fractured and tribalistic? Values clarification without social cohesion is meaningless (cf. Geras, 1995, Ch. 3).

Instead of appealing to rational abstractions, or to the social order, I argue for an ontological paradigm rooted in animate nature. The rationale for human action is reverence for life on earth, respect for the organic realm in which human civilization is situated. The Age of Science defined nature as spiritless materiality. This reductionism to matter and motion enabled the technological revolution to prosper. Material reality as inert substance could be manipulated at will, in Cartesian terms we were considered masters and possessors of nature. Or, in another historical reading, the neutral paradigm laid the foundation for an Enlightenment political economy.

> *Bourgeois political economy—child of eighteenth-century thought—articulated the view of nature as "resource" and attributed to itself the prime theoretical task of determining the rational allocation of resources that were scarce. To this end it appealed…to the centrality of money as the common means to measure…elements and processes "in nature". (Harvey, 1996, p. 150)*

The "history of how humans have valued their natural world is long and intricate" (Harvey, 1996, p. 150), but at least these two dominant views cannot account for the purposiveness of life itself. In its own reproduction, living nature gives evidence of a determinate goal. The ethics of being reads the natural world in contradiction to the Age of Science, and sees within the natural order a moral claim on us for its own sake and in its own right.

Our duty to preserve life is similar in kind to parental obligation for their offspring. When new life appears, the progenitors do not debate their relationship to it as though their responsibility is a matter of calculating the options. The forbears' duty to children is an imperative outside subjectivity that is primal, timeless and nonnegotiable (cf. Jonas, 1984, Ch. 4). Nurturing life has a taken-for-granted character outside subjectivity. Reverence for life on earth is the philosophical foundation of the moral order. From the sacredness-of-life perspective: "The natural world provides a rich, variegated, and permanent candidate for…universal and permanent values to inform action and to give meaning to otherwise ephemeral and fragmented lives" (Harvey, 1996, p. 157). Our human livelihood is rooted in the principle that "we have inescapable claims on one another which cannot be renounced except at the cost of our humanity" (Peukert, 1981, p. 11). Given the oneness of the human species, universal solidarity is the basic principle of ethics.

The primal sacredness of life is a protonorm—similar in kind to the proto-Germanic language, our reconstruction of a lingual predecessor underlying the Germanic languages as we actually know them in history. Reverence for life on earth bonds us universally into an organic whole. Our obligation to sustain one another defines our human existence. One ethical principle inscribed within this protonorm is human dignity. And on the basis of our unassailable sacred status as human beings, we begin to formulate a systematic ethics of social justice.

In our study (Christians and Traber, 1997) of ethical foundations in 13 countries on five continents, the sacredness of life is consistently affirmed as bonding us universally into an organic whole. Our obligation to sustain one another is seen as defining our human existence. And entailed by this protonorm, in addition to human dignity, are such ethical principles as nonviolence and truthtelling: *likute* (respect) in Zambia; Judeo-Christian humans as divine image bearers; *ahimsa* (nonviolence) in Hinduism; reverence for life in the Osage nation; truthfulness in Arab-Islamic communication; cultural identity in Latin America, and so forth.

In articulating such protonorms as the sacredness of life, communication ethics must respond to the simultaneous globalizing of communications and the reassertion of local identities. We are caught now in the contradictory trends of cultural homogenization and cultural resistance. Therefore, theoretical models must be explicitly cross-cultural.

Projects for worldwide ethics litter history like tanks abandoned in the desert.... There is surely great need for caution about slogans invoking common values, often so glibly used to disguise efforts to proselytize and subdue. It is nevertheless urgent to seek out fundamental moral values on which to base cross-cultural dialogue and choice, given the nature and scope of the challenge societies now confront together. (Bok, 1995, p. 1)

A multicultural comparative ethics is needed to supplant the dominant canons, most of them North Atlantic and patriarchal. A new axis is necessary to replace the monocultural one of rationalism and the contextualism of narrative.

We need a comparative ethics that places Western and non-Western societies, and those North and South, on a level playing field. A comparative model presumes that all philosophies of culture can offer unique insights into the fundamental principles of communication ethics and can thus make substantial contributions to normative discourse. Protonorms are possible because every culture depends for its existence on norms which order human relationships and social institutions. This is a universalism from the ground up, not subject to the postmodern critique of universals. Ontological ethics makes no appeal to essentialist human nature or to universal reason (the primary assumptions of rationalistic ethics).

The primal sacredness of life establishes a level playing floor for cross-cultural collaboration in ethics. Representatives of various societies articulate this protonorm in different terms and illustrate it locally, but each brings to the table a fundamental respect for the others gathered around it. Without a starting point, ethical imperatives are always indeterminate. If moral claims are assumed to be presuppositionless, the possibility of doing communication ethics at all is jeopardized.

Without primal norms, how can we despise Rodney King's assailants and support him instead? "How is government to be carried on, if, lying behind it, there is no consensus morality? If there is...no general shared sense of what is right and wrong, how are laws to be enacted?...And, if enacted, how are they to be enforced?" (Warnock, 1992, p. 85). If, following Michel Foucault, we conclude that moral discourse is rhetoric for securing power, then we undercut our opposition to sexism, military megamachines, torture, and our favorite list of obvious evils. Without a commitment to universal solidarity, our moral claims are merely emotional preference.

Over the last decade, the social ethics of Agnes Heller, Charles Taylor, Cornel West, and

Edith Wyschograd, and the feminist ethics of Nel Noddings, Carol Gilligan, and Seyla Benhabib, have made a major impact on ethical theory. For all their apparent achievements, why consider them intellectual advances? Why not endorse a cynical will of the stronger like Nietzsche? Why not be content with a quandary ethics of a minimalist sort? Without their contributions to human solidarity, we might as well insist on maintaining the rationalist canon instead. Obviously not every community ought to be celebrated. Through a moral order we resist those social values which are exclusivistic and divisive.

The quest for protonorms responds to the human yearning for a lever long enough to move the earth.

REFERENCES

Benhabib, S. (1992). *Situating the self: Gender, community and postmodernism in contemporary ethics.* Cambridge, UK: Polity Press.

Bok, S. (1995). *Common values.* Columbia: University of Missouri Press.

Cassirer, E. (1951). *The philosophy of the enlightenment.* Princeton, NJ: Princeton University Press.

Christians, C. G. (1995). The naturalistic fallacy in contemporary interactionist-interpretive research. In N. K. Denzin (Ed.), *Studies in symbolic interaction* (Vol. 19, pp. 125–30). Greenwich, CT: JAI Press.

Christians, C. G. & Traber, M. (Eds.). (1997). *Communication ethics and universal values.* Thousand Oaks, CA: Sage.

Cortazzi, M. (1993). *Narrative analysis.* Bristol, PA: Taylor & Francis.

Denzin, N. K. (1997). *Interpretive ethnography: Ethnographic practices for the twenty-first century.* Thousand Oaks, CA: Sage.

Dewey, J. (1948). *Human nature and conduct.* New York: Henry Holt and Company. (Original work published 1922).

Ellos, W. (1994). *Narrative ethics.* London: Blackwell.

Fackler, M. (1992, May). Debates in contemporary theory: Richard Rorty versus Charles Taylor. *Conference proceedings of the second national communication ethics conference.* Annandale, VA: Speech Communication Association, pp. 26–34.

Fisher, W. R. (1987). *Human communication as narration: Toward a philosophy of reason, value, and action.* Columbia: University of South Carolina Press.

Geras, N. (1995). *Solidarity in the conversation of humankind: The ungroundable liberalism of Richard Rorty.* London: Verso.

Glasser, T. L. (1991). Communication and the cultivation of citizenship. *Communication, 12* (4):235–48.

Harvey, D. (1996). *Justice, nature and the geography of difference.* Oxford, UK: Blackwell.

Hume, D. (1739). *Treatise of human nature.* London: J. Noon.

Hume, D. (1963). *Enquiries concerning the human understanding and concerning the principles of morals.* Oxford, UK: Clarendon Press (Original work published 1748 and 1751).

Jonas, H. (1984). *The imperative of responsibility.* Chicago: University of Chicago Press.

Outka, G. & Reeder, J. P., Jr. (Eds.). (1993). *Prospects for a common morality.* Princeton, NJ: Princeton University Press.

Paul, E. F., Miller, F. D., & Paul, J. (Eds.). (1994). *Cultural pluralism and moral knowledge.* Cambridge, UK: Cambridge University Press.

Peukert, H. (1981). Universal solidarity as goal of communication. *Media Development, 28* (4): 10–12.

Richter, D. H. (Ed.). (1996). *Narrative-theory.* New York: Longman.

Rorty, R. (1988). The priority of democracy to philosophy. In M. D. Peterson & Robert C. Vaughn (Eds.), *The Virginia statute for religious freedom* (pp. 257–82). Cambridge, UK: Cambridge University Press.

Rorty, R. (1989). *Contingency. irony, and solidarity.* Cambridge, UK: Cambridge University Press.

Rosaldo, R. (1989). *Culture and truth: The remaking of social analysis.* Boston: Beacon Press.

Vico, G. (1948). *The new science of G. Vico* (T. G. Bergin & M. H. Fisch, Trans.). Ithaca, NY: Cornell University Press.

Warnock, M. (1992). *The uses of philosophy.* Oxford, UK: Blackwell.

West, C. (1989). *The American evasion of philosophy: A genealogy of pragmatism.* Madison: University of Wisconsin Press.

When the Mass Media Have Strong Effects: Intermedia Processes

Everett M. Rogers

University of New Mexico

"Mass communication ordinarily does not serve as a necessary and sufficient cause of audience effects, but rather functions among and through a nexus of mediating factors and influences, [but] there are certain residual situations in which mass communication seems to produce direct effects...."

Joseph Y. Klapper (1960, p. 8),
The Effects of Mass Communication.

The purpose of this chapter is to analyze situations in which the mass media have strong effects. We seek to identify when and why such relatively rare but important situations occur. We argue that the finding of strong or weak media effects may depend in part on the research designs and the research methods used in the investigations. Further, intermedia processes (also called "media-stimulated interpersonal communication") often considerably magnify the effects of direct exposure to the media messages.

WHEN DO THE MEDIA HAVE STRONG EFFECTS?

Research on mass media effects has been the most popular single issue for mass communication researchers since this scholarly specialty got underway with the pioneering works of Harold D. Lasswell and Paul F. Lazarsfeld in the 1930s (Rogers, 1994). Lasswell studied the effects of propaganda, mainly through content analysis, while Lazarsfeld originally investigated the effects of the then-new medium of radio via survey research methods. As techniques for studying media effects gradually became more precise, in part due to the methodological advances pioneered by Lazarsfeld,

mass communication investigators concluded that the media have only minimal direct effects (the most cited statement of the minimal effects of the media is Joseph Klapper's generalization, which appears at the top of the present chapter). On the relatively rare occasions when the media were found to have strong effects, they were thought to occur due to massive exposure to media messages by a particularly vulnerable audience (such as the effects of violent television programs on children).[1]

The media were often found to have strong *indirect* effects, such as the agenda-setting process through which the media tell their audience what news issues are most important (Dearing & Rogers, 1996). But communication researchers have found that *the mass media have very limited effects for most individuals under most circumstances.* Even though the occasions in which the media have strong effects may be relatively rare, these occasions can be quite important.

BACKGROUND OF RESEARCH ON MEDIA EFFECTS

Several classic communication "milestones" (Lowery & DeFleur, 1989) are scholarly studies of the relatively unusual circumstances in which the media have strong effects. Examples are (1) the investigation by Hadley Cantril with others (1940) of the widespread panic resulting from Orson Welles's "War of the Worlds" radio broadcast in 1938, and (2) the study by Robert K. Merton with

---

[1] A recent meta-analysis of 217 studies by Paik and Comstock (1994) concluded that television violence has an effect on aggressive behavior by children.

others (1946) of the 1943 Kate Smith radio marathon to sell War Bonds during World War II. These two media events were characterized by:

1. Highly unusual radio messages whose effects were easily discernible from those of the regular content of radio news, music, and other entertainment. A dramatic end-of-the-world show and a patriotic marathon fund-raiser by a popular singer, respectively, served as "markers" for Cantril, Merton, and their fellow scholars who traced the effects of these two radio programs. These unique radio programs stood out starkly from the backcloth of other radio programming of the day.

2. A specific, measurable type of individual-level behavior resulting from the media event, which served as a distinctive indicator of the media's effects. For example, the effects of the Kate Smith marathon were measured by individuals' purchases of, and pledges to buy, U.S. War Bonds, which totaled an amazing $39 million (two earlier radio marathons had raised only $1 million and $2 million, respectively). Merton with others (1946) used the variable of whether or not their survey respondents made telephone pledges as their dependent variable indicating media effects. Orson Welles' "Invasion from Mars" radio broadcast panicked an estimated one million (16 percent) of the approximately six million individuals who listened to the radio broadcast (Cantril, Gaudet, & Herzog, 1940/1966). As Lowery and DeFleur (1989, p. 55) stated: "What occurred that October night was one of the most remarkable media events of all time. If nothing else was proved that night, it was demonstrated to many people that radio could have a powerful impact on its audience."

These early, influential media effects studies of 50 years ago helped form the central elements in the paradigm (Kuhn, 1962/1970) for scholarly research investigating media effects: (1) select an unusual media event for study, (2) gather data from audience individuals about its behavioral effects (for example, buying War Bonds or panicking), and (3) analyze the message content in order to understand how the media effects occurred. For example, Merton with others (1946, p. 142) concluded that the perceived genuineness of Kate Smith's patriotic appeals in the radio fund-raiser were actually a carefully engineered kind of "pseudo-Gemeinschaft," defined as the feigning of personal concern for another individual in order to manipulate the individual more effectively.[2] The paradigm for the early media effects research represented (1) a combination of audience survey methods and message content analysis, (2) both qualitative and quantitative data,[3] and (3) "firehouse research" in which the data were gathered immediately after the media event of study.[4]

Both the Cantril and colleagues (1940/1966) and the Merton and colleagues (1946) investigations were closely associated with Paul F. Lazarsfeld, the main founder of mass communication research (Rogers, 1994). Hadley Cantril, a Prince-

---

[2]This concept of pseudo-Gemeinschaft led to later research (1) by Beniger (1987) on pseudo-community and the mass media, and (2) by Horton and Wohl (1956), and many others, on *para-social interaction,* defined as the degree to which an individual perceives a media personality as someone with whom they have an interpersonal relationship. Carl Hovland, the founder of experimental research on persuasion, said that he became interested in investigating the attitude change effects of source credibility because of the Kate Smith radio marathon (Rogers, 1994, p. 375).

[3]For example, the Merton with others (1946) investigation was based on 100 focused interviews with New York respondents, 75 of whom had called in pledges to buy War Bonds, plus survey interviews with another sample of 978 respondents in New York. A generally similar procedure was followed by Cantril with others (1940) in their study of the effects of the "War of the Worlds" broadcast on panic behavior. So both studies used a combination of quantitative and qualitative data-gathering methods.

[4]Paul F. Lazarsfeld, then Director of the Radio Research Project, telephoned Frank Stanton, Director of Research at the CBS radio network, on the morning after the "War of the Worlds" broadcast on CBS to request funding for a "firehouse research project" (Hyman, 1991, p. 193). Stanton also provided immediate funding for the Merton with others (1946) study of the effects of the Kate Smith radio fund-raiser. Firehouse research is today referred to as "quick-response" research. The advantage of such immediate investigation of media effects is (1) that cause–effect relationships are less likely to be clouded by intervening factors, and (2) that respondents are better able to report on their media effects.

ton University psychologist, was an Associate Director of the Rockefeller Foundation-supported Radio Research Project, which Lazarsfeld directed. Lazarsfeld played an influential role in designing the 1938 "War of the Worlds" study, and in raising funds for its conduct. Robert K. Merton was Lazarsfeld's faculty colleague in the Columbia University Department of Sociology, and also served as the Associate Director of Lazarsfeld's Office of Radio Research, the research institute through which the 1943 War Bond study was conducted. So the scholars who conducted the early two communication researches that found strong media effects constituted a small network of like-minded individuals.

Shortly thereafter, Lazarsfeld designed the well-known Erie County voting study (Lazarsfeld, Berelson, & Gaudet, 1944) in order to test the strong media effects model. However, the research findings did not support this model, and led instead to the limited effects paradigm that has dominated mass communication thinking to this day. *Later scholars discarded, along with the powerful media effects model, the special methodology utilized by Cantril, Merton, and their colleagues for investigating media effects.* Today's scholars of media effects seldom concentrate on tracing the impacts on a specialized audience of a particular and spectacular media event or message. For instance, the body of communication research on the effects of exposure to violent television programs focuses on violent television shows in general, rather than on a particular television program or a specific television episode.

The present chapter urges a return to a contemporary version of the earlier Cantril–Merton approach to investigating media effects. Here we look at the effects on specialized audiences of specific media messages through a combination of quantitative and qualitative data-gathering that is conducted immediately after the media event of study. This more disaggregated approach has seldom been used in most media effects studies.[5]

---

[5]This more disaggregated research strategy has been found to be useful in agenda-setting research (Dearing & Rogers, 1996).

THE PRESENT METHODOLOGY

My interest in reconsidering mass communication research on media effects began when I read a brief research report by Gellert and colleagues (1992) in the *New England Journal of Medicine*. These scholars traced the effects of five AIDS-related news events (for example, Rock Hudson's death in October 1985; Magic Johnson's announcement of his HIV-positive status in November 1991, etc.) on the number of AIDS blood tests in Orange County, California. These data suggested strong media effects. I identified four distinctive aspects of the Gellert and others (1992) research methodology:

1. The focus of study was on an important media event that had occurred at a specific point in time.
2. The event received major news coverage.
3. The media effects were measured by data available from an independent source (clinic records) about overt behavior changes on the part of individuals (AIDS blood tests).
4. The data on the overt behavioral effects of the media were obtained rather immediately after the media coverage, and at a specific point in time, and thus it could be assumed that the effects were caused by the media messages about the media event (for example, Magic Johnson's announcement that he was HIV positive).

The methodology utilized by Gellert and others (1992) is remarkably similar to that used by Cantril and Merton and their colleagues 50 years previously. Gellert and others are not communication professionals, nor did they know of the media effects research on the Invasion from Mars broadcast and the Kate Smith War Bond marathon that had been completed four decades previously. So they quite naively discovered powerful effects. A communication scholar, trained and experienced in the paradigm of mass communication effects research, might have missed the opportunity.

I began to search for other data sets or studies characterized by similar research methodologies to those used by Gellert and others (1992). I located the following studies:

1. Data on the number of calls made to the National AIDS Telephone Hotline (provided by Dr. Fred Kroeger, Centers for Disease Control and Prevention) at the time of such specific media events as basketball player Magic Johnson's announcement that he was HIV positive on November 7, 1991. Some 118,124 telephone call-attempts were made the day following Magic Johnson's announcement, then an all-time record for the Hotline, up from an average of 7,372 call-attempts for the 90 previous days.

2. The January 26, 1986 *Challenger* disaster and its effects on the American public's participation in memorial events for the *Challenger's* crew, as measured in a national sample survey conducted by Dr. Jon D. Miller (1987) at Northern Illinois University's Public Opinion Laboratory.[6]

3. The diffusion of a highly unusual news event in New Delhi, India, in 1995: That stone and metal statues of Hindu deities were drinking milk (Singhal, Sood, & Rogers, 1996).

4. An investigation of the effects of an entertainment-education radio soap opera to promote family planning and HIV/AIDS prevention in Tanzania from 1993–1995 (Rogers et al., 1997).

MAGIC JOHNSON AND CALLS TO THE AIDS HOTLINE

The Federal government established the National AIDS Hotline in February, 1983 through a contract by the Centers for Disease Control and Prevention (CDC) with the American Social Health Association to provide a toll-free telephone system 24 hours a day, seven days a week. The Hotline furnishes information on how HIV is spread and how its transmission can be prevented. Access is provided to the English-speaking population, the Spanish-speaking population, and to the deaf community (through TDD/TTY) by calling 1–800–342–AIDS. The CDC's National AIDS Hotline is by far the most important of numerous AIDS hotlines in the United States, and is the only service provided to the entire nation.

Earvin "Magic" Johnson, a professional basketball player for the Los Angeles Lakers, announced that he was seropositive, and that he was retiring as an active player, at a press conference on November 7, 1991 (the story had leaked to certain media on November 6th). Magic Johnson was perhaps the most famous sports figure in America at the time of his announcement, and was the first African American celebrity to disclose seropositivity.[7] The media gave massive coverage to this news event: The *New York Times,* for example, devoted 300 column inches to the Magic Johnson story on November 8–10, 1991. As is the usual pattern for most issues (Dearing & Rogers, 1996), however, media attention then fell off, with the *New York Times* devoting 140 column inches to Magic Johnson's disclosure the following week (November 11–17th), 35 column inches in the week of November 18–24th, and no coverage the following week. This rise-and-fall of a news issue usually occurs because newer issues push the earlier issue out of its high priority on the media agenda (Dearing & Rogers, 1996).

The National AIDS Hotline was immediately deluged with telephone calls following Magic Johnson's November 7th disclosure (Figure 1). During the preceding 90 days, the National AIDS Hotline averaged 7,372 call-attempts, about half of which could be answered. On November 7, 1991,

---

[6]The *Challenger* accident caused a 20 percent drop in the price of Morton-Thiokol stock on the New York Stock Exchange within the 30 minutes immediately following this event (the Morton-Thiokol Company manufactured the rocket boosters whose O-rings failed). Obviously, the investment community was immediately affected by media coverage of the *Challenger* disaster.

---

[7]Movie actor Rock Hudson and schoolboy Ryan White played a major role in putting the issue of AIDS on the media agenda in the United States by disclosing their HIV/AIDS status. For the three years prior to their disclosures in October, 1985, there were an average of 14 news stories about AIDS in six national media (like the *New York Times* and CBS News) per month. During the four years thereafter, the average number of news stories per month increased to 143 (Rogers, Dearing, & Chang, 1991).

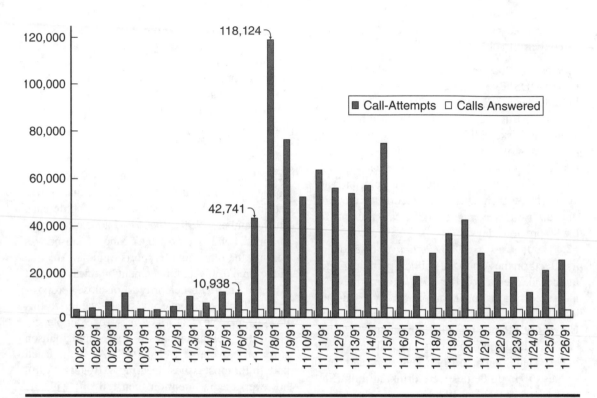

FIGURE 1   The Effects of Magic Johnson's News Conference on November 7, 1991, on the Number of Call-Attempts Made to the National AIDS Hotline (only English-language calls are shown here).
Source: CDC National Aids Hotline.

when news of Johnson's HIV infection was carried by the media, the number of calls jumped by a factor of 6 times to 42,741. The following day, when Magic Johnson's announcement was the major news item in the United States (in terms of the amount of news coverage), the number of call-attempts to the National AIDS Hotline surged to 118,124, 19 times the average number of calls previously and a then-record for the Hotline.[8] During the 60 days immediately following Magic

Johnson's announcement, 1.7 million call-attempts were made, an average of 28,333 per day, or four times the average number of call-attempts for the preceding 90 days.[9] No other important HIV/AIDS-related events occurred during this five-month period, so it seems clear that *most of the increase in calls to the CDC's National AIDS Hot-*

---

[8]The slowly decreasing effects over time of the Magic Johnson disclosure on the number of call-attempts to the National AIDS Hotline presumably is a function of the decreasing media coverage of this news event (such as in the case of the *New York Times,* cited previously).

[9]As is evident in Figure 1, this deluge of call-attempts completely swamped the Hotline's capacity to respond, with only about 3,000 of the 118,124 call-attempts answered on November 8, 1991. A few months later, the National AIDS Hotline added staff, telephone lines, and call-intercept capacities so as to better address the enormous volume of call-attempts that occurred due to celebrity disclosures and to other media events like Oprah Winfrey's television program on AIDS on April 8, 1992, in which she broadcast the telephone numbers for the National AIDS Hotline.

line was due to mass media reports of Magic Johnson's disclosure of seropositivity.[10]

This conclusion is supported, and amplified, by several other investigations of the effects of Magic Johnson's disclosure of his HIV status:

1. A comparison of 186 patients at an STD (sexually-transmitted disease) clinic in the Washington, DC suburbs during the 14 weeks prior to November 1, 1991, versus 97 patients at this clinic during the 14 weeks following Magic Johnson's announcement (Boekeloo et al., 1993). The patients were predominantly African American and male. The main impact of the Johnson disclosure was a decrease in the number of sexual partners, and fewer "one-night stands," rather than in increased condom use. These effects fit with the message-content of Magic Johnson's announcement, in which he told of his promiscuous sexual behavior, but said relatively little about practicing safe sex by using condoms.

2. Wanta and Elliott (1995) interviewed 366 Illinois respondents in March 1991, prior to Johnson's announcement, and 307 respondents 10 days after the November 7th disclosure. Correct knowledge that sneezing does not transmit the virus increased from 77 percent to 91 percent. Knowledge that using the same restroom as someone with AIDS cannot transmit the virus increased from 80 percent to 93 percent. Further, the respondents reported a major increase in knowing the difference between HIV and AIDS, which is consistent with the content of the Johnson announcement (he disclosed that he had the virus but did not have AIDS). The difference between HIV and AIDS was stressed in news stories about Magic Johnson.

3. Kalichman and Hunter (1992) gathered data from 361 men waiting for mass transportation in downtown Chicago, before and after the Magic Johnson announcement. A marked change oc-

curred in perceptions of AIDS, with an increased concern about AIDS, greater interest in AIDS-related information, and more frequent interpersonal discussion about AIDS. All of the men heard about Magic Johnson's HIV infection, and 86 percent discussed his disclosure with their friends during the three days following his news conference (100 percent had talked about it by 10 days after November 7, 1991). The percentage of the respondents who reported they "often" talked with friends about AIDS increased from about 24 percent prior to the Johnson disclosure, to 37 percent three days after, and to 48 percent ten days after.

One of the important effects of mass media messages about Magic Johnson's HIV infection was to encourage interpersonal communication about the issue of AIDS (a crucial matter to which we shall return in our later discussion of intermedia processes).

THE *CHALLENGER* DISASTER

Miller (1987) conducted three sets of telephone interviews with samples of the U.S. adult population: (1) an initial telephone survey of 2,005 interviews about a week prior to the *Challenger* disaster on January 26, 1986, which fortunately included a battery of questions about the U.S. space program, (2) a news event diffusion survey of 1,557 respondents conducted three days after the disaster, and (3) a follow-up survey of 1,111 respondents conducted six months later, after the Rogers Commission Report was released. The 1986 news event attracted spectacular audience attention: 18 hours after the disaster (which occurred at 10:00 a.m. EST), 95 percent of U.S. adults had seen television pictures of the exploding shuttle. Such exposure had strong emotional effects:

1. Some 90 percent talked to family members about the accident, and 73 percent talked to friends or colleagues at work or at school about the accident.

2. Some 78 percent watched all or part of a televised memorial service for the astronauts

---

[10]Unfortunately, the characteristics of the callers to the National AIDS Hotline, such as whether they were especially likely to be African Americans or males, could not be determined, as the Hotline only began to interview a 2 percent sample of callers in June, 1992.

broadcast from the Johnson Space Center in Houston.

3. About 6 percent (more than 10 million adults) attended a local memorial service for the astronauts. In addition, many others attended regular religious services which included a prayer for the *Challenger* astronauts and their families. Some 54 percent of the respondents said they cried or felt like crying.

4. Some 4 percent contacted their senator or congressman about the accident, and 1 percent wrote to NASA or to the U.S. president about the accident.[11]

Compared to the usual news event diffusion study, which only focuses on the dependent variable of awareness-knowledge of the news event (Rogers, 1994; DeFleur, 1987), media messages about the 1986 *Challenger* disaster had strong effects on the overt behavior of the U.S. public. Further, the impact of the *Challenger* disaster news coverage had a stronger, long-term effect on the American public than any of 480 other major news events (including the 1995 O. J. Simpson trial, the 1989 San Francisco earthquake, and the 1995 bombing of the Federal Building in Oklahoma City).[12]

FEEDING MILK TO HINDU DEITIES

Singhal and colleagues (1996) gathered data by telephone interviews from a sample of 199 residents of Delhi, India, about a spectacular news event a few days after it occurred in the very early morning of September 21, 1995: That statues of Hindu deities were drinking milk! Some 87 percent of the respondents said that upon hearing the news, they told an average of 21 others. Word-of-mouth channels were particularly important be-

cause the mystery surrounding this event led to a high degree of personal involvement with the event, and thus to a social construction of the meaning of the milk drinking. Upon initially hearing the news that the Hindu gods were drinking milk, only 17 percent believed this divine miracle and 36 percent were unsure. The news set off an unprecedented devotional frenzy, with 74 percent of the 199 respondents trying to feed milk to the deities, either at a Hindu temple or at an altar in their home. This experimental behavior convinced 68 percent of the individuals that the deities consumed the milk.

By the late morning of September 21st, milk supplies were exhausted in all major cities in India and by midday, police had to intervene in order to maintain order as crowds at Hindu temples became unmanageable. Newspaper headlines proclaimed: "Deities Drink Milk in Tonnes," "Divine Miracle Stuns the World," and "Miracles Claimed in Temples Abroad." Soon, Indians living abroad in England and the United States were feeding milk to Hindu gods. Scientists and others dismissed the milk drinking by the gods as a hoax, "perpetrated on gullible and devout people of a deeply religious country" (*Hindustan Times*, 1995, page 1). Some doubters explained the miraculous events as due to such processes in physics as surface tension or capillarity. The controversy over the milk drinking was reported in the mass media for several weeks after September 21, 1995.

As in the previous two media events of study, mass media coverage of an important event set off interpersonal discussion, which led to overt behavior change (feeding milk to the Hindu gods in this case).

A RADIO SOAP OPERA
AND FAMILY PLANNING
IN TANZANIA: INTERMEDIA PROCESSES

Both theoretical models and empirical research (Rogers, 1994) suggest that the mass media often have effects in changing human behavior through stimulating interpersonal communication about a message-topic. *Intermedia processes* occur when a

---

[11]Note the evidence of a hierarchy-of-effects here, with 90 percent of the respondents talking to someone, 78 percent watching the televised memorial service, 6 percent attending a memorial service, and 1 percent writing a letter.

[12]According to the Times Mirror Center for the People and the Press (now the Pew Research Center for the People and the Press). Some 75,000 people in 54 national sample surveys were asked which news events they had paid most attention to (according to an AP press release dated December 29, 1995).

mass media message leads to interpersonal communication among peers, which in turn influences behavior change.[13] Rogers and others (1997) investigated the effects of a two-year entertainment-education[14] radio soap opera in Tanzania that was designed to promote the adoption of family planning methods. The soap opera was planned around a dozen main characters who represented positive and negative role models for family planning. For instance, one popular character is Mkwaju, a truck driver who is promiscuous, a male chauvinist, and who displays strong son preference. He is punished in the soap opera's storyline.

Data were gathered via personal interviews from about 3,000 respondents in mid-1993, prior to broadcast of the twice-weekly episodes of the soap opera, *Twende na Wakati* (*Let's Go with the Times*). Another sample of 3,000 respondents were interviewed following the soap opera's broadcasts in 1995. The radio program was not broadcast in the Dodoma region of Tanzania, which served as a control group, in order to remove the effects of contemporaneous changes.

While the degree of exposure to the radio soap opera was highly related to adoption of family planning methods, *most individuals adopted family planning as the result of interpersonal communication stimulated by the entertainment-education radio soap opera* (Rogers et al., 1997). The degree of listening to *Twende na Wakati* was related to spouse/partner discussions of family planning; the frequency of such interpersonal communication was related to the adoption of family planning; and married women who were

both exposed to the radio soap opera, and who talked about it with their spouse/partner, were especially likely to adopt family planning.[15]

In general, *direct exposure to* Twende na Wakati *was less important in influencing the adoption of family planning than was interpersonal communication (especially with a spouse/partner) about family planning.*[16]

CONCLUSIONS

The present paper recommends returning to a research methodology pioneered 50 years ago by Paul Lazarsfeld and his colleagues at Columbia University's Bureau of Applied Social Research, in which data are gathered (1) about an important media event (2) by tracing its effects on the overt behavior of individuals exposed to the media messages, (3) whose contents are analyzed, and (4) whose effects are ideally evaluated by means of data gathered rather immediately after the event occurs. Here, we summarized the results of four investigations: Magic Johnson's 1991 disclosure of his HIV infection on calls to the National AIDS Hotline, diffusion of news of the 1986 *Challenger* disaster, diffusion of news of feeding milk to Hindu gods in 1995, and the effects of an entertainment-education radio soap opera on the adoption of family planning in Tanzania. These studies show that *the media can have strong effects, especially when the media messages stimulate interpersonal communication about a topic through intermedia processes.*

One distinctive aspect of the entertainment-education strategy is that the educational messages, because of their entertaining aspect, often

---

[13]*Intermedia processes,* a term coined by Gumpert and Cathcart (1986), were referred to as "mass media-generated interpersonal communication" by Valente, Poppe, and Merritt (1996).

[14]*Entertainment-education* is the strategy of placing educational content in entertainment messages in order to change the overt behavior of audience members concerning the educational issue. This entertainment-education strategy has been utilized to promote family planning, female equality, adult literacy, and HIV/AIDS prevention in 75 different projects, mainly in developing countries of Latin America, Africa, and Asia.

[15]Another possible reason for the strong effects of *Twende na Wakati* may have been the great frequency of audience individuals' exposure to the educational content, which occurred because of the popularity of the radio soap opera. As DeFleur and Dennis (1991, pp. 560–565) pointed out, strong media effects can occur due to the accumulation of minimal effects.

[16]Similar evidence for this statement is reported by Valente and others (1996) for family planning adoption in Peru, and by Rao and colleagues (1996) for HIV/AIDS prevention in Tanzania.

cause people to engage in peer communication as they seek to make sense out of what is happening. For example, the Tanzanian respondents often discussed the characters in the radio soap opera with their friends and family, relating the role models' behavior to their own lives (Rogers et al., 1997).

Our present analysis shows that intermedia processes (Gumpert & Cathcart, 1986) are a basic reason why the mass media sometimes have strong effects. The notion that media messages have their effect through peer communication raises basic questions about the dichotomy of interpersonal versus mass media communication that pervades communication study (Reardon & Rogers, 1988; Hawkins, Wiemann, & Pingree, 1988). Past research has often "created a false competition between mass and interpersonal communication" (Chaffee, 1986). Perhaps this false dichotomy is created because communication scholars in the academy divide themselves into two subdisciplines (Reardon & Rogers, 1988). Then the world that they perceive consists of *either* mass media or interpersonal communication, rather than the two types of channels working together to have effects.

We conclude that *past mass communication effects research may have supported a minimal effects model, in part, because of the methodology with which it was conducted.* Tracing a specific and spectacular message content that is conveyed by the mass media to audience individuals, and taking into account their interpersonal communication about the media message event, represent fruitful means for media effects research in the future.

REFERENCES

Beniger, J. R. (1987). Personalization of mass media and the growth of pseudo-community. *Communication Research, 14(3),* 352–371.

Boekeloo, B., Schiavo, L., Rabin, D., Jordan, C., & Matthews, J. R. (1993). Sexual risk behaviors of STD clinic patients before and after Earvin "Magic" Johnson's HIV-infection announcement: Maryland, 1991–1992. *Morbidity and Mortality Weekly Report, 42(3),* 46–48.

Cantril, H., Gaudet, H., & Herzog, H. (1940/1966). *The invasion from Mars: A study in the psychology of panic.* Princeton, NJ: Princeton University Press; New York: Harper and Row.

Chaffee, S. H. (1986). Mass media and interpersonal channels: Competitive, convergent, or complementary? In G. Gumpert and R. Cathcart, (Eds.), *Inter/Media: Interpersonal communication in a media world.* New York: Oxford University Press.

Dearing, J. W., & Rogers, E. M. (1996). *Agenda-Setting.* Newbury Park, CA: Sage.

DeFleur, M. L. (1987). The growth and decline of research on the diffusion of news. *Communication Research, 14,* 109–130.

DeFleur, M. L., & Dennis, E. E. (1991). *Understanding mass communication* (4th ed.). Boston: Houghton Mifflin.

Gellert, G. A., Weismuller, P. C., Higgins, K. V., & Maxwell, R. M. (1992). Disclosure of AIDS in celebrities. *New England Journal of Medicine, 327(19),* 1389.

Gumpert, G., & Cathcart, R. (Eds.). (1986). *Inter/Media: Interpersonal communication in a media world* (3rd ed.) New York: Oxford University Press.

Hawkins, R., Wiemann, J., & Pingree, S. (Eds.). (1988). *Advancing communication science: Merging mass and interpersonal processes.* Newbury Park, CA: Sage.

Horton, D., & Wohl, R. R. (1956). Mass communication and para-social interaction: Observations on intimacy at a distance. *Psychiatry, 19(3),* 215–229.

Hyman, H. H. (1991). *Taking society's measure: A personal history of survey research.* New York: Russell Sage Foundation.

Kalichman, S. C., & Hunter, T. L. (1992). The disclosure of celebrity HIV infection: Its effects on public attitudes. *American Journal of Public Health, 82,* 1374–1376.

Klapper, J. Y. (1960). *The effects of mass communication.* New York: Free Press.

Kuhn, T. S. (1962/1970). *The structure of scientific revolutions.* Chicago: University of Chicago Press.

Lazarsfeld, P. F., Berelson, B., & Gaudet, G. (1944). *The people's choice: How the voter makes up his mind in a presidential campaign.* New York: Duell, Sloan and Pearce.

Lowery, S. A., & DeFleur, M. L. (1989). *Milestones in mass communication research* (2nd ed.). White Plains, NY: Longmans.

McCombs, M. E., & Shaw, D. L. (1972). The agenda-setting function of mass media. *Public Opinion Quarterly, 36,* 176–187.

Merton, R. K., Fiske, M., & Curtis, A. (1946/1958/1971). *Mass persuasion: The social psychology of a War Bond drive.* New York: Harper and Brothers.

Miller, J. D. (1987). *The impact of the* Challenger *accident on public attitudes toward the space program.* DeKalb: Northern Illinois University, Public Opinion Laboratory, Report to the National Science Foundation.

Paik, H., & Comstock, G. (1994). The effects of television violence on antisocial behavior: A meta-analysis. *Communication Research, 21(4),* 516–546.

Rao, N., Svenkerud, P. J., Sood, S., & Alford, K. L. (1996). Mass media effects through interpersonal communication: The effects of *Twende na Wakati* on the adoption of HIV prevention in Tanzania. Unpublished paper. Albuquerque: University of New Mexico, Department of Communication and Journalism.

Reardon, K. K., & Rogers, E. M. (1988). Interpersonal versus mass media communication: A false dichotomy. *Human Communication Research, 15(2),* 284–303.

Rogers, E. M. (1994). *A history of communication research: A biographical approach.* New York: Free Press.

Rogers, E. M., Dearing, J. W., & Chang, S. (1991). *AIDS in the 1980s: The agenda-setting process for a public issue* (Journalism Monographs 126).

Rogers, E. M., Vaughan, P. W., Swalehe, R. M. A., Rao, N., Svenkerud, P., Sood, S., & Alford, K. L. (1997). *Effects of an entertainment-education radio soap opera,* Twende na Wakati, *on family planning and HIV/AIDS prevention in Tanzania* (POFLEP Research Report). Albuquerque, NM: University of New Mexico, Department of Communication and Journalism; Arusha, Tanzania.

Singhal, A., Sood, M., & Rogers, E. M. (1996). The Gods are drinking milk! Word-of-mouth diffusion of a major news event in India. Unpublished paper. Athens: Ohio University, School of Interpersonal Communication.

Valente, T. W., Poppe, P. R., & Merritt, A. P. (1996). Mass-media-generated interpersonal communication as sources of information about family planning. *Journal of Communication, 1,* 247–265.

Wanta, W., & Elliott, W. R. (1995). Did the "Magic" work? Knowledge of HIV/AIDS and the knowledge gap hypothesis. *Journalism and Mass Communication Quarterly, 72(2),* 312–321.

NOTE

The data reported in the present paper were made available by Fred Kroeger of the Centers for Disease Control and Prevention, Atlanta; Dr. Arvind Singhal, Ohio University; and Dr. Peter Vaughan, consultant to the Department of Communication and Journalism, University of New Mexico.

CHAPTER 12.

AT THE HELM IN MEDIA STUDIES

Introduction

David L. Swanson
University of Illinois

Of all of the areas of research that are featured in this volume, media studies probably has the least distinct identity. In part, this reflects youth. Scholars and students have studied media for quite a long time, and the term "media studies" has been used for many years in various local contexts where it has taken on many different meanings. But it is only in the last few years that media studies has come to be used more generally as though it were a formal rubric that identifies a commonly understood domain of teaching and scholarship. Yet, there is not much agreement about what the rubric refers to. Indistinct identities are not unusual in young and emerging areas, and they are no great cause for concern. To the contrary, interest in clarity of definition and boundary-setting seems out of place in today's academy of fluid disciplinary boundaries and transdisciplinary communities. The more important fact about media studies is that students and scholars have been attracted to this domain in large and growing numbers. The quality of their best scholarship has established media studies as an area where important questions can be tackled in imaginative ways that yield valuable results of broad interest. It is this fact, rather than an unseemly preference for tidiness in the organization of disciplinary subfields, that leads us to try to identify what this area is and why it offers such promise.

Despite the celebrated plainness and precision of the English language, media studies is not, in fact, studies of media. At least, not simply. Elsewhere in this volume will be found a set of papers that represent the study of mass communication. The reasoning that led the editor to include two different sets of papers that bear on media probably has to do with a distinction that often is made between the social-scientific study of mass communication, usually called mass communication research, and the more humanistic and critical study of mass communication, frequently referred to as media studies. But this distinction is not universally accepted. In an important volume of essays entitled *Defining Media Studies,* editors Mark Levy and Michael Gurevitch (1994) suggested that the terms "mass communication" and "mass media" have been rendered obsolete by the rise of new communication technologies such as cable television, computer networks, and home video systems (p. 7). Hence, according to Levy and Gurevitch, the term "media studies" has emerged as simply today's equivalent of the older "mass communication." As can be seen, some people regard these two terms as synonymous while others believe they describe rather different domains of work.

We may get more purchase on the subject by comparing media studies to some other "studies" that are popular in communication research, cultural studies and women's studies. Cultural studies are not simply studies of culture. Within our field, only studies of culture that employ particular concepts, theories, and methods are regarded as cultural studies. Similarly, women's studies refers not to studies about women but rather to the more narrowly defined domain of feminist studies. Here is a key difference among media studies, cultural studies, and women's studies. The latter two domains are defined by particular and rather closely drawn approaches to their subject matter, whereas media studies is a more intellectually open domain that welcomes a whole range of concepts, theories, and methods. In most usages, the range of approaches associated with media studies is limited to broadly humanistic (as opposed to social-scientific) ways of doing intellectual work, but this limitation is quite expansive.

Because of its intellectual openness and unlike the other "studies" domains found in the field of communication, media studies is one of only a few areas of communication research where scholars representing such diverse intellectual traditions as rhetorical studies, cultural studies, and media history all find room to work. The exchange of insights and viewpoints that occurs gives the area a particular vitality where contributions are judged on their demonstrated merits rather by their conformity to some orthodoxy.

Media studies is energized as well by its subject matter, which invites the best students and scholars to pursue questions of substantial scope and importance. The world of media and the roles of media in shaping individual, social, political, and cultural life are constantly changing. Understanding this complex subject is a daunting undertaking, but no one doubts that it is vital as well.

The following papers present an opportunity to explore media studies as exemplified in the work and views of three major scholars whose contributions are closely associated with the area. In his work, each panelist has ranged across several different fields and subfields, illustrating the interdisciplinary spirit that seems to be a central tendency of media studies. These papers also illustrate the intellectual diversity found in media studies. Each author has approached the subject

somewhat differently, drawing on somewhat different intellectual traditions, and focusing on different sets of questions. But there are also common themes across these authors: in their shared interests in the relationship between communication and culture, in understanding communication as cultural practice, in their efforts to direct attention to symbolic processes and forms. If media studies has a defining core of concerns, perhaps it is found in these themes.

One particular problem that scholars of media studies and related areas have thus far been unable to get much traction on concerns how to understand conceptually, and therefore how to analyze, the visual elements that are such an important part of many media messages. The difficulties of dealing with visual content are so dismaying that most scholars concentrate on verbal content and offer only a few, often vapid, generalizations about visual elements. In his paper, Bruce Gronbeck grapples with this daunting subject in a way that is characteristic of his work in media studies. Operating from within the rhetorical studies tradition, Gronbeck's scholarship has elaborated a sociocultural perspective on the role of the media, and has applied a wide range of theoretical viewpoints to media content. His contributions to media studies include well-known works on such subjects as politics and the media, popular culture, rhetoric and the media, television criticism, and the views of Walter Ong.

James Carey enlarges the focus of discussion to media systems and speculates about change, transitions, and transformations. Carey's advocacy of a cultural approach to media studies has been one of the formative ideas which have shaped this field. Consistently, his analyses have displayed an intellect of great breadth, devoted to a vision of the social and cultural responsibility of the media, and committed to a conception of the media as the nexus of cultural processes and practices.

James Chesebro widens the discussion still further to consider culture and media as symbolic systems. Within this general subject, Chesebro has long pursued an interest in dramatistic theory, methods, and criticism, with specific applications to contemporary culture, particularly television. Over the last 15 years, this orientation has been extended to include all media systems, with special attention devoted to media literacy and media technologies as communication and cognitive systems.

These papers thus exemplify some of the best characteristics of media studies scholarship: They raise fundamental questions of great scope; they range across a broad theoretical terrain; they are imaginative but not intellectually reckless or casual; they are provocative. It is easy to see why, as a domain of teaching and scholarship, media studies is moving ahead so rapidly, confidently, and well.

REFERENCE

Levy, M. R., & Gurevitch, M. (Eds.). (1994). *Defining media studies*. New York: Oxford University Press.

Reconceptualizing the Visual Experience in Media Studies

Bruce E. Gronbeck
University of Iowa

I take my text from a statement made by Maurice Merleau-Ponty a third of a century ago. Said he: "Perception is…paradoxical. The perceived thing is itself paradoxical; it exists only in so far as someone can perceive it" (Merleau-Ponty, 1964, qtd. in Jenks, 1995, p. 2). The paradox articulated by Merleau-Ponty, I would argue, has the status of being the central problematic of the twentieth-century human sciences, a problematic we inherited from John Locke. It is this: What is the relationship between the external world and the internal lives of human beings, or, if you prefer, between objectivity and subjectivity? And, for people gathered in this room, I assume that problematic has a corollary: what is the role of human communication processes and coding systems in framing and negotiating that relationship?

One half of Merleau-Ponty's paradox—the "someone" who can "perceive it"—certainly has been subject to much commentary among students of media studies over the last fifteen or twenty years. Audience studies exploded unto the scene in the late 1970s, and made a series of names—Charlotte Brunsdon, Dorothy Hobson, David Morley, Ien Ang, James Lull, John Fiske—regular occupants of footnotes in *Critical Studies in Mass Communication.*

The other half of the paradox—the "thing" that is perceived—has been with us even longer. Since the early 1950s, there has been considerable controversy over what the "thing" we call "television" actually is: does the word "television" refer to the industry, the box in your living room, the electronics of the technology, individual programs, or the sequence—what Raymond Williams called the flow—of those broadcast materials? Television understood as an industry spawned work on the polit-ical economy. The box itself has come in for renewed study, for example in an essay by David Morley (1995; cf. Boddy, 1984; Geller & Williams, 1990) just last year. The electronics of television—more particularly, its combination of vocal, visual, and verbal coding—have fertilized innumerable semiotic studies (e.g., Seiter, 1987; Fiske, 1985).

But, it has been the television program, the usual "texts" of television, that has been featured in most of the critical work in the United States. Horace Newcomb, first with his *TV, The Popular Art* (1974) and then with his anthology, *Television: The Critical View* (1976), led the way into textual criticism of television, drawing from generic criticism in literary studies in his first effort, and from American cultural studies for his later works. From the continental side of the Atlantic, 1974 also introduced TV scholars to Raymond Williams's *Television: Technology and Culture Form* (1974/1975), which argued that we cannot understand television as a personal and social experience without also understanding it as a governmentally regulated and economically framed communications technology. Television's texts thus were positioned within their social, political, economic, and technological contexts. Williams's ideas came to condition British textual analysis, as can be seen in John Fiske and John Hartley's *Reading Television* (1978). While they focused their analyses of programs or texts on psychoanalytic, semiotic, and generally sociocultural understandings, yet Williams's political and economic frames for texts and flow were visible in their work.

The simple conclusion I would draw from these first remarks is that we have done a good job in media studies of investigating especially the texts of television and the people who read or view them. What we have done less well is to bring those two kinds of study together. I say "less well" because I certainly would recognize that investigations of so-called "active audiences"— that is, of viewers making meanings out of the texts that they've been offered on television—are important. The notion of audience meaning-making so central to a series of works following in the wake of Stuart Hall's enormously important article on encoding and decoding in 1980,[1] tended to focus studies, however, on the meaning-makers more than the texts out of which meanings were made. That is, while the theory of active audiences highlighted relationships between texts and their consumers, in fact the consumers were probed a good deal more thoroughly than the texts. This even has led to the near-beatification in recent years of ethnography, which is to say, of investigation of so-called socially situated readers and their constructions of the world following exposure to televisual texts.[2] In our rush to study active audiences— essentially, in the world of John Fiske (e.g., 1987), to study oppositional readings that audiences can build—some have come to view television's texts as but vehicles for liberation, often not probing deeply the connection between particular characteristics of those texts and the act of empowerment or liberation that a John Fiske believes can result from an encounter with TV.

The more complicated conclusion I would draw from those first remarks, therefore, is this: we as yet lack ways of reconciling what Ien Ang (1996) in her most recent book has called the sociological and the semiological approaches to television, or what is also referred to as the "text/context problematic." Most of the work on the text/context problematic has gone on at the macro level, following David Morley's lead (1980) by examining various viewers' decoding of the same text or Charlotte Brunsdon's lead (1981) by looking at confrontations between particular kinds of texts and their habitual audiences. For a full reconciliation between audience-centered and text-centered analysis to occur, though, I think that such research must move into the dirty little world of micro-analysis.

And hence, when I call in my title for a reconceptualizing of the visual experience, I am urging that we move into explicitly psychocultural realms of thought, armed with the tools of close textual analysis and cognitive research and with conceptualizations of ocularcentrism as a mark of western intellectual life. Let me devote a few minutes to these topics in order.

First, close textual analysis. In our rush to offer ideological critiques of domination in race/class/gender studies, for example, media critics seldom take the time and space needed to disassemble particular scenes to demonstrate that domination. So, someone analyzing the medical drama *Chicago Hope* might wish to argue that the show's construction of professional relationships between male doctors and female nurses conditions and reinforces a male domination of females in their social relationships. Fine, but such a critic is likely to describe two or three scenes generally, say, something in an operating theatre that seems paralleled by a male–female conversation in the hall, using those descriptions as evidence for the claim. Seldom will such a critic dissect the shots that comprise the scenes. If seeing is believing, then we ought to spend more time talking in specific ways about how seeing is controlled by shot selection, framing, set direction, reinforcing audio and verbal cues, and all of the other production values that Fiske talks about in Chapter 1 of *Television Culture* (1987) or that Ellen Seiter exposes in her analysis of *The Cosby Show* (1987; cf. Schwichtenberg, 1983). I will return to this theme in a couple of minutes.

---

[1]Certainly the centrality of semiotics to the study of communication predated Hall's essay, and had been all the rage especially in film studies for well over a decade by 1980. But, Hall's genius was to see the text, the coded discourse, as a site of struggle between encoders and decoders, offering an analysis of three different sorts of decodings (dominant, negotiated, and oppositional readings) that could result from the encounter between producers and audiences.

[2]For the television critic, ethnographic study has been interesting, I suspect, largely because it turns audiences into texts, thereby making them accessible to analysis via the same sorts of critical methods by which programs themselves are analyzed.

Next, some thoughts about cognitive research's utility for the critic. I am no expert on this sort of research, which has seized film studies. I do know, however, that dimensions of cognitive theory and research can provide innovative accounts for media effects. The 1994 Super Bowl ad for the then-new Chrysler product, the Neon, for example, absolutely fascinated me. The first 49 seconds of that ad were recognizable to most viewers—even when I showed it in Finland the following year—as a remake of the film *Close Encounters of the Third Kind.* While almost none of the 43 shots making up the *Close Encounters* section of the ad were lifted from the movie, yet the feeling created by their selection and sequencing, as well as by their depictive analogy to shots moviegoers might remember, combined to evoke that film. The last 11 seconds of the ad, where the smiling little white car saying "Hi" drove out of an airplane hangar as strongly backlit as were the aliens in *Close Encounters,* was an auto sales talk: "Introducing...Neon...89–75 for starters, 12–5 nicely loaded." It was as though we had faded from one set of memories to another. Likewise, the audio channel segued from the orchestrated chase-and-danger music of the first 49 seconds to synthesizer-stroked chords of funky, terminally cute sounds appropriate to a smiling car saying "Hi."

While I don't have time to repeat the detailed analysis I did of this ad in last year's Alta proceedings (Gronbeck, 1996), I can indicate that visually and acoustically, the ad mixes imagaic memories of danger, excitement, fear of death, joy of living, adventure, and sex, all the while offering rational appeals for purchasing the car in its verbal discourse.

I would suggest that we must have in place a theory of memory—even of repressed memory of the sort associated with the admittedly controversial research of Elizabeth Loftus (Loftus & Ketcham, 1994)—to understand meaning-making as it is occurring in that 1994 ad for the Neon. Loftus argues that we call up and reassemble into new experiences—even new "memories"—events from our past to frame and justify present thought and action. Likewise, many of our engagements with

television programs draw upon our fragmented memories of past viewing and other life experiences as we encounter new events, affecting how we understand those events. Even our viewing of local news, I will argue in *The Sociological Quarterly* this winter (1997, in press), is conditioned by previously understood social frames for interpreting the world. Even the "news" is "old," a product of reconstituted memory.

All I'm really suggesting here is that media studies complete its escape from the tyranny of the information model of human communication that we have flirted with at least since Colin Cherry's monumental book *On Human Communication* (1957/1978), now in its fortieth year of circulation. To understand television viewing as a kind of surveillance project wherein we scan our environment for danger, promise, and new information is to forget the experiential base of human comprehension. The very familiarity we have with content and form, that is, with traditional themes and their technological formalization within particular media, can and should provide the starting point for a retheorization of television viewing.

Let me take up the third topic: ocularcentrism. The ocularcentrisim thesis is the assertion that the western world, especially, possesses a visually based epistemology. Heidegger blamed Plato for this, seeing the allegory of cave as a prime example of visuality in the service of knowledge (see Levin, 1993). Ivins (1973, quoted in Jenks, 1995, p. 2) captures the importance of a visually-oriented theory of knowledge when he says:

> At the very beginning of human history men discovered in their ability to make pictures a method for symbolization of their visual awareness which differs in important respects from any other symbolic method that is known. As distinguished from purely conventional symbols, pictorial symbols can be used to make precise and accurate statements even while themselves transcending definition.

As Ivins makes clear, what is at issue in the ocularcentrism thesis is more than the idea of observation as it is understood within traditions of science. To observe is to look at some aspect of the external world so as to consciously record and explicitly interpret that world. Observation is a planned activity that recognizes the distance between the observer and the observed. Observation is the search for what Mitchell (1986, quoted in Jenks, 1995, p. 4) called "the innocent eye," that is, a kind of mechanically purified process "uncontaminated by imagination, purpose, or desire." In theories of observation, seeing is not only believing but also knowing in objective ways.

The socially and culturally sensitive theory of ocularcentrism, however, recognizes that ways of seeing are partial in two important senses of that word—a fragment of the environment, never totalized, and partial as well in the sense of having an interest in what is seen. What we come to know about the world visually is conditioned by how we are taught to see and what we are taught to look at—that is, by culturally based formalizing processes and by culturally contoured content. And hence, while seeing and comprehending are in fact cognitive processes, yet that cognitive processing is a psychocultural activity, wherein the psychological acts occur within frames given to us by others who are insuring that we see in socially approved ways.

If you'll grant that I could expand and ground these notions so briefly stated here, I can get to my central call for work: I am convinced that we need to retheorize the viewing experience by exploring what it is that people actually see when they watch television and how that seeing process is conditioned by culturally sanctioned modes for interpreting television's codes. A micro- rather than macro-analytic investigative process is called for, I think, because social epistemology comes into play at a much more concrete and subtle level than we usually work on.

And so, in the Neon ad I mentioned earlier, I think the individual shots need to be studied: what are the socially based ideas and attitudes encoded in those shots? How are they arranged? What iconic signs are juxtaposed to other icons? Are icons of danger edited near to icons of death or icons of curiosity? How about the voiceover of the female announcer? What is the place of the sexual play evoked in her tonal patterns as she says "It's capable of extrasensory communication" early on and "no one has ever seen anything quite like it" near the end? At any given moment in the ad, how do the emotionality of paralinguistic tone, visual icon, and verbal argument overlay each other, and to what effect on viewers who have been conditioned to think of, say, danger, sex, and automobile safety as unrelated dimensions of living?

The visual experience of those millions of viewers looking at a Dole–Clinton debate, an episode of *Third Rock from the Sun,* or the Weather Channel represents a full amalgamation of cognitive and social activity, in fact a psychocultural experience. To find in acts of mass communication an amalgamation of consciousness and culture, self and society, is to find a way out of the paradox Merleau-Ponty articulated 32 years ago.

Critical-cultural approaches to media studies have evolved in interesting ways since the 1950s, from normative judgments about television's shortcomings to cultural celebrations of the medium in the McLuhan era to text- and audience-based analyses of viewing over the last two decades. While I will continue, certainly, to teach all of these conceptions of the medium technology we love to hate, I also will ask my students to take the helm, to explore visual experience via what is now called technocriticism (Woodward, 1994) understood within a distinctively ocularcentric framework via close textual and cognative analysis. That is our next challenge: to rivet together perceptual, social, and technological frames for thought.

REFERENCE.S

Ang, I. (1996). *Living room wars: Rethinking media audiences for a postmodern world.* New York: Routledge.

Boddy, W. (1984). The shining centre of the home: The ontology of television. In proceedings of the *International television studies conference.* London: N.p.

Brunsdon, C. (1981). The Nationwide audience—A critical postscript. *Screen Education, 22*(4), 32–37.

Cherry, C. (1957/1978). *On human communication.* Cambridge, MA: MIT.

Fiske, J. (1987). *Television culture.* New York: Methuen.

Fiske, J., & Hartley, J. (1978). *Reading television.* London: Methuen.

Geller, M., & Williams, R. (Eds.). (1990). *From receiver to remote control: The TV set.* New York: New Museum of Contemporary Art.

Gronbeck, B. E. (1996). Unstated propositions: Relationships among verbal, visual, and acoustic languages. In S. Jackson (Ed.), *Argumentation and communication: Proceedings of the ninth biennial conference on argumentation* (pp. 876–882). Annandale, VA: SCA.

Gronbeck, B. E. (1997, in press). Technology and tradition in local news: The social psychology of form. *The Sociological Quarterly.*

Gronbeck, B. E. (1997, in press). Technology and tradition in local news: The social psychology of form. *The Sociological Quarterly.*

Hall, S. (1980). Encoding/decoding. In S. Hall, D. Hobson, A. Lowe, & P. Willis (Eds.), *Culture, media, language* (pp. 128–139). London: Hutchinson.

Ivins, W. M. (1973). *On the rationalization of sight.* New York: Da Capo.

Jenks, C. (1995). The central of the eye in western culture: An introduction. In C. Jenks (Ed.), *Visual culture.* pp. 1–25. New York: Routledge.

Levin, D. M. (1993). Introduction. In D. M. Levin (Ed.), *Modernity and the hegemony of vision* (pp. 1–29). Berkeley: University of California Press.

Loftus, E., & Ketcham, K. (1994). *The myth of repressed memory. False memories and allegations of sexual abuse.* New York: St. Martin's Press.

Merleau-Ponty, M. (1964). *The primacy of perception.* Evanston, IL: Northwestern University Press.

Mitchell, W. J. T. (1986). *Iconology: Image, text, ideology.* Chicago: University of Chicago Press.

Morley, D. (1980). *The "Nationwide" audience: Structure and decoding.* London: BFI.

Morley, D. (1995). Television: Not so much a visual medium, more a visible object. In C. Jenks (Ed.), *Visual culture.* New York: Routledge. pp. 170–189.

Newcomb, H. (1974). *TV, the popular art.* New York: Anchor.

Newcomb, H. (1976). *Television: The critical view.* New York: Oxford University Press.

Schwichtenberg, C. (1983, Fall). *Dynasty:* The dialectic of feminine power. *Communication Studies, 34,* 151–161.

Seiter, E. (1987). Semiotics and television. In R. C. Allen (Ed.), *Channels of discourse: Television and contemporary criticism* (pp. 17–41). Chapel Hill, NC: University of North Carolina Press.

Williams, R. (1974/1975). *Television: Technology and culture form.* New York: Schocken.

Woodward, K. (1994). From virtual cyborgs to biological time bombs: Technocriticism and the material body. In G. Bender & T. Druckery (Eds.), *Culture on the brink: Ideologies of technology* (pp. 47–64). Seattle: Bay Press.

Everything that Rises Must Diverge: Notes on Communication, Technology, and the Symbolic Construction of the Social Self

James W. Carey
Columbia University

My title is a play on a remarkable collection of short stories by Flannery O'Connor, *Everything That Rises Must Converge.* Her stories, in turn, provided an ironic gloss on the work of the late Jesuit paleontologist Pere Teilard de Chardin, who experienced five minutes in the intellectual sun thanks to publicity given one of his books, *The Phenomenon of Man,* by Marshall McLuhan. McLuhan, scavenging for support for the notion of a "global village" evolving through modern electronic communications, appropriated Teilard's concept of a noosphere, a moment in the evolution of human knowledge in which the globe was engirdled by a dematerialized belt of human intelligence lifting us to an "omega point," outside history, where everything had risen and converged.

The spare and ironic intelligence of Flannery O'Connor was the necessary corrective to Teilard and McLuhan's redemptive vision, to any "fatuous happiness" in abstractions, for, in story after story of cruelty and suffering, she gave to the forces of chaos and disorder, disintegration and death, the power they actually possess in life. In episode after episode, in the world as in ourselves, they won. She reminded us that while we may have evolved a noosphere of human understanding, we have not reached an omega point. Everything has risen but diverged.

We have our noosphere. The earth is now engirdled, thanks to satellite technology, with an organized belt of intelligence. Words and images, converted by the magic of our lingua franca, plus and minus, zero and one, circulate endlessly through space. Pop on a computer, or a television screen, appropriately wired, and such images emerge from everywhere and nowhere; pop it off and they disappear while still circulating in space. Words and images created on one continent are processed on another and returned to their original home. Human intelligence has lodged itself, extrasomatically, in the very atmosphere that surrounds and supports us. Yet, back at home, we have a surplus of disorder and disarray.

My take on the phrase "Everything That Rises Must Converge" was inspired by some lines in the proposal for this conference:

> However, the convergence of communication forms and channels that characterizes the information age in which we live goes beyond engineering and hardware…The fragmentation of society, the emergence of new communities of interest and newly articulate ethnic and linguistic groupings offer serious threats to social well-being.

However, we were encouraged to "examine options within the context of convergence.…" This theme encapsulates certain exhausted ideas, which, to use an expression of William Pfaff (1989), are like "dead stars" in the cultural atmosphere yet remain central to the way communications is discussed and to the formulation of national policy. These are ideas that people want or need to be true merely because it would be bewildering to be without them. I have in many other places (Carey, 1989) characterized this way of talking and thinking about communications and technology as the "rhetoric of the electrical sublime": the hope, against all odds, that the dual elixirs of communications and technology will dissolve our troubles and transport us to a new plane of economic advance, social harmony, and human understanding.

The opposite is the case. Cultural fragmentation and postmodernist homogenization, to rename divergence and convergence, are not opposing views of what is happening but two constitutive trends of a single global reality (Appadurai, 1990). Divergence is not some random and unfortunate occurrence, a snake in our idyll of convergence, but a necessary consequence of the technological change we so eagerly support. We are living, engineering and hardware notwithstanding, in a period of enormous disarray in all our institutions and in much of our personal life as well.

We exist in a "verge" in the sense Daniel Boorstin gave that word: a moment between two different forms of social life in which technology has dislodged all human relations and nothing stable has as yet replaced them. Media may be converging, as we are continuously told these days, but only in a minor sense: All modern media are rooted in the power of the computer to convert words and images into numbers, analog models into digital ones. Social convergence does not follow the technical convergence, however. Alas, the only social convergence about these days is found in simulated electronic cottages such as MIT's Media Lab. Out on the streets, in the cities, in our neighborhoods, things continue to fall apart.

Another, more useful though whimsical gloss on this subject, comes from the 1992 Republican convention in Houston. Patrick Buchanan, one-time challenger for the Republican nomination and full-time polemicist, painted a vivid picture of the Democratic convention that had been held in June of that year in New York. The delegates to the Democratic convention were, he said, liberals and radicals "dressed up as moderates and centrists in the greatest single exhibition of cross-dressing in American political history." (The *New York Times,* never to be outdone, gravely interpreted Buchanan's remarks as homophobic but was disappointed that he had overlooked and thereby taken a swipe at "the largest group of cross-dressers in the United States, women.") The larger significance of Buchanan's remark is pursued, albeit indirectly, by

Marjorie Garber in *Vested Interests: Cross Dressing and Cultural Anxiety* (1992).

Professor Garber's book poses this question: "Why have cultural observers today been so preoccupied with cross-dressing?[1] Why is it virtually impossible to pick up a newspaper or turn on television or go to the movies without encountering, in some guise, the question of sartorial gender-bending?" She tells us that in the previous two years Phil Donahue had 16 programs on cross-dressing and transsexualism and Geraldo Rivera more than 7. Movies of the 1980s (*Tootsie, Yentl, Victor/Victoria*) were based on the theme; indeed transvestism and transsexuality are issues of intense popular and academic interest.

She claims that the distinct figure of the transvestite fills an important role in all cultural life. The cross-dresser signals a category crisis, a moment when established cultural boundaries of any kind, not only sexual, are being crossed or put in doubt. The transvestite thus stands for or "marks" any transgressive leap and creates a crisis of category itself. She means by "category crisis" a failure of definitional distinction, a borderline that becomes permeable and permits crossings from one distinct category to another: between black and white, noble and bourgeois, master and slave. The binary distinction male and female, fundamental to the categorical structure of all cultures, is put into question by transvestism.

Admittedly this is post-structuralism gone round the bend. However, the notion of a category crisis, an historical moment when the distinction between male and female (and with it all other binary categories) is put in question, has an independent usefulness. We may have thought at one time that people came in two types, plain and fancy, but all that has been placed in doubt, is under erasure. We no longer can take the established categories of the culture for granted, whether they are seen as constructed, biological, or cultural. The prominence of cross-dressing represents a melt-down in

---

[1]I have taken some of this formulation from Anne Hollander (1992).

the established categories of the culture, the categories through which we normally make sense of the world. Old binaries are displaced or radically conventionalized without new ones replacing them. This represents a displacement of fixed and given identities and subjectivities and sets in motion a restless search for new ones that can act as the countersigns of new practices, sexual and otherwise. In turn, the category crisis sets in motion the search for new meta-narratives with which to tell the story of our lives. The story of progress, of the melting pot, of freedom and liberation, the American story, no longer seems capable of catching what is going on today in our lives.

We live then in a moment of divergence, when things fall apart and the center will not hold, when all that is solid melts into air. It is not only genres that are blurred, to invoke Clifford Geertz (1983), but all cultural categories are gauzy, losing their sharp-edged distinctiveness. We are having a displacement and transgression of the symbolic, but it is unclear what will replace the terms on which we have navigated our sense of the world and our own nature for at least the last hundred years.

Despite those apocalyptic lines, I am not suggesting that we are living in an "imaginative proximity to revolution," to appropriate Perry Anderson's useful phrase. This is all rather normal, even predictable, just about what one would expect when existing patterns of communications and social relations are displaced, existing structures of community life dissolved under the impact of new forms of communications technology and yet another phase of capitalist expansion. It is not so different than what was experienced one hundred years ago when the modern system of communications was put into place. We are at the end of a long cycle of communications, a cycle which for lack of a better name and in order to have a stick with which to beat it, we might call the cycle of the modern. The cycle stretches from the birth of the national magazine in the 1890s through the disintegration of the network era in television which occurred sometime in the late 1970s. In framing this as a long cycle of some

eighty to ninety years duration, I do not wish to deny the profound changes wrought by the introduction and growth of motion pictures, radio, and television but only to characterize these changes as elaborations and intensifications of a common secular trend: the development, institutionalization, and later disintegration of what Gilbert Seldes called the "great audience." The long cycle of the modern, the cycle that formed the now dissolving great audience, is, in turn, composed of shorter epicycles revolving around the introduction of motion pictures, radio, and television.

In the 1890s a fundamentally new, national system of communications was put into place. Since then, this structure has been refined and improved, corrected and completed, through successive waves of invention in motion pictures, radio, and television without disturbing the basic underlying pattern. Along this extended axis continuous adjustment has occurred such as the important changes that took place when television replaced radio and film, as the central medium in the national system. However, these shorter cycles have moved around a long secular trend: the formation of an ever larger and more inclusive mass audience, the deeper penetration of the media into every corner of the national system and the progressive displacement of other forms of social relations that were not mediated by technology. In the late 1970s a structure that had persisted across time and technology started to unravel. The national, mass audience was fractured by cable television and transcended with the creation of the first effective system of international communication. The key technological ingredients in both the splintering and the transcendence were the satellite and computer. A long cycle appears now to be complete and we face a wave of technological and social change in which the scalar dynamic is tied, not to the nation, but to the globe, or least a globe divided into the three parts dictated by satellite technology.

The convergent order of the information society may appear from a safe distance as a neat geometric order with straight lines running into the future. However, on the streets this convergent order of the information society dissolves into ceaseless and disorderly flows: new people and new things flowing to new places along new routes; flows of migrants, guest workers, tourists, entrepreneurs and itinerants; new flows of capital, factories, messages, products, ideas, images, and currencies. Things are flowing from new places to new places, upsetting established patterns of geography, trade, and communications, imploding and exploding at the same time.

The central problem in these interactions which today occur as never before on a global scale, is the tension and contradiction between cultural homogenization and cultural fragmentation, between the order of technology and commerce and the disorder of migration, messages, and settlements.

It was within a similar conjuncture, contained within a different scalar dynamic, that of the nation and the city (rather than the globe), that the modern system of communications was created.[2] In the nineteenth century western countries were hit with two successive waves of change, separated in time but tied in logic. The first was the industrial revolution which reorganized the nature of work and the structural basis of class and community and set loose a worldwide movement of migrants from low to high industry areas. The second was a change in communication and culture which reorganized the basis on which art, information, and culture were made available and the terms on which experience was worked into consciousness. These were not independent events but successive moments in the same social process. The timing, interrelationship, speed, and extensiveness of these changes varied considerably from country to country but both the direction and major implications of the changes were everywhere the same.

The industrial and cultural revolutions of the modern era were remarkably telescoped in the United States. The full tide of industrialization struck between 1840 and 1860. The communications revolution, presaged by the growth of the

telegraph and the penny press in the decades before and after the Civil War, decisively began in the 1890s with the birth of the national magazine, the development of the modern mass, urban newspaper, the domination of news dissemination by the wire services, and the creation of early, primitive forms of electronic communication. The latter constituted the infrastructure of a nationwide system of signalling tied to a largely local network of telephony. By the 1920s the dominant tendencies of this revolution were clear, although they continued to work themselves out even into the 1970s.

The most explored dimension of the cultural revolution was the rise of national or mass media communication—media that cut across structural divisions in society drawing their audiences independent of race, ethnicity, occupation, region, or social class. This was the creation of a new collectivity, a great audience, in which we were destined to live out a major part of our lives. The great audience was both a new social formation and a new body of lived experience. This was the first national audience and the first mass audience and, in principle, it was open to all. Modern communications media allowed individuals to be linked, for the first time, directly to the imagined community of the nation (at least for nations as large as the United States) without the mediating influence of regional and other local affiliations. Such national media laid the basis for a mass society, understood in its most technical and least ideological sense: the development of a form of social organization in which intermediate associations of community, occupation, and class did not inhibit direct linkage of the individual and primary groups to the state and other nationwide organizations through mass communications.

The rise of national media represented a centripetal force in social organization. Such media greatly enhanced the control of space by reducing signalling time (the gap between the time a message is sent and received as a function of distance) in communication, by laying down direct lines of access between national centers and dispersed audiences, and by producing a remarkable potential for the centralization of power and authority.

---

[2]I have drawn some of the material that follows from two earlier essays (Carey, 1969, 1989)

However, there was a second dimension to this communication revolution, one that acted in precisely the opposite fashion, creating a centrifugal force in social organization. Specialized media of communication transformed inchoate groups into national but specialized audiences organized around ethnic, occupational, class, religious, racial, and other affiliations and interests. These minority media were in many ways more crucial forms of communication because they were the foundation stones upon which the social structure was built up and they served as intermediate mechanisms linking local and partial milieus to the wider national community.

Specialized or minority media indexed the progressive differentiation of social structures. They mirrored a process whereby groups formerly dependent upon face-to-face contact were transformed into audiences, and audiences were, in turn, devolved into groups. More importantly, such media created entirely new groups by providing collective symbols that transcended space, time, and culture. Finally, while such media addressed themselves to narrow dimensions of their audience's life, they created national communities of interest by allying themselves with national bureaucracies and selecting their audiences on a national basis. The formation of national economic and ethnic communities is one dimension of this process; the formation of national racial and sexual communities is another.

Collectively, then, the first two dimensions of the communications revolution represented centripetal and centrifugal forces, the systolic and diastolic beats of the social, creating a national mass audience while at the same time creating new groups, transforming existing groups into audiences and nationalizing the sentiments and interests of everyone in virtually every dimension of their lives. They were simultaneously moments of universalism and fragmentation, moments when a common though mass-produced culture was created and moments of intense cultural differentiation and fragmentation as well.

In 1892 it was announced that the frontier had closed, that the society had been fully enclosed in space. The expansion of the railroad and telegraph had, first of all, connected the major cities into a national system of transportation and communication and, then, in the later years of the nineteenth century, the vacant spaces were "backed and filled," hooking "island communities" into a national society. This process everywhere met local resistance but the "system was the solution" and communities everywhere were either integrated into it or circumvented by it and left to die.

The closing of the frontier represented larger closings and transformations. Space was enclosed in two senses: first the nation was enclosed, reaching its manifest destiny as a prelude to a leap beyond its own borders in imperial expansion. Second, space was enclosed institutionally as national networks of communication invaded the space of local institutions. That is, local institutions of politics, commerce, and culture were reconfigured as end points or nodes in national structures. Local political organizations became outposts of national parties; local business became elements in chains; local newspapers, lectures, performances, concerts, and educational institutions became stops on, in a manner of speaking, a national circuit. They lost their autonomy and, increasingly, their local identity.

Time was also transformed and opened as a new frontier. Time was, first of all, standardized into a national grid so that everyone was on the same clock of awareness. The telegraph organized and controlled time zones so that organization and activity could be coordinated nationally. But new "times" were also opened as commercial and other forms of activity broke into the Sabbath and then upward, via the electric light, into the nighttime. It began with the Sunday newspaper invading the Sabbath in the 1880s. Eventually, nationally produced communications would occupy every space and every time: every office, home, street, city, and institution; every time, sacred and secular, seasonal and annual, daytime and nighttime: we would never be out of earshot or eyeshot of national media. This imperialism of images spread the representation of the national into all geographic times and spaces and into all cultural times and spaces as well. The system represented an imperative that every social time and space should be filled by commerce and communications. The national system, the system of the modern, was, for "advanced" nations such as the United States, enclosed in the 1890s, and subsequent developments in communications—motion pictures, radio, television—from this perspective were protracted and relentless mopping up operations.

There were other, concomitant changes that must be noted. The urban milieu, which was the center of the social drama in which the national society took on its existence, was the scene of parallel change: explosive growth fueled by two forms of migration. The first was the emptying out of rural areas as migration from the farm and small town accelerated. The second was the international migrations which largely had the city as their terminus and which filled these spaces with new faces. The city, then, was the site of conflict and accommodation as new groups struggled with one another to occupy the turf of urban areas. There were three kinds of ecology involved here. The first was a purely physical ecology as groups radiated out over the transportation system of the city and created new patterns of settlement and new forms of community life. There was a struggle for physical space. However, this struggle was transformed into a symbolic ecology as groups cast their experience in dramatic form: friends and enemies had to be named and identified, competitive groups had to be characterized and their motives represented. Third, there was a media ecology which overlaid both of these processes as newspapers, magazines, and eventually radio and television stations articulated to the underlying physical and symbolic struggles. The city, at one level a purely physical world, contained an imaginative world of social relations as well. For example, each ethnic group had to define itself, which meant each had to know, understand, compete, name, and struggle against other ethnic groups inhabiting contested physical and symbolic space. The media were overlaid on these baser ecologies producing yet another imaginative world of the city, one articulated to and integrated with the national community.

The communities of the city were in every case transmuted or diasporic communities of two kinds. Some were formed out of the physical diaspora of migration—nationally and internationally. In their native habitat people were known only as country people or rural folk or had subnational identities deriving from clans, provinces, or dialects. In the cities they became hillbillys or hicks, Italians or Irish: identities and subjectivities made within the migratory process itself rather than being formed in advance of it. Other groups were formed by imaginative diaspora—cosmopolitans and the new professionals who lived in the imaginative worlds of politics, art, fashion, medicine, law, etc. These diasporic groups were twisted and knotted into one another within urban life: given form by the symbolic interactions of the city and the ecology of media who reported on and defined these groups to one another, fostered and intensified antagonisms among them, and sought forms of mutual accommodation.

The new communications technologies of the 1890s were a force of social disorganization, if we understand that term technically rather than morally as referring to a moment when established routines, institutions, and identities ceased to offer enough structure to conduct social and psychological life. Disorganization was a temporary state however; this was not a mass society aborning. Eventually new identities, new routines, and new institutions established themselves and took on the illusory permanence and stability of those recently displaced. The social may have gone opaque resisting representation at that moment, but the very opaqueness of the social motivated the intellectual and cultural work necessary to map and configure a new urban world. Out of it came the structures of ethnic, racial, occupational, and class groups, the new "progressive" institutions of the economy and polity, and the new routines of love, marriage, and child raising that were the predominant features of the "modern."

The ethnic and other groups were creations of a process of symbolic interaction, and to understand these formations required a sociology of border crossings, of migration across the semipermeable membranes of social life that constituted the disorderly fronts of urban living.

Surrounding the structural changes of modern society were a variety of cultural and social movements that were both responses and assertions: progressivism, populism, the creation of ethnic groups, nativism, the know-nothings, women's suffrage, temperance, the Grange. There was also the creation of a new class structure organized around the plutocrats, a structure Henry Adams lamented and Charles Beard described. These movements—some modern, some antimodern, some even postmodern—expressed a restless search for new identities and for new forms of social and cultural life. Taken together these movements offered new ways of being for a new type of society. The 1890s appear to be a moment when people actively shed their past, shed ways of being and belonging, and created a society in motion that lacked a clear sense of where it was going or what it would be when it got there. These were movements organized by media, and defined by media, commented upon by media, and formed within media, or at least as responses to new conditions of social life brought about in part by new media.[3]

The 1890s also involved kicking over the narrative structures of the past, of searching for a new metanarrative within which to tell the story of the modern. This required, above all, displacing and deconstructing the story through which Americans had told themselves about themselves. The story of the small town as either barren or romantic is one of achievements of this period. The image of the American small town, the country town, as a seat of unrelieved bigotry, Babbitry, and philistinism, a site of class conflict and exploitation is

an achieved image despite the fact that it is now an unquestioned one. The attack on the small town was a necessary part of the modern movement. The emergence of the national society depended in part on a burning over its predecessor, the agricultural society and the small town credo that justified it. Just as the emergence of the postmodern depends on the destruction of the modern in all its forms, the emergence of the modern relied upon the denigration of that phase of history that preceeded it.

The struggle to create a modern society was simultaneously a displacement of an older way of life. The creation of new groups and social structures depended on a complex reconstruction of the past, a reconstruction that delegitimated an older order so as to pave the way for a new world of industry, the city, the professions, and modern lifestyles. Metanarratives do not simply end; they are actively attacked and destroyed within the complex actions that move the social from one phase to another.

I have described the interlinked changes—social, political, and intellectual—of the 1890s as the creation, in Benedict Anderson's (1983) useful phrase, of the "imaginary community of the nation": the formation of a national economy, a national polity, and a national culture. Since the late 1970s, we have been undergoing a similar communications revolution but one whose scalar dynamic is at the global rather than the national level, a revolution producing in the words of the former chairman of Citicorp, "the twilight of sovereignty" (Wriston, 1992). However, it has produced similar phenomena: a category crisis or cultural meltdown in which established conceptual schemes no longer make adequate sense of the world; a frenzied attempt to build new conceptual schemes to account for changed circumstances; an attempt to deconstruct the meta-narrative of the modern and build a new historical understanding through the category of the postmodern; a destruction of fixed subjective identities and the search for new forms of self-understanding and new forms of social relations; a reconstruction of the dimensions of space and time through the agency of new communications tech-

---

[3]Many of the movements typical of the city spilled over into the international arena as a wave of romantic nationalism swept over Western societies leading up to World War I. In that conflict the slogan was every nation deserved a state and that ancient people—Celts, Slavs, Turks—would be restored to their rightful identity in social life. These movements, as with domestic counterparts, can hardly be understood without reference to the spread of international communication, particularly via high speed shipping and underwater cable.

nologies; the eruption of new social movements attempting to reconstruct politics, economics, and social life, a new migration that has unsettled the established social fronts of the city and, even more, the nation and, of course, the international expansion of multinational capitalism which is the ingredient that has kept the pot boiling. We are living through yet another crisis of representation, another episode in our attempt to produce a knowable society and a livable community. The global village turns out to be an unstable and in many ways an unfriendly place in which ethnic nationalisms again occupy the center of the stage. Everywhere state and nation are pitted against one another; primordia have been globalized and identity politics is practiced on a world scale. A new informational class, represented by Walter Wriston (1990, p. xii) as a figure with the skills to write a complex software program that produces a billion dollars of revenue and can walk past any customs officer in the world with nothing of "value" to declare, has replaced an old plutocracy.

This story could be told as the tale of the satellite and computer, the key instruments of the transformation, or, as the tale of postmodernism, the process and ideology through which we are living or as a story of yet another rebirth of capitalism. In closing, however, I want to take up but one aspect of the contemporary situation, the one troubling most institutions these days, namely the question of diversity.

In an early essay (Carey, 1967) I suggested that human diversity was disappearing, at least in a spatial sense. Communications, technology, and economic modernization were reducing variations in conduct, culture, and human institutions throughout the world. The contrasts that remained were paler and softer than those detailed in the anthropological texts. All of us were increasingly living one uniform way of life under very similar economic and political circumstances. However, I also suggested that the end of diversity was not yet at hand. As spatial diversity decreased, temporal diversity increased. As differences among people in space declined, differences among people in generational terms increased. The axis of diver-

sity, in other words, had shifted from space to time, from differences between societies to differences between generations within societies. The sharpest evidence of this is the development of new age segregated patterns of living and, more importantly, the generational styles of popular culture that bear new and discontinuous outlooks and sensibilities.

In other words, we are living in a world where under the force of communications and transportation—all the imperialisms of which we are daily reminded—it is getting rather hard to find headhunters, people who climb mountains on their knees, and others that predict the weather from the entrails of a pig. The good old days of cannibalism and ritual sacrifice of virgins may be gone forever. Moreover, the strangest tribes we face these days may not be in Borneo where the people look familiar but in our living rooms where we confront the strange ways of thinking, believing, and understanding current among our own children.

But that argument misses something of vital importance relative to the diversity of people in both space and time. As Clifford Geertz (1985), from whom I am rather freely drawing, has suggested, it is not that spatial differences are being eliminated, but they are being relocated from there to here. The age of large undifferentiated total societies facing off against one another is, relatively speaking, gone. The old comparisons of East versus West, primitive versus modern, developed versus underdeveloped, anthropologist versus native do not work anymore. There is no longer an East here and a West there, a primitive in Malaysia and a modern in New York. The natives, if you will forgive me, are everywhere and so are we. If someone is predicting the weather from the entrails of a pig, chances are he is living next door. If there is widow burning going on, it is like to occur outside of town rather than halfway around the world. The most recent cases of cannibalism I have encountered have not been in darkest Africa but in relatively enlightened Milwaukee.

The force of this change was caught by Marshall McLuhan's suggestion that the period of explosion, when the West sailed forth to convert the

Natives, was over. The communication and transportation system was now running in reverse, cultures were imploding, taking up residence next to one another on the television screen and in the housing subdivision. You can now sample many of the tribes of the world by taking a one hour stroll through the neighborhoods of most cities or grazing through cable television channels.

But if space has imploded so that what was once out there is now in here (next door, around the corner, in the next office, on channel 51) so has time. The differences in generations are still substantial and our first contact with the mysteries of the Orient may occur when our son shaves his head and takes up the sitar. But even with those differences, it remains true that the French, despite all the upheavals in the world, remain cussedly the French, whether you find them in Paris, Quebec City, or Woonsocket, Rhode Island. Or to give the same matter a different spin, despite the rise of heroic atheism, it is still necessary to ask the unbeliever whether he is a Protestant atheist, a Catholic atheist, or a Jewish atheist. Ancient cultural differences remain, in paler and softer tones, even if we rename them.

Finally, our capacity to reawaken the past, to reclaim all sorts of ancient traditions, customs, crafts, and habits, has reached new heights in postmodern culture. The past appears more than ever to be less like a solid glacial deposit than an infinite and discontinuous set of geological layers, all of which are accessible for mining for whatever strange purpose. The "way we live now" is not only a pastiche of the cultures of the world but of the cultures of history. This pastiche quality is nicely caught in Hannah Davis's (1990) description of life in a small Moroccan agricultural town where

symbols from different worlds overlap; a picture of the king of Morocco hangs next to a poster of the Beatles. The sounds of a religious festival outside…mingle with the televised cheering of soccer fans…in the morning we watch a holy man curing a boy, then stop off at the fair where we see a woman doing motorcycle stunts; in the evening

we watch an Indian fairy tale or a Brazilian soap opera or an Egyptian romance. (p. 13)

She remarks, "It is not the contrast between the elements that is striking; it is the lack of contrast, the clever and taken-for-granted integration" (p. 12). As Annabelle Sreberny-Mohammadi (1991, p. 133), from whom I am quoting the quotation, comments: "The transcultural mix of symbols is apparent when one young girl organizes a traditional religious feast yet defiantly appears wearing a denim skirt and earrings; thus, such symbols may be used in personal struggles to 'define, test or transform the boundaries' of local lives." The same description can be applied, with an inversion or two, to any street on virtually any day, in Manhattan.

If I can shift the metaphor to an aesthetic one and work toward a conclusion, we can no longer understand the world as a still life through the standing back of perspectival painting; rather, it is a collage of conflicting and randomly assorted elements in which the artist is absorbed into the art. From the penthouse of the informational society this may look all rather peaceful, calm, and progressive but down in the streets, where most people have to live, it is really rather messy. We live amidst enormous cultural and social diversity, part of it the persisting traces of older ways of life, and part of it generated on new axes of differentiation such as those of gender and sexuality. There seems to be no end to the delicacy and invidiousness with which we can describe, impute, and elaborate human difference. We can no longer count the number of tribes—old and new—that array themselves before us.

As I said at the outset, the global village created by communications technology has turned out to be a rather peculiar place. It is not a place of convergence where the cultures of the world arrive at some omega point of agreement and identity. Everything has risen: communications and transportation have uprooted human cultures and set them in motion once again. However, nothing has converged: these cultures are in motion in their infinite variety and painful diversity. There are days when we wish for the dangerous certitude of squared off countries pitted against one another: the United States versus the Soviet Union. However, today we encounter collage societies barely hanging together where host and migrant cultures leak into one another. The very technology which is bringing us together physically and imaginatively is just as assuredly driving us apart.

Our temptation at moments like this is to chant mantras like race, class, and gender, another kind of talisman, a modern crucifix, to ward off postmodern vampires. Such invocations do not signal, for all the bluster, a settled analysis of a settled word but only that our inherited notions have dissolved and we have nothing with which to replace them; we live in a world of nameless things and thingless names. We are all transvested.

We do not know how to describe this transvested society we are creating willy-nilly at a new conjuncture of a physical ecology, a symbolic ecology, and a media ecology. To call this an information society of convergent media is but to express the puritanism of the decracinated. To believe that we have a purchase on a new world of diversity is a delusion of those who visit difference armed only with spiritual travellers checks. We are as confused, though often as arrogant, as the first anthropologists encountering the first natives. And we have a critical problem. Because in the midst of these unsettling changes we stubbornly cling to the hope of forming a democratic world, we wish to retain amidst globalized diversity a public space for citizenship. But what can public space or citizenship mean when Time Warner proclaims that "the world is our audience"? Having failed to create a national public space, we now are charged with the problem of creating an international one. And, closer to home, our received notions of democracy are tested by forms of public diversity they were never created to contain. The recovery of a public space for citizenship can only occur if we can describe the social differences being produced and reproduced in what we often naively call the information society. For public spaces are only recovered from the interstices where difference collides with

difference and where both collide with the global. There is a fragile, fugitive moment between these forces where we might, with the right language and the right descriptions, and with a lot of luck, recover something of value. For only if we can describe difference in an intelligible and mutually acceptable way, only if we can humanely articulate difference to difference, can we produce a public space and a public sphere. Only then can we insert between the global and the fragmented, a public space of citizenly discourse.

REFERENCES

Anderson, B. (1983). *Imagined communities: Reflections on the origins and spread of nationalism.* New York: Verso Books.

Appadurai, A. (1990). Disjuncture and difference in the global cultural economy. In M. Featherstone (Ed.), *Global culture: Nationalism, globalization and modernity* (pp. 295–310). Newbury Park, CA: Sage.

Carey, J. W. (1967). Harold Adams Innis and Marshall McLuhan. *Antioch Review, 27, 2,* 5–37

Carey, J. W. (1969). The communications revolution and the professional communicator. *The Sociological Review Monograph, No. 13,* 23–38.

Carey, J. W. (1989). *Communication as culture.* New York: Routledge.

Carey, J. W. (1989). Communications and the progressives. *Critical Studies in Mass Communication, 6,* 264–282.

Davis, H. (1990). American magic in a Moroccan town. *Middle East Report, 159, 4,* 12–18, 19.

Garber, M. (1992). *Vested interests: Cross dressing and cultural anxiety.* New York: Routledge.

Geertz, C. (1983). *Local knowledge.* New York: Basic Books

Geertz, C. (1985). *The uses of diversity.* The Tanner Lectures on Human Values delivered at the University of Michigan, November 8, 1985.

Habermas, J. (1970). *Toward a rational society.* Boston: Beacon Press.

Hollander, A. (1992). Dragtime. *The New Republic.* August 31, 34–41.

Sreberny-Mohammadi, A. (1991). The global and the local in international communications. In J. Curran and M. Gurevitch (Eds.), *Mass media and society* (pp. 118–138). London: Edward Arnold.

Media as Symbolic and Cognitive Systems

James W. Chesebro
Indiana State University

For the last 25 years, if not 75 years, critics of communication have focused on the content and the style of verbal and nonverbal presentations. Indeed, they have tended to treat the content and style of a presentation as the totality of the message being conveyed. In this regard, communication critics have traditionally failed to give the channel, format, and medium of communication the same attention they have devoted to the ideational presentation of a message.

Granted, communication critics might readily agree that technologies create messages, but the rhetorical analyses they have offered have bypassed a consideration of how technologies themselves serve as message-generating sources of messages. In more traditional terms, the influence of the channel has been slighted, if not ignored. For example, fantasy theme and narrative analyses have both served as profoundly creative methods for rhetorical critics. Yet, regardless of the classification and interpretative modes involved, contemporary rhetorical critics have made content and style their objects of study when using these methods. While some exceptions[1] are noteworthy, essentially all of the methods currently available to contemporary rhetorical critics have been used as content analysis techniques.

In this presentation, I want to explore an alternative view. I want to suggest that how a message is conveyed is as important as what the content of the message is. Information derived from computing is different than information derived from face-to-face encounters which is different than televised or printed information. These formats function as independent and significant variables affecting meaning. They cannot be equivocated. The format, medium, or technology exerts unique influences on what is understood and therefore on what meaning is.

Particularly, in this presentation, I will be specifically examining: (1) how technologies themselves can generate messages; and (2) the kinds of relationships that can exist between communication technologies and cultural systems. Given the size of the current project,[2] it is necessary to condense certain sections in a preliminary fashion. I want to deal with this condensation initially as background in the form of five assumptions. Following these assumptions, I want to detail how technologies and cultural systems interact. So, first the assumptions which provide a foundation and background for the more detailed analysis.

FIVE CRITICAL ASSUMPTIONS

At this point, I list these assumptions here as an introduction to the more detailed analysis. I don't mean that we must bypass these assumptions. If you wish, we can talk about these assumptions in the subsequent question and answer period. But, for now, I plan only to specify these assumptions.

Assumption 1: Any one of the communication variables can function as a message-generating system. In terms of a traditional model

[1]For an outstanding example of one of these scholarly efforts to understand communication technologic see: Bruce E. Gronbeck, Thomas J. Farrell, and Paul A. Soukup, Eds., *Media Consciousness, and Culture: Explorations of Walter Ong's Thought* (Newbury Park, CA: Sage Publications, 1991).

[2]For a more detailed analysis of the thesis developed in this presentation, see James W. Chesebro and Dale A. Bertelsen, *Analyzing Media: Communication Technologies as Symbolic and Cognitive Systems* (New York: The Guilford Press, 1996).

of the communication process, the verbal or linguistic act, source, receiver, context, feedback system, and channel are each capable of generating distinct, and potentially contradictory, messages.

Assumption 2: The verbal or linguistic act can be over-emphasized when accounting for meaning or what people understand during communicative exchanges. In his now famous study in 1968, Albert Mehrabian reported that the words or what is verbally expressed accounted for only 7 percent of the meanings conveyed to an audience. Likewise, in a series of studies conducted between 1980 and 1987, Jacoby and Hoyer reported that the average American forgets or misunderstands 23 to 36 percent of televised information when asked to recognize information immediately after a viewing (Jacoby, Hoyer, & Sheluga, 1980). Misinformation analyses of readers of print information have also suggested that approximately one-third of average Americans forget or misunderstand the content they read (Jacoby & Hoyer, 1987). And, some media critics have reached similar conclusions. For example, Everett M. Rogers (1986, p. 31) has concluded that "a large percentage of Americans" absorb "little of the message content." More specifically, using TV news as one of his examples, Rogers has noted that, "When asked to recall certain salient facts from a TV news broadcast within a few hours of viewing it, few can do so."

Assumption 3: A medium of communication is an active determinant of meaning. In his now classical analysis of *The Process of Communication* in 1960, Berlo identified the channel or medium of communication as one of the six primary determinants of communication outcomes. He specifically maintained that the channel functions as the "encoding and decoding apparatus" and determines which "external physical" stimuli are "translated internally." Berlo therefore concluded that "the choice of channels often is an important factor in the effectiveness of communication."

Assumption 4: Every medium of communication constructs its own conception of reality. Every medium of communication is highly selective, designed to respond to and record certain external stimuli, but not all external stimuli. As Wachtel (1978, pp. 376–377) has maintained, "Every medium has a bias toward space and time. Each, in its own way, imposed a...[different] order and a coherence on the world." Or, as Carpenter (1960, p. 162) has put it, each medium "codifies reality differently."

Assumption 5: Every medium of communication creates a unique knowledge base. Krugman's (1965 and 1971) neurophysiological findings function as an excellent example of how each medium creates and presents a unique view of reality. Krugman has argued that television is five times less involving than print, a form of "passive learning," and generates fewer spontaneous thoughts, fewer links to the content of the viewer's personal life, and generally "unformed and shapeless" responses. Accordingly, television creates a general "orientation and awareness" rather than the particular role-specific behaviors, computational skills, or logical analyses created by other kinds of media. A massive accumulation of research can be compiled to support these assumptions.

With these five assumptions in mind, let me illustrate the kind of communication research which embodies these assumptions and begins to outline the perspective I wish to develop about technology and culture. The example is provided by Michael Pfau in his spring 1990 essay, "A Channel Approach to Television Influence," in the *Journal of Broadcasting & Electronic Media.* In this essay, Pfau has explored the degree to which "media" function "as a distinct variable in social influence," focusing specifically upon "whether television, as a result of unique channel characteristics, is more similar to interpersonal communication than to public address, print, and radio in the manner that it exercises influences." Pfau first sought to create equivalent verbal messages across five channel conditions of television, radio, print, interpersonal communication, and public address. Pfau specifically wanted the verbal message to "remain constant across all communication modalities," with only the "intrinsic channel features" of each medium able to exert influence. Using a series of adjustments in the verbal messages in each medium,

Pfau created message equivalence across media in terms of length, comprehension, and language intensity, and care was also taken to use the same verb tense, modifiers, and metaphors under all five channel conditions. Several additional measures were also employed to determine that equivalency had been achieved, including Likert-type scales of the perceived quality of presented information and the perceived strength of the case made.

Yet, even with these equivalencies across media established, Pfau found significant differences when groups of subjects were exposed to two commercials, two political messages, and two social action messages on television, on radio, in print, under an interpersonal communication condition, and in the form of a public address. Differences were measured in terms of attitudes toward the object of the message (business/product, candidate, or cause), the persuasiveness of the position raised in the message, and on a probability of acting scale. Measured by the degree to which person variables were elevated in the process of influence, he concluded that television is significantly more frequently viewed as "interpersonal communication,' than radio, print, or public address in terms of commercial, political, and social action persuasion messages. Pfau concluded that all channels can be persuasive, but he also concluded that channel choice alters the way in which audience members are persuaded (or, in terms of which dimensions of an attitude are affected as well as the readiness to act upon altered beliefs).

In all, such research findings suggest that channel choice affects how attitudes are changed and the willingness to act upon newly created attitudes. Such findings suggest that technologies might appropriately be examined for their potential as communication variables.

THE TECHNOCULTURAL DRAMA: THE NATURE OF THE TECHNOLOGY-CULTURE INTERACT

I employ the term *technocultural drama* to capture the dynamic relationship which exists whenever both technology and culture interact and ulti-

mately create a system which defines the nature of the human experience. In this conception, both technology and culture are treated as active determinants of human meanings. Let me first suggest how technology can function as a communication or message-generating variable, then how culture functions as a communication variable, and finally how technology and culture interact and mutually define what is understood to be the nature of the human experience. First, then, a consideration of technology as text.

As we have already implied, the concept of technology as text shifts attention from the content of a communication technology to the structural features of the technology itself. In greater detail, three meanings are embedded in the notion of *technology as text* (cf. Woolgar, 1991).

First, the concept of *technology as text* emphasizes the unique instrumental functions of a technology itself, regardless of its content. In this sense, technologies are not "simply docile objects with fixed attributes (uses, capabilities, and so on)" (Woolgar, 1991, p. 37). The meaning of the technology—or, the text of the technology—is not revealed by examining the intentions of designers of technology. The designers of a technology may provide little indication of the instrumental functions of a technology. In this context, computer technologies function as an appropriate example. Waltz (1982, p. 130) has noted that, "In many cases the [computer] programmer does not know what his program can do until it is run on a computer." Similarly, several computer programs—such as heuristic, planning, backward-chaining, and concept-learning programs—are intentionally designed to alter the inputs provided by human beings and to generate "unique results with a minimum of guidance from the user" in which the "outcome of one of these computer runs is unknown" (Chesebro and Bonsall, 1989, pp. 179–180). As Williams (1982, p. 108) has noted, computers "can qualify as communication technology" because they are capable of taking our messages and giving them back to us or others," but "unlike any other communications device, they are capable of *acting upon* them in a manner defined by an extension of our own human intelligence." And, as Miller (1978, p. 229) has maintained, a technology is different than a tool. Tools, Miller has maintained, "extend the immediate biological capabilities" of human beings, while by definition technologies lose their original purpose and begin to function independently of the human being. For example, after outlining an expert system for "speech composition," Phillips and Erlwein (1988, p. 258) concluded by noting that, "No argument is made that the composition program itself operates in human fashion." Ultimately, the instrumental functions or meaning of the text of a technology are determined by examining the full range and permutations of the production capabilities of the technology, not the intentions of those creating the technology.

Second, the concept *technology as text* emphasizes the interpretative function of a technology. A technology organizes the environment in which it operates by drawing upon selective resources from its environment and impacting upon selective features of its environment. The technology creates its own "organizational structure, management style, beliefs, and culture" (Woolgar, 1991, pp. 37–38). To function effectively within a technology's environment, practitioners must accommodate or adjust to the technology by establishing functional connections between the technological environment and their practices. Ultimately, the interpretative functions or meanings of the text of a technology is determined by identifying the coding system or the organizational form used to construct the "reality" to which a technology can respond.

Third, the concept of *technology as text* emphasizes the reflexive functions of a technology. Cultural systems can theoretically respond to and use a technology in an infinite number of ways. A cultural system might, for example, seek to avoid any kind of interaction with a technology. However, if a cultural system utilizes the services or products generated by a technology, the use reduces the range of potential responses possible, if the full capabilities of the technology are to be realized. In essence, when a technology is used, the reflexive functions of a technology constrain the possible range of human responses. Ultimately, the reflexive functions or meanings of the text of a technology are determined by the range of response sets that are possible if outcomes of a technology are to be realized.

In these three senses, a technology can be said to possess a text. For the text to be "read," the restrictions created by the technology itself must be accommodated. A technology possesses instrumental, interpretative, and reflexive functions that regulate how human beings can respond to a technology.

At the same time, technologies are a product of cultural systems. A definition of culture is appropriate, and Goodenough provides a common conception: "*Culture, then, consists of standards for deciding what is, standards for deciding what can be, standards for deciding how one feels about it, standards for deciding what to do about it, and standards for deciding how to go about doing it*" (Goodenough, 1971, pp. 22).

The cultural standards and norms (or values) of a societal system stimulate the development of and foster the use of technologies. Indeed, a cultural system is also capable of determining how a technology is and is not to be utilized. As Woolgar (1991, p. 30) has stated the case, "society plays an important part in deciding which technologies are adopted." As Woolgar has explained, "there are many instances when devices judged useful and even essential were not taken up or were effectively resisted" (p. 30). In all, "determining the effects of a technology" requires "an understanding of the overall dynamics of society" (Woolgar, 1991, p. 30).

Theoretically, the text of a technology and the norms and values of a cultural system can each be viewed as deterministic. Technology and culture might further be viewed as dialectically related. On one hand, as a text, a technology can restrict human actions and responses. On the other hand, as the system which generates a technology, a culture can restrict if and how technologies are and are not used. In practice, the text of a technology and the norms and values of a culture frequently interact, creating an outcome which reflects the deterministic capabilities of both technology and culture.

The term *technocultural drama* seems to capture the dynamic relationship which exists whenever both technology and culture interact and ultimately create a system in which technology and culture mutually define the nature of the human experience. Any number of explanations might be posited for this technology–culture interaction. For example, Hughes (1983, pp. 3–4) has speculated that these technocultural dramas are a "natural" outgrowth of the human experience, for he has maintained that human beings are "technological" and can be characterized by a "creative spirit manifesting itself in the building of a human-made world patterned by machines, megamachines, and systems" which grow from a value system of "order, system and control that [has been purposefully] embedded in machines, devices, processes, and systems."

While discussions regarding the origins of the technological impulse are interesting, the stages governing the nature of the dynamic and "corrective" relationship which exists between technology and culture are definitionally more salient. Again, several schemes exist to characterize how technology and culture interact over time. For example, using the term "technological drama" to reflect his concern (which we equate to our use of the term "technocultural drama"), Pfaffenberger (1992, p. 285) has argued that, "A technological drama is a discourse of technological 'statements' and 'counterstatements,' in which there are three recognizable processes: technological regularization, technological adjustment, and technological reconstitution. "A technological drama begins," Pfaffenberger has argued, "with technological regularization" in which the designer of a technology "creates, appropriates, or modifies a technological production process" so that the technology's "technical features embody a political aim" or "intention to alter the allocation of power, prestige or wealth in a social formation" (p. 285). This period of technological regularization if followed by a period of technological adjustment in which, Pfaffenberger has argued, "the

people who lose when a new production process" is introduced begin to "engage in strategies that try to compensate for the loss of self-esteem, social prestige, and social power that the technology has caused" (p. 286). The period of technological adjustment is followed by a period of technological reconstitution in which "impact constituencies try to reverse the implication of a technology through a symbolic inversion process" which frequently leads to the fabrication of counterartifacts, such as the personal computer or "appropriate technology," which embody features believed to negate or reverse the political implications of the dominant system (p. 286). Pfaffenberger concluded that, "I choose the metaphor *drama* rather than *text* to describe these processes," because the processes "draw deeply from a culture's root paradigms, its fundamental and axiomatic propositions about the nature of social life, and in consequence, technological activities bring deeply entrenched moral imperatives into prominence" (p. 286).

CONCLUSION

In all, this view posits that a relationship exists between technology and culture, and it specifically holds that the relationship is dramatic and ultimately governs human communication. There are, however, several kinds of technocultural dramas. We are convinced that orality, literacy, telecommunication, and interactive communication systems each constitute a distinct type of technocultural drama. As this study evolves, an analysis of each of these technocultural dramas will be provided. For now, you have a sense of the reasoning which will govern these applications.

REFERENCES

Berlo, David K. (1960). *The Process of Communication: An Introduction to Theory and Practice.* New York: Holt, Rinehart and Winston.

Carpenter, Edmund. (1960). "The New Languages." In Edmund Carpenter and Marshall McLuhan, Eds.,

Explorations in Communication: An Anthology (pp. 162–179). Boston, MA: Beacon Press.

Chesebro, James W. and Donald G. Bonsall. (1989). *Computer-Mediated Communication: Human Relationships in a Computerized World.* Tuscaloosa, AL: The University of Alabama Press.

Goodenough, Ward H. (1971). *Culture, Language, and Society.* Reading, MA: Addison-Wesley.

Hughes, Thomas P. (1983). *American Genesis: A Century of Innovation and Technological Enthusiasm, 1870–1970.* New York: Penguin Books.

Jacoby, Jacob and Wayne D. Hoyer. (1987). *The Comprehension and Miscomprehension of Print Communications: An Investigation of Mass Media Magazines.* New York: Advertising Educational Foundation, Inc.

Jacoby, Jacob, Wayne D. Hoyer, and David A. Sheluga. (1980). *The Comprehension and Miscomprehension of Televised Communication.* New York: American Association of Advertising Agencies.

Krugman, Herbert E. (1965). "The Impact of Television Advertising: Learning Without Involvement," *Public Opinion Quarterly, 29,* pp. 349–356.

Krugman, Herbert E. (1971). "Brain Wave Measures of Media Involvement," *Journal of Advertising Research, 11,* pp. 3–9.

Mehrabian, Albert. (1968, February). "Communication Without Words," *Psychology Today, 2,* pp. 53–55.

Miller, Carolyn R. (1978). "Technology as a Form of Consciousness: A Study of Contemporary Ethos," *Central States Speech Journal, 29,* pp. 228–236.

Pfaffenberger, Bryan. (1992). "Technological Dramas," *Science, Technology, and Human Values, 17,* pp. 282–312.

Pfau, Michael. (1990, Spring). "A Channel Approach to Television Influence," *Journal of Broadcasting and Electronic Media, 34,* pp. 195–214.

Phillips, Gerald M. and Bradley R. Erlwein. (1988). "Composition on the Computer: Simple Systems and Artificial Intelligence," *Communication Quarterly, 36,* pp. 243–261.

Rogers, Everett M. (1986). *Communication Technology: The New Media in Society.* New York: The Free Press/Macmillan.

Wachtel, Edward. (1978). "Technological Cubism: The Presentation of Space and Time in Multi Image," *Etc., 4,* pp. 376–382.

Waltz, David L. (1982, October). "Artificial Intelligence," *Scientific American,* pp. 118–133.

Williams, Frederick. (1982). *The Communications Revolution.* Beverly Hills, CA: Sage Publications.

Woolgar, Steve. (1991). "The Turn to Technology in Social Studies of Science," *Science, Technology, and Human Values, 16,* pp. 20–50.

CHAPTER 13

AT THE HELM
IN PERFORMANCE STUDIES

Introduction

Sheron J. Dailey
Indiana State University

When I was in San Diego last summer, I walked out to the Embarcadero and stared—as everyone does—at the ocean, the horizon, the sky. Probably no one is capable of standing at the edge of the Pacific without thinking about new worlds, vast continents, and infinite spaces; and no one who has read Keats's "On First Looking into Chapman's Homer" can stand there without remembering "stout Cortez" and his "wild surmise." So I did—until my companion said, "Shall we go?" I turned to leave and, of course, the Marriott Hotel and Marina exploded into my vision. So there I was, balanced between the old and the new, between the poetic and the prosaic, between the second and third millennia, between infinity and reality. I blurted out to my companion, "Now I know how Judith Trent got the idea for the 'At the Helm' Series!"

My companion said, "Huh?"

"Ah, never mind," I said.

Surely it was a similarly astonishing moment that led Dr. Trent to envision this significant series for which she invited 61 leading scholars from 17 areas of communication to "take the helm" in "mini-plenary sessions."

The two scholars chosen from performance studies are well known not only to the division but also to the association—so well known, in fact,

that introducing them seems almost redundant. But perhaps a few comments will refresh your memories.

Our first speaker is Mary Susan Strine. Dr. Strine is Professor of Communication at the University of Utah. Dr. Strine's capacious mind and eclectic interests make it impossible to narrow her scholarly accomplishments to a few areas. Clearly supporting this statement are the varied research areas of the students whose work she has supervised ("Imagery in Selected Poems by Wallace Stevens," "Narrative Semiotics in France," "Stand-Up Comedy as Cultural Representation," and "Domesticating Modernization: The Rhetorical Construction of Identity in Victorian American House Design and Decoration," to mention only a few). Her own research includes essays focusing on writers such as Joseph Conrad, Flannery O'Connor, Williams Styron, and Adrienne Rich. Indeed, her essay entitled "The Politics of Asking Women's Questions: Voice and Value in the Poetry of Adrienne Rich" received the Speech Communication Association 1990 Golden Anniversary Monograph Award. Equally distinguished are her explorations of intersecting links between performance studies and other disciplines including organizational communication, critical theory, and cultural studies. Dr. Strine received the Lilla

Heston Award for Distinguished Scholarship in Performance Studies (1995), and the Performance Studies Division's Distinguished Service Award (1993). Dr. Strine probably could not tell us what moment in her distinguished career has been the high point, but somewhere near the top must be the "Spotlight on Scholarship" program at the 1993 SCA Convention when her former students discussed her extraordinary influence on them. From that program, we can all understand why the University of Utah chose her for its Presidential Teaching Scholar Award in 1994.

Our final speaker is Lynn Christine Miller from the University of Texas at Austin. Dr. Miller first distinguished herself as an undergraduate at the University of North Dakota where she was elected to Phi Beta Kappa with double majors in English and Theatre. Dr. Miller's scholarly work includes not only the publication of over 30 ssays and reviews, but also extensive work as a performer, director, and creative writer. She brought together all of these talents in her first one-person show *Gertrude Stein as Gertrude Stein*, which she researched, wrote, performed, and directed. Interestingly enough, this production also combined all of her current research interests: It was (1) a feminist performance, which included (2) the performance of autobiography (3) using contemporary performance theory (4) in adapting "fiction" to the stage and film. For this prodigious effort she received grants from the Tulsa Arts and Humanities Council and the New Mexico Endowment for the Humanities. Her performances of "Gertrude" have taken her to North Dakota, Colorado, Indiana, Illinois, Oklahoma, and New Mexico. In addition, she has written extensively about Stein's work in performance as well as adapted and directed a number of her writings for stage. A few years ago Dr. Miller began research for another one-person show focusing on Edith Wharton, which materialized this summer at the Tulsa Chautauqua as the splendidly itled *Edith Wharton: Inside the House of Fiction*. Most recently, her new play, *Video Love* premiered at the 1996 FrontcraFest in Austin. She is also the author of numerous poems, short stories, and a novel. In 1996 the University of North Dakota recognized that Dr. Miller had lived up to her undergraduate promise by bestowing on her their 1996 Maxwell Anderson Award for excellence in Arts and Letters.

Articulating Performance/Performativity: Disciplinary Tasks and the Contingencies of Practice

Mary S. Strine
University of Utah

Performance studies in each of its historical per-mutations has been extraordinarily sensitive to the institutional contexts and sociocultural currents in which those studies occur. Since the early twenti-eth century, as a formative and sustaining aspect of the developing field of speech, and then speech communication, performance-centered scholar-ship has grown, undergoing various shifts in em-phasis or "turns" from elocution, to oral interpretation, to interpretation and the study of literature in performance, to its most recent and inclusive designation, performance studies. Each "turn" has reflected and shaped changes that are both disciplinary and more broadly cultural in scope. At its best, each "turn," in responding to new contingencies,—to historically emergent is-sues and questions,—has acknowledged and built upon, thereby adding to, the strengths of the evolving disciplinary tradition.

Currently, multidisciplinary appropriations of "performance" and "performativity" as analyt-ical tools or critical tropes abound, giving rise to an invigorating if unsettling sense that work in performance studies is at the cutting-edge of post- or anti-disciplinary scholarship.[1] While we might wholeheartedly welcome the newfound solidarity that widespread interest in performance and per-formativity has generated, it is important that we not lose our sense of connectedness and purpose as academic professionals. Arguably, the most valuable resources we bring to an interdiscipli-nary alliance of performance studies scholars arise from the skills honed and the insights devel-oped through our own disciplinary work—our "conventional and obligatory routines" that liter-ally constitute us as practicing scholar/teachers[2] in departments of speech, communication, and theatre. What follows is an effort to advance that disciplinary work first, by clarifying some impor-tant distinctions between "performance" and "performativity" as these terms circulate in cur-rent scholarly discourse; second, by suggesting how, once conceptually distinguished, perfor-mance and performativity articulate, coming to-gether to form a dialectical tension at the center of expressive culture; and finally, by relating this cul-ture-performance matrix[3] to the renewed impor-tance of one of the strengths of our disciplinary tradition, the study of literature in and through performance.

In recent scholarly discussions, the term "per-formance" refers to a widely diffused spectrum of activities, events, and processes, all of which share the common dimension of "restored behavior" or expressive (re)presentation of experience for some-one, typically for an audience (Schechner, 1985, 1988; Carlson, 1996, pp. 1–6).[4] Folklorist Richard Bauman (1992) provides a cogent extension of this idea of performance, one that emphasizes its dis-tinctive features and also reflects the performance studies tradition developed within the field of com-munication. According to Bauman, "performance" may in a limited sense refer to all communicative activity as opposed to mere communicative poten-tial, but the term more typically designates "an aesthetically marked and heightened mode of com-munication, framed in a special way and put on dis-play for an audience." Bauman adds that "[t]he analysis of performance—indeed, the very conduct of performance—highlights the social, cultural, and aesthetic dimensions of the communicative process." He elaborates further on what is entailed in this understanding of performance as a "specially marked mode of action" as distinct from performance understood as "any doing of an act of communication." Bauman writes:

> In this sense of [marked] performance, the act of communication is put on display, objectified, lifted out to a degree from its contextual surroundings and opened up to scrutiny by an audience. Performance thus calls forth special attention to and heightened awareness of the act of communication and gives license to regard it and the performer with special intensity. Performance makes one communicatively accountable; it assigns to an audience the responsibility for evaluating the relative skill and effectiveness of the performer's accomplishment. (p. 44)

Bauman's depiction of "an aesthetically marked and heightened mode of communication" touches on several interdependent aspects of performance that I want to underscore because together they offer a conceptual grounding for performance studies. First, *performances are in a certain sense always contractual with provisional outcomes;* that is, in "call [ing] forth special attention to and heightened awareness of the act of communication, and giv[ing] license to the audience to regard it and the performer with special intensity," participation in performances "makes [both performer and audience] communicatively accountable." It entails mutual risk-taking and responsibility, implicating performers and audiences—even seemingly passive spectators—cognitively, emotionally, and ethically in the outcome of the performance event.[5] Second, in "highlight[ing] the social, cultural, and aesthetic dimensions of the communicative process," *performances become privileged spaces of social reflexivity* (Turner, 1986, pp. 24–25) *and occasions of intense critical scrutiny and evaluation.* Through the collective pressures and energies, conflicts and constraints that performances display a particular form of embodied thinking gets done; in this sense, performances function as

praxis, or thinking-in-action. Third, in noting that even for conventionally scripted performances there is "always manifest an emergent dimension, as no two performances are exactly the same" (p. 42), Bauman pinpoints *the radically contextual, improvisational, and transformational character of performances generally.* As a result of performances, societies and cultures do change, often imperceptibly and seldom in a predictable manner. In short, the historically situated interplay of performance's contractual, provisional nature; its condition of social reflexivity and critique; and its improvisational and transformational potential forms the energizing, destabilizing center of performance as a focus of study, aptly described by performance historian Joseph Roach (1996b, p. 219) in these terms:

> Performance…entails a compact between actors and audience (even when their roles are rapidly handed back and forth, as in carnival), a compact that promises the production of certain mutually anticipated effects, but the stipulations of the compact are often subject to negotiation, adjustment, and even transformation. The range of human interactions defined within these limits delineates the field of performance studies.

Whereas performance encompasses a broad range of social behaviors, forms, and effects, performativity refers more specifically to the complexities of discursive practices, to the often unconscious investments and desires that circulate in all discourses, and to the decisive effects that various modes of discursive action have on individual and group subjectivities and identity formations. The term "performativity," as it recurs in recent critical scholarship, takes its meaning in part from the foundational work of ordinary language philosopher J. L. Austin, and in part from the extensions of that work by poststructuralist theorists. In his pathbreaking series of lectures, *How to Do Things With Words* (1962), Austin identifies a particular type of utterance that he calls "performative." Performatives constitute a special class of speech acts whereby "to say something is to do something;" for example, to promise *performs* promising, to affirm *performs* affirmation, to deny *performs* denial, and so forth. In being appropriate to their context of utterance, performatives exercise a conventionalized force; that is, by promising, affirming, denying, and so forth, performatives actually produce or bring into existence, rather than simply refer to, particular forms of social reality. Thus, with the concept of performative, Austin was able to move beyond a strictly referential view of language as descriptive statements about preexisting conditions (saying as stating) to a view of language as constitutive of the conditions within which language operates (saying as doing).

Austin, however, did not fully appreciate the revolutionary potential of his anti-essentialist claims and reserved the name "performative" for a limited set of formal utterances under a restricted set of conditions, thus opening his theory to later poststructuralist critique. For example, while Austin denies performative status to mimetic or fictional types of utterance on the grounds that they are "non-serious," poststructuralist philosopher Jacques Derrida (1982) argues powerfully against the restricted application of "performative" to a limited set of utterances. All utterances, Derrida claims, exercise the productive function of performatives. He reasons that, in order to be at all intelligible, *every* utterance must display some degree of "citationality" or reiterability and is therefore, to some degree, imitative of prior utterances. Derrida gives the notion of citationality another turn, reasoning that, since "[e]very sign, linguistic or non-linguistic, spoken or written…can be *cited,* put into quotation marks; thereby it can break with every given context, and *engender infinitely new contexts in an absolutely nonsaturable fashion*" (p. 320).[6]

In a similar vein, poststructuralist critical theorist Judith Butler (1993, p. 2), argues that "performativity must be understood not as a singular or deliberate 'act,' but rather as the reiterative and citational practice by which discourse produces the effects that it names." Notable here is the implicit claim that the performativity of discourse per se in its many forms and variations rather than the extra-linguistic reality of social relations and

material practice is the principal site of political and ideological struggle. For many of those committed to politically engaged textual analysis, such as Butler, the concept of "performativity" opens new possibilities for critical intervention, an emancipatory way of rethinking the dynamics of oppression and marginalization, especially totalizing cultural categories of race, gender, and sexuality, and of pushing beyond the impasse of "identity politics,"—at times, by writing back performatively against hardened discursive forms and practices (see, for example, Phelan, 1993).

I

If, as the foregoing discussion has shown, performance and performativity are separable entities and distinct in the scholarly agendas they advance, in what ways are they related? In what sense can studies of performance and performativity be thought of as interdependent, mutually challenging enterprises? What can the purposeful articulation of performance and performativity—the disciplinary "production of unity on top of difference"[7]—contribute to an enlivened and deepened understanding of the cultures in which they occur?

Brought together within the disciplinary frame of performance studies, work on performance and performativity might be thought of as complementary projects that interrelate dialectically, providing each other with invaluable critical perspective. On the one hand, the often profound insights of poststructuralist thought that fund scholarship on performativity might usefully complicate the study of performances. Through deconstructive unraveling of essentialist categories, such as those of race, gender, and sexuality, and analysis of the impact of discursive practices on human subjectivity, the perspective of performativity could foreground what is fundamentally at stake but not always conscious or visible in the performance process itself. On the other hand, in its emphasis on material embodiment, historical situatedness, and experiential immediacy, attention to performance might ground and sharpen the deconstructive analysis of discursive performativity. Reflecting on the contribution that performance-centered analysis might make to the deconstructive agenda, critical theorist Elin Diamond (1996, p. 5) observes,

Performance...is precisely the site in which concealed or dissimulated conventions might be investigated. When performativity materializes as performance in that risky and dangerous negotiation between a doing (a reiteration of norms) and a thing done (discursive conventions that frame our interpretations), between someone's body and the conventions of embodiment, we have access to cultural meanings and critique. Performativity ...must be rooted in the materiality and historical density of performance.

As Diamond's observation suggests, culture exists dynamically in the tension between performativity and performance, in the interplay between conventionalized forms of expression or discursive practice and the contingent and infinitely revisable (re)presentations of thought and value through which social groups struggle to understand and orient their collective lives (Chaney, 1994, Roach, 1996b). Social theorist David Chaney argues at length that performances are a principal means of communication in late twentieth-century culture, and that meanings produced through participation in cultural performances are inherently ideological, politicized, and unsettled; that is, "they serve to sustain forms of socially structured inequality" and, at the same time, "they provide a basis for [empowering and emancipatory] struggle over terms of collective identity" (Chaney, 1994, p. 43). Performance studies, in its embrace of the culture-performance matrix with the interplay of performance–performativity at its core, occupies a unique position for understanding (and critically intervening in) the ways that culture produces, maintains, and transforms relations of identity and difference.

II

Despite the lingering tendency to separate art from real world exigencies, aesthetic forms, in particular literary genres, remain among the most significant, if contested, sites of cultural performances.[8] Early modern aestheticism set in place an intractable dualism whereby art, including literature, was valorized and studied as an order of reality "naturally" different from the instrumentality of social and political life and therefore unaccountable for its political and ideological entailments. With the collapse of aestheticism beginning in the late 1960s and the subsequent rise of poststructuralist theory, literature lost favor with many sectors and became an embattled site of "culture wars," roundly condemned by outspoken liberal critics as ideologically elitist, racist, or sexist and, as a predominantly First World cultural practice, deeply implicated in Western imperialism. In turn, entrenched conservative critics ardently championed literature as a preserve of "universal" aesthetic norms and values, and a beacon to the greatness of Western civilization generally.

More recently, important scholarly efforts have been made to rethink the study of literature and the aesthetic in a measured way, recognizing that literature, in being imaginatively responsive to its social and historical location, is at once an always politically inflected cultural form and a uniquely engaging and empowering social practice.[9] Critical and cultural theorist George Levine (1994, p. 3) exemplifies the impulse behind this revisionary work when he writes: "I am trying to imagine the aesthetic as a mode engaged richly and complexly with moral and political issues, but a mode that operates differently from others and contributes in distinctive ways to the possibilities of human fulfillment and connection."[10]

Levine goes on to identify the distinctive features of the literary aesthetic mode as he sees it, and he does so in terms consistent with the performance–performativity dynamic described above: First, he argues that the literary aesthetic realm is a "much contested utopian space" where [as with the specially marked space of performance] the political and ethical pressures of daily life can be at least momentarily suspended and held up for reflection, scrutiny, and evaluation (p. 17). Second [as with participation in performance generally], literary engagement provides an occasion for thinking and feeling beyond the contingencies of everyday life and for imaginatively entering into the lives of others. Levine explains: "As the aesthetic provides a space where the immediate pressures of ethical and political decisions are deferred, so it allows sympathy for, and potential understanding of people, events, things otherwise threatening.... [T]he aesthetic reception of literature and art allows, even if it only occasionally achieves, a vital sense of the other" (p. 17). Lastly, in its irreducible complexity, even ambivalence, literary discourse plays out its imaginative vision performatively, both resisting and affirming its own ideological grounding, thereby "test[ing] the limits of community." In Levine's words, literary experience "is one means to some larger sense of community, to the awareness of the necessity of personal compromise and social accommodation.... Part of the value of the aesthetic is the way in which it can provide spaces and strategies for exploring [and rehearsing] the possibility of conciliations between the ideosyncratic and the communal" (pp. 17–18).

Literature and the aesthetic, then, serve an essential and unduplicated cultural function in late modern society. Postcolonial minorities and marginalized groups worldwide have been especially sensitive to the ways that literary representation functions performatively as a site of global struggle for cultural recognition, self-determination, and community rebuilding.[11] In the broad scheme of current methods available for literary study, performance-centered scholarship remains ideally positioned for exploring the dynamic features of literature as the complex interworkings of understanding, pleasure, and power having far-reaching social consequences. As we near the twenty-first century faced with increasing cultural diversification and fragmentation, coupled with growing demands for public accountability from higher education, the disciplinary tasks of performance studies should include a vigorous recommitment to the study of literature in performance, a uniquely productive way of understanding and appreciating culture as unity within the simultaneity, interanimation, and negotiation of differences.

NOTES

1. See, for example, Marvin Carlson's (1996, pp. 187–99) cogent summation of this trend.
2. Stanley Fish (1995, p. 41) provides an incisive analysis and critique of "conventional and obligatory routines" that constitute and sustain the discipline of English.
3. I have discussed the notion of a culture-performance matrix in "Mapping the 'Cultural Turn' in Performance Studies" *The Future of Performance Studies: The Next Millenium,* ed. Sheron J. Dailey, forthcoming. Parts of my foregoing argument were first developed in this essay.
4. Beyond this common feature, references to "performance" seem highly divergent. For example, in the introduction to their edited volume, *Performativity and Performance,* literary theorists Andrew Parker and Eve Kosofsky Sedgwick (1995, p. 1) conceive of performance narrowly as a "loose cluster of theatrical practices, relations, and traditions." In contrast, performance theorist Richard Schechner, in one of his latest books, *The Future of Ritual* (1993, p. 20), identifies four inclusive and interactive spheres of performance: entertainment, healing, education, and ritualizing.
5. Parker and Sedgwick (1995, p. 8) call attention to the ethical dimension of the context of performative utterances as "the tacit requisition of a third person plural, a 'they' of witness—whether or not literally present."
6. Derrida (1982), emphasis added. Marvin Carlson (1996, pp. 56–65) provides a detailed and useful discussion of the issues inherent in linguistic approaches to performance/performativity.
7. Grossberg (1992, p. 54).
8. Joseph Roach (1996b, p. 218) argues that "literature itself (and not just dramatic literature) may be understood as the historic archive of restored behavior, the repository and medium of transmission of performative tropes..."
9. Although tracking this theme within our disciplinary literature is beyond the scope of this essay, it is important to note that the study of literature in performance has and continues to serve as vehicle for realizing this potential. See, especially, Bacon (1966), Geiger (1963, 1967), and Long and Hopkins (1982).
10. In a parallel vein, philosopher Martha Nussbaum (1995, p. xvi) makes an impassioned and eloquent case for the social importance of the literary imagination as "an ingredient of the ethical stance that asks us to con-

cern ourselves with the good of other people whose lives are different from our own."

11. For example, Kenyan novelist, playwright, and cultural activist Ngugi wa Thiong'o (1986) argues compellingly for renewed attention to "orature," the living oral traditions at work in resisting colonization. Ngugi explains: "Orature has its roots in the lives of the peasantry. It is primarily their compositions, their songs, their art, which forms the basis of the national and resistance culture during the colonial and neo-colonial times"(p. 83). The popular reception of written literature among African villagers, Ngugi remarks, occurs often through "the appropriation of the novel into the oral tradition," having the book read aloud in families and in public gathering places.

REFERENCES

Austin, J. (1975). How to do things with words [1962] (2nd. Ed.). Cambridge, MA: Harvard University Press.

Bacon, W. A. (1966). *The art of interpretation.* New York: Holt, Rinehart and Winston.

Bauman, R. (1992). Performance. In R. Bauman (Ed.), *Folklore, cultural performances, and popular entertainments: A communication-centered handbook* (pp. 41–49). New York: Oxford.

Butler, J. (1993). *Bodies that matter: On the discursive limits of "sex."* New York: Routledge.

Carlson, M. (1996). *Performance: A critical introduction.* New York: Routledge.

Chaney, D. (1994). *The cultural turn: Scene-setting essays on contemporary cultural history.* New York: Routledge.

Derrida, J. (1982). Signature event context. In J. Derrida, *Margins of philosophy* (Alan Bass, Trans.). (pp. 307–30). Chicago: University of Chicago Press.

Diamond, E. (1996). Introduction. In E. Diamond (Ed.), *Performance and cultural politics* (pp. 1–12). New York: Routledge.

Fish, S. (1995). *Professional correctness: Literary study and political change.* New York: Oxford.

Geiger, D. (1963). *The Sound, sense, and performance of literature.* Chicago: Scott, Foresman.

Geiger, D. (1967). *The dramatic impulse in modern poetics.* Baton Rouge, LA: Louisiana State University Press.

Grossberg, L. (1992). *We gotta get out of this place: Popular conservatism and postmodern culture.* New York: Routledge.

Levine, G. (1994). Introduction: Reclaiming the aesthetic. In G. Levine (Ed.), *Aesthetic and Ideology* (pp. 1–28). New Brunswick, NJ: Rutgers University Press.

Long, B. W., and Hopkins, M. F. (1982). *Performing literature: An introduction to oral interpretation.* Englewood Cliffs, NJ: Prentice-Hall.

Ngugi wa, T. (1986). *Decolonizing the mind. The politics of language in African literature.* Portsmouth, NH: Heinemann.

Nussbaum, M. (1995). *Poetic justice: The literary imagination and public life.* Boston, MA: Beacon Press.

Parker, A., and Sedgwick, E. (1995). Introduction: Performativity and performance. In A. Parker and E. Sedgwick, (Eds.). *Performativity and performance* (pp. 1–18). New York: Routledge.

Phelan, P. (1993). *Unmarked: The politics of performance.* New York: Routledge.

Roach, J. (1996a). *Cities of the dead: Circum-atlantic performance.* New York: Columbia University Press.

Roach, J. (1996b). Kinship, intelligence, and memory as improvisation. In E. Diamond (Ed.), *Performance and cultural politics* (pp. 217–236). New York: Routledge.

Schechner, R. (1985). *Between theater and anthropology.* Philadelphia: University of Pennsylvania Press.

Schechner, R. (1988). *Performance theory* (Revised Ed.). New York: Routledge.

Schechner, R. (1993). *The future of ritual: Writings on culture and performance.* New York: Routledge.

Turner, V. (1986). *The anthropology of performance.* New York: PAJ Publications.

Witness to the Self: The Autobiographical Impulse in Performance Studies

Lynn C. Miller
University of Texas at Austin

AUTOBIOGRAPHY AND THE SEARCH FOR SELF

Over the past five years, I've watched with great interest as, increasingly, colleagues in performance studies have developed and toured in extensive solo performances based on experiences and situations from their own lives. At performance festivals and conferences twenty years ago, featured artist/scholars might have performed Robert Frost or T. S. Eliot or Wallace Stevens; certainly they would have showcased performances by others, prominent writers of fiction, poetry, or nonfiction. At present, the same events frequently include solo performance of self-generated texts such as Barnard Down's "An Unsolicited Gift," Linda Park-Fuller's "A Clean Breast of It," Jacqueline Taylor's "On Being an Exemplary Lesbian: My Life as a Role Model," Craig Gingrich Philbrook's "Refreshment," Tami Spry's "Skins: A Daughter's (Re)construction of Cancer," and Joni L. Jones' "Sista Docta."[1] Performers of autobiography, having once performed texts by others (projections of themselves as constructed through someone else's viewpoint), are now performing their own stories (idealized projections of themselves as constructed by themselves). On the surface, this autobiographical turn in performance mirrors trends in our larger culture toward performing self, from the popularity of talk radio and talk t.v., to the proliferation of performance art in theatrical venues, to the very recent explosion in publishing of the memoir by both recognized and first-time authors.

At one time only "celebrities" published or performed their autobiographical stories, actors like Lauren Bacall or figures like Colin Powell or Bill Gates, people who had previously acquired national prominence—and name recognition. But in the 1990s the push to express one's personal story has accelerated: in cyberspace chat rooms, in self-help groups, in coffeehouses and theatres, in books, magazines, and on television. However, the focus on autobiography in Performance Studies has little do with the currents driving the popularity of an Oprah Winfrey or a Ricki Lake. Rather, there are clear theoretical developments in the field that underlie this use of the self as performance text.

Academically, Performance Studies has steadily moved away from the single focus on traditional printed literature (texts of critically-acclaimed poetry, fiction, and drama), a focus our field largely maintained for more than three decades; this focus has broadened in the past twenty years to include analyzing and performing political and cultural phenomena and traditions, and the events of everyday life and conversation. Notions of performance have shifted from a strictly aesthetic realm into a more integral paradigm for explaining, critiquing, and experiencing how contemporary life is lived.

The centrality of canonical literature in the teaching and practice of oral interpretation from the '40s through much of the '70s paralleled the primacy of new critical models and object-centered theories of aesthetics. Though they emerged in the '30s, it wasn't until the latter part of the '70s that perceiver-centered aesthetics challenged the prevailing formalist perceptual schema when reader-response criticism and poststructuralist theories began to be widely taught in graduate classrooms. The adoption of reader-response critical models stripped away the inviolate position of "great art" and in our field, great books, by shifting the perceptual locus (and the creation of meaning) from the object of art to tlhe perceiver/audience. The act of performance itself emerged as significant apart from its text, as did the dynamic transaction of text, performer, and audience; contexts—including environments and rhetorical situations, historical milieus, cultural prescriptions, and biases—were increasingly examined.

The emphasis on the perceiver as reader, viewer, or participant naturally resulted in an increased scrutiny of self in general and of various kinds and qualities of response in particular throughout aesthetic, political, psychological, and social spheres. This increased attention to self from the 1970s on has been hailed as self-awareness by some observers and as narcissism by others.

The decentering of the text coincided with the decentering of many of the tenets, traditions, and inherent meanings of American cultural life. The proliferation of technological innovations in communication has broadened our notions of community and vastly enriched our interactions into regional, national, and global spheres (even while at times we feel enslaved by the proliferation of messages). The immediacy and accessibility of electronic information allows material from vastly disparate sources to be juxtaposed and recombined in a kind of fluid, electronic collage. As John Berger (1972) writes, speaking of visual art:

In the age of pictorial reproduction the meaning of paintings is no longer attached to them; their meaning becomes transmittable: that is to say it becomes information of a sort, and, like all information, it is either put to use or ignored; information carries no special authority within itself. When a painting is put to use, its meaning is either modified or totally changed.... It is not a question of reproduction failing to reproduce certain aspects of an image faithfully; it is a question of reproduction making it possible, even inevitable, that

an image will be used for many different purposes and that the reproduced image, unlike an original work, can lend itself to them all. (pp. 24–25)

We are continually aware of the idiosyncracies and the limits of perception. In our postmodern world, any pretense to objectivity is seen as just that, and the multiplicity of subjectivities regularly challenges what we once saw as core beliefs about gender, sexuality, ethnicity, and morality. Not only great texts and great works of art have lost their absoluteness, their authority; poststructuralism, deconstruction, postmodernism have decentered other sources of authority in our lives as well, and institutions of government, family and education, codes of behavior and notions of civility are no longer seen as inviolate.

Similarly, the notion of an essential self has also been challenged. Our knowledge of the diverse roles we occupy and the selves we perform in various situations at times destabilize the process of decision-making, particularly on moral or ethical grounds. As Kenneth Gergen (1991) notes in *The Saturated Self:*

This bursting of postmodern consciousness into the academic sphere is paralleled by a rich set of trends emerging within the broader cultural realm.... Of particular interest is the loss of identifiable essences, the increasing sensitivity to the social construction of reality, the erosion of authority, the growing disregard for rational coherence, and the emergence of ironic self-reflection. Each of these trends, traceable to the saturation of society by multiple voices, both contributes to and is supported by the breakdown of the knowable self. (pp. 16–17)

Accompanying this uncertainty about self and selves, and the recognition that particular situations impinge upon our reactions and behaviors, the "knowable self" is precisely what is most sought after. Even while essences disappear, giving way to situational characteristics or reactions, most of us still cling wistfully to some version of the Romantic notion of an integrated, whole self. We want to know as fervently as Barbara Walters does as she relentlessly queries her guests for the real truth, what we are *really* like underneath the surface and the rumors and the roles and the facades, what do we really think? what do we really feel? We yearn for what seems most elusive, to truly know ourselves and those around us.

THE SIGNIFYING WITNESS

In the 1995 satiric film *To Die For,* the characters don't really feel they exist unless they appear on television. No stakes are too high, no risks are too great—even that of committing murder—to prevent them from seeking their moment in the spotlight, their mediated and thus authentic moment of "real" life. The television audience becomes the ultimate judge of worth, and even more important, the ultimate witness. While Nicole Kidman's character truly is on the edge—of sanity, if not believability—the notion of witnessing indeed possesses great power. In a world where beliefs and decisions and meanings are relative, substantiation and validation arise from a community's consensus. In therapeutic communities, from group counseling to 12-step programs to groups focused around bereavement or loss, the healing power of the witnesses has long been acknowledged. Much contemporary storytelling, from professional performance art to less structured sharing of personal narratives, relies on the interaction of storyteller, story, and audience to acknowledge—in some way make real or palpable—the teller's emotional pain and experience and to provide a space for healing and communal acceptance or redress. Joni L. Jones (1993) mentions aspects of healing in performance when she writes about the redressive power in performed stories revealing the tension between black men and black women: "Performance as healing is an essential feature of the African-based productions with which I have worked; the healing is the way in which such performances achieve efficacy" (p. 237).

Grotowski's great theatrical experiments of the 1960s and early '70s employed the witness as an integral part of the performance. He chose to limit his ideal audiences to only 30 members in an attempt to ensure the intimate, spiritual, almost religious contact of the performer with the witness; his goal was a performance with the potential to spiritually and psychologically transform actor and audience member alike. In Grotowski's theatre the actor stripped away all masks to reveal raw human feeling in order for the spectator "to undertake a similar process of self-penetration" (Grotowski, 1968, p. 34). Grotowski's theories remain alive in contemporary performance art, in works by artists such as Holly Hughes, Karen Finley, Tim Miller, Rachel Rosenthal, where struggles about gender, sexuality, ethnicity, and personal crisis call upon the audience to examine their own beliefs. The witness and the storyteller share an emotional territory as well as a physical space for a limited, but intensely charged, period: "The potential engagement of self and other makes possible an evolving, revelatory dance between performer and spectator in productions of performance art" (Miller, 1995, p. 49).

The civil rights movement, the women's movement, the gay and lesbian rights movement, therapeutic, and religious communities have all built momentum and community through the testifying and the witnessing of personal stories and struggles. In the July 1996, issue of *The Women's Review of Books,* Vivian Gornick confronts the enormous current popularity of the literary memoir in "Why Memoir Now?" She writes:

> *In this culture the idea of the self is vital to the conventional wisdom. Today, millions of people consider themselves possessed of the right to a serious life. A serious life, by definition, is a reflective life; a life to which one pays attention; a life one tries to make sense of and bear witness to. The age is characterized by a need to testify. Everywhere in the world women and men are rising up to tell their story out of the now commonly held belief that one's own life signifies. (p. 5)*

AUTOBIOGRAPHY AND COMMUNITY

Many of the voices testifying most powerfully in recent decades are those of women, minorities, lesbians and gays, and others whose physical and personal uniqueness now or at some time classified them as Other. The mantle of otherness is dissipated in a room where speakers/performers relate their subjective selves to witnesses; experience, however idiosyncratic, cannot remain marginalized if it is shared. And this construction of shared history is a vital impetus to the writing and performing of autobiography now, particularly in a time where so much of our lives seem impersonal, our particulars recorded in vast data banks, in a time when the proliferation of people and problems seems to render the individual even more minuscule and invisible. I see a direct relationship between the increase in depersonalization in our society—from automated bank tellers to computerized solicitation on the telephone—to the increase in spoken word performance, storytelling, the simple interactions between a particular individual (actor, speaker) and a participating audience—what Grotowski called the essence of theatre. As our daily lives deprive us of the kind of reassuring personal contact that used to be part of community life, we are finding other venues for participation and connection.

Rather than an act of narcissism, the urge to perform the self is a way to examine the one constant in an increasingly destabilized, chaotic, and rapidly-transforming environment. For while the self may have many selves, while the psyche is saturated and shattered and scattered, each of us nonetheless is rooted in a body, brain, and spirit that we cannot separate from. As radically changing as this bundle is (at the very least the aging process alone forces us to greet an increasingly unfamiliar succession of personae), it may be the only fixed point of reference each of us has. What we loosely call the self, in all its complexity, filters perception and meaning; it fundamentally constitutes our primary site of performance.

In addition, performance allows us a fixed point of reference within the self. As the self feels increasingly shattered, we feel more compelled to gather up the fragments to proclaim "this is the self" for that performative moment or in that particular instance, only to go "no, not that, *this* is the self" as we construct another. By creating a performance text around a particular circumstance, we mark that peculiar confluence of time and space with characteristics, a script, of our emotional/physical/intellectual presence. This script remains fluid, and presumably is altered with each subsequent performance and set of witnesses as new responses and new insights are gathered. As Linda Park-Fuller (1995) noted in writing about her performance piece, "Clean Breast of It": "Having composed and performed this narrative, my experience with breast cancer has been reconfigured within the context of my life. I look at that experience differently having storied it and shared it publicly. I see it less as a trauma and more as a learning experience" (p. 65).

Performing autobiography allows one's life stories to signify and resonate within multiple layers of consequence: marking the private, spiritual configurations of self in a public arena and creating a space for new possibilities for transformation and communion between performer and audience.

NOTE

1. These performances have had multiple productions, including the following: "An Unsolicited Gift," "A Clean Breast of It," and "Skins" were all presented at the national meeting of the Speech Communication Association in New Orleans, November 1994; "Refreshment," "Sista Docta," and "On Being an Exemplary Lesbian" were presented at the Northwestern University Performance Studies Conference, March 1996.

REFERENCES

Berger, J. (1972). *Ways of Seeing*. London: British Broadcast Corporation and Penguin Books.

Gergen, J. G. (1991). *The Saturated Self: Dilemmas of Identity in Contempory Life*. New York: Basic Books.

Gornick, V. (1996, July). Why Memoir Now? *The Women's Review of Books, XIII*, 5.

Grotowski, J. (1968). *Towards a Poor Theatre*. New York: Simon & Schuster.

Jones, J. L. (1993). Improvisation as a Performance Strategy for African-Based Theatre. *Text and Performance Quarterly, 13,* 233–251.

Miller, L. C. (1995). "Polymorphous Perversity" in Women's Performance Art: The Case of Holly Hughes. *Text and Performance Quarterly, 15,* 44–58.

Park-Fuller, L. M. (1995). Narration and Narratization of a Cancer Story: Composing and Performing "A Clean Breast of it." *Text and Performance Quarterly, 15,* 60—67.

CHAPTER 14

AT THE HELM IN SOCIAL THEORY

Introduction

Jimmie D. Trent
Miami University

Today's program is titled "At the Helm in Social Theory." I teach communication theory and when social theory started gaining prominence in interpersonal communication, I studied it with an attitude that I was an old dog learning new tricks. Somewhere along the way, I discovered that I was constructing a new dog. I anticipate the continuation of my self construction today as I listen to four of the people who most influenced my personal growth.

Dr. Barnett Pearce first came to the attention of many in the discipline as an undergraduate student when he and his colleague, representing Carson Newman College, won the National Debate Tournament in 1965. He has distinguished himself many times in the 30 years that followed. He has authored or co-authored eight books including his first (in 1975) *Communicating Personally: A Theory of Interpersonal Communication and Human Relationships, Communication and the Human Condition* (in 1989), which was translated into Italian and published in Italy in 1993, and *Making Social Worlds: Interpersonal Communication,* a basic textbook adapting the concepts of social constructionism for beginning students in my and many others' classes. In addition, he has authored or co-authored 31 book chapters, 58 refereed articles, 2 communication modules, and 2 videotapes. In the 1970s, he co-authored what I and many others thought was the best rules theory, the *Coordi-*

nated Management of Meaning, which by the middle 1980s was being revised consistent with a social constructionist view of meaning. He has been a featured speaker, seminar faculty member, Senior Visiting Fellow, and presented a workshop in Denmark, Colombia, Argentina, Nigeria, Italy, England, Portugal, India, Turkey, Martinique, Yugoslavia, Japan, and Costa Rica. He is presently Professor and Chair of the Department of Communication at Loyola University of Chicago. Today, his presentation is titled "'Do No Harm' or 'Make It Better'? Some Implications of Transcending the False Dichotomy between Theory and Practice."

Although others had previously introduced social theory to the study of interpersonal communication, Dr. Wendy Leeds-Hurwitz significantly advanced its application as Editor of the "Forum on Social Approaches to Communication" when it was published in two issues of *Communication Theory* in 1992. She expanded the series in a 1995 book titled *Social Approaches to Communication,* one of five books Dr. Leeds-Hurwitz has written or edited. In addition, she has presented 51 refereed papers at professional conferences and authored or co-authored 56 book chapters, articles, essays, or reviews. Her most recent book chapters include "The Concept of Context in Social Communication" in James Owen's forthcoming *Context and Communication Behavior* and "A Social Account of Symbols" in John Stewart's soon to be published *Beyond the Symbol Model: Essays on the Nature of Language.* Many of her publications have been printed or reprinted in French language publications in France. In addition to her numerous writings on social theory and communication, her topics have included intercultural communication and folklore. Dr. Leeds-Hurwitz is currently Professor and Chair of the Department of Communication at the University of Wisconsin–Parkside. Her topic for today is "Social Interpretations, Social Theories."

I am sure that I am not alone in having my first introduction to the work of Dr. John R. Stewart come from the highly popular interpersonal communication textbook *Bridges, not Walls.* While that book has had six editions between 1973 and 1995 with each revision containing 40 to 50 percent new material, Dr. Stewart has published nine other books. Among the most recent is a SUNY University Press publication titled *Beyond the Symbol Model: Reflections on the Representational Nature of Language.* In addition to the most recent edition of *Bridges...* in 1995, he had another university press publication titled *Language as Articulate Contact: Toward a Post Semiotic Philosophy of Communication.* In addition, he has 14 book chapters, 17 articles, 39 guest lectures, and 57 scholarly conference presentations on a wide variety of topics. In his spare time, he has maintained "an active consulting practice, providing communication assessment, coaching, and training services to a variety of technical organizations, especially consulting engineering and architectural firms." Dr. Stewart is Professor of Speech Communication at the University of Washington. The topic of today's address is "Social Theory and Dialogue."

Dr. Arthur R. Bochner has been honored for his scholarship by his own College of Arts and Sci-

ences, which awarded him its Scholar of the Year Award, and by the Florida Speech Communication Association, which named him the state's Outstanding Research Scholar. He has also been honored for his teaching. The National Communication Association awarded him the NCA Teachers on Teaching Award for contributions to the philosophy and methodology of teaching and the University of South Florida Graduate Communication Council has twice awarded him its Outstanding Graduate Professor Award. His work with minority students was recognized when he was selected by the McKnight Foundation for the William R. Jones Most Valuable Doctoral Mentor Award. Another fact in which he can take pride is that two students whose doctoral dissertations he directed, Mary Anne Fitzpatrick and William Rawlins, are also presenting papers in the "At the Helm" series. Dr. Bochner now lists his research methodologies as interpretive studies, qualitative research, and narrative inquiry but such was not always the case. Like many who now accept the social perspective, among his 22 refereed articles is one published in 1972 titled "A Multivariate Investigation of Machiavellianism and Task Structure in Four-Man Groups." And among his 22 book chapters is 1 published in Peter Monge and Joseph Cappella's 1980 book titled *Multivariate Analysis in Communication Research.* But by the end of the decade, he was selected to write the preface for Dr. Leeds-Hurwitz's *Social Construction.* The most recent of his five books, co-edited with Carolyn Ellis, is titled *Composing Ethnography: Autoethnography, Sociopoetics, Reflexivity.* Dr. Bochner is currently Professor of Communication at the University of South Florida. The title of his paper is "Storied Lives: Recovering the Moral Importance of Social Theory."

"Do No Harm" or "Make It Better"? Some Implications of Transcending the False Dichotomy between Theory and Practice

W. Barnett Pearce
Loyola University

"...a world that theory could fully grasp and neatly explain would not, I suspect, be a pleasant place " (Waltzer, 1997, p. 8).

Early last year, Judith Trent invited me to be a part of the "At the Helm" series of panels she was organizing for the 1996 annual convention of the National Communication Association. Flattered to be invited, I quickly accepted and then thought little more about it until, in early summer, pressured to meet the deadline for printing the convention program, she insisted that I give her the title of my paper, notwithstanding the fact that it was not yet written. Still basking in the pleasure of being included on the panel and flattered to be named among the others on the panel, I responded by sending her the title which appears on this page.

As the date for the convention drew nearer, I did write a formal paper, but wished that I were not permanently committed to the title that seemed so attractive in the heat of summer. As I pondered what to do, I hit upon the idea of writing the paper as an extended meditation on what the title might have been had I the chance to choose again. So in September, I wrote a paper which, as it turned out, bore little resemblance to what I subsequently said at the convention in November. Two months later, I was asked to put the paper into proper form according to the appropriate style manual, and prepare it for publication in this book.

This story about how this paper came to exist serves the function of calling to attention the historical situatedness of the preparation and delivery of papers, whether as part of convention programs or as journal articles or book chapters. I invite you to scan the table of contents of any of our journals and ask a series of questions about how the titles listed there came to be formulated in the way that they appear. What was going on in the life of the authors when they chose that title? Is the title that appears in print the first idea that they had? If not, how does this one differ from others that were rejected or displaced? With whom was the author having important conversations when she chose this title? How was the decision made to use the vocabulary that appears rather than some other? The point of this exercise is to see scholarship as a form of practice, and the theories which emerge out of that practice as human artifacts rather than inscriptions of eternal truths that might better be written on God's Own Chalkboard In The Sky.

Nothing is said or written out of a context, and what is said and written means something different if it is brought into a new context. I decided to write this third version of the paper like the first, as an extended meditation on the titles I might have chosen, and as an invitation for you, the reader, to join me in thinking about the implications of the relationships between theory and practice which give rise to them. Let's start with the original title that I submitted:

"Do No Harm" or "Make It Better"? Some Implications of Transcending the False Dichotomy between Theory and Practice

This title grew out of the concerns that I was wrestling with at the time. My colleague Shawn Spano (San Jose State University) and I had just finished a full day briefing the Council of the City of Cupertino about the results of Phase I of the Cupertino "Community Project: Voices and Visions," which was organized and led by members of the Public Dialogue Consortium. By conducting 10 focus group interviews involving almost 100 residents, we had identified five issues which the residents were concerned about. One of these was described as potentially explosive but not being adequately discussed. The issue involved the rapid change of the ethnic composition of the residents. We deliberately chose to name this issue "cultural richness" rather than any of the other, more commonly available terms. Not only was this issue underrepresented in the public conversations in the city, many citizens thought it "undiscussable" because any attempt to discuss it would set off unproductive and undesirably confrontational patterns of communication. Based on our research, theory, and commitments as practitioners (see Pearce and Littlejohn, 1997), we proposed a second phase of the Cupertino Community Project which would create new places for discussing this topic and new forms of communication in which to discuss it.

As you might expect, the members of the Council were not surprised at the issue (although none of them had mentioned it to us before our project found it!) and, sharing the other citizens' concern that the issue was undiscussable without initiating a firestorm of ethnic opposition, they sought reassurance that we would not "make it worse" by exacerbating tensions only barely suppressed. Specifically, they asked if we really knew what we were doing; if we had experience doing this before; and if we had thought about how we would respond to various contingencies. Shawn and I found ourselves assuring the Council members that our first criterion was "to do no harm" and that we thought that we might, possibly, "make it better."

These conversations were very much in my consciousness when I developed the title I gave to Judith last summer. I was mulling over the meanings of "harm" and "better," wondering about the concepts of agency and the efficacy of the PDC

project, and quite in a quandary about how one could pledge not to do harm without renunciating action altogether. However, when I read the title in the cold print of the program, it was hard not to see the distinction between "do no harm" and "make it better" in the context of theory rather than practice, and particularly in some major strands of the philosophy of science. It looked as if I was posing the question in the old terms of a dichotomy between "ought" and "is" and were going to rehash yet once again the fact that there are no "oughtless ises." But this issue has been sufficiently developed and I do not have anything useful to add to it. Rather, I am going to articulate a different set of assumptions that undermine the distinction between practice and theory and then explore some of their implications.

1. I assume that all of us have good intentions. That is, our practice and our theories emerge from the desire to make things better.[1]
2. I assume that there is a reciprocal but asymmetrical relationship between practical action and the action that is comprised of doing theory. That is, making, teaching, and/or testing a theory is a form of doing a social action, but while all social action presumes a theory, much social action does not lead to theory.
3. I assume that doing social theory is a powerful form of social action. Just as all research observations are theory-laden, so all forms of communication practice are shaped by social theory. Those social theories may be implicit or explicit; rigorous or sloppy; private or shared, but they are influential. In this context, it is good to explore one's theories, to articulate them, and to develop them in conversations with others.[2]

---

[1] I'm not particularly concerned about whether this assumption is "true" or not, if "true" is understood in a "representational" sense. I am taking a more "pragmatic" perspective and reporting that, in my experience, the *consequences* of assuming that people have good intentions is enabling and the alternative disabling. I am not so much concerned about what they "really" think, whatever that might mean.

4. I assume that social theories are seen as *praxis,* in which the theorist takes the perspective of a person acting into contingent situations with care for the consequences of those actions.[3]

5. I assume that communication theories deal with transpersonal, temporally extended patterns of interaction by embodied persons in which the events and objects of our social worlds, including ourselves and our knowledge of those patterns themselves, are created, shaped, and sometimes transformed.

As one way of describing the implications of these assumptions, I might have titled the paper:

The Ethical Responsibilities of the Theorist as a Creative Artist

But would the participants in the NCA convention have foregone the pleasures of San Diego and the intellectual delights of other concurrent sessions to hear a paper with that title? What sense do you have for the notion that social theorists can be seen as creative artists, and that ethical responsibilities derive from that role?

You have to love irony to enjoy intellectual history. The Enlightenment's separation of "ought" from "is" brought with it a great liberation (Toul-

---

[2]In this discussion, I am presuming a particular notion of "theory" and "practice" consistent with that developed more rigorously by Craig and Tracy (1995, p. 248): "Within a practical discipline perspective, theory is conceived as a rational reconstruction of practices for the purpose of informing further practice and reflection." Craig and Tracy's article moves to the question of how to evaluate such grounded practical theories; in this paper, I move to the dialectical partner of that concern: how to evaluate practices which are reconstructed in such theories and which emerge from such reconstructions. My thought is even more explicitly grounded in Cronen's (1994) notion of "practical theory."

[3]There is a rich historical development of the idea of praxis, but I am using it as I understand it from Aristotle. In the *Nicomachean Ethics,* Aristotle differentiated *praxis* (which operates within a contingent social framework on the basis of *phronesis,* or practical wisdom) from *theoria* (which operates within a framework in which things have to be what they are on the basis of *episteme*) and *poesis* (which operates in a domain of made-things on the basis of *techne*).

min, 1990). One way of describing the Medieval context to which the Enlightenment was a response is to say that "oughts" and "ises" had been fused. What we would call moral or aesthetic answers were given to what we would call questions of fact. One of the great contributions of the Enlightenment was to distinguish among ethics, aesthetics, and what Kant called "pure reason." These distinctions enabled people to describe "inconvenient" or even "revolutionary" facts, and there is a kind of heroism in Copernicus' and Galileo's refusal to let ideological orthodoxy blind them to the perception of elliptical orbits or the moons of Jupiter. But there is an important difference between making a distinction and treating things as dichotomies.. The dualism which resulted from the Enlightemnent's extremists led many theorists to treat the description of facts (what Aristotle would call *episteme*) as if they were the only "reality," dismissing aesthetics and practical reason as outmoded residues of the pre-scientific era. Ken Wilbur calls the result a "flatland" in which only facts exist and there is no room for significance, value, or beauty (Wilbur, 1996).

Of course this "flatland" view cannot withstand closer scrutiny, even by those who espouse it most wholeheartedly. At first, the fact that all observations are theory-laden was taken to be a "problem" for epistemology ("Gosh! How can we ever REALLY know the truth?") to be solved by eliminating, as much as possible, the subjective elements of perception. This is really embarrassing: distinguished scholars were seen by students and other innocent bystanders wrestling with the question of what they "ought" to do with the fact that "oughtness" is inevitably involved in our perception of what "is," and concluding, in weighty scholarly tomes, that we "ought" to eschew "oughtness" and be as "is-y" as possible! (Perhaps a historical context for our topic favors an appreciation for self-reflexive paradoxes as well as the enjoyment of irony!)

Another way of looking at the situation is to take seriously the notion that social theorists necessarily nominate themselves as mythmakers; we tell tales of "what if," "what is," and "just so," and these tales are deeply embedded in moral orders of what people ought to do. We now know that there are any number of stories (theories) which can be supported by any cluster of facts (Pearce, 1995; Shotter & Gergen, 1994). As a result, social theorists are inevitably "creative artists," constructing one of any number of possible stories which correspond in some way with inconclusive (and incomplete and corrigible) sets of data. Since each of these stories has implications for what people ought to do, the act of constructing, presenting, publishing, and testing social theories has ethical implications, and so the theorist, in the process of rationally reconstructing one form of practice within another set of practices, is a creative artist, shaping what some (e.g., Pearce, 1994) might call the "social worlds" in which theorists and others of God's creatures live.

Surely there is an ethical responsibility implied within such an aesthetic act of artistic creation; perhaps one which would reward more attention than is often given to it. But how can we come to grips with these ethical issues without falling into all-too-familiar forms of imposing "my" values on "your" theory or simply wrapping my prejudices in the rhetorical form of theory? Perhaps a clue might come from some mulling about the nature of truth—or at least about the nature of truth-claims. Another title for this paper might have been:

PRESERVING THE TENSIONS AMONG THE THREE SIDES OF TRUTH

Had you been at the San Diego NCA convention, would you have come to a presentation with this title? (Honesty counts, but please be kind.)

One of the key terms in this version of the title describes "tensions" which should be preserved rather than dichotomies to be respected (or even transcended!); another key term is the notion that truth has (at least) three sides. What are we to do with terms like this?

I believe that we should not attempt to find a single, clear, and distinct notion of truth, because the world as we know it does not fall into atomis-

tic nuggets. Arthur Koestler (1978) suggested that we think of the world as consisting not of atomistic units but of "holons," each of which is a systemic "whole" comprised of other holons and itself one of the holons comprising a larger whole.

Ken Wilbur (1996, p. 107) provided a playful way of thinking of holons as having both an "inside" and an "outside" and being capable of being viewed from an individual perspective (that is, the holon as a "whole") or from a collective perspective (that is, the holon as one among many, a part of a holarchical organization of larger "wholes"). This makes a 2 by 2 matrix in which the right side consists of seeing things from the "outside" whether as things in themselves (their objective "truth") or as parts of more complex systemic relationships (their "functional fit" in Wilbur's terms); and the left side consists of seeing things from the "inside" whether as things in themselves (their "truthfulness") or as parts of more complex systemic relationships (their "justness"). This 2 by 2 matrix decomposes into three perspectives: the events and objects of our social worlds, including ourselves, can be seen as "I's", "we's," or "it's" (which can be seen as either wholes in themselves or as complex systems of holons) and these are roughly equivalent to Popper's distinctions among objective, subjective, and cultural worlds; Habermas' distinctions among objective truth, subjective sincerity, and intersubjective justness as validity claims; and Kant's distinctions among pure reason, practical reason, and judgment (Wilbur, 1996, pp. 122–123).

Is it possible to describe any piece of our social worlds from only one of these perspectives? Of course! But the more interesting question is why would one want to? Why would a social theorist be so fatally attracted to just one of these language games when others are available? When what is lost and what is gained by using these as complementary perspectives is assessed, I believe that we will conclude that it is important to maintain the tensions among them in our descriptions and practices. Any description of a holon which is limited to only one or two of these perspectives is incomplete. In fact, I think that any consistent description of our social worlds *must* be incomplete,[4] but these three "dimensions" provide a touchstone for comparing degrees of incompleteness.

The attempt to preserve the tensions among the three sides of truth—objective accuracy, subjective truthfulness, and collective justice—leads to yet another potential title for the paper:

FOUR MAXIMS FOR SOCIAL THEORISTS

Please hear the following four maxims in the context of the lower left quadrant of Wilbur's matrix: looking at ourselves from the "inside" as a collectivity. This is the quadrant that deals with "intersubjective justice" or "judgment;" that is, it is the area in which we can at least raise the question of whether we are "making it better" when we engage in the practice of social theorizing or the theorizing of social practice. So let us, as social theorists and practitioners:

1. Stay in the tensions among all three faces of truth.   Do not try to, or fall prey to the temptation to, reduce the world to any one of these. The world is complex and so are we. In fact, the world must be more complex than we are since it includes us as holons, and our description of wholes of which we are a part should be characterized by an essential humility.

2. Stay in the "conversation."   I think that this maxim is slightly different from the more familiar "keep the conversation going." Life and the universe goes on and changes as it does. So should we. The question is not whether the conversation will continue but whether we will remain in it or find some way to drop out.

Etymologically, "conversation" means "to turn with" someone or something else. I have in mind two conversations. One conversation is temporally extended, a recurring cycle of different sorts of practices in which each of us might engage as social theorists. We act into a variety of social contexts in an attempt to improve them, and

then we rationally reconstruct those practices in order to evaluate them and prepare ourselves to act yet again, and so on.

The other conversation is horizontally extended. It engages all of us who do social theory in patterns of turn-taking as listeners and speakers with people who do not devote a significant amount of their time to producing formal rational reconstructions of their experience. To ignore this conversation, which includes us "theorists" but extends far beyond us, is to give an unwarranted priority to the "upper left" quadrant of Wilbur's model, which describes ourselves as individuals from the inside.

3. Be reflexive.   Use what Gregory Bateson called "double description." The characterization of theorizing as one sort of practice which is "about" other sorts of practice already presupposes some sort of reflexivity. We should take into account our own actions as part of the ontogenesis of reality-as-we-know-it.

I am certain that my decision to write this paper as a reflexive meditation will elicit frowns of disapproval from many readers, and to them I apologize. I do not apologize, however, for insisting that both theory and practice are human artifacts and that any honest description of each must include an account of the theorist-artist or the practitioner-artist as well as the artifact. My apology extends only to the clumsiness of my attempt to do so, and my regrets that any attempt to write in this vein seems to counter so much of the contemporary standards of practice. I am not the first to note that the style manuals which govern our professional writing are themselves not neutral; they embed a "behaviorist" perspective which makes it hard for us to write in a way which constitutes a different worldview (Bazerman, 1987). In addition to my apology, I invite those more skilled than I to experiment with more eloquent discursive forms that include double description.

4. Be open to the possibility of transformations of our consciousness in ways that expand our horizons so that what we had thought of as "wholes" in themselves are seen as parts of larger "wholes."   This not only expands our view

---

[4]There is an echo of Godel's Proof in this, as well as Heisenberg's Principle of Complementarity.

of the world, it expands that with which we view the world. To fully expect to be surprised in ways that transform the very categories in which we perceive the world is the most modest attempt to honor the complexity of the world, and it is the surest way to transcend egocentric perceptions/descriptions and be able to encounter others who are not like us. If we have any affinity for social justice at all, we will need to be open to continual transformations of our consciousness, and if our affinity for social justice is not to become just another self-serving form of self-righteousness, we need to experience the effects of these transformations (Frey et al., in press).

AND IN CONCLUSION...LET US CONTINUE

As a social theorist, I have disquieting thoughts. I believe that *any* way of saying what we think or know crystallizes some aspects of what might have been said equally truly and equally importantly, and obscures others. Furthermore, any re-telling confronts a choice of whether to compound this crystallization and obscuring function, or to shift to a new pattern of crystallization and obscuring. (I try to be clear about the inherent futility and perversity of clarity in Pearce, 1989, pp. 77–87.) If theory is thought of as a representation of objective, immutable reality, successive re-tellings of the same story may be applauded as consistent and hoped to become more coherent and clear. But if theory is a form of practice as suggested here, telling the same story the same way in different contexts seems lazy or evidencing a perverse fascination with one product of the obscuring/crystallizing process.

Again because of the necessity of publication deadlines, Judith asked for what turned out to be only the first draft of this paper to be written by September 1, 1996, and the convention in which it (or something like it) was presented did not convene until November. Heeding the maxims I just proposed, in November I wanted to talk about something other than what was on my mind in September. As those who attended the session will attest, I did talk about something else because I had learned/become something then that I did not know/was not in September.[5] And here I am in another transient "now," re-writing what I did not say in November and what I wrote in September for a very different time, place, and purpose.

This business of transcending the false dichotomy between theory and practice has important implications. It affects both the content and the clarity of purpose for what and how one presents papers at conventions as well as how one does work in the world such as our project in Cupertino. In both cases, aesthetics and ethics are fully as much a part of the process as objective accuracy, and this points clearly to the area in which further work needs to be done.

We have well-developed ways of evaluating theory and practice in the "objective accuracy" face of truth. I'm thinking here of the criteria of reliability, validity, generalizability, replicability, etc. In addition, we have well-worked out vocabularies for first-person accounts of truthfulness, sincerity, etc. But we have much less well-developed vocabularies for "we" talk about good judgment in the ethical responsibility of ourselves as creative artists in theory and in practice (Chen and Pearce, 1995). Like those who are not communication theorists and practitioners, we co-construct the events and objects of our social worlds. Unlike these others, we are committed to an evolving process in which we rationally reconstruct our practices. It seems to me that we would be well served by efforts that increase the sophistication of the vocabulary and grammar for the "we" perspective that involves aesthetics, judgment, and justice and that allows us to focus on the systemic relationships among the events and objects of our social world seen from the "inside."

REFERENCES

Bazerman, C. (1987). Codifying the social scientific style: The APA *Publication Manual* as a behaviorist rhetoric. In J. S. Nelson, A. Megill, & D. N.

---

[5]I proudly declared that "I don't know a thing about communication" and asked those attending the session to join me in this affirmation. My point was that communication is not "a thing" and the cognitive process of apprehending it is not what we usually think of as "knowing."

McCloskey (Eds.), *The rhetoric of the human sciences* (pp. 125–144). Madison: University of Wisconsin Press.

Chen, V. & Pearce, W. B. (1995). Even if a thing of beauty, can a case study be a joy forever? A social constructionist approach to theory and research. In W. Leeds-Hurwitz (Ed.), *Social approaches to communication* (135–154). New York: Guilford.

Craig, R. T. & Tracy, K. (1995) Grounded practical theory: The case of intellectual discussion. *Communication Theory,* 5, 248–272.

Cronen, V. E. (1994). Coordinated management of meaning: Theory for the complexities and contradictions of everyday life. In J. Siegfried (Ed.), *The status of common sense in psychology* (pp. 183–207). Norwood, NJ: Ablex.

Frey, L., Pearce, W. B., Pollock, M. Artz, L., & Murphy, B. O. (in press). Looking for justice in all the wrong places: On a communication approach to social justice. *Communication Research.* In press.

Koestler, A. (1978). *Janus: A summing up.* New York: Random House.

Pearce, W. B. (1989). *Communication and the human condition.* Carbondale: Southern Illinois University Press.

Pearce, W. B. (1994). *Interpersonal communication: Making social worlds.* New York: HarperCollins.

Pearce, W. B. (1995). A sailing guide for social constructionists. In W. Leeds-Hurwitz (Ed.), *Social approaches to communication* (pp. 88–113). New York: Guilford.

Pearce, W. B. & Littlejohn, S. W. (1997). *Moral conflict: When social worlds collide.* Thousand Oaks, CA: Sage.

Shotter, J. & Gergen, K. J. (1994). Social construction: Knowledge, self, others, and continuing the conversation. In S. Deetz (Ed.), *Communication yearbook/17* (pp. 3–33). Thousand Oaks, CA: Sage.

Toulmin, S. (1990). *Cosmopolis: The hidden agenda of modernity.* Chicago: University of Chicago Press.

Waltzer, M. (1997). The idea of civil society. *Kettering Review. (Winter),* 8–22.

Wilbur, K. (1996). *A brief history of everything.* Boston: Shambhalla Publications.

Social Interpretations, Social Theories

Wendy Leeds-Hurwitz

University of Wisconsin, Parkside

One response to all of the discussion within the discipline of communication the past few years about how to define communication, about what name our association should have, about whether we should properly be described as a field or a discipline, is to suggest that we need to take the time to discover what common ground cuts across all the different approaches to the study of communication, to learn what it is that we all share. I would suggest that we begin at a basic level by making explicit the major components of social theory that we hold to be self-evident. (I take social theory to be a term referring to large ideas about how people act with other people.) We will each bring different interpretations, but perhaps we can discover the similarities underlying superficial distinctions. Such a conclusion should contribute to a better integration of knowledge within the discipline; it will serve a "taking stock" function as we ask what it is that we share, and how the different questions pursued by communication researchers over the past few decades are related. As there is a time for pursuing separate interests, there must also be a time for synthesis.

This would have a secondary benefit: there has been a continued, if quiet, discussion over the past few decades about the need to minimize the significance of borders between disciplines, increasing the exchange of knowledge and the development of interdisciplinary research projects (Leeds-Hurwitz, 1994; Klein, 1990). At best, interdisciplinary research is designed to take into account what has been learned in not just one but several fields of study; as a result, it should generally be broader in scope than research based upon the questions and answers of a single discipline. Clearly people who cannot cross within-discipline boundaries are not good candidates for crossing more substantial disciplinary boundaries. Communication cannot usefully contribute to an interdisciplinary conversation about social theory if it remains impossible even to talk to colleagues across very narrow theoretical groupings within the discipline. And we will make our interests more obvious to others if we are able to clarify what ideas, themes, topics, questions, we hold in common.

I would like to contribute in both of these ends today by proposing a series of topics that seem to be central to social theorizing in the field, regardless of particular theoretical approach. These are underlying issues central to the development of the larger theories that spark specific research questions. These topics may seem obvious, and they may seem quite broad, but they should at least be familiar to everyone. In this instance, at least, I would prefer to provoke the comment "well, of course," rather than "what a novel idea!"

1. MEANING CREATION

How people create meaning for themselves and for others in the social world can be studied anywhere, any time, for it is the primary human activity. As such, it should be, and often actually is, a central topic for communication researchers. As Pearce (1989) suggests, "Making 'meaning' is not an optional activity in which persons sometimes engage; it is part of what it means to be a human being" (p. 65). Viewing meaning as a central topic in communication implicitly requires an assumption of at least some version of the social construction of reality. That is, it implies that people can create meaning for themselves, just as they can create other elements of the social world.

Concern with the creation of meaning in the social world leads to the following questions: Just how do we create meaning? If we say that we construct meaning jointly with others, how do we actually do this? Can it be observed in process? If so, how is it best observed? For me, the production of meaning is most readily studied through detailed observations of actual behavior, especially when matched to extended interviews intended to encourage discussion of intention, although I understand that others have found other ways to study meaning creation.

The attempt to observe the creation of meaning incorporates a secondary question: How are small behaviors used to convey larger values and ideas; how are even the smallest, most mundane choices understood to convey meanings? That people create social meanings even for the most minor details implies investigation of how even small, seemingly insignificant, details of language, behavior, or material culture stand for and convey ideas that are important to us and to those we know. As Geertz (1973) points out, "Small facts speak to large issues" (p. 23). Concern for nonverbal behavior does not imply ignoring verbal behavior, for it is partially through verbal descriptions of what was done and what it meant to the participants that we come to understand nonverbal behavior. However, language is notoriously slippery, easily permitting slightly different interpretations by each of the participants. It is harder for material culture to be so open to diverse readings; generally an object, a particular food, an item of clothing, is either present or not, and mere presence or absence can convey some meaning.

2. CULTURE/COMMUNICATION

The connections between culture and communication can be studied in any context, for our culture always influences our communication choices. We can only act on what we know, and culture is, among other definitions, a cover term for all that we know. The link between culture and

communication is most obvious at those times when cultures overlap, influencing one another, as on occasions when people of different cultural backgrounds come together. For me, this is potentially the central issue in the study of intercultural communication, but one which often has been skirted (Leeds-Hurwitz, 1992). In communication, as in anthropology and sociology, until recently it was common to study each subculture, each ethnic group, each community, apart from others, an isolated unit. This is now changing, and it is more common to study the combination of subcultures, ethnic groups, communities, and their mutual influences.

There has been a recent push for research combining the study of the influence of culture with the study of interpersonal communication or social interaction in general (see Carbaugh [1990]; Cooley [1983], among others), a push which is long overdue. As Sapir pointed out many years ago, "The true locus of culture is in the interactions of specific individuals" (1949, p. 515), so we must base our discussions of the abstract concept culture on observations of actual behavior.

Concern for the connection between culture and communication leads to the following questions: What is the role of culture in shaping our expectations of communicative behaviors? What happens when individuals with different cultural understandings interact? How do we resolve the difficulties and misunderstandings that result? In an increasingly multicultural world, these are critical questions requiring answers.

3. INDIVIDUAL/GROUP

The connections between the individual and the larger group or society can be studied in any context where some individual statement or display draws heavily on societal expectations, or where the individual acts out a particular societal role. We act by turns as interpreters of the discourse of others in the society or as producers of discourse ourselves for others (Greimas, 1987, p. 201), whether for rituals or for less formal examples of text, such as conversation. People learn first from interpreting what others do, and later contribute new and unique behaviors to the range of what is understood as possible. Each individual contributes to the larger community expectations: taking what they understand to be the norms of the groups within which they function, revising as necessary, and re-introducing the revised versions back into the larger society. Tambiah points out that "no one performance of a rite, however rigidly prescribed, is exactly the same as another performance" (1985, p. 125). This is true of mundane secular rituals as well as true of elaborate religious rites. Each individual simultaneously draws upon and expands the societal norms, contributing their originality to the group's traditions.

This concern for the fact that we are each simultaneously individuals, doing what we want, and members of some larger group or society, doing what is expected and required of us by others, leads to the following questions: How is the influence of the larger society actually experienced by particular individuals? To what extent do we take into consideration what we want to do versus what others expect of us? What happens if we lean too heavily in either direction?

4. TRADITION/CREATIVITY

Although the social world appears as something real, existing in its current form for others as well as for us, it is in fact built out of our own actions. Every time we act, we contribute to either the continuity of old traditions or the creation of new traditions (or, often, simultaneously to both). This can be studied in any context, for each individual always stands between what has occurred in the past and what will happen in the future. It is especially important in a context where the forces for continuity are confronted by forces requiring the creation of something new and different. As Hsu (1985) points out: "If everyone acts as individualized individuals, no society is possible. If everyone acts in complete conformity with others, there will be no differences between human beings and bees. Human ways of life are obviously somewhere in between these extremes" (p. 25). In most contexts

of interaction, participants attempt to design a path somewhere between chaos and bees.

Orchestrating an organized event (for example, the celebration of a rite of passage such as a wedding) is an intensely creative act, requiring much knowledge of the past in order to recreate it anew for the present; creativity does not come from nowhere, but most often is an expansion of the expected. We need to learn more of cultural creativity of this sort, to learn more of how social actors manipulate what they have experienced in the past in order to create a new present (Leeds-Hurwitz & Sigman with Sullivan, 1995). Culture is often assumed to be static, yet it is actually dynamic, always in a state of flux. To continue my example, each wedding is an opportunity for a particular couple to "talk back" to their own traditions, to make their own unique contribution to the cultural dialogue. All traditions are open to change by all participants; this change is appropriately described as cultural creativity.

Concern for the connections between tradition and change leads to the following questions: Given that the world constantly changes, how does the tension between doing what is considered normal and right and doing what is new and innovative actually play out? Each event is unique, yet each contributes to our understanding of what is traditional; how does this actually work? How do people decide what to change and what to keep the same? And whose version of tradition comes to be followed?

5. PROCESS/PRODUCT

Social products have no less reality than physical products, and are no less dependent upon a process of creation. Geertz (1971) tells us that "meaningful forms…have as good a claim to public existence as horses, stones, and trees, and are therefore as susceptible to objective investigation and systematic analysis as these apparently harder realities" (p. x). An evening of dinner and conversation may not leave much in the way of a physical structure for later analysis, but it exists and can have an impact on our ideas and behaviors, thus we treat it as a concrete thing; currently we even have the technology to record it if we so choose, making it yet more tangible.

Bourdieu (1990) demonstrates another sense of the connection between process and product:

> *Social functions are social fictions. And the rites of institution* create *the person they institute as king, knight, priest or professor by forging his social image, fashioning the representation that he can and must give as a moral person, that is, as a plenipotentiary, representative or spokesman of a group. But they also create him in another sense. By giving him a name, a title, which defines, institutes, and constitutes him, they summon him to become what he is, or rather, what he has to be; they order him to* fulfill *his function, to take his place in the game, in the fiction, to play the game, to act out the function. (p. 195, his emphasis)*

In the field of communication there has been a recent shift from a focus on product to an emphasis on process. Certainly when the topic is an aspect of social interaction, it is generally far more important to study how that interaction happened than to study the end product alone. Hobart (1990, p. 314) refers to the desire to freeze the society under study as a "cryogenic trend," a marvelous metaphor. But it is the combination of the two that is most significant: we study what is stable (structure, product) because that is what we can most readily perceive; this is one way of coping with the instability of what is more essential to study (process).

Concern for both product and process leads to the following questions: How does the process, the constantly changing moment, create a product, something that can be pointed to as having particular boundaries? Where are the boundaries of the event set? Who sets them?

6. CONFLICT/CONSENSUS

In a group of individuals, what one person wants is not always the same as what every other person wants, leading to inevitable conflicts, small or large. Groups generally manage to come to some sort of resolution, to reach consensus at least with those considered to be significant members of the group. Berger and Kellner (1964) point out that "sufficient similarity in the biographically accumulated stocks of experience…facilitate the described reality-constructing process" (p. 67). In other words, it is easier to establish a relationship, to reach agreement on ground rules, when the individuals concerned share a large number of expectations, though we generally learn more from those with whom we do not share as much.

Given a concern for the resolution of conflicts, the following questions are implied: How are conflicts expressed, and how are they resolved? How is it possible to do what everyone wants, when they want different things? Given the diversity of experience and opinion with most groups, how is consensus ever achieved?

7. IDENTITY

Identity refers to who we view ourselves to be, who others view us to be, and how these two are reconciled. For the majority of our lives, we are accepted as private individuals, but on a few particular occasions we put ourselves on public display, and our identity (jointly with ideas, behaviors, assumptions) may become a topic for public discussion. This is sometimes referred to as the constitution of the public self (Lessi, 1993). On most occasions familiarity with group expectations remains under the control of the individual, and so is essentially private, but public events are carefully planned in advance, and consciously given a particular structure and design, thus they are particularly interesting as deliberate statements of identity: "As the flow of living so often is not, public events are put together to communicate comparatively well-honed messages" (Handelman, 1990, p. 15).

An interest in how identity is displayed in the connections between private opinions and public events leads to the following questions: How does a physical individual develop a unique social identity? Since all of us are members of multiple groups, how do we learn to display appropriate membership signs to one group at a time? Can we display membership signs to multiple groups simultaneously? What is the connection between the private and the public persona?

CONCLUSION

Meaning creation; culture/communication; individual/group; tradition/creativity; process/product; conflict/consensus; identity. These are only a beginning, the barest bones of a start to a discipline-wide conversation about what issues, topics, questions hold sufficient interest to bind us together. Obviously not everyone will agree with this list, but perhaps it will begin some productive discussions about what list would be more appropriate. Even this brief proposal will have value if it encourages others to continue the conversation.

REFERENCES

Berger, P. and H. Kellner. (1964). Marriage and the Construction of Reality: An Exercise in the Microsociology of Knowledge. *Diogenes, 46,* 1–21.

Bourdieu, P. (1990). *In Other Words: Essays Towards a Reflexive Sociology.* Stanford, CA: Stanford University Press.

Carbaugh, D. (Ed.). (1990). *Cultural Communication and Intercultural Contact.* Hillsdale, NJ: Lawrence Erlbaum Associates.

Cooley, R. E. (1983). Codes and Contexts: An Argument for their Description. In W. B. Gudykunst (Ed.), *Intercultural Communication Theory: Current Perspectives* (pp. 241–251). Beverly Hills, CA: Sage Publications.

Geertz, C. (1971). Introduction. In C. Geertz (Ed.), *Myth, Symbol, and Culture* (pp. ix–xi). New York, NY: Norton.

Geertz, C. (1973). *The interpretation of cultures.* New York, NY: Basic Books.

Greimas, A. J. (1987). *On Meaning: Selected Writings in Semiotic Theory.* Translated by Paul J. Perron and Frank H. Collins. Minneapolis, MN: University of Minnesota Press.

Handelman, D. (1990). *Models and Mirrors: Towards an Anthropology of Public Events.* Cambridge, England: Cambridge University Press.

Hobart, M. (1990). Who do you think you are? The authorized Balinese. In R. Fardon (Ed.), *Localizing strategies: Regional traditions of ethnographic writing* (pp. 303–338). Edinburgh/Washington DC: Scottish Academic Press/Smithsonian Institution Press.

Hsu, F. L. K. (1985). The self in cross-cultural perspective. In A. J. Marsella, G. DeVos, & F. L. K. Hsu (Eds.), *Culture and self: Asian and Western perspectives* (pp. 24–55). New York & London: Tavistock.

Klein, J. T. (1990). *Interdisciplinarity: History, Theory, & Practice.* Detroit, MI: Wayne State University Press.

Leeds-Hurwitz, W. (1992). *Connecting Interpersonal to Intercultural Communication by way of Ethnography.* Keynote address delivered to the Ethnography of Communication Conference: Ways of Speaking, Ways of Knowing, Portland, Oregon.

Leeds-Hurwitz, W. (1994). Crossing Disciplinary Boundaries: The Macy Foundation Conferences on Cybernetics as a Case Study in Multidisciplinary Communication. *Cybernetica: Journal of the International Association for Cybernetics, 3/4,* 349–369.

Leeds-Hurwitz, W., & S. J. Sigman, with S. J. Sullivan. (1995). Social Communication Theory: Communication Structures and Performed Invocations, A Revision of Scheflen's Notion of Programs. In S. J. Sigman (Ed.), *The Consequentiality of Communication* (pp. 163–204). Hillsdale, NJ: Lawrence Erlbaum Associates.

Lessi, T. M. (1993). Punctuation in the constitution of public identities: Primary and secondary sequences in the Scopes trial. *Communication Theory, 2,* 91–111.

Pearce, W. B. (1989). *Communication and the Human Condition.* Carbondale, IL: Southern Illinois University Press.

Sapir, E. (1949). Language. In D. Mandelbaum (Ed.), *Selected writings of Edward Sapir* (pp. 7–32). Berkeley, CA: University of California Press. (Original work published 1933)

Tambiah, S. J. (1985). *Culture, Thought, and Social Action: An Anthropological Perspective.* Cambridge, MA: Harvard University Press.

Social Theory and Dialogue

John R. Stewart
University of Washington

My first response to the announcement of this panel was, "What shall we agree 'Social Theory' means?" I notice, for example, that a recent Social Theory catalogue from one scholarly press features books on philosophy of ecology, an analysis of the links between gender relations and the organization of household space, a report on the spread of Public Journalism, and a book arguing that "reinvigorated democratic politics can and should supersede conventional economic reasoning as a basis for decisions about technology." On the other hand, published work by the members of this panel indicates that we see Social Theory including relational approaches to interpersonal communicating, conceptual and practical ways to enhance public dialogue, narrative in social practice, and social theorizing about language. In some venues the term "Social Theory" labels abstractions about social processes, and in others it highlights the claim that theorizing itself is a social accomplishment. But whether the emphasis is on social content or social process, and whether the researcher is a philosopher, critical theorist, feminist, architect, journalist, political theorist, literary analyst, management theorist, linguist, or communication scholar, social theory across the human studies implicates a view of humans-in-relation, and this is why the topic is an important one for communication scholars to address.

One increasingly prominent term in many social theorists' accounts of humans-in-relation is "dialogue." In the last decade this construct has enjoyed a remarkable renaissance. For example, in 1990 the University of Chicago Press published anthropologist Tullio Maranhao's collection, *The Interpretation of Dialogue,* which surveys meanings and uses of this construct in classical philosophy, literary theory, political theory, and what Maranhao calls "Dialogical Anthropology" (Maranhao, 1990). Since about the same time, British theoretical physicist David Bohm has been focusing on closely related practical matters in books and seminars that urge managers to cope with the challenges of globalization and continuous geometric change by learning how to create spaces in their organizations for dialogue. In his role as organizational theorist and consultant, Bohm emphasizes that the *"dia"* in *dia-logos* means not "two" but *"through,"* so that "dialogue" in his lexicon is a term for the co-creation of meaning through and among up to 30 or 40 interlocutors (Bohm, 1990, p. 1). William Isaacs at MIT's Sloan School of Management has applied Bohm's thinking in the Dialogue Project within the Center for Organizational Learning there (Isaacs, 1994), and Peter Senge (1990) has similarly made dialogue the centerpiece of his design for what he calls "learning organizations," a corporate culture that Ford Motor Company and Boeing are currently attempting to develop. Among academics, philosopher Calvin Schrag has prominently featured dialogue in his response to the postmodern deconstructions of subjectivity (Schrag, 1986) and rationality (Schrag, 1992), and psychologist Edward Sampson has integrated dialogic theory and feminism in his radical challenge of contemporary psychological thinking called *Celebrating the Other: A Dialogic Account of Human Nature* (Sampson, 1993). Complementary projects are underway in western Europe, Canada, and Australia. For example, for more than a decade, Norwegian communication theorist Ragnar Rommetveit has been developing what he calls a "dialogically-based social-cognitive approach to human cognition and communication" (Rommetveit 1988, 1990), and Scandinavian University Press recently published a collection of works elaborating Rommetveit's perspective entitled *The Dialogical Alternative: Towards a Theory of Language and Mind* (Wold, 1992). In Cambridge, Massachusetts, family therapists Laura and Richard Chasin, Sallyann Roth, Margaret Herzig, Carol Baker, and their colleagues have anchored their conceptually and praxically-innovative Public Conversations Project on the distinctions between public conversation as debate and public conversation as dialogue, and have had a remarkable impact on some advocates on both sides of such inflammatory disputes as the ones involving homophobia and pro-life versus pro-choice forces (Roth, 1993; Roth, Chasin, Chasin, Becker, and Herzig, 1992). Even closer to home, New Hampshire communication scholar John Shotter is becoming increasingly known for his rhetorical-dialogic version of social constructionism (Shotter, 1992, 1993a, 1993b), and recently Guilford Press released Leslie Baxter and Barbara Montgomery's innovative account of interpersonal communication entitled *Relating: Dialogue and Dialectics* (Baxter & Montgomery, 1996). Clearly, the notion of dialogue is central to many current theoretical and practical social theory projects across the human studies.

Like many dialogic social theorists, Rommetveit claims that his approach to dialogue integrates ideas from several intellectual traditions. Rommetveit (1992) mentions William James' pragmatism, Mead's social interactionism, Berger and Luckmann's social constructivism, Wittgenstein's account of language, Habermas' critical-emancipatory social science, Gadamer's philosophical hermeneutics, and the linguistic semantics of Naess and Uhlenbeck (p. 24). Sampson explains why the work of several feminist scholars, most prominently Harding (1986, 1991), and Code (1991), also belong on this list of seminal thinkers. But the most influential contributors to this approach to social theorizing were two early twentieth-century thinkers with the initials MB; every contemporary social theorist of dialogue I've read at least partly anchors his or her dialogical theorizing in the works of Mikhail Bakhtin

and/or Martin Buber. In the last two or three decades, Buber's influence on social theorists has been diminished by his sometimes-impenetrable prose, his self-identification as an "arch Jew," and the fact that his work was associated with such intellectually-suspect programs as humanistic psychology and encounter groups. But Bakhtin and his collaborator Volosinov are currently the darlings of dialogic social theorists. Maranhao, Rommetveit, Sampson, Shotter, and Baxter and Montgomery directly and liberally credit Bakhtin, and several other social theorists develop ideas derived from Bakhtin's writing. As a contribution to the clarification of where this version of social theory is currently moving, I think it would be useful briefly to identify the primary insights from Bakhtin[1] that dialogic theorists appropriate.[2] Although these insights will be of obvious relevance to speech communication theorizing, teaching, and training, space limits will prevent me from doing more than mentioning applications here.

A PRÉCIS OF SEVEN PRIMARY ELEMENTS OF DIALOGIC SOCIAL THEORY

1. The Centrality of Meaning and Response

Although "beginning" points always depend on punctuation, all social theory could be said to begin with the recognition that humans live in worlds of meaning, not worlds of things. Rommetveit (1992) offers a dialogic version of this claim in three of his 24 "basic theses" of his perspective:

> **(3)** *Different potential aspects of our "external" world (i.e. of objects, events, actions and other* not-yet-verbally described *states of affairs) are generated when states of affairs are made sense of and "brought into language" from different positions.*

---

[1]The question of authorship of materials attributed to Bakhtin, Volosinov, and Medvedev is not yet finally answered. For a review of some comments on this issue, see Stewart (1995), pp. 165–167. In this paper I treat Bakhtin's corpus and *Marxism and the Philosophy of Language,* attributed to Volosinov by Harvard University Press, as Bakhtinian.

[2]Along the way, it will be possible to discover whether and how Buber's work is still relevant to this thinking. But space limits prevent any development of this point here.

(4) *Aspects of that "external world"…tend to become objectified and acquire the status of shared social realities.*

(5) *Such…background conditions constrain the range of possible human perspectives…, yet themselves as a rule remain unacknowledged….(p. 22)*

Shotter (1993b) makes the same point when he notes that "…there are no extralinguistic 'somethings' in the world merely awaiting precise or accurate description" (p. 182). And, as Baxter and Montgomery (1996) put it, "…social life exists in and through people's communicative practices" (p. 4). The point all these authors make is that the basic realities that social theory works with are meanings negotiated communicatively, that is, in verbal-nonverbal language, not objective phenomena in some "external world."

Bakhtin (1986) underscored an enormously important feature of this meaning-making when he noted that "all real and integral understanding is actively *responsive*" (p. 69, italics added). No human participant in meaning-making is Eve or Adam, Bakhtin reminded his readers; none is "after all, the first speaker, the one who disturbs the eternal silence of the universe" (p. 69). Thus, "there can be no such thing as an isolated utterance. It always presupposes utterances that precede and follow it. No one utterance can be either the first or the last. Each is only a link in the chain…"(p. 136).

Why is this point so significant? First, because it anchors dialogism's rejection of the Cartesian-Kantian concept of subjectivity that still dominates much of Western thinking, despite the challenges by virtually every postmodern thinker, from Heidegger (1962), through Derrida (1974), Foucault (1972), Gadamer (1989), and Lyotard (1984), to Wittgenstein (1953) and Rorty (1979). Descartes, Kant, and other Enlightenment thinkers viewed subjects as *initiators* of *actions,* and this punctuation of social reality facilitated the development of concepts of individuality, intentionality, responsibility, and control that still pervade Western systems of philosophy, politics, jurisprudence, psychology, linguistics, and communication. Bakhtin underscored the narrowness of this Enlightenment

view of subjectivity by simply reminding his readers of the obvious point that every human is born of a mother and into a physical setting, relationship network, and linguistic-communicative soup that constrains (without determining) *everything* the human thinks and does. This altered understanding of the nature of humanity has enormous consequences, perhaps the most important of which was originally identified by the Greek term, *hubris.* That term originally meant forgetting-that-you're-not-a-god. Cartesian-Kantian subjects are much more likely to suffer from hubris than are subjects who recognize themselves as responders; in fact, some of the former have actually believed that they can predict and control and that their investigations can achieve certainty and closure, whereas responders do not. So some of the most hallowed tenets of what has come to be known as the western scientific world view are called into question by the acknowledgement by dialogic social theorists of the responsive nature of human being. This cornerstone of dialogic understanding and acting renders the human forever a *co*-participant in meaning-making, rather than an initiator or controller.

The second reason Bakhtin's notion of response is so important is that it compels systemic thinking. If every human event is responsive, then it is impossible to understand any of them without attending as closely as possible to all-that-which-is-responded-to, namely *context.* Social theorists, of course, highlight the importance of the *human* context that frames all meaning-making, and dialogical social theorists pay primary attention to the verbal-nonverbal *communicative* elements of context. Research preferences for *in situ* data gathering—as in participant observation and ethnographic studies—and ecological validity—as in other forms of interpretive or qualitative research—are just two outcomes of this recognition of the importance of context. Two additional important results of this orientation are Gadamer's (1989) insight that every text can best be understood as a response to a central question, and the disinclination of social theorists to apply linear causal analyses to human events because such analyses inevitably oversimplify the contributions of context.

2. Critique of Monologist Assumptions

Although most dialogical theorizing is affirmative, there is also a critical component, and it focuses on the reductive oversimplifications of monological thinking. As Baxter and Montgomery (1996) summarize, Bakhtin's "intellectual project was a critique of theories that reduced the unfinalizable, open, and heterogeneous nature of social life to determinate, closed, totalizing concepts" (p. 24). Shotter (1993) appropriates this critique when he insists throughout his treatment of conversational realities that the human world of meaning is a "diffuse…unordered hurly-burly or bustle" (p. 7). An important implication of this basic assumption about the human world is that understandings of, or knowledge claims about this hurly-burly world cannot coherently be more determinate or absolute than the phenomena they describe. This means that a dialogical stance is necessarily indeterminate, anti-teleological, and in one sense "relativist." I say, "in one sense," because the construct "relativism" can only be meaningful if one assumes the possibility of a completely "non-relative" or absolute human reality that can be used to define what is "relative." Since dialogic social theory fundamentally denies this possibility, the term loses much of its coherence. On the other hand, social theorists and practitioners are as concerned as other serious researchers about credible findings. "Anything and everything" certainly does not "go" in dialogical social theory; there are constraints, but they are clearly topic- and field-dependent. As Rommetveit (1992) puts it, "Human cognition and communication are, within limits set by such constraints, characterized by perspectival relativity" (p. 22). This sense in which social theory is relativist raises important ethical and research issues that dialogical theorists continue to address.

3. The Dialectic of Unity and Difference

Both Buber and Bakhtin emphasized that dialogue consists simultaneously of division and fusion, individuality and meeting, uniqueness and contact.

For Buber (1965) this meant in part that interpersonal conflict is dialogic whenever the parties actively confirm their opponents and their positions while continuing to maintain their own position *and* to construct meaning together (pp. 35– 39), in this way working the unresolvable tension between individuality and contact. Bakhtin used the terms "centripetal and centrifugal" to label these forces of division and contact, and similarly emphasized their simultaneity. Centripetal forces are those that heighten difference and centrifugal forces promote sameness. As Bakhtin (1981) summarized, "Every utterance participates in the 'unitary language' (in its centripetal forces and tendencies) and at the same time partakes of social and historical heteroglossia (the centrifugal, stratifying forces)" (p. 272). Baxter and Montgomery (1996) insist that only Bakhtin's both-and, yin-yang theoretical perspective is adequate for understanding social life. Consistent with its rejection of monologic oversimplifications, dialogic social theory attempts to understand and describe both the dividing and the unifying dimensions, aspects, or moments of the human events on which it focuses.

4. Chronotope

"Chronotope" is another prominent term in Bakhtin's corpus. As a literary theorist he used the construct in descriptions of the form and substance of the novel. He defined chronotope, "(literally, 'time space') [as] the intrinsic connectedness of temporal and spatial relationships that are artistically expressed in literature" (Bakhtin, 1981, p. 84). Bakhtin noted that his sense of the term borrowed from Einstein's Theory of Relativity in that chronotope "expresses the inseparability of space and time" (Bakhtin, 1981, p. 84). For Bakhtin, the significance of chronotope to meaning-making is global and profound: "Every entry into the sphere of meaning," he wrote, "is accomplished only through the gates of the chronotope" (1981, p. 258). Context and meaning, in other words, are mutually determinative. The space-time world of a text is socially constructed, maintained, and changed in the dialogue between co-participants (author and reader), and chronotope functions both to enable and to constrain this dialogue.

I have already noted how Bakhtin's foregrounding of response compels systemic thinking; chronotope is the specific construct he used to operationalize this move. John Shotter follows Bakhtin when he labels chronotopes "providential spaces" in order to emphasize their enabling/constraining functions. Shotter explains, for example, how arguments over both conceptual and practical issues take place in a *living tradition* that "is rooted both in peoples' embodied knowledge and in their embodied evaluative attitudes" (1993a, p. 153). One cannot follow, participate in, or critique such arguments without understanding how they simultaneously emerge out of and contribute to the development of these living traditions. Shotter's appropriation of Bakhtin's treatment of context and application to the ethics of communication are apparent when he explains the linguistic nature and function of these providential spaces.

> It is the socio-cultural, socio-historical nature of *this* intralinguistically created *textual context, as it is temporally (and spatially) developed by what is said, that everyone involved must take into account (when it is their turn to speak or act)—if, that is, their actions are to be judged as appropriate to it. It is this, the realization that as one speaks, a temporal-spatial network of intralinguistic references is developed into which one's future speech* must *be directed, that I think is the key to the further understanding of the ethical nature of our mental processes. For this network is a "providential space" of joint action with two major properties: first, it carries within it the traces of one's socio-cultural history, and one* ought *to act within it in such a way as to sustain the resources it contains; but second, in* responding *to the "invitations," etc., available to one from one's place or position within it, one acts in it in one's own unique, creative, novel way. However, if one respects its providential nature, then one's creativity is always intelligible creativity, because it takes place within* the *forms of the "providential space" in question. (Shotter, 1993a, p. 118)*

For dialogic social theorists, in short, chronotope is a useful way to operationalize the praxical dimensions of context.

5. Utterance as Molecule

Sampson (1993) makes a great deal of the differences between the monologic orientation of the traditional approaches to psychology that he is attempting to replace and his dialogic orientation. One key distinction between these orientations is the site or location of the primary phenomenon that the theorist, researcher, or clinician investigates. Monologic psychology celebrates the "self" as an individual, bounded container located "inside" the human and thus accessible only indirectly and inferentially. Dialogic psychology takes as its primary phenomenon conversation, talk, or addressed utterance, because it is precisely here that humanity happens. As Sampson (1993) summarizes, "Because we have become so intent on searching deeply within the individual's psyche for the answers to all our questions about human nature, we usually fail to see what sits right before us, a dominating feature of our lives with others: conversations. It is time now to take conversations seriously" (p. 97).

Rommetveit (1992) makes the same point in slightly different terms. If one wants to study cognition, he argues, one must study dialogue. Developmentally, "the human infant is…dyadically embedded and dialogically operative," and "the developing human mind is hence dialogically constituted" (p. 22). Here Rommetveit is echoing both Bakhtin and his contemporary Vygotsky who maintained that thinking, minding, or meaning-making is first social and only later gets construed as *intra*personal. Vygotsky (1978) cited as an example a child's pointing gesture:

> The child's unsuccessful attempt [at pointing] engenders a reaction not from the object he [sic] seeks but from another person. Consequently, the primary meaning of that unsuccessful grasping movement is established by others…. It becomes a true gesture only after it objectively manifests all

*the functions of pointing for others and is under-
stood by others as such a gesture (p. 56).*

*Every function in the child's cultural develop-
ment appears twice: first, on the social level, and
later, on the individual level; first between people
(interpsychological) and then inside the child (in-
trapsychological). (p. 57)*

The child's first meaning-making is not linguistic,
but it is communicative, and this is the root sense
of the key term, "utterance." In dialogic social theory, "utterance" labels the basic unit of verbal and/
or nonverbal communicative behavior that embodies the human's fundamentally social way of
being-in-the-world.

6. Addressivity

Addressivity is one prominent term dialogic social
theorists use to highlight the "aimed," contact-
functioning quality of this behavior. As Baxter and
Montgomery (1996) note, Bakhtin argued that, because of its addressivity, "the expression of an utterance was constructed as much by the listener as
by the particular speaker. In this sense, an utterance can never be 'owned' by a single speaker; utterances exist at the boundaries between a person
and the particular other and the generalized other"
(Baxter & Montgomery, 1996, p. 29). Shotter
(1993a) also makes the point that "the 'voice' of
the other whom one is addressing is always present
in one's own utterance," a phenomenon which,
Shotter notes, Bakhtin labelled being "internally
dialogized." In Bakhtin's (1981) words, "The word
is born in a dialogue as a living rejoinder with it;
the word is shaped in dialogic interaction with an
alien word that is already in the object.... Every
word is directed toward an *answer* and cannot escape the profound influence of the answering word
that it anticipates" (pp. 279–280).

Rommetveit's (1992) term for addressivity is
"attunement to the attunement of the other." He
identifies this quality as "a distinctive and pervasive feature of the prototypical human discourse
situation" (p. 22). From Rommetveit's perspective, "mutual understanding on the part of conversation partners is contingent upon reciprocally

adjusted perspective setting and perspective taking." And this "reciprocal adjustment of perspectives is achieved by an 'attunement to the
attunement of the other' by which states of affairs
are brought into joint focus of attention, made
sense of, and talked about from a position temporarily adopted by both participants in the communication" (p. 23).

Parenthetically, Buber also underscored the
importance of addressivity when he contrasted the
"basic movement of the life of dialogue" as "turning towards the other," as contrasted with the "re-
flexion" that characterizes monologue (Buber,
1965, pp. 20–23), when he argued that "the importance of the spoken word is grounded in the fact
that it does not want to remain with the speaker. It
reaches out toward a hearer, it lays hold of him
[sic], it even makes the hearer into a speaker, if perhaps only a soundless one" (Buber, 1965, p. 112),
and when he summarized that dialogue ends when
address "breaks off or breaks down."

Dialogic speech, all these authors agree, is directed speech, speech meant-for-another, utterance that is oriented-for, focused, aimed, or
addressed.

7. Utterance and Self as Relational

I have already noted Sampson's (1993) argument
that, following Mead, Vygotsky, Wittgenstein, and
Bakhtin, the human self can only be understood
accurately when it is understood relationally. Bakhtin's (1986) metaphor for this point is especially
poignant. "Just as the body is formed initially in
the mother's womb (body)," he writes, "a person's
consciousness awakens wrapped in another's consciousness" (p. 138). Bakhtin (1986) is similarly
unambiguous about utterance. *Everything* that is
said, he maintains,

*is located outside the 'soul' of the speaker and
does not belong only to him [sic]. The word cannot
be assigned to a single speaker. The author
(speaker) has his own inalienable right to the
word, but the listener also has his rights, and those
whose voices are heard in the word before the author comes upon it also have their rights (after all,*

there are no words that belong to no one).
(pp. 121–122)

The expression of this idea attributed to Volosinov (1973) is just as clear:

> *In point of fact,* word is a two-sided act. *It is determined equally by* whose *word it is and* for whom *it is meant. As word, it is precisely* the product of the reciprocal relationship between speaker and listener, addresser and addressee...*A word is a bridge thrown between myself and another. (p. 66)*

CONCLUSION

This expression of the Bakhtinian view of self and utterance brings the account of dialogic social theory full circle, back to the centrality of response: "Any utterance—the finished written utterance not excepted—makes response to something and is calculated to be responded to in turn. It is but one link in a continuous chain of speech performances. Each...carries on the work of its predecessors, polemicizing with them, expecting active, responsive understanding, and anticipating such understanding in return" (Volosinov, 1973, p. 72).

This is the spirit in which I offer this panel contribution. Given the available space, I've only been able to summarize Bakhtin's central constructs, hint at similarities between his dialogicism and Buber's, and nod in the direction of some implications for communication theorizing, teaching, and training. But this paper will have succeeded if it prompts your response.

REFERENCES

Bakhtin, M. M. (1981). *The dialogic imagination.* (M. Holquist, Ed., C. Emerson & M. Holquist, Trans.). Austin, TX: University of Texas Press.

Bakhtin, M. M. (1986). *Speech genres and other late essays.* (V. W. McGee, Trans.). Austin, TX: University of Texas Press.

Baxter, L. A. & Montgomery, B. M. (1996). *Relating: Dialogue and dialectics.* New York: Guilford.

Bohm, D. (1990). *On dialogue.* Ojai, CA: David Bohm Seminars.

Buber, M. (1965a). *Between man and man.* (R. G. Smith, Trans.). New York: Macmillan.

Buber, M. (1965b). *The knowledge of man.* (R. G. Smith and M. Friedman, Trans.). New York: Harper.

Code, L. (1991). *What can she know? Feminist theory and the construction of knowledge.* Ithaca, NY: Cornell University Press.

Derrida, J. (1974). *Of grammatology.* (G. C. Spivak, Trans.). Baltimore: Johns Hopkins Press.

Foucault, M. (1972). *The archeology of knowledge.* (A. M. Sheridan, Trans.). London: Tavistock.

Gadamer, H. G. (1989). *Truth and method.* Second, rev. ed. (J. Weinsheimer & D. G. Marshall, Trans.). New York: Crossorad.

Harding, S. (1986). *The science question in feminism.* Ithaca, NY: Cornell University Press.

Harding, S, (1991). *Whose science? Whose knowledge? Thinking from women's lives.* Ithaca, NY: Cornell University Press.

Heidegger, M. (1962). *Being and time.* (J. Macquarrie & E. Robinson, Trans.). New York: Harper & Row.

Isaacs, W. (1994). Dialogue. *The fifth discipline fieldbook: Strategies and tools for building a learning organization* (pp. 357–364). (P. Senge, A. Kleiner, C. Roberts, R. B. Ross, & B. J. Smith, Eds.). New York: Doubleday.

Lyotard, J. F. (1984). *The postmodern condition: A report of knowledge.* Manchester: Univ. of Manchester Press.

Maranhao, T. (Ed.) (1990). *The interpretation of dialogue.* Chicago: University of Chicago Press.

Rommetveit, R. (1988). On human beings, computers, and representational-computational versus hermeneutic-dialogical approaches to human cognition and communication. In *Artificial Intelligence and Language: Old Problems in a New Key.* (H. Sinding-Larsen, Ed.). Oslo: Tano.

Rommetveit, R. (1990). *On axiomatic features of a dialogically based social-cognitive approach to language and mind.* In I. Marikova and K. Foppa (Eds.), *The dynamics of dialogue.* (pp. 82–104). Hemel Hempstead: Harvester Wheatsheaf.

Rommetveit, R. (1992). Outlines of a dialogically based social-cognitive approach to human cognition and communication. In *The dialogical alternative: Towards a theory of language and mind.* (A. H. Wold, Ed.). London: Scandinavian University Press.

Rorty, R. (1979). *Philosophy and the mirror of nature.* Princeton, NJ: Princeton Univ. Press.

Roth, S. (1993). Speaking the unspoken: A work-group consultation to reopen dialogue. In *Secrets in Families and Family Therapy.* E. Imber-Black, (Ed.) New York: Norton.

Roth, S., Chasin, L., Chasin, R., Becker, C., & Herzig, M. (1992). From debate to dialogue: A facilitating role for family therapists in the public forum. *Dulwich Centre Newsletter,* No. 2, 41–48.

Sampson, E. E. (1993). *Celebrating the other: A dialogic account of human nature.* Boulder, CO: Westview Press.

Schrag, C. O. (1986). *Communicative praxis and the space of subjectivity.* Bloomington, IN: Indiana University Press.

Schrag, C. O. (1992). *The resources of rationality: A response to the postmodern challenge.* Bloomington, IN: Indiana University Press.

Senge, P. M. (1990). *The fifth discipline: The art and practice of the learning organization.* (New York: Doubleday).

Shotter, J. (1992). Bakhtin and Billig: Monological vs. dialogical practices. *American Behavioral Scientist.* 36: 8–21.

Shotter, J. (1993a). *Cultural politics of everyday life.* Toronto: University of Toronto Press.

Shotter, J. (1993b). *Conversational realities.* London: Sage.

Volosinov, V. N. (1973). *Marxism and the philosophy of language.* (L. Matejka & I. R. Titunik, Trans.). Cambridge, MA: Harvard University Press.

Vygtosky, L. S. (1978). *Mind in society: The development of higher psychological processes.* Cambridge, MA: Harvard University Press.

Wittgenstein, L. (1953). *Philosophical investigations.* (G. E. M. Anscombe Trans). Oxford: Blackwell.

Wold, A. H. (Ed.) (1992). *The dialogical alternative: Towards a theory of language and mind.* London: Scandinavian University Press.

Storied Lives: Recovering the Moral Importance of Social Theory

Arthur P. Bochner
University of South Florida

…when you weigh the good and the bad the social novelists have done against the good and the bad the social theorists have done, you find yourself wishing there had been more novels and fewer theories.

Richard Rorty

I couldn't fall asleep that night. I tossed and turned and felt unusually anxious. Sometimes I have trouble sleeping when I'm away from home or when I'm apprehensive about a presentation. But this was different. It wasn't the hotel room or the upcoming convention that was keeping me awake. I felt that something was terribly wrong, but I didn't know what it was—this undefined nervousness in the pit of my stomach. Finally, at about 7:15 a.m., I got out of bed and headed for the shower.

I don't recall how long I had been standing under the water when I heard the phone ring. A few seconds later, my roommate and dear friend, Herb Simons, called to me. "Art, it's your secretary. She wants to speak to you. She says it's very important."

My secretary would not call me at an NCA Convention unless the roof was caving in. I knew instantly that this call was personal not departmental. I grabbed a towel and ran to the phone, my heart beating rapidly, my mind sorting possibilities.

The voice on the other end was calm and deliberate. "Art, I don't know how to tell you this. Your father died last night. Your sister called. I thought I should tell you as soon as possible."

I don't remember what I said next. I recall putting the receiver down, standing naked, drops of water dripping down my body, forming a small pool at my feet; and Herb looking pale and puzzled, rising from his bed. "My father died last night," I muttered quietly. "I don't know details."

Herb saw instantly that I was in a state of shock. He sensed the terrible struggle I was having as my mind raced to organize what had to be done next, while my body yielded to the undeniable emotional reality of death and loss. I felt dazed and confused, like a boxer who is shocked by the first powerful blow from a stronger opponent. Stunned by the blow, he hears competing voices, one inside his head whispering, "ignore the pain, stay with the game plan," the other calling from the site of his body's pain and injury, rejecting the authority of consciousness over bodily experience.

I knew I had to get home to Tampa as soon as possible. My mother would need me. I would be expected to take the helm, be in control, arrange the funeral, keep the family from falling apart. Suddenly, the three papers I was to present at the convention had little significance. But I was too responsible to miss sessions without forewarning. I should contact the chair of each program, get someone to substitute if possible, give people a chance to prepare for my absence. But I couldn't silence the voice of my suffering body or break its intrusion on my cognitive processes. I felt tears trickling down my face and a void in my gut. It didn't matter that as a child my relationship with my father had been so troubled, hurtful, and destructive, or that he had grown old and fragile before I could come to terms with the fierce and violent father of my youth. The chance to rise above these circumstances was gone now. I could never prove any better as a son than he had been as a father. Our relationship would live on in my mind, but conversation between us had ended. He was gone. We were gone.

Suddenly I was numb. I couldn't think straight. I couldn't even hold the phone in my hand, let alone complete all the tasks begging for attention. How grateful I was to have Herb there. He overlooked my confusion and incompetence, gave me emotional support, and brought a semblance of order to the chaos surrounding me. Herb didn't talk about his mother's death, but when he looked at me I felt the kind of communion that can only occur when two people are woven into the same fabric of experience. For many years, I had thought of Herb as a mentor and a friend; now I knew him as a brother. Within two hours he had me on a plane back to Tampa comforted by the knowledge that details of my departure from the convention would be communicated to people who needed to know.

On that long plane ride home I realized as never before that I was a human being. It sounds strange to say that, but I believe it's true. What I had known in my head, I began to feel in my body. I started to grasp the significance of how contingent, limited, and relative human experience can be and to understand how different human problems are from scientific or academic ones. At the university, or at conferences, I normally move in and out of analytical or conceptual frames without experiencing anything akin to an experiential shock. But when my father died while I was attending an NCA Convention, I was stunned to learn how tame the academic world was in comparison to the wilderness of lived experience. Life had a different shape and texture than the ways it was sculpted in the classroom. Now the academic man in me stood face-to-face with the ordinary man. What did they have to say to each other? Could they get in touch with each other? Integrate? Harmonize?

The sad truth is that the academic self frequently is cut off from the ordinary, experiential self. A life of theory can remove one from experience, make one feel out of touch, unconnected. All of us inhabit multiple worlds. When we live in the world of theory, we usually assume that we are inhabiting an objective world. There, in the objective world, we are expected to play the role of spectator. It is a hard world for a human being to feel comfortable in, so we try to get rid of the distinctively human characteristics that distort the mythological beauty of objectivity. We are taught to master methods that exclude the capriciousness of immediate experience. When we do, we find ourselves in a world devoid of spirituality, emotion, and poetry—a scientific world in which, as Galileo insisted, there is no place for human feelings, motives, or consciousness. In the objective world, the goal is to speak nature's language without the intrusions of human subjectivity. In some quarters, this kind of world is the only rational world, and the only world that can produce knowledge that makes a difference.

I have no bone to pick with scientists. I suspect there are as many kind, decent, and loving people inhabiting the objective, scientific world as there are in any other reality. But there is nothing inherent in the scientific method that requires these traits. Findings do not become less scientific if the scientist who reports them has undesirable personality traits or character flaws. Remember the Milgram (1963) experiments on obedience. They were ingenious and elegant exemplars of social scientific research, but they also were spiritually offensive. As R. D. Laing (1982, p. 22) declared, "what is scientifically right may be morally wrong." Science may improve our predictions, but it does not necessarily tell us what we should do. When we know how to predict and control behavior, we do not consequently know how to deal with a person justly or empathically (Rorty, 1982).

My personal struggle after my father's death was not a scientific crisis but a moral one. And the moral questions that were raised cast a long shadow over both my personal and my academic life. No matter that I had studied, theorized, and taught about loss and attachment. I didn't really know loss until I experienced it. And the more I thought about my own experience of loss, read other people's accounts, and reviewed the theoretical and research literature, the more I began to understand that the academic world was not normally in touch with the everyday world of experience, the ordinary world. This was true not only for the topic of loss but for many of the profound emotional experiences of everyday living. The academic world was long on conceptualizations and short on details; long on abstractions, short on concrete events; long on analysis, short on experience; long on theory, short on stories. I had no desire to get rid of concepts, abstractions, analysis, or theory. Like most academics, I know them as the tools of my trade. It was the imbalance that troubled me—how quickly we turn lives and experiences into texts and concepts (Jackson, 1995).

Perhaps I was mistaken to want to inhabit a different world of inquiry. Referring to philosophers, Richard Rorty (1991, p. 71) says: "We all hanker after essence and share a taste for theory as opposed to narrative. If we did not, we should probably have gone into some other line of work." When a person considered to be one of the most important writers of this generation suggests that I may have chosen the wrong line of work, it's more than a little disconcerting. Yet in the same essay, Rorty also recommends a healthy dose of detailed narrative as an antidote to the essentializing proclivities of social theorists: "Earlier I said that theorists like Heidegger saw narrative as always a second-best, a propeaedeutic to a grasp of something deeper than the visible detail. Novelists like Orwell and Dickens are inclined to see theory as always a second-best, never more than a reminder for a particular purpose, the purpose of telling a story better. I suggest that the history of social change in the modern West shows that the latter conception of the relation between narrative and theory is the more fruitful" (Rorty, 1991, p. 80).

Let me return, then, to my story. After my father's death, I had a renewed appreciation for contingency, chance, and time. I realized that no one really is at the helm. Control is an illusion, at least insofar as we think that control frees us from choices, exempts us from accidents, or protects us from the uncertainty of the future. Adam Phillips (1994) says that we all have lives inside us competing to be lived; the accidents that happen to

most of us remind us that we are living too few of them. To understand an event in one's life as an accident that was meant to happen, much like a Freudian slip, to see the course of one's life under the influence of coincidence rather than control, and to treat contingency as something not to overcome but to be used, is to give oneself the freedom to take chances (Phillips, 1994).

The epiphany of my father's death was a turning point in the conversation between my academic self and my ordinary self. Something very *personal*—my father's death—had unintentionally intruded upon my public, professional life. When I began receiving sympathy cards from people in the field who barely knew me, I was reminded that the split between these worlds often is severed. So why is it, then, that you rarely hear anyone talk about their personal lives in the papers they give at conventions, or see the personal self mix with the professional self on the pages of *Communication Monographs, Communication Theory,* or *Human Communication Research?* Obviously, because we've been conditioned to separate the personal and professional domains of experience. And why is that the case? Because it helps us maintain the illusion that the academic self hasn't been prejudiced by the interests of the ordinary, personal self. When we insulate the academic from the personal we imply that the personal voice is, as Jane Tompkins (1989, p. 122) observes, "soft-minded, self-indulgent, and unprofessional," while the academic voice is exalted as the voice of reason, objectivity, and rigor. So we learn to hide our personal self behind the veneer of academic and theoretical detachment, fostering the misconception that it has no influence, no place, no significance in our work.

We pay a steep price for this illusion. Our work is under-read; undergraduates find many of our publications boring; graduate students say our scholarship is dry and inaccessible; seasoned scholars confess they don't finish half of what they start reading; and the public hardly knows we exist (Richardson, 1994). Oh, we've learned to rationalize these responses, but we know in our hearts we would like them to be different. We do a good job of protecting our secrets—hiding our embarrassment—but we are troubled by how few of us carry a passion for theory and research into our forties and fifties and sixties. We've seen the casualties of an alienated workforce up close, etched on the blank faces of colleagues who caved in, gave up, stopped caring. This too is a moral crisis—our crisis. We turn the other cheek, keep quiet, pretend the moral crisis isn't there, but that doesn't make it disappear.

I think it's about time we wrestled more openly and collectively with these problems. Instead of hiding the pain many of us feel about the ways we are unfulfilled by the life of the mind, we need to muster the courage to speak the truth about "the emotional fallout" of a lifetime of teaching and research (Tompkins, 1996, p. 57). We need to face up to the ways we use orthodox academic practices to discipline, control, and perpetuate ourselves and our traditions, stifling innovation, discouraging creativity, inhibiting criticism of our own institutional conventions, making it difficult to take risks, severing academic life from emotional and spiritual life. No matter how much change may threaten us, we need to consider alternatives—different goals, different styles of research and writing, different ways of bringing the academic and the ordinary into conversation with each other.

One alternative that I favor is narrative inquiry (Bochner, 1994; Ellis and Bochner, 1996). Stories ask readers to *feel* their truth and thus to become fully engaged—morally, aesthetically, emotionally, and intellectually. Stories invite us to enter horizons of the human condition where lived life is shown as comic, tragic, and absurd, and where endless opportunities exist to create a reality and live it. "How to encompass in our minds the complexity of some lived moments of life?" asks Robert Coles (1989, p. 128). "You don't do that with theories. You don't do that with a system of ideas. You do it with a story."

A narrative approach to social theory—what I call *storied lives*—seeks to show how people breach canonical conventions and expectations, how they cope with exceptional, difficult, and transformative crises, how they invent new ways

of speaking when old ways fail them, and how they turn calamities into gifts. Stories activate subjectivity and compel emotional response. They long to be used rather than analyzed, to be told and retold rather than theorized and settled. And they promise the companionship of intimate detail as a substitute for the loneliness of abstracted facts, touching readers where they live and offering details that linger in the mind.

After my father's death, I struggled to bring my academic and personal worlds closer together. I had yearned to do so for a long time; now I felt I had no choice. Twenty years earlier I had been drawn to communication studies because I thought it could help answer deep and troubling questions about how to live a meaningful, useful, and ethical life. Somewhere along the way these questions gave way to smaller, more precise, more professional questions. But I found, when I began listening more closely, that students were still coming with many of the same searching questions. They express a lot of concern about how to understand the life that is in them and around them. They want to lead decent and honorable lives, even in the face of the hypocrisy, shame, and betrayal they've already experienced in life. I know I don't have the answers, but I also feel an obligation to help students address the moral contradictions they feel, bring their dilemmas out into the realm of public discourse, name the silences, make them discussable issues. What is education if not an intense, probing scrutiny of moral choices and dilemmas (Coles, 1989)? What does communication studies (or social theory) have to offer students if we strip away emotional experience, avoid questions of moral contradiction, or act as if duties, obligations, desire, and imagination are outside the scope of what we teach because they can't be grasped as hard data?

Shortly after I published "Theories and Stories" (Bochner, 1994), I got calls and letters from concerned colleagues in the field who wanted to know whether I really was opposed to theory (and whether I'd lost my mind). I tried to explain that I had not juxtaposed stories *against* theories, that I only wanted to create a space for appreciating the value and uses of stories. Now the time is right to revise that explanation.

What I want to say now is that there is nothing as theoretical as a good story. The split between theory and story is false—and it's not false. It's not false when theory is viewed in the terms I have used above—objective, scientific, detached, value-free, beyond human consciousness. Described in these terms, theory becomes an end in itself, divorced from its consequences, politics, and uses. This is the taken-for-granted sense of theory I heard from a colleague at a tenure-review hearing, when she observed, "He's published enough, but his work isn't theoretical." It is also the sense of theory promoted by those who see the purpose of communication research as the development of middle-range (Burleson, 1992) or general theories of communication (Berger, 1991), but who do not consider the ways in which describing or explaining reality is different than dealing with it. As Rorty (1989, p. 383) queries, "What is the point?" "What moral is to be drawn from our knowledge of how we and the rest of nature work?" or "What do we do with ourselves now that we know the laws of our own behavior?" When we don't ask questions like these we run the risk of forgetting that theorizing is not an activity devoid of context or consequences. Consider the plight of the kin of Europeans killed in the July 1996 crash of TWA Flight 800. Stuck for seven days and nights in uncomfortable hotel rooms in an unfamiliar city, frustrated by the cross-purposes of theory and experience, and bewildered by the insensitivity of officials to their emotional trauma, the kin of victims had reached their limits. At a hastily called news conference, a spokesman for the French contingent expressed the feelings shared by many in the group: (paraphrased) "We don't care about your theories or your examination of the causes of the crash. We want our bodies and we want to go home."

But the split between theory and story is false when theorizing is conceived as a social and communicative activity. This is what I mean when I use the term *social theory*. In the world of social theory, we are less concerned about representation and more concerned about communication. We give up the illusions of transcendental observation in favor of the possibilities of dialogue and collaboration. Social theory works the spaces between history and destiny. The social world is understood as a world of connection, contact, relationship. It also is a world where consequences, values, politics, and moral dilemmas are abundant and central.

As social beings, we live storied lives. Our identities—who we are and what we do—originate in the tales passed down to us and the stories we take on as our own. In this sense, stories constitute "our medium of being" (Schafer, 1981). Storytelling is both a *method* of knowing—a social practice—and a way of telling about our lives (Richardson, 1990). As an academic practice, narrative inquiry changes the activity of theorizing from a process of thinking *about* to one of thinking *with*. Theory meets story when we think with a story rather than about it. As Arthur Frank (1995, p. 23) points out: "To think about a story is to reduce it to content and then analyze the content…To think with a story is to experience its affecting one's own life and to find in that effect a certain truth of one's life." Thus, we do not turn stories into data to test theoretical propositions. Rather, we link theory to story when we think with a story, trying to stay with the story, letting ourselves resonate with the moral dilemmas it may pose, understanding its ambiguities, feeling its nuances, letting ourselves become part of the story (Ellis, 1995). We think *with* a story from the framework of our own life. We ask what kind of person we are becoming when we take the story in, how we can use it for our own purposes, what ethical directions it points us toward, what moral commitments it calls out in us (Coles, 1989).

Narrative ethicists say, if it's time to end and you're not sure you've made your point, don't try to explain, just tell another story (Frank, 1995). So I end with one more story, an aging tale passed down by Gregory Bateson (1979, p. 13):

A man wanted to know about mind, not in nature, but in his private large computer, He asked it (no doubt in his best Fortran), "Do you compute that you will ever think like a human being?" The machine then set to work to analyze its own computational habits. Finally, the machine printed its answer on a piece of paper, as such machines do. The man ran to get the answer and found, neatly typed, the words:

THAT REMINDS ME OF A STORY

REFERENCES

Bateson, G. (1979). *Mind and nature: A necessary unity.* New York: Dutton.

Berger, C. (1991). Communication theories and other curios. *Communication Monographs,* 101–113.

Bochner, A. (1994). Perspectives on inquiry II: Theories and stories. In M. Knapp and G. R. Miller (Eds.), *Handbook of interpersonal communication* (pp. 21–41). Beverly Hills, Ca.: Sage.

Burleson, B. (1992). Taking communication seriously. *Communication Monographs, 59,* 79–86.

Coles, R. (1989). *The call of stories: Teaching and the moral imagination.* Boston: Houghton Mifflin.

Ellis, C. (1995). *Final negotiations: A story of love, loss, and chronic illness.* Philadelphia, Pa.: Temple University Press.

Ellis, C. and Bochner, A. (Eds.). (1996). *Composing ethnography: Alternative forms of qualitative writing.* Walnut Creek, Ca.: AltaMira.

Frank, A. (1995). *The wounded storyteller: Body, illness, and ethics.* Chicago: University of Chicago Press.

Jackson, M. (1995). *At home in the world.* Durham, N.C.: Duke University Press.

Laing, R. D. (1982). *The voice of experience.* New York: Pantheon.

Milgram, S. (1963). Behavioral study of obedience. *Journal of Abnormal and Social Psychology, 67,* 137–143.

Phillips, A. (1994). *On flirtation.* Cambridge, Mass.: Harvard University Press.

Richardson, L. (1990). Narrative and sociology. *Journal of Contemporary Ethnography, 19,* 116–135.

Richardson, L. (1994). Writing as a method of inquiry. In N. Denzin and Y. Lincoln (Eds.), *The handbook of qualitative research* (pp. 516–529). Beverly Hills, Ca.: Sage.

Rorty, R. (1979). *Philosophy and the mirror of nature.* Princeton, N.J.: Princeton University Press.

Rorty, R. (1982). *Consequences of pragmatism (essays 1972–1980).* Minneapolis: University of Minnesota Press.

Rorty, R. (1991). *Essays on Heidegger and others: Philosophical papers* (Vol. 2). Cambridge: Cambridge University Press.

Schafer, R. (1981). Narration in the psychoanalytic dialogue. In W. Mitchell (Ed.), *On narrative* (p. 31). Chicago: University of Chicago Press.

Tompkins, J. (1989). Me and my shadow. In L. Kauffman (Ed.), *Gender and theory: Dialogues on feminist criticism* (pp. 121–139). Cambridge: Blackwell.

Tompkins, J. (1996). *A life in school: What the teacher learned.* Reading, Massachusetts: Addison-Wesley.

CHAPTER 15

AT THE HELM IN ETHNOGRAPHY AND COMMUNICATION

Introduction

Thomas R. Lindlof
University of Kentucky

Had the NCA At the Helm series been held 20 years ago, a session devoted to ethnography and communication would likely *not* have been chosen, and probably would not have made it to the program planner's short list. The basis for this conjecture is neither mysterious nor complicated. Very simply, the appearances of ethnography in communication journals circa mid-1970s were few and very far between. Without studies regularly entering the canon, there can be no sustained development of knowledge, no agenda of pressing issues, not even a commonly recognized language in which to begin discussing an agenda of research—and, therefore, no "helm" to speak of.

Certainly there were dispersed groups of communication faculty and graduate students alert to the interpretivist buzz coming out of sociology (ethnomethodology, dramaturgical analysis), postcolonial (reflexive) anthropology, semiotics, feminism, organizational-culture studies, and other areas. Many of them followed these interests to whatever next pursuit or project made sense. For the broad sweep of scholars trained in and dedicated to the social-scientific study of communication, however, ethnography and other qualitative approaches were usually a blank zone. If known at all, they were probably perceived as a tradition of sociological inquiry associated with a place and time (e.g., the University of Chicago in the 1920s),

or as a kind of expedient craftwork that anthropologists use to find their way around non-Western settings—little of which seemed especially vital for the ascendant aspirations of communication science. Notions of ritual, performance, lived experience, cultural practice, and the social construction of reality seemed to reside in an altogether different universe than concerns with the effective or functional use of messages by aggregated individuals. The fit was not good. Experimental social psychology—not cultural hermeneutics—was communication science's intellectual bloodline.

The story of how and why ethnographic inquiry began to make inroads in the communication discipline through the 1980s and into the 1990s is vastly more complex than the tale told above (which itself is vastly simplified), and has yet to be written. My own interpretation, like everyone else's, is selective and uniquely situated, but may have some themes, moments, and people held in common with others. Certain people's work was memorable, and induced a cognitive reorganization on my part of what it was possible to do as a communication researcher. Gerry Phillipsen (1975), with his telling analysis of urban speech performance, James Lull (1980), with his groundbreaking work on the interpersonal nexus of family TV viewing, and Tom Benson (1981), deliberately at play in the fields of empirical fiction, were scholars whose work told me that something new was definitely happening, and the fact that it was happening dangerously along the edges of what was then considered proper theory and technique made it all the more seductive. Others began to produce important work that relied on close analysis of contextual discourse and social action. A very incomplete list would include David Morley, Janice Radway, Klaus Bruhn Jensen, and James Anderson in media studies; Michael Pacanowsky, Nick Trujillo, Mary Hellen Brown, and George Cheney in organizational studies; and Donal Carbaugh, Dwight Conquergood, Carolyn Ellis, and Tamar Katriel in interpersonal and intercultural studies. And, of course, the authors featured in this section. This work was alive with the exciting prospect of being able to understand "everyday communication" up close and through multiple frames: as process, as emergent and negotiated, as artful event, as subcultural style, as articulation of identity, as politically conflicted, as institutional routine, and as cultural performance.

One of the great strengths of ethnography, in all of the disciplines in which it is prominent, is its capacity to reveal the *particularity* of social life, telling us about *these* people, *these* voices, *these* forms of conduct, *these* meanings. Ethnographic inquiry enables us to study how communication actually gets accomplished in culturally specific circumstances, and how meanings proliferate through social and moral orders. These richly detailed studies can then be employed as exemplars in developing the constructs and theoretical arguments of social action or cultural interpretation. They can also be used to speak to many other audiences about the power and diversity of communication in people's experience.

It is probably accurate to say that communication ethnographers as a whole now work in a more theory-driven, self-critical fashion. There are now "invisible colleges" of researchers, spanning national and disciplinary borders, that engage on issues of theory development, critique, method, ethics, narrative, and application. We have graduate programs that include an interpre-

tive/cultural component, special symposia, book series, adequate (if not always continual) representation of work in national communication journals, and, yes, even methods texts—all of the material apparatus of a mature professionalism, though hopefully not achieved at the cost of openness, eclecticism, and a spirit of risk-taking.

It may even be an expectation on the part of many that, whenever a Helm-like series comes along at a major conference, "ethnography and communication" should legitimately claim a place. Such expectations, if they are widespread, are one succinct "measure" of how far we have traveled the last 20 years. The occasion of programs like this one allows members of the communication community to ask: How has the practice of ethnography made a difference in our knowledge of the nature and process of communication, as well as in issues of praxis? On what grounds do we now explain, justify, and extend the value of this form of scholarship?

This section's three authors have all made significant contributions in the area of ethnography and communication over the last 15 years. Stuart Sigman, from the State University of New York at Albany, is well known for his social communication approach to social conduct in a variety of interpersonal and institutional contexts, as well as his writings on methodological issues of ethnography. His theoretic ideas have been articulated more prominently in the book, *A Perspective on Social Communication.*

William K. Rawlins, from Purdue University, has devoted most of his career to studying the communicative dimensions of friendship formation and maintenance, using an interpretive framework. His 1992 book, *Friendship Matters,* represents a synthesis of his thought and research in this area. It was selected as an Outstanding Academic Book for 1993 by the editors of *Choice,* and also received the Gerald R. Miller Book Award for 1994 from the Interpersonal and Small Group Interaction Division of the National Communication Association.

H. L. Goodall, Jr., from the University of North Carolina at Greensboro, is best known for his investigations of narrative, drama, mystery, and culture in organizational contexts. Among his many books are *Casing a Promised Land* and *Living in the Rock n Roll Mystery,* each of which develops a distinctively reflexive approach to ethnographic fieldwork and writing.

REFERENCES

Benson, T. W. (1981). Another shooting in Cowtown. *Quarterly Journal of Speech, 67,* 347–406.

Lull, J. (1980). The social uses of television. *Human Communication Research, 6,* 197–209.

Philipsen, G. (1975). Speaking "like a man" in Teamsterville: Culture patterns of role enactment in an urban neighborhood. *Quarterly Journal of Speech, 61,* 13–22.

A Matter of Time: The Case for Ethnographies of Communication

Stuart J. Sigman

University of Albany SUNY

This paper provides a vision for ethnographic work in communication; it is less a rationale for ethnography per se, and more a rationale for a particular view of the potential role of ethnography in communication studies. First, I define ethnography in terms of a values framework for the process of data collection and analysis; and second, I explore the important role that ethnography can play in our discipline. Throughout this discussion, but especially in the latter portion, I emphasize ethnography's ability to situate observable behavior in multi-laminated temporal streams. I argue that more detailed consideration of the relationship between time and behavior than is currently afforded this is needed, and that ethnography provides a suitable methodology.

First, a definition of ethnography. Ethnography is less a collection of particular techniques for data collection and analysis than a framework for thinking about the social world and the researcher's attempts to understand it. Neither observation nor interviewing, nor the combination, alone defines ethnography. Rather, ethnography comprises a belief that the social world should be approached naturalistically, in terms of behavior that members of a community themselves typically engage in and witness; holistically, with an understanding that any datum can be situated and understood within more encompassing streams of behavior (contexts); and emically, so that the meanings of behavior that are most relevant are those that are lived and generated by the members themselves, not by the researchers.

Observational and interview work support these values in a number of ways. For example, ethnographers tend to search out already existing activities, communities, institutions, or scenes—i.e., those which are independent of the researchers—rather than create them. Second, a single observation of an event is usually not sufficient for ethnographic purposes; while the "internal" composition of an event may be studied, the "external" relationship of this event to other community events is important. This requires that ethnographers observe multiple iterations of an event and multiple event-types, and attempt to articulate their structural and semantic connections. Finally, the ways in which community members themselves witness, respond to, and talk about their events and behavior are crucial to the vocabulary that ethnographers use when describing or analyzing these. Emphasis is placed on both observational and informant meaning for behavior; the researchers' initial descriptive vocabulary—an "etic" framework—should ultimately give way to "emic" vocabulary and understanding.

With the advent of relatively inexpensive and readily available video-recording equipment, one might reasonably ask whether fieldwork's contribution has been diminished. Is ethnographic fieldwork really necessary? Moreover, are extensive periods of fieldwork really necessary? The availability of transcription machines, computer arrayed video and audio recordings, and qualitative software packages might lead some to conclude that ethnography has become obsolete. I certainly hope this is not the case, and I also think it need not be so. While permanent records of observations and interviews permit a previously unimagined micro-analysis of behavior, ethnographers would claim that the selection of events for recording and transcription requires considerable long-term exposure and familiarity with the people, places, and activities associated with the field. Ethnographic fieldwork is still an essential component of social science research.

To illuminate this point further, allow me to briefly contrast the approach taken by conversation analysts, as I understand this, and ethnographers on the issue of data generation. Harvey Sacks is credited with having suggested that the conversation analyst must approach each project "unmotivated," without any particular hypotheses, inclinations, or interests in what might be revealed by repeated viewings and hearings of recordings and transcripts. "The way to investigate a phenomenon was not to begin from conclusions about what the study of it would have to yield, but to begin by examining the phenomena itself to see what kind of character it has and what conclusions it could actually support" (Sharrock & Anderson, 1986, p. 64). Ethnographers, too, approach the field in an unmotivated fashion. As their goal is to produce an emically meaningful study, they must be willing to forgo premature "operationalization" of the behaviors to be studied. However, ethnographers conceive of the unmotivated nature of their work at an earlier stage of the research enterprise. Ethnographers generally do not engage in extensive taping of behavior until they have developed some familiarity with the repetitive scenes and activities, and the overarching goals and values, that define the culture. As I expressed this in a previous publication, ethnographers tend to leave the creation of permanent recordings for micro-analysis to fairly late in the research sequence, at a point in time when the behavior captured on tape has some meaning and contextualization (Sigman, 1985).[1]

Before moving on to the main thesis of this paper, I do want to acknowledge that several writers recognize the value of integrating conversation analysis and ethnography. While he was not the first to combine micro-analytic and cultural methodologies, Moerman (1988) has provided the clearest statement about the value and potential of doing so. He labels such an approach "culturally contexted conversation analysis." (For a discussion of the reactions to Moerman's proposal, see Nelson, 1994.) My goal here has been to point out some affinities between conversation analysis and ethnography, and to acknowledge the different senses of relevant time employed by the two qualitative methods.

To conclude this initial discussion, then, ethnography is a methodology defined less by a set of unique data collection and analysis techniques and practices, and more by a set of values informing the use of these. Three of these values are naturalism, holism, and emic orientation. All three infuse an interest in balancing the reliance on micro-analyzable and more macro data.

Next, I wish to take up a vision of the relationship between communication behavior and time. In the process, I explore the role that ethnography can play in providing temporally rich data and temporally rich insights about data. Ethnography, it strikes me, is the only methodological vehicle in the social sciences capable of taking account of extended durations of time. Communication can be thought of as a process that exists "here in the moment," in local contexts of its occurrence, yet it can also be profitably viewed for its historical antecedents and projections. These are the themes for the remainder of this presentation.

The anthropologist Clifford Geertz (1973) suggests that ethnography provides a kind of "thick description" of cultural events. He writes: "What the ethnographer is in fact faced with...is a multiplicity of complex conceptual structures, many of them superimposed upon or knotted into one another, which are at once strange, irregular, and inexplicit, and which he must contrive somehow first to grasp and then to render" (p. 10). This rendering is in the form of thick description. Such thick description enables the researcher to distinguish observations about the appearance of behavior (e.g., an eye

---

[1]I have tried to phrase the above contrast in such a way as to avoid sounding partisan. The value of conversation analysis and similar tools for the study of actual communication behavior, as opposed to social psychological variables associated with it and/or idealized reconstructions and reports of it, cannot be stressed enough. My own thinking on this subject is reflected in the notion that we must study the consequentiality of communication, and conversation analysis provides a useful means for accomplishing this (see Sigman, 1995a, b).

twitch or the stealing of some sheep) with analyses of the "web of signification" in which that behavior accomplishes something culturally meaningful (e.g., "practicing a burlesque of a friend faking a wink to deceive an innocent into thinking a conspiracy is in motion" [p. 7]). Elaborating on this notion, Wolcott (1995) cautions that ethnography not be defined by the amount of data presented, but rather by the interpretive frames used with the data. He writes: "This confusion between degree (level of detail) and kind (direction one takes with the interpretation) has fostered the mistaken idea that ethnography is achieved by staying on site longer, taking 'more complete' notes, or conducting extra interviews" (p. 91). For Wolcott, research is "more ethnographic" to the extent that a cultural interpretation infuses whatever data are presented.

If ethnographies are characterized by thick description, then the social-cultural world itself can be thought of as thickly describable. In what ways is this so? Three considerations about the relation between communication and time are offered here as partial answers.

First, events unfold over time, and indeed what constitutes a particular event may not be immediately apparent either to participants or researchers, but may develop over time. Events may only come to "be" through the passing of time. Contributing to this perspective, Latour writes that "by itself a given sentence is neither a fact nor a fiction; it is made so by others, later on" (quoted in Taylor et al., 1996, p. 18). Similarly, in a critique I provided a few years back of a semiotic model of the relationship between media viewing and interpersonal relationships, I suggested that the significance of a particular moment of media exposure might be negotiated and renegotiated by people and various others (both those who were and were not in attendance at the media event) across numerous subsequent conversations (Sigman, 1990). These conversations serve to delineate and define the earlier event as an event and as an event with a particular significance. If we think of the function of a behavior as being rooted in the "uptake" afforded it by others, then I am encouraging the recognition that such uptake does not al-

ways occur immediately subsequent ("adjacent") to the behavior's production, and that even when it does this is subject to further actions during later encounters (cf. Scheflen, 1973).

Second, an event always derives from (or can meaningfully be placed within) a structure defining what does not occur and what does. A behavior's meaning may not be discernible without consideration of the background expectations and variations brought to encounters by the participants. Comparison of the presence and absence of behavior, or of the variations in the presence of behavior, may be indispensable in this regard. A good example can be found in Katriel's (in press) study of Israeli folk museums. Katriel examines tour guides' narratives while hosting either Hebrew or Arab visitors to two museums. There are striking differences in the stories told, the language used, and the material objects highlighted during the tours. Of course, there are also discursive similarities—in the way the guides lead the visitors through the museum and structure the tours. But Katriel's main point is that the contrast of the several performances is significant. Each Hebrew tour is also a non-Arab tour, and each Arab tour a non-Hebrew one. This implies that any particular tour performance is part of a more inclusive system of meanings—about Israeli history, identity, and Arab–Hebrew relations—and that a political structure exists which delineates which party(ies) defines these meanings for all. We are unable to understand this more encompassing system if each tour is treated individually, and we do not approach the depth of meanings within each tour without consideration of what transpires in the others. Both the larger system of meanings and the particular meanings generated within each performance are implicated in the other. Each depends on the other for what it is (and for what it is not).

Finally, communicative acts and events are situated within an ever-developing set of historical texts. Prior behavior establishes the semantic groundwork for subsequent behavior; the former may prospectively establish the salience of the latter, and it is the latter which serves to uphold or negate commitments made earlier by the parties involved. As Taylor writes: "A conversation is not just a succession of disjoint individual productions, in alternation, but knits together to make a much denser fabric, where one intervention is woven with others to make a structure of talk" (1995, p. 25). Also: "A conversation is thus an interplay of texts, fusing in an interpretation old knowledge (previous texts) and new, the old or 'given' now becoming the *con*text of the new" (Taylor et al., 1996, p. 20). This recognizes that the social-cultural world constructed in and through communication contains an accretion of textual meanings, that communicators both produce a world by behaving and behave in a world that is more encompassing than their individual and collective behaviors.

What the above discussion suggests is that some methodology is needed which enables the communication researcher to keep track of behavior and its multiple patterns of connection across time. Here I am advocating not simply that ethnography is just such a method, but that communication researchers must be willing to use ethnography in this way, to tackle the difficult task of studying behavioral trajectories. There is evidence that the patterning and meaning of communication come not only from the production of behavior in an existential moment, but across larger expanses of space and time. Communicators project the significance of "current" events onto "future" ones; they rely upon knowledge generated in "previous" encounters; and they retrospectively define the presence and meaning of "past" events. They also produce behavior repetitively, and it is against the background of expected repetitions that absences are noteworthy and that unique performance iterations can be explained.

A concept from pre-Chomskyan structural linguistics may help develop these ideas further. There a distinction is drawn between the "internal" and "external" grammar of a linguistic unit (Hockett, 1958; Wells, 1957). The internal structure of behavior consists of the arrangement of its components, while its external patterning refers to its relations with behavior of a comparable size and its contribution to larger and still larger units of behavior. Of course, these terms are relative not absolute; the analysis of the external patterning of one unit might be similar to that of the internal composition of some superordinate unit. Thus, internal and external perspectives on behavior do not remain fixed on any particular level of behavioral organization, but vary with each unit under consideration (cf. Sigman, 1987).

It seems to me that the thick describability of communication obligates researchers to examine both the internal and external features of a behavior, activity sequence, or event. Analyses of the patterning of communication must account for both the structural arrangements of the units that comprise the behavior, activity sequence, or event being studied, as well as for the relationship of those units to other behavior, activity sequences, or events that have occurred in the near or distant past and that are projected to occur some time in the future. Because ethnographers do not study isolated behavior units, but the arrangements of those units into larger and larger contexts, their method is most suited to the needs of communication scholars as I have articulated them. Because ethnographers attempt to write thick descriptions, they are sensitive to the forces that shape human communication experience and the production of meaningful behavior across time. Stated differently, they are sensitive to influences and patterning of behavior not always apparent within or during any particular communication event.

Communication may be defined as the ongoing production of meaningful behavior that is "locally" occasioned and situated. In addition, however, it may also be thought of as thickly contexted, as part of and fitting within larger, more extensive networks of behavior. Thus, I encourage communication scholars—communication ethnographers more particularly—to study behavior across time.

REFERENCES

Geertz, Clifford. *The Interpretation of Cultures.* New York: Basic Books, 1973.

Hockett, Charles. *A Course in Modern Linguistics.* New York: Macmillan, 1958.

Katriel, Tamar. *Performing the Past: A Study of Israeli Settlement Museums.* Mahwah, New Jersey: Erlbaum, in press.

Moerman, Michael. *Talking Culture: Ethnography and Conversation Analysis.* Philadelphia: University of Pennsylvania Press, 1988.

Nelson, Christian K. "Ethnomethodological Positions on the Use of Ethnographic Data in Conversation Analytic Research," *Journal of Contemporary Ethnography,* vol. 23, no. 3 (1994), 307–329.

Scheflen, Albert. *Communicational Structure: Analysis of a Psychotherapy Transaction.* Bloomington: Indiana University Press, 1973.

Sharrock, Wes & Anderson, Bob. *The Ethnomethodologists.* London: Tavistock, 1986.

Sigman, Stuart J. "Some Common Mistakes Students Make When Learning Discourse Analysis," *Communication Education,* vol. 34, no. 2 (1985), 119–127.

Sigman, Stuart J. *A Perspective on Social Communication.* Lexington, Massachusetts: Lexington Books, 1987.

Sigman, Stuart J. "Toward an Integration of Diverse Communication Contexts: Commentary on the Chapter by Fry, Alexander, and Fry." In James A. Anderson (ed.), *Communication Yearbook 13.* Newbury Park, California: Sage, 1990, pp. 554–563.

Sigman, Stuart J. (ed.). *The Consequentiality of Communication.* Hillsdale, New Jersey: Erlbaum, 1995a.

Sigman, Stuart J. "Question: Evidence of What? Answer: Communication," *Western Journal of Communication,* vol. 59, no. 1 (1995b), 79–84.

Taylor, James R. "Shifting from a Heteronomous to an Autonomous Worldview of Organizational Communication: Communication Theory on the Cusp," *Communication Theory,* vol. 5, no. 1 (1995), 1–35.

Taylor, James R.; Cooren, François; Giroux, Hélène; & Robichaud, Daniel. "Are Organization and Communication Equivalent?" Paper presented to the Conference on Organizational Communication and Change: Challenges in the Next Century, Austin, Texas, 1996.

Wells, Rulon. "De Saussure's System of Linguistics." In Martin Joos (ed.), *Readings in Linguistics I.* Chicago: University of Chicago Press, 1957, pp. 1–18.

Wolcott, Harry F. "Making a Study 'More Ethnographic'." In John Van Maanen (ed.), *Representation in Ethnography.* Thousand Oaks, California: Sage, 1995, pp. 79–111.

From Ethnographic Occupations to Ethnographic Stances

William K. Rawlins
Purdue University

I use "ethnography" in this essay to refer to an array of investigative practices in which inquirers use their embodied selves as their primary research instruments in seeking to understand other persons and cultures. For some time now persons interested in ethnography from a variety of disciplines have been vigorously questioning its existential, ethical, methodological, practical, and political attributes and implications (Clifford, 1986; Conquergood, 1991; Geertz, 1988; Kauffman, 1992; West, 1993). With no space here to discuss their historical evolution, I want to touch on selected themes emerging in recent debates about ethnography that I consider important for communication scholars to ponder. After I briefly discuss the inherently communicative character of ethnography, I explore connotations of "ethnographic occupations" and pose questions concerning being and learning with others derived from the self-questioning of contemporary ethnographers. I suggest that embracing the core tensions composing these quandaries reflects and implies an ethnographic stance for communicating in a world of differences.

Ethnography is intrinsically communicative praxis. That is, ethnographers symbolically shape and are shaped by the contexts of their own activities. People develop initial ideas and proposals for projects in concert with other beings-in-the-world and/or in-the-academy. On location they discursively generate data principally through interacting face-to-face and writing field notes, sometimes supplemented by other communication technologies. Additional written, audio, visual, or filmic text-making practices, or embodied performances, then represent the work for various audiences (Conquergood, 1992). The enterprise is communicative, hence rhetorical, through and through (Conquergood, 1991; 1992).

The phrase, "ethnographic occupations," evokes multiple meanings. In one sense it refers to the professional contexts where people are paid to do ethnographic work, including professors and research scholars in various academic fields, as well as people hired to do applied ethnographic research in health care, educational, marketing, and industrial contexts, to name a few examples. Such individuals make their livings employing ethnographic practices to investigate and represent targeted individuals and cultural settings.

Meanwhile the phrase may have critical connotations as well. One of the most criticized heritages of ethnography is its use by colonial powers to gather information and de facto to aid in the identity manipulation, plundering, and subjugation of people in the reaches of their empires who were/are minimally able to defend or define themselves (Clifford, 1986; Conquergood, 1992; Said, 1989). "Ethnographic occupations" can thereby signify uninvited and controlling presences in the lifeworlds of others. Accordingly, many ethnographers have become duly concerned about the extent to which they are imposing themselves on others and the degree to which the understandings they seek serve only the interests of their culture of origin or sponsorship—be it an interest group of the National Communication Association or the board of directors of a prosperous corporation—to the neglect or detriment of the people they are actually studying (Fiske, 1991; Rose, 1990). In a post-colonial spirit, ethnographers cross-examine themselves about the motives and ethical principles guiding their efforts, the existence and extent of power disparities inherent in their projects, the degree to which they are altering or speaking for rather than amplifying indigenous voices, in short, the extent to which their projects mutually benefit themselves and the scrutinized persons and cultures.

But "ethnographic occupations" can also imply some of the dominating presences patrolling, interrogating, and sequestering ethnography itself. Rose (1990) argues that the values and practices of corporate capitalism overdetermine the contours and horizons of ethnographic projects. To be a professional ethnographer is to conform to the "legal-formal" demands of copious hours of laboring in the field or the office, hidebound standard-publication-format-driven conventions for timely, acceptable writing, and strategic and cost-effective decisions about teaching and research interests as befitting a rational career trajectory. West (1993) considers ethnography further marginalized by its often awkward alignment with the production-oriented worldview of traditional hypothetico-deductive social science. He observes, "Especially in graduate programs where graduate students are used as cheap migrant laborers to help harvest data, ethnography is often viewed as too time consuming and incapable of being appropriated within the relations of power between graduate students and professors" (p. 217).

Values endemic to and enforced by traditional social scientific reviewers, such as objective detachment, reliability through interceder agreement, operationalization of variables, mutually exclusive categories, and "author-absent" writing, are not shared by many ethnographers (Atkinson & Hammersley, 1994). Indeed, some would find such social scientific imperatives repugnant (West, 1993). Closely connected, feminist critics have noted the masculinist cast of much ethnography, critiquing the historic tendency for another principally male occupation (Harding, 1987; Kauffman, 1992; Wolf, 1992). Finally, growing camps of postmodern writers have occupied ethnographers with their decrees regarding the primacy of writing in ethnographic inquiry and the "crisis of representation" (Clifford & Marcus, 1986; Van Maanen,

1995). With the ethics and the very possibility of writing about other cultures forcefully contested, increasing numbers of inquirers are focusing more on their own experiences of studying and writing about others because they feel compelled to question the legitimacy of describing others (Bochner & Ellis, 1992; Crawford, 1996).

Recognizing and resisting the detrimental characteristics of these diverse ethnographic occupations has spawned critical self-reflection and questioning that tug at the heart of ethnography. Such questions include: Since we construct and judge ourselves and others with every meaning we make, how do we arrive at these appraisals? How does each of us experience and communicate the multiple discourses informing our evaluations? How aware are we of producing and consuming them? For what purposes do we make them? What forms do they or should they assume? How cooperative or conflictual are the contexts of their creation? How much say do we have about the time and place of their production? Their distribution? Are there any discursive fields that are level? Who are the audiences for representations of our encounter(s)? Would we recognize ourselves in our own and others' descriptions of us? How can we learn with, about, and from each other in just and edifying ways? What does it mean to live well?

These questions acknowledge that everybody everywhere is simultaneously a potential ethnographer and subject of ethnographic inquiry. Indeed, ethnography can be perceived as offering ways of living, ways of relating, and ways of being (Rose, 1990). Interpersonal communication itself can thus be framed as ethnographic praxis. Conceived in this way, a crucial issue becomes how and to what extent we achieve understanding or at least acknowledgment of the differences striating our personal identities and everyday interactions with others. How do we assert and appreciate what makes us distinctive to each other? While admitting alternatives, I turn now to what I consider an edifying "ethnographic stance" toward social learning and living that addresses this concern. I believe that the current reflections and self-questioning of ethnographers can remind and teach us about dilemmas and possibilities shaping our social lives. They provide the basis for the following ethnographic stance toward being with others.

Other persons are participating subjects of discourse; they are not objects of knowledge (Kauffmann, 1990). Ethnographers have had difficulties reaching this conversational position, especially if they subscribe to the classic agon of scientism, the subject/object split. When seeking objectivity in knowing others, distance and detachment are virtues. However, from such a remove, self may merely project self's qualities onto others and arrogantly find the others lacking (e.g., "primitive"), or in a spirit of false friendship idealize them (e.g., the "noble savage"). And even if the others are discovered to resemble self (despite apparent differences), self is the center from which all things are measured. Yet in wanting to get closer to others, immerse oneself in their culture, and try to tap their meanings, self may now fear too much identification with the other and losing self's identity. Worse yet, "going native" is the bane of objectivity.

The ethnographic stance of which I speak does not consider people objects; so objectivity, disembodied and disconnected from subjectivity, seems a demeaning if not distorting quest. Moreover, ethnographers have recognized that to objectify others is to objectify self, and that every version we create of others also constructs complementary selves (Clifford, 1986; Laing, 1971). We are seeking conversation, not classification.

Being a person requires relating with others; there is an avowedly relational cast to ethnographic living and learning (Bateson, 1972; Rose, 1990). We continue to understand others in part through projections of ourselves; we continue to understand ourselves based largely on others' responses to us. Meanwhile, as Bakhtin (1981) has taught us, we cannot remedy the fact that each of us occupies specific spatio-temporal coordinates. From our unique, embodied vantage points we address and are addressed by a world of others (Holquist, 1990). There are limits to our knowl-

edge and understanding of self and others. This is a reason for humility. But whatever we know we have learned with others. This can be a reason for good will toward others (Bateson, 1993).

The ethnographic stance I describe here involves an appreciation of the differences composing our lives and the challenges of defining relationships. Such a stance notices that differences are the basis for self- as well as other-recognition, and that all differences arise from and are only possible in relationships (Bateson, 1972; 1979). Consider persons, colors, moments, moods, temperatures, and musical tones—none of these can be different (or even similar) in and of itself at one moment in time. For every way in which the other is different from self, there are ways self is different from the other. Viewed in this way, all meaning making between people involves potential struggles to express and deal with their manifold and manifest differences. Two related questions become important in mutually defining communicative relationships under these conditions (the human condition). Who determines the "differences which make a difference" (Bateson, 1972, p. 456)? And to what degree does "each person possess the other's otherness" (Holquist, 1990, p. 51)? Both are questions of power and point of view.

The pinch is that we are not merely talking about empathy here, where self employs self's categories, frames of reference, and temporal orientations in trying to see self through the other's eyes. The other's differences make little difference in this scenario. Instead, self seeks the other's point of view and images of self's being, without necessarily relinquishing self's point of view or converting the other's point of view into self's. As Rose announces, this "reversal, the space of discourse and counterdiscourse, is a political space in which voices are raised that remain incommensurable; they do not map to one another, they do not share the same sensibilities" (1990, p. 50). In other words, radical differences are sustained; they are not transcended or merged through empathy or other domesticating practices.

Ethnographic conversation can foster the relationally constituted yet distinctive subjectivities of self and other, facilitating co-learning while and by preserving differences. Even so, it requires respect for others, respect for self, and for the differences that enliven the space between persons (Buber, 1958; Rose, 1990; Todorov, 1984). Yet it also demands humility, through reflexive awareness of one's indebtedness to others in the ongoing construction of selfhood; one's limited abilities to achieve absolute knowledge of others or self; and one's temporal and spatial finitude despite the enlarging capabilities of symbolic systems. An ethnographic stance requires the renouncing of "self-privileging positions" (Rose, 1990, p. 53), and a deep affinity for "the canon of human experience" (Bateson, 1993, p. 118), the wealth of ways in which people make sense of being alive. Finally, while assuming this stance and speaking together in light of these concerns may be enriched and encouraged by good will, participants must make every attempt to address and redress power disparities to prevent their interactions from being hollow exercises. The ethnographic stance mandates speaking as equals as a means-to-a-beginning and a beginning-in-itself.

REFERENCES

Atkinson, P. & Hammersley, M. (1994). Ethnography and participant observation. In N. K. Denzin & Y. S. Lincoln (Eds.), *Handbook of qualitative research* (pp. 248–261). Thousand Oaks, CA: Sage Publications.

Bakhtin, M. M. (1981). *The dialogic imagination: Four essays.* Austin: University of Texas Press.

Bateson, G. (1972). *Steps to an ecology of mind.* New York: Ballantine Books.

Bateson, G. (1979). *Mind and nature: A necessary unity.* New York: E. P. Dutton.

Bateson, M. C. (1993). Joint performance across cultures: Improvisation in a Persian garden. *Text and Performance Quarterly, 13,* 113–121.

Bochner, A. P. & Ellis, C. (1992). Personal narrative as a social approach to interpersonal communication. *Communication Theory, 2,* 165–172.

Buber, M. (1958). *I and thou.* New York: Macmillan.

Clifford, J. (1986). Introduction: Partial truths. In J. Clifford & G. E. Marcus (Eds.), *Writing culture: The poetics and politics of ethnography* (pp. 1–26). Berkeley: University of California Press.

Clifford, J. & Marcus, G. E. (Eds.). (1986). *Writing culture: The poetics and politics of ethnography.* Berkeley: University of California Press.

Conquergood, D. (1991). Rethinking ethnography: Towards a critical cultural politics. *Communication Monographs, 58,* 179–194.

Conquergood, D. (1992). Ethnography, rhetoric, and performance. *Quarterly Journal of Speech, 78,* 80–123.

Crawford, L. (1996). Personal ethnography. *Communication Monographs, 63,* 158–170.

Fiske, J. (1991). Writing ethnographies: Contribution to a dialogue. *Quarterly Journal of Speech, 77,* 330–335.

Geertz, C. (1988). *Works and lives: The anthropologist as author.* Stanford, CA: Stanford University Press.

Harding, S. (Ed.). (1987). *Feminism & methodology.* Bloomington: Indiana University Press.

Holquist, M. (1990). *Dialogism: Bakhtin and his world.* London: Routledge.

Kauffman, B. J. (1992). Feminist facts: Interview strategies and political subjects in ethnography. *Communication Theory, 2,* 187–206.

Kauffmann, R. L. (1990). The other in question: Dialogical experiments in Montaigne, Kafka, and Cortazar. In T. Maranhao (Ed.), *The interpretation of dialogue* (pp. 157–194). Chicago: University of Chicago Press.

Laing, R. D. (1971). *Self and others.* Middlesex: Penguin.

Rose, D. (1990). *Living the ethnographic life.* Newbury Park, CA: Sage Publications.

Said, E. W. (1989). Representing the colonized: Anthropology's interlocutors. *Critical Inquiry, 15,* 205–225.

Todorov, T. (1984). *Mikhail Bakhtin: The dialogical principle.* Minneapolis: University of Minnesota Press.

Van Maanen, J. (Ed.). (1995). *Representation in ethnography.* Thousand Oaks, CA: Sage Publications.

West, J. T. (1993). Ethnography and ideology: The politics of cultural representation. *Western Journal of Communication, 57,* 209–220.

Wolf, M. (1992). *A thrice-told tale: Feminism, postmodernism, and ethnographic responsibility.* Stanford: Stanford University Press.

Transforming Communication Studies through Ethnography

H. L. Goodall, Jr.
University of North Carolina, Greensboro

THE TRUTH ABOUT ETHNOGRAPHY

Ethnography is a natural academic activity for any reasonably curious person, but, in some academic circles, it is considered a merely curious activity done by spurious persons. In part this is because ethnography itself is considered a "radical" research method derived (or stolen) from anthropology and/or sociology, whose actual fieldwork practices are located in an ambiguous, seemingly boundaryless set of participant-observer interactions that are themselves recorded in odd fieldnote scrawl which place someone (who, if not a licensed academic engaging in research, might well be considered a *voyeur*) in close, sometimes strikingly intimate, and always self-reflexive position relative to his or her subjects, collaborators, or (and here even the politically correct spelling is considered off-putting) Others. The result is termed "a text of experience" that often reads—or in the case of ethnographic films, looks—pretty much like anything the ethnographer (and her or his publisher, journal editor, or sponsor) thinks it ought to read or look like, from (im)pure social science to a learned, if personal, diary, to creative nonfiction, to something very much like—and in some cases, indistinguishable from—a novel, a documentary, or even a book of short stories (see Conquergood and Segal, 1990; Denzin, 1997; Ellis and Bochner, 1996; Goodall, 1989, 1991, 1996).

This abusive view of ethnography as a curiosity in communication studies does, indeed, make the activities that constitute it appear unusual enough, but the truth about what ethnographers do—as well as why they do it—is admittedly stranger still. This is because the true practice of ethnography,[1] while found in relatively ordinary, sometimes tedious, and usually everyday experiences and analytical considerations of the complex meanings of persons, places, and things, is in fact, *extraordinary*, which is to say, *transformative*. In the remainder of this brief essay I will outline a case for why this essential strangeness is so vital, and what this extraordinary practice can teach the disciplines that comprise what we these days call "communication studies."

THE NATURE OF TRANSFORMATION, THE NURTURING OF LIVED EXPERIENCE

Transformation is a term—very much like "communication"—that is largely misunderstood, often misused, and therefore generally undervalued. Articles appear before us in newspapers and popular magazines touting "the transformation of global business" via some new software package (marketed no doubt by Microsoft), or "the transformation of day-time television" based on the appearance of yet another cable all-news, all-sports,

---

[1] Anyone using audacious language such as I just have in the phrase "the true practice of ethnography" owes the reader some form of postmodern explanation (e.g., the "true" is different from the Truth in that the former is a loose contextual signifier while the latter is a modernist dream) as well as an outright apology to the critical theorists who might otherwise perceive such a statement as a rhetorical grab for power via definitional dominance and textual control. Sigh. That said, what I do mean here is that when excellence in ethnography is attained, the process and product are very much akin to bringing to life works of art, in and through which the transformation via the ordinary—for the artist as well as for the audience—takes place; for a fuller explanation of this perspective, see Wolcott (1995); for an explication of how this artful work is deeply related to a moral imperative, see Denzin (1997). For some examples of writing experiments drawn from autobiographical materials, see Ellis and Bochner (1996).

or altogether-too-much television channel. Romance is "transformed" by a new fragrance for men (highly unlikely); fashion is "transformed" by a new look, always, and always seasonally. One result of this commodity-based rhetoric of transformation is a general devaluing of the term; another is an increasing inability to appreciate the nature of transformation as a deeply dramatic, often terribly poetic, always ontologically moving life experience that alters, fundamentally, our approach to and understandings of who we are, what we are here for, and how the awe and all of it *means*. Put a little more simply, transformation occurs not on the surfaces, but in the *soul* of life.

This, then, is what ethnographers do (see Anderson & Goodall, 1994; Goodall, 1996). We seek to discover the soul in the ordinary, the everyday, and the otherwise obvious; we are on a quest for clues to some greater mystery, some evolving, perhaps even final, pattern in communication that yields "a sacred unity" (Bateson & Donaldson, 1991; McPhail, 1996). When you set out with that sort of destination, *everything counts* (Goodall, 1989, 1994). Unlike our socially scientific brethren within the communication faith, our guiding (or confining) metaphor is not "behavior" but "culture," so our interest is less in repeatable findings than in finding in the repeatable patterns what is otherwise purposefully being left unsaid, underspoken, or that which suggests the taken-for-granted done within the presence of what is ineffable. We read cultures from the inside out, then from the outside back in, by which I mean from conversational experiences, interpretive observations, and semiotic readings of signs to the mythic and narrative tensions that exist in between those always contested lines. Clues to a culture are a deep and dialogic duality, at once locked within the hermeneutically sealed worlds made of their metaphors as well as within larger world dialogues that go on outside of them (see Conquergood & Segal, 1990).[2]

Through all of these acts of perceptual and linguistic association, these connective rhetorical and semiotic practices, we are simultaneously (and often, relentlessly) engaged as well in a *self-*defining process. For us it is a way of temporally and epistemically centering ourselves, however improbably, in the inevitable swirl and collective mix of this sensual, collaborative scene. It serves as a way of finding and articulating a point of view from which to further engage the ongoing dialogue, but it may appear to those searching for well-defined methods or additive findings too much like the unnecessary leaves of self-disclosure that simply obscure the damned trunk of the tree from clear, panoptical view. For those of us struggling to find our way to meaning through an ecology of lived experiences, this self-defining process of dialogic engagement feels a lot more like coming to terms not only with the metaphorical trunks of trees and the arguable beauty of such leaves, but moreover with the very roots of scholarly and personal authenticity.

So it is that our *lived experiences* within a given cultural space form and define our exploratory boundaries (see Goodall, 1991; Jackson, 1989). Our lived experiences situate our selves within a context of Others. Necessarily, the dialogic tensions between researcher and researched establish many of the meaningful patterns that are used to piece together various clues to the overall puzzle, but the third partner to every dialogue is the *place,* or context, in which meanings occur, the living space of experiential realities. One of the early clues for disciplinary transformation currently available to communication researchers that is drawn from ethnographic inquiries concerns the general contextual weakness in most studies of relationships, groups, or even organizations. Persons interact within real and imagined places, and what goes on in the imagination of relational partners is often as meaningful (if not more so) than what actually gets recorded in a behaviorally oriented transcript.

---

[2]I am thinking here of Dwight Conquergood's work with the Hmong people and with the Chicago street gang "The Latin Kings"; in both cases the conversations that form the dominant ethnographic texts are further inflected with political, economic, and cross-cultural meanings derived from larger world issues. His documentary film *Heart Broken in Half* (1991) is a vivid rendering of these complexities.

Communication is only in part "observable" behavior. It is also—some might say more so—both source and vehicle for the imagination, wherein part of what can be imagined seems always to be a dialogic interplay between real and metaphorical contexts that are themselves lived out within a specific place, community, context, or locale. Ecocritics have recently argued that "place" deserves equal status with race, class, and gender in cultural studies, and Christopher Tilly (1994; see also Sennett, 1990) makes an impressive argument for constructing a phenomenology of place to inform any study of human meaning-making. Ethnographers—at least ever since Malinowski—have always done this. Lived experience is lived *somewhere,* after all. It's just that where that "somewhere" is carries a mindful body into and through it.

All of this leads up to the hardest part of being an ethnographer, which is also the *Tao* of ethnographic lived experience: discovering, sometimes creating, the meaningful *questions* that open up and expose the real and imagined tensions in everyday life within a context occupied by bodies, voices, imaginations, and minds; of acquiring the authentic habits of hanging out; of doing the routine work of collecting the experiences of culture as well as of imagining it; of dialogic participation in what I call "the plural present" (1991, pp. 211–215); of making entries into—and exits from—the presence and absence of conversations with and about Others within such a land—and mind—scape. Collectively, these activities are the "how-tos" of *nurturing* lived experiences. Of nurturing the soul of communication through ethnographic practice. Maybe just nurturing the soul, period.

MAKING SPACE FOR THE SOUL IN COMMUNICATION STUDIES

Transformation is a highly creative experience. Drawing its many energies from mythic forms of change, its experiential and narrative path is part silence and part drama, part ritual and part personal mastery, part desire and part fulfillment of that desire—these tensions always mixed and con-

fluent in ways that could not have been fully anticipated (see Goodall, 1996; Whyte, 1994). Transformation begins in the middles of things and seemingly ends at the beginnings, thus confounding and redefining any sense of linear time. It is perhaps the most influential form of communication known.

What I've just described as transformation is analogous to the "universal story" of fieldwork experience. Ethnographers enter the field to conduct *in vivo* studies of something we pretty much believe we already understand; after all, we have read the appropriate books, attended lectures, tracked down theoretical subtleties and various nuances of academic interpretation. However, we soon learn that what we are confronting is *different.* In part this difference is derived from the stark realization that although people in any culture may resemble theories about that culture, they aren't necessarily bound by those theories. And in part it is the even starker realization that we are "there"; that what we discover, create, or learn is highly dependent upon who we are, and *how* we are (see Ellis and Bochner, 1996; Geertz, 1988). Instead of interpreting our experiences as data about behavior, we learn to see them as lessons about the cultural and personal connections in and among lives that hold within them clues to a deeper, coherent mystery (see Denzin, 1997; Goodall, 1989, 1991, 1996). Eventually, if we are lucky, we are transformed through our experiences and by the new and complex knowledge that we acquire, and with that transformation comes changes to the shape and content of the stories we have to tell.

Making room for those stories is making room for the soul in communication studies. It is to re-think what "communication" is *about,* as well as *for.* As I have argued elsewhere (Goodall, 1993), it is to learn to see what we have known and studied as "communication" as the evolution of a partial and partisan account of the essential role of communication in the lives of human beings. It is as if we have effectively defined human beings as "soulless sacks of behaviors, suspended by calcium skeletons and driven by something called cognitions" (op. cit., p. 41) instead of viewing the ability to communicate as a sign of why we are here as well as the principal way of understanding our individual and collective purpose. When viewed alternatively from the experiential core of ethnographic transformation, the soul of communication studies (as represented by the vast majority of our scholarly work, textbooks, and teaching) is, simply put, *lost*. To continue the ecology metaphor begun earlier, it is as if by concentrating so hard and so long on figuring out the behavior of trees, we have missed the point of the existence of a forest altogether.

Communication is and can be about many facets of human experience, from the behavioral and rhetorical to the cognitive and contextual, as well as the larger question of coherence in an ecology of the cosmic. By focusing communication studies on the movements of bodies and/or the cull and pull of cognitions, we have sacrificed the soul for knowledge about the body and mind, a Faustian equation if ever there were one. Yet the ability of human beings to find transformative connections between and among ourselves as well as with and through nature persists in everyday places, as ordinary people discover extraordinary connections and use communication to coach and urge their lives into meanings. They explicitly practice communication as the everyday activity, sometimes the art, of divining signs and symbols, of treating the voice as the breath of the soul and the eyes as its beautiful windows. By devaluing the soulful contributions of communication, we marginalize what is, for most people, most important about what we say we study, which is how they create meanings for their lives.

Transformative ethnographic experiences teach us that the stories we have been telling about human communication are, at best, incomplete, and at worst, incoherent. Neither modernist social science nor postmodern pastiche critique is likely to recapture what is missing, which is the soul—call it the Spirit—in communication studies. While each in its own right has something of value to offer to our understanding of the hows and whats and wherefores of communicating, it is the *why* question that ethnographic transformations produce

and that rediscovering issues of human communicative purpose—the soul of communication studies—can best address.

When this happens, if it happens, it is the narrative representation of what constitutes a legitimate "communication study" that must also be altered. As everyone in this field knows, we are—to borrow Max Weber's metaphor—"suspended in webs of our own significance," these days thought to be the narrative wraps that cover the disciplinary self. Journals in our field still tend not to be very much interested in work that does not adhere to the page limitations of social science or rhetorical studies, a move on behalf of the ideology of the bottom line that severely impacts how ethnographic interpretation can be rendered, which in turn effectively restricts what constitutes our "professional literature." Curiously, with increased public scrutiny about the merits of academic publication, it seems far more likely that the worth of our disciplinary storyline, and not the disciplinary bottom line, will be that which most matters.

It is often said when you choose an ethnographic life, you must do so aware of the challenges I've just discussed. That's true, but I've also learned that the choice to become an ethnographer is one that, alternatively, may be thought of as "visited upon" a scholar because of her or his place in the overall order of persons, places, and things. Ethnography chooses *you*. By extension, the inroads of ethnographic practice and the need—as I see it—for alternative storytelling in communication studies seems to me to have arrived simultaneously at the same propitious moment: our discipline has never been more in need of transformation, in part because it has never before had to bear the public weight of so much accumulated scholarly knowledge adding up to so relatively little coherent public news, and in part because even within our own disciplinary ranks the audience for any work of scholarship is dangerously fragmented and increasingly small. Although we applaud a kind of diversity—more and more interest groups can author scholarship done in mostly traditional and always narrowly defined texts—there are fewer and fewer common texts of communicative knowledge, fewer and fewer widely shared principles or beliefs about communication, such that the research stories we are telling are at risk of becoming irrelevant even to ourselves.

Ethnographies reestablish public relevance because they place the study and practices of communication directly into the rich, lived experiences of cultures. Because they reveal transformations, because they are personal as well as professional, and because they tend to be good reads for intelligent lay people as well as for subdisciplinary loyalists, they can and do connect the academic study of communication to important issues and lessons in the various localized complexities of our everyday world. When they are done well, ethnographies search for, grapple with, and sometimes find the soul of communities and relationships, in which "communication"—or its absence—figures in as the operant tender. We must, therefore, promote and sustain such work, curious as it may appear to be.

REFERENCES

Anderson, J. A., and Goodall, H. L. (1994). Probing the body ethnographic: From an anatomy of inquiry to a poetics of expression," in F. L. Casmir (Ed.), *Communication theories: A socio/cultural approach* (pp. 87–130). Hillsdale, NJ: Erlbaum.

Bateson, G., and Donaldson, R. (1991). *A sacred unity: Further steps toward an ecology of mind.* New York: HarperCollins.

Conquergood, D., and Segal, T. (1990). *Hearts broken in half.* [ethnographic documentary film]

Denzin, N. (1997). *Interpretive ethnography: Ethnographic practices for the 21st century.* Thousand Oaks, CA: Sage Press.

Ellis, C., and Bochner, A. P. (Eds.). (1996). *Composing ethnography: Alternative forms of qualitative writing.* Walnut Creek, CA: AltaMira Press.

Geertz, C. (1988). *Works and lives: The anthropologist as author.* Palo Alto, CA: Stanford University Press.

Goodall, H. L. (1989; 1994). *Casing a promised land: The autobiography of an organizational detective as cultural ethnographer.* Carbondale, IL: Southern Illinois University Press.

Goodall, H. L. (1991). *Living in the rock n roll mystery: Reading context, self, and others as clues.* Carbondale, IL: Southern Illinois University Press.

Goodall, H. L. (1993). Mysteries of the future told: Communication as the material manifestation of consciousness. *World Communication, 22,* 40–49.

Goodall, H. L. (1996). *Divine signs: Connecting spirit to communities.* Carbondale, IL: Southern Illinois University Press.

Jackson, M. (1989). *Paths toward a clearing: Radical empiricism and ethnographic inquiry.* Bloomington, IN: Indiana University Press.

McPhail, M. (1996). Spirituality and the critique of epistemic rhetoric: A coherentist analysis. *Journal of Communication and Religion, 19,* 48–60.

Sennett, R. (1990). *The conscience of the eye.* New York: Basic Books.

Tilly, C. (1994). *The phenomenology of landscape: Places, paths, and monuments.* Oxford: Berg Press.

Whyte, D. (1994). *The heart aroused: Poetry and the preservation of the soul in corporate America.* New York: Currency/Doubleday.

Wolcott, H. F. (1995). *The art of fieldwork.* Walnut Creek, CA: AltaMira Press.

CHAPTER 16.

AT THE HELM IN INTERCULTURAL AND CROSS CULTURAL COMMUNICATION

Introduction

Deborah F. Atwater

Pennsylvania State University

Good morning, Jambo, Buenos Dias, I am Deborah F. Atwater and I am serving as Chair of one of seventeen programs for the "At the Helm" series. I am currently Head of the Department of African and African American Studies, Associate Professor of Speech Communication at Penn State University. As a past President of the Eastern Communication Association and longtime member of the National Communication Association, I have seen the importance of intercultural and cross cultural communication grow within the field of communication as our global world diminishes in size but increases in its complexity.

On the eve of the twenty-first century, the United States is experiencing a dramatic shift in its demographic composition, which includes a greater percentage of people of color. In 20 years, African Americans, Latinos, and Asian Americans will comprise more than one-third of the nation, and about one-half of the nation by the year 2050. We must recognize that each group brings its own norms for language, communication behavior, thinking patterns, and learning styles to what may be defined as the "New American Mosaic." (Orlando Taylor, 1991, p. i in Dandy's *Black Communications: Breaking Down the Barriers*).

The way we interact, react, and think comes from our culture and culture may be defined as the values, symbols, interpretations, and perspectives that distinguish one group of people from another. Culture is transmitted within the group through expressive means: language, music, dance, and even food. Using intercultural communication effectively requires an open mind, and a recognition of different language styles, rules, norms, and behaviors. By valuing diversity in our interactions, we contribute to a positive environment for all parties involved. The American mosaic or quilt really is a work of communicative art.

This morning our three panelists will share their unique and thought-provoking perspectives on issues and trends in the field of intercultural and cross-cultural communication. You might say that I have the opportunity to weave or sew a diversity quilt or kente cloth with different ideas from people with different backgrounds whose common thread or binding tie is an interest and expertise in intercultural communication.

Professor Dolores V. Tanno earned her Ph.D. from the University of Southern California and is currently Visiting Associate Professor in the Department of Communication at California State

University, San Bernadino. Professor Tanno's research centers on the ethical implications in multicultural communication studies.

She has published widely in the journals in the field and she serves on the editorial boards of *The Howard Journal of Communications, Western Journal of Communication, Women's Studies in Communication,* and has been a reviewer for *Communication Monographs.*

Professor Tanno's topic is "At the Helm" in Graduate Education: Service as Preparation for and Practice of Intercultural Communication Theory.

Professor Carolyn Calloway-Thomas earned her Ph.D. from Indiana University and is Associate Professor of Speech Communication and Adjunct Associate Professor of Afro-American Studies at Indiana University, Bloomington. Professor Calloway-Thomas's research focuses on communication in Black America, intercultural communication, and historical and contemporary public address.

She has published in *Southern Speech Communication Journal, Quarterly Journal of Speech, The Howard Journal of Communications, Communication Quarterly,* and the *Journal of Black Studies,* has several books and serves on several editorial boards. She is also past President of Central States Communication Association, has ex-

tensive NCA service, and has lectured in Barbados, Nigeria, Puerto Rico, and Senegal. But what she really wants me to say is that she loves lively conversation and has some flair for gardening. She savors the grace notes of life culled from elegant minds. One of her favorite quotes is "Do the best you can with what you have" (Thurgood Marshall). Her topic is "Cheer the Weary Traveler: Reframing Conversation and Ethnicity."

Professor Alberto Gonzalez received his Ph.D. from Ohio State University and is an Associate Professor in the Department of Interpersonal Communication at Bowling Green University. His research deals with a wide range of areas and interests, including popular music, technology, political rhetoric, and the impact of culture on communication. He has published in many of the journals in the field and has served on the editorial boards of *The Howard Journal of Communications, Quarterly Journal of Speech, Women's Studies in Communication,* and the *New York Communication Annual.*

Lastly, Professor Gonzalez is the 1995 winner of the Distinguished Scholarship Award (International and Intercultural Division of NCA). His topic is "My Back Pages: Confessions of a Fugitive Interculturalist."

"At the Helm" in Graduate Education: Service as Preparation for and Practice of Intercultural Communication Theory

Dolores V. Tanno
California State University, San Bernadino

There are many reasons why a discipline would want to position itself "at the helm." Some of these reasons include, but are not limited to, the maintenance of programmatic and curricular order; the promotion of the simultaneous conduct of theory and practice; the conviction that we have accumulated some knowledge of the world as it is or, perhaps more accurately, how we think it should be; or simply because we think we have a better view of what lies ahead. The academy has a long history of being unfettered in these pursuits and in the process we have developed a relatively clear academic identity. That identity is increasingly being challenged by society at large, by students, by government, and even by some within the academy and rightly so. No institution should ever be immune to challenges. We have been pushed to answer for our processes and our values and our place in society. Accurately or not, we are being perceived as distant from the world around us. Perhaps it is not too far fetched to say that the academy, long accustomed to defining itself as being at the center of society, is now being defined by others as being close to or at the social margins. In discussing a "European Perspective on Multiculturalism" Francis Crawley (1994) describes this challenge to academic identity as being confronted "with feelings of no longer being home, of being confused, of having lost our way" (p. 38).

Of all the challenges facing the academy perhaps the most significant has been the shift from a monocultural perspective to a multicultural perspective of the world. This shift of perspective has expanded our understanding of the definitions, forms, and purposes of communication in cultural contexts. This has in turn led us to a concomitant shift in our ideas about what is or is not "effective" or "correct" or "persuasive" or "respectful" or "informative" communication behavior. Within the academy we have attempted to meet the challenge inherent in this perspectival shift. We have revised curriculum, introduced graduate programs in intercultural communication, and created journals and annuals that emphasize the study of multicultural communication. As faculty, especially those who left graduate school before the advent of the multicultural perspective, we have educated ourselves in the theories and processes of multiculturalism. However, one area seems to me to have remained firmly rooted in the past and it is in that area that our discipline should strive to be "at the helm."

I refer to the graduate education process. Many of the challenges to higher education have come because the world around us has dramatically changed. Although we have acknowledged these changes in various ways, the process and philosophy of graduate education has remained fixed. We continue to concentrate on teaching information gathering, critical evaluation, and methodologies; we continue to encourage writing that targets others like us; we continue to inculcate in students the attitude of expert "other"; and we continue to emphasize theory over praxis. All of these are arguably good and necessary, but in our world now they are no longer sufficient. One measure of insufficiency is the increasingly negative view by society of the time-honored myth of the ivory tower.

The ivory tower has been a defining narrative in academia. Within the ivory walls we have pursued knowledge often for its own sake, often a far remove from the world surrounding us. This myth still looms large in graduate education, although the shadow it casts is dimmed with each passing year as graduate students increasingly question the value of an education devoid of "real-world" connections. As long as we keep this myth alive, we will continue to provide graduate students with ideas and theories and communication visions that expand their academic minds, but seldom their social minds, and there is a difference between the two. Our academic minds are often confined to the abstract and theoretical contexts; our social minds seek a larger context, more concrete, more practical, more attuned to everyday living in a social context. More than merely attuned to everyday living, our social minds seek ways of producing something that will alleviate the problems that assault our senses at seemingly every turn.

I have been intrigued and gladdened at the rather steady production of publications by those within the academy who have raised questions about the academy's place in society. For the past 20 years, we have had such publications as Corry's (1970) *Farewell the Ivory Tower: Universities in Transitions,* in which he addresses the roles of universities in Canada; Bok's (1982) *Beyond the Ivory Tower: Latino Professors in American Universities,* in which he advocates that universities must assume social as well as academic responsibilities; Padilla and Chavez's (1995) *The Leaning Ivory Tower: Latino Professors in American Universities,* in which they bring together a collection of essays that challenge the continuing hegemonic practices within colleges and universities; Herriot's (1984) *Down From the Ivory Tower: Graduates and Their Jobs,* in which he focuses specifically on the graduate recruitment process and advocates for a recruitment process that forces the universities to leave the safety of academia and venture out into the social world; and Lempert's (1996) *Escape From the Ivory Tower,* in which he describes an educational process grounded in responsiveness and accountability to community.

This collection of authors make it clear that the relationship between social issues and processes and academic issues and processes can no longer be one of polite reserve and distance. Neither can we expect that our future graduate

students will so easily accept what may appear to them to be an unrealistic process. As Cristina Gonzalez (1995) has argued, "if we continue to teach our graduate students in ways that perpetuate the systems that have contributed to their personal infernos, then we can never expect to remedy the problems we so eloquently and frequently lament" (p. 88).

There are always options, of course. We could fortify the ivory walls as we deny that change is necessary. We can opt for retreat, confining ourselves within the tower, hoping to ride out the current sociopolitical climate that "allows" those outside the academy to define what education *is* and what education *is for.* Or we can participate fully in the envisioning of higher education for the future.

It becomes clearer to me with each passing year that future students will be bringing quite different worldviews to the graduate education process. These will be the individuals who most likely will have experienced multicultural education throughout their student careers. These will be the students who most likely will have participated in what Lempert (1996) has called "democratic experiential education" (p. 69), some features of which include teachers as facilitators, and more importantly, responsiveness and accountability to the community as I mentioned previously, as well as multiculturalism, and ethics. What will these students do when they reach graduate school and discover a process that provides them with information about and practice in critical thinking and research methodologies, but little about the individual and social impact of what they do and their way of doing it? How are they to maintain and also implement the skills they will presumably bring with them, skills of responsiveness and accountability to the community, of thinking about the ethical aspects of their work, of practicing the facilitating dimension of teaching? Can we hope to retain these students in a graduate training environment that does not give emphasis to these skills? How can we build on the multiculturalism that will have been part of their educational experience at the elementary and high school and undergraduate levels?

And were we to build on it, what would graduate education look like?

In my view, *one of the most prominent components of graduate education in the twenty-first century should be community service.* In graduate school we were given the opportunity to teach and to observe others who teach. We were taught to do research (and I will return to this component a bit later). Only on rare occasions were we encouraged to serve our social communities and rarer still taught to do so as an important and necessary part of our graduate training. Yet it is these communities that will become the source of working information for those graduates who choose to focus on intercultural communication. Intercultural communication principles and theories make some sense in the classroom but their true meanings and values are not really made apparent until they are placed in the larger communal context. Where better than in graduate school to be reminded that we are of the world and not only of the academy? When students make community service a part of their lives, that service becomes a preparation for the development of multicultural communication theories and principles based on experience as well as study. When students make community service a part of their lives, that service also provides them with opportunities to practice the theories and principles of multicultural communication.

This vision of community service as a required component of graduate education in the future is still quite new to me, its shape not yet clearly outlined, its foundation only half conceived. I am selfishly using this opportunity to articulate what I do envision, inviting you to join me in refining this vision, working out the details together, as we move to a new era in the academy's place in society. Having made that confession and having issued the invitation to re-envision the future of graduate education, let me move on to a series of questions meant to help clarify the value of introducing community service into the graduate education process.

These questions have to do with the research component of graduate education and how it might be impacted by introducing service into the process. The critical reading of books and journal articles and the development of our own ideas and studies represent one way our view of the world is clarified and broadened. As students develop studies, we encourage them to ask: Why am I doing this particular research? Why do I choose a particular methodology? Why do I focus upon a particular cultural group? What are my biases and prejudices? What do I hope to accomplish? What are the implications? They seek answers to these questions as a matter of course and we have a label for it: we call it "providing a rationale." These questions are often asked either in the context of the study itself and/or in the context of the broader discipline.

There are other ways of clarifying and broadening our worldview. Adding the service component to graduate education would, I think, make us better critics and researchers. This would provide the larger social context within which we might ask the same questions. Consider how the meanings might change when students ask these questions with the larger social context in mind and with a background rich in community service. Why am I doing this particular research, choosing this particular methodology, focusing on this particular cultural group? What are my biases and prejudices? What do I hope to accomplish? Within this larger context, the answers will come from a more intimate understanding of the daily lives of the people within the communities they study. Such understanding may help all of us realize that beyond the ivory tower, we are not so much experts as mediators. We mediate between people's cultural experiences and the formal bodies of knowledge created by those experiences. As students place the research process in the communal context, they also become aware of the ethical aspects of their work. What impact does my work have on my discipline, on a given cultural group, on the larger social group, on me? What responsibilities do I have and to whom am I accountable?

One responsibility that occurs to me is that of communicating what we know or think we know to communities, to the general public, as well as to narrower audiences of our discipline and/or our interest groups. I do identify with Henry Perkinson (1969) who wrote about the difficulties he faced when preparing a talk about the future of education. "I was at a loss to go about describing the future," Perkinson wrote, "all the more so since I belong to that congregation of historians who regard it as a sin not to use the past to predict what will happen in the future. We call it historicism and excommunicate any who practice it." He went on to explain, "My (academic) upbringing…had been so rigid that I found myself unable to use the history of education to forecast the future of education" (p. 1). Like Perkinson, I have belonged to a congregation of academics who have traditionally considered it "unacademic" if not altogether sinful to be of the world first and then of the academy; to emphasize praxis over theory; to write in the first person or to use story telling as a matter of course; or to rely on experience as a credible source of knowledge. We have traditionally considered it suspect to write for a general audience. All of these have not been considered "intellectually respectable." Yet, if we are to successfully leave the ivory tower (and here I am assuming we want to leave the ivory tower), we have to make these respectable, intellectually as well as socially.

Let me return to Perkinson. True to his academic training, he operationalized his problem: "My problem was to find some way to make my dreams and visions and hopes intellectually respectable. I finally hit upon the methodological device of a single-factor explanation.…The joy of a single-factor explanation is that it can be pushed and pulled in various and intricate ways.… In what follows I will be using a single factor to try to inject some coherence into my own very personal notions about the future" (p. 1). Perkinson's single-factor explanation was "information explosion"; mine has been incorporating community service into graduate education. I, too, wanted to inject some coherence into my own personal emotions about the future of graduate education. I am well aware that graduate education is only one factor among many that identify our academic mission and our academic identity. Our methodologies, our pedagogical theories and practices, our reasons for pursuing knowledge, our visions of ourselves as researchers and critics, and the types of writing we declare to be intellectually respectable—all of these are factors. In my single-factor mode, however, I have chosen community service as the inroad to all of these. My point is that in the graduate education process of the future, we might want to teach the value of community service by making service an important and necessary aspect of graduate training. In that way, future researchers and critics may be more motivated to write for the general public and for cultural communities, to write *stories* of understanding as well as *studies* of understanding, to be as comfortable writing in the first person as in the third person, to recognize the us/them component in jargonistic writing, and recognize equally that other types of writing can erase that separation. More importantly, the theories and principles of multicultural communication developed by students such as these are bound to provide a greater understanding of cultural communities.

It is my argument that the incorporation of community service into the graduate process has great potential. I would summarize that potential this way: Community service can help place ideas and knowledge into a larger social context; it can remind us that we are in this world together, to survive or to perish; it can help in the examination of motives for being researchers and critics and to appreciate the value of writing for the general public; and it can also help in enhancing our awareness of the ethical impact of what we do.

There is a measure of vision, a greater measure of courage, and an enormous measure of responsibility to being "at the helm." Vision gets us there, courage helps us move forward, and responsibility ensures that both our vision and our courage are grounded in ethical principles. If we want to be at the forefront, where better than in the incorporation of community service into graduate education processes in and for the future?

REFERENCES

Bok, D. (1982). *Beyond the ivory tower.* Cambridge: Harvard University Press.

Corry, J. A. (1970). *Farewell the ivory tower: Universities in transitions.* Montreal: McGill-Queens University Press.

Crawley, F. P. (1994, Summer). Absolute truth, radical relativism, and the Euroversity: A European perspective on multiculturalism. *International Educator, 22–38.*

Gonzalez, C. (1995). In search of the voice I always had. In R. Padilla & R. Chavez (Eds.), *The leaning ivory tower: Latino professors in American universities* (pp. 77–90). Albany, NY: State University of New York Press.

Herriot, P. (1984). *Down from the ivory tower: Graduates and their jobs.* New York: John Wiley & Sons.

Lempert, D. H. (1996). *Escape from the ivory tower.* San Francisco: Jossey-Bass.

Padilla, R. V. & Chavez, R. C. (1995). *The leaning ivory tower: Latino professors in American universities.* Albany, NY: State University of New York Press.

Perkinson, H. J. (1969). Education in the twenty-first century. In H. London & A. Spinner (Eds.), *Education in the twenty-first century* (pp. 1–11). Danville, IL: Interstate Printers & Publishers, Inc.

Cheer the Weary Traveler: Reframing Conversation and Ethnicity

Carolyn Calloway-Thomas
Indiana University

Of the many issues that have lately commanded the public's attention, perhaps none has been more hotly debated than the issues of affirmative action, feminism, and multiculturalism. Issues such as these, and the debate over the Western canon, once moved author Saul Bellow to say "When the Zulus produce a Tolstoy we will read him," and Houston Baker to say that choosing between Pearl Buck and Virginia Woolf is "no different from choosing between a hoagy and a pizza." On June 18, 1996, I presented a lively seminar at Indiana University titled "Under Cherry Trees There Are No Strangers: Communicating Interculturally." Following my presentation, I invited my delightfully attentive audience to ask questions and make comments. Things proceeded as expected until a gentleman named Calvin made an observation that is of the greatest pertinence today: "I don't understand why people refer to themselves as African American, Asian American, or Hispanic American. *We are all Americans!*"

Bellow's and Baker's famous quotes, along with Calvin's implied suggestion that recognition of a person's ethnic identity is irrelevant to who we are as Americans, all are compelling examples of issues that lie at the heart of the present struggle over ethnicity. We deduce many lessons from Calvin's comment, such as that our nationhood and identity must be "taken very seriously," that specific references to ethnicity challenge our thinking and way of life, and that public references to ethnicity should be discouraged.

Indeed, I am struck by how well Calvin's comments reflect the tensions inherent in the way Americans talk to one another about matters of multiculturalism nationwide. Today, we all too often lose our bearings and talk at cross-purposes.

An underlying reason for our wrenching public conversations concerning multiculturalism is an issue that philosopher Charles Taylor (1992) terms the "politics of recognition."

If Taylor's presence is so conspicuous in this essay, so are memories and stories of cultural tensions that have mounted in public discourse: Roger Kimball's (1990) characterization of black studies as "this war against Western culture" (p. xi), Leonard Jefferies's description of white Americans as "ice people," Alan Bloom's (1987) view of liberal teachers as "intellectual barbarians" and "culture peddlers" (p. xii), talk show host Rush Limbaugh's characterization of feminists as "feminazis," as well as the chants at Stanford University that accompanied the debate over the Western canon ("Down with racism, down with Western culture, up with diversity," "Hey, hey, ho, ho, Western culture's got to go"). These are only a handful of examples of an unrestrained character in public discourse concerning multiculturalism.

Why are there such acrimonious disagreements over ethnicity? Rodney King's searing question, "Why can't we just get along?" has become cliché precisely because it mirrors so well our public frailties and difficulties. The overarching question we face is simply this: How can individuals with conflicting purposes and agendas articulate their concerns to one another constructively and civilly, using public argument? Because the conflicting concerns, issues, and debates over multiculturalism are related in very complex ways and go to the heart of who we are as Americans, we cannot so easily dismiss advocates and opponents of multiculturalism as simply "racists," or "crazy" individuals who have ventured into "Cloud-Cuckooland."

To understand some of the issues which frame our moral disagreements over multiculturalism, let us first look briefly at historical origins. According to Taylor (1992) and Hannerz (1992), modern debates about identity and recognition that are raging across the land today are in part "an offshoot of the decline of hierarchical society" (p. 31). In earlier societies hierarchies were the basis for honor and were intrinsically linked to "inequalities" (Taylor, 1992, p. 27). Titles such as Duke, Duchess, Emperor, and Queen are vivid reminders of the relationship that once obtained between one's social position and the duties and responsibilities that accompanied status. During the feudal period, for example, public disputes over issues of recognition were largely muted because identity was fixed by one's social position. Because people knew who they were by virtue of their titles or position in society, questions such as "What does it mean to be a person?" and "What constitutes personal identity?" were hardly, if ever, raised.

When hierarchies truly mattered, however, they reflected preferential status, as in the case of bestowing honor on individuals, for example, the Order of Canada. It was reasoned that an individual who received such an honor was worthy and that "worth would be removed if tomorrow we decided to give it to every adult Canadian" (Taylor, 1990, p. 27).

My point is that in earlier times people were comfortable with hierarchy. Today, however, the modern notion of "dignity" has superseded the old notion of honor. Herein lies some of the current problems in public argument today over multiculturalists' insisting upon "recognition." This insistence upon "recognition" carries with it divided sentiments concerning interpretations of "equal recognition."

Proponents of egalitarianism and equal dignity have met with strong opposition. Pulitzer Prize–winning critic William A. Henry III (1994) argues persuasively in *In Defense of Elitism* that egalitarianism is a myth, "a vital lie," and that the defense of elitism "is ultimately nothing more than the defense of common sense" (pp. 31–32). Other writers (Himmelfarb, 1994; Ravitch, 1973) also argue sim-

ilarly. While proponents of equal rights put a premium on the idea that all cultures have something worth knowing, the elitist view serves to show the embeddedness of the current conflicts.

A decline in hierarchy also helps to explain why public arguments concerning ethnicity are framed around the dignity of human beings or to use Taylor's (1992) phrase—"the politics of recognition" (pp. 25–73). By identity I mean "who we are, where we're coming from" (Taylor, 1992, p. 33). Taylor perfectly catches the distinctive qualities of "the politics of recognition," that is, the way that recognition frames who we are. If we accept the notion that our identity is partly shaped by recognition or its absence, a person can, as Taylor notes, "suffer real damage, real distortion if the people of a society around them mirror back to them a confining or demeaning or contemptible picture of themselves" (p. 36).

Asante (1987) and Dates and Barlow (1990) argue that a negative portraiture derides, belittles, and robs African Americans of public virtue. Thus, minority group demands for recognition are deeply rooted in their claims to public virtue. Minorities' search for recognition clearly forces to the foreground the double agenda that characterizes current conflicts between multiculturalists and their opponents. These cultural tensions arise not from small disagreements or mundane matters. Rather they arise from strong notions of who we are as Americans, as well as from one side's claim that recognition should not be based upon ethnic identity but upon individual achievement in keeping with the ideals of democracy. The other side argues for recognition, elevating (implicitly and/or explicitly) ethnic origins and identity as, for example, in the case of most African Americans.

There are also other forces undergirding the cultural clash over ethnicity. I am referring to the eighteenth century notion that individuals are endowed with a moral sense. If one is in tune with one's moral sense, then one has a sense of what is right and wrong, good or bad, and so on. As Taylor (1992) notes, "being in touch with our feelings takes on independent and crucial moral significance" (p. 28). A moral sense, then, is another fundamental basis for multicultural groups' demands for equal treatment. President Clinton's statement in 1992 that he wanted a Cabinet that reflected America's multiethnic makeup is a striking example of the *"because something is good"* moral argument that is a source of much cultural hostility.

A final factor undergirding "the politics of recognition" is the dialogical quality of the human condition. Because we achieve our sense of humanity through interactions with others, that is, dialogically, this characteristic presupposes a connection between identity and recognition. This means, therefore, that our identity is also formed dialogically as George Herbert Mead (1934) notes in his book, *Mind, Self, and Society*. Mead introduces us to the concept, "significant others," to indicate that our sense of identity crucially depends upon our dialogical relations with others. Since this is the case, all of us—including African Americans, Latinos, Native Americans, and Asian Americans—depend upon *significant others* for an image of who we are. In the case of minorities, however, a demeaning or inferior image of them has been created and promoted by the larger society. This negative image can come not just from active misrepresentation, but from simple refusal of acknowledgement. As Taylor states, "Not only contemporary feminism but also race relations and discussions of multiculturalism are undergirded by the premise that the withholding of recognition can be a form of oppression" (1992, p. 36).

The point of this albeit brief sketch of the historical genesis of the worrisome debate over multiculturalism is to show that the movement from honor to identity and claims to the better side of our nature are the very foundation of one side's (multiculturalists) use of universal arguments and their accompanying symbols and meanings, and the other side's (opponents of multiculturalism) use of particularism and its accompanying symbols and meanings. As one might expect, among other reasons, minorities claim recognition on the basis of universal human identity and potential. Opponents of such beliefs uphold a different conception, however. They argue from a particularistic perspective and maintain that elevating race or

ethnic origin weakens the foundation of liberal democracy. For example, Henry (1994) reconciles democracy with elitism by claiming that America is "not a democracy pure and simple," but rather a *"representative* democracy" (p. 21). He reasons further that our elected officials represent such a norm because they are chosen "by virtue of superior talent, intellect, and drive," and that that expectation is evident in the aphorism "May the best man win" (p. 21). Thus, "this persistent if unarticulated elitism is compelling evidence for differentiating between egalitarianism and democracy" (p. 21).

Considering these opposing points of view (and there are many more that space will not permit me to articulate here), several questions beg to be answered: Is political recognition of ethnicity essential to a person's dignity? How can these competing arguments be reconciled for the good of society? What form should such resolution take?

As I have emphasized from the start, the spectrum of values, views, and arguments surrounding ethnicity is indeed wide. At issue are "competing moral visions" of what America *should be or do,* to use Hunter's phrase (1991, p. 107). It bears repeating that these competing visions of what *should* define America are taken very seriously by their respective adherents. Indeed, each group is motivated by its own "sources of moral authority"; that is, each group's views are firmly grounded in its own ideas of what is right or wrong, good or bad, appropriate or inappropriate, relevant or irrelevant, and important or unimportant.

Each source of moral authority has associated with it a line of argumentation. For example, multiculturalists argue that the Western canon should be expanded to include historical, artistic, and literary contributions that they have made to society. The opposition argues that some standard of judging the quality of *"the to be included"* works must be used. According to the opposition, high school and university students should not be assigned to read works such as Frederick Douglass's "Fourth of July Oration" and Louise Erdrich's *Love Medicine* based solely upon claims to ethnicity. Of course, most minorities agree with such sentiments as well. Asante (1987), however, asks compellingly "Whose standards of judging will be used?" The opposition, in turn, argues that it is possible to measure standards of beauty and brilliance, using Matthew Arnold's provocative phrase, "the best that has been thought and said," as a guide. Opponents respond by noting that Arnold's phrase represents an exclusively Western model of thinking and judging standards of beauty and brilliance. In this way, the arguments shift back and forth with little commonality between the two opposing groups.

Is it possible, then, given "competing moral visions," and given the difficult issues surrounding multiculturalism, for these disparate groups to resolve the cultural and social tensions that exist between them?

Underlying my argument about resolving quarrels between the two opposing groups is the idea that however different our ethical paths are through the wilderness, we must find a way to function well and harmoniously within our civic culture. We must know what is essential to interacting with others across the divide. We must know collectively what our society is and is not. These suggestions are motivated by my belief that humans are naturally inclined to seek the good, and that there are enough things that we share in common as humans to guide our collective paths (Berlin, 1991; Morris, 1994; Selznick, 1992; Wilson, 1993; Wright, 1994).

The first way that we might reframe the debate over multiculturalism and begin to foster a more harmonious public culture is to *change the environment of public discourse.* Hunter (1991) argues sensibly that media technologies are primarily responsible for passing along the *content* of debates that flow between opposing groups. Because the contending parties to a quarrel rely heavily on bits and pieces of information that flow back and forth via television, for instance, the parties rarely confront each other face-to-face. Giving groups along the great divide an opportunity to confront one another face-to-face should resurrect old-fashioned modes of discursive discourse, which would encourage a serious and rational public conversation.

I have in mind here an environment that would discourage rhetorical excess. All of us know very well that television invites sound bites and bombastic generalities. Changing the environment in which debates over ethnicity and race occur should help debaters to draw upon complex, rich sources of language, such as rebuttal, cross-examination, and presentation of evidence, in addition to predisposing individuals to civility. Would, for instance, a discussion between Leonard Jefferies and Diane Ravitch concerning the relative merits of "ice" cultures versus "warm" cultures degenerate in a face-to-face rhetorical environment free of television? Perhaps. However, the rules governing what can and cannot be said, when and where, should mitigate against the development of a hostile rhetoric. My point is that a change from a media environment to an environment more conducive to discursive talk should promote civility, community, and goodwill.

A second factor that would seem essential to framing a new dialogue between competing voices is *finding appropriate language with which to argue differing perspectives.* For example, to what extent can an ethnic white American be critical of black studies and Jewish studies, and other aspects of black and Jewish life, while at the same time avoiding charges of racism or anti-Semitism? I am searching for an increased human understanding. It is the kind of understanding that we invoke when we say things like, "*I understand what makes him or her tick,*" or "*Now we understand each other.*" What should the grammar and style of such language look like? What should it *be* and *do?*

If we are to expect anything bordering on congeniality, then we must find some way of checking our polarizing impulses or tendencies. Of course I am not suggesting the elimination of vigorous discussion and debate. Rather, I am concerned with ways of managing talk so that versions of our better selves will triumph in discussions and debates. As we grapple with these overarching issues, however, we must not fail to address the historical antecedents in the rhetorical environment, such as slavery, distrust, racism, and cultural differences. Indeed, one could argue that

America's pre-Civil War history of slavery and racism is a primary culprit in disputes over multiculturalism, not only because history depends upon memory, experience, and powerful cultural, political, and economic legacies, but also because the very nature of arguments over ethnicity is presumed to grow out of—at least in some measure—the question of nationality or "identity."

In fact, Derrick Bell's (1992) message in *Faces at the Bottom of the Well: The Permanence of Racism* is that "once-bright expectations for racial progress" are dimming and "will not alter the deeply entrenched components of racism" (pp. xi–xii). Such conclusions, however, diminish opportunities for using dialogue as *a way out* of the messiness of current discussions concerning multiculturalism. "If racism is permanent," some individuals ask, "then why discuss its very nature and remedy?"

Admittedly, reconciling extreme positions is no easy undertaking, despite my firm belief that common ground can be achieved. Hans-Georg Gadamer's (1975) notion of "fusion of horizons," which is akin to Taylor's (1990) notion of *perspicuous contrast,* offers some hope. Suppose, for example, that antiaffirmative action and proaffirmative action groups, with great effort and understanding, could articulate a language in which their differences could be *undistortively expressed to the satisfaction of both sides.* Broader understanding could be achieved by employing *comparison and contrast,* for example, which is a starting point with which we ought to approach analyses of difference. This way if and when opposing forces join together for an airing of differences for the good of the community, we might develop new vocabularies with which to understand the other's perspective. By *undistortively* transferring our private experience of empathy into language that the other can appreciate, by giving up isolation of views and separation in favor of becoming part of an organic community, we might begin to participate fully in a world where there exists no inside and outside, no "I" and "they" or "we" and "they." These are moments of bliss that we all can yearn for and that can indeed cheer the weary traveler.

REFERENCES

Asante, M. (1987). *The Afrocentric idea.* Philadelphia, PA: Temple University Press.

Bell, D. (1992). *Faces at the bottom of the well: The permanence of racism.* New York: Basic Books.

Berlin, I. (1991). *The crooked timber of humanity.* New York: Alfred A. Knopf.

Bloom, A. (1987). *The closing of the American mind.* New York: Simon & Schuster.

Dates, J. & Barlow, W. (Eds.). (1990). *Split image: African Americans in the mass media.* Washington, DC: Howard University Press.

Gadamer, H. (1975). *Truth and method.* New York: Seabury Press.

Hannerz, U. (1992). *Cultural complexity: Studies in the social organization of meaning.* New York: Columbia University Press.

Henry III, W. (1994). *In defense of elitism.* New York: Doubleday.

Himmelfarb, G. (1994). *On looking into the abyss: Untimely thoughts on culture and society.* New York: Alfred A. Knopf.

Hunter, J. (1991). *Culture wars: The struggle to define America.* New York: Basic Books.

Kimball, R. (1990). *Tenured radicals: How politics has corrupted higher education.* New York: Harper & Row, Publishers.

Mead, G. (1934). *Mind, self, and society.* Chicago: University of Chicago Press.

Morris, D. (1994). *The human animal.* New York: Crown Publishing Company.

Ravitch, D. (1973). *The great school wars: The public schools as a battleground for social change.* New York: Basic Books.

Selznick, P. (1992). *The moral commonwealth: Social theory and the promise of community.* Berkeley, CA: University of California Press.

Taylor, C. (1992). *Multiculturalism and "the politics of recognition."* Princeton, NJ: Princeton University Press.

Taylor, C. (1990). Comparison, history, truth. In F. Reynolds & D. Tracy (Eds.), *Myth and philosophy* (pp. 37–50). Albany: State University of New York Press.

Wilson, J. (1993). *The moral sense.* New York: The Free Press.

Wright, R. (1994). *The moral animal.* New York: Pantheon Books.

My Back Pages: Confessions of a Fugitive Interculturalist

Alberto González
Bowling Green State University

We must *mistake ourselves.*

Friedrich Nietzsche,
from *The Genealogy of Morals* (p. 149)

Fugitives run in my family. First there was José Luis González, my grandfather. He was in love with Librada Uribe, a young woman who delivered lunches to her father and brothers in a silver mine near Mexico City, Mexico. Tired of placating the Uribe family, whose daughter he wanted to marry, he masterminded her kidnapping. By the time the Uribes discovered what had happened to their daughter, José had crossed the northern border into the U.S. Not only was he a fugitive from the Uribes and Mexican law, he was a fugitive from the INS. Eventually, he traded the silver mines of central Mexico for the steel mills of Detroit.

My father, Silverio Uribe González, was a fugitive from Catholicism and the precepts of traditional Mexican culture. An avowed assimilationist, he read to his uninterested children British history, the philosophies of Dewey and Thoreau, and the folk wisdom of Franklin. That his co-existing mysticism, individualism, and skepticism revealed his Mexican sensibility was completely invisible to him. To this day, he claims to disdain the surrender to passion performed by his outlaw father and seeks to read the workings of the universe in the mowing of his lawn and the trimming of his tree branches.

My brother, Silverio, Jr., was a fugitive from sanity. Having internalized the assimilationist perspective of my father, he failed to reconcile the discrepancies between the media life of his hero, Ricky Nelson, and the irrepressible remnants of our Mexican heritage. There was little in anglo popular culture that seemed to fit the way we lived and it perplexed and embittered him. His subse-quent induction into the U.S. Army during the Vietnam era provided another contradicting life-style, and this experience guaranteed for the remainder of his too-short life powerful medications and periodic stays in hospital mental wards.

And that is only the male side of my family....

Compared to these epic dramas, my own sense of fugity is unremarkable. Nonetheless, there are parallels, and though many of the struggles of fugitives I have known seem remote, the fugitive concept helps me to understand and live with what I have done as an interculturalist in communication.

Fugity presupposes the breach of law. It also presupposes an ongoing evasion of capture and adjudication. It is a social drama where redress is in perpetual abeyance.

BREACH AND CONFESSION

Being there. Clifford Geertz, in his celebrated book (aren't all of them celebrated?) *Works and Lives: The Anthropologist as Author* (1988), distinguishes between being there and being here. Being there refers to the ethnographer's practice of living within the community whose members have been deemed to possess an approach to living that will become riveting upon its narratization. Being here refers to the academic settings within which concluding and writing take place. The challenge, of course, is to prevent the being there to get lost in the being here. As Geertz states, "The gap between engaging others where they are and representing them where they aren't, always immense but not much noticed, has suddenly become extremely visible. What once seemed only technically difficult, getting 'their' lives into 'our' works, has turned morally, politically, even epistemologically, delicate" (p. 130).

A confession: In communication studies, I hold myself partly responsible for making "delicate" discussions of and conclusions about intercultural interactions. In my own studies of Mexican Americans, and in the *Our Voices* (1997) anthology that Marsha Houston, Victoria Chen, and I edited, community inhabitants speak back. Put another way, we are the natives who were once studied who are now also generating cultural interpretation. Where before the researched communities remained remote, now we bring our communities with us as we encounter and respond to interpretations about us.

Until graduate school, it had never occurred to me that research on intercultural communication could be conducted without an experience of being within a cultural community. Yet, the research I read and the research I was encouraged to design took me farther and farther away from the ambivalences and embarrassments of participant observation. With the exception of two very powerful courses, I was immersed in the world of being here. Only recently have I understood the power of being here: Everyone in academe knows what here is. Only recently have I understood why, as I prepared to write a Master's thesis on Mexican American political activists, when I asked an African American professor, "For whom should I be writing?" he responded by saying, "Your committee. They grant the degree." That was good advice, but he had the same worn look in his eyes when he said it as my brother after his military discharge.

With all its dangers of going native, going paternal, and going showman, I have adhered to being there. And I have marveled at the courage of others as they retrieved moments that are forever carved on the post of memory—one example: the immigrant tenants of Big Red working together until midnight to restore water that had been shut off due to the landlord's neglect and indifference (Conquergood, 1992).

My confession is twofold. First, my objection to traditional intercultural research is to its fore-

grounding of the theory-validating here over the descriptive there.

Second, it is not out of any deeply moral or political mission to excavate and liberate Mexican American cultures that I have written, and continue to write about them. That is not to say that the political and the moral have no place in what I write, this just isn't my starting point. Being there is simply more interesting than being here.

In the realm of the history queen. (With apologies to Anna Tsing, author of the elegant critical ethnography, *In the Realm of the Diamond Queen* [1993].) If there is such a thing as local knowledge, then there is also such a thing as local history. By local history, I do not mean the history found abstracted in Chamber of Commerce brochures. Nor do I mean the often romantic histories spun on front porches by aging matriarchs and patriarchs that are recorded by eager interviewers who are obsessed with all things alternative. Instead I mean those interpretations of the past that are performed in daily life, interpretations that are given expression in community conversation and ritual.

This is another breach with conventions that prescribe adherence only to historical narratives that themselves have stood the test of time. As researchers, we have been taught to prefer accounts written by our academic kin. As with the professor who steered me toward disciplinary values, this position on history has merit and should be followed. However, I have chosen to understand first, and believe most, the social invocations of history that advance themselves with complete conviction.

The inspiration to do this is frequently sustained. At a recent visit to the New York Museum for African Art, I saw a wonderful exhibit on memory and Luba art. The Luba chiefs "remembered" events with the use of a "memory board." Pieces of wood, *lukasa*, have embedded upon them beads and carvings that tell the past. What the exhibit made clear is that central to the presentation of history are the articulations of the present. History is abstract; history is symbolic. As noted African historian, Jan Vansina (1996), states, "Even the main Luba kingdom was first and foremost a construction of the mind. Regional communities belonged to it because they *proclaimed*[1] that they belonged to it. They shared in its historical consciousness and believed in its contents" (p. 13). For me, gaining insight into the dynamics by which communities create and perform (or *proclaim*) a history is at once thrilling and foreboding.

But this breach does not endure without generating crisis. Recently, I was chastised for referring to the *cumbia* as a "distinctly Mexican" dance. Didn't I know that the *cumbia* originated in Africa and came to Mexico via South America? Didn't I know history? Yes, I do know this. But, when I ask tejanos about the *cumbia*, they say, "*Cumbia*. Sensuous, hip moving, from Mexico."[2] What I will not do is contradict a native's historical understanding when the purpose is to present and interpret the orienting meanings within a cultural community. The accounts I present may not satisfy the historian or the ethnomusicologist. Only later might other questions arise: What are the historical relations between Mexico and Africa? Why might Mexico submerge South American and African cultural meanings? How do tejanos read their Mexican cultural history?

My confession is this: I have no particular regard for official historical visions or revisions.

Sightings.   I am skeptical of any rubric I might devise for charting the future of intercultural communication research. My first test of such a rubric would be to determine if it could have forecast me—mutiny—had it been available 10 years ago.

First, intercultural studies have taken a decisively critical turn. From the cultural rhetoric of William Starosta to the critical rhetoric of Raymie McKerrow; from the critical ethnographies of Dwight Conquergood to the critical organizing of Stanley Deetz; from the postcolonial rap of Wen Shu Lee to the womanist vision of Marsha Houston; all of these authors anticipate a conceptual piñata that will rain vitality onto research in intercultural communication.

Second, I believe that another future for intercultural communication studies is only now coming into view. It is a future that will be played out by those now entering high schools. Oddly, I am not intimating highly technologized perspectives on research, though the saturation of technology into our everyday lives may have something to do with it. I believe that future researchers will be asking questions that are largely precluded by present communication values. It is a future that is guided more by puzzles on the edge of our understanding than by the politics of method.

In intercultural communication research, as in most communication research, we have sought to understand and mediate differences, build consensus, and improve problem solving, etc. We move into populations to study how these things are done, what it means to do them, and how others might learn from having descriptions and interpretations of community practices. We look for domains of life that are amenable to examination by our Western analytical methodologies.

But this won't hold for long. There are many domains of community experience that are beyond these methods, even critical methods.

I utter the sacred claims:

Reality is socially constructed.

Knowledge is contingent.

Inquiry is political.

Yet these claims do not make me sweat, as they once did; nor do they ease my pain, which they never could. Now these claims challenge us to look *beyond* them, and they challenge us to look *before* them.

Tsing (1993) tells of her first encounter with Uma Adang—a Meratus seer and occasional social movement leader: "Her voices, she said, had begun to instruct her in all the languages of the world. Then she dreamed of my coming; she had experienced the high winds, she said, of America, and she had known that I would retrace the steps of the Diamond Queen, who had come once before in ancient time to restore prosperity to this isolated realm" (p. 6). We cannot profitably understand intercultural interactions until our interpretations take into account the voices people hear, the miracles they see performed, visions that appear before them, and the dreams they recount. To banish these events from everyday experience is to create an investigation of partial humans. To banish these events from our interpretations is an act of cowardice.

I remember when I taught at the University of Minnesota at Morris. During one cold winter, the students began to complain of mysterious events. Students saw dresser drawers open and the contents scattered. They saw objects sail across the rooms. At first, everyone attributed these events to cabin fever. In Minnesota, you take cabin fever seriously. But the reports of events persisted and the students grew increasingly afraid.

One night my telephone rang. It was a student from one of my communication courses. "Someone was in my apartment," she said in a half whisper. Her voice was calm and very intent.

"Did you hear them run away?" I asked.

"No."

"Are they there now?"

"No."

"Well, why are you calling *me?*"

The student later told this story: She awoke to see a young Sioux child leaning over her. The child was laughing but there was no sound. The child was peering into the student's eyes like children do when they are looking for a response. The child then silently withdrew to a circle of adults floating in the upper corner of the bedroom. All the Sioux quickly faded out of sight. The student thought she was dreaming, but when she looked at the clock she could clearly see the digital numbers change. The entire episode lasted about two minutes.

I take this student's experience as an intercultural interaction that is as legitimate for examination as re-entry shock, acculturation among expatriates, and discontent in multiethnic workplaces. Yet what conceptual frame must be devised to gain access to these rare events? I met my daughter as a clever eight-year-old three years before she was born. I attribute this event to my heritage, but what interpretive base allows me to understand its significance? We'll have to wait. But the interpretive turn toward the magical and

mystical domains allows critics to confront what we in communication studies have rendered anathema: fantasy, contradiction, simultaneity, ambivalence, and equivocation.

My confession is this: I have participated in sustaining the Western analytical perspective even as I seek to avoid it. One example: Sometimes people will say, "I really liked the *Our Voices* book, but the essays are uneven."

"Yeah," I reply lamely, "we'll try to do something about that in the next edition." But in my mind I'm screaming that cultures are uneven, and we are trying to reveal the diverse expressions of cultural voices. It is unclear to me why interculturalists cling to uniformity and evenness when nothing they know resembles that except possibly their own thinking. But I remain silent—civil—and another chance for dialogue is closed.

CONCLUSION

It has been exactly 10 years since I received the Ph.D. Some of my earliest ideas are still the best. In my first convention paper, I compared intercultural interaction to the colliding of galaxies. Some collisons are traumatic as the galaxies destroy each other. Other galaxies simply pass through each other and emerge unscathed. Intercultural interactions are like that. There is no predicting. There is no healing. There is only the possibility of understanding.

My career has been made on bringing unlikely factions together, of putting myself in places that I didn't belong, and by creating a space for the expressions of those who might otherwise be overlooked. My career has been made by approaching communication through the side door of inquiry. All of these activities have required me to break the rules, violate conventions, and unmeet expectations. But for the fun of it all, and the encouragement of allies, it would have ended long ago.

My challenge, and it is a challenge I direct to you, is to keep our projects fresh and to keep our projects moving. After all, the fugitive must flee at a moment's notice.

REFERENCES

Conquergood, D. (1992). Life in the Big Red. In L. Lamphere (Ed.), *Structuring diversity: Ethnographies and the new immigrants.* Chicago: University of Chicago Press.

Dylan, B. (1985). *Lyrics: 1962–1985.* New York: Alfred A. Knopf.

Geertz, C. (1988). *Works and lives: The anthropologist as author.* Stanford: Stanford University Press.

González, A., Houston, M., and Chen, V. (Eds.). (1997). *Our voices: Essays in ethnicity, culture, and communication* (2nd ed.). Los Angeles: Roxbury Publishing Co.

Nietzsche, F. (1887/1956). *The genealogy of morals.* Trans. F. Golffing. New York: Doubleday.

Tsing, A. L. (1993). *In the realm of the diamond queen.* Princeton, NJ: Princeton University Press.

Vansina, J. (1996). From memory to history: Processes of Luba historical consciousness. In M. N. Roberts and A. F. Roberts (Eds.), *Memory: Luba art and the making of history* (pp. 12–14). New York: Museum for African Art.

NOTES

1. Italics retained.
2. This is the verbatim response of a tejano asked about the *cumbia* in Oct. 1996.

CHAPTER 17

AT THE HELM IN CULTURAL STUDIES AND COMMUNICATION

Introduction

Thomas Rosteck
University of Arkansas

By now it has become conventional—a ritual trope—to assert that American academia is in the midst of something called "a cultural studies boom." And boom it is: During recent years, this culture studies movement has generated considerable academic heat over what might be the right relations of communication studies with cultural studies, and in the intersection of these two metadiscourses. You need only mark the recent National Communication Association conference, "Communication and Culture Studies," the burgeoning number of panels on communication and cultural studies at the annual meeting, at those of the International Communication Association, and the American Studies Association, and of course, this plenary session today. But not only that, works that begin to explore the parallels of culture and communication have found their way onto publishers' lists and more are on the way. Taken all together, these events nurture the conclusion that communication studies and cultural studies not only intersect, but also that this NEW relationship at that intersection marks a site of redefinition and of potential gain.

But it's an old relationship really. Almost 25 years ago, Raymond Williams defined "communication as cultural science" in his essay of the same name; and James W. Carey described the relation-

ship sometime ago as "European" in its emphasis upon the "ritual or cultural" work of communication in contrast to what he called the "American," and more empirical, social science perspectives. Yet even today, the issues which surface as we speculate about communication and culture are exciting, invigorating, and urgent.

First, there are important matters of critical practice, including how one might rightly study culture, and the interaction or borrowings which could occur between communication studies and cultural studies. But more than that, such matters also include the more immediate issues of current academic practice, assessing the future of communication studies in the (postmodern) university, and the challenges which culture studies presents for the discipline of communication. Thus the intersection might well illuminate issues of history, society, textuality, and reception in provocative ways.

Second, there are crucial matters concerning the formation of academic disciplines. Implicit in cultural studies is the recognition that the best work questions traditional disciplinary boundaries seeks to create a new language of cultural critique, that such work decenters authority and redraws the institutional borders as a way of making clear the relations between agency and power. And so, the intersection before us must address anew central issues of identity, subjectivity, and academic disciplinarity and pedagogy.

Finally, we should remember that these essays we shall hear this morning are cultural/political practices themselves. They each will give new demonstration to the broader implications of intellectuals as cultural workers and of communication studies/cultural studies as a form of discursive challenge to a variety of political, academic, and cultural spheres.

So what we have before us are three monographs that pursue much more than middling pedantic controversy. These papers are presented by three leading scholars—Lawrence Grossberg, Della Pollock, and Phillip Wander. Each paper is positioned differently in relation to the formation that is cultural studies and communication studies; each cuts into the formation from a different angle. Taken together, they contribute to definitions about who we are, about where we ought to be tending as a discipline, and how, in the end, we can all make the world a more humane place to live and to work.

Doing without Culture or, Cultural Studies in Helm's Country[1]

Lawrence Grossberg
University of North Carolina, Chapel Hill

1. CROSSROADS IN CULTURAL STUDIES; CULTURAL STUDIES AT A CROSSROADS

I cannot think cultural studies today without thinking of "Crossroads Blues" and the legend of Robert Johnson, who sold his soul to the devil to become the greatest blues musician of all time, although he did not get to play for very long. Notice the peculiar economic logic operating here: Robert Johnson got to keep his soul as long as he lived; after all, you can't play the blues without a soul. I have the feeling that those of us who claim a commitment to cultural studies, especially in the United States, are making our deal with the devil in order to gain a new place and with it, a certain legitimacy and power. But I fear that we are giving up our soul before we get to do anything with this new place.

In too many spaces, cultural studies is being institutionalized in ways that merely reproduce the structure of area studies, or of the English and communication departments in which so many of us were educated and are located. One result is that "interdisciplinarity" is often used as a rhetorical weapon against the disciplines instead of a productive challenge to build new relations and to change our own research practices. A second result is that, too often, the "knowledge" we are producing seems merely to rediscover what we already know, and to reinscribe in our pedagogical practice what we already do. I certainly do not mean to "bash" theory or to blame the fact that it is often (necessarily) inaccessible for the current situation. On the contrary, I think theory is absolutely necessary. But I do want to criticize aspects of the practice of some contemporary theorizing.

I want to defend a different practice of theorizing, a different way of politicizing theory and theorizing politics.[2] This is what I call "cultural studies." Let me begin then by making clear what I mean by cultural studies, since it is becoming less obvious what its referent is: it stretches out into an umbrella term for the study of culture or collapses into the name of a particular theoretical paradigm or research practice. I do understand the reasons why the term "cultural studies" has been appropriated for the broader of these uses, but I also want to hold onto to what is unique about cultural studies.[3] I do not mean to legislate here (and I doubt that I have either the power or the rhetorical skills to do so). But I do want to describe what I took from my experience at the CCCS (and why I think Birmingham has played and continues to play a central—but not founding—role in the history of cultural studies), what I continue to see in the very best examples of cultural studies, many of which have no obvious links to Birmingham.

As a research practice, cultural studies leads us to reflect on where the questions driving our researches are coming from, and to refuse to take either our theory or politics for granted, as if they could be assumed in advance. Cultural studies is a scene for an ongoing battle between theoretical resources and political realities. It is not about interpreting or judging texts or people, but about describing how people's everyday lives are articulated by and with culture, how they are empowered and disempowered by the particular structures and forces that organize their lives, always in contradictory ways, and how their everyday lives are themselves articulated to and by the trajectories of economic and political power. It is about the historical possibilities of transforming people's lived realities and the relations of power, and about the absolutely vital contribution of intellectual work to the imagination and realization of such possibilities. In this sense, I want to defend cultural studies as an academic, knowledge-producing activity. Cultural studies believes that intellectual work matters!

Thus cultural studies has to be disciplined enough to use the best and most rigorous resources available to it, and at the same time, it has to be willing to take the risk of being interdisciplinary. But its interdisciplinarity is always practical and strategic, called into existence by the fact that the study of culture requires one to examine the relations between culture and everything that is not culture. Hence, cultural studies is not merely the expansion of the notion of the text nor textual methods.[4] But I would add that cultural studies is also not simply (i.e., neither always nor only) the study of the relations between texts and audiences, or between audiences and everyday life, or the application of ethnographic methods to culture.

Practicing cultural studies involves constantly redefining it in response to changing geographical and historical conditions, and to changing political demands; it involves making a home for it within specific disciplines even as it challenges the legitimacy of the disciplinization of intellectual work. But how cultural studies is to be defined and located in any particular project can only be determined by doing the work of cultural studies, by mapping/reconstructing the relations between discourses, everyday life, and the machineries of power. This is the peculiar logic of cultural studies: it begins with a context that has already posed a question; yet the question itself defines the context. Thus, cultural studies always has to begin again by turning to discourses as both its productive entrance into and a productive dimension of that context. In the end, it is not interested in the discourse per se but in the articulations between everyday life and the formations of power. Thus, it ends with a different understanding of the context than that with which it began, having gone through the mediations of both culture (discourse) and theory.

Cultural studies attempts to strategically deploy theory to gain the knowledge necessary to reconstitute the context in ways that may enable the articulation of new or better political strategies. While it puts knowledge in the service of politics, it also attempts to make politics listen to the authority of knowledge (and hence, it is not relativist). I do not believe this "definition" installs a new mythology which proposes cultural studies as the new salvation for the humanities, the university, or the world; rather it is a modest proposal for a flexible and radically contextual intellectual and political practice, one which tries to make the connections between the politics of culture and what Meaghan Morris (1988) has called the politics of politics.

But this already locates a paradox at the heart of cultural studies: for on the one hand, it is always an attempt to respond to the questions of power and domination posed to the intellectual by the "real" material and discursive context in which he or she operates. Thus, cultural studies is committed to a sense of intervention—to enabling new forms, sites, and relations of agency—and even, in both the broad and narrow senses, to policy. On the other hand, cultural studies refuses to give in to the increasingly common effort to reduce all intellectual work to a single functionalist logic, as if all scholarship operated within the same temporality. On the contrary, cultural studies not only believes in the necessary intervention of theory, it believes as well in the almost (but not quite) inevitable displacement of the effects of any cultural practice, including its own. The effects of cultural practice are always somewhere else, at some other time. While it would be nice if the effects of intellectual work (interventions) were always as immediate and obvious as other forms of political interventions, it is unfortunately not usually the case.

2. ON THE CHALLENGE OF THE CONTEMPORARY

The obvious question, then, the starting point for a reflection on cultural studies, must involve an exploration of the contemporary context. Here I can only briefly propose that we might see the contemporary context as the articulation of a number of historical developments (and theoretical challenges):

1. the globalization of culture and the need to avoid assuming that contemporary forms of globalization are simply more intense forms of older spatial relations. Cultural studies must confront the globalization of culture, not merely in terms of the proliferation and mobility of texts and audiences, but rather, in terms of the movement of culture outside the spaces of any (specific) language. Consequently, analysts can no longer confidently assume that they understand how cultural practices are working. The new global economy of culture entails a deterritorialization of culture and its subsequent reterritorialization, which challenges culture's equation with location, place, or locale. Not only must cultural studies rethink the relation of the local and the global, it must begin to find ways to think about culture as an ecumenical structure, much the same as capital.[5]

2. the economization (capitalization) of everything, which suggests not only that cultural studies must return to the economic issues it has often bracketed, but that it must seek it own approach to political economy, one which does not automatically slot the economy into the bottom line, and which does not simply treat the economics of culture as a matter of commodification and industrialization.[6]

3. the growing power of and investment in, and the increasingly obvious limits of a politics organized around notions of identity and theories of difference,[7] and predicated on an identification of subjectivity and agency. We need to analyze the geohistorical mechanisms by which relations have been constructed as differences and politics organized by identities. The category of identity needs to be deconstructed, but not necessarily in the sense that postmodernists, postcolonialists, and post-structuralists theorize. Identity becomes more of a political category to be mobilized and laid claim to, a matter of belonging, of the claim to be somewhere and hence, with someone.

4. the increasing importance, both theoretically and politically, of the a-signifying, whether understood as the material, the body, or affect. Here we might begin simply by recognizing how little theorizing has been done of these planes of existence.

When they are talked about, they are either immediately reconfigured into the realm of representation, or they are treated as the concrete, the particular, the a-theoretical. Interestingly, much of contemporary cultural theory and criticism seems to assume a binary opposition between affect/the body/materiality and the concrete on the one side, and ideology, subjectivity, consciousness, and theory on the other. This question is, it seems to me, connected to one of the most striking lacunae in contemporary cultural theory: its inability to address the politics of ecology in significant and compelling ways.

5. the reconstitution of a complex, contradictory, and highly self-reflective and strategic conservative movement and ideology which has already had significant effects, not only on politics, culture, and everyday life in the U.S., but around the world.[8]

6. the collapse of any shared sense of the nature, effectivities, and modalities of agency (or, in cultural studies terms, articulation).

7. the challenge of periodization: The debate between postmodernists and those who would describe contemporaneity as, e.g. late modernity, points to the need for a theoretical vocabulary which would allow us to decide what if anything is "new" about the contemporary mechanisms of culture and power. But more deeply—and connected to the previous issue—perhaps we need to rethink "the very basis of modern thinking about what constitutes change." (Morris, 1994)

8. the need to rethink the relations among the politics of culture, the politics of everyday life, and the politics of the State. This will require us to rethink notions of political transformation and struggle in relationship to questions of policy and "revolution," and to find new ways of linking political struggle with acceptable and effective ethical discourses.

3. ON THE VICTORY OF CULTURE

Obviously, these are all issues that demand significant empirical researches. But even more importantly, I believe that they demand not only theoretical but also philosophical work. I do not take philosophy to involve a move away from the real (as if the conceptual were less real than the particular) but as a way of touching the real, as an active intervention. Cultural studies has to begin to examine its own cultural categories and how they are implicated in modern structures and technologies of power. To what extent are we, as cultural analysts, locked into the very systems of power we are attempting to change? Now I am not suggesting that all other work must await the results of some total rethinking of the philosophical foundations of cultural studies, but I am suggesting that cultural studies continue to do what it has always done, move forward, little by little, on the grounds of politics, analysis, and theory, together, unevenly, in different spaces and at different speeds. In particular, I am also suggesting that some of that work must question our inherited philosophical common sense. I believe that cultural studies rests on three philosophical logics: a logic of identity and difference (as a way of conceptualizing belonging and exteriority or otherness);[9] a logic of temporality;[10] and a logic of mediation.[11] For the present, I want to consider only the last of these.

I believe that part of the challenge facing cultural studies lies in its very constitution as the study of *culture,* and in the particular way in which "culture" has been understood in cultural studies, an understanding with its roots in European modernist philosophy (especially German idealism) in general, and Kantian philosophy in particular.[12] Raymond Williams (1958) has argued that the very power of the concept, as it emerged in Europe depended on its ambiguity—e.g., culture as a product (art), a state ("a cultured person") and a process (creativity). While it is not unusual for words to have multiple and even contradictory meanings, it is more unusual for that ambiguity and even contradiction to be the source of its productivity and thus, to be sustained without challenge for centuries.[13]

That ambiguity is of course most commonly expressed in terms of the distance between the anthropological conception of culture as a whole way of life of a people, and an aesthetic-textual concept of culture. Both of these have recently come under serious attack. Notions of a "whole way of life," especially insofar as these are spatialized and ethnicized, constructing a singular culture in a limited space, are increasingly seen (especially within critical race theory and postcolonial theory) as the product of the colonizing and imperialistic projects of modern Europe. Aesthetic notions of culture have been "deconstructed" as it were by Bourdieuians and feminists (among others) who argue that, rather than being a distinct group of practices with inherent value, such groupings produce and embody distinctions of value and power. This undermines our ability to assume, not only the existence of qualitative distinctions (between high and low) within the domain of culture, but also the existence of a self-contained category of creative, textual, aesthetic practices such as literature or art existing outside of their institutional laws of regulation.

But the ambiguous figure of culture is much more than the sum of its parts, for according to Williams, the notion of culture that animates much of what he calls "the culture and society tradition" involves a double articulation: on the one hand, the projection of a position, constituted by a temporal displacement from some other (e.g., tradition), from which change can be comprehended; and, on the other hand, the equation of that position with a standard of judgment from which one can offer a "total qualitative assessment" of such changes. "The idea of culture is a general reaction to a general and major change in the conditions of our common life." That is, the very act of producing the concept of culture involves the construction of a place which allows one to both describe and judge the changes in everyday life; it requires at the very least a "court of human appeal," some locatable "higher" standard, to be set over the processes of practical social change.

A partial solution may be found in Williams' refusal to locate himself within the "culture and society tradition." He argued that the concept of culture was invented as the recognition of "a practical separation of certain moral and intellectual activities from the driving force of a new kind of society," i.e., that the modern is partly constituted by the separation of culture and society. For those authors whom Williams located in the culture and society tradition, the separation is taken for granted; culture is simply appropriated and transformed into a position from which that very separation can be described and judged. But Williams refused such a separation. Cultural studies had to reinsert culture into the practical everyday life of people, into the totality of a whole way of life. Yet Williams was never able to actually escape this separation—both in his privileging of certain forms of culture (literature) and in his desire to equate culture with some sort of ethical standard of judgment (enabled by the "structure of feeling"). How then was Williams able to avoid the contradiction: by postulating a third term—that of culture as a process ("the community of process"), the most human of all processes, the process of communication which, it turns out, is the process of meaning production, which is the process of mediation (in the Kantian sense).

This dialectical ambiguity is, I believe, constitutive of the history of cultural studies and now, a stumbling block to its continued intellectual force. In other words, like other intellectual developments of the nineteenth and twentieth century such as various theories of sociology and anthropology, the notion of culture was an attempt to define the specificity of the modern. Unlike many other theories of the emergence of the modern (including the "culture and society" tradition), the dialectic of culture in cultural studies is driven less by a vision of a total qualitative transformation of society (e.g., from the traditional to the modern, or from community to mass society)—cultural studies was never about the destruction of community—than by a concern for the consequences of new forms and degrees of mobility. Or to put it differently, it was always a question about the changing nature of a universal human process. But there is a specific and peculiar logic to this concept of culture, for the concept of culture as a dialectic (the anthropological and aesthetic notions mediated by a notion of expression or communication) reproduces the dialectical role of culture in which, as Bill Readings (1996) has argued, culture

as individual development mediates between individual relationships to ethnic nationality or identity and the modern state.

This dialectical structure also enables the concept of culture to become a magical solution to the problem of the specificity of human existence by defining all expression as mediation and then absolutizing the category of mediation. By implicating culture in a logic of lack and mediation, culture is close to if not identified with consciousness as the middle space of experience and human existence. According to Rosaldo (1989), modern thought conceives of culture within the "stark Manichean choice between order and chaos;" culture is the medium of information—the supplement—which substitutes for some lack (e.g., of genetic coding, of access to the real). Culture is the agency by which the chaos of reality is transformed into the ordered sense of human reality. Without culture, reality would be simply unavailable, nothing more than James' booming buzzing confusion. Within culture, reality is always already sensible. Both Rosaldo (1989) and Bauman (1987) have suggested that the invention and victory of the concept of culture, its particular internal logic and its power, have to be located in the context of the rising power of Europe, modernity, and the new middle class intelligentsia (and I might add with Readings, the modern university).

The victory of culture is, then, built upon the victory of Kantian philosophy, which inserted the realm of experience between the subject and the real, thus effectively erasing any possible reference to the real as anything but a regulative ideal. I believe, then, that one philosophical inheritance of Kantian philosophy is the taken-for-granted assumption of mediation, and its subsequent expansion into the variety of positions that have come to be described as the social construction of reality.[14] Social constructionism asserts that all experience of the world (and hence, any possible relation to reality) is:

1. mediated (i.e., always involving three terms)
2. by "human" (perhaps subjective?) structures
3. which are spatially and temporally specific

4. and which are expressive (or meaningful) in the broadest sense
5. and which are signifying in the narrow sense (involving cognitive signification, representation, semantic-referentiality, ideological, semiotic, or narrative meanings)

Of course, different versions of social constructionism will assent to and interpret these assumptions in various ways and combinations. The totality of these assumptions, the most common version of social constructionism in contemporary thought, not only makes culture the "essence" of human existence, it ends up equating culture with communication.[15] Thus the dialectic of culture not only erases the real but predefines every possibility of production (or articulation) as **a particular kind** of—a semantic—social construction. By identifying mediation with communication, all cultural practices necessarily involve the production of meanings and representations, of subjectivities and identities (making it into little more than the form of ideology or the content of common sense). This notion of culture as a plane of cognitive meanings makes every practice an instance of the communicational relationship between text and audience and all critical analysis into a question of individuated (although often defined through social identities) and psychological interpretations and tastes.

Opposing the last assumption (#5), cultural studies should hold onto a more contextual notion of discursive practices and effects, locating both texts and audiences within broader contexts that articulate the identity and effects of any practice. Without denying that cultural practices enable us to "make sense" of the world (or at least to navigate within a sensible world), such a contextualism contests the reduction of sense-making to cognitive meaning and interpretation, and the model of culture as somehow standing apart from—and between—other planes which it interprets. Instead cultural practices always operate on multiple planes, producing multiple effects that cannot be entirely analyzed in the terms of any theory of communication, ideology, consciousness, or semiotic.

But if culture is not simply a matter of meaning and communication, then the struggle over "culture" is not merely a struggle over interpretive or cognitive maps available to the different and differently subordinated fractions (which in the contemporary world includes the vast majority of the population). Rather than asking what texts mean or what people do with texts, culture studies should be concerned with what discursive practices do in the world, with "how these cut across and organize the various time/spaces in which the labor, as well as the pleasure, of everyday living is carried out." (Morris, forthcoming) Discourses are active agents, not even merely performances, in the material world of power.

While this is obviously a philosophical argument, it is not that in the first instance, for it is above all an attempt to respond in part to the conditions of the contemporary context. Thus, for example, Frow and Morris (1993) have argued that such (social constructionist) conceptions of culture are simply inadequate descriptions of the ways "culture" is being articulated and deployed in contemporary politics. They argue that "changing the culture" has become "a shorthand but expansive way of challenging the conduct of other people's lives." It is all about controlling people's behavior—no room for ethics or aesthetics here except as a disciplining strategy.

But if the demands of the contemporary context seem to push us in a certain direction—away from social constructionism, we must also distinguish various counter-theories by how they assent and dissent from the set of assumptions listed above. A post-anthropological (Gilroy, 1993) and post-aesthetic (Bennett, 1992, and Hunter, 1988) theory of culture would have to deny not only social constructionism but mediation itself (thus rejecting the first, second, and fifth assumptions). Ironically, I believe that this returns us to earlier, albeit somewhat vague, attempts to define cultural studies in the work of Richard Hoggart and Raymond Williams. Although both of them were certainly writing within the logic of social constructionism, their work can be read as opening up or at least pointing to a more materialist and contextualist notion of cultural studies as the study of "all the relations between all the elements." I am afraid that the task of describing what such a practice of cultural studies might look like will have to wait for another occasion.

4. THE RETURN OF THE POLITICAL

Of course, my description of the context within which cultural studies must produce itself has been too dispassionate, for there is little sense of the very real stakes in the struggle. Cultural studies scholars need to begin to seriously confront the dystopian trajectories that are leading us, all together, whatever our politics, identity, or status, into the next millennium. And we need to try to understand how the different trajectories and their different successes are being constructed. We need to understand the mechanisms and contexts of the contemporary transformations and of their articulations to specific relations of power. While we should constantly remind ourselves that people are active and struggling, we also should remember that they are suffering. We need to understand the specific forms in which domination is organized, how it is lived, mobilized, and empowered, without assuming that domination (or even hegemony) is always and everywhere the same. We cannot take for granted that the political effects of particular cultural practices are somehow guaranteed in advance, or even guaranteed across contexts. We need to ask how modes that empower people or serve as tools of resistance in one place can disempower people in another place, and vice versa.

We need to consider that the possibilities for progressive political struggle, especially one that extends beyond the micropolitics of everyday life, is being actively deconstructed, for particular fractions of the populace, at (at least) three sites: first, the impossibility of investing in the political (i.e., of believing, whether in the government or "the people" as agents of change, or in some utopian field of political and ethical values); second, the active discouragement of any imagination of the possibility of political community (i.e., of rethinking the relation of the individual to the group,

and of identity to struggle); and third, the impossibility of articulating a theory and practice of agency (of reconsidering how people make history but not in conditions of their own making).

These are, in the first instance, problems of everyday life, constructed in struggles in and over the popular. They are also problems at the intersection of everyday life and the larger, long-term "tendential" forces struggling to determine it. But they are also challenges for the intellectual, and I believe we will have failed if we cannot find ways to address them outside of the limits of our own theoretical and political positions, if we cannot speak, as intellectuals, through the popular, in order to connect everyday life and culture with the very real struggles against economic and political injustice. In fact, too often, the very battles we have chosen to fight, and the ways we have chosen to fight them, have contributed to the weakening of the very institutions we are supposedly fighting for. I hope you will forgive my rhetorical excesses here, but I think it is time that we admitted that much of what we (progressive academics and intellectuals) are doing is not working. And it is time we asked, why not?

NOTES

1. This paper is written for an invited "At the Helm" session of the Speech Communication Association meeting, San Diego, 1996. An expanded version was given at the Crossroads in Cultural Studies conference, Tampere Finland, June 1996, as "The Cultural Studies Crossroads Blues." I am grateful to the organizers of both events for their invitations and support. This paper draws heavily on Grossberg (in press)
2. Rather than thinking of theory as a canon, cultural studies thinks of it as a strategic resource (although this does not mitigate the existence of a body of resources from which to choose). Rather than thinking of theory of therapeutic, or truth-producing, or subject-producing, cultural studies thinks of theory as enabling agency and action. Thus, cultural studies has had, and continues, to wrestle with the theoretical (and political) agendas of Marxism, feminism, critical race theory, queer theory, etc., without thereby identifying itself with the totality of such bodies of work.

3. The discomfort that often accompanies attempts to define cultural studies is easily understood, for precisely what distinguishes cultural studies is its openness, but it is not the anarchic openness of "anything goes" but the strategic openness of "no guarantees."

4. Cultural studies does not treat a text as if it inscribed meaning on a single plane or embodied the essence of an epoch. It offers no quintessential insight, and provides no way of reading a social totality off the event of the text. It is not the exemplary or proper human event. See Frow and Morris (1993).

5. The notion of an ecumenical structure describes a material body capable of moving across borders. See Deleuze and Guattari (1977).

6. See Grossberg.

7. Difference is "a logic whereby the consolidation of the self entails the assimilation/exclusion of the object/ Other by the subject." It assumes "that individual and collective identity is always and necessarily founded on a same/other dialectic and produced by a logic of exclusion or sacrifice." Weir (1996).

8. See Grossberg (1992).

9. See Grossberg (1996a).

10. See Grossberg (1996b) and (forthcoming).

11. Obviously, these three logics intersect around the notion of culture: e.g., consider the complex appropriations and debates around "multiculturalism."

12. At least for the present argument.

13. One need only consider the ease with which the concept of culture is appropriated and deployed by and against competing political positions in contemporary struggles.

14. Kant's project was to demonstrate the "man" [sic] was self-legislating and therefore could not be an object of scientific knowledge, by establishing the conditions of possibility (and hence, the limits) of all knowledge and experience. Obviously, this project failed precisely insofar as it opened the space, not only of philosophical anthropology but also of the sciences of man. As Foucault has argued, the epistemology of modernity is one in which man is both subject and object of knowledge.

Let me add three important caveats. First, Kant serves here only as a figure of a much broader discursive change which cut across many discursive domains and regimes. But Kant was a particularly important crystallization of such changes, in part perhaps because he knew that the logics he was establishing would necessarily lead to antinomies which, as Ian Hunter (1988) has argued, produce a certain kind of person. Second, I am not

claiming to seek a better philosophy per se nor am I attempting to reject modernism across the board. In fact, I am not claiming to have effects on anything but the contextual practice of cultural studies, i.e., the effort to understand the context in relation to discursivity. And finally, to repeat myself, I am not saying that we should not or cannot not do cultural studies until such philosophical work is completed. On the contrary, as I have said, cultural studies is always done with the best resources available. And I have no doubt that valuable work in cultural studies will go on even if such philosophical work is never undertaken.

15. Note that none of this denies the existence of the world—that would be a version of subjective idealism—nor does it deny the continuing function of that reality as a regulative principle or transcendental term.

REFERENCES

Bauman, Z. (1987). *Legislators and interpreters*. Cambridge: Polity.

Bennett, T. (1992). Useful culture. *Cultural Studies* 6.

Deleuze, G. & Guattari, F. (1977). *Anti-Oedipus: Capitalism and schizophrenia*. R. Hurley, M. Seem, & H. R. Lane (Trans.). New York: Viking Press.

Frow, J. and Mooris, M. (1993) Introduction. In J. Frow and M. Morris (Eds.), *Australian cultural studies: A reader*. Urbana: University of Illinois Press.

Gilroy, P. (1993). *The Black Atlantic: Modernity and double consciousness*. Cambridge: Harvard University Press.

Grossberg, L. (1995). Cultural studies and political economy: Is anybody else bored with this debate? *Critical Studies in Mass Communication* 12: 72–81.

Grossberg, L. (1996a). Identity and cultural studies: Is that all there is? In S. Hall & P. duGay (Eds.), *Questions of cultural identity* (pp. 88–107). London: Sage.

Grossberg, L. (1996b). The space of culture, the power of space. In Iain Chambers & L. Curti (Eds.), *The postcolonial question* (pp. 169–188). London: Routledge.

Grossberg, L. (forthcoming). Cultural studies, modern logics and globalization. In A. McRobbie (Ed.), *New directions in cultural studies*. Manchester: Manchester University Press.

Grossberg, L. (in press). Introduction: Birmingham in America? In *Bringing it all back home: Essays on Cultural Studies*. Durham: Duke University Press.

Hunter, I. (1988). *Culture and Government: The Emergence of Literary Education,* London: Macmillan.

Morris, M. (1988). Tooth and claw: Tales of survival, and *Crocodile Dundee*. In *The pirates fiancee: Feminism reading postmodernism* (pp. 241–269). London: Verso.

Morris, M. (1994). 'Too soon too late': Reading Claire Johnston, 1970–1981. In C. Moore (Ed.), *Dissonance: Feminism and the arts 1970–90*. St. Leonards, NSW: Allen and Unwin/Artspace.

Morris, M. (forthcoming). *Upward mobility: Popular genres and cultural change*. Bloomington: Indiana University Press.

Readings, B. (1996). *The university in ruins.* Cambridge: Harvard University Press.

Rosaldo, R. (1989). *Culture and truth: The remaking of social analysis.* Boston: Beacon.

Weir, A. (1996). *Sacrificial logics: Feminist theory and the critique of identity.* New York: Routledge.

Williams, R. (1958). *Culture and society 1780/1950.* New York: Harper and Row.

Performance, Feminist Subjects, Cultural Studies

Della Pollock
University of North Carolina, Chapel Hill

Performance and cultural studies are increasingly interlocked—mutually entangled and struggling to define their commonalities/differences. The primary questions I want to address briefly are: what is—or should be—the relation between performance and cultural studies? and how are the actual and possible relations between performance and cultural studies informed, shaped, animated by feminist theory and studies? This second question reflects a third current of work that draws on both performance and cultural studies and draws them up into a centrifugal swirl of ludic feminisms, performative nationalities, and grotesque bodies.[1] Much recent feminist theory/practice tests, extends, and exceeds the respective and common limits of performance and cultural studies. It runs between cultural studies and performance, connecting and swelling the banks that define it.

What I want to consider here are the feminist subjects—the issues, motives, positions, and agencies—at the heart of something like performance/cultural studies. I will proceed in three, short stages. First, I want to claim my primary identification with or "position" within performance studies and to explore the implications of thinking through the relation between performance and cultural studies from that perspective. I then want to suggest a homologous relation between performance and cultural studies that makes their affiliation relatively unique within the larger field of communication studies. Finally, I will suggest three preliminary lines of (cross-)current development, three paths down which feminist subjects may lead, which I will provisionally call: engendering subjects, dis/play, and performance praxis.

WRITING FROM HOME

I come to this panel from a primary sub-disciplinary identification with performance studies, itself a hybrid formation that, like cultural studies, rests uneasily within the disciplinary formations to which, in a conference context like this one, it is called. Identifying with performance studies as I understand it, I am not disposed to draw lines or to stipulate differences that I nonetheless happily, lovingly, accept. Nor do I wish to suggest that these differences are secondary, that performance studies should be *or* subsume cultural studies. Rather, I want to entertain, to perform, the entanglements of performance studies and cultural studies one with the other, recognizing that for me desire is itself shaped by identification with performance.

Cultural studies is what it is for me, is what it may be, because at its best (at what I take to be its best), it is performative. It is, as Mary Russo (1994) has said of what she calls "ordinary feminism": "heterogeneous, strange, polychromatic, ragged, conflictual, incomplete, in motion, and at risk" (p. vii). It is a ragged enterprise that takes its shape from affiliation and instigation—from the *practice* of distinct intellectual interests on the stage of disciplinary formation. It is precisely because cultural studies lacks a stabilizing object or defining method that its status within the academy is peculiarly heightened, contested, inflamed (characteristics we often identify with performance or performance contexts). All too often smoothed into interdisciplinary paste, cultural studies entails the active engagement of difference around issues

[1]See for instance Bhaba (1994); Case, Brett, and Foster (1995); Ebert (1996); Parker, Russo, Sommer, and Yaeger (1992); Parker and Sedgwick (1995).

conventionally safeguarded by disciplinary boundaries. It performs the trickster's function of removing issues surrounding, for instance, the status of the "nation," or the gendered body, or economies of consumption, from subordination to given and/or privileged methodologies, simultaneously exposing those issues and their disciplinary keepers to cultural/political investigation.

In turn, then, cultural studies and performance studies are neither absolutely co-equal nor distinct fields. To talk about performance studies *and* cultural studies is, to my mind, to describe an operative rather than a definitive or *a priori* difference. It is to position performance and cultural studies in dialogue, in the hardest, most dynamic sense of dialogue as agonistic, inter-cursive, counter-active. As dialogic partners, performance and cultural studies write each other in ongoing, rough, and contested (re)productivity. They perform each other. They permeate each other's form, keeping their respective fulfillment in form—or performance—always already partial.[2]

I don't want either to force or to collapse a structural binarism between performance and cultural studies (a problem that has, to some extent, plagued the so-called rhetoric-cultural studies debates). Both structural definitions by negation and poststructural negations of definition rely on logics of opposition. They assume a true or false distinction between performance studies or rhetorical studies or communication studies, for that matter, and cultural studies that in turn determines possible conclusions—or conclusions about their *possible* relations. Beginning in the realm of the possible, in the realm of performance, I assume instead that performance studies and cultural studies are bound together in a restless, active, shifting, e/motional process of co-transformation, to which the critic/scholar is in turn bound to yield, to *give in*—imaginatively, rhetorically, bodily.

What I propose to do then is not to define performance and/or cultural studies or their common territories or even to review the abundance of work that has already emerged at the nexus of performance/cultural studies but to identify some ignition points: a few modes or moments of work that seem to me to engage the possible with particular acuity. What is or what has been done is positioned here "as if" it were indicative of the course of performance/cultural studies. I perform its implications in the present, constructing the possible as the real. In so doing, I reconstruct the real as performance: as the provisional, emergent, heterogeneous, and trace effects of the combustive co-venture of performance/cultural studies.

STRUCTURAL RELAYS

In a recent challenge to what she calls the "culturalism" that has dominated cultural studies since Raymond Williams characterized culture as "a whole way of life," Virginia Dominguez (1994) argues that cultural studies often simply assumes that culture is a "thing" and that it is something of value:

> While we are arguing over the content of canons of knowledge, disputing the value or need for canons, and pointing out the patterns of exclusion evident in curriculums, publishing practices, funding agencies, and museums, we are ironically reinforcing the perception that there is such a "thing" as culture and that it is something of value. But why is culture something of value? Perhaps more important, why does so much of cultural politics around the world stop short of asking that question?

But to stop short of asking why or whether culture is something of value is, for Dominguez, to reify assumptions about its value and ultimately to homogenize diverse cultural practices by locating them all under the general rubric of "culture." Dominguez (1994) argues:

> To understand what is involved we need to shift the question we're asking. We need to move away from asking about culture—what belongs, what doesn't belong, what its characteristics are, whose characteristics are being imposed and whose are being

---

[2]The difference between "performance" and "performativity" has been the subject of extensive discussion. See Conquergood (1995), Diamond (1996), Parker and Sedgwick (1995), all following Butler (1990, 1993).

excluded—and toward asking what is being accomplished *socially, politically, discursively when the concept of culture is invoked to describe, analyze, argue, justify, and theorize. (pp. 238–239)*

In this light, what cultural studies is or should be *about* is the concept of culture or *what happens* when the concept of culture is used/deployed. Cultural studies should investigate the performative status of culture conceptually and practically, with the implication that we can then evaluate cultural discourses and bypass both relativism and the kind of culturalist imperialism Dominguez describes. To refocus cultural study on the discourses that constitute "culture" is, above all, to resist the reduction of "culture" to a dead-end ("transcendental") signified.

In her charges against culturalism, Dominguez echoes Jill Dolan's (1993) complaints about "contemporary theory's promiscuous citation of the performative" (p. 430). For Dolan, performance studies, like culturalism, is at risk of imperializing the very practices it wants to engage/critique not by being too broad or appearing in too many places at once but by doing so unreflexively, by repeating without (re)producing the implications of its key terms. This is not simply a matter of defining terms but of accounting for their use-value in any particular scene. Assuming the reference-value of "performance" and "performativity" and ignoring their peculiar agency/effectiveness at a given moment, in a given context, actually limits the contextual flexibility of the terms (what we can *do* with them) and, at best, sustains a contradictory division between performance study and practice. It freezes performance as a "thing" (*the* "thing") within what Dominguez would call the wrong question. Following Dominguez, we need to move away from asking *about* performance—what belongs, what doesn't belong, what its characteristics are, whose characteristics are being imposed and whose are being excluded—and toward asking *what is being accomplished* socially, politically, discursively when the concept of performance is invoked to describe, analyze, argue, justify, and theorize.

In this light, performance studies and cultural studies are not primarily analogous but homologous formations. They are corresponding types. Their ends and effects may differ but both take (or should take) their momentum from identification with the social processes ("cultural," "performative") they describe, commensurate reflexivity, disciplinary instability, and a sense that both culture and performance are, if anything at all, joint sites of production: spaces for the imaginative reproduction of the forms, style, and implications of what would be the "objects" of more removed modes of analysis and explanation.

UNSTABLE CHEMISTRIES

Feminist theory/practice enters those spaces like a light to unstable chemistries, setting issues surrounding the status of the subject, visual economies, and opportunities for praxis into rapid motion. I do and don't mean to privilege feminist theory here. I will refer to "feminist" quite broadly but recognize that other interventions in more specific forms (e.g. queer theory, critical race theory, postcolonial critique, new geographies, critical legal studies) also work the interstices of performance/cultural studies. I have selected the three tropes represented here rather arbitrarily, as suggestive of *what happens,* what is accomplished, by the peculiar mix of feminist/performance/cultural studies. Each is represented, very briefly, by a selected text.

Engendering Subjects

Performance studies takes from cultural studies an analytic and praxical appreciation of the politics of cultural production and exchange; cultural studies takes from performance/feminist studies an appreciation of the excessive, embodied subject and erotic subjectivities so often weirdly absent in discussions, say, of popular culture and critical pedagogy, or held, as in the early work of Dick Hebdige (1979) or Stallybrass and White's (1986) important work on transgression, to conventional distinctions between "high" and "low" (even as each author purports to cross those borders). Anne Balsamo (1991) recently hailed feminist cultural studies for investigating "the way that social and cultural practices gender the material body" and for demonstrating "how the body is culturally constructed and not 'naturally given'" (p. 64). In so doing, however, she also indicated the preoccupation of much feminist cultural study with the social construction of the embodied self, with the ways in which gendered selves are "mapped" onto subject-bodies.

As important as it may be, the question of how the body is sexed/gendered still tends to eclipse emerging, performance-centered work on how and what the body engenders. Assuming that agency is itself constructed, Mary Russo (1994), for instance, nonetheless asks, "In what sense can women really produce or make spectacles of themselves" (p. 60)? Extending Bakhtin through Kristeva and Irigaray, through abjection and mimicry, Russo dwells in the *excesses* of social construction—in what's "too much," left over, or cut out. In what is normally/normatively contained or degraded is, for Russo, the possibility not only of reconstructing femininity but of going over/beyond construction itself. For Russo, the embodied subject, especially in the act of self-spectacularization or putting on femininity "with a vengeance," is not only always already in excess of construction but poised to re-identify by alliance with others at the material limit of the performing body (1994, p. 70). As Russo suggests, at the limit of material bodies are other bodies and the consequent possibility of founding a new, co-generative politics:

> What appeals to me about this vamping onto the body...is that it not only grotesquely de-forms the female body as a cultural construction in order to reclaim it, but that it may suggest new political aggregates—provisional, uncomfortable, even conflictual, coalitions of bodies which both respect the concept of 'situated knowledges' and refuse to keep every body in its place. (1994, p. 179)

Display

Feminist cultural/media studies have conventionally focused on how women have been represented in film/media, on how spectators have been positioned to receive those representations, and, most recently, on how audiences have made media representations meaningful in their own terms, "raiding" and "poaching" on the field of consumer production.[3] But, at the risk of oversimplifying, this history is strung between distrust of visual pleasure (figured in Laura Mulvey's important work on the "male gaze" and Kaja Silverman on the cinematic "suture" effect), on the one hand, and what John McGuigan (1992) has called happy populism on the other.[4] Performance enters and transforms the discourses of display and visualism largely through pleasure, recovering pleasure with desire to *seeing again*, to re-seeing—revising, re-sighting, re-*citing*, or seeing as itself refigured within the defining dynamic of performance/performativity: repetition.

Judith Butler (1990) has perhaps done more than any other critic/theorist to popularize discourses of performativity by characterizing gender as precisely an effect of repetition, as a citational practice constrained by history and discipline to repetition. And yet performativity is for Butler a matter of temporal disjunction. It signifies the tension between history and time enacted in the moment when one repetition of identity stumbles into another—and performance fails. Time proves performance imperfect. It shows the stains and seams in the reiteration of gender/sex norms. Performance, in turn, achieves performativity precisely at the moment that it fails history and falls, as it were, into time: into imperfection, loss, disappearance, laughter, and desire.

Following Butler, Elin Diamond (1996) identifies performativity with the constraints of (textual) history on the immediacies of everyday life. She insists nonetheless that performativity materializes as performance: it manifests as a "risky and dangerous negotiation between a doing (a reiteration of norms) and a thing done (discursive conventions that frame our interpretations), between

---

[3]Re: the latter, see for instance de Certeau (1984), Fiske (1989), Jenkins (1992).

[4]The idea that Fiske's early work, for example, favors an uncritical deployment of popular forms has been popularized by esp. McGuigan (1992).

someone's body and the conventions of embodiment." Performativity is, for Diamond, a material analytic. Whereas for Butler performativity and performance are to some extent at odds—the latter realizing the former when it fails to "do" what it is supposed to do, when it confounds the reiteration of norms of action, identity, and interpretation by parody or excess, for Diamond performativity and performance collapse in the specificities of negotiating historical norms and the conventions of embodiment. In-between, in the space opened by the act of negotiating itself, Diamond argues, "we have access to cultural meanings and critique." (1994, p. 5).

In this light, performativity is something more than the Derridean citationality with which Butler's work is typically identified. It has distinctively temporal and material dimensions that are not only inseparable from but gain their significance in the act of performance. In the light of their work, I think of performativity as something like the tension that joins what is done (the reiteration of norms) and the practices of doing (the conventions of embodiment) in a broken ramble across the stages of everyday life, as an encompassing term that privileges neither the past (textual histories) nor the present (in a rough recoding of "presence") but insists on their often awkward, criss-crossing. Performance entails the material reiteration of historical norms; it works through conventions of bodily display, expression, action. But in so doing, it also requires the negotiation of historical norms and bodily conventions in action, opening a critical, fluctuating space "in-between" one claim and another—and it goes beyond textual embodiment towards a new materiality, towards a space of both incompleteness and excess that is indeed "outside" the text that Buter's own theory of performativity continues to repeat.

One implication of crossing performance and performativity in this way is that we have to re-see seeing, we have to reiterate visualism in excess of those disciplinary codes by which women are conventionally the object of scopic desire and control, and to recast sight itself as fragile, contingent, and always already about to break open into the space/time of embodied interaction—as it does, for instance, in Carol Mavor's (1995) recent work, *Pleasures Taken: Performances of Sexuality and Loss in Victorian Photographs.*

In Mavor's work, the looker and looked-at momentarily collapse in the multi-sensual act of looking.[5] Conventional subject-object relations give way to delicate rites of corporeal exchange. Taking her cue from Roland Barthes' *punctum*, the place where a visual image breaks through its frame into the viewer's experience, Mavor sees herself in a subject-subject relation with the images she literally takes up. Writing about the photographs of the maid-of-all-work, Hannah Cullwick, collected by the late Victorian poet, Arthur Munby, for instance, Mavor begins with the act of removing them from the collector's box stored in the Wren Library at Cambridge. She fingers an image of Cullwick's rough, working hands, laid open and blackened with soot before her. Their hands touch. In Mavor's hand/eye, the image takes on its own, material agency. It performs her and through her, us, now caught in a kind of *ménage à trois* of looking/feeling/wanting. Mavor draws us in as the images, in her description, "pop out of their small drawer" and then catch her red-handed, in the scene of her own (now our own) desire: "Hannah's big, disconnected hands mirror my own as I fondle the tiny pictures of hard-working woman [sic] that have been fetishistically frozen in a lovely miniature museum" (1995 pp. 89–90). The image turns back on Mavor, suggesting Mavor's own fetishistic enchantment, but more importantly engaging Mavor in Cullwick's subversive performance of sexuality. Rather than re-boxing Cullwick in print and containing her sexuality within more conventional object-analysis, Mavor subjects herself to Cullwick's performance. She performs viewing as an act of being performed, in turn achieving a marginal sexuality at the margins of art history.

---

[5]See also Cooke and Wollen (1995).

Material Praxis

The cultural practices to which cultural studies is devoted are, as Stuart Hall has noted, "interwoven with all social practices; and those practices, in turn, [with] sensuous human praxis, the activity through which men and women make their own history" (quoted in Diamond, 1996, p. 6). And yet so long as those practices remain objects of argument and analysis and not the pivot on which cultural studies examines and pursues its own praxical implications, they remain dead history. From my perspective, feminist/performance studies push cultural studies to praxical claims through the embodied act of performance (or what Diamond calls *doing* culture), as well as through performative writing, or abandoning textual self-containment for the open, material process of making history/making meaning in writing.[6]

In his recent performances of "The X-Syndrome," Dick Hebdige does both.[7] Hebdige's performance work represents a particularly compelling case of one of the leading critic-theorists of music subcultures seeking alternative modes of intervening in the chains of signification he otherwise so eloquently describes. Enacting and extending the double-voiced, densely layered approach to cultural theory that he takes, for instance, in his 1996 essay, "The Impossible Object: Toward a Sociology of the Sublime," in "The X-Syndrome," Hebdige "dubs" a multitextual performance event. He mixes and remixes life texts, figured in elementary school notebooks, Scrabble games, music, memory-dream fantasies, and a vast image-landscape of postwar masculinity, twining them in an urgent, at once intimate and oversized reflection on the experience of a psychotic epi-

sode. The performance is relentless. Loud, brash, searingly, even voluptuously funny, it proceeds with measured, centrifugal force—water spills over a bare arm, ping-pong balls fly, Scrabble pieces fall in a great, welcome rush to the ground. As personally as it is theoretically driven, the performance/presentation engages an open dialectic between political and erotic agencies. In its pounding rhythms and quick, twisting ironies, it positions itself against other performances (of medical care, masculinity, theory) and invites the viewer into (re)play and fury. It enacts Diamond's sense that "to study performance is not to focus on completed forms, but to become aware of performance as itself a contested space, where meanings and desires are generated, occluded, and of course multiply interpreted" (1996, p. 4). But more importantly and directly, it contests space, generates desires, avails the body's text (the performer's, the viewer's, the viewer-as-performer's) of multiple, interpretive claims, and thus to mobilize the affective structures of social knowledge formation.

I was at first disconcerted by the comments that followed Hebdige's performance (which I first saw in short form at the New York University Performance Studies conference in 1995 and then in a longer version at the University of North Carolina in the spring of 1996). The response was vigorous, vehement even. It gained momentum over the weeks and months that followed. Initially shell-shocked, I was doubly overwhelmed by the array of responses: *say more about what actually happened; tell me about healing; define the transgression here; replay the Gramscian aesthetic; I too felt...I dreamt...I can't stop thinking...*But when I finally rose to meet this response, I realized that here was the performance, the "reckoning," the trace of the object long gone, gone long before Hebdige began to dub and mix, lost forever to memory and the broken, intimate fits and starts of re-membering.[8] Here, I began to think, in this interweaving of one (social) body with another, one

---

[6]On performative writing, see Florence and Reynolds (1995), Phelan (1993, 1995), Pollock (in press).

[7]Presented in part at the Performance Studies Conference, New York University, March 1995, and in a longer version at the University Program in Cultural Studies' "Vertigo" Conference, University of North Carolina at Chapel Hill, March 1996, as well as at multiple other sites, in other forms, over an approximately four-year period.

[8]On performance as "reckoning," see Phelan (1993), Ch. 7.

memory-text with another, one utterly contingent attempt at making meaning with another, was at least one, but surely a preeminent, affective/extensive site of cultural studies praxis.

These are only preliminary tropes, images for what performance/cultural studies might accomplish. All three however are prefigured in Angela McRobbie's (1992) call for identity ethnography. "What is now required," McRobbie argued, "is a methodology, a new paradigm for conceptualizing identity-in-culture, an ethnographic approach which takes as its starting point the relational interactive quality of everyday life and which brings a renewed rigor to this kind of work by integrating into a keen sense of history and contingency" (1992, p. 730). Within the field of Speech Communication, scholars as widely divergent as Ruth Bowman, Dwight Conquergood, Craig Gingrich-Philbrook, Judith Hamera, Shannon Jackson, and Soyini Madison (to name only a few), have repeatedly shown what is at stake in taking the status of culture for granted. They not only move away from asking *about* performance toward asking *what is being accomplished* socially, politically, discursively when performance is invoked: they do, accomplish, *perform* the very conditions of agency, affiliation, and praxis that their work describes. In such scholarly performances, they moreover renegotiate the boundaries of action, generate multiple meanings and desires, reckon with the textual remains of performance, and *make possible* a new configuration of feminist/performance/cultural studies.

REFERENCES

Balsamo, A. (1991). Feminism and Cultural Studies. *Journal of Midwest MLA, 24,* 50–73.

Bhaba, H. (1994). *The Location of Culture.* New York: Routledge.

Butler, J. (1990). *Gender Trouble: Feminism and the Subversion of Identity.* New York: Routledge.

Butler, J. (1993). *Bodies That Matter: On the Discursive Limits of 'Sex.'* New York: Routledge.

Case, S. E., Brett, P., & Foster, S. L. (Eds.). (1995). *Cruising the Performative: Interventions into the Representation of Ethnicity, Nationality, and Sexuality.* Bloomington, IN: Indiana University Press.

Conquergood, D. (1995, February). *Beyond the Text: Toward a Performative Cultural Politics.* Paper presented at Indiana State University, Terre Haute, IN.

Cooke, L., & Wollen, P. (Eds.). (1995). *Visual Display: Culture Beyond Appearances.* Seattle, WA: Bay Press.

de Certeau, M. (1984). *The Practice of Everyday Life.* Berkeley, CA: University of California Press.

Diamond, E. (Ed.). (1996). Performance and Cultural Politics. New York: Routledge.

Dolan, J. (1993). Geographies of Learning: Theatre Studies, Performance, and the 'Performative.' *Theatre Journal, 45,* 417–441.

Dominguez, V. (1994). The Messy Side of 'Cultural Politics.' In M. Torgovnick (Ed.), *Eloquent Obsessions: Writing Cultural Criticism* (pp. 237–259). Durham, NC: Duke University Press.

Ebert, T. L. (1996). *Ludic Feminism and After: Postmodernism, Desire, and Labor in Late Capitalism.* Ann Arbor, MI: University of Michigan Press.

Fiske, J. (1989). *Understanding Popular Culture.* Boston: Unwin Hyman.

Florence, P., & Reynolds, D. (Eds.). (1995). *Feminist Subjects, Multi-media: Cultural Methodologies.* New York: Manchester University Press.

Hebdige, D. (1979). *Subculture: The Meaning of Style.* New York: Methuen.

Hebdige, D. (1996). The Impossible Object: Towards a Sociology of the Sublime. In J. Curran, D. Morley, and V. Walkerdine (Eds.), *Cultural Studies and Communications* (pp. 66–95). London: Arnold.

Jenkins, H. (1992). *Textual Poachers: Television Fans and Participatory Culture.* New York: Routledge.

Mavor, C. (1995). *Pleasures Taken: Performances of Sexuality and Loss in Victorian Photographs.* Durham, NC: Duke University Press.

McGuigan, J. (1992). *Cultural Populism.* New York: Routledge.

McRobbie, A. (1992). Post-Marxism and Cultural Studies: A Post-script. In L. Grossberg, C. Nelson, & P. Treichler (Eds.), *Cultural Studies* (pp. 719–730). New York: Routledge.

Parker, A., & Sedgwick, E. K. (Eds.). (1995). *Performativity and Performance.* New York: Routledge.

Parker, A., Russo, M., Sommer, D., & Yaeger, P. (Eds.). (1992). *Nationalisms and Sexualities.* New York: Routledge.

Phelan, P. (1993). *Unmarked: The Politics of Performance.* New York: Routledge.

Phelan, P. (1995). Thirteen Ways of Looking at *Choreographing Writing.* In S. L. Foster (Ed.), *Choreographing History* (pp. 200–210). Bloomington: Indiana University Press.

Pollock, D. (in press). Performing Writing. In P. Phelan & J. Lane (Eds.), *The End(s) of Performance.* New York: New York University Press.

Russo, M. (1994). *The Female Grotesque: Risk, Excess and Modernity.* New York: Routledge.

Stallybrass, P., & White, A. (1986). *The Politics and Poetics of Transgression.* Ithaca, NY: Cornell University Press.

Freeing a Leafhopper: A Note on Rhetorical Contextualization and Cultures

Philip C. Wander
San Jose State University

Late one morning, I walked into the kitchen and there, clinging to the screen on the window, was a bright green leafhopper. I turned and walked over to the sink, opened the door underneath, and got my special glass. Clear, sloping, with little scalloped indentations at the bottom, it is the glass I use to capture little creatures in the house. I walked back to the window and placed it against the screen over the leafhopper. Flurry of leaps, pingings against the glass, and then quiet. I slowly pulled the glass away, angling it slightly, and slipped my free hand over the opening. I carried the glass across the living room, out the door into the back yard, and laid it gently on a bench attached to the wooden deck. The leafhopper crept out of the glass, paused for a moment, and then took flight. Its wings whirred, an iridescent, day-glow green against the sunlight as it flew toward the smoke tree.

THE SELECTION PROCESS

Why am I here talking about culture? There are several scholars addressing this topic in our field. Marsha Houston, Dwight Conquergood, Carole Blair, Ramona Liera-Schwichtenberg, Ray McKerrow, Bill Starosta come to mind. There are a number of younger scholars who live these issues. People like Lisa Flores, Dilip Goankar, Richard Morris, Mary Garrett, Fernando Delgado, Chen Kuan-Hsing, Mark McPhail, Tom Nakayama, Dolores Tanno, Barbara Biesecker, and Kent Ono. These folks, and I could have added others, are changing the direction of our field. I am honored to be here, but there is a sense in which I wish one of them were in my place talking about culture.

Who Was Selected

Who are we up here sitting on this platform? I look at Larry Grossberg, whom I have known for twenty years, and Della Pollack whom I am getting to know. Larry is a founding figure in cultural studies in this country and has introduced the work of a truly profound theorist, Stuart Hall, to our field. Della is the Director of a Center for Cultural Studies. She has just had a manuscript accepted by the Columbia University press which is and will be a ground breaking work. Clearly they belong.

Maybe I can learn something about the selection process from them. They have both been issued passes to leave North Carolina. Maybe under the assumption that this was a panel celebrating Jessie Helms. Larry's paper hints at this. Both teach at the University of North Carolina. Both are raising young children (when I first spoke with Della about this panel, her two children were recovering from chicken pox; later, talking with Larry about this paper, he mentioned how much fun it was staying home and watching his little two-year-old grow up). Both are Jewish Americans.

There are differences. One is female, and one is male. One is a lot older than the other, though I think he still has a charming, youthful aspect about him. Although it is true that both work in culture studies, one of them comes out of what used to be called British cultural studies and the other from performance studies. Della in her paper expands on some of the differences here.

I still don't see how I fit into this. I am white, male, middle class, straight, Euro-American (French, German, English, and Irish, etc.), born and raised in the Middle West and living in California. Charming perhaps, but my youthful aspect is slipping away into that great unnamed which a magazine being sent to me assures me is populated by happy, active retirees.

Whiteness: An Observable Dimension

Still there are similarities. Look carefully at the three of us sitting up here: we are all white. There is an irony about this, if you know your history. There was a time, during the great waves of immigration reaching the East Coast in the nineteenth and early twentieth centuries, when some nativists did not think of the Irish and the Jews as white, much in the way some nativists in California think about Mexican Americans and everyone in this country thinks about African Americans (recall the one-drop theory of race), though even here lightness of skin color is often prized.[1]

I marked the whiteness and wondered whether this panel was an exception. So I did a little checking. Of the 14 Helms panel chairs, ten are men, four are women, and I could not identify any minority scholars. Of the featured speakers, 44 are men, 18 are women. Out of the combined 62 speakers, there are 3 minority speakers, 2 Hispanics and 1 African American. Rendered statistically, roughly 70 percent the participants are male, 30 percent are female; 96 percent are white, 4 percent are "nonwhite" people. Statistics can be revealing.

Professional Identity:
An Unobserved Dimension

There is another similarity that may not be apparent. We come from different parts of the field of communication studies—Della from performance studies, Larry from British cultural studies, and I from rhetorical studies. There are some who think

these fields are in conflict. There is stodgy old, elitist rhetoric, there is Foo-who (the joke about Foucault) and the Gramsci (it sounds like Hootie and the Blow Fish, if you say it quickly enough), and there is the artsy-fartsy crowd.[2] I will however confine myself to rhetorical studies, a culture I know something about, approaching it critically and offering few comparisons between and among our various studies at the end of my remarks.

RHETORICAL STUDIES AND ME

My Teachers

I have a history in rhetorical studies, and part of it includes having left it for ten years. I got my degree in what was called rhetoric and public address from the department of speech at the University of Pittsburgh in 1968. My teachers were Otis Walter, Robert P. Newman, and Edwin Black. They also included Ted Cleavenger who passed away recently, a victim of an AIDS infected blood transfusion and who, because the hospital, following the advise of consultants, decided to keep it a secret, also infected his wife, Charlotte.

I saw him for the last time in Miami Beach at an NCA panel in his honor. To give you some idea of Ted and the intellectual climate at Pitt, I thought of asking him about his views about modern science and Hans Reichenbach's, *The Rise of Scientific Philosophy,* which he assigned so many years ago. He would have had no trouble thinking it through, but when I shook his hand and he said, "Good to see you, Phil. Glad you could make it," tears welled up in me, and all I could say was the truth, "I wouldn't have missed it, Ted."

Jack Daniels, Ted's student at Pitt, was on the panel that day. John Angus Campbell, another of

---

[1]Garry Wills writes that "the Christian Identity theology behind militia groups like the Freemen of Montana treats Jews as the quintessential blacks" (1996, p. 67). For a historical treatment of the Irish struggle to become "white," see David Roediger (1991).

[2]A local politician was invited to hear a famous communication scholar speak. After she finished talking about national campaigns, one of her questioners pressed her on the political theories of Michele Foucault. Hearing Foucault's name mentioned several times, she, somewhat peeved, declared that Foucault had not been a candidate in the recent Presidential election. Afterward, the local politician turned to some other audience members and is alleged to have asked, "Foo-who?"

his students, was in the audience. They, along with Irving Rein, Steven Jenkins, Keith Sanders, a friend of mine from my undergraduate days at Southern Illinois University, Tom Kane, and I made up the better part of Ted's seminars.

Early Scholarship

Edwin Black, who is at this very moment about to speak on another Helm's panel, directed my dissertation. It had to do with the way race was used to justify slavery in three movements in this country—pro-slavery, colonizationist, and abolitionist—in the decade prior to the Civil War. I wrote it in the context of the civil rights movement which had inspired me during the 1950s and 60s. I published early, but when Vietnam became unbearable, I began to shift from my dissertation to the war. I sent an early draft of the rhetoric of American foreign policy to a journal I admired, *Philosophy and Rhetoric*. It was rejected, and an anonymous reviewer wrote: "What if one shoved Nixon's Vietnam speech of 1969 in Wander's face."

I was already feeling frustrated about "scholarly writing." So I started writing criticism of TV and film, minus the footnotes, hoping to reach a larger audience. I sent my work to the *Journal of Communication*. The editor there was Marsha Siefert. Over the years, she taught me that an editor can support good work and that changes can actually improve the writing. She was one of the finest editors I ever worked with, and I owe her more than I can say. She also taught me another lesson, one that has to do with the future of this field. When she was the editor, articles from the *Journal* diffused into other disciplines: the *New York Times,* the *Chronicle of Higher Education,* the *Woodrow Wilson Quarterly,* the CBS, ABC, NBC news programs, and the *Congressional Record.*

An Accidental Return

I returned to rhetorical studies by accident. A distinguished rhetorical scholar, Lawrence Rosenfield

(whom I had read and admired in graduate school and whose work still deserves to be read) commented on my work in print. He said I was argumentative, ignorant, and should read Martin Heidegger and Hannah Arendt, so that I might someday hope to do "appreciative" criticism. He got my attention. I brooded on this for a few years and then, on an NCA panel, I wrote a response. Michael Calvin McGee, who was the critical respondent, liked the work. He commended it to Bruce Gronbeck who was, at that time, editor of *Central* (now called *Communication Studies*). Encouraged by Michael, I sent it to the *Quarterly Journal of Speech* where it was politely rejected as not central to the field. I turned it around and sent it to Bruce where it was accepted. His editing improved it greatly, and he had students working overtime correcting my footnotes, which I appreciated.

Bruce asked me if it was all right to send it out to get responses. With the understanding I would get the last word, I agreed. Between 1981 and 1984, I published a long article on cultural criticism (Wander, 1981), an essay on the aesthetics of fascism (Wander, 1983a), "The Ideological Turn" (Wander, 1983b) an introduction to Henri Lefevbre's *Everyday Life in the Modern World* (Wander, 1984c), a radically revised version of "The Rhetoric of American Foreign Policy" (Wander, 1984a), and "The Third Persona" (Wander, 1984b). Together these constituted my own ideological turn and my inadvertent return to rhetorical studies.

"Unintended" Exclusions

Yet while I am back in rhetorical studies, I am still not quite of it. I am a middle class, late middle-aged, straight, widely published white male. I have been supported by many folks who look a lot like me, but I am not from a big school, my politics rankle, and I like spicy, garlicky, Chinese food. Whatever the reason, a non-Ph.d. granting institution, left-wingism, or bad breath, I still do not get invited to those little mini-conferences that occur in places like Evanston, Des Moines, Bloomington, and Champaign-Urbana (the Big Ten schools) on topics like public address, prudence, and rhetoric criticism.[3]

You may not know the kind of conference I am talking about. They are by invitation only, you know, "RSVP." These are semi-private affairs that have traditionally excluded women, ethnic minorities, and gays and lesbians. Why? It just turns out that way. If you asked them, the organizers would tell you that they did not know you were interested; your work (or, pause, lack of it) does not quite fit the theme; the conference has to be limited to folks already working on the topic; there are only a few slots. Unless you are a white, male, full professor, you might not want to ask. With no inquiry though, they can, in all honesty, conclude "those people have never really expressed any interest."

And why would you want to go, anyway? A few papers get read, future panels are planned, book series are hatched. And if that is not enough, you might have to chitchat with a journal editor and editors in waiting, not to mention several associate editors and referees. So what's to make a fuss about?

RHETORICAL CONTEXTUALIZATION AND CULTURES IN RHETORICAL STUDIES

Method

Being inside and outside rhetorical studies has enabled me to identify several cultures in rhetorical studies. Culture here refers to processes of communication and their characteristics or predictable inclusions and exclusions. I will employ a method for doing this called "rhetorical contextualization," a method spelled out in an article called "Marxism, Postcolonialism, and Rhetorical Contextualization" (Wander, 1996). This method uses an oral model for getting at questions of meaning and sig-

nificance. Instead of fixing on the speakerless and audienceless text favored by most literary and linguistic theorists, this method includes speaker/s, text/s, *and* audience/s. Rhetorical contextualization fixes on two dimensions related to the production of culture. One is the empirical/historical dimension: Who gets to speak? What was said? And who constituted the audience/s. The other is the critical dimension: Who did not or does not get to speak? What did not and does not get said? And who did not or does not constitute the audience?

Meta-Levels of Analysis

This method also deals with meta-communication, that is talk about talk, talk about talk about talk, etc. Theory and criticism are terms used to specify meta-talk. Rhetorical contextualization asks who gets to do criticism and theory? Who does not? What gets said in critical and theoretical texts? What does not? What are the audiences included in such events? And what are the audiences left out? Rather than inter-subjectivity (speakers without text or audience) or inter-textuality (text without speakers or audience), this method advances the conception of inter-rhetoricity.

Inter-rhetoricity includes presence and voids in speakers, texts, and audiences. Inter-rhetoricity, in relation to different levels of talk, may be further labeled as *laminated inter-rhetoricity,* which is to say rhetorical contextualization does not stop with the speaker, but continues to contextualize what the critic says about the speaker, text, and audience. The critic/theorist speaks, but who is she (and who is she not), what appears (and what does not appear), and what audiences are included (and excluded)? The object of criticism may be a text, but who produced the text (and who did not), what does it say (what does it not say), and who was included in the audience (and who was not)?[4]

---

[3]My informants tell me that the most recent public address conference at the University of Illinois had a few white female and minority scholars in attendance, and that some of them actually got to speak. The decision to hold the next one in Iowa City and to include mediated public address caused some of the established members to threaten a boycott.

[4]I owe this entire formulation and the language used to express it to my colleague (and wife) Wenshu Lee (1996). Portions of this theory appear in Lee (1994) and Lee, Ching, Wang, and Hertel (1995).

Two Cultures

Broadly speaking, there are two large groupings in rhetorical studies. There are others and, as this essay progresses, their importance will become obvious. But these two have had a major influence on its production of cultures. They are well organized, identifiable groups of people. They hold separate panels at conventions, maintain separate lines of research and writing (though this is becoming more permeable), and socialize in ways that tend to exclude each other. One is a men's culture, and the other is a women's culture. In the next section, we will contextualize men's and, in the following section, we will contextualize women's culture. This order reflects their order of appearance in our field.

CULTURE, IDEOLOGY, AND "HUMANISM"

Men's culture in our field may be (and often is) called "humanism." Rhetoric you may recall is a humanistic study. Humanism, as an ideal, is not confined to men. It includes everyone—men, women, the human race. Humanist motives are pure and good, because they are grounded in the categorical imperative which calls on us to universalize our actions. Historically, humanistic ideas have offered a shelter from religious dogma on one side and scientific objectification on the other.

Humanism, like any other ideal, has an ideological dimension. In our field, humanism tends to be celebrated by white men. Remember the mini-conferences. Read the journals. Count the number of non-white rhetoricians or humanistic rhetoricians. Recalling our method, the speakers tend to be Euro-American males. Let's turn to the text. When we look at humanist texts in our field, what do they not talk about? Among other things, they rarely talk about the brutalization of women and minority peoples. If they do, they most certainly do not relate it to humanists, humanist texts, or the history of humanism.

Some Stories

I mark this silence by breaking it. Early on in my career, I was told by two women friends (who are now well known scholars) that they had been propositioned during job interviews. I was dumbfounded. "You're kidding," I said, and they laughed at my innocence. Years later, two of my female colleagues asked me to call someone I knew at a major university and tell him to tell his friend that "joking" about requiring one of my colleagues, if she got the job, to fuck him first, John second, and Steve third was unacceptable.

Over the years, I have heard women talk about being made to feel like prostitutes in order to make it. Another friend told me that her professor at a major Ph.d. granting program walked with her into a suite where their university party was in full swing, boasting that he had fucked every woman in the room. And humanists participated in this. Like me, they enjoyed the "game." Like me, they fell silent, even when they disapproved. Like me, they did not know quite what to do when Julia Wood finally spilled the beans in her special issue on sexual harassment in the *Journal of Applied Communication Research* in 1992.

When that issue came out, I scanned it to see if any of the protocols were about me. They weren't, so far as I could remember. I felt guilt and remorse, but on the inside of the glass, I remained silent. I did not move. No more!

The Debate

Humanism, in our field, may be understood as an ideology protecting the interests and advancing the fortunes of white men. I do not say this to shock. This proposition ought to be debated in a form that raises all the issues. Let me suggest the following: [*Resolved that humanism advances the interests and careers of successful, established, upwardly mobile men who are, for the most part white, straight, middle class, and English only speakers.*]

Portions of this proposition appear inside our field in the work of feminist and, more recently, postmodern critics. Outside our field, postcolonial theorists are raising some of the issues.[5] Hear me

---

[5]Raka Shome (1996) has recently called for a postcolonial turn in rhetorical studies.

clearly, though. I said it should be *debated,* not that it should be *ratified.* Humanism is not just what appears in our field and, though one may invoke the authority of Martin Heidegger in announcing its demise, both the authority and the claim are open to question. Edward Said, surveying the wreckage of Western colonialism, reminds us that some of the values advanced against domination were "Western values," and they remained useful in the struggle for human liberation, after the colonial troops left.

Humanism does not live in hypothetical space. If it is to be other than a master narrative or a learned allusion, it must be interrogated in the here and now, and that is why we ought to debate the proposition: [*Resolved that humanism advances the interests and careers of successful, established, upwardly mobile men who are, for the most part, white, straight, middle class, and English only speakers.*]

CULTURE, IDEOLOGY, AND "FEMINISM"

There is a women's culture in rhetorical studies. Women's culture in rhetorical studies is called "feminism." Feminism, as an ideal, includes all women. Feminism offers shelter from male values, male domination, and male brutality. Feminist motives are pure and good.

As an ideal, feminism, like humanism, has an ideological dimension. In our field, feminism tends to be celebrated by and talked about by white women. Feminist or "gender" conferences are run by white women and tend to be about white women.[6] If minority women are invited, they are invited by white women. The speakers tend to be Euro-American females. What about their texts? Feminist texts, in our field, rarely speak about the humiliation and brutalization of women by women, certainly not about humilia-

tion and brutalization of younger women by older women, or women of color by white women, or novice women by established women.

A Story

In rhetorical studies, there is an unspoken rule that men are not supposed to talk about women and certainly not about feminism. I will break this rule, and I will do it by telling a story. Once upon a time there were three middle-aged, well-meaning, white men who decided to organize a seminar. The seminar would feature the works of women, minorities, gays and lesbians, people from the third world, and other social and ideological dissenters. Already it sounds like a fairy tale, I know, but hear me out.

Where, these fellows asked themselves, would be a good place to issue an invitation for such an event? The best place, they thought, would be at a workshop on these same issues at a regional conference that one of the sponsors had co-organized with a third-world woman. So, at the workshop, the woman and one of the sponsors pitched the seminar.

There were 50 or so folks at the workshop. There were a few white males present (and some of them were straight), but the vast majority were white women, and men and women of color. This was a remarkable workshop. Fifty people spent the day, even ate lunch together, and hashed out their differences—gays, Latinas, environmentalists, Marxists, lesbians, etc. No one was packing (a street term for carrying a weapon). No one got punched out. At the close of the workshop, everyone left with a glow.

Or so it seemed. The next day, another of the seminar sponsors, who had also attended the workshop, was running from his last panel to catch a plane. Rushing through the lobby of the hotel, his path was suddenly blocked. A small group of women, two of whom had been in the workshop the day before, would not let him leave. They surrounded him. They shouted. They cried. "The seminar is dominated by men! It erases prominent feminist rhetorical scholars' work. You must withdraw and appoint one of us in your

---

[6]A shift, though, is occurring. The 1997 Gender Conference will be organized by women, most of whom are minorities, and the theme will be "Interrogating Feminism." The key-note speaker will be Dr. Joni Jones, an African American female scholar specializing in performance studies.

place," they said, "and if you don't we will wreck your seminar."

This little drama which began in the lobby and ended sometime later curbside did not go unnoticed. Word got back to the other sponsor. He heard stories from people sitting in the lobby, coming through the doors, and waiting out front for cabs. He pieced them together. He grew more and more dumbfounded. He could not imagine such a thing, but then he began to imagine it. He became upset, then baffled once again. He slept on it. A few days later, having returned from the conference, he called some women friends in the field to ask for advice.

Another Turn

At this point the story takes an even more bizarre turn. The women called, after hearing the story, and said that they were not surprised. Each of them then told him a personal story. One recalled being shouted down at panel presentations, another being screamed at during a gender workshop for arguing the importance of class and race in relation to feminist scholarship, another being run down when she was going up for tenure. One woman framed the problem in this way. "The young women in our field are afraid," she said. If they do not follow the party line in writing about feminism, they take their careers into their hands."

He was shaken by the stories. Even more shaken by the fact that each of these women, independent of the others, had her own story and that, despite the fact that he had known some of them for a long time, they had never breathed a word about it before. He knew that younger scholars often felt oppressed and that somewhere there was a party line. He was on a few review boards now. He now "knew" it was not as monolithic as it appeared (at least he thought he knew this). He was more baffled than ever.

The Victims

Our story threatens to get away from us—too much us versus them. So let's step back for a mo-

ment and ask ourselves: Who are the victims in this narrative? One might answer: the sponsor who was surrounded and ordered to step down! But he survives, unbruised. One might answer: the female scholars who, over the years, have received abuse. But the ones he talked to are established and have quite distinguished careers. One might answer: the young women who fear to say what they think. Surely, they have been policed. Maybe not. They will have to stop suffering in silence, talk about the problem with each other, and organize. They will do this, if they want to stand up for what they believe, and believe what they have to say is worth saying. They will be the better for it in the long run.

One might conclude from this that there are no victims. But what about the women in the lobby who brow beat an old friend? They are, I would argue, the real victims. How, you may ask, can they be considered the victims? Aren't they the victimizers? To make sense of their victimage, we have to recover an unwritten history, a history having to do with male, humanistic rhetoricians discussed earlier. Our field has, over the years, been dominated by men in graduate seminars, conference sessions, journal publication and association politics, and tenure/promotion decisions. Everywhere men were in control—tall men, short men, old men, young men, bright men, stupid men, married men and not-so-married men, men who liked women, men who were still fighting their mothers. The struggle was ongoing, and there were casualties.

What has this to do with the women in the lobby, any more than any other women? Over the years, women who remained politically active, who made the struggle against the patriarchy the cornerstone of their work, heard many stories. They heard them from generations of young women trying to make their way through a system offering them no justice and no opportunity publicly to protest, except in special panels, workshops, or quiet dinners at the conventions. Such women, dealing with their own wounds and knowing about the wounds of many others, may come to feel the rage.

An Empathic Response

Confronting the intolerable, they find themselves in a struggle against the forces of darkness. Embattled, embittered, isolated, their cause becomes more desperate. They frantically send out pleas, issue invitations, confront their friends with what is really happening. They gather their troops about them knowing that they are few and the enemy many. Suddenly a little ray of light appears, but it does not shine on them. They stay up all night trying to figure out what to do. They will not be victimized one more time. They will not be erased, not after all that has happened over the years.

Through an empathic response, and I am here referring to my effort to understand what happened, what occurred in the hotel lobby was *not bullying*. It was an expression of outrage, a sincere and passionate protest against an oppressive system. Through an empathic response, I can get beyond the melodrama drummed into me, since I was a boy—the story pitting the all-virtuous us against an all-evil, treacherous, and malevolent them. An empathic response takes us beyond Manicheanism, and this is to the good (Condit, 1993).

Empathy and Activism

An empathic response does not require us to ignore our principles or prevent us from drawing a line. That is if empathy does not confine us to the purely psychological. In our everyday world as academic scholars, we may be able to understand why confronting people in hotel lobbies, on panels, in workshops makes sense in light of personal experience and party ideology but still decide to resist it.

We could object on moral grounds: "Shame on you! You know that scholars should not bully other scholars. Screaming at and threatening people who do not agree with you is not only wrong. For us, it also constitutes a professional violation!"

Yet if they thought it was wrong, they presumably would not be doing it. Clearly it is not wrong for those who see themselves in a struggle with the forces of darkness. Morality aside, screaming at, threatening, and bullying other people is often bad politics. In this instance, it is not at all clear how using such strategies can create a scholarly community, save through one party rule. The political problem here is that the more successful such efforts become, the closer one party rule is to becoming a reality, the more likely other parties will band together in opposition. The outlines of this story appear in Thucydides, but it is a lesson that can be learned in departmental, university, and movement conflicts, even in our little association.

The Larger Debate

Some good did in fact come out of the conflict. You will recall our three well-meaning, hopelessly naive middle-aged white boys. After the demonstration in the lobby, they got together and, while they had wanted to show that even white men can change, they agreed, in retrospect that they would have been better off including non-white, non-males in the beginning. They decided to enlarge their number. They called a few female scholars to see if they were interested in co-leading the seminar. Pressed by the deadline, two accepted, one of whom was a Latina.

Another benefit: It is not likely that these old guys would have gone much beyond liberal self-satisfaction had they included a woman in the first place. With their "feminist," they would have remained ignorant of feminisms. Had the lobbyists succeeded in placing one of their own as a sponsor, what feminist/womanist views might have been shut out? This question would not have occurred to the original sponsors. It would now!

Still another benefit: One of the women in the lobby wrote a letter of apology. The letter, in the context of the local conflict, called for addressing their differences honestly and openly. In the larger conflict, it calls for addressing differences in and among feminisms honestly and openly. To this end, with the knowledge that affirmative action and the future of feminism in this country is in doubt, one of the sponsors concluded that he should not set aside personal conflicts but understand them in relation to larger issues.

Returning to our discussion of rhetorical cultures, I urge consideration of the following proposition: [*Resolved that feminism, in rhetorical studies, functions ideologically to advance the interests and careers of successful, established, upwardly mobile women who are, for the most part, white, straight, middle class, and English only speakers.*]

As with humanism, I am calling for a debate not for mindless ratification. As with humanism, I have framed the proposition to insure that a variety of viewpoints can be legitimately brought into play. Unlike humanism, however, some feminisms are fervently believed to be good and true in a religious sense. Given this, one might conclude that our proposition, as it now stands, is insensitive, mean-spirited, and potentially disruptive. A related concern has to do with current, right-wing attacks on feminism. However honest and useful the suggestion, might it not play into the hands of those whose reading and thinking about the issues gets summed up in the term "femi-nazis"?

This last consideration weighed upon me. It is one thing to be critical, quite another to be a simple-minded reactionary. Beyond this, the foundations for our proposition are already beginning to be laid in our field, most recently in Julia Wood's review (1996) of three current, popular books on feminism. They have also been articulated at Gender Conferences, particularly in the "Difficult Dialogues" organized (and initiated) by Marsha Houston (1994).

Variations on this proposition have also been vigorously and publicly debated outside our field, and this has gone on for nearly two decades. *This Bridge Called My Back,* a book of poems, stories, and polemics about women's differences and community building marks a beginning (Moraga & Anzaldua, 1983).

The debate has come to include some very powerful and persuasive theorists—Adrienne Rich, a lesbian poet and social critic, for example, and Audre Lorde, whom I have already alluded to, an African American, lesbian feminist, whose "Letter to Mary Daly" on these issues has achieved canonical status among lesbian feminists. It also includes bell hooks.

Bell hooks, is, in my view, one of the finest socio-literary critics now writing. Movies, rap, art, history, she ranges over contemporary life and culture. But central to her vision as a feminist is the fact that not only gender, but also race and class make huge differences in people's lives, especially in the lives of women.

The differences between and among women, however, in hooks's view, are being obscured by what she calls "white power feminists," white women who claim to speak for all women, who cannot say that they are white and know what that means, and who, in their lives and in their writing, ignore women of different racial and sexual backgrounds.[7] The problem is especially acute in places where white power feminists dominate—in academe, for example. "What I find very saddening," writes hooks,

> *is the number of feminist thinkers, particular white feminist thinkers, who continue to be the majority group within academe, who draw on the work of people of color in a way that is blatantly disrespectful; that is to say, they utilize that work to inform their own scholarship in such a way as to make it seem like they are the 'real' theorists (hooks & McKinnon, 1996, p. 828).*

One cannot, following hooks, be a serious feminist and ignore the importance of race and class in dividing women (and men). One cannot be a serious feminist and fail to acknowledge the importance of lesbians and women of color. One cannot be a serious feminist and not take seriously the work of nonstraight, nonwhite, nonwealthy, nonacademic, nonfemale feminists and "womanists."[8] The reason is simple: Ignoring such people and their is-

---

[7]Some sense of the historic origins of the women's movement in this country places it directly in the context of movements to liberate people of color. Margaret Fuller, for example, links it to the abolitionist movement (1971, pp. 25–28). The women's liberation movement in the 1960s and 70s, with its emphasis on equality, grew out of and often echoed the civil rights movement of the 1950s and 60s.

[8]The "womanist" movement among African American theorists does not break along racial lines. Womanist differences are to be found among African American women.

sues will destroy the feminist movement in this country.

Carolyn Allen and Judith A. Howard (1996), the new editors of *Signs,* a leading journal in women's studies and a model for engaged scholarship, share hooks's concerns. They identify race and class as pivotal issues in the contemporary women's movement. They point to a groundbreaking article on exclusionary practices in women's scholarship published 12 years earlier by Maxine Baca Zinn, Lynn Weber Cannon, Elizabeth Higginbotham, and Bonnie Thornton Dill as a starting point (1986). Ignored at the time, this article details the ways feminist scholarship privileges the work of white theorists working at upper class universities and ignores the work of women of color and lower class women working outside the Ivy League and the big research institutions.[9]

Wake up! This matter of difference and the debate over the theoretical limits and political disabilities of dogmatic essentialism—the insistence on woman as one—is well under way. It will not go away because we, in rhetorical studies, remain oblivious to the critical scholarship written by smart, sharp, articulate women (and men) arguing for a more inclusionary theorizing of women's differences. It will not stop, because we place our hands over our ears, persuading ourselves and others that debate over these issues is somehow unbecoming and that we should not listen.

We do ourselves a favor by taking part in this debate. It has implications for our work, our personal relationships, and how we seize up and respond to public issues. Each and every one of us— men and women, old and young, black and non-black, nationals and immigrants, first-world and third-world women, and so forth—has a stake in this debate. Like humanism, feminism and its formulations in our field need to be debated. All the moreso, given our professed interest in argument, debate, and public issues.

A Personal Note

One might want to but be reluctant to ask the question: Where does a middle-aged, white male get off talking like this about women's issues? It's a fair question. I have been called many things— argumentative, ignorant, polemical, Marxist, even postmodernist. I have not been called a feminist, at least not to my face. But I would call myself a feminist, a male feminist.[10] I believe in full equality for women. I believe not only in equality for women, however, but also in equality for people of color, poor people, immigrants, people in other nations, people of different generations and sexual preferences, and for men as well as women.

Granted we have to start somewhere, yet if our moral, social, and political concerns stop with gender, or class, or race, clan, tribe, or profession, our limits will come back to haunt us. It's a brutal historical lesson and it can be said succinctly: Liberatory movements, refusing to examine issues of equality and justice in relation to their own members or in relation to peoples they oppose, themselves become instruments of oppression.

---

[9]Historical research is beginning to open up important issues. Rivka Polatnik (1996) maps out radical differences in attitudes toward motherhood between a black women's collective and a white women's collective in the late 1960s.

---

[10]Male feminists are not a party. There are no titles, no committee meetings, and no salaried positions. Historically they have been confined to the private sphere. They are the grandfathers, fathers, uncles, friends, and comrades that female feminists love and cherish. They are the friends and lovers they could talk to. They come in all ages and all colors. First wave male feminists went into barber shops, pool halls, and town councils to urge men to vote for women's suffrage. Second wave male feminists sat on all male boards of directors, clubs, and university tenure committees arguing the merits of bright, hard-working, young women who now are the cornerstone of our profession. They are the ones female feminists ask to take on the hard core who only listen to their own kind. Male feminists are the ones who do not ask for special favors in return. They are invisible, but every female feminist knows a few of them. By their very nature, crossing gender, class, and color lines, and remaining more or less outside the ideological struggles, male feminists tend, borrowing a term advanced by African American feminist theorists, to be womanists. Third wave male feminists are individuals who support and fight for gender equality and other forms of equality without being constrained by their hereditary characteristics. This issue is difficult but the effort is proceeding. See Jardine and Smith (1987).

A CASE FOR RHETORICAL STUDIES

Humanism is not obliged to ignore women and minorities (those others who belong to the human race). Feminism is not obliged to ignore race, class, and nationality in its rhetoric, its processes of selection, or its topical concerns. Obvious outside academe, it is also obvious outside this country. Women in other countries, Charlotte Bunch (who has a great deal of international experience) tells us, have "made more use of the concept of human rights as an ethical basis for feminism than women in this country have. It has proven, for many women, to be the primary moral backing they use to counter cultural religious right language" (Hartmann et al., 1996, p. 944).

Theory

Rhetorical theory compassing men and women, of every color (note: white is a color too!), the poor as well as the rich and the powerful, American and non-American, non-Buddhists and Buddhists does more than probe fissures, clashes, and divisions. It touches on living issues, and it stands to enrich our understanding of argument in the process. Read Alice Walker, bell hooks, Trinh T. Minh-Ha, and Gayatri Spivak carefully—these women, women of color, make arguments brilliantly, they challenge the propositional logic which logical positivists early in this century equated with rationality.

Their arguments challenge not so much logic as the ground of logic, or what passes for rationality in concrete situations. Their struggle to contest fundamental premises recalls Ernesto Grassi's analysis of the ground of argument (1980). Ground, he says, is a metaphor. "Ground" is not the soil my grandfather scooped up from his freshly plowed field to show me what loam looked like. Ground is a metaphor like foundation or base or premise. What this means is that, while rationality includes the consistent drawing of inferences, it also depends on the givens. These "givens"—the presuppositions and assumptions made in actual arguments—find their force in the willingness of audiences to use them as a basis for collective efforts at reasoning.

Logic, rationality, and reasoning, therefore, depend on the predispositions of actual audiences. This becomes apparent, Grassi argues, in moments of crisis. Here metaphors, authority, and habitual inferences no longer suffice. If they did, we would not call it a crisis. Instead, we would call it an exercise in logic. When everyday assumptions become irrelevant—during fire, or flood, or a terrible reversal, what remains is what we together, in the here and now of a collective problem, can see, hear, smell, and feel.

In moments of crisis, argument—verbal forms used to explore differences of opinion—leaves the hypothetical space of logic, grammar, and "the text." It enters a world inhabited not by the body, but by people present, active, talkative; people with friends and places to go; people confused and hopeful; people shaped by social forces and historical accident; people with names. In this world, we can hear other people, voice our disagreements, see other points of view, feel the closeness, and sometimes smell a rat. Here, instead of studying Venn diagrams, identifying warrants and backings, or explicating a text, we find ourselves puzzling through important issues, as we are doing now on this Helms Panel at NCA in San Diego!

Practice

I like the expansiveness of such talk, and the burst of energy that comes from entering into a here and now where things get done. And I have always believed that, despite his affinity for Latin texts, Grassi expands the range of rhetorical theory, especially in relation to the impasse between humanism, postmodernism, and feminisms informed by postcolonial critiques. In part, this is because Grassi, unlike most theorists, reminds us of the historical context—including fascism and a world war—within which his work emerged (and to which it may be considered a response).[11]

But rhetorical studies is not just theory, it is also a practice. In communication departments, it is associated with courses in public speaking and debate. Historically, it has affirmed the importance of these skills in a democratic process. Our students actually stand up and speak in our classes. In the speech of relatively powerless people, in this case students making themselves heard in a classroom (often for the first time), is an implicit critique of anti-democratic processes going on in our schools, our workplaces, and in other political spheres. In our fear of public speaking is a reminder of how we have been conditioned not to speak up.[12] In our excitement about communicating with others as real people over issues of importance are the claims of modern, electronic democracy refuted.

Political Realism

Even so, departments of communication in the future may do away with rhetorical studies. Some have already done so, arguing that students no longer understand the term, that rhetoric is elitist, old fashioned, non-progressive, etc. These arguments may seize on some of the problems I have been talking about. These same departments, however, in an era of distance learning and downsizing, will sooner or later be called upon to justify their existence, and survival will often turn on those public speaking courses.

---

[11]See Grassi's discussion of Gentile and Heidegger in the formation of his thought and in relation to a "Latin tradition" (1980, pp. 1–17).

[12]Speaking is required in such courses, and speakers are graded and sometimes humiliated by teachers. The contradictions and abuses must not overshadow the extent to which students are *required* to remain silent in most other courses, in their families, and at work. The contrast is astounding and student response toward the end of the course and afterward is often gratifying.

When that occurs, they will reinvent the values embraced in rhetorical studies. They will search out, perhaps even hire people who teach, write about such things, hoping that they can find someone to perform effectively in front of college and university committees. In its ideals and in its pedagogical practices if not in its scholarship, rhetorical studies resonates with general education, training for citizenship, and the ideals of multiculturalism. As such, it speaks to audiences outside our field. It speaks to parents, to corporate leaders, to people in state legislatures, to college administrators, and often, when their fear subsides, to students themselves.

CONTEXTUALIZING OUR VARIOUS "STUDIES": SOME CONCLUDING REMARKS

Rhetorical studies is not more basic than performance and cultural studies. Philosophically, they cannot be disentangled. Rhetoric is a practice. Arguments cannot be understood apart from cultural differences.

As fields of study, however, they do offer some instructive contrasts. For example, broadly speaking: (a) more ethnic minorities, including minority men, women, straight and gay, from nations other than the Americas and the U.S. get to write, speak, and perform in performance and cultural studies than in rhetorical studies; (b) rhetorical scholars are less likely than performance and cultural scholars to debate issues raised by bell hooks, Audre Lorde, Cherrie Moraga, Gayatri Spivak, Edward Said, Cornel West, and Stuart Hall; (c) performance and cultural studies scholars are more likely than rhetorical scholars to play with form, that is to break through, transcend, or ignore the theory-case study-two-hundred item bibliography essay that passes for righteous form in rhetorical studies; (d) performance and cultural studies scholars and texts are more likely to reach out to interdisciplinary and even non-academic audiences than are scholars and texts in rhetorical studies; (e) rhetorical studies scholars are more likely to talk about the values of argumentation, debate, and democracy, through the exploration of controversy; (f) rhetorical and performance studies are more inclined to value embodied practices in their teaching and classes than is cultural studies.

There is also something to be gained from contextualizing our various "studies"—rhetorical, performance, and cultural—as academic activities. How might we answer the questions of who does not get to speak, what does not get said, and the audiences ignored in rhetorical, performance, cultural, and an insurgent postcolonial studies?

The speakers in these four areas, for example, tend not to be poor, illiterate, or other than academics. The texts tend to be silent about political practice in general, but especially about racism, sexism, classism, and homophobia in the departments, colleges, universities, and the cities in which the writers live and work. The audiences for our "studies" tends to exclude those too poor to read academic journals and scholarly books, the illiterate, and in some cases high school, junior college, four year college, and university teachers who are unable to fly to conferences in "foreign" cities.

Contradictions confound us all, however progressive our views and our reading lists. Iain Chambers and Linda Curti, in a recent and excellent anthology of conference papers *The Post-colonial Question,* tried to justify holding their conference in Naples, Italy. Naples, they enthuse, bears traces of cosmopolitan encounters in previous periods in its language, dress, and food. How appropriate a place it is for people who want to discuss famine, poverty, genocide, migration, religious sentiments and nationalist identities appearing on TV in different parts of the world (Chambers & Curti, 1996, pp. xi-x).

"Come to Naples; denounce poverty!" I can almost see it on T-shirts and hear the snorts it would elicit outside the convention circuit. I read Chambers and Curtis's introduction on my return from an argumentation conference in Venice and having just put down David Lodge's novel, *Small World,* a satire about the annual migrations of ac-

ademics in search of fun, sun, and profit. I recollect that moment here at an SCA conference held in San Diego, California, one of the loveliest vacation spots in the United States. I can never tell at these luxury hotels, especially at the top having a margarita and looking out over the city, whether I am holding the glass or the glass is holding me.

Have I freed the leafhopper, or is it still clinging, taking the hard, smooth surfaces around me and the soft indirect lighting overhead for reality itself? But if you have ever seen or heard the green, iridescent wings whirring and found yourself inert, afraid, take courage: Life is short, and the time is now.

REFERENCES

Allen, C., & Howard, J. A. (1996). Editorial: Moving forward in proactive times. *Signs, 21,* ix–xv.

Chambers, I., & Curti, L. (Eds.). (1996). *The postcolonial question.* London: Routledge.

Condit, C. (1993). The critic as empath: Moving away from totalizing theory. *Western Journal of Communication, 57,* 178–190.

Fuller, M. (1971). *Women in the nineteenth century.* New York: W. W. Norton & Company. [Orig. pub. 1845].

Grassi, E. (1980). *Rhetoric as philosophy: The humanist tradition.* University Park: The Pennsylvania State University Press.

Hartmann, H., Bravo, E., Bunch, C., Hartsock, N., Spalter-Roth, R., Williams, L., & Blanco, M. (1996). Bringing together feminist theory and practice: A collective interview. *Signs, 21,* 917–951.

Hooks, b., & McKinnon, T. (1996). Sisterhood: Beyond public and private. *Signs, 21,* 814–829.

Houston, M. (1994). When black women talk with white women: Why dialogues are difficult. In A. Gonzalez, M. Houston, & V. Chen (Eds.), *Our voices: Essays in culture, ethnicity. and communication* (pp. 133–139). Los Angeles, CA: Roxbury Publishing Company.

Jardine, A., & Smith, P. (Eds.). (1987). *Men in feminism.* New York: Routledge.

Lee, W. S. (1994). On not missing the boat: A processual method for inter/cultural understanding of idioms and lifeworld. *Journal of Applied Communication Research, 22,* 141–161.

Lee, W. S. (1996). Women, "other" women, and emancipatory oppression: Laminated inter-rhetoricity as a key to inclusionary theory and practice. Manuscript under journal review.

Lee, W. S. (1997). One whiteness veils three uglinesses: from border crossing to a womanist interrogation of colorism. A book chapter under review, in T. Nakayama & J. Martin (Eds.), *Whiteness: Communication perspectives.* CA: Sage.

Lee, W. S., Ching, J., Wang, J., & Hertel, E. (1995). A sociohistorical approach to intercultural communication. *Howard Journal of Communications, 6,* 262–291.

Moraga, C., & Anzaldua, (Eds.). (1983). *This bridge called my back.* New York: Kitchen Table Press.

Polatnik, R. (1996). Diversity in women's liberation ideology: How black and white group in the 1960s viewed motherhood. *Signs, 21,* 679–706.

Roediger, D. (1991). *The wages of whiteness: Race and the making of the American working class.* New York: Verso.

Shome, R. (1996). Postcolonial interventions in the rhetorical canon: An 'other' view. *Communication Theory, 6,* 40–59.

Walker, A. (1983). *In search of our mothers' gardens: Womanist prose.* New York: Harcourt Brace Jovanovich.

Wander, P. (1981). Cultural criticism. In D. Nimmo & K. R. Sanders (Eds.), *Handbook of political communication* (pp. 497–538). Hollywood: Sage.

Wander, P. (1983a). The aesthetics of fascism. *Journal of Communication, 33,* 70–78.

Wander, P. (1983b). The ideological turn in modern criticism. *Central States Speech Journal, 34,* 1–18.

Wander, P. (1984a). The rhetoric of American foreign policy. *Quarterly Journal of Speech, 70,* 339–361.

Wander, P. (1984b). The third persona: An ideological turn in rhetorical theory. *Central States Speech Journal, 35,* 1–28.

Wander, P. (1984c). Introduction, *Henri Lefebvre: Everyday Life in the Modern World,* trans. S. Rabinovitch (Rutgers University Press/Transaction Books, 1–28).

Wander, P. (1996). Marxism, postcolonialism, and rhetorical contextualization. *Quarterly Journal of Speech, 82,* 402–426.

Wills, G. (1996, September 19). A tale of three leaders. *New York Review of Books, 43,* 67.

Wood, J. T. (1996). Dominant and muted discourses in popular representations of feminism. *Quarterly Journal of Speech, 82,* 171–205.

Zinn, M. B., Cannon, L. W., Higginbotham, E., & Dill, B. T. (1986). The costs of exclusionary practices in women's studies. *Signs, 11,* 290–303.